More Praise for How to Reach and Teach All Children in the Inclusive Classroom, Second Edition

"Motivating and educating today's students requires an artful blend of science and time-proven strategies. Sandra Rief and Julie Heimburge's new book stands as a testament to the very best of this model. This wise and practical resource for educators committed to developing the best in every student is superb."

—Dr. Sam Goldstein
Co-author of *Understanding and Managing Children's Classroom Behavior, 2nd Edition*

"After reviewing several books on inclusion, I decided *How to Reach and Teach All Children in the Inclusive Classroom* had all I was looking for. The activities, lessons, and strategies are modified for various learners with diverse learning styles. This book is a must-have for all educators!"

—Michelle Hammer
Middle School Inclusion Class Teacher

"Rief and Heimburge's new work provides the novice/beginning and experienced professional educator with a plethora of valuable ideas and techniques for promoting prosocial behaviors in school, and raising the academic achievement of all learners."

—Dr. Bob Bayuk, school psychologist and past president of Wyoming School Psychology Association

JOSSEY-BASS TEACHER

Jossey-Bass Teacher provides K–12 teachers with essential knowledge and tools to create a positive and lifelong impact on student learning. Trusted and experienced educational mentors offer practical classroom-tested and theory-based teaching resources for improving teaching practice in a broad range of grade levels and subject areas. From one educator to another, we want to be your first source to make every day your best day in teaching. *Jossey-Bass Teacher* resources serve two types of informational needs—essential knowledge and essential tools.

Essential knowledge resources provide the foundation, strategies, and methods from which teachers may design curriculum and instruction to challenge and excite their students. Connecting theory to practice, essential knowledge books rely on a solid research base and time-tested methods, offering the best ideas and guidance from many of the most experienced and well-respected experts in the field.

Essential tools save teachers time and effort by offering proven, ready-to-use materials for in-class use. Our publications include activities, assessments, exercises, instruments, games, ready reference, and more. They enhance an entire course of study, a weekly lesson, or a daily plan. These essential tools provide insightful, practical, and comprehensive materials on topics that matter most to K–12 teachers.

HOW TO REACH AND TEACH
ALL CHILDREN
in the INCLUSIVE
CLASSROOM

Practical Strategies, Lessons, and Activities

Second Edition

SANDRA F. RIEF • JULIE A. HEIMBURGE

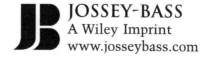
JOSSEY-BASS
A Wiley Imprint
www.josseybass.com

Published by Jossey-Bass
A Wiley Imprint
989 Market Street, San Francisco, CA 94103-1741   www.josseybass.com

Jossey-Bass books and products are available through most bookstores. To contact Jossey-Bass directly call our Customer Care Department within the U.S. at 800-956-7739, outside the U.S. at 317-572-3986 or fax 317-572-4002.

Jossey-Bass also publishes its books in a variety of electronic formats. Some content that appears in print may not be available in electronic books.

Library of Congress Cataloging-in-Publication Data

Rief, Sandra F.
  How to reach and teach all children in the inclusive classroom : practical strategies, lessons, and activities / Sandra F. Rief, Julie A. Heimburge. — 2nd ed.
        p. cm.
  Includes bibliographical references and index.
  ISBN-13: 978-0-7879-8154-9 (pbk.)
  ISBN-10: 0-7879-8154-0 (pbk.)
  1. Inclusive education—United States. 2. Mainstreaming in education—United States. 3. Elementary school teaching—United States. 4. Cognitive styles in children—United States. 5. Lesson planning—United States. 6. Motivation in education—United States. 7. Learning disabled children—Education—United States. I. Heimburge, Julie A. II. Title.
  LC3981.R54 2006
  371.9'046—dc22
                            2006014173

Printed in the United States of America
SECOND EDITION
PB Printing   10 9 8 7 6 5 4 3 2 1

DEDICATION

In loving memory of Benjamin, my precious son and inspiration; and Edie Katz, my wonderful and extraordinary mom

—Sandra

To Jaime and Cory, for filling my life with love, joy, and happiness

—Julie

ACKNOWLEDGMENTS

Our deepest thanks and appreciation to:

- Neil and Itzik, our loving, supportive husbands.
- Our precious and wonderful kids: Jaime, Cory, Ariel, Jackie, Jason, Gil, and Sharon. We are so proud of all of you.
- Brian, for his skill and expertise with technology.
- Friends and colleagues who contributed ideas and student samples: Linda Lemen, Janet Manen, Bill Patterson, Michele Janette, Linda Sheeler, Kathy Aufsesser, David Van Slyck, Jan Armstrong, Steve Guadarrama, Carolyn Hasselbar, Marian Jacobs, Pat John, Mary Smith, Terri Knight, and Sharon Landacre.
- The many other teachers who shared their strategies, perspectives, and insights with us.
- Arlyne and Fred Skolnik for their exemplary programs and contribution to Chapters Eight and Nine.
- Our many students over the years for making us so happy we chose teaching as our profession and for inspiring and challenging us to keep learning, growing, and developing as educators. We give special thanks to all the students who have created their own survival math activities and have shared them with other teachers, students, and visiting teachers. These quality projects have lifted the level of student products tremendously.
- Our editors at Jossey-Bass for their help and guidance in writing this new edition.

ABOUT THE AUTHORS

Sandra Rief, M.A., is a leading educational consultant, author, and speaker on effective strategies and interventions for helping students with learning, attention, and behavioral challenges. Sandra presents seminars, workshops, and keynotes nationally and internationally on this topic. She received her B.A. and M.A. degrees from the University of Illinois. Sandra is formerly an award-winning teacher (California Resource Specialist of the Year) with over twenty-three years' teaching experience.

Sandra is the author of several books including: *How to Reach & Teach Children with ADD/ADHD, Second Edition* (2005); *The ADHD Book of Lists: A Practical Guide for Helping Children & Teens with Attention Deficit Disorders* (2003); *The ADD/ADHD Checklist: An Easy Reference for Parents & Teachers* (1998); *Alphabet Learning Center Activities Kit* (2000, coauthored with Nancy Fetzer); and other books/publications.

Sandra also developed and presented these acclaimed educational videos: *ADHD & LD: Powerful Teaching Strategies and Accommodations; How to Help Your Child Succeed in School: Strategies and Guidance for Parents of Children with ADHD and/or Learning Disabilities; ADHD: Inclusive Instruction & Collaborative Practices,* and together with Linda Fisher and Nancy Fetzer, the videos *Successful Classrooms: Effective Teaching Strategies for Raising Achievement in Reading and Writing* and *Successful Schools: How to Raise Achievement & Support "At-Risk" Students.*

Sandra is an educational expert for the Web site www.adhdbalance.net and is an instructor for continuing education courses offered through California State University, East Bay, and Seattle Pacific University. For more information, visit her Web site at www.sandrarief.com.

Julie Heimburge is a native San Diegan and earned her standard teaching credential from San Diego State University and her M.A. in Person-Centered Studies at United States International University. She has been an elementary teacher in the San Diego Unified School District for more than thirty years. Julie has served as a mentor teacher, demonstration teacher, guest lecturer, curriculum writer, and a staff developer for her district. She has also been a featured presenter for conferences in other parts of the United States—sharing innovative instructional practices designed to motivate diverse learners in the general education classroom. Julie is a supervising teacher for student teachers and has trained new teachers for the Beginning Teacher Support and Assessment Program (BTSA). She coauthored *How to Reach and Teach All Children in the Inclusive Classroom, First Edition.*

CONTENTS

Part 2
REACHING STUDENTS IN THE CLASSROOM AND AT HOME

Part 3
DESIGNING CURRICULUM TO HOOK IN STUDENTS

13 *Revvin' Up the Content Areas* 275

14 *Motivating Students to Be Successful Mathematicians* 337

FOREWORD

I have been fortunate to speak with thousands of teachers throughout the United States each year at my workshops. I am frequently asked which books I consider most useful in guiding teachers to create a positive school climate for all students. Whenever I recommend a book, I do so because I believe that the contents provide an educational framework that makes sense and offers teachers sensible ideas together with realistic, practical strategies. Ten years ago I enthusiastically wrote the Foreword for the first edition of the remarkable book *How to Reach and Teach All Children in the Inclusive Classroom* by Sandra F. Rief and Julie A. Heimburge. At that time I emphasized that I would place the book at the top of the list of publications I would recommend for teachers, parents, and other professionals interested in learning more about the ways in which we educate our children.

Sandy and Julie have now written the second edition of the book. This new edition does not simply represent minor changes from the first edition. While maintaining the informative, easy-to-read style of the first edition, Sandy and Julie have impressively incorporated research findings and educational practices that have evolved during the past ten years. Not only does the second edition include a wealth of new material but it also conveys this material in a manner that captures Sandy and Julie's respect for educators, students, and parents. Their ability to blend educational theory and strategies with the joy, excitement, and humanity of the teaching process is to be highly commended. They continue to take the position that educational practices are most effective when housed within interpersonal relationships, and they spotlight the significant role of the teacher.

The book includes a wide spectrum of topics and issues that Sandy and Julie address and capture, but what must also be emphasized is that within each chapter there are numerous examples and strategies for achieving educational goals. In addition, the book includes many forms to help educators reach their goals as well as references should educators wish to do additional reading in a particular area of interest.

An important message throughout the book is that if students are not learning and succeeding in school, then we, as educators, must have the courage to ask, "What is it that I can do differently to help students to experience success and accomplishment in the school environment?" As I have often emphasized in my dialogues with teachers, this question should not be interpreted as blaming educators but rather empowering them. I ask, "Isn't it better to focus on factors over which we have control or influence rather than continuing to apply ineffective techniques, hoping that our students will change first? If our teaching techniques are not working, then why continue to use them?"

This book truly assists teachers to feel empowered, not only providing many worthwhile ideas, but also stimulating teachers to develop their own very creative strategies to meet the particular needs of their students. As I read this book, I thought of many students with whom I have worked and the ways in which Sandy and Julie's ideas might be applied to enhance their learning, their hope, and their resilience.

As was true of the first edition, this book is a treasure, to be read and then read again. It is a resource that will be enormously beneficial in providing information about specific topics such as discipline or teaching math, or taken in its entirety. It is a book that makes a major contribution to the field of education, which articulates the key components of the educational process, which offers us a plethora of useful techniques and strategies, and which reminds us of the interpersonal foundation involved in learning and of the excitement and gift of teaching. This book is must reading.

Robert Brooks, Ph.D.
Newton, Massachusetts
Author of *The Self-Esteem Teacher*
Coauthor of *Raising Resilient Children* and *Handbook of Resilience in Children*

INTRODUCTION

As an educator, you are in a position of great privilege: every day you have the opportunity to make a positive difference in the lives of children. The manner in which you interact with your students, the environment you create, and the curriculum, learning activities, and methods you use to teach greatly affect how motivated and successful your students will be. It also affects how willing your students will be to take risks, work cooperatively together, and be kind to and supportive of one another. Not only do you teach students countless academic skills and behaviors, but you also have great influence on how your children accept and appreciate the differences and diversity among all of us. It is important that all teachers ensure that students feel they are vital to their classroom community and valued and respected for their individuality. You need to make the connection with your students, stimulate in them the desire to learn and participate, and do everything in your power to build and earn their confidence and trust.

This philosophy, and above all else the fundamental belief that all children can learn—that we can and must find the means to reach and teach every one of our students—is the underlying theme of this book. It is with great joy that we are able to once again work together to coauthor this new edition. We were teaching colleagues at the same elementary school in San Diego Unified School District (Julie in general education and Sandra in special education) for sixteen years and have been close friends for over two decades. While teaching at the same school, we often shared students who had individualized educational programs and were placed in Julie's classroom while receiving special education services. The school we taught at (and where Julie still is teaching) has historically had a strong commitment to the individual child. This school has a diverse student population, with many students bused in from communities and neighborhoods throughout San Diego. It has always been a high-performing school with a reputation for high achievement and a caring, nurturing, child-centered program. There is strong parental support and involvement, and a dedicated staff well trained and on the cutting edge of innovative teaching practices.

This school always has had a firm commitment to heterogeneous groupings of students in every classroom. When classrooms are formed, they are carefully structured to be multiethnic, multicultural, and multiracial, with the full spectrum of high- and low-performing students and those with learning and behavioral challenges. Every effort is made to balance each classroom so that students identified as gifted and talented, as well as special education students and others with special needs, are integrated throughout.

Within a classroom of thirty-three students, for example, it is common to find a cluster of gifted students and students with various disabilities or special needs (including children with learning disabilities, attention deficit hyperactivity disorder, Asperger's syndrome, speech and language disorders, health impairments, and other disorders), students with limited English proficiency (English-language learners), and children who have significant issues in their personal and home lives. Observers would have a difficult time distinguishing students who have disabilities and special needs from the other children in the class and typically find that students are happy and comfortable in their learning environment, working together cooperatively, and achieving success. This is the case in classrooms anywhere throughout the country where good and inclusive teaching is taking place.

Teachers who are skilled in and committed to differentiating instruction will find the means and channels to motivate and reach diverse learners in their classrooms. It will be hard to pick out the "average" learner from the "exceptional" learners in their classroom. All teachers each year have some students with various disabilities or neurobiological disorders in their classrooms, so it is important to understand these children and how they learn and perform best. Fortunately, instructional and management strategies that are vitally important for reaching and teaching those with learning and behavioral challenges are good and effective teaching practices for all students.

Since we wrote the first edition of this book, published in 1996, there have been monumental changes in the field of education due to what we have learned from the abundance of research that has come to light and now guides instructional practices. Much has been learned about how we acquire literacy skills and prevent reading problems, the brain and brain-compatible teaching strategies, learning in general that affects all content-area instruction, and brain-based (neurobiological) disorders such as attention deficit/hyperactivity disorder, learning disabilities, and Asperger's syndrome (one of the autism spectrum disorders that is more commonly found in a child placed in a general education classroom). It is important for educators to keep current with the new research to guide their practice, and we all must make it a priority to collaborate with each other in identifying and addressing our children's individual needs.

Among the changes we have seen take place in classroom instruction, the following are some of the most significant:

- Almost everything in content-area instruction and curriculum now centers around teaching the "big idea"—the major focus, message, or theme—and teaching through a variety of sources, media, and means of expression.
- The importance of student "talk": that is, teaching students to share ideas and explain or "unpack" their thinking and listen to one another's perspectives has new importance.
- There are now varied and alternative means of assessment.
- Classroom teachers are being trained in differentiating instruction: learning and understanding the need to have scaffolding and supports in place to enable all diverse learners to access the curriculum and information at whatever level they are at.
- Research-based strategies found effective for teaching literacy, math, and other content areas are recognized as being important and working for all students, although we need to make accommodations and modifications for various learners.
- There has been shift in how we teach to a focus on getting to the meaning and depth of understanding.
- There are now more opportunities for student choice and options, hands-on experiential learning opportunities, and the use of technology.

- Standards-based instruction and curriculum and challenging demands for all students to achieve or exceed grade-level standards are commonplace.
- There is a greater understanding of and commitment to providing a range of targeted academic and behavioral supports and interventions and the importance of early intervention whenever possible.

Cumulatively, the two of us have over fifty years of experience teaching in public schools in both general and special education. It is our intent to share lessons, activities, and successful teaching practices that are powerful and effective with a full spectrum of diverse learners. The focus of this book is on how all students can learn and be successful if the proper techniques are employed and when instruction is motivating, engaging, and relevant. The activities in this book are carefully structured to provide active, high-interest learning and address the multiple intelligences and wide range of learning styles of all students. The lessons are designed to be used for instruction with all students in your classroom. There are also tips to share with parents for helping their children achieve success, and the learning activities can become an extension or reinforcement of the classroom at home.

We wish to clarify one important point in our reference to "reaching and teaching all children in inclusive classrooms," as we do not want to mislead any readers. It is not our intent to imply that all children, including those with more severe disabilities, can be taught effectively in the general education classroom. We believe in a full spectrum of service and placement options to students in need of special education. Not every student is able to function in a regular classroom, even with a maximum amount of support from special education. The regular classroom setting is not the best or most appropriate placement for every student. Children with various disabilities are entitled to appropriate placements and supports that will provide them with the best-suited and beneficial educational program to meet their needs.

What we *will* be addressing throughout this book is how school personnel can effectively reach and teach all of the children who are generally placed within the mainstream, general education classroom. This may include students with learning disabilities; attention deficit disorders; speech and language needs; various social, emotional, and behavioral difficulties; health impairments; and those who are at risk due to any number of other factors. This also includes children who are linguistically diverse and may be limited in English proficiency, and gifted students, with their own unique and exceptional needs. Inclusive classrooms are respectful of and take into account the wide range of background experience, ability, and developmental levels of students. We firmly believe that most students with mild to moderate disabilities and various learning and behavioral differences can be successful in general education classrooms through the collaborative efforts and partnership of the classroom teacher, special education staff, other student support personnel, and parents.

We hope that this new edition provides the necessary information and specific techniques to help ensure the success of every child in the classroom. It is designed to provide complete guidance for educators, parents, administrators, school counselors, and other school personnel seeking to create a school truly supportive and inclusive of all children. The specific activities and engaging activities across the curriculum are designed to be adaptable for grades 3 to 8. We will be referring to students within the third- through eighth-grade range interchangeably as either "upper graders" (meaning upper elementary grade), "older students," or "upper/middle school students." Some of the chapters focus on specific topics, such as creating learning environments and instruction that build on students' strengths, interests, multiple intelligences, and learning style preferences; differentiating instruction; motivating and hooking in reluctant readers and writers; motivating students to be successful mathematicians; increasing home-school communication and collaboration; building students' organization, time management, and study skills; proactive classroom management; positive behavioral supports and interventions; classroom and schoolwide programs designed to enhance students' resiliency and self-esteem; how to make accommodations and modifications; and numerous user-friendly strategies, tools, activities, and ready-to-use materials across the curriculum.

Sandra F. Rief and *Julie A. Heimburge*

Part 1

RECOGNIZING STUDENT DIFFERENCES

Chapter 1

REACHING ALL STUDENTS THROUGH DIFFERENTIATED INSTRUCTION

Educators have heard a lot over the past few years about "differentiating instruction" as well as "brain-based" teaching strategies. This chapter explores what these terms mean and the importance of such instructional efforts by teachers in order to reach and teach all students in an inclusive classroom. In this chapter, we begin with an explanation of differentiated instruction and how to go about it in our classrooms, and we address some of the components under the umbrella of differentiated instruction and brain-based teaching strategies, such as multisensory instruction and cooperative learning. Chapter Two addresses other components of differentiated instruction, such as teaching through students' learning styles and multiple intelligences.

DEFINITIONS, DESCRIPTIONS, AND KEY COMPONENTS

To address the learning differences in all students and maximize their levels of performance and achievement, teachers need to differentiate instruction in the classroom. Differentiated instruction is a way of thinking about teaching and learning that recognizes the fact that one size does not fit all learners. Some students are not successful in school because there is a misfit between how they learn and the way they are taught (Association for Supervision and Curriculum Development, 2002). This concept or awareness certainly is not new for teachers, particularly special educators. But the term *differentiated instruction* is relatively new, and so is the recognition in the general education community that teaching must change in order to fulfill our responsibility to reach and teach all of the diverse learners in our classrooms.

Carol Ann Tomlinson, associate professor at the University of Virginia, Charlottesville, is one of the key educational leaders who speaks and writes extensively about the subject. According to Tomlinson (2001), differentiated instruction is:

- *Proactive.* Teachers plan a variety of ways to get at and express learning and that are planned to be robust enough to address the range of learner needs.

- *More qualitative than quantitative.* Teachers adjust the nature, not necessarily the length or quantity, of the assignment.

3

- *Student centered.* Learning experiences are engaging, relevant, and interesting.
- *Rooted in assessment.* Throughout the unit of study, teachers assess students' developing readiness levels, interests, and modes of learning in a variety of ways—and adjust instruction accordingly.

For struggling learners, differentiated instruction means setting important goals of understanding and then figuring out how to build scaffolding leading to success in those goals, not diluting the goals. *Scaffolds* are supports needed for a student to succeed in challenging work, defined as assignments or tasks that are slightly beyond the student's comfort zone, not overwhelming and frustrating assignments (Tomlinson, 2001). Scaffolds may include more modeling and structure, guided instruction and practice opportunities, reteaching, provision of study guides, graphic organizers, and other learning tools. They also include the numerous strategies and accommodations throughout this book that help make learning more accessible to students.

Some students need more time and opportunity to learn the basic content and material through various means, and with additional explanation, review, and practice. Other students need less time on the core content and opportunities for extended, advanced learning. Adjusting time and degree of support provided are components of differentiated instruction.

Heacox (2002) further defines differentiated instruction as:

- Changing the pace, level, or kind of instruction provided in response to individual learners' needs, styles, or interests
- Rigorous: Providing challenging instruction to motivate students to push themselves and base learning goals on a student's unique capabilities
- Relevant: Focused on essential learning, not on "side trips" or "fluff"
- Flexible and varied
- Complex: Challenging students' thinking and actively engaging them in content that conveys depth and breadth [p. 5]

Differentiation is based on the beliefs that (Tomlinson, 2000):

- Students who are the same age differ in their readiness to learn, interests, styles of learning, experiences, learning profiles, life circumstances, and levels of independence.
- The differences in students are significant enough to make a major impact on what students need to learn, the pace at which they need to learn it, and the support they need from teachers and others to learn it well.
- Students will learn best when supportive adults push them slightly beyond where they can work without assistance.
- Students will learn best when they can make a connection between the curriculum and their interests and life experiences.

"Curriculum," Tomlinson (2000) writes, "tells us *what* to teach. Differentiation tells us *how* to teach the same standard to a range of learners by employing a variety of teaching and learning modes" (p. 6).

HOW, WHAT, AND THROUGH WHICH MEANS DO WE DIFFERENTIATE?

There are numerous ways to differentiate instruction, and they are illustrated throughout this book—for example:

- Materials, tasks, and learning options at varied levels of difficulty
- Multiple and flexible groupings of students

- Multisensory instruction
- Lessons, assessments, and projects that take into account students' varied learning styles and preferences, interests, talents, and multiple intelligences
- Varying degrees of supports and scaffolds
- Choices of where, how, and with whom students may work
- Choices about topics of study, ways of learning, and modes of expression
- Assignments, projects, and student products that draw on students' individual strengths and interests
- Adaptations, modifications, and multiple approaches to instruction
- A variety of assessments (for example, portfolios, written and oral exams, learning logs, and demonstrations)
- Tiered assignments, which vary the level of complexity or challenge, the process or product

We can differentiate content, presentation and instructional strategies, activities, performance tasks, and assessment tools (Chapman, 2000). Differentiated instruction typically involves multiple approaches and adaptations in the areas of content (what students learn), process (the ways students learn and how the content is taught), and product (how students present or demonstrate their learning).

Content can be differentiated by complexity based on readiness level. For example, if a writing lesson is focused on dialogue, one student might be ready to create a single dialogue exchange between two characters, and another may be ready to write four to five exchanges (Pettig, 2000). As Pettig describes, students in a math class might be working problems of varying complexity based on their readiness or skill level. For example, the class may be studying long division, but students who are more advanced may be solving problems with two- and three-digit divisors, while others are solving problems with single-digit divisors.

When teachers differentiate by readiness level, they can do so through varied texts or supplementary materials by reading level, varied scaffolding, tiered tasks or products, small group instruction, homework options, and negotiated criteria for quality (Tomlinson, 2001)

It is important for teachers to preassess prior knowledge—what students already know and can do (for example, through performance tasks, surveys, and interviews—in order to be able to challenge all students at their appropriate readiness level. In addition, teachers should be assessing students' interests related to the topic (Chapman, 2000).

Differentiating the process will include the wide array of strategies for engaging students' attention and active participation, and questioning strategies that incorporate the full range of Bloom's Taxonomy (knowledge, comprehension, application, analysis, synthesis, and evaluation) levels of questions (see Chapter Seven). It also involves designing lessons and activities that tap into students' strengths, interests, and multiple intelligences, as well as their learning style preferences (see Chapter Two and the numerous activities through this book).

Flexible grouping is another aspect of process differentiation. The teacher structures an array of grouping opportunities best suited for the activities: whole class, teams, cooperative groups, partners, or independent; by interest, preferred learning modality, or readiness level; heterogeneously, homogeneously, teacher assigned, or self-assigned. Grouping formats for varying purposes may involve:

- The whole class (for preassessment, introduction of concepts, planning, sharing, and wrap-up of explorations)
- Small groups (pairs, triads, quads) for sense making, teaching skills, directed reading, planning, and investigation
- Individualized for practice and application of skills, homework, interest centers, products, independent study, and testing (Tomlinson, 2001)

Chapter Two discusses the diversity in individual learning preferences (for example, modality preferences, environmental preferences, cognitive style preferences) and students' multiple intelligences.

Differentiating the process can also be accomplished by tapping into students' diverse learning styles, strengths, and interests and incorporating a variety of options in how students are able to access the curriculum. Teachers need to present information through multiple modes and provide students with choices in how they learn the curriculum. There are countless ways of doing so—for example:

- Interest or instructional learning centers or stations
- Projects (individual, partner, or group)
- Technology
- Choices of or built within activities
- Tiered assignments
- Books on tape

Another key aspect of differentiating instruction is differentiating the output or the product—that is, how students demonstrate mastery of the content and their learning that has taken place. There are numerous ways to differentiate the product, including oral presentations, dramatic performances, demonstrations, designing a creative product, constructing or building something, and analyzing something. Chapter Two contains more on this topic, as do the activities throughout the book, which provide many examples of how to differentiate student products.

When differentiating the product, teachers encourage all students to draw on their personal interests and strengths. At the same time, they retain focus on the curricular components they deem essential to all learners (Tomlinson, 2001). Some teachers design project menus based on multiple intelligences. Others provide a project menu based on Bloom's Taxonomy (Heacox, 2002), which involve students in activities at various levels of cognitive domain.

Layered curriculum (Nunley, 2001) is an excellent source of practical ideas and ways to differentiate instruction based on a three-layered triangular-shaped learning model. Each layer represents a different depth of study of a topic or unit of learning, and students can choose how deep they wish to examine a topic, thereby choosing their own grade as well. The bottom layer, which is the largest, covers general content designed around meeting the district and state's core curriculum and standards. The middle layer is smaller and asks students to apply concepts learned in the bottom layer. The top layer is the smallest and requires a higher critical thinking assignment (Nunley, 2001).

According to Nunley, to earn, for example, a C in a biology class, students must select from a unit menu of learning activities for that topic of study. This section may offer a choice of fifteen activities, each worth approximately 10 to 15 points. Students can select from those choices and earn up to a maximum of 65 points through performance of activities at the C level. To be able to earn a B, students must also perform a lab. Students may choose one lab from a choice of three or four lab activities for 15 points. In order to earn an A, students must also do one A-level activity. A few A-level choices are provided, each worth 20 points. In this example, a student may earn a grade of D (40–55 points), C (56–70 points), B (71–85 points), or A (86 or more points). The author and creator of this model, Kathie Nunley, provides a wealth of strategies and guidance in layering curriculum in any subject or grade level to address the diverse range of learners in any classroom. We highly recommend visiting her Web site (www.Help4Teachers.com).

THE CHALLENGE OF DIFFERENTIATING INSTRUCTION

Teachers face enormous pressure to raise achievement and test scores, and for all students—the full range of diverse learners in classrooms—to somehow manage to meet or exceed grade-level standards. There is no question that this is a daunting task and expectation. Examining our teaching practices and making an effort to incorporate the components of differentiated instruction is one of the best means to achieve this goal. We can manage to tailor instruction to effectively reach and teach all of our students. However, teachers will be overwhelmed and discouraged if they try to do all of this at once in all areas of the curriculum. This is a process, and there is a learning curve in gaining the competence and comfort level at differentiating curriculum and instruction. We recommend starting by integrating some of these methods and techniques into instruction, and to do so in stages. Experiment with some units of study, and incorporate more and more strategies as you feel ready to do so.

MULTISENSORY INSTRUCTION

We must make every effort to teach the curriculum through multimodal approaches. Multisensory instruction is necessary to reach the diverse learners in classrooms. It involves incorporating a combination of auditory, visual, tactile, and kinesthetic strategies in teaching methods and in the ways students can learn the content.

For most of us, the five primary senses do not all contribute equally to our learning. Each of us has sensory preferences, that is, we favor one or two senses over the others when gathering information to deal with a complex learning situation. We can still process with the other senses, but most of us rely more on our preferences when we face a complex task (Sousa, 2001a).

Studies of sensory preferences in U.S. school children in grades 3 to 12 in the mid-1990s showed that nearly half (46 percent) have a visual preference, over one-third (35 percent) have a tactile-kinesthetic preference, and just under one-fifth (19 percent) have an auditory preference (Sousa, 2001a; Swanson, 1995).

Sousa (2001b) notes that retention of information also depends on the type of teaching method used. Studies in the 1960s by the National Training Laboratories of Bethel, Maine (now the NTL Institute of Alexandria, Virginia), provided these interesting statistics with regard to how well people on average recall material twenty-four hours after being taught through the following teaching methods:

Lecture	5 percent
Reading	10 percent
Audiovisual	20 percent
Demonstration	30 percent
Discussion group	50 percent
Practice by doing	75 percent
Teach others/immediate use of learning	90 percent

The obvious implications are that we need to present lessons using a combination of methods. Students need hands-on experience. They also need the opportunity to verbalize their understanding frequently during the school day. Cooperative learning situations with partners, triads, or groups of four are very effective for getting students to discuss their learning—to verbalize, share, and teach each other.

Students who have the opportunity to work together and discuss ideas with peers and are actively and physically involved and participating in the lesson will have the most success in learning and retaining the information taught to them. The activities and strategies throughout this book incorporate these learning principles.

THE ADVANTAGES OF COOPERATIVE LEARNING

The crux of differentiated instruction requires that teachers employ methods and strategies that enable all students, with their diverse learning abilities and differences, to be able to master the curriculum and content and performance standards. This is achieved through instruction, assessment, and learning activities that are meaningful and engaging. Cooperative learning is one of the best means of doing this, with decades of research that validates its efficacy. All teachers should be trained in best practices for implementing cooperative learning in the classroom. Teachers may mistakenly believe they are using cooperative learning when they simply have students working together in groups. This is not cooperative learning. In fact, students, particularly those with attention deficit hyperactivity disorder (AD/HD), often have difficulty learning and functioning productively in unstructured group work. Cooperative learning encompasses a high degree of careful planning and structuring and is an excellent vehicle for students to learn, including those with AD/HD. When students are taught how to work as a team and given the opportunity to learn and produce cooperatively with peers supporting one another in their learning, all can make significant academic and social gains (Rief, 2005).

Roger T. Johnson and David W. Johnson—researchers, professors, and codirectors of the Cooperative Learning Center at the University of Minnesota, Minneapolis—are national authorities and leaders on cooperative learning. They explain that all learning situations can be structured so that students either compete with each other ("I swim, you sink; I sink, you swim"), ignore each other and work independently ("We are each in this alone"), or work cooperatively ("We sink or swim together"). There is a positive correlation among goal attainment when they work cooperatively. Individuals in the group work together to achieve shared goals and maximize their own and each other's learning. Cooperative learning is supported by a vast amount of research as the most beneficial structure in the classroom (Johnson, Johnson, & Holubec, 1998).

According to Johnson et al. (1998), there are five elements of cooperative learning:

1. *Positive interdependence.* This is the most important element: that group members perceive that they need each other to complete the task and cannot succeed unless everyone in the group is successful. Positive interdependence can be structured by establishing and including mutual goals, joint rewards, shared resources, and assigned roles.

2. *Individual accountability.* Each member of the group must be accountable for contributing his or her share of the work. There are various ways to provide for individual accountability, including giving each group member an individual exam, observing and recording the frequency of each member's contribution, or randomly calling on one member to answer questions or present his or her group's work to the teacher or the whole class.

3. *Face-to-face promotive interaction.* Several children (usually three or four) are grouped together and arranged facing each other (eye to eye, knee to knee). Team members promote each other's productivity by helping, sharing, and encouraging each other's efforts to produce and learn.

4. *Interpersonal and small group skills.* Students do not come to school with all the social skills they need to collaborate effectively. Teachers must teach teamwork skills as purposefully and precisely as they do academic skills.

5. *Group processing.* Group members need to discuss how well they are achieving their goals and maintaining effective working relationships. Give time and procedures for students to evaluate how well their group is functioning. For example, after each session, have groups answer: "What did we do well in working together today? What could we do even better tomorrow?" In addition, teachers monitor groups, providing feedback on how well the members are working together.

BRAIN-COMPATIBLE RESEARCH AND STRATEGIES

In the past decade or so, we have gained vast amounts of knowledge and understanding of the brain, its functioning, and how we learn. New technologies developed by neuroscientists have enabled researchers to study and verify what many educators always "knew" to be important factors in learning and retention of information taught: that students learn, understand, and remember best when they:

- Are actively engaged and participating in the learning experience
- Are taught through multisensory instruction
- Are interested

- Feel the material or lesson is relevant and meaningful
- Connect what they are learning that is new to what they already know
- See the pattern and connections
- Experience an emotional reaction (emotions are engaged)
- Feel safe and comfortable rather than stressed
- Have time and opportunity to grapple with problem-solving situations

Also, an abundance of research supports the importance of and need for music and physical activity in schools. We know the positive effects of different types of music and rhythm on learning, memory, and emotions. We also know that movement breaks and physical activity are important for students. They raise and lower the levels of various brain chemicals and consequently have impacts on our brain states, including energy levels, mood and emotions, and level of stress. Physical activity aids learning and memory.

According to Eric Jensen (2003), one of the leaders in brain-based learning strategies:

An average teacher may be reaching, at any given time, 50–70% of students. A great teacher may be reaching at any given time 50–70% of his or her students, but a different 50–70% each time! In other words, the great teacher uses a variety of activities and instructional methods to ensure that they reach different learners at different times. Over the course of a week or a month, the great teacher will eventually reach all the learners. The average teacher, however, will still be reaching the same learners over and over again. The average teacher, too, will lump learners by ability into a bell curve at grading time, convinced that the differences among learners are because of differences in effort or ability, not because of the teaching! [p. 22].

Much of what we will be sharing throughout this book addresses the various components of differentiated instruction and brain-compatible teaching and learning strategies. This will include the content in many of the chapters, as well as the student activities that are differentiated for diverse learners. Let us strive to be great teachers, managing to reach and teach all of our students.

HELPFUL WEB SITES

Following are two interesting Web sites for brain information:

- Dana Alliance for Brain Initiatives, www.dana.org.

  The Dana Alliance is a nonprofit organization of more than two hundred preeminent scientists dedicated to advancing education about the progress and promise of brain research.
- Neuroscience for Kids, http://faculty.washington.edu/chudler/neurok.html.

  This Web site has been created for students and teachers who would like to learn about the nervous system. It is a tremendous resource, with interesting information about the brain, experiments, links, and much more. This site was developed by Eric Chudler, a research associate professor in the Department of Anesthesiology at the University of Washington in Seattle, Washington.

REFERENCES

Association for Supervision and Curriculum Development. (2002). *At work in the differentiated classroom: Facilitator's guide.* Alexandria, VA: Author.

Chapman, C. (2000). *Sail into differentiated instruction.* Thomson, GA: Creative Learning Connection.

Heacox, D. (2002). *Differentiating instruction in the regular classroom*. Minneapolis, MN: Free Spirit Publishing.

Jensen, E. (2003). *Tools for engagement*. San Diego, CA: Brain Store.

Johnson, D., Johnson, R., & Holubec, E. (1998). *Cooperation in the classroom* (7th ed.). Edina, MN: Interaction Book Company.

Nunley, K. (2001). *Layered curriculum*. Kearney, NE: Morris Publishing.

Pettig, K. L. (2000). On the road to differentiated practice. *Educational Leadership, 58*(1), 14–18.

Rief, S. (2005). *How to reach and teach children with ADD/ADHD* (2nd ed.). San Francisco: Jossey-Bass.

Sousa, D. (2001a). *How the special needs brain learns*. Thousand Oaks, CA: Corwin Press, Inc.

Sousa, D. (2001b). *How the brain learns* (2nd ed.). Thousand Oaks, CA: Corwin Press.

Swanson L. J. (1995, July). *Learning styles: A review of the literature*. (ERIC Document Reproduction Service No. ED 387067)

Tomlinson, C. (2000). Reconcilable differences: Standards-based teaching and differentiation. *Educational Leadership, 58*(1), 6–11.

Tomlinson, C. A. (2001). *How to differentiate instruction in mixed-ability classrooms* (2nd ed.). Alexandria, VA: Association for Supervision and Curriculum Development.

REACHING STUDENTS THROUGH THEIR LEARNING STYLES AND MULTIPLE INTELLIGENCES

How do children understand that it is all right to learn, think, and approach problems in different ways? How do they come to accept others and recognize that we all have strengths in some areas and weaknesses in others? Children learn that we all have our differences, which are to be respected, appreciated, and celebrated, by what significant adults in their lives model, communicate, and teach about diversity. This may indeed be one of the most important lessons parents and teachers can ever teach so our children will grow up to be tolerant, empathic adults who are capable of developing positive relationships in their lives and work successfully in a global society. One of the best ways to instill this understanding in students is to teach them that we each have our own uniqueness, comprising, among many other things, varying learning styles and multiple intelligences.

LEARNING STYLES

Students need to develop an understanding that we all learn differently and that there is no right or wrong way to learn. It is helpful if from the first week of school, teachers communicate to their students something like this: "Each of us has our own unique way of learning and may need some different kinds of help in order to do our best at school. Therefore, I will probably treat each of you differently throughout the year to make sure you all get what you need to be successful in this class." This kind of statement also addresses the common concerns teachers have about fairness issues when they provide accommodations, either academic or behavioral, for individual students or do something for one student that is not typically done for the rest of the class. Fairness does not mean treating everyone the same; it means providing the support, help, and opportunity each individual needs in order to have an equal chance to achieve success (Rief, 2005).

We all have different learning styles that affect our way of thinking, how we behave and approach learning, and the way we process information. Identifying our own learning style is an important first step for us as teachers to take in order to be most effective in reaching and teaching a classroom of diverse learners. A variety of instruments are available that may be used for learning style assessments by which we can glean insight into own functioning as learners—our own propensities, strengths, weaknesses, and preferences. It is enlightening to see the variety of styles among us—to better understand ourselves and our colleagues. This awareness of and sensitivity to learning styles helps us in the effort to reach and teach all kinds of learners, especially students who struggle academically, emotionally, and behaviorally in the classroom.

We all benefit from being exposed to a variety of strategies and approaches to learning. It is a wonderful discovery that there are many ways to do things, not just one right way. Teachers who plan instructional methods and activities, the classroom environment, and so forth by taking into account the diversity of learning styles in their classroom will be most effective in reaching all of their students. This is all part of what is involved in differentiating instruction.

There are a number of definitions of *learning style*. Rita Dunn (1988) defines it as "the way in which each learner begins to concentrate on, process, and retain new and difficult information" (p. 6). Learning styles have also been described as how each of us deals with ideas and day-to-day situations, our learning preferences and propensities, how we approach thinking, and how we best perceive and process information.

Modality (Sensory) Preferences

Not everyone learns in the same way. Our learning styles encompass a number of factors, such as cognitive styles and sensory modality preferences (visual, auditory, or tactile-kinesthetic, for example). *Modality preferences* are the sensory channels through which it may be easier for each of us to learn and process information. It does not mean that we have an impairment or weakness in the other modalities or channels, but that we favor a particular means of receiving information (input) or showing understanding (output) (Rief, 2003, 2005).

By far the majority of students prefer and perform better with visual and tactile-kinesthetic techniques. Yet in many classrooms, particularly at the secondary level, the primary mode of instruction is through lecture and discussion (auditory means) with minimal visual or tactile-kinesthetic strategies employed.

In this section, we examine what it means to be a visual learner, an auditory learner, or a tactile-kinesthetic learner. Again, it does not mean that students learn only through that particular modality but that is the channel or modality through which they may learn best. It is important for teachers to recognize the different types of learners, as well as the need to use a variety of teaching strategies that address students' diverse learning styles and draw on their different strengths.

The following descriptions of modality preferences and the characteristics that signal strengths in that area are accompanied by teaching strategies that address those areas of strength and allow students to learn more effectively.

Auditory Learners

These types of students learn best through verbalizing, listening, explaining, discussing, verbal instruction and lecture, read-alouds, studying with a partner or small group, and any cooperative learning format (partner, triad, small group). Encourage and provide opportunities for these students to participate in creative dramatics, speeches, debates, and reader's theater. They should be encouraged to use self-talk or verbalizations to help talk themselves through various tasks (motor activities, organization, problem solving, and review information such as written notes). Usually they do well with rhyming, blending, and word games. They learn well when information is reinforced through melodies, beats, and rhythms. Use a lot of poems, verse, songs, and jingles.

It is helpful to give directions and questions orally and have children repeat them. Practice spelling words orally, and use phonetic approaches in reading/decoding. Provide many opportunities to use listening centers, listen to books on tape, and participate in discussions. These are the students who should always be involved in small and large group discussions, partner talk, and other oral activities prior to independent work (for example, silent reading, projects, writing assignments). Provide verbal explanations (the what, why, and how) when modeling tasks or sharing your expectations.

During silent reading, auditory learners are often observed to subvocalize, that is, read aloud to themselves. They may need the auditory input to hold their attention or get meaning, so it should be permitted if it is not loud and distracting to others. Some students may use special devices that enable them to talk quietly to themselves without disturbing other students. The commercial product Toobaloo (available at www.superduperinc.com) is one such device. Use auditory cues to alert, get attention, and remind students—for example, use a brief verbal message such as "Listen . . . this is important" and nonverbal auditory signals such as chimes, a xylophone, or a clap pattern. A student with reading disabilities may also benefit from access to talking software and computers with speech synthesizers (Rief, 2005).

Visual Learners

These students learn best by seeing, watching, and observing, and they are strong in remembering visual detail. They often learn to read best through recognition of visual patterns in words (for example, word families such as *date, fate, grate, state, equate* or *ink, pink, wink, clink, shrink, blink*), structurally, and through the configuration or shape of words. Color cues are very helpful, and when these students need to recall information and the salient, most important points, we recommend using color highlighting, framing with a heavy line or boxing in, or any other visual symbols near or around that information you want them to attend to. For assisting these students with word recognition and spelling, draw lines around the configuration or shape of words and then color-code structural elements such as prefixes, syllables, suffixes, and vowels.

Visual learners remember best through pictures and images. Information should be written for them to refer to, and graphics, pictures, key words, or phrases in writing should accompany verbal presentations and directions. Use the overhead projector with colored pens, a dry-erase whiteboard with colored pens, or other such instructional tools. Visual learners need instruction to include many graphic organizers such as charts, webs, outlines, story maps, and diagrams. They benefit from writing things down, circling information, underlining, color-highlighting their texts, note taking, and practicing with flash cards. Use maps, puzzles, computers, PowerPoint, DVDs, and a lot of illustrations. Provide models, visual examples and exemplars, and a lot of demonstration. Teachers with access to images and video clips through Discovery Education unitedstreaming (www.unitedstreaming.com) have a very powerful visual tool for the classroom and ideal means of reaching and teaching students. Have available many books with pictures that accompany text, such as reference books with illustrations, even at the secondary level. Use sentence strips or index cards with information to sequence appropriately, word cards to arrange into sentences, and letter cards to arrange into words for this type of learner. Teach and encourage visualization techniques to aid comprehension.

In addition, be sure to provide a lot of visual prompts as reminders of expectations, procedures, and routines. For example, refer frequently to charts of expected classroom rules and behaviors, or placing a small card on a student's desk, with small pictures showing a student in his or her seat and working and a child raising his or her hand. The teacher can walk by the desk of an off-task student or one who blurts out without being called on, and tap on that picture as a cue or reminder (see figure on page 14). Prompt students visually: "Can you see what I mean? Look at this . . ."

Tactile-Kinesthetic Learners

These learners learn best by doing, touching, moving, assembling objects, and direct involvement. They are hands-on learners who need to be involved physically with projects and activities. They need to use manipulatives and have many objects to touch and use to help lock in learning through their sense of touch. They need many opportunities to participate in learning games, labs, drama and performance experiences, crafts, drawing, various arts, construction, and use of computers and other technology.

REMEMBER TO . . .

1

Raise hand.
Don't call out.

2

Stay seated.

3

Keep on task.

Provide for tactile-kinesthetic learning needs through experiential learning, role playing, simulations, field trips, and frequent movement opportunities.

Teach concepts with concrete examples that students can act out in the classroom. For example, the concept of conflict between protagonists and antagonists in literature can be demonstrated through arm wrestling. The symbols of greater than (>) and less than (<) can be demonstrated through use of a crocodile puppet or similar animal with a big mouth that opens up wide to face the larger number because it only "eats" the larger number.

Tactile-kinesthetic learners do well when they can tap out or clap out the sounds or syllables they hear in words. This often assists them through decoding and spelling. Provide number lines and a variety of writing materials. Tracing and using their finger to write letters and numbers on sandpaper, carpet, and other textures and surfaces are all beneficial techniques with this type of learner.

Kinesthetic learners do best when information to be learned is tied to movement. Try having these students study information by reciting and rehearsing while in motion (walking, riding a bicycle, bouncing a ball, jotting down notes). Use tactile-kinesthetic cues (for example, hand on shoulder) to alert, get attention, and remind student. Provide many movement breaks throughout the day and as much physical activity and active learning opportunities as possible.

Cognitive Style Preferences

Analytical/global learners and left/right hemisphere preferences are cognitive learning styles. The terms *left-brain* or *left-hemisphere dominant/right-brain* or *right-hemisphere dominant, analytical/global,* and *inductive/deductive* have been used in the literature for years to describe individuals' learning styles. For the most part, the left hemisphere of the brain governs the right side of the body and the right hemisphere, the left.

Left-Hemisphere-Dominant Learners

In most cases, the left cerebral hemisphere of the brain controls the functions of language, sequential thinking, literal thinking, logical and rational thinking, reasoning, and analysis. Reading, writing, and speaking, as well as time awareness and orientation, are generally left hemisphere functions.

Left-hemisphere analytical learners tend to be logical, sequential, linear processors who learn best by:

- Working from parts to the whole
- Making lists
- Using words and language to process information
- Following written directions
- Following schedules
- Following step-by-step instructions in a process

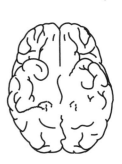

Right-Hemisphere-Dominant Learners

Right-hemisphere global learners tend to be simultaneous, intuitive, holistic processors of information who learn best by:

- Seeing the big picture (given examples of the end product)
- Focusing on the whole or main concepts first and then tackling the details
- Clustering, webbing, mind mapping, and similar other techniques
- Seeing patterns
- Using images and graphics
- Discussing the relevance and making connections, particularly at an emotional level

In most cases, the right cerebral hemisphere controls the following functions: simultaneous processing, imagination, sense of color, musical abilities, pattern thinking, spatial tasks, and intuition. This is the creative and emotional side of the brain. These individuals tend to be spontaneous, intuitive, creative, and random, and typically they have visual, tactile-kinesthetic learning styles.

Specialization Versus Exclusivity

Although research supports that the left and right hemispheres of the human brain have specialized functions, processing and storing information differently, both usually work together when learning as an integrated whole. Also, specialization does not mean exclusivity. These functions are not always exclusive to one hemisphere. Research shows that most people have a preferred hemisphere and that this preference affects personality, abilities, and learning style. The preference runs the gamut from neutral, with no preference, to strongly left or right (Sousa, 2001). Once again, preference for either hemisphere does not mean that we do not use both hemispheres. In tackling a simple task, we use the hemisphere that will accomplish it more efficiently. When we are faced with a more complex task, the preferred hemisphere takes the lead, although the nonpreferred hemisphere will likely get involved as well (Weisman & Banich, 2000).

MULTIPLE INTELLIGENCES

In his book *Frames of Mind* (1983), Howard Gardner, a professor of education at Harvard University, posed the theory that people use at least seven relatively autonomous intellectual capacities—each with its own distinctive mode of thinking—to approach problems and create products. According to Gardner's theory, called *multiple intelligence (MI) theory*, every normal individual possesses varying degrees of each of these intelligences, but the ways in which intelligences combine and blend are as varied as the individuals themselves (Gardner & Blythe, 1990).

Gardner's Eight Multiple Intelligences

When Gardner proposed his theory in 1983, he introduced seven distinct intelligences. In 1996, he added an eighth intelligence, naturalist, and is currently researching at least one other (existential intelligence) at this time. The first eight intelligences are as follows.

Linguistic Learners

These *word smart* individuals are adept in verbal and language skills (reading, writing, speaking). Lawyers, journalists, broadcasters, and writers are some professions that require this aptitude. Linguistic learners appreciate and use metaphors, analogies, and various forms of humor, and they play with language through word games, tongue twisters, and puns. People with strength in this intelligence are often good at playing games such as Scrabble, Wheel of Fortune, Boggle, and crossword puzzles. They may be skilled in debating, learning languages, and oral and written communication. They generally do well in school because they learn and can express themselves best through oral and written language.

Logical-Mathematical Learners

These *number smart* individuals are skilled at manipulating numbers, problem solving, and analytical reasoning; they are good at interpreting data, figuring things out, and exploring abstract patterns and relationships. Mathematicians, scientists, and engineers are some professions that require this aptitude. These individuals learn best through the opportunity to experiment, search for patterns, and make their own discoveries. They typically enjoy games of strategy such as card games, Rummicube, and Battleship.

Spatial Learners

These *art smart* individuals are skilled at visualizing, perceiving, and recreating aspects of the spatial world. They use their mind's eye to make mental pictures and are adept at drawing, constructing, designing, creating, building, painting, and imagining. Sculptors, painters, navigators, architects, and interior designers are some professions that require this aptitude. These individuals learn best through visual presentation (the use of images, color, pictures, and charts and graphs) and the opportunity to engage in artistic activities.

Bodily-Kinesthetic Learners

These *body smart* individuals are adept in physical activities and executing goal-oriented movements with their bodies; surgeons, athletes, dancers, actors, craftspeople, and mechanics are professions that fit into this category. They learn best by doing through active learning, movement, and hands-on activities. Bodily-kinesthetic learners often report that they need to be in movement to process new information, for example, by walking or pacing, acting out a concept, or manipulating objects. Sports, dance, crafts, and games such as charades address this intelligence.

Musical Learners

These *music smart* individuals appreciate, recognize, and are attuned to rhythm, melody, pitch, and tone. Musicians, singers, instrument makers, conductors, and composers are professions that require this aptitude. They should have the opportunity to listen and respond to, produce, and express themselves through music. They learn best through music (for example, melody, rhythm, and songs that teach). They often seek background music or engage in humming, tapping, and so forth when they work.

Interpersonal Learners

These *people smart* individuals are sensitive and attuned to others' feelings, moods, and desires and motivations. They are empathic and understanding of other people's needs and often are the mediators of conflicts and leaders. Teachers, therapists, clergy, social workers, salespeople, and politicians are some professions that require this aptitude. These individuals enjoy and learn best through interaction with others (for example, cooperative learning, collaborative activities, and working with partners and in groups).

Intrapersonal Learners

These *self-smart* individuals understand and know themselves well. They are introspective, often dreamers, and are able to recognize and pursue their own interests and goals. This important intelligence enables a person to use self-knowledge to guide actions and make decisions. Philosophers and theologians have strength in this intelligence. These people often prefer to work alone and independently and have ample time and opportunity for reflection and intro-spection. They tend to learn best when they work at their own pace, in their own space, and on individualized projects of choice.

Naturalist Learners

These *nature smart* individuals, recognized later than the original seven as having a special intelligence, appreciate, recognize, and understand flora, fauna, rocks, clouds, and other natural phenomena. They enjoy collecting, analyzing, studying, and caring for plants, animals, and environments. They are sensitive to interdependence within ecologies and to environmental issues. Ecologists, farmers, biologists, zoologists, landscapers, and botanists are some professions that require this aptitude (Kagan, Kagan, & Kagan, 2000; Nicholson-Nelson, 1998).

Impact of Gardner's Multiple Intelligence Theory

Gardner's MI theory of multiple intelligences has had enormous impact, affecting educational practice in classrooms throughout the United States and elsewhere. It speaks to what educators intuitively understand about children: that each individual is unique, with his or her own areas of relative strengths and weaknesses in various skills and abilities. Incorporating MI theory and practice into instruction and assignments is part of differentiating instruction and how we can best reach and teach all students. It is our job as teachers to recognize and capitalize on each student's strengths to motivate and enable him or her to learn. At the same time, we must provide the opportunities and training to develop and strengthen their competencies in other areas.

Numerous resources are available to teachers that address MI theory and practices. A few recommended books on this topic include:

- Armstrong, T. (2000). *Multiple intelligences in the classroom* (2nd ed.). Alexandria, VA: Association for Supervision and Curriculum Development.
- Campbell, L., Campbell, B., & Dickinson, D. (2003). *Teaching and learning through multiple intelligences* (3rd ed.). Needham Heights, MA: Allyn & Bacon.
- Gardner, H. (2000). *Intelligence reframed: Multiple intelligences for the 21st century.* New York: Basic Books.
- Nicholson-Nelson, K. (1999). *Developing students' multiple intelligences (Grades K–8).* New York: Scholastic.
- Teacher Created Materials. (1999). *The best of multiple intelligences activities.* Teacher Created Materials. Huntington Beach, CA.

Activities to Teach About Multiple Intelligences

Everyone has abilities in varying degrees in all of the multiple intelligences. Student Activity 2.1, The 100 Percent Smart Activity, at the end of this chapter is a powerful means of sensitizing students to the vari-ations among themselves and their classmates. Through this activity, after they learn about Gardner's theory of multiple intelligences, students identify their own perceived areas of relative strength and weakness among the eight intelligences. The activity illustrates through student-made individual pie graphs that we are all intelligent (100 percent smart), but that areas of smartness are different for each of us. In this activity, after class time is spent learning about Gardner's MI theory, everyone (including the teacher) makes a pie or circle graph using a paper plate. As noted on the activity page, there are two versions for carrying out the assignment: pie graphs with percentages determined and those without. Teachers may assign the version they want students to follow or allow students to make their own choice.

The pie graphs are designed to show the degrees of aptitude or strength students feel they possess in each of the eight areas to make up the whole. These "We Are 100 Percent Smart" pie graphs can be used to create a fascinating display for the classroom. When all the individual graphs are displayed on the wall, students can view the profiles of their classmates and various distributions of strengths and weaknesses among their peers.

Parents can also be asked to participate by making a graph of their own. They can make their own profile, and they can make one for their child showing how they perceive their child's relative areas of strength and weakness. This can then be compared with the one the child made of himself or herself. At a back-to-school night parent meeting, teachers may want to present some information about learning styles and multiple intelligences and then engage the parents in the 100 Percent Smart activity.

Throughout the school year, have discussions about being smart or skilled in different areas and help students to recognize areas of strength in the eight intelligences among their peers. One way to do this is to have students list a person in class whom they think is logical-mathematically smart. They have to write why they think that student is number smart and give evidence. Do the same for the other intelligences.

You may also consider making a chart with eight columns across the top—one column for each of the eight intelligences. Students place a sticky note with their name on it under the intelligence they consider to be their primary area of strength or smartness. Then they write paragraphs beginning, "I think I am best at . . ." about why they think they are strong in that intelligence and give examples.

Graphs can be generated with regard to the various multiple intelligences. For example, one graph could be "My Primary Intelligence"; another could be "Which Smartness Do I Want to Work on Developing This Year?" Use either a photo of each student or a sticky note with their name to place on the graph. These types of graphs can and should change throughout the year.

Giving students many choices of activities and projects rather than requiring everyone to do the same is an important way of differentiating to address the multiple intelligences of children.

Individual Choices for Individual Students

Allowing students to choose projects that tap into their various intelligences can enable them to work successfully. As part of a unit on World War II in Julie's classroom one year, students read one or two novels related to life during World War II and then chose a project to complete from a menu of some twenty options. Each project was intended to extend the student's understanding of this period of history, but the different possibilities drew on different intelligences and required the use of different modalities, such as interviews, writing, illustration, maps, reports, locating, watching, and researching. Following are examples of projects completed by three students with learning or behavioral challenges. Each student experienced great motivation and success when given this assignment:

- Josh, a sixth grader with AD/HD and learning disabilities, had a passion for music and ran his own business as a disc jockey at children's parties. Josh struggled significantly with written projects so wisely chose a project that tapped into his area of strength. The activity he selected required that he look for songs of that time period (around 1940) and compare them with songs of today. Building on his strong interest in music, Josh eagerly and actively participated in the project. He made meaningful connections between the music of then and now and brought in music for the class to listen to together. He became the class expert of the musical period of World War II.

- Peter generally took little pride in his classroom work. He rarely turned in his assignments, and when he did, they were generally sloppy or done with little apparent effort. His attitude was often one of, "Why do I need to do this?" For the World War II project, Peter selected an activity requiring him to draw aircraft of that time period and tell about each of the aircraft. Although he was not particularly strong in art, Peter was so interested in this project that he executed it with high quality and care and took great pride in his accomplishment.

- Amy was a student with learning disabilities in the resource program. She was also a very popular, social young lady with strong interpersonal abilities. Although she had difficulty in a lot of the academics in the classroom, when given a choice to engage in a project that capitalized on her strengths, she participated fully and eagerly. Amy interviewed a neighbor who was a Holocaust survivor. In spite of her aversion to writing, she wrote the responses to this most extraordinary interview. The presentation she made was so powerfully moving that no one who heard it will likely forget.

As we illustrate throughout this book, providing students with a variety of choices and options in their learning is critically important to motivate and engage them. Attention to individual learning styles, student preferences, and multiple intelligences must be addressed and practiced in classrooms if we are to reach and teach all of our students.

Classroom Jobs for the Multiple Intelligences

Part of establishing an engaging classroom environment is to ensure that all students learn to take responsibility for making the classroom run smoothly. Along with starting the school year by talking about Gardner's multiple intelligences, it is also beneficial to start discussions about employment opportunities. Tell students why you decided to be a teacher. Then introduce how they will all be given the opportunity to apply for classroom jobs. Following is a list of twenty-seven jobs aligned with the theory of multiple intelligences. Children should be able to choose something of interest that they would like to do. For instance, a student who loves to work with words and is a good speller might put down the Word Wizard job as a first choice, whereas a child who loves art might be most interested in the Interior Designer or the Awesome Artist position. A child who enjoys sports might select the job of Enthusiastic Energizer.

We recommend that the jobs be assigned for several months or a trimester rather than the entire year. If children know that they have choices and will be able to change jobs in a few months, they will become proficient and motivated in the tasks required for their choice. Sometimes a child becomes so busy in his or her job assignment that some personal assistants need to be assigned as helpers. More than one job can be assigned to one person, and several of the jobs require at least two people. Over the years, students and other teachers have contributed to the names and the responsibilities aligned with these jobs. These are only possibilities; some of the jobs may not fit in at all with your classroom management style, and maybe there are too many jobs that would be overwhelming in your classroom. Think about what is manageable for you, try to elicit thoughts and suggestions from your students, and make the jobs personal and fun. The more that students participate in deciding on the jobs, the more ownership they will take in making things work.

Have students choose the jobs that they think they would like and then apply for them. Learning how to fill out a job application takes instruction, and it is never too early to provide occasions for students to learn this skill. Early exposure to the application format can build confidence and enhance writing, spelling, and organizational skills. Have students fill out the application form in Activity 2.2 at the end of this chapter. Remind students that they should spend time thinking through their choices and writing neatly. Establish a standard of excellence, and stress the importance of making a good first impression.

When you read the applications, make sure the students have met your standards, and let them know what helped you make up your mind in "hiring them" for certain jobs. Remember not to assign jobs and then forget about them; the children need to feel that they are an integral part of the classroom and that their job is important. If someone is not fulfilling his or her responsibility, go over the job description with the student and give him or her a little more time. Only then change the child's position if it is not going well, especially if it is a job someone else is eager to do. Usually there is a place on a report card that indicates if a student has taken responsibility, and this gives some accountability and offers an assessment tool for just that.

Following are the multiple intelligence job descriptions for twenty-seven jobs. This list is composed of various jobs that have evolved over the years with student input from upper grade students in Julie's classroom.

Multiple Intelligence Job Descriptions

Job #1: Awesome Artist: Loves art and is willing to organize and locate art supplies when needed. Is responsible for the art center books and will offer suggestions as to what books might be added to the basket. Responsible for helping the art teacher with organization and cleanup. Assists teacher in organization of artwork for display. Is responsible for introducing a new artist to the class each month. Helps others with drawing for display boards and posters. Must be willing to help others, as well as be skilled and interested in art.

Job #2: Book Boaster: Reads extensively. Monitors the classroom library. Gives short book talks when new books come in. Assists with book orders and their distribution. Makes suggestions of new books that the class should purchase. Makes sure new books are marked with the genre label and placed in the correct basket. Oversees the teams that are in charge of maintaining certain sections of the library. Must be an avid and enthusiastic reader with good organizational skills.

Job #3: Classroom Communicator: Answers the telephone and is able to take messages correctly. Must make calls to the school secretary and outside locations. May be asked to call students who are absent from school to see how they are feeling and when they might return. Must be willing to help others call for classroom services and gives permission to use phone if the teacher is unavailable. Must be polite, have good manners, and be respectful using the phone.

Job #4: Computer Whiz: Has expertise in computers. Is in charge of computer rules, maintenance, and setup. Helps others who are having difficulty. Sets a schedule for computer use. Helps with computer instruction in the classroom. May be asked to help with PowerPoint presentations. Is patient and willing to assist in use and understanding of technology.

Job #5: Conservationist: Is willing to help in the recycling effort with paper, cans, and cleanup of the playground. Makes posters to remind students not to litter and to conserve water and electricity. Looks for books and articles about saving our environment and pollution control. Appreciates the need to protect and preserve the environment and is motivated to encourage others to do so.

Job #6: Culinary Caterer: Enjoys planning food preparation and serving food. Sets up a plan for an orderly, fair, and well-managed disbursement of food and makes sure that there are adequate supplies such as napkins, plates, and utensils. Assists students who bring in food for a party or celebration and helps the teacher when food is sent in by parents. Keeps track of needed supplies. Talks with school nurse about nutrition and food choices and shares those ideas with the class. Must have good skills in attending to details involved in planning food preparation, as well as attention to food-handling hygiene.

Job #7: Enthusiastic Energizer: Plans and leads simple exercises when the class needs to release stress or on rainy days. Leads the class in jogging around the field. Looks for sports books to add to the sports book basket. Watches for playground problems and reports them to the teacher. Will be in charge of choosing fair teams for sports activities. Must enjoy physical activities and have good leadership and people skills.

Job #8: **Equipment Expert:** Knows how to operate the video camera, digital camera, VCR, and television/listening center. May be asked to assist the computer expert with changing the screen saver and making sure all computers are working. Must have technological know-how and problem-solving skills.

Job #9: **Financial Adviser:** Assists in collecting money for classroom field trips and special occasions. Assists an adult with counting the money. Checks off names of students who have paid and labels and marks envelopes in which to place returned notices and money. Must be skilled in arithmetic and have efficient organizational skills.

Job #10: **Gracious Greeter:** Meets visitors and new students when they arrive. Helps them adjust to the classroom and feel welcomed. May be asked to give tours of the classroom or school or assist a visitor with supplies. Must be personable, friendly, and polite.

Job #11: **Helpful Housekeeper:** Is willing to do extra cleaning and pickup that is not done by classmates. Jobs might include cleaning up the teacher's desk, vacuuming the floor, wiping down the sink area, dusting the blinds, putting up chairs, moving desks, or washing off the desks. Is responsible for picking up team or individual point cards from tables and helping the teacher make a new seating chart. Must be willing to do manual labor.

Job #12: **Homework Helper:** Checks in and records all homework on a daily basis. Writes down names of students on the whiteboard who did not hand in work. Must have good organizational skills.

Job #13: **Interior Designer:** Is good at putting colors together and likes to arrange things artistically. May be asked to help with bulletin board design and door or window displays, or help classmates design, glue, or staple projects that are eye appealing. Knows how to use the paper cutter and teaches others the correct way to use it. May help with special schoolwide projects. Must be skilled in artistic design and willing to help others.

Job #14: **Mail Manager:** Sorts through all the special bulletins and mail from the office. Places all mail in student mailboxes and goes to the office to retrieve more if there are not enough. Places extra bulletins in reading center basket. Glances over each bulletin and gives a brief summary of what each is about to the entire class. Is responsible for organizing returned mail in paper-clipped or rubber-banded piles. Must have good organizational skills.

Job #15: **Math Aide:** Enthusiastic in assisting students who are having difficulty in math. Must be patient, understanding, and proficient in math.

Job #16: **Math Center Manager:** Keeps the math center resources, books, and materials organized. Introduces new book, activities, and games that are purchased for the center. Looks through catalogues for new items that could be added to the math center. Must be interested in and good at math.

Job #17: **Math Computer Researcher:** Researches Web sites and computer programs that will be supportive of students in math that might be used by classmates. Records listings of interesting Web sites at the math center. Checks with the computer lab teacher for computer resources and assistance. Must be interested and skilled at researching and computer literate.

Job#18: **Math Materials Distributor:** Hands out math manipulatives, graph paper, protractors, rulers, compasses, calculators, and other math materials as needed. Makes sure math materials are in working order and informs teacher if items need to be repaired or replaced. Must be willing to check and deliver materials in a timely manner.

Job #19: **Music Master:** Loves music and is in charge of setting up the CD or tape player for work and music sessions. Makes a schedule for open mike experiences. (For open-mike opportunities, students sign up for time to do a creative presentation in front of the class, for example, sing a song, read a poem, do a dramatic reading, tell a joke, or give a dance performance.) Maintains the music center and offers suggestions of what resources can be added. Hands out musical instruments and leads patriotic songs in the morning. Assists music resource teacher as needed. May be asked to locate music for class activities and ideas for musical experiences. Introduces different kinds of music to the class. Encourages others to bring in their music instruments for demonstration. Must have musical background and knowledge, and be motivated to share love of music with others.

Job #20: **Performance Director:** Helps organize readers' theater scripts and presentations, poetry parties, author's teas, and open mike. Announces upcoming assemblies, gives an overview of the performances, and writes brief summaries of the performances. Looks for plays and scripts in magazines and books for classmates to perform. Must be interested in theater and performing arts and capable of planning, organizing, and overseeing such events.

Job #21: **Rippin' Reporter:** Is interested in writing articles for the school or community newspaper about class activities. May be asked to write summaries of class activities for the school Web site. Must be a strong writer and excellent speller who is willing to put time and energy into representing the class to the outside world.

Job #22: **Science Sleuth:** Keeps a lookout for books and materials that could be added to the science basket. Helps others prepare and organize materials for science investigations. Must enjoy science and discovery activities and be willing to assist others in this area.

Job #23: **Sensational Secretary:** Takes messages to the office. Writes thank-you letters to visitors and consultants and reminder messages to students. Changes the date on the board each day. Assists the Homework Helper with assigned tasks (as needed). Must be a strong and neat writer and excellent speller. Must also be polite and willing to assist.

Job #24: **Serious Scribe:** Likes to write and is neat at lettering, printing, and cursive writing. Must be organized and be able to use a ruler to draw straight lines on unlined posters. Might be asked to rewrite charts, sentence strips, poster lettering, and word wall entries so they are exemplary for bulletin board and window displays. Might be asked to type up and format items for formal display. Must have neat penmanship and able to pay close attention to detail.

Job #25: **Squad Leaders** (two people): Act as line leaders and make sure that lines are well managed for movement throughout the school. Will stop at teacher-directed locations to realign their squads if necessary. Will make sure that the squads are well behaved and quiet as they walk through the school if the teacher is not visible when they move to library, computer, or physical education class. Must be able to take a leadership role and be respected by classmates.

Job #26: **Substitute Assistant:** Is responsible for helping the substitute teacher, student teacher, or other adult when the teacher is not in the classroom. Will be clear and concise in communicating with the adult so must know procedures, locations of items, and management techniques. Must be polite and helpful and interact well with adults.

Job #27: **Word Wizard:** Is a good speller and likes to use the thesaurus, dictionary, and spell-checker on the computer. Assists in teaching others how to use these tools as well. Classmates will rely on this person to know how to spell a word or help them look it up. They may ask the Word Wizard to proofread their work for spelling mistakes. Must have strong spelling, editing, and vocabulary skills and be willing to help classmates.

LEARNING STYLE ELEMENTS

Among the leaders in learning styles are Rita and Kenneth Dunn, professors and researchers who have developed a well-known model of learning style elements. The Dunn and Dunn Learning Style Model (2003, which can be viewed in its graphic form at www.learningstyles.net) describes twenty-one elements that comprise a person's individual learning style, organized into these categories:

- *Environmental elements*—an individual's preference regarding *sound, light, temperature,* and *design* in the learning environment
- *Emotional elements*—a person's level or type of *motivation* for learning (for example, intrinsic/extrinsic), *persistence* on a learning or instructional task, *responsibility* (independent worker or needing supervision or feedback), and need for *structure*
- *Sociological elements*—refers to how an individual prefers to work on a learning task (working by *self*, in *pairs*, in *small groups, teams*, with *adults*, or *varied*)
- *Physiological elements*—includes *perceptual* modality preferences, *intake* (need to eat, drink, or chew while engaged in learning activities), *time* (preference for time of day to work on tasks requiring high concentration or effort), and *mobility* (need to move while involved in concentration)
- *Psychological elements*—*global-analytical* preferences in learning, *hemispheric* preferences, and *impulsive-reflective* style

These learning style elements are important considerations when planning instruction, assignments, and classroom environment. For example, a student with a neurobiological disorder such as AD/HD is affected in his or her learning and behavioral functioning by some of these elements and needs careful planning and adjustment of those key elements to ensure that child's school success. The section later in this chapter on environmental adaptations and accommodations highlights some of those adjustments that are beneficial for a student with attention difficulties or difficulty regulating his or her behavior. Other elements of significance for a child with neurobiological disorders would be the physiological elements. A hyperactive child, for example, has a strong need for mobility, and teachers must build in many movement opportunities during instruction to accommodate this need. A student with AD/HD, who has an impulsive style by nature, needs many opportunities to practice reflection, with reflective, self-monitoring activities built into instruction.

We recommend taking all of these elements into consideration to reach and teach all students effectively. Plan with these elements in mind when designing lessons and instructional formats, the daily schedule, classroom structure, room environment, and so forth.

Student Learning Style and Interest Interview

There are various ways for teachers to learn more about their students' learning style preferences, interests, and motivators. A number of surveys, questionnaires, inventories, and learning-style assessments are commercially available. They can provide valuable insight as to how one learns best. These methods are the most time-efficient tools for obtaining learning style information about all students in the classroom. If a teacher wishes to delve deeper and obtain information and hear directly from an individual child or teen about his or her learning style preferences, an interview format such as the following is helpful. Students taking such an interview tend to enjoy the one-to-one attention from their teacher and responding to questions about their likes and dislikes. The interviewer will need to record responses in direct notes, on a tape recorder, or a combination of both, and adapt the questions as appropriate (Rief, 1998, 2005).

Learning Style Interview

1. Think back over the past few years of school. Whose class did you feel most comfortable in? Tell me a little about your favorite classes—ones you felt successful in. What did you particularly like about those classes or teachers?

2. What are some of the best school projects you remember doing? Is there any project you did or activity that you participated in that you are especially proud of?

3. Do you prefer working in a classroom that is warmer or cooler in temperature?

4. When you are trying to concentrate in class or read silently, do you need the room to be completely quiet? Do you mind some noise and activity during these times when you are trying to concentrate, study, or read silently? Do you think it would help to use earphones or earplugs to block the noise? Would it help to have some music in the background or would that distract you? [More questions may be asked regarding music preferences and dislikes.]

5. I want you to imagine that you can set up the perfect classroom any way you want. Think about it, and tell me or draw for me how you would like the classroom to be arranged. Would you like the tables or desks in rows? Tables or desks in clusters? Tell me [show me] where you would choose to sit in order to learn best in this room. Where would you want the teacher to be standing when giving instructions?

6. Do you like to do school projects alone, or do you prefer to work with others?

7. When you have to study for a test, do you prefer to study alone? With a friend? With a small group? With a parent or teacher helping you?

8. In your classroom, if you had a study carrel [private office area or partition] available, would you choose to do your seat work in it if some other students in your class were also using them?

9. When do you feel you are able to do your best work and concentrate best: In the morning before recess? After recess but before lunch? After lunch in the afternoon?

10. Do you usually get hungry and start wishing you could have a snack during the school day? What time of day do you usually start getting hungry?

11. If your teacher assigned a big project, giving you choices of how to do it, would you prefer to:
    - Make an oral presentation in front of the class?
    - Tape-record something?
    - Act it out?
    - Build something (for example, from clay or wood)?
    - Draw something?
    - Write something or keyboard it (or have someone else keyboard it)?

12. Do you think you are good at building things? Taking things apart and putting them back together?

13. Do you like listening to stories?

14. Are you good at learning words to songs?

15. Do you like to read? Write stories? Do math? Do science experiments? Do art projects? Sing? Dance? Play an instrument? Play sports and, if so, which ones? Use the computer?

16. What school subjects and activities do you usually do best in? What do you like about those subjects and activities?

17. What are the subjects and activities that you usually have the hardest time doing at school? What don't you like about those subjects and activities?

18. What kind of school assignments do you dread, or hate having to do?

19. Tell me what you think you are really good at. What do you think you are not so good at?

20. Do you ever feel you cannot concentrate in class and have problems paying attention? What kinds of things distract you?

21. How is it easier for you to learn: When someone explains something carefully to you or when someone shows you?

22. If you have to give directions to go somewhere or instructions for how to do something, is it easier for you to tell that person, draw a map, or write it down?

23. When do you concentrate best and prefer to do your homework: Soon after you get home from school? Have a break (play first) after getting home from school but before dinner? After dinner?

24. What are your favorite things to do at home?

25. If you had a chance, what would you love to learn to do? For example, if you could take special lessons or have someone work with you to teach you, what would you choose?

26. At home, where do you usually do your homework? If you had your choice, where in the house would you like to do your homework and study?

27. Pretend that your parents would build you or buy whatever you needed in your home for a good study space. What would it look like and have in it?

28. Do you like to be alone or with someone else around you when studying and doing homework? Do you need it to be quiet? Do you like having some music or background noise when studying?

29. Name five classmates you prefer to work with in partner activities. Don't name your best friends; give me names of students with whom you can productively get work done well.

30. If you were to work toward earning a special privilege, activity, or other reward at school, what are some things you would like to be able to earn?

31. What do you think is important for me to know about you?

32. If you were promised a special trip with your family and a thousand dollars for spending money if you got an A on a very difficult test (for example, a social studies test covering four chapters, with lots of information to memorize and learn):
    - How would you want me to teach it to you?
    - Tell me exactly what you would like me to do in class so that you can learn the information.
    - How would you go about memorizing all the information you were taught?
    - How would you need to study at home?
    - What kind of help would you want your parents to give you?
    - Do you want to study alone? With someone? Tell me as much as you can.

Environmental Adaptations to Accommodate Learning Styles

Environmental factors are an important element of learning style (Rief, 1998, 2003, 2005). Following are some strategies that are essential to effective classroom management and preventing behavioral problems. They also address the needs of diverse learners and accommodating individual learning styles.

Strategic Seating Arrangements

Seating is a big environmental factor for some students, for example, those with AD/HD. Providing preferential seating is an important accommodation. In most cases, a preferred choice of seating for a distractible, inattentive student is:

- Within close proximity to the teacher and the center of instruction
- Within easy access for cueing, prompting, monitoring, and supervising
- Desk positioned so the teacher can easily and frequently make eye contact with student
- Surrounded by well-focused peers (if possible)
- Away from (whenever possible) distracting locations or high-traffic areas such as doors, windows, learning centers, pencil sharpeners, and heating or air-conditioning units

Disruptive or distracted students often do better sitting at an individual desk rather than at a group table. Physically arrange the classroom with options for seating, for example, single-desk options as opposed to two-person desks or tables for students who need more buffer space.

In many classrooms, the desks are arranged in clusters with students facing each other to facilitate teamwork and cooperative activities. Distractible or disruptive students may do better with other desk formations, such as: E-shaped, U-shaped or horseshoes, or staggered rows (for example, groups of four students per row in the center and slanted groups of two students per row on the peripheries).

The key to furniture arrangement is the ability of the teacher to easily access (with as few steps as possible) each student without obstruction. The best classroom management strategy is teacher proximity: moving among the students, monitoring, cueing, and giving feedback.

If you are able to have some flexibility in providing choices and options as to where and how students do their work, it is very helpful for some students. For example, some students, such as those with AD/HD, have difficulty working in their seats at their desks. Here are some options that have been found helpful and can increase student productivity and on-task behavior:

- Allowing a child to sit on a beanbag chair with paper attached to a clipboard may increase productivity and motivation.
- Provide an alternative desk or chair in the room (two-seat method).
- Permit a student who cannot sit for very long to stand near the desk while working at certain times (if this is productive).

In addition:

- Be open, flexible, and willing to make changes in seating when needed. Be responsive to student complaints about their seating, and honor reasonable requests to move.
- Have variation in desks, seats, and tables (single and double desks, rounds), and allow some students more desktop space.
- Allow students to move to a quiet corner or designated area of the room if needed.
- Provide "office areas" or "study carrels" for seating options during certain times of the day as needed.

Structure to Reduce Auditory and Visual Distractions

Permit students to use earphones to block out noise during seatwork, test taking, or other times of the day (Rief, 2003, 2005). Some teachers purchase sets of earphones to be used for this purpose or allow a child to bring to school his or her own earphones, earmuffs, or earplugs (which is preferable for sanitary purposes). It is encouraged that *all* students, not just students with special needs, experiment with and be allowed to use these tools.

One of the best environmental modifications for distractible students is provision of study carrels or office areas. It is very helpful to have at least three or four "office areas" in the classroom for use during seat work or other concentration time, particularly test taking. By making these areas desirable and available for anyone who requests using them, you are preventing them from being viewed by the class as areas of punishment.

Purchase or construct privacy boards to place on tables while taking tests or other times of the day to block visual distractions and limit the visual field. Construct desk-size, collapsible privacy boards with two or three pieces of heavy chipboard and duct tape.

Addition of Visual and Auditory Cues

The use of visual and auditory cues and strategies is important for reaching students of varying learning styles and for adding structure to the environment.

- Use colored signals (red, yellow, and green cards) to indicate the noise level permitted in the class at that time. For example, "red zone" means silence is required (for example, for test taking). Green zone may mean that quiet, inside voices are permitted.
- Use similar visual cues to indicate the degree of movement permitted—for example, "must be in seats" or "quiet, purposeful movement around the room is permitted."
- Use private visual cues: "look at me," "time to listen," and "no talking."
- Post all schedules, calendars, and assignments.
- Have pictures or a list of rules and daily routines (or use both).
- Provide a lot of visual prompts, models, and displays for student reference, including visual depictions of procedures, routines, and rules.
- Use tools such as timers or bells for signaling changes of activity. The visual CD Time Timer (available at www.timetimer.com), the overhead timer TeachTimer by Stokes Publishing Company (www.stokespublishing.com), and Time Tracker, the stoplight-designed timer by Learning Resources (www.learningresources.com), are highly recommended (Rief, 2003, 2005). See Chapter Ten for information about timers.

Using Music

Using music in the classroom is another environmental consideration. Music can be used during transitions to calm and settle a class, particularly after recess, physical education, or lunch. Music can be played quietly during work periods. For some students, music increases productivity. Music can be used for arousal and activating (when the class needs energizing, particularly in the afternoon). Many students enjoy and benefit from having music in the classroom; others do not and cannot tolerate it. Make provisions for both groups.

Experiment with background music at different times of the day and for various activities and purposes (for example, to calm and relax, motivate, and stimulate thinking). Try a variety of instrumental cassettes or CDs, including environmental sounds (for example, of a rain forest) and different kinds of music: classical, jazz, and show tunes, for example. (More about music in the classroom is discussed in Chapter Fifteen.)

Accommodations to Support Physical and Sensory Needs

Be sensitive to the physical needs of students that may interfere with learning: the need for a drink of water, snacks, use of the restroom. Consider allowing students to bring a bottle of water to school. Some teachers ask students to keep their water bottle in a sock cut to fit around the bottom of the bottle. This helps identify whose bottle it is and reduces leaks. Teachers may also want to keep some healthy snack food available.

Provide for students' physiological need for mobility. Build in many movement opportunities throughout instruction. Try to avoid using the loss of recess time as a consequence for misbehavior or incomplete work. Also, build in stretch breaks or exercise breaks after the students have been sitting any length of time (Rief, 2003, 2005).

Other Sensory Input in the Environment

Colors are known to have effects on behavior. Teachers may want to consider use of certain colors for specific purposes. For example, orange, purple, and red raise levels of alertness. For relaxation, pale blue or green, light pink, lavender, peach, or rose are recommended. In general, cool hues such as blue are relaxing (Karges-Bone, 1996).

There has been research in aromatherapy regarding the use of scent to create or change behavior. The following are scents that apparently are good for alertness or attention: peppermint, wintergreen, pine, lemon, eucalyptus, and spearmint. Aromatherapists say the fragrances of chamomile, jasmine, lavender, sandalwood, marjoram, and honeysuckle have positive effects on relaxation or reflection (Karges-Bone, 1996).

Because of individual sensitivities to different scents or possible allergies, teachers have to use these cautiously in the classroom. However, they could also give parents information for experimenting with some of the fragrances that enhance alertness at homework time.

REFERENCES

Dunn, R. (1988). Introduction to learning styles and brain behavior: Suggestions for practitioners. *Association for the Advancement of International Education, 15*(46), 6–7.

Dunn, R., & Dunn, K. (2003). *Dunn and Dunn Learning Style Model.* Center for the Study of Learning and Teaching Styles at St. John's University, New York. Retrieved Dec. 17, 2003, from http://www.learningstyles.net/n3.html.

Gardner, H. (1983). *Frames of mind: The theory of multiple intelligences.* New York: Basic Books.

Gardner, H., & Blythe, T. (1990). A school for all intelligences. *Educational Leadership, 47,* 33–37.

Kagan, S., Kagan, M., & Kagan, L. (2000). *Reaching standards through cooperative learning—English/language arts.* Port Chester, NY: National Professional Resources.

Karges-Bone, L. (1996). *Beyond hands-on.* Carthage, IL: Teaching and Learning Company.

Nicholson-Nelson, K. (1998). *Developing students' multiple intelligences.* New York: Scholastic.

Rief, S. (1998). *The ADD/ADHD checklist: An easy reference for parents and teachers.* San Francisco: Jossey-Bass.

Rief, S. (2003). *The ADHD book of lists.* San Francisco: Jossey-Bass.

Rief, S. (2005). *How to reach and teach children with ADD/ADHD.* San Francisco: Jossey-Bass.

Sousa, D. (2001). *How the brain learns* (2nd ed.). Thousand Oaks, CA: Corwin Press.

Weisman, D., & Banich, M. (2000). The cerebral hemispheres cooperate to perform complex but not simple tasks. *Neuropsychology, 14,* 41–59.

Activity 2.1

THE 100 PERCENT SMART ACTIVITY

In class we have been discussing the ideas and theory of Howard Gardner, a professor at Harvard University. He believes in the theory of multiple intelligences—that every person is smart in different ways. We all vary in our strengths and weaknesses in the eight areas of intelligence. We are 100 percent smart with varying degrees of smartness in each of the eight areas of multiple intelligence. As we have learned in class, those eight intelligences are:

- Logical-mathematical (math smart)
- Spatial (art smart)
- Linguistic (word smart)
- Musical (music smart)
- Bodily-kinesthetic (body smart)
- Intrapersonal (self smart)
- Interpersonal (people smart)
- Naturalist (nature smart)

Here are two circles, each divided into eight segments. They are examples of how two different people look at their own intelligences using Gardner's theory:

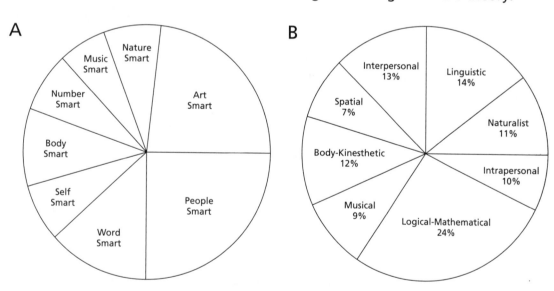

100 Percent Smart Activity Steps

1. Talk with your parents, and come to some agreement as to how much of each intelligence you possess. Decide how strong you are in each of the eight intelligences that make up the whole circle or pie chart. Sometimes your parents see you differently from how you see yourself.

31

THE 100 PERCENT SMART ACTIVITY *(continued)*

2. Choose one of two ways to present this information:

   Version 1: You will be given a white paper plate in class. Decide the proportion of each of your eight intelligences. Then shade in each segment using colored pencils, and label each in thin black marker with the names of the eight intelligences. (See circle A on page 31 as an example.)

   Version 2: Use a protractor and ruler with your paper plates. Show precisely the percentage of how you view your intelligences in the eight areas. When you make your graph using the protractor, you will end up with degrees for each of the eight sections. Make a ratio for each section using 360 percent as your bottom number (because there are 360 degrees in a circle). Then use your calculator to figure out what percentage of 360 makes up each of your individual intelligences. Your percentages should add up to 100 percent. Shade in each area with colored pencils. Label your intelligences, and write in the percentage for each of those eight areas. (See circle B on page 31 as an example.)

3. Have at least one member of your family design a multiple intelligence paper plate of his or her own. Discuss the similarities and differences between yours and his or hers.

4. Write a paper explaining why and how you came up with your conclusions about your 100 percent smart profile. It helps to do this after you have discussed your thoughts with your parents.

   - Include a paragraph about your area (intelligence) of greatest strength. Tell how you think this strength or smartness helps you in your life.
   - Comment on your area (intelligence) of least strength. Tell how this might be a hindrance in your life. Explain what you think you can do to strengthen this intelligence.
   - Compare your paper plate with your family member's. Tell how they are alike and different.
   - Look at your classmates' paper plates. Try to explain how you compare with them and your teacher. Discuss your uniqueness and why you are glad to be you.
   - Display your paper plate on the bulletin board in the student section for everyone to see. You may also include your family member's plate in the section labeled "Family Members."

Although many of us have one or two intelligences that are stronger than the others, our goal should be to seek ways to balance ourselves and build strength in other areas as well.

Most important, we should enjoy our uniqueness as well as appreciate and respect the differences in others.

THE 100 PERCENT SMART ACTIVITY *(continued)*

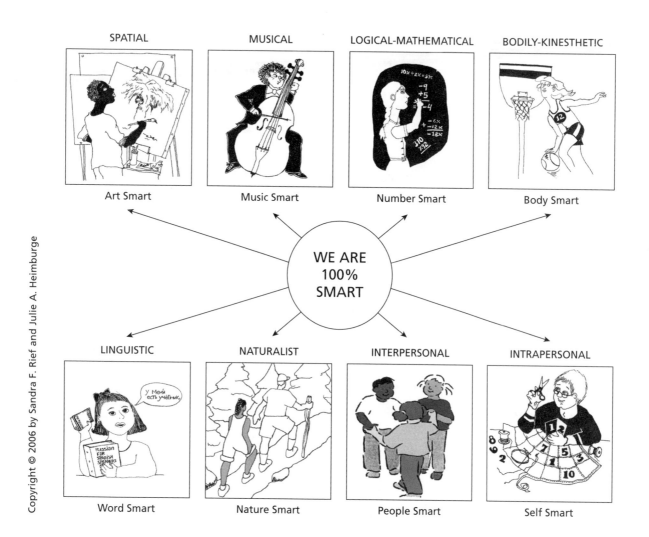

SPATIAL — Art Smart

MUSICAL — Music Smart

LOGICAL-MATHEMATICAL — Number Smart

BODILY-KINESTHETIC — Body Smart

WE ARE 100% SMART

LINGUISTIC — Word Smart

NATURALIST — Nature Smart

INTERPERSONAL — People Smart

INTRAPERSONAL — Self Smart

Activity 2.2
JOB APPLICATION

Room _____

Personal Data

Name: _____ Date: _____
Room: _____
Teacher's Name: _____

Please review all the possible positions and list your top three choices:

Choice 1: _____
Choice 2: _____
Choice 3: _____

Important Skills and Experiences

What makes you best qualified for this position?

_____
_____
_____
_____

What experiences, interests, and skills make you the best candidate for this position?

_____
_____
_____
_____

List memberships in any organizations or clubs that you participate in.

_____
_____
_____
_____

List any honors, awards, certificates, or personal achievements that you are proud of.

_____
_____
_____
_____

Chapter 3

UNDERSTANDING AND REACHING SPECIAL POPULATIONS OF STUDENTS

To be an effective teacher, it is imperative to have awareness, sensitivity, and understanding of the academic, behavioral, and social and emotional difficulties of some of our students. We need to be able to teach and adapt our instruction for all levels of ability and learning differences. We need to create a learning environment that will be motivating and comfortable for the full range of diversity among students. In today's classrooms all teachers will have students with attention-deficit/hyperactivity disorder (AD/HD), with learning disabilities (LD), and other disabilities, neurobiological, medical, and mental health disorders. In many classrooms there are students who are gifted and talented, and immigrant students who are English language learners (ELLs).

Teachers need to learn the instructional strategies, structure, environmental modifications, curriculum adaptations, and support that will allow all students, those with and without special needs, to achieve. First and foremost, we need to see our students as children. They are all unique, special individuals, but they are all just children, with far more similarities than differences. Some, such as those with disabilities, may present more challenging behaviors and learning difficulties that require more than average support and intervention. Teachers will need to dig deeper into their bag of tricks in order to reach them and help them learn. However, all students can learn. They all want to be successful in school. They all want to have fun, make friends, be accepted, and feel part of the community.

In this chapter, we focus on some of the research and information, common characteristics, specific needs, and educational interventions important for the success of the following populations of children and teens:

- Students with learning disabilities
- Students with AD/HD
- Students with other mental health disorders
- Students with Asperger's syndrome (an autism spectrum disorder)
- Students who are English language learners (also referred to as *limited English proficient* and *second-language*)

- Students who are gifted and talented
- Students with dual or multiple exceptionalities

It is important that if we have not found the best avenues through which to reach some of our individual students, it is our responsibility to seek assistance, learn more about their special needs, and keep on trying tenaciously and persistently until we do.

LEARNING DISABILITIES

The highest percentage of students identified as having a disability impairing their learning and school performance requiring special education and related services are children and teens with learning disabilities (LD). Most students with LDs who qualify for special education will be educated inclusively in the general education classroom.

Learning disabilities is a term used to describe a neurological disorder and set of conditions that interfere with the ability to receive, process, store, respond to, or produce information. It affects somewhere in the range of 5 to 15 percent of the population. According to the U.S. Department of Education (2001), approximately 5 percent of all children enrolled in public schools have a learning difficulty. These disabilities can cause difficulty with language, memory, listening, conceptualization, speaking, reading, writing, spelling, math, and motor skills—in various combinations and degrees. Each individual is unique in the combination of strengths and weaknesses and the degree of impairment.

Learning disabilities can be quite mild and subtle and may go undetected, or they may be quite severe, greatly affecting the ability to learn many academic, communication, functional, and social skills. Specific learning disabilities have been described as affecting individuals in ways similar to a telephone switchboard that has problems in the circuitry of the system, causing difficulties with incoming or outgoing messages, or both.

Learning disabilities may affect any combination of the reception or input of information into the brain (visual or auditory perception), the integration of that information in the brain (processing, sequencing, organization), the retrieval from storage (auditory or visual memory), and the output or expression of that information (communicating through motor skills or through oral or written language). Most children with LDs have deficits in their language-based skills: reading, writing, listening, word retrieval, and use. There are also nonverbal types of LDs, such as those affecting social perception and awareness, mathematics, and coordination.

Learning disabilities create a gap between a person's true capacity and his or her day-to-day performance and functioning in various ways. Individuals with LD have at least average intelligence yet underachieve to their potential in one or more academic areas, such as reading, math, or written language. This significant discrepancy between the person's ability and performance is not due to mental retardation, emotional disturbance, environmental deprivation, or sensory impairment such as vision or hearing problems.

Learning disabilities are considered hidden disabilities because they are not visible or apparent to others in most cases—at least on the surface. People with LD present with a puzzling picture because they appear normal and capable. Because of that, others may have difficulty understanding when and why certain skills and concepts are so frustrating for these children, teens, or adults to grasp and such a struggle for them to learn.

As a result, many people with LDs have been unfairly mislabeled as "slow learners" or "lazy," and they are often misplaced in the educational system. Over the past three decades or so, there has been much more awareness regarding LDs and far more recognition and understanding that these individuals are not lacking in intelligence and are not lazy or unmotivated. In spite of their learning differences, many are intellectually, artistically, musically, or athletically gifted.

Children who are evaluated and meet eligibility criteria under the federal special education law, the Individuals with Disabilities Education Improvement Act (IDEA), under the category of "specific learning disabilities," are eligible for a range of special education programs and services. Most students with

LD who receive special education and related services do so because of reading and language disabilities and are educated in the general education classroom.

Generally children are not identified or diagnosed with LDs until they are school aged. However, parents may suspect their child has some specific LDs even before he or she begins school. Listed below are some areas in which a person may have specific LDs and how weaknesses in those areas affect learning and functioning. Every individual with LD has his or her own profile of strengths and weaknesses. No one has impairment in all of the areas, just some, and to varying degrees of severity. The best approach in teaching children with LDs is to teach them through their areas and channels of strengths, while also providing direct intervention and support to build their skills, compensate, and bypass (when possible) their areas of weakness.

Visual Processing Disorders

There are several types of visual processing deficits (Rief, 2001), each affecting different aspects of visual information processing, that is, how the brain perceives and processes what the eyes see (National Center for Learning Disabilities, 1999–2005a). Any of the following areas may or may not be areas of weakness.

Visual Figure-Ground

This is the ability to recognize or identify a specific object or shape against a background. Children who lack visual figure-ground ability often lose their place while reading, skip lines, have difficulty locating a specific item or information on a printed page, or have trouble finding letters or words written on charts, lists, or the chalkboard. They typically have trouble completing work presented on crowded pages, often skipping or omitting sections. It helps to present these children visual information with an uncluttered background and to color-highlight specific information on the page.

Visual Discrimination

This is the ability to differentiate likenesses and differences in objects, shapes, and so forth. Visual discrimination is essential to reading, writing, and arithmetic. Young children who lack visual discrimination struggle with tasks such as matching letters, numbers, shapes, patterns, and designs and recognizing the difference between symbols or shapes that look similar. Students in third grade and higher may still have trouble recognizing and distinguishing between some print or cursive letters (b/d; m/n, v/w), mathematical signs (+/×), numerals with decimal points, and similar other visual symbols and information.

Spatial Relations or Position in Space

This is the ability to perceive objects in space and in relation to other objects. A child with difficulty in this area makes numerous reversals and inversions and typically has trouble differentiating between and remembering letters, numbers, and shapes that look very similar—the difference being how they are positioned or rotated in space (for example, b/d/p/q, 6/9, u/n, mom/wow, was/saw). Students in third grade and higher who have this weakness may still make reversals and inversions, have trouble with place value in math, and make errors in directionality (left/right; north/south/east/west) and spatial awareness (judging and planning spatially). For example, they may have messy project boards and written work that is illegible or poorly spaced and organized.

Visual Closure

This is the ability to anticipate and supply missing visual elements by using context clues—recognizing a symbol or object when all of it is not visible. Children lacking this ability may have difficulty in visualizing a whole and omit portions or details from objects or symbols when they write or draw. When younger, these children may have had trouble with dot-to-dot activities, identifying what an object is if part of the picture is missing (for example, a picture of half or two-thirds of a house or bird). Older students with this difficulty are probably weak at tasks such as putting together puzzles and spelling and writing because of their poor ability to visualize the whole word or product.

Visual Sequential Memory

This is the ability to recognize, recall, and reproduce visually presented materials in the correct order. Weakness with visual memory makes it hard to remember how to write letters or numbers without models to refer to and look at. When these children were younger, they had difficulty recognizing and recalling the same word on the page even if it appeared numerous times; they approached it as a new word each time they had to read it. Nonphonetic high-frequency words—those that are learned by visual recognition and not by sounding them out (for example, *from, of, said, where*) may still not come automatically for older students with this difficulty. These students, even in upper grades, may be observed to have sequencing errors in spelling (for example, *gril* for *girl*) and when reading multisyllabic words, as well as numerals when writing a series of numbers. In the upper grades, these students may still need a visual model of the cursive alphabet and frequently have difficulty learning and being able to recall information such as multiplication facts.

Visual-Motor Integration

This is the ability to use visual cues to guide physical movements. The child with difficulty in visual-motor integration may be clumsy and uncoordinated, but gross motor activities may not be a challenge. Typically students with this weakness have trouble copying material from the board or book onto paper. The younger LD child likely struggled when learning to write on and within the lines and align numbers when doing math problems. The older child with this weakness will probably still have poor spacing and organization when writing and computing. Paper and pencil tasks tend to be tedious and frustrating for them.

Visual Association

This is the ability to make sense out of or relate visual symbols in a meaningful way. Children with problems in this area may have difficulties reading and interpreting graphs, maps, and charts and seeing how objects that are related go together.

Auditory Processing Disorders

Auditory processing disorders (Rief, 2001) affect how the brain perceives and processes what the ear hears (National Center for Learning Disabilities, 1999–2005b). Auditory processing deficits include several specific types. Some may be areas of weakness, while others are not.

Phonological Awareness

This is the awareness and understanding that speech is composed of parts (strings of separate words; words comprising a sequence of syllables; syllables made up of smaller units of sound called phonemes). Phonemes are the distinct, individual, smallest units of sound that are put together to form the words we speak. Phonemic and phonological awareness is a fundamental prerequisite to learning how to read and write. Children with phonological awareness difficulties have a hard time learning letter-sound association, and this difficulty impairs their ability to decode words with ease, so necessary for reading with fluency. It also affects encoding (spelling) skills.

Auditory Reception

This the ability to understand the spoken word. At any age, those with auditory reception difficulties are not adequately receiving information that is presented auditorily (in lecture, read-alouds, or verbal directions, for example). These students need supplementary modes of presentation and frequent clarification and comprehension checks.

Auditory Discrimination

This is the ability to distinguish one sound from another. Children with difficulty in this area cannot tell when some sounds or words that sound similar are the same or different (for example, pin/pen, fan/van, bus/buzz, mad/mat). Of course, it is common and typical for individuals for whom English is not their primary language to have some difficulty discriminating various sounds in the English language. Students with LD who have auditory discrimination difficulties are poor spellers.

Auditory Closure

This is the ability to anticipate and identify the whole when only part of the auditory information is presented. It involves tasks such as supplying missing words (for example, at the end of a rhyme) or word parts. It also includes the skills of auditory blending. When presented with individual sounds or phonemes of a word (for example, /m/. . . /a/. . . /n/), the child will not recognize that the word is *man*. A child with this difficulty cannot easily blend sounds into syllables and words. For example, when reading the word *fast,* the child may correctly sound the word out /f/a/s/t/, but not be able to then blend the sounds together to say the whole word. Or on hearing the word ham . . . bur . . . ger, the child may not recognize that word as being *hamburger.*

Auditory Sequential Memory

This is the ability to recognize, remember, and reproduce a sequence of auditorily presented (verbal) data in the correct order after hearing it. Children with this weakness have great difficulty remembering and following a series of directions, remembering telephone numbers and messages, learning months of the year in sequence, memorizing multiplication tables, and so forth. A deficit in this area often causes difficulty in reading and spelling because words consist of sequences of sounds. It is typical for children with this difficulty when reading or in spelling to sound out the word in the wrong order; all the letters or sounds may be there but out of sequence. Young children with this deficit often have difficulty learning and saying in sequence the alphabet, the days of the week or months of the year, and counting to 100 and higher.

Auditory Association

This is the ability to relate spoken words in a meaningful way to classify and categorize information heard. Children with difficulty often have trouble with listening comprehension—that is, making sense out of what they hear. They may have difficulty with riddles, analogies, idioms, reading comprehension, and so forth.

Verbal Expression

This is the ability to express ideas in spoken language. A student may be verbal but have weaknesses in vocabulary knowledge and use and various expressive language skills.

Nonverbal Learning Disabilities

This LD category is much less familiar and understood than language-based LDs. Individuals with nonverbal LD (NLD) often have excellent verbal skills and skills in decoding and spelling. Their cluster of symptoms involves dysfunctions in: motor skills (for example, lack of coordination, balance, fine-motor, handwriting), visual-spatial organizational skills (for example, poor visual recall, spatial relationships), and social skills (poor social judgment and interaction resulting from lack of awareness, comprehension, and use of nonverbal communication). The student with NLD has poor attention to visual and tactile input (Thompson, 2005).

Individuals with NLD do not accurately process information that is not verbal/linguistic in nature. They rely almost exclusively on their interpretation of the spoken or written word. This interpretation tends to be concrete and often appears to be rigid and lacking in flexibility, likely as a result of failure to incorporate information of a nonverbal nature into their understanding (Foss, 2005).

It has other symptoms as well:

- Focus on details, and not seeing the whole picture or understanding the main idea
- Tendency to process information in a linear, sequential fashion, not seeing multiple dimensions
- Not able to read facial expressions and body language and gestures, therefore missing the subtleties, and nuances of communication (Foss, 2005)

Dyslexia and Other Reading Difficulties

Chapter Four contains information about dyslexia, a common LD that impairs reading and other language-based skills, and addresses the research about learning to read and reading difficulties.

Strategies and Interventions for Students with Learning Disabilities

The most important first step is a thorough psychoeducational evaluation. Then use the following guidelines when teaching students with LD.

- Know the profile of the student's strengths and weaknesses.
- Capitalize on the student's strengths when differentiating instruction.
- Provide intensive, direct instruction in skill areas of weakness.
- When teaching students with LDs, incorporate explicit, systematic, structured instruction.
- Teach concepts and skills through multiple channels (multisensory strategies).
- Provide necessary scaffolds and supports.
- Explicitly teach learning strategies, such as study skills, mnemonics and other memory strategies, note taking, organization, and time management.
- Tailor instruction to the student's learning style whenever possible.
- Provide a high rate of guided practice and corrective feedback.
- Provide the necessary accommodations and modifications to access the classroom curriculum and meet grade-level standards.

ATTENTION DEFICIT/HYPERACTIVITY DISORDER

Attention deficit/hyperactivity disorder is the most common neurobehavioral disorder of childhood (Rief, 2003, 2005). It is also among the most prevalent chronic health conditions affecting school-aged children (American Academy of Pediatrics, 2000). AD/HD refers to a family of related chronic neurobiological disorders that interfere with an individual's capacity to regulate activity level (hyperactivity), inhibit behavior (impulsivity), and attend to tasks (inattention) in developmentally appropriate ways (National Institute of Mental Health, 2000; National Resource Center on AD/HD, 2003a). Estimates of the number of school-age children with AD/HD vary from 3 to 12 percent (American Academy of

Pediatrics and National Initiative for Children's Healthcare Quality, 2002; American Psychiatric Association, 2000). There are degrees of AD/HD ranging from mild to severe and types of AD/HD with a variety of characteristics; no one has all of the symptoms or displays the disorder in the exact same way. Symptoms vary in every child, and even within each child with AD/HD the symptoms may look different from day to day.

AD/HD is not new. It has been recognized by clinical science and documented in the literature since 1902 (having been renamed several times). Some of the previous names for the disorder were *minimal brain damage, minimal brain dysfunction, hyperactive child syndrome,* and *ADD with or without hyperactivity.*

There has been a lot of inaccurate information about this disorder and controversy over treatment. What is clearly known from an abundance of research is that AD/HD is not a myth. It is not a result of poor parenting or lack of caring, effort, and discipline. AD/HD is not laziness, willful behavior, or a character flaw. There is also no quick fix or "cure" for it.

Many children and teenagers with AD/HD slip through the cracks without being identified or receiving the intervention and treatment they need. This is particularly true of ethnic minorities and girls.

AD/HD exists across all populations, regardless of race or ethnicity. There are racial and ethnic disparities in access to health care services. As such, ethnic minorities with AD/HD are often underserved and do not receive adequate help and treatment (Satcher, 2001).

Types of AD/HD

The fourth edition of the *Diagnostic and Statistical Manual of Mental Disorders* (DSM-IV), published by the American Psychiatric Association (APA) in 1994 and more recently the DSM-IV-TR (text revision) in 2000, is the source of the official criteria for AD/HD, as well as other mental health disorders (Rief, 2003, 2005).

There are three distinct types of AD/HD:

- *Predominantly inattentive type.* This type is now understood to be more common than previously thought, and it is most prevalent in girls with the disorder. Those with this type may have some but not a significant number of the hyperactive/impulsive symptoms. Since these children and teens do not exhibit the disruptive behaviors associated with the disorder, it is easy to overlook them and misinterpret their behaviors and symptoms (for example, as "not trying" or "being lazy").

- *Predominantly hyperactive/impulsive type.* This type is rare but found most typically in early childhood when developmentally the inattention has not yet emerged as a significant problem.

- *Combined type.* This is the most common type of the disorder. A significant number of symptoms are found in all three core areas: inattention, impulsivity, and hyperactivity.

Part of the diagnostic criteria is that the child or teen displays a significant number of symptoms within the inattentive category, the hyperactive/impulsive category, or both of those categories. The symptoms must occur often, be evident from childhood, not be better accounted for by another diagnosis, and are maladaptive and inconsistent with the child's developmental level. In addition, the symptoms must be causing impairment in the child's life and affecting his or her successful functioning in more than one setting: at home, school, and social situations in other environments. The lists in the following boxes contain the symptoms or behaviors found in the DSM-IV (1994) and DSMIV-TR (2000).

DSM-IV Characteristics and Symptoms of Inattention That Occur Often

- Easily distracted by extraneous stimuli (for example, sights, sounds, and movement in the environment)
- Does not seem to listen when spoken to directly
- Difficulty sustaining attention in tasks and play activities
- Forgetful in daily activities
- Does not follow through on instructions and fails to finish schoolwork, chores, or duties in the workplace (not due to oppositional behavior or failure to understand instructions)
- Avoids, dislikes, or is reluctant to engage in tasks requiring sustained mental effort such as schoolwork or homework
- Loses things necessary for tasks or activities such as toys, school assignments, pencils, books, or tools
- Fails to pay attention to details and makes many careless mistakes, for example, with math computation, spelling, and written mechanics such as capitalization and punctuation
- Has difficulty organizing tasks and activities (for example, in planning, scheduling, and preparing)

DSM-IV Characteristics and Symptoms of Hyperactivity and Impulsivity That Occur Often

- "On the go" or acts as if "driven by a motor"
- Leaves seat in classroom or in other situations in which remaining seated is expected
- Runs about or climbs excessively in situations in which it is inappropriate (in adolescents or adults, may be limited to subjective feelings of restlessness)
- Fidgets with hands or feet or squirms in seat
- Difficulty playing or engaging in leisure activities quietly
- Talks excessively
- Interrupts or intrudes on others (for example, butts into conversations or games)
- Blurts out answers before questions have been completed
- Has difficulty waiting for his or her turn in games and activities

Other Common Characteristics in Children and Teens with AD/HD

Following are some additional behaviors common in individuals with AD/HD that are related to the core symptoms of inattention, hyperactivity, and impulsivity; their difficulty with self-regulation; and the use of their "executive functions," which are the goal-directed, management functions of the brain. Some of the executive functions that are often weak in children with AD/HD involve planning, prioritizing, activation (getting started on tasks), sustaining alertness and effort (to get through tasks), and working memory—which is holding information in mind long enough to act on it (Rief, 2003, 2005). Many of these behaviors interfere with academic productivity, peer and adult interactions, and the ability to work and play cooperatively with classmates:

- Off-task behavior; lack of productivity and work production
- Not getting started on assigned tasks or getting very little work done without someone monitoring and focusing to the task
- Poor goal-directed behavior

- Forgetful; poor working memory
- Poor listening and communication (for example, does not follow directions, is easily pulled off topic in conversations, does not focus on the speaker)
- Difficulty sustaining level of alertness to tasks that are tedious, perceived as boring, or not of one's choosing—hence, many incomplete, late, or undone assignments
- Tunes out, daydreams, may appear "spacey"
- Gets bored easily
- Inconsistent performance; one day is able to perform a task and the next day cannot; the student is "consistently inconsistent"
- Cannot sit still (jumps up and out of chair, falls out of chair, sits on knees, or stands by desk)
- A high degree of unnecessary movement (paces, taps feet, drums fingers)
- Intrudes in other people's space; difficulty staying within own boundaries
- Cannot wait or delay gratification; wants things now
- Knows the rules and consequences but repeatedly makes the same errors or infractions of rules
- A greater challenge to motivate and discipline: gets bored easily; does not respond as well to rewards and punishments effective for most other students
- Gets in trouble because he or she cannot stop and think before acting—in other words, responds first and thinks later
- Difficulty standing in lines; keeping hands, feet, and objects to self; and being in situations where he or she must wait patiently
- Does not think or worry about consequences, so tends to be fearless or gravitate to high-risk behavior—hence, a high frequency of injuries
- Difficulty inhibiting what he or she says and making tactless comments; says whatever pops into his or her head and talks back to authority figures
- Constantly drawn to something more interesting or stimulating in the environment
- A high degree of emotionality: temper outbursts, quick to anger, gets upset, irritable, moody
- Becomes easily overstimulated and excitable and has difficulty calming self and settling down
- Poor coping skills and handling of negative emotions (frustration, anger)
- Overreactive: easily provoked to fighting and inappropriate means of resolving conflicts

Statistics and Risk Factors

AD/HD is associated with a number of risk factors. Compared to their peers of the same age, youth with AD/HD experience more serious accidents, hospitalizations, and significantly higher medical costs than children without the disorder (Centers for Disease Control and Prevention, 2005). Numerous studies suggest that children and teens diagnosed with AD/HD but are *untreated* for their disorder compared to those of the same age and developmental level who do not have AD/HD have more school failure and dropout; underachievement and underperformance at school and work; rejection, ridicule, and punishment; trouble socially and emotionally; delinquency and altercations with the law; engagement in antisocial activities; teen pregnancy and sexually transmitted diseases; and earlier experimentation and higher use of alcohol, tobacco, and illicit drugs (Barkley et al., 2002; Barkley, 2002).

With regard to the academic impact of AD/HD, Russell Barkley (2000) points out that almost 35 percent of children with AD/HD quit school before completion, up to 58 percent have failed at least one grade in school, and at least three times as many teens with AD/HD as those without have failed a grade, been suspended, or been expelled from school. Clearly, without early identification, appropriate treatment, and necessary supports and accommodations, AD/HD can result in serious consequences. When it comes to academics, every child or teen with AD/HD presents a unique profile of learning strengths and weaknesses. AD/HD-related symptoms may or may not be problematic, and if so to varying degrees. Due to the core symptoms and executive functioning weaknesses associated with AD/HD, however, children and teens with attention deficit disorders often display some or many of the following challenges.

Reading Difficulties

- Cannot stay focused on what he or she is reading (especially if the text is difficult, lengthy, boring, or not reading material of the student's choice), resulting in having to read the same material several times to sink in; losing place when reading; missing important details, causing spotty comprehension
- Forgets what he or she is reading (limited recall) and needs to reread frequently

Writing Difficulties

- Difficulty planning and organizing for the writing assignment
- Off topic as a result of losing train of thought
- Minimal written output and production
- Slow speed of output or production, often taking two or three times longer (or more) to execute on paper what is typical for the average student of that age or grade
- Written work lacks attention to details (for example, incorrect capitalization, punctuation, or spelling; incomplete sentences) and poor editing skills
- Poor fine motor and handwriting skills
- Written work is messy and difficult to decipher (poorly organized and spaced)
- Struggles with and avoids paper-and-pencil tasks

Difficulties with Mathematics

- Numerous computational errors because of inattention to operational signs ($+$, $-$, $\times$, $\div$), decimal points, and so forth
- Poor problem solving due to inability to sustain the focus to complete all steps of the problem with accuracy
- Math weaknesses in holding information long enough to work through multiple steps of a problem; learning and retrieving quickly and accurately the basic facts and multiplication tables; remembering procedures and algorithms

Difficulties with Organization and Time Management

- Being unprepared with materials and textbooks needed for school work and homework
- Disorganized work space, locker, and notebooks; loses or misplaces important materials and belongings
- Poor planning for assignments and projects
- Lack of awareness or sense of time; hence, poor estimation of time required to pace self adequately to complete tasks
- Procrastination; therefore misses deadlines and due dates
- Poor study skills and habits, which significantly affect classwork and homework success

Making the Diagnosis: A Comprehensive Evaluation for AD/HD

The diagnosis of AD/HD is not a simple process (Rief, 1998, 2003, 2005). It is made by a qualified professional by gathering and synthesizing information obtained from multiple sources in order to determine if there is enough evidence to conclude that the child meets all of the criteria for having AD/HD. A critical part of the diagnostic process is taking a thorough history. The history is obtained through interviewing the parents, use of questionnaires (generally filled out by parents prior to office visits), and review of previous medical and school records.

Another key part of the diagnostic process is reviewing information supplied by the school that indicates past and current student academic, behavioral, and social performance. No one is in a better position than the teacher to report on the child's school performance compared to other children of that age and grade. This includes the teacher's observations, perceptions, and objective information regarding the child's academic productivity and social, emotional, and behavioral functioning. Teachers may be asked to report their observations about the child through behavioral rating scales, questionnaires, narrative statements, telephone interviews, or other measures. Information from the student's cumulative records is a good source of data indicating the existence of symptoms in previous school years.

Other components of a comprehensive evaluation for AD/HD generally are observing the child in various settings, a physical exam to rule out other possible medical conditions that could produce AD/HD symptoms, and sometimes other measures.

If the student is exhibiting learning difficulties and struggles academically, a full psychoeducational evaluation needs to be done to determine ability, academic achievement levels, and information about how the child learns. Approximately 30 to 50 percent of students with AD/HD also have coexisting LDs. Because of this high correlation between AD/HD and LD, if the child is having significant difficulty learning or with academic performance, it should be suspected that the child may have a learning disability, and a psychoeducational assessment needs to be administered.

The AD/HD evaluation and diagnosis may be performed by a clinician with information from the school to help make this diagnosis. But the school has the responsibility of initiating and following through with a comprehensive evaluation by school professionals if the child is suspected of having any disability impairing his or her educational performance. The school can provide support and services to an eligible child under either of two federal laws: IDEA, the federal special education law, or Section 504 of the Rehabilitation Act of 1973, a civil rights statute protecting individuals with disabilities from discrimination.

Multimodal Treatments for AD/HD

Once a child is identified and diagnosed with AD/HD, there are many ways to help him or her and the family (Rief, 2003, 2005). It is important to realize that AD/HD is not something that can be cured, but it can be treated and managed effectively. The best way in most cases is through a multifaceted approach: a multimodal plan of interventions tailored to the needs of that individual child and family (American Academy of Pediatrics, 2001). This typically includes a combination of medical, behavioral and psychosocial, and educational interventions, implemented as needed at different times in the child or teen's life. Children with AD/HD often do best with a combination of structuring of their environment (home, school, and other settings), medication, behavior modification and specific behavior management strategies implemented at home and school, educational supports and accommodations, and counseling of some kind, for example, parent counseling and training, family counseling, or individual (Goldstein, 1999; Rief, 2003).

An effective multimodal management plan is accomplished by a collaborative partnership of parents, educators, and clinicians (medical and mental health professionals). All parties involved in the care and education of the child must communicate and work together in establishing target outcomes, plans to reach those goals, and monitoring the effectiveness of any interventions.

AD/HD is recognized as a chronic condition such as asthma and follows a chronic care plan of action (American Academy of Pediatrics and National Initiative for Children's Healthcare Quality, 2002). This means looking at the long-term picture. Various supports and treatments may be needed throughout the person's lifetime or employed at different times of life as needed (assistance from educators, physicians, counselors and therapists, tutors, coaches). In addition, because of the long-term management, the treatment plan needs vigilance on the part of parents, educators, and health providers in monitoring and following up on the effectiveness of the plan. A multimodal treatment program may have the following components.

Behavior Modification and Specific Behavior Management Strategies

Behavioral intervention implemented at home and school has been validated by research as effective intervention for children with AD/HD (Hinshaw, 2000). Training teachers and parents in behavioral techniques, structuring the environment, contingency management systems, and home-school plans are very beneficial in effective management of AD/HD. The classroom and individualized behavioral supports and interventions such as those described in Chapter Six are recommended for students with AD/HD.

Medical/Pharmacological Intervention

Well-managed and monitored medication therapy, most commonly with stimulant medications, has been proven by an abundance of research to be a highly effective intervention for managing symptoms and improving the functioning of children and teens with AD/HD (MTA Cooperative Group, 1999; Adesman, 2003). In fact, stimulants are highly effective for 75 to 90 percent of children with AD/HD according to a report of the surgeon general (U.S. Department of Health and Human Services, 1999).

Counseling

Counseling can help the child, parents, and other family members understand, cope with, and learn new skills to better manage the problems related to living with AD/HD.

Educational Support

A variety of possible school accommodations and interventions (for example, environmental, academic, instructional, behavioral) can be implemented to enable the child to have better academic and social and behavioral success. This includes educational planning to address the child's individual needs and may involve classroom strategies and supports, plus other safety nets that may be available as part of the general education program at the school (for example, homework assistance, mentoring, academic tutorials, computer labs). It may also involve special education and/or related services (IEP) or a 504 accommodation plan to eligible students. (Students with AD/HD who qualify for special education often do so under the IDEA disability category of "Other Health Impaired.")

Physical Outlets

Examples are swimming, martial arts, gymnastics, wrestling, track and field, bicycling, dance, hiking, and sports. Children with AD/HD may benefit particularly from getting involved in a physical activity as a way to channel energy, increase motivation, and practice focus and self-discipline. There are also other physical and mental health benefits of exercise that are important for everyone. Team sports can also provide the opportunity to practice social skills and cooperative behaviors.

Support Groups

It is often helpful for parents to interact with other parents who have children with AD/HD. Parent support groups are excellent sources of information, assistance, and networking

Instructional Strategies and Accommodations to Improve Performance

See Chapter Seven for more strategies and accommodations to address inattention and distractibility. In addition, see Rief (1998, 2001, 2003, and 2005) and the video *ADHD and LD: Powerful Teaching Strategies and Accommodations* (2004). There are many teaching strategies that can be employed to enable students with AD/HD to be more successful in the classroom. Following are some ways to enhance the academic and behavioral performance of students with AD/HD.

Difficulties with Inattention, Distractibility, and Off-Task Behavior

- Employ strategies to engage students' attention and active participation in lessons.
- Differentiate instruction to boost interest and motivation.
- Provide multimodal lesson presentation.
- Provide environmental and learning style accommodations, such as preferential seating and use of tools such as privacy boards and earphones, to minimize distractions and optimize attention to task.
- Make high use of visual prompts, cues, and redirection to task.
- Increase the use of supportive partners or buddies to help students with AD/HD through, for example, reminders, focusing attention to task, and clarifying directions.

Difficulties with Inhibition and Self-Control

- Use proactive classroom management, for example, by providing clear rules, expectations, and procedures; anticipating problems; and structuring and planning for prevention.
- Carefully structure the student's seating among well-focused, tolerant peers or locations where the teacher can frequently and discretely prompt and cue the student.
- Use more frequent monitoring, feedback, and reinforcement through positive and negative consequences that are meaningful to the student or shortened time intervals to earn rewards for desired target behaviors.
- Use relaxation strategies, music, and other calming and diversionary techniques.
- Provide individualized behavioral supports and interventions. Examples are the use of notes between home and school, daily or weekly report cards, contingency contracting, response cost techniques, strong efforts to build a positive relationship with the student, and close communication between home and school.
- Provide specific training, for example, in anger management, conflict resolution, and social skills. Sometimes the school counselor, psychologists, or other school support professional provide such training. If it is not available through the school district, parents may be referred to other professionals or agencies in the community.
- See Chapters Five and Six for more strategies and accommodations to address issues with behavior and self-control.

Difficulties with Organization and Time Management

- Explicitly teach and provide tools for organization. For example, require the use of a binder, a backpack, a planner or assignment calendar, and color-coding strategies.
- Organize the classroom environment using designated areas, trays, files for turning in work, and storing materials, and provide direct assistance in organizing notebooks, desks, lockers, and filing important papers, for example.
- Teach, model, and consistently use daily assignment sheets, planners or agendas, or calendars.

- Check that the student has the materials, books, and recorded assignments needed before leaving the classroom at the end of the day. The teacher does this directly or assigns a responsible peer or partner to make the check.

- Provide structure and monitoring of any long-term assignments and projects—for example, by chunking them into a series of shorter assignments with incremental due dates, check points, and teacher feedback along the way.

- See Chapter Ten for more organization and time management strategies, supports, and interventions.

Difficulties in Other Academic Areas and Study Skills Due to Weaknesses with Executive Functioning

- Explicitly teach learning strategies (for example, how to use resource and reference materials, note taking, and test taking) and use of metacognitive strategies (for example, journal responses, learning logs) that engage the learner in thinking about learning, responding, and monitoring his or her own comprehension and production.

- Build in goal setting and self-evaluation in assignments and projects.

- Teach mnemonic devices, association strategies, melody, rhythm, and other ways to aid memory and recall of information.

- See Chapters Five and Ten for a host of academic and study strategies, scaffolds, and accommodations.

OTHER MENTAL HEALTH DISORDERS IN CHILDREN

There are a number of medical and mental health disorders that afflict students. As many as 20 percent of children and teens in the general population will experience a significant mental health problem (Office of the Surgeon General, 2000). Those statistics are significantly higher among children who have another diagnosed disorder such as LD or AD/HD. Among those diagnosed with AD/HD, by far the majority (estimated around 75 percent) have or will at some point have a coexisting condition such as depression, anxiety disorder, or oppositional defiant disorder, in addition to their AD/HD. These coexisting disorders often go undiagnosed, misdiagnosed, and undertreated. Part of the problem is that symptoms overlap for various disorders, and in many cases it is complicated and difficult to differentiate, diagnose properly, and treat.

It is important that teachers have awareness of these disorders, their symptoms, and ways to intervene to ensure children obtain the help they need. Classroom teachers need to be able to recognize symptoms that students in need of a psychiatric evaluation might display. When concerned about a student's school functioning (academic, social, behavioral, or emotional) and his or her possible mental or physical health, teachers need to share their concerns and observations. Consulting with the school psychologist, counselor, social worker, nurse, or administrator or requesting to be scheduled for a student support team meeting is recommended as one of the first steps.

In some cases, children with mental health disorders will be eligible for special education and related services (for example, if tested and their symptoms are to the degree that it is considered an emotional disturbance causing significant impairment in their learning and functioning). In other cases they will not meet eligibility criteria for special education.

Following are a few of the mental health disorders in children and teens who may be in inclusive classrooms (with or without special education services).

Oppositional Defiant Disorder

Oppositional defiant disorder (ODD) is a "disruptive behavioral disorder" (as is AD/HD) that is diagnosed according to the criteria in the DSM-IV. Five to 15 percent of all school-age children have ODD, according to the American Academy of Child and Adolescent Psychiatry (1999). It is a common coexisting disorder in children and adolescents with AD/HD. The prevalence of ODD in children and youth diagnosed with AD/HD is estimated to be from 30 to 60 percent (American Academy of Pediatrics, 2000; Children and Adults with Attention Deficit Disorders, 2001b).

Children and teens with ODD have a pattern of ongoing and frequent hostile, uncooperative, negative, and defiant behaviors that significantly exceed what is normal in children of the same age and developmental level. These behaviors must impair their functioning and significantly interfere with day-to-day functioning to be diagnosed with this disorder. Behaviors and symptoms may include hostility, defiance to authority figures, temper outbursts, noncompliance with requests made by adults, belligerency, inflexibility, disobedience, blaming others for his or her mistakes or misbehavior, persistent arguing with adults, bullying, often touchy or easily annoyed, spiteful, and deliberately annoying others (American Psychiatric Association, 1994, 2000; American Academy of Child and Adolescent Psychiatry, 1999).

It can be very difficult to teach (or parent) children or teens who have ODD and deal with their challenging behaviors. Teachers need the direct support and intervention of other school personnel in managing a student with this disorder. Often these are children who may have a diagnosis of AD/HD, and the ODD is not recognized or diagnosed. Children and teens with AD/HD who have not had effective treatment and intervention in many cases end up developing ODD, moving up the scale of disruptive behavioral disorders. Mental health interventions outside school, such as counseling (individual, family therapy), social skills training, parent training and supports, behavior modification programs, and other psychosocial interventions are generally recommended. Medication for AD/HD sometimes helps with the symptoms of ODD as well.

What Teachers Can Do

Students with ODD demonstrate behaviors that impede learning and social success and are at high risk for developing conduct disorder and delinquency and a number of other negative outcomes without appropriate intervention. The school should take steps to refer for a clinical evaluation when it appears that a student may have this disorder. Parents of children with AD/HD should be made aware that ODD is a common coexisting condition. When there are indications from parent and teacher reports that disruptive, aggressive, and oppositional behaviors are not improving with the AD/HD treatment plan, ODD should be suspected as a possibility. The child should be referred to a specialist with expertise in AD/HD and coexisting mental health disorders.

At school, behavior modification and contingency management techniques and individualized behavioral plans to motivate and reinforce contingently for cooperative behaviors will be important in managing the ODD student. For example, the use of a daily or weekly report card between home and school or response cost techniques described in Chapter Six should be implemented. In addition, many strategies and accommodations suggested earlier for AD/HD would be appropriate. A functional behavioral assessment is recommended for these students, as is a behavioral intervention plan based on the assessment.

It is very important to work in collaboration with the parents in home-school reinforcement systems to better manage the student's school behaviors. Teachers need support and perhaps training in how to avoid escalation of the student's behaviors. They need to recognize the stages of an acting-out behavior cycle and escalating behavior changes, and apply appropriate strategies at various phases of the cycle. For example, some behaviors can be prevented by planning to avoid various triggers, such as changes in routine, certain task demands, or seating next to certain students, or reduced by noting signs of agitation and acceleration and intervening accordingly. It is very difficult for adults to learn how to avoid and disengage from power struggles, respond in a thinking and not emotional mode, and so forth. Chapter Six offers suggested strategies for dealing with a behaviorally challenging student. Mentoring and relationship-building efforts are also recommended.

Depression

Depression is one of the mood disorders. Those who suffer from depression have what is referred to as internalizing symptoms rather than the externalizing symptoms of ODD or those who have the hyperactive-impulsive symptoms of AD/HD. Because they are not disruptive and generally do not disturb others, the fact that they are troubled and in need of help may go unnoticed, especially in a large classroom.

The incidence of severe depression in children is probably about 5 to 6 percent, although exact figures are not known (Saklofske, Janzen, Hildebrand, & Kaufmann, 1998). Among those already diagnosed with AD/HD, depression coexists in about 10 to 30 percent of children and between 10 and 47 percent of adolescents (American Academy of Pediatrics, 2000; Children and Adults with Attention Deficit Disorders, 2001b).

Some signs and symptoms to watch for that may indicate depression include a drop in grades and school performance, pervasive irritability, withdrawing from friends, sadness, self-criticism, change in appetite, feelings of worthlessness or inappropriate guilt, abnormal sleep patterns, poor concentration, fatigue, loss of interest or pleasure in almost all activities, disinterest in school, labeling of everything as boring, recurrent thoughts of death or suicide, significant weight gain or loss, increased anger or hostility, drop in school attendance, physical complaints (stomachache, headache), or drug or alcohol abuse (American Psychiatric Association, 2000; Cash, 2001; Zionts, Zionts, & Simpson, 2002). Many people think of social withdrawal and sadness as key symptoms of depression, but sadness is not always one of the symptoms. Be aware that anger and hostility can be symptomatic of depression in children and teens as well.

What Teachers Can Do

When you are concerned that a student may be depressed or if you notice an unexplained, significant change in behavior, communicate those concerns to parents and other school professionals (for example, the counselor, school psychologist, school nurse, social worker, or an administrator). Sharing your observations and any work samples that may be indicators, such as student writings or art work, to alert others is an important step in obtaining the necessary intervention. The school can help facilitate a referral for a clinical evaluation and provide the student and family with supports. Intervention for depression comes in many forms. A treatment plan may involve counseling, psychotherapy, medication, or involvement of community professionals and agencies.

At school, it is very important that the student has someone to talk to—at least one adult who will listen to the student and build a connection. Place the student in situations that are supportive and prevent feelings of failure, rejection, and stress. For example, seat the student near and partner in activities with friends or kind, supportive peers. Provide the structure and assistance to enable the student to do class assignments. Adjust the environment as needed, and make any accommodations you feel may be beneficial—academic, organizational, or behavioral. Provide the opportunity for the student to have some exercise during the day and positive social interaction. Take the time and make the effort to speak with and listen to the student frequently; perhaps have breakfast or lunch together, or meet at other times together outside class. Monitor the student's mood and behavior, and consult with support staff. It is also appropriate to request a student support team meeting to communicate your concerns with the team and parents. If there is any mention, threat, or concern about suicide, be sure to communicate this immediately.

Anxiety Disorders

These are other mood disorders with internalizing symptoms that affect children and teens as well as adults. About 13 of every 100 children and adolescents ages nine to seventeen experience an anxiety disorder, and girls are affected more than boys (U.S. Department of Health and Human Services, 1999). The following various behaviors or symptoms may signal anxiety disorders: excessive and persistent worries, fretting about everything, restlessness, irritability, health or somatic complaints, edginess, stress, fatigue, difficulty concentrating, sleep disturbances, and dread of doing things wrong. Although everyone gets anxious at times, when a child is overly concerned and worried so frequently and to the degree that it affects his or her ability to function, this may be indicative of an anxiety disorder.

There are various types of anxiety disorders: general anxiety disorder, separation anxiety disorder, panic disorder, specific phobia or social phobia, obsessive-compulsive disorder, and posttraumatic stress disorder. Depending on the type of anxiety disorder, children and teens experience significant anxiety and stress related to certain situations, such as separation from parents and social situations.

What Teachers Can Do

Anxiety disorders can impair children's school functioning—both academic and social performance. If you are concerned about a possible anxiety disorder, bring this to the attention of school support personnel and the child's parents so an appropriate referral can be made, if indicated. Clinical treatment for anxiety disorders may involve counseling and other psychosocial interventions and perhaps medication.

At school there are a lot of strategies, supports, and interventions that can be implemented to reduce the student's stress and calm his or her intense worries. Depending on the specific anxieties that are observed, preventive and supportive measures can be provided. For example, for social anxieties, set up buddy systems or peer partners with care, matching with classmates who may potentially become friends and who are most likely to be supportive. Orchestrate games and activities that will encourage but not demand participation in social interactions that the student may find overwhelming. Provide reassurance, direct teacher or peer assistance, and whatever accommodations might help to alleviate this student's worries about classwork and homework assignments. An anxious student needs to be in a structured environment with procedures, routines, and expectations that are clear and predictable. Music that is calming and relaxing might help, as well as movement and exercise opportunities during the school day. School counseling is recommended and other frequent student interactions with a caring, empathic adult.

Bipolar Disorder

Bipolar disorder, previously referred to as manic-depressive disorder, is now known to be far more prevalent among children than was once the belief. This disorder sometimes mimics AD/HD, resulting in an AD/HD diagnosis first, or can co-occur with AD/HD. The research suggests a 10 to 20 percent overlap of children with AD/HD having bipolar disorder (Biederman et al., 1996; Benoit, 2005), and some pooling of data suggests that between 57 and 98 percent of children who have bipolar disorder also have AD/HD (Geller et al., 2002; Benoit, 2005).

Diagnosis and clinical treatment are very important. Because many children with bipolar disorder are diagnosed with this disorder after they may have received another diagnosis first (for example, for AD/HD, oppositional defiant disorder, depression, or anxiety disorder), medications prescribed for treatment of other disorders, such as stimulants or antidepressants, may exacerbate their bipolar symptoms.

Bipolar disorder in children may look different than it does in adults. In children, there are rapid mood shifts, referred to as cycling, sometimes within hours, between extreme highs (manic states) and lows (depressive states). Children with bipolar disorder may display explosive, sudden mood changes, rages that last for hours, and psychotic behavior. Symptoms may include irritability, anger, snappiness, aggression, hyperactivity, a level of distractibility and inattentiveness, agitation, impulsivity and poor judgment, sleep difficulties (sometimes needing too little and at other times too much), periods of laughing fits, silliness, giddiness, extreme sensitivity to stimuli, prolonged temper tantrums, delusions and hallucinations, and signs of depression such as withdrawal from activities previously enjoyed, pervasive sadness, change in appetite, low energy, or thoughts of death and suicide. There are also periods between manic and depressive episodes during which the child is well and not experiencing such behaviors (Papolos & Papolos, 2002; Child and Adolescent Bipolar Foundation, 2002).

What Teachers Can Do

Help facilitate diagnosis and treatment by observing and documenting your observations. Indicate in anecdotal records or another recording system when you notice a student's mood shifts during the day and what types of behaviors the student engages in during times that might signal a manic or depressive state. As with any other concerns about a possible disability or medical or mental health disorder you have about a student, it is important to share these observations and concerns with parents and school support personnel and administrators.

The hope is that this student will be referred for a clinical evaluation in a timely manner and that your documentation and observations will be important in the diagnostic process. Be prepared to share objective information about what you observe: the duration, frequency, and intensity of specific behaviors; times and situations; your response and ways you address various behaviors and symptoms; and strategies and interventions you have tried. School intervention often includes special education and related services. Educational needs (programs, services, accommodations) depend on the individual child.

Because those with bipolar disorder have such extremes in their behaviors, you will need the direct support of and assistance from various school support personnel in modifying the classroom environment, designing and implementing behavioral support plans, and other interventions to enable the student to function in the school setting. When the student is in the low state, employ strategies we have already recommended for depression and anxiety. When the student is in the agitated and manic state, strategies such as those described for students with AD/HD and oppositional defiant disorder are recommended.

ASPERGER'S SYNDROME

Asperger's syndrome was first identified in 1944 by Austrian pediatrician Hans Asperger. Until fairly recently, there was little awareness or understanding about this disorder or the puzzling symptoms these children and teens display. As with some of the other brain-based disorders of which the child has no differing physical characteristics and has average to above-average cognitive ability (such as LD or AD/HD), students with Asperger's syndrome are typically among the mainstream in the general education classroom and may or may not as yet be diagnosed. The prevalence of this syndrome has been estimated by research as approximately one in three hundred (Stokes, 2006).

To someone who is not aware of the symptoms, a child or teen with Asperger's may just seem "different" or "quirky" and socially delayed or awkward. Frequently viewed as eccentric or peculiar by classmates and inept in social skills, they are vulnerable to being teased and scapegoated by other students (Williams, 1995).

Although the DSM provides a definition of Asperger's syndrome (American Psychiatric Association, 1994, 2000), many view it as providing an inadequate list of symptoms. Among the possible symptoms are indicators of a qualitative disability in social interaction (such as serious impairments in peer relationships, social or emotional reciprocity, nonverbal behaviors) and some restricted, repetitive, and stereotyped behaviors or rituals, such as rigid adherence to rules or routine, preoccupation with a narrow interest or parts of objects, or repetitive motor movement (American Psychiatric Association, 1994; Safran, 2002).

Asperger's syndrome falls under the category of pervasive developmental disorders (PDDs) in the DSM-IV, which also includes autism, Rett's syndrome, childhood disintegrative disorder, and PDD-not otherwise specified (Autism Society of America, 2004). Asperger's syndrome is recognized as a separate and distinct clinical entity from autism but is within the autistic spectrum of disabilities (Richard & Hoge, 1999). Although many of the symptoms of autism and Asperger's syndrome are similar, there are important differences. Both are classified as PDDs, which means impairments exist in social interaction, communication, and the range of interests and activities. Differences in the two conditions are found primarily in the degree of impairment (Sousa, 2001).

What distinguishes Asperger's syndrome from autism is the severity of symptoms and the absence of language delays. Children with autism are frequently seen as aloof and uninterested in others. This is not the case with Asperger's syndrome. Individuals with Asperger's syndrome usually want to fit in and have interaction with others; they simply do not know how to do it. They may be socially awkward, not understanding conventional social rules, or they may show a lack of empathy (Kohrt & DuMond, 2004).

Because autism is a spectrum disorder, with symptoms in individuals ranging from mild to severe, there are individuals who have "high-functioning autism." Many people still consider Asperger's syndrome to be synonymous with "high-functioning autism," but there are differences. Asperger's syndrome characteristics are more consistent with right-hemisphere deficits, such as a nonverbal learning disability, while high-functioning autism characteristics are more consistent with left-hemisphere language and communication deficits (Trevarthen, Aitken, Papoudi, & Robarts, 1996; Richard & Hoge, 1999).

Common Characteristics of Students with Asperger's Syndrome

Following are symptoms and characteristics of Asperger's syndrome (American Psychiatric Association, 1994, 2004; Richard & Hoge, 1999; Safran, 2001, 2002). As with other disorders, each individual is different. The child or teen has some but generally not all of the symptoms, and they vary in degree, severity, and resulting impairment. The characteristics listed below include areas of strength and early development that are often observed in children with Asperger's syndrome, as well as the skills and behaviors that are commonly areas of weakness.

Communication Skills

- Normal to above speech, vocabulary, and other verbal skills—with the exception of abstract language. Individuals with Asperger's syndrome interpret language literally. They often do not pick up on the subtleties of language, such as words with multiple meaning, jokes and puns, inferences and implied meanings, and figurative language such as idioms.
- Voice and speech patterns are monotone or stilted, sometimes sounding robotic.
- Poor conversational skills, with a lack of reciprocating in conversation (for example, listening, asking questions, responding appropriately).
- Poor eye contact and nonverbal communication such as body language.

Behavior

- A significant deficit in social interaction skills with peers. Individuals with Asperger's syndrome do not understand social nuances and frequently misinterpret social situations. For example, their skills of recognizing and correctly interpreting verbal and nonverbal cues used to communicate (such as intent, feelings, and emotions) are deficient, resulting in social errors and often inappropriate behavior.
- Specific and often unusual topics of interests that the child is extremely knowledgeable about, fixates on, and talks about incessantly, to the exclusion of almost everything else.
- May have sensory issues and react to sensory overload (for example, noise in the environment, tactile sensations such as the feel of certain fabrics or clothing).
- May have outbursts.
- Inflexible to changes in routine.
- A variety of socially inappropriate behaviors.
- May show a lack of empathy.

Learning and Academic Abilities

- Motor skill difficulties are common (clumsiness and stiff, awkward movements, fine-motor and handwriting problems).
- Often off task and internally distracted.
- Poor organization, time management, and study skills.
- Often excellent rote memory.
- Typically strong reading decoding skills; learned to read at an early age.

- Reading comprehension difficulties, particularly for abstract concepts, and making inferences and connections.
- Thinking patterns can be very rigid: concepts are viewed as black or white, with subtle variations almost impossible for them to understand. They tend to see situations from their perspective only (Richard & Hoge, 1999).
- Poor problem-solving skills.
- Often function at grade level or above.
- Typically exhibit strengths in visual processing skills, with weakness in the ability to process information auditorily (Williams, 1995).

According to Safran (2002), academic performance usually ranges from adequate to exceptional, but children and youth with Asperger's syndrome are likely to flounder and fail in possibly more important ways. With increasing emphasis on teaching methods that favor social interaction (for example, cooperative learning and other group work), the child with poor interpersonal skills and inability to read social cues will continuously test the patience of teachers and peers and be admitted to groups last, if at all.

Key Educational Supports, Strategies, and Interventions

There are many ways that educators can better reach and teach students with Asperger's syndrome and reduce the academic, social, and behavioral impairment resulting from their disorder. Teachers can maximize the learning and school success of these children by teaching through and using their areas of strength. Teachers can teach and model the skills the children are deficient in and provide the supports, services, and accommodations that address and improve their areas of weakness.

Social Skills

- Direct, explicit training in social skills and appropriate social interaction. Social skills training may be part of a student's IEP, provided by a special service provider. Social skills taught may include how to read social cues (facial expressions to convey emotions, body posture), social manners, the nuances of social behavior, and friendship skills (for example, sharing, taking turns and being reciprocal, giving compliments).
- Social skills should be directly taught through demonstration, role playing, and daily routine practice (Richard & Hoge, 1999).
- Classroom teachers will need to be explicit and provide demonstration and practice of behavioral expectations during cooperative learning activities and games that require social interaction among students.
- Teachers should seek opportunities to foster involvement of this student in social, interpersonal activities.
- Use of "social stories," such as those developed by Carol Gray (http://www.thegraycenter.org/ Social_Stories.htm), are helpful for individuals with Asperger's syndrome in learning how to respond to social situations. These teach a variety of social expectations and the reasons behind them. They are an effective technique for providing social information the child may be lacking.

Speech and Language Skills

These skills are often taught by speech and language therapists. Classroom teachers should follow recommended strategies and prompts provided by the speech-language therapist for carry-over in the classroom.

- Teach aspects of verbal discourse, for example, topic initiation, maintenance, and termination, and conversational turn taking (Richard & Hoge, 1999).
- Therapy may address the robotic speech through attention to rate, rhythm, pitch, and inflections in speech.
- Directly teaching the nuances of language (for example, idioms, expressions, words with multiple meanings).

Environmental, Behavioral, and Social-Emotional Support

- Provide preferential seating near helpful, tolerant peers.
- Reduce anxiety by providing a structured environment with clear expectations.
- Allow the student to use earplugs or headphones if he or she wishes.
- Consult with the occupational therapist regarding strategies, tools, and supports to address sensory issues and sensitivities that seem to be bothering the student.
- Provide for the need to "escape" sensory overload and stress from social challenges. For example, allow the student to access a "take a break" area—voluntary time away to a calming location.
- Teach calming and relaxation techniques.
- Use a lot of visual prompts and cues with regard to behavioral expectations.
- Prepare the student for transitions and changes in routine.
- Teach, model, and practice problem-solving skills.
- Watch for signs of other possible conditions, such as anxiety or depression. Share your observations with special educators and support personnel, and request consultation if the student is having difficulty coping.

Learning and Academic Supports and Accommodations

- Provide accommodations for fine-motor and handwriting difficulties.
- Provide frequent comprehension checks.
- Do not assume that the student comprehends because he or she reads the words with fluency or can repeat information back to you (Williams, 1995).
- Break down assignments, and provide frequent feedback.
- Provide organization, time management, and study skill assistance.
- When planning cooperative group or partner activities, carefully pair or group the student for best chances of social success.

ENGLISH LANGUAGE LEARNERS

Our schools are filled with many children for whom English is not their primary language and who are limited in their English proficiency. Statistics indicate that there were approximately 3.5 million limited-proficient students in K–12 U.S. schools in 1997–1998 (Macías et al., 2000). In many school districts throughout the United States, English is not the primary language for the majority of students.

These children are somewhere in the process of acquiring English-language skills and proficiency and are often referred to as English language learners (ELLs), English learners (ELs), or limited English proficient (LEP) students. In order to reach and teach these students effectively, teachers need to have basic awareness of how a second language is acquired, be knowledgeable about recommended practices for instructing ELL students, and provide the educational supports and programs to enable this population of students to achieve success.

Stages of Second Language Acquisition and Development

One of the most accepted approaches to teaching second-language acquisition (English to non-English proficient students) is the natural approach described by Tracy Terrel (1977, 1981). According to Terrel, there are four stages of second-language acquisition: preproduction, early production, speech emergence, and intermediate fluency.

The first stage, *preproduction,* is a silent period for the ELL student. During this time, the student is dependent on modeling, visual aids, and context clues to obtain and convey meaning. According to Salend and Salinas (2003), students at this stage process what they hear but refrain from verbalizing, which is sometimes misinterpreted as indicating a lack of cognitive abilities, disinterest in school, or shyness. Stephen Krashen (1981), another leading expert on language acquisition, developed several important hypotheses on the acquisition of language. According to one of his hypotheses, everyone learning a language goes through this silent period. This is the period before speech is produced in either the first or second language, when the child must listen and develop an understanding of the language before beginning to speak. There is a focus at this time on listening comprehension and building the student's receptive vocabulary.

During the *early production stage,* students begin to speak using single words and short phrases or sentences, two to three words in length. Activities in class should be designed to motivate students to produce vocabulary they already understand. The *speech emergence stage* occurs when students start to speak in longer phrases and complete sentences. Lessons and activities are designed to develop higher levels of language use and expand their receptive vocabulary. During this stage, the student is able to respond to literal questions that have been made comprehensible. *Intermediate fluency* is the stage students reach when they are able to engage in conversation and produce full sentences. At this stage they should be challenged to extend their language and use more complex sentence structure. Salend (2001) describes the additional stage of *extension and expansion,* during which students are developing even further in their language comprehension, employing more complex sentence structures, and making fewer errors when speaking.

Krashen (1981) also posed other hypotheses, including the "natural order hypothesis"—that grammatical structures are acquired in a predictable sequence, with certain elements usually acquired before others—and the "affective filter hypothesis" (1985)—that several affective variables are important in second language acquisition, which include low anxiety in the learning situation, high motivation, and self-confidence.

Krashen (1985) is also responsible for the *comprehensible input hypothesis,* which states that growth in language occurs when the learner receives comprehensible input, or input just beyond what he or she already understands. According to this hypothesis, it is the teacher's responsibility to provide speech modified to the point that the listener can understand the message and get the message across using visual or contextual clues, by dealing with familiar topics, using body language, and so forth. The input needs to be interesting and motivating and embedded in context so that the ELL student can move easily through the different natural stages of language acquisition.

There are levels of proficiency based on developmental stages of acquiring a second language. The California Department of Education (1999) delineates five proficiency levels of English language development (ELD):

ELD 1	Beginning
ELD 2	Early Intermediate
ELD 3	Intermediate
ELD 4	Early Advanced
ELD 5	Advanced

For example, third- through fifth-grade California ELD standards for listening and speaking comprehension include the following at each of the five proficiency levels:

- *Beginning.* (a) Begin to speak with a few words or sentences, using some English phonemes and rudimentary English grammatical forms (e.g., single words or phrases); (b) Answer simple questions with one- to two-word responses; (c) Retell familiar stories and participate in short conversations using appropriate gestures, expressions, and illustrative objects.

- *Early Intermediate.* (a) Begin to be understood when speaking, but may have some inconsistent use of standardized English grammatical forms and sounds (e.g., plurals, simple past tense, pronouns [he/she]); (b) Ask and answer questions using phrases or simple sentences; (c) Restate and execute multi-step oral directions.

- *Intermediate.* (a) Ask and answer instructional questions with some supporting elements (e.g., "Is it your turn to go to the computer lab?"); (b) Listen attentively to stories/information and identify key details and concepts using both verbal and non-verbal responses; (c) Make oneself understood when speaking by using consistent standard English grammatical sounds and forms; however, some rules may not be followed (e.g., third-person singular, male and female pronouns).

- *Early Advanced.* Listen attentively to more complex stories/information on new topics across content areas, and identify the main points and supporting details.

- *Advanced:* (a) Listen attentively to stories and subject area topics, and identify the main points and supporting details; (b) Demonstrate understanding of idiomatic expressions by responding to and using such expressions appropriately (e.g., "It's pouring outside.") [pp. 21–27].

Social and Academic Language

There is a distinction between social language and oral fluency, and academic language. According to the research, social language skills are acquired in about two years (Collier, 1987). It often takes up to seven years for children to develop and use the language skills that relate to literacy, cognitive development, and academic development in the classroom (Salend & Salinas, 2003). The term often used in reference to social, oral, and conversational skills is *basic interpersonal communicative skills*; *cognitive academic language proficiency* is the level of second-language proficiency that students need to perform the more abstract and cognitively demanding tasks of a classroom (Cummins, 1980, 1991).

Bilingual Education

Several types of bilingual education programs exist. These vary by state but typically include these (Harris & Hodges, 1995; New York State Education Department, 1989; Office of Bilingual Education, University of the State of New York, 1999):

- *Transitional bilingual education programs,* in which the primary language of the student is used for instructional support until some prescribed level of proficiency in the second language is reached.

- *Maintenance bilingual education programs,* in which the primary language of the student is first used, with a gradual transition toward the use of the primary language in some subjects and the use of the second language in others.

- *Two-way bilingual programs,* also known as *dual-language programs,* in which two languages are employed, one of them English, for the purposes of instruction, and which involve students who are native speakers of each of these languages. Both groups of students, English-language learners and native English speakers, have the opportunity to become bilingual and biliterate.

Terminology and Definitions

Various terminology is used in different states and districts related to second-language acquisition and programming. The following are a few of the more common terms:

- *English language development (ELD).* Refers to instruction designed especially for English learners to develop their listening, speaking, reading, and writing skills in English (California Teacher Association, 2004). ELD instruction aims to teach students to communicate in social settings, engage in academic tasks, and use language in socially and culturally appropriate ways (Linquanti, 1999). It follows a developmental scope and sequence for learning English systematically, moving from concrete to abstract and more complex levels of language. Students are grouped by proficiency level for ELD, based on assessment, during this period of instruction.

- *First language (L1).* The first or initial language learned by a child; also known as *native language* or *primary language.*

- *Language proficiency.* The ability to use the English language for both academic and basic communicative tasks (Loide, 1991).

- *Second language (L2).* Refers to the less used language, that is, the language that is not the mother tongue.

- *Sheltered English instruction.* Teaching of grade-level subject matter in English in ways that are comprehensible and engage students academically while also promoting English-language development.

- *Specially designed academic instruction in English.* Refers to instruction in a subject area, delivered in English, that is specifically designed to provide ELL students with access to the curriculum (California Teacher Association, 2004). It involves the scaffolding and strategies employed to provide comprehensible input so that ELLs can more readily grasp the content and master grade-level standards. In some states, such as California, sheltered English instruction is often called Specially Designed Academic Instruction in English (Linquanti, 1999).

- *Front-loading language.* Refers to deliberately preteaching the language demands of an upcoming lesson so that ELL students can access the content instruction (Dutro & Moran, 2003; Dutro, 2003). In California schools, front loading is an important component of a comprehensive program to build the English-language proficiency of students. It might involve preteaching vocabulary or sentence structures that will be needed for comprehension and participation in the lesson or activity.

Literacy Development in Native and Second Languages

Based on the literature reviewed on language literacy for LEP/ELL students, the research suggests a number of interesting points. There are universal aspects of literacy acquisition that are essentially similar for all languages. A strong and positive correlation exists between literacy in the native language and learning a second language, as skills and knowledge can transfer from one language to another. Students with the highest levels of native language literacy are those who eventually become the strongest readers in their second language. Valuing the native language and building on the existing knowledge of ELL students will enhance their cognitive and academic development. It is also important to provide interactive and collaborative learning environments with meaningful language and literacy experiences for these students that involve their higher-level thinking skills (Office of Bilingual Education, University of the State of New York, 1999).

Strategies for Increasing Comprehensible Input

It is important to be aware of our delivery of instruction and communicate in a way to make comprehension easier. Consider the following strategies.

- Provide multisensory instruction using manipulatives, hands-on activities, realia (real objects), and visuals (such as graphic organizers, charts, maps, and pictures).
- Slow the rate of speech, build in longer pauses, and repeat as needed.
- Paraphrase and rephrase.
- Use fewer idioms and pronouns.
- Modify language to be more comprehensible for the proficiency level of the student.
- Speak naturally but slowly.
- Provide a great deal of background information to increase comprehension.
- Draw illustrations and pictures to define.
- Teach through relevant familiar topics.
- Label objects in the classroom.
- Use gestures, body language, pantomimes, demonstrations, dramatization, and role play.
- Supplement oral directions with visuals.

Additional Strategies and Instructional Considerations

Use these instructional practices, as well, to enhance ELL/second-language students' learning and success in the classroom.

- Increase wait time for the student to process and respond to questions (give at least five seconds).
- Provide numerous opportunities to work with partners and in triads. In cooperative learning groups, mix the ELL student with English speakers or bilingual speakers as a team.
- Assign a student buddy to help whenever additional assistance is needed to understand directions.
- Foster a comfortable, low-anxiety environment that encourages risk taking.
- Provide peer tutoring.
- Preview and review material and lessons.
- Provide students with many opportunities to respond to questions and verbalize without ridicule.
- Use questioning techniques appropriate to the stage of language acquisition.
- Do not teach vocabulary in isolation; use several examples and move from example to definition, and back to more carefully prepared examples.
- Check frequently for understanding.
- Create an environment that gives the message to children that all linguistic and cultural backgrounds are respected, honored, and valued.
- Facilitate the ELL student's involvement in sports, games, and group activities. Through playing a game, for example, students soon acquire the rules as well as the vocabulary in context.
- Encourage communication attempts, accepting the student's effort. Give feedback on errors made in ways that are respectful and will avoid student embarrassment. For example, you may try correcting indirectly by restating the student's response using the correct form or provide corrective feedback regarding the error made at another time when you can do so more privately.
- Tap into the student's prior knowledge and background experiences.
- Teach directly (front-load) the language needed that we may assume the student comprehends but in fact does not. There are many such words (for example, *compare and contrast, describe, summarize, predict, sequence*) that we use throughout the school day that are essential for academic success.
- Provide specific learning support and accommodations to meet students' cultural, linguistic, and learning style needs.

One of the strengths of our nation is the diversity of our population. Immigrant children bring with them a wealth of strengths, talents, global perspectives, and motivation to learn and with great potential for educating us and enriching all of our lives. They also face communication barriers and cultural and academic challenges as they enter our schools and adjust to life in a new country and community. Educators must do all they can to help these students overcome the many obstacles, meet the challenge, and achieve success.

GIFTED AND TALENTED STUDENTS

Gifted and talented is defined differently in states throughout the United States. Each state may have its own criteria for which students can be considered gifted and talented. For example, according to the California state education code:

Each district shall use one or more of these categories in identifying pupils as gifted and talented (GATE). In all categories, identification of a pupil's extraordinary capability shall be in relation to the pupil's chronological peers.

   a. Intellectual Ability: A pupil demonstrates extraordinary or potential for extraordinary intellectual development.

   b. Creative Ability: A pupil characteristically: 1) Perceives unusual relationships among aspects of the pupil's environment and among ideas; (2) Overcomes obstacles to thinking and doing; (3) Produces unique solutions to problems.

   c. Specific Academic Ability: A pupil functions at highly advanced levels in particular subject areas.

   d. Leadership Ability: A pupil displays the characteristic behaviors necessary for extraordinary leadership.

   e. High Achievement: A pupil consistently produces advanced ideas and products and/or attains exceptionally high scores on achievement tests.

   f. Visual and Performing Arts Talent: A pupil originates, performs, produces, or responds at extraordinarily high levels in the arts.

   g. Any other category which meets the standards set forth in these regulations [California Code Regulations title 5, § 3822].

There are various definitions of giftedness in children, such as "a school-aged person whose intellectual ability, paired with subject matter aptitude/achievement, creativity/divergent thinking, or problem-solving ability/critical thinking is so outstanding that special provisions are required beyond the general education program" (Belcher & Fletcher-Carter, 1999, p. 22). A gifted student as defined by Florida Department of Education (1999) is one with "superior intellectual development who is capable of high performance" (as cited in Gibson & Efinger, 2000, p. 48). Renzulli's definition (1978) brings together the three features of ability, task commitment (as observed through teacher nominations and recommendation), and creative expression (through work sampling) and requires that all three be jointly applied to a valuable area of human endeavor (Gibson & Efinger, 2001).

Identification

Belcher and Fletcher-Carter (1999) describe assessment for giftedness as involving these characteristics:

- *Intellectual ability* (evidenced by very superior performance on an individually administered intelligence measure)
- *Subject matter aptitude/achievement* (standardized measure or documented evidence)

- *Creativity/divergent thinking* (evidenced by observation, portfolios of work, reports from qualified individuals knowledgeable about the student's performance, or outstanding performance on a test of creativity or divergent thinking)
- *Problem solving/critical thinking* (evidenced by observation of the student's superior problem-solving/critical thinking ability, or outstanding performance on a test of problem-solving/critical thinking)

Common Characteristics

Students who are gifted differ from other students their age in behavior, creativity, and learning. The following are some common characteristics (Winebrenner, 1992; Rhode Island State Advisory Committee on Gifted and Talented Education, 2004):

- Commonly learn basic skills quickly and with less practice than other children
- Have well-developed powers of abstraction and conceptualization
- Quickly perceive similarities, differences, and anomalies
- Learn to read early
- Have interests that are both wildly eclectic and intensely focused
- May prefer the company of older children and adults to that of their peers
- Are highly inquisitive and curious
- Readily see cause-and-effect relationships
- Often have a large storehouse of information about a variety of topics, which they can recall quickly
- May show keen powers of observation and a sense of the significant, with an eye for important details
- Are fluent thinkers who are able to generate possibilities, consequences, or related ideas
- Are original thinkers, seeking new, unusual, or unconventional associations
- Can see relationships among seemingly unrelated objects, ideas, or facts
- Are flexible thinkers, able to use many different alternatives and approaches to problem solving
- Have an extensive vocabulary
- Are extremely sensitive
- Discuss in detail and with elaboration
- Enjoy challenging academic activities
- Are self-motivated in areas that interest them
- Are often intense
- Are highly self-critical
- Achieve very high in one particular subject
- Have unusual insight or perception
- Creative and inventive

Keep in mind that not all characteristics apply to any individual student. Also, some students have specific disabilities impairing certain functioning (for example, reading skill, academic performance in various areas) while they are still gifted.

According to Tomlinson (2001), sometimes gifted or advanced learners do not achieve their full potential because they may become hooked on the trappings of success (good grades, praise) and avoid taking intellectual risks. Others may be perfectionists and avoid or do not learn struggle and failure. Some fail to develop a sense of self-efficacy that comes from stretching to achieve a goal that they first believed was beyond their reach or may fail to develop study and coping skills. In many cases, advanced learners make good grades without learning to work hard. Then when hard work is required, they become frightened, resentful, or frustrated.

Instruction and Programming Options

Gibson and Efinger (2001) describe the Schoolwide Enrichment Model, which was developed by Joseph Renzulli (1994–1995). This model focuses on the development of gifted behaviors in a specific area of learning and human expression. It uses concept rather than skill learning, interdisciplinary curriculum and theme-based studies, student portfolios, performance assessment, cross-grade grouping, alternative scheduling patterns, hands-on learning, firsthand investigations, and application of knowledge and thinking skills to complex problems. Among other options are these:

- *Curriculum compacting* (Renzulli & Purcell, 1995) is a popular strategy for gifted students. It enables students who can demonstrate previous mastery of material to spend less time with the regular curriculum and more time with extension, enrichment, and acceleration opportunities. Curriculum compacting has a number of steps. Initial assessment (formal or informal) is done prior to a unit of study to determine what a student knows and does not know about a particular topic or chapter. If the student can demonstrate reasonable mastery of a good portion of the content, he or she is exempt from participating in those class activities and lessons and is provided the time for learning more challenging, accelerated, and extended material. A plan is developed to ensure the student learns the skills he or she did not show mastery of in the initial assessment, as well as for the extension tasks and in-depth study the student will be working on (Tomlinson, 2001).

- *Contracts.* These are written agreements between teachers and students that outline what students will learn, how they will learn it, in what period of time, and how they will be evaluated (Parke, 1989; Winebrenner & Berger, 1994).

- *Acceleration.* Students are placed in grades or classes more advanced than those of their chronological age group and receive special counseling or instruction outside the regular classroom in order to facilitate their advanced work. There are potential downsides to this option, particularly when a student is accelerated by skipping grades. In spite of the child's intellectual or academic advancement, he or she may have difficulty fitting in socially with older students and making friends. Also, although advanced in some academic areas, the gifted child may be missing learning skills of the grade level he or she is skipping.

- *Independent projects.* This programming option allows a student or small group of students to pursue an area of interest.

- *Independent study.* This program allows a student to pursue a study of any area of interest for school credit. The student often works with a special tutor or mentor.

- *Subject acceleration/telescoping curriculum.* A student takes the next level of a particular subject at an earlier age or grade level than normal.

- *Enrichment activities.* Students remain in regular classrooms but participate in supplemental educational activities planned to augment their regular educational programs.

- *Advanced Placement classes.* This nationally recognized program consists of college-level courses and examinations for high school students.

- *Cluster classes.* These classes are developed by placing gifted and talented students in a specially designed class at the elementary or secondary level or grouping students in accelerated classes or honors classes.

- *Cluster grouping.* Students are grouped within a regular classroom setting and receive appropriately differentiated activities from the regular classroom teacher.

- *Part-time grouping and pull-out programming.* Students attend classes or seminars organized to provide advanced and specially designed enrichment activities for part of the school day or a few hours per week.
- *Compacted courses.* Two or more courses in a given subject area are compressed into one course or a one-course (or shorter) time frame.
- *Dual enrollment.* Students at any grade level are allowed to simultaneously take courses at the next school level.
- *Early entrance.* This is an acceleration strategy whereby students enter elementary, middle, or high school (or college) earlier than the age usually prescribed.
- *Honors/advanced classes.* Advanced classes are offered in any discipline at the middle or high school level.

Although this book focuses on educating students in heterogeneous inclusive classrooms, we recognize that various instructional programs, grouping of students homogeneously at times, and service delivery options need to be provided to best meet the diverse learning needs of students. At the elementary school where we taught for many years, there historically have been a significant number of students identified as GATE. To enable us to provide heterogeneous classrooms throughout the school, all upper-grade teachers were trained to differentiate instruction and certified to teach GATE students. Therefore, we could have clusters of gifted students distributed in different classrooms.

Strategies for Gifted Learners

Tomlinson (2001) recommends continually raising the ceilings of expectations so that advanced learners are competing with their own possibilities rather than with a norm. She advises that as you raise ceilings of expectations, to raise the support system available to the student to reach his or her goals because high-end learners need teacher support and scaffolding to achieve genuine success just as other learners do. It is important to balance rigor and joy in learning and to differentiate the materials, assignments, and products in level of complexity, abstractness, and depth in order to enable these students to maximize their potential.

With gifted and advanced students it is important to allow and encourage higher levels of thinking and processing, such as through open-ended activities that stimulate further thinking and investigation. Use discovery approaches, which enable students to use their inductive reasoning processes, and provide students many opportunities to express their reasoning and how they went about solving problems.

These students need to be presented with challenging tasks, complex ideas, and sophisticated methods. It is particularly important in inclusive classrooms that teachers differentiate instruction to meet the educational needs of gifted students through accelerated pacing, choices in activities and projects, tiered assignments, telescoping the common core curriculum, and using interdisciplinary, thematic teaching and project-oriented curriculums. In addition, the school (and parents) must extend the learning opportunities for these students—through field trips, seminars, technology and information access, and use of community resources and mentors.

DUAL OR MULTIPLE EXCEPTIONALITIES

There are a number of students who are puzzling and often misunderstood and whose educational needs are not fully identified or addressed because they have more than one exceptionality. For example, there are students who are gifted intellectually, musically, artistically, or athletically, but also have AD/HD, LD, Asperger's, Tourette's syndrome, or another neurobiological, developmental disorder or disability. A high percentage of children and teens have coexisting disorders, which makes diagnosis, treatment, and educational interventions more complex. For example, as discussed earlier in this chapter, the majority of students with AD/HD also have a coexisting disorder or condition, such as ODD, LD, depression, anxiety or other mood disorder, or Tourette's syndrome. Many children and teens diagnosed with one disorder have at least one other (diagnosed or undiagnosed) coexisting condition as well. And among English-language learners are some who are gifted and talented or may have a disability or disorder of some type.

The Challenges of Recognizing and Addressing Dual Exceptionalities

It is unfortunate that due to lack of awareness and understanding, students with dual exceptionalities often fall through the cracks in the system. They are often misplaced, underserved, and have either inadequate or inappropriate expectations placed on them. Gifted children with disabilities are often functioning at grade level (or above) but may be significantly underachieving to their potential. Often, for example, those with AD/HD have adequate or above academic skills, but due to their executive functioning disorders, they have serious difficulty with organization, time management, memory, and work production and require much external support from teachers and parents. Without such intervention, they would be doing poorly in school. So it is important to be aware that "bright" students with AD/HD, LD, or other disabilities may perhaps be eligible for special education or accommodations, and it requires an evaluation and input from all parties, including parents and student, to make that determination by the multidisciplinary team.

According to Susan Baum (1989, 1994), children who are both gifted and LD can be grouped into three categories: (1) identified gifted students who have subtle learning disabilities, (2) unidentified students whose gifts and disabilities may be masked by average achievement, and (3) identified LDs who are also gifted. Those in the first group are often labeled as lazy, not trying, and underachievers when they do not perform well in school. Many times, these students do well in school in younger grades, but as the workload (such as reading and written language requirements and demands) increases, they have increasing difficulty achieving. In the second group, these individuals are often diagnosed later in life, in college or even adulthood. Their superior intellectual ability has worked throughout their life in overtime—overcompensating for their undiagnosed LD. They have appeared to be average students, when in fact they have been functioning significantly below their potential. Students in the third group may be receiving support and help for their LDs, but their strengths and abilities are often not sufficiently recognized and nurtured. They are often rated by teachers as the most disruptive students at school. All of these students are at risk for social and emotional problems when either their potential or their disabilities go unrecognized (Sousa, 2001).

In addition to dual exceptionalities, students' symptoms frequently overlap, and it is not uncommon to be misidentified and misdiagnosed. For example, Webb and Latimer (1993) point out some similarities and differences when distinguishing AD/HD from giftedness. Gifted children may present with some of these traits: poor attention, boredom, daydreaming in specific situations, low tolerance for persistence on tasks that seem irrelevant to them, judgment that lags behind development of their intellect, an intensity that may lead to power struggles with authorities, and questioning of rules, customs, and traditions (Webb, 1993). In the classroom, a gifted child's perceived inability to stay on task is likely to be related to boredom, curriculum, mismatched learning style, or other environmental factors. Those with AD/HD have a neurobiological basis for their inattention and difficulty sustaining attention to many tasks.

Gifted children may spend a great deal of their day in the regular, heterogeneously grouped class waiting for others to catch up. Their level of academic achievement is often two to four grade levels above their actual grade placement. Such children often respond to nonchallenging or slow-moving classroom situations by off-task behavior, disruptions, or other attempts at self-amusement, which may look like symptoms of AD/HD. Webb and Latimer (1993) strongly suggest that careful consideration and appropriate professional evaluation are necessary before concluding that bright, creative, intense youngsters have AD/HD.

Students from some races and ethnicities continue to be underrepresented in programs for the gifted relative to their proportions in the population. The problems of underrepresentation are compounded for students who have not acquired oral and written proficiency in English (Kitano & Espinosa, 1995). Ford and Thomas (1997) note that some minority groups of gifted learners, particularly African American, Hispanic American, and Native Americans, may be underrepresented by as much as 30 to 70 percent, with an average of 50 percent (Ross, 1993).

As a group, gifted ELL students share some common characteristics related to their high abilities, as well as differences in culture and language. The literature suggests that keys to increased access include recognizing that students who do not speak English can be gifted; involving in identification procedures qualified bilingual personnel familiar with the student's culture and any risk factors; and ensuring proportionate referral for assessment as potentially gifted (Kitano & Espinosa, 1995).

Recommended Strategies and Interventions

Children with dual or multiple exceptionalities have many special needs that must be addressed. It is important to be aware of ways to help and be willing to try the following tips and suggestions:

- Be alert to signs of dual or multiple exceptionalities.
- Do not be thrown off-course because of some children's highly discrepant abilities.
- Share your observations with parents and school team members, and refer the child for appropriate evaluations and assessment.
- Attend to the student's areas of weakness. Provide whatever adaptations, accommodations, and supports may be necessary for success.
- Nurture and enable students to showcase their strengths (their gifts, talents, and areas of competence). Provide the enrichment and allow the student to participate in areas of strength and interest (art, physical education, music). Try not to deprive them of these activities as a general consequence for incomplete or unfinished class work.
- Do not assume that because the student has the "ability" that he or she can perform the tasks or do expected work without assistance or with consistency. In spite of how intelligent and capable a student may be, if he or she has LD, AD/HD, or another neurobiological disorder, support and scaffolds are almost always necessary.
- Differentiate instruction, and provide for learning style differences.
- Help students use their strengths to compensate for their weaknesses, while providing intervention to build their skills in those areas of difficulty.
- Provide mentors and role models.
- Address emotional and self-esteem issues that often arise.

TIPS FOR PARENTS OF CHILDREN IN SPECIAL POPULATIONS

Parents of a child with a disability or who suspect their son or daughter may have a disabling condition or disorder impairing his or her school functioning (academically, behaviorally, or social-emotionally) should note the following:

- Request an evaluation. This is a necessary step to identifying and addressing your child's educational needs.
- Meet with your school's multidisciplinary team to discuss concerns. If you would like to request an assessment, do so in writing, stating the reasons that you want your son or daughter evaluated by the school district.

- Ask the school district to provide you with information about the federal laws protecting children with disabilities: Individuals with Disabilities Education Act (IDEA, the federal special education law), and Section 504 of the Rehabilitation Act of 1973 (a civil rights statute protecting individuals with disabilities from discrimination). All school districts have this information available to distribute to parents informing them of their educational rights under the law and what the process is for evaluation and due process.

- Explore reputable Web sites for information and resources, such as those listed in this section—for example, www.chadd.org for AD/HD, www.ldonline.org for LD and AD/HD, and www.schwab learning.org for LD and AD/HD.

Parents of a student who is an English-language learner or of a gifted student should be familiar with the program options and your child's classroom placement. If you have any questions or concerns, meet with the teacher and other school or district personnel.

It is very important when you have a child with special learning needs to be a close participant in your child's education. Know your son or daughter's teachers. Establish a positive working relationship and teamwork. If you feel the school is not adequately addressing your son or daughter's special needs, act on your concerns and try to problem-solve appropriate solutions with the school team. See Chapter Nine for more suggestions.

HELPFUL WEB SITES

Following are some online resources pertaining to topics addressed in this chapter of special populations and other related information in support of students with diverse learning needs. Some sites are listed in more than one category.

Learning Disabilities

Council for Exceptional Children,
www.cec.sped.org

Council for Learning Disabilities,
www.cldinternational.org

Division for Learning Disabilities,
www.dldcec.org

Hello Friend: The Ennis William Cosby Foundation,
www.hellofriend.org

International Dyslexia Association,
www.interdys.org

LD Resources,
www.ldresources.com

Learning Disabilities Association of America,
www.ldanatl.org

Learning Disabilities Information and Education Center,
www.ldiec.net

Learning Disabilities Online,
www.ldonline.org

National Center for Learning Disabilities,
www.ncld.org

Nonverbal Learning Disorders—NLDLine,
www.nldline.com

Parents of Gifted/Learning Disabled Children,
www.geocities.com/Athens/1105/gtld.html

Recordings for the Blind and Dyslexic,
www.rfbd.org

Schwab Foundation for Learning,
www.schwablearning.org

Attention-Deficit/Hyperactivity Disorder

ADDitude Magazine,
www.ADDitudemag.com

ADDvantaged,
www.ADDvantaged.com

ADHD Balance,
www.ADHDbalance.net

Children and Adults with Attention Deficit
Disorders,
www.chadd.org

Council for Children with Behavioral
Disorders,
www.ccbd.net

Hello Friend: The Ennis William Cosby
Foundation,
www.hellofriend.org

Learning Disabilities Information and Education
Center,
www.ldiec.net

Learning Disabilities Online,
www.ldonline.org

National Attention Deficit Disorder Association,
www.add.org

National Resource Center on AD/HD,
www.help4adhd.org

Schwab Foundation for Learning,
www.schwablearning.org

Other Mental Health Disorders

Anxiety Disorders Association of America,
www.adaa.org

Federation of Families for Children's Mental
Health,
www.ffcmh.org

National Alliance for the Mentally Ill,
www.nami.org

National Institute for Mental Health,
www.nimh.nih.gov

National Mental Health and Education Center
for Children and Families,
www.naspcenter.org

Research and Training Center on Family Support
and Children's Mental Health,
www.rtc.pdx.edu

UCLA School Mental Health Project,
http://smhp.psych.ucla.edu

Asperger's syndrome

Asperger Syndrome Coalition of the United
States,
www.asperger.org

Asperger Syndrome Education Network,
www.aspennj.org

Asperger Syndrome Organization,
www.aspergersyndrome.org

Autism Network International,
www.ani.ac

Autism Society of America,
www.autism-society.org

MAAP Services for Autism and Asperger
Syndrome Coalition of the United States,
www.maapservices.org

Online Asperger Syndrome Information and
Support,
http://www.udel.edu/bkirby/asperger

Tony Attwood (a leading expert on Asperger's),
www.tonyattwood.com

English-Language Learners

Center for Applied Linguistics (CAL),
http://www.cal.org/

Center for Language Minority Education
and Research,
www.clmer.csulb.edu

ERIC Clearinghouse on Languages and
Linguistics,
http://www.cal.org/ericcll

Linguistic Minority Research Institute,
http://lmrinet.gse.ucsb.edu/

National Association for Bilingual Education,
http://www.NABE.org

National Clearinghouse for Bilingual Education,
http://www.ncbe.gwu.edu/

National Clearinghouse for English Language
Acquisition,
www.ncela.gwu.edu

Office of Bilingual Education and Minority
Languages Affairs,
http://www.ed.gov/offices/OBEMLA/

Office of English Language Acquisition,
Language Enhancement,
http://www.ed.gov/about/offices/list/oela

Gifted and Talented

Center for Gifted Education Policy,
www.apa.org/ed/cgep.html

Center for Talented Youth—Johns Hopkins
University,
www.jhu.edu/gifted

ERIC Clearinghouse on Disabilities and Gifted
Education,
http://ericec.org/gifted/gt-menu.html

National Association for Gifted Children,
www.nagc.org

Other Organizations and Resources for Professionals and Parents

American Occupational Therapy Association,
www.aota.org

American Speech-Language-Hearing Association,
www.asha.org

Children's Medical Library,
www.childmedlib.org

Disability Resources on the Internet,
www.disabilityresources.org

EDLAW,
www.edlaw.net

Education Resources Information Center,
http://www.eric.ed.gov/

ERIC Clearinghouse on Disabilities and
Gifted Education,
http://ericec.org/gifted/gt-menu.html

Federation for Children with Special Needs,
www.fcsn.org

Internet Resources for Special Children,
http://www.irsc.org

Kid Source OnLine,
www.kidsource.com

Laws and Regulations: A Composite of Laws
Database Search Engine,
http://eit.otan.dni.us/speced/laws_search/search
Laws.cfm

National Academy for Child Development,
www.nacd.org

National Association of School Nurses,
www.nasn.org

National Association of School Psychologists,
www.nasponline.org

National Dissemination Center for Children with
Disabilities,
www.nichcy.org

National Institute of Child Health and Child Development,
www.nichd.nih.gov

No Child Left Behind Act,
http://www.ed.gov/nclb/landing.jhtml

Office of Special Education Programs,
http://www.ed.gov/about/offices/list/osers/osep/index.html

Office of Special Education and Rehabilitated Services,
www.ed.gov/offices/OSERS

Parent Advocacy Coalition for Educational Rights (PACER Center),
http://www.pacer.org

Technical Assistance Alliance for Parent Centers,
www.taalliance.org

Tourette Syndrome Association,
www.tsa-usa.org

Williams Syndrome Association,
www.willliams-syndrome.org

Wrightslaw (regarding rights under IDEA and Section 504),
www.wrightslaw.com

REFERENCES

Adesman, A. (2003). Effective treatment of attention-deficit/hyperactivity disorder: Behavior therapy and medication management. *Primary Psychiatry, 10,* 55–60.

American Academy of Child and Adolescent Psychiatry. (1999). *Children with oppositional defiant disorder.* Retrieved Dec. 29, 2005, from http://www.aacap.org/publications/factsfam/72.htm on.

American Academy of Pediatrics. (2000). Clinical practice guideline: Diagnosis and evaluation of the child with attention-deficit/hyperactivity disorder. *Pediatrics, 105,* 1158–1170.

American Academy of Pediatrics. (2001). *Understanding ADHD: Information for parents about attention-deficit/hyperactivity disorder.* Elk Grove Village, IL: American Academy of Pediatrics.

American Academy of Pediatrics and National Initiative for Children's Healthcare Quality. (2002). *Caring for children with ADHD: A resource toolkit for clinicians.* Chicago: American Academy of Pediatrics.

American Psychiatric Association. (1994). *Diagnostic and statistical manual of mental disorders* (4th ed.). Washington, DC: Author.

American Psychiatric Association. (2000). *Diagnostic and statistical manual of mental disorders-IV-TR* (text rev.). Washington, DC: Author.

Autism Society of America. (2004). *Asperger syndrome.* Retrieved July 30, 2005, from http://www.autism-society.org/site/PageServer?pagename=Aspergers.

Barkley, R. A. (2000). *Taking charge of ADHD* (rev. ed.). New York: Guilford Press.

Barkley, R. A. (2002). Presentation at Schwab Foundation for Learning. Retrieved Aug. 10, 2002, from http://www.schwablearning.org/pdfs/2200_7-barktran.pdf.

Barkley, R., Cook, E., Dulcan, M., Prior, M., Gillberg, C., Halperin, J., Pliszka, S., et al. (2002). International consensus statement on ADHD. *Clinical Child and Family Psychology Review, 5*(2), 89–111, Retrieved Nov. 4, 2002, from www.additudemag.com/additude.asp?DEPT_NO=201&ARTICLE_NO=8&ARCV=1Full-Text:http://www.kluweronline.com/issn/1096–4037/contents.

Baum, S. (1989). *Gifted but learning disabled: A puzzling paradox.* Reston, VA: Council for Exceptional Children/ERIC Clearinghouse on Handicapped and Gifted Children.

Baum, S. (1994). Meeting the needs of gifted/learning disabled students. *Journal of Secondary Gifted Education, 5,* 6–16.

Belcher, R. N., & Fletcher-Carter, R. (1999). Growing gifted students in the desert: Using alternative, community-based assessment and an enriched curriculum. *Teaching Exceptional Children, 32*(1), 17–25.

Benoit, M. (2005). Bipolar disorder with AD/HD: A case study. CHADD: *Attention, 12*(2), 38–44.

Biederman, J., Faraone, S., Mick, E., Wozniak, J., Chen, L., Quellette, C., Marrs, A., Moore, P., Garcia, J., Mennin, D., & Lelon, E. (1996). Attention-deficit hyperactivity disorder and juvenile mania: An overlooked comorbidity? *Journal of the American Academy of Child and Adolescent Psychiatry, 35*(8), 997–1008.

California Department of Education Standards and Assessment Division. (1999, July). *English Language Development Standards for California Public Schools.* Retrieved May 5, 2006, from http://www.cde.ca.gov/re/pn/fd/documents/englangdev-stnd.pdf.

California Education Code Regulations. Gifted and Talented Pupil Program. Title 5, § 3822.

California Teachers Association. Department for Instruction and Professional Development. (2004). *QuickGuide: English learners.* Sacramento: California Teachers Association.

Cash, R. E. (2001). *Depression in children and adolescents—Information for school personnel.* Bethesda, MD: National Association of School Psychologists, Guidance Channel, and National Association of School Psychologists.

Centers for Disease Control and Prevention. (Sept. 20, 2005). *ADHD and risk of injuries.* Retrieved July 13, 2006, from http://www.cdc.gov/ncbddd/adhd/injury.htm.

Child and Adolescent Bipolar Foundation. (2002, Oct.). *About pediatric bipolar disorder.* Retrieved Jan. 6, 2006, from http://www.bpkids.org/site/PageServer on.

Children and Adults with Attention Deficit Disorders. (2001a). *The disorder named AD/HD.* Retrieved Aug. 30, 2003, from http://www.chadd.org/fs/fs1.htm.

Children and Adults with Attention Deficit Disorders. (2001b). *AD/HD and co-existing conditions.* Retrieved Sept. 4, 2003, from www.chadd.org/fs/fs5.htm.

Children and Adults with Attention Deficit Disorders. (2003). *Evidence-based medication management for children and adolescents with AD/HD.* Retrieved Jan. 7, 2004, from http://www.chadd.org/fs/fs3.htm.

Collier, V. P. (1987). Age and rate of acquisition of second language for academic purposes. *TESOL Quarterly, 21,* 617–641.

Cummins, J. (1980). The construct of language proficiency in bilingual education. In J. E. Alatis (Ed.), *Georgetown University Round Table on Languages and Linguistics 1980.* Washington, DC: Georgetown University Press.

Cummins, J. (1991). Conversational and academic language proficiency in bilingual contexts. *AILA Review, 8,* 75–89.

Dutro, S. (2003). *A focused approach to English language instruction: Teacher's handbook.* Sacramento: California Reading and Literature Project.

Dutro, S., & Moran, C. (2003). Rethinking English language instruction: An architectural approach. In G. Garcia (Ed.), *English learners: Reaching the highest level of English literacy.* Newark, DE: International Reading Association.

Florida Department of Education. (1999). *Florida statutes and state board of education rules.* Tallahassee: Author.

Ford, D. Y., & Thomas, A. (1997, July). *Underachievement among gifted minority students: Problems and promises.* Reston, VA: ERIC Clearinghouse on Disabilities and Gifted Education.

Foss, J. M. (2005). *Students with nonverbal learning disabilities.* Retrieved Apr. 7, 2005, from http://www.ldonline.org/ld_indepth/nonverbal/students_with_nonverbal_ld.html.

Geller, B., Zimerman, B., Williams, M., Delbello, M. P., Bolhofner, K., Craney, J. L., Frazier, J., Beringer, L., & Nickelsburg, M. J. (2002). DSM-IV mania symptoms in a prepubertal and early adolescent bipolar disorder phenotype compared to attention-deficit hyperactive and normal controls. *Journal of Child and Adolescent Psychopharmacology, 12*(1), 11–25.

Gibson, S., & Efinger, J. (2001). Revisiting the schoolwide enrichment model—An approach to gifted programming. *Teaching Exceptional Children, 33*(4), 48–53.

Goldstein, S. (1999). *The facts about ADHD: An overview of attention-deficit hyperactivity disorder.* Retrieved Nov. 14, 2001, from http://www.samgoldstein.com/articles/9907.html.

Harris, T. L., & Hodges, R. E. (Eds.). (1995). *The literacy dictionary: The vocabulary of reading and writing.* Newark, DE: International Reading Association.

Hinshaw, S. (2000). Psychosocial interventions for ADHD: How well does it work? CHADD: *Attention, 6*(4), 30–34.

Hoekman, L. A. (2005). *Identifying the child with ASD.* Retrieved Apr. 7, 2005, from http://www.thegraycenter.org/autism_spectrum_disorders.htm on.

Kitano, M. K., & Espinosa, R. (1995). Language diversity and giftedness: Working with gifted English language learners. *Journal for the Education of the Gifted, 18*(3), 234–254.

Kohrt, B., & DuMond, R. (2004). Interventions at two school districts successfully serve ASD students. *CASP Today: Quarterly Newsletter of the California Association of School Psychologists, 53*(4), 1–11.

Krashen, S. D. (1981). *Bilingual education and second language acquisition theory: Schooling and language minority students—a theoretical framework.* Sacramento: Office of Bilingual Bicultural Education, California State Department of Education.

Krashen, S. D. (1985). *The input hypothesis: Issues and implications.* New York: Longman.

Linquanti, R. (1999). *Fostering academic success for English language learners: What do we know. Section 1: Definitions and terms.* Retrieved Feb. 17, 2005, from http://www.wested.org/policy/pubs/fostering/definitions.htm.

Loide, M. (1991). *LDS exam prep.* Davis, CA: Praxis Publishing.

Macías, R. F., with Cobarrubias, A., Arredondo, G., de Jesús Gutiérrez San Miguel, J., Huerta, M., & Martínez, A. (2000). *Summary report of the Survey of the States' Limited English Proficient Students and Available Educational Programs and Services, 1997–98.* Washington, DC: National Clearinghouse for Bilingual Education.

MTA Cooperative Group. (1999). Fourteen-month randomized clinical trial of treatment strategies for attention-deficit hyperactivity disorder. *Archives of General Psychiatry, 56,* 1073–1086.

National Center for Learning Disabilities. (1999–2005a). *Visual processing disorders—Challenges and strategies by age group.* Retrieved Apr. 7, 2005, from http://www.ncld.org/LDInfoZone_FactSheet_VisualPD.cfm on.

National Center for Learning Disabilities. (1999–2005b). *Auditory processing disorders—challenges and strategies by age group.* Retrieved Apr. 8, 2005, from http://www.ncld.org/LDInfoZone/InfoZone_FactSheet_AudioryPD.cfm on.

National Institute of Mental Health. (2000, Mar.). Attention deficit hyperactivity disorder (ADHD)—Questions and answers. Retrieved Nov. 14, 2001, from www.nimh.nih.gov/publicat/adhdqu.cfm.

National Resource Center on AD/HD. (2003a). *About AD/HD: The science of AD/HD.* Retrieved Aug. 31, 2003, from http://www.help4ahd.org/en/about/science.

National Resource Center on AD/HD. (2003b). *Statistical prevalence.* Retrieved Aug. 31, 2003, from www.help4adhd.org/en/about/science/statistics.

New York State Education Department. (1989). *Regents policy paper and proposed action plan for bilingual education.* Albany, NY: Author.

Office of Bilingual Education, University of the State of New York. (1999). *The teaching of language arts to limited English proficient/English language learners: A resource guide for all teachers.* Albany, NY: Author.

Office of the Surgeon General. (2000). *Report of the Surgeon General's Conference on Children's Mental Health: A national action agenda.* Washington, DC: Department of Health and Human Services.

Papolos, D., & Papolos, J. (2002). *The bipolar child.* New York: Broadway Books.

Parke, B. N. (1989). *Gifted students in regular classrooms.* Needham Heights, MA: Allyn & Bacon.

Renzulli, J. S. (1978). What makes giftedness? Reexamining a definition. *Phi Delta Kappan, 60*(3), 180–184.

Renzulli, J. S. (1994–1995). Teachers as talent scouts. *Educational Leadership, 52*(4), 75–81.

Renzulli, J. S., & Purcell, J. H. (1995). A schoolwide enrichment model. *Educational Digest, 61*(4), 14–16.

Richard, G. J., & Hoge, D. R. (1999). *The source for syndromes.* East Moline, IL: LinguiSystems.

Rhode Island State Advisory Committee on Gifted and Talented Education. (2004). *Characteristics and behaviors of the gifted.* Retrieved Oct. 10, 2005, from http://www.ri.net/gifted_talented/character.html.

Rief, S. (1998). *The ADD/ADHD checklist.* San Francisco: Jossey-Bass.

Rief, S. (2001). *Ready, start, school—Nurturing and guiding your child through preschool and kindergarten.* Upper Saddle River, NJ: Prentice Hall.

Rief, S. (2003). *The ADHD book of lists.* San Francisco: Jossey-Bass.

Rief, S. (2004). *ADHD & LD: Powerful teaching strategies and accommodations.* (video). San Diego: Educational Resource Specialists.

Rief, S. (2005). *How to reach and teach children with ADD/ADHD* (2nd ed.). San Francisco: Jossey-Bass.

Ross, P. (1993). *National excellence: A case for developing America's talent.* Washington, DC: Office of Educational Research and Improvement, Programs for the Improvement of Practice.

Safran, S. P. (2001). Asperger syndrome: The emerging challenge to special education. *Exceptional Children, 67*(2), 151–160.

Safran, J. S. (2002). Supporting students with Asperger's syndrome in general education. *Teaching Exceptional Children, 34*(5), 60–66.

Saklofske, D. H., Janzen, H. L., Hildebrand, D. K., & Kaufmann, L. (1998). Depression in children: A handout for teachers. In National Association of School Psychologists, *Helping children at home and school: Handouts from your school psychologist.* Bethesda, MD: Author.

Salend, S. J. (2001). *Creating inclusive classrooms: Effective and reflective practices* (4th ed.). Columbus, OH: Merrill.

Salend, S. J., & Salinas, A. G. (2003). Language differences or learning difficulties: The work of the multidisciplinary team. *Teaching Exceptional Children, 35*(4), 36–43.

Satcher, D. (2001). *Mental health: Culture, race and ethnicity.* Rockland, MD: U.S. Department of Health and Human Services.

Sousa, D. A. (2001). *How the special needs brain learns.* Thousand Oaks, CA: Corwin Press.

Stokes, S. (2006). *Children with Asperger's syndrome: Characteristics/learning styles and intervention strategies.* Retrieved Jan. 10, 2006, from http://www.cesa7.k12.wi.us/sped/autism/asper/asper11.html on.

Surgeon General of the United States. (1999). *Mental health: A report of the Surgeon General.* Retrieved March 8, 2006, from http://www.surgeongeneral.gov/library/mentalhealth/chapter3/sec4.html.

Terrel, T. D. (1977). A natural approach to second language acquisition and learning. *Modern Language Journal, 61,* 325–337.

Terrel, T. D. (1981). *The natural approach in bilingual education—Schooling and language minority students: A theoretical framework.* Sacramento: Office of Bilingual Bicultural Education, California State Department of Education.

Thompson, S. (2005). *Nonverbal learning disorders revisited in 1997.* Retrieved Apr. 7, 2005, from http://www.ldonline.org/ld_indepth/nonverbal/nld_revisited.html on.

Tomlinson, C. A. (2001). *How to differentiate instruction in mixed-ability classrooms* (2nd ed.). Alexandria, VA: Association for Supervision and Curriculum Development.

Trevarthen, C., Aitken, K., Papoudi, D., & Robarts, J. (1996). *Children with autism: Diagnosis and interventions to meet their needs.* London: Jessica Kingsley Publishers.

U.S. Department of Education. (2001). *Twenty-third annual report to Congress on the Implementation of IDEA.* Washington, DC: Author.

U.S. Department of Health and Human Services. (1999). *Mental health: A report of the surgeon general.* Rockville, MD: U.S. Department of Health and Human Services.

Webb, J. T. (1993). Nurturing social-emotional development of gifted children. In K. A. Heller, F. J. Monks, & A. H. Passow (Eds.), *International handbook for research on giftedness and talent* (pp. 525–538). Oxford: Pergamon Press.

Webb, J. T., & Latimer, D. (1993). *ADHD and children who are gifted.* Reston, VA: Council for Exceptional Children. Retrieved Apr. 11, 2005, from http://www.kidsource.com/kidsource/content/adhd_and_gifted.html.

Williams, K. (1995). Understanding the student with Asperger Syndrome: Guidelines for teachers. *Focus on Autistic Behavior, 10*(2), 47–52.

Winebrenner, S. (1992). *Teaching gifted kids in the regular classroom.* Minneapolis: Free Spirit.

Winebrenner, S., & Berger, S. (1994, June). *Providing curriculum alternatives to motivate gifted students.* Reston, VA: Council for Exceptional Children. Retrieved Apr. 12, 2005, from: http://www.kidsource.com/education/motivate.gifted.html.

Zionts, P., Zionts, L., & Simpson, R. (2002). *Emotional and behavioral problems: A handbook for understanding and handling students.* Thousand Oaks, CA: Corwin Press.

UNDERSTANDING READING AND WRITING DIFFICULTIES IN STUDENTS

During the past few decades, a great deal of research has taken place with regard to normal reading development, identifying risk factors, and means of prevention and intervention for reading difficulties. In the late 1990s, the converging evidence based on over thirty years of reading research became available through the National Institute of Child Health and Human Development (NICHD), National Institutes of Health (Lyon, 1998a, 1998b).

PREVALENCE OF READING PROBLEMS AND RESEARCH RESULTS

The high rate of illiteracy and reading difficulties in the United States (roughly 17 to 20 percent of the population) has been considered not only an educational problem but a major public health problem. To address this issue, the NICHD has supported scientific research continuously since 1965 to investigate how children learn to read, why some children struggle in learning to read, and what can be done to prevent reading difficulties. NICHD developed a research network consisting of forty-one research sites in North America (and other parts of the world) that conducted numerous studies on thousands of children—many over a period of years. The findings from this wealth of research were presented as testimony by G. Reid Lyon, chief of the Child Development and Behavior Branch of the NICHD, National Institutes of Health, to the Committee on Labor and Human Resources, U.S. Senate, in 1998.

In addition, more research findings on this topic came from the Committee on the Prevention of Reading Difficulties in Young Children, National Research Council. This committee was entrusted by the National Academy of Sciences to conduct a study of the effectiveness of interventions for young children who might be predisposed to reading difficulties. This committee reviewed several factors: normal reading development and instruction, risk factors useful in identifying groups and individuals at risk of reading failure, and prevention, intervention, and instructional approaches to ensuring optimal reading outcomes. The results of their research findings are found in *Preventing Reading Difficulties in Young Children* (Snow, Burns, & Griffin, 1998).

As a result of this abundance of research, we now know the following based on the scientific evidence from these sources (Lyon, 1998a, 1998b; Snow et al., 1998):

- Failure to read proficiently is the most common reason that students drop out, get retained, or are referred to special education.

- Approximately 50 percent of reading difficulties can be prevented if students are provided effective language development in preschool and kindergarten and effective reading instruction in the primary grades.

- There is a strong association between a child's ability to read and his or her ability to segment words into phonemes (that is, hear and separate a spoken word into its individual sounds, such as *pig* as /p/ /i/ /g/).

- Kindergarten children's phonemic awareness can predict their levels of reading and spelling achievement even years later. It is a more powerful predictor of reading progress than IQ.

- By providing explicit instruction in alphabetic code, sound-spellings, and phonemic awareness, we may prevent many children from needing to enter special education programs. (As many as 80 percent of referrals to special education involve reading difficulties.)

- Learning letter-sound correspondence, necessary for reading and spelling, requires an awareness that spoken language can be analyzed into strings of separable words. These words comprise sequences of syllables, made up of smaller units of sounds (phonemes).

- Most children with severe reading difficulties have substantial weakness in auditory-related skills such as phonemic awareness and associating those sounds with the printed letter (sound-symbol relationships).

- The most frequent characteristic observed among children and adults with reading disabilities is a slow, labored approach to decoding, or sounding out, unknown or unfamiliar words and frequent misidentification of familiar words.

- Children who are most at risk for reading failure enter kindergarten limited in their awareness of sound structure and language pattern, phonemic sensitivity, letter knowledge, and the purposes of reading and have had little exposure to books and print.

- Effective prevention and early intervention programs can increase the reading skills of 85 to 90 percent of poor readers to average levels.

Louisa Moats (2001), another leader in the field, provides the following abysmal statistics: about 42 percent of fourth graders score below basic in overall reading skill on the National Assessment of Educational Progress (NAEP). In some communities, the proportion of students beyond third grade who cannot read well enough to participate in grade-level work is between 60 and 70 percent, depending on the grade and year of assessment (Moats, 2001). According to McCormick (2003), U.S. Department of Education data show that approximately 3.5 percent of school-age youngsters in the United States are enrolled in learning disability classes because of reading difficulties (Snow et al., 1998). If it had considered students with mild delays as well as those with moderate and severe problems, as many as 15 percent of students probably warrant special instruction in reading (Spache, 1981)

Moats (2001) describes the challenge with regard to teaching older students who are poor readers: "They cannot read, so they do not like to read; reading is labored and unsatisfying, so they have little reading experience; and, because they have not read much, they are not familiar with the vocabulary, sentence structure, text organization and concepts of academic 'book' language. Over time, their comprehension skills decline because they do not read, and they also become poor spellers and poor writers. What usually begins as a core phonological and word recognition deficit, often associated with other language weaknesses, becomes a diffuse, debilitating problem with language—spoken and written" (p. 1).

THE GENDER GAP IN READING

Boys are known to be more at risk for poor reading achievement than girls. William Brozo (2004) cites some of the research with regard to this gender discrepancy. Studies show that boys in elementary through high school score significantly lower than girls on standardized measures of reading achievement (Donahue, Voelkl, Campbell, & Mazzeo, 1999). Because boys of all ages fail in reading more often than girls, they are more numerous in corrective and remedial reading programs (National Center for Education Statistics, 2000). In addition, boys are far more likely to be retained at grade level (Byrd & Weitzman, 1994) and are three to five times more likely than girls to have a learning or reading disabilities placement (National Center for Education Statistics, 2000).

Brozo (2004) points out that in order to address the needs of failing boys and reverse the trend of their lower reading achievement, creative programs and instruction (such as book clubs) are needed. Chapter Eleven focuses on such creative programs and instructional strategies to hook in reluctant and struggling readers and raise the reading achievement of boys. Our book, *How to Reach and Teach All Students Through Balanced Literacy* (forthcoming), details how to establish and manage book clubs in third through eighth grade.

This gender gap has become apparent in recent years in other areas as well. Posnick-Goodwin (2005) notes a U.S. Department of Education study released in December 2004 that found that the academic edge boys once held has vanished and boys now seem to be falling behind girls. And the July 2003 NAEP writing results show boys scoring, on average, twenty-four points lower than girls.

READING DISORDERS

There are a number of reasons that students are poor readers and deficient in their reading skills that are not brain based in nature. However, a significant number of students who are struggling readers do have neurobiological impairments that cause a reading disorder or specific difficulties that interfere with their reading.

Dyslexia

Among the various learning disabilities, reading disorders are the most common. Some children with reading disabilities have specific processing deficiencies (for example, in auditory or visual perception, short-term memory, phonological awareness, orthography) that affect their acquisition of reading skills. Determining if a child or teen has a learning disability impairing reading requires a psychoeducational evaluation. (Chapter Three provides information about learning disabilities.)

Dyslexia is a language-based learning disability. It refers to a cluster of symptoms that result in people having difficulties with specific language skills, particularly reading. Students with dyslexia may experience difficulties in other language skills such as spelling, writing, and speaking. Current studies suggest that 15 to 20 percent of the population has a reading disability. Of those, 85 percent have dyslexia (International Dyslexia Association, 2000).

Joseph Torgeson (2003), professor at Florida State University, has identified these instructional features needed for effective intervention for children with reading disabilities:

- Systematic and explicit instruction on whatever component skills are deficient
- A significant increase in the intensity of instruction
- Ample opportunity for guided practice of new skills in meaningful contexts
- Appropriate levels of scaffolding as students learn new skills

- Systematic cueing of appropriate strategies in context
- Teachers who are relentless in their efforts to build students' reading competency

Kevin Feldman (2001), director of reading and early intervention in the Sonoma County Office of Education (Santa Rosa, California), believes that older struggling readers must fill in the holes and build the literacy foundations they have missed such as:

- Phonological and phonemic awareness
- Grapheme and phoneme matching
- Decoding of single and polysyllabic words
- Reading fluency
- Word structure (for example, syllable complexity, morphology)
- Word study and layers of the English language
- Comprehension and text-handling strategies
- Study skills, habits, and strategies in content-area reading and writing

For students with reading disabilities who do not have phonologically based problems (the core problem for most), orthographic processing may be the key deficit. These are children who have weakness in the visual processing areas (see Chapter Three). These learners typically have difficulty in recognizing letters and words, recognizing and recalling the sequence of letters within words, and using productive cues to help them visually distinguish word patterns (Stanovich & West, 1989; McCormick, 2003).

Other Common Reading Difficulties

Some students, for example, many with AD/HD (who may have average or strong skills in decoding and word recognition and be able to read fluently), may have reading difficulties to varying degrees. Due to inattention and "executive functioning" weaknesses, these students often have difficulty sustaining focused attention, which affects their recall of text and comprehension of reading material. They frequently need help learning how to become strategic readers—knowing how to read actively, with a purpose, and self-monitoring to ensure comprehension of the text.

Many students with AD/HD and/or learning disabilities have difficulties with the following (Rief, 2003, 2005):

- Failure to use metacognitive strategies. This refers to the practice of self-monitoring comprehension while reading the text by addressing errors in comprehension as soon as they arise. They are not actively engaging while reading (for example, predicting, making connections, self-questioning) and making sure that they are comprehending the text as they read.
- Lacking a schema, or structure, to guide them in figuring out the critical elements and main ideas of what they are reading. They need, for example, more explicit instruction in expository and narrative text structures.
- Poor memory skills. This results in limited recall of the reading material. It also affects their comprehension of the text, such as the ability to summarize, retell, and respond to questions related to the reading.
- Inattention (that is, distractibility and difficulty sustaining attention to a task). When they are drawn off-task while reading, they miss words and important details, which consequently impedes their comprehension. Many individuals with AD/HD report having difficulty maintaining their train of thought while reading. Their high level of distractibility interferes with their ability to concentrate on the text and process the information. This problem is compounded if the student is

presented with dry, uninteresting, or difficult material. Many also lose their place as their attention drifts when they are reading.

- Silent reading is often difficult for many children and teens with AD/HD or learning disabilities. They frequently need to subvocalize or read quietly to themselves aloud in order to hear their voice and maintain attention to what they are reading. These readers often need the auditory input to stay focused as they struggle to process the text through silent reading.

Reading Interventions

Chapter Eleven addresses numerous strategies and interventions for struggling or reluctant readers. (Our other book, *How to Reach and Teach All Students Through Balanced Literacy,* forthcoming), also offers many suggestions.) The following are instructional tips to keep in mind:

- Explicitly teach and involve students regularly with strategies such as paraphrasing, summarizing, reciprocal teaching, and self-questioning, using techniques that require active involvement with regard to thinking about and responding to what is being read. This helps students maintain their focus and attention and increases their comprehension of the text. Teach students how to become strategic, active readers and thinkers.
- Some struggling readers benefit from the use of various tools while reading. For example, reading frames, windows, or markers enhance visual focus.
- Use research-validated intervention materials for students with significant reading difficulties. (See the suggestions at the end of this chapter.)

STRUGGLES WITH WRITING

Writing is an area of weakness for many students, particularly those with neurobiological disorders such as learning disabilities and AD/HD (Rief, 2003, 2005). These children are often knowledgeable but unable to communicate on paper what they know. Written language is a common area of difficulty because the process of writing is complex. It involves the integration and often simultaneous use of several skills and brain functions: organization, planning, memory, language processing, spelling, graphomotor skills (handwriting and fine-motor skills), self-monitoring, and processing speed. Writing difficulties are often manifested in one or more of the following areas.

Preplanning and Organization

This requires being able to generate, plan, and organize ideas. This stage of the writing process is often the most challenging and neglected, especially for those who experience difficulties with written expression. When given a written assignment, some students, particularly those with learning disabilities or AD/HD, often get stuck here. They do not know what to write about, how to organize and begin, or how to narrow down and focus on a topic that will be motivating to write about.

Memory

Working memory is necessary in order to juggle the many different thoughts that one might want to transcribe onto paper. It involves:

- Keeping ideas in mind long enough to remember what one wants to say
- Maintaining focus on the train of thought so the flow of the writing will not veer off course
- Keeping in mind the big picture of what to communicate, while manipulating the ideas, details, and wording

The process of writing also requires the retrieval of assorted information from long-term memory (for example, facts and experiences) to share about the writing topic, as well as recall of vocabulary words, spelling, mechanics, and grammar (PBS, 2002).

Spelling

Children with learning disabilities are typically weak in spelling due to:

- Deficiencies in phonemic awareness and phonological processing (for example, learning letter-sound correspondence, discriminating between sounds, and having the ability to segment and blend sounds into words).
- Auditory-sequential memory deficits, which cause much difficulty in remembering and writing the sounds of a word in the correct order. Children with learning disabilities often missequence sounds when spelling and insert or delete sounds within a word.
- Difficulty comprehending spelling rules, patterns, and structures (Currie & Wadlington, 2000; International Dyslexia Association, 1998).
- Difficulties with orthographic processing. They may have visual-sequential memory deficits causing them difficulty recalling the way a word looks and getting it down in the correct order or sequence. This results in misspelling common high-frequency words (for example, *said, they, where, does, of, because)* that cannot be sounded out phonetically and must be recalled by sight.

The International Dyslexia Association (2000) points out that "the visual memory problems of poor spellers are specific to memory for letters and words. A person may be a very poor speller, but be a very good artist, navigator, or mechanic; those professions require a different kind of visual memory" (p. 1).

Students with learning disabilities generally progress through the same series of stages in the acquisition of spelling as other children, but at a slower rate than their peers without learning disabilities (Weiner, 1994; Rhodes & Dudley-Marling, 1988; Mather & Roberts, 1995; Moats, 1995).

Children and teens with AD/HD may not have a processing problem causing spelling difficulties but may misspell words due to inattention to detail, and therefore not noticing or paying attention to the specific letters, sequence, or visual patterns within words, or a tendency to make many careless mistakes resulting from inattention and impulsivity (Rief, 2005).

Language

Writing requires the ability to express thoughts in a logical, cohesive, and coherent manner. Individuals with learning disabilities, in particular, frequently have some kind of language disorder (phonological, morphological, syntactical, semantic). Impairments in one or more of these areas can significantly affect writing ability. Good writers generally have facility with the language (for example, vocabulary, word use, sentence structure, mechanics). They are able to use a wide vocabulary to express themselves and write descriptive sentences while maintaining proper sentence and paragraph structure. Each writing genre (such as persuasive, response to literature, or personal narrative) has its own structural components. The writer must know the structure and specific language and vocabulary to use (for example, in order to persuade or convince an audience or compare and contrast). Students with learning disabilities and English-language learners often have difficulty with some of the following aspects of language:

- *Syntax.* This is the structure of language (grammar or word form), that is, the structure or order of words in a sentence. It is common for students who have delays in their awareness and understanding of syntax to write many run-on sentences, use too many conjunctions (such as the connecting word *and*), make errors in verb and pronoun use, and get confused with structurally complex sentences (Mercer & Mercer, 1993; Mather & Roberts, 1995).

- *Morphology.* A morpheme is the smallest meaningful unit of language. Morphology has to do with the understanding and use of root words and affixes (prefixes and suffixes), verb tense, regular and irregular verbs, possessions, plurals, compound words, and rules for word formation.
- *Semantics.* This relates to the meaning of words and the way words are used to relate meaning. It involves knowledge and use of vocabulary and the subtleties of language such as idioms, similes, metaphors, and words with multiple meanings. Individuals who do not have facility with precise and colorful vocabulary use are hampered in their writing.

Graphomotor Skills

Many children with AD/HD or learning disabilities have impairments in graphomotor skills that affect the physical task of writing and organization of print on the page. They often have trouble in these areas:

- Forming letters correctly
- Writing neatly on or within the lines
- Spacing and organizing their writing on the page
- Copying from the board or book onto paper
- Executing print or cursive with precision or speed

Handwriting is particularly difficult and complex for many children, particularly those with neurobiological disorders. Many struggle with handwriting due to poor fine motor coordination, limited memory (remembering with automaticity the sequence of fine motor movements needed in forming the letters), and slow processing speed. The act of handwriting for some children and teens is inefficient, fatiguing, and frustrating. Children with fine motor and handwriting problems often have poor pencil grip, exert too much or too little pressure while writing, and have illegible written work. Some children also reverse or invert letters well beyond what is normal developmentally and form numerals and letters in strange, awkward ways (Rief, 2003, 2005).

Written Expression

Due to any number of difficulties in the areas described, students may have poor written expression and struggle to write to grade-level standards. To produce written compositions, a combination of all of these skills is involved. Students who have challenges in any of the language areas, trouble with planning and organization, memory weaknesses, or trouble staying focused and on task can have difficulty when it comes to written production and composition. Many of the strategies and activities in Chapter Eleven are highly effective in improving students' written expression skills.

Self-Monitoring

Fluent writing requires:

- Thinking and planning ahead
- Keeping the intended audience in mind and writing to that audience with a clear purpose
- Following and referring back to the specific structure of a writing genre (for example, steps of a complete paragraph, narrative account, persuasive essay, friendly letter)
- Knowing how to read their own work critically in order to make revisions and develop ideas more thoroughly

Some students, particularly those with learning or attention difficulties, do not effectively self-monitor during the writing process.

Mechanics

The accurate use of capitalization and punctuation is an area of weakness for many students, particularly those with learning disabilities and with AD/HD. Some children lack the skills and awareness for application of proper capitalization and punctuation. Others are inattentive to details such as the use of proper mechanics and do not notice their errors in use.

Editing

Students who struggle in the writing process generally have particular difficulty, and sometimes exhibit resistant or oppositional behavior, when asked to revise and edit their work. Because writing is so tedious and effortful for some of them, they often want to go directly from the initial draft to their final draft without making revisions (unless they are provided with the use of assistive technology and other supports). For these students, proofreading their work without assistance and being expected to revise and edit without direct help is an unrealistic expectation.

Speed of Written Output and Production

Some students rush through writing assignments, often leading to illegible work with many careless errors. Others write excruciatingly slowly. For example, many students with learning disabilities or AD/HD may know the correct answers and be able to verbally express their thoughts and ideas articulately, yet may be unable to put more than a few words or sentences down on paper. Needless to say, this is extremely frustrating to both the child and the teacher. Part of the problem with speed of output may be due to impairments in impulsivity and inhibition, difficulty sustaining attention to task and maintaining the mental energy required in written expression, or graphomotor dysfunction.

Being aware of the particular difficulties students may experience in their reading and writing enables teachers to observe students more carefully (with a diagnostic eye) and to better prepare and provide literacy instruction and intervention. This understanding allows us to more effectively differentiate instruction to address individual learning strengths, weaknesses, and developmental stages. This awareness can alert teachers to individual students showing signs of what may be a brain-based disorder or disability impairing their reading or writing development. Teachers may then request a student support team meeting to discuss appropriate strategies and early interventions for these students.

RESEARCH-BASED LITERACY INTERVENTION PROGRAMS

The following are research-based programs proven effective with children who have reading, writing, and language difficulties:

- Johnson, G., & Engleman, Z. (1999). *Corrective Reading.* This program provides intensive intervention for below-grade level readers (third–twelfth) in general or special education. Through tightly sequenced, carefully planned lessons and direct instruction, the program is designed to increase students' reading accuracy, fluency, and comprehension. (New York: SRA/McGraw-Hill). www.sra4kids.com.

- Herman, R. (2007). *The Sopris West Herman Method for reversing reading failure.* Herman Method Reading Institute. A multisensory program based on the Orton-Gillingham philosophy is a remedial program for struggling readers at all grade levels. (Longmont, CO: Sopris West Educational Services). www.hermanmethod.com or www.sopriswest.com.

- Fell, J. (2007). *Language! The Comprehensive Literacy Curriculum.* This program teaches literacy explicitly, sequentially, and cumulatively. It is designed for differentiated instruction, is strategic in its use of assessment and technology, and is based on teacher input, testing, and review. This curriculum is appropriate for grades 4 to 12. (Longmont, CO: Sopris West). www.so;priswest.com.

- Lindamood, P., Lindamood, P., & Bell, N. *Lindamood-Bell Learning Processes.* The Lindamood-Bell programs teach children and adults to read, spell, comprehend, and express language. All are designed to stimulate basic sensory functions related to learning, and are recognized as being effective in the instruction of those with dyslexia, autism, and learning disabilities. (San Luis Obispo, CA). http://www.lindamoodbell.com.

- *Orton-Gillingham Failure Free Reading Program,* produced by the Institute for Multi-Sensory Education (2002), is based on the Orton-Gillingham method of reading instruction developed by Samuel T. Orton and educator Anna Gillingham. The methodology utilizes phonetics and emphasizes visual, auditory, and kinesthetic learning styles. Instruction begins by focusing on the structure of language and gradually moves toward reading. The program provides students with immediate feedback and a predictable sequence that integrates reading, writing and spelling. www.ortongillingham.com.

- Enfield, M., & Greene, V. (2005). *Project Read—Language Circle.* This program has five curriculum strands: phonology, linguistics, reading comprehension report form (expository), reading comprehension story form (narrative), and written expression. Project Read follows the principles of systematic learning, direct concept teaching, and multisensory strategies. (Bloomington, MN: Language Circle Enterprise). www.projectread.com.

- Hasselbring, T., Kinsella, K., & Feldman, K. *Read 180 Reading Intervention Program.* This program utilizes a teaching system that provides a clear instructional path, integrated professional development, and resources for assessing students and differentiating instruction. Instructional materials are provided for systematic instruction in reading, writing, and vocabulary to the whole class, resources for differentiating instruction to small groups, and Read 180 software for independent, intensive skills practice, as well as modeled and independent reading of paperbacks and audiobooks. http://teacher.scholastic.com/products/read180.

- Arbogast, A., Bruner, E., Davis, K. L., Englemann, O., Englemann, S., Hanner, S., Osborn, J., Osborn, S., & Zoraf, L. (2002). *Reading Mastery Plus.* This direct instruction comprehensive program provides systematic, explicit instruction and instant feedback to develop reading skills. (New York: SRA McGraw-Hill). www.sra4kids.com.

- Ihnot, C., & Ihnot, T. *Read Naturally.* The Read Naturally line of products are designed to improve reading fluency and measure student progress. Fluency is built through teacher modeling, repeated reading, and progress monitoring. (St. Paul, MN). www.readnaturally.com.

- Archer, A. L., Gleason, M. M., & Vachon, V. (2006). *REWARDS—Reading excellence: Word attack and rate development strategies.* The REWARDS reading intervention programs have been research-validated in schools across the country and proved to efficiently and effectively improve decoding, fluency, vocabulary, comprehension, test-taking abilities, and content-area reading and writing. REWARDS can be used as interventions in general and special education, remedial reading, summer school, and after-school programs for grades 4 to 12. (Longmont, CO: Sopris West). www.sopriswest.com.

- *The Slingerland Multisensory Structured Language Instructional Approach* is an adaptation for classroom use of the Orton-Gillingham method. This structured, sequential, simultaneous multisensory teaching approach is designed to teach dyslexic students and others the integrated skills of speaking, reading, writing and spelling. (Bellevue, WA: Slingerland Institute for Literacy). www.slingerland.org.

- Spalding, R. B. The Spalding method is a total language arts approach for pre-K to 8 that provides explicit sequential, multisensory instruction in spelling (including phonics and handwriting), writing, and listening/reading comprehension. www.spalding.org.

- Wilson, B. The Wilson Reading System is a research-based reading and writing program and a complete curriculum for teaching decoding and encoding (spelling). It provides an organized, sequential system with extensive controlled text to help teachers implement a multisensory structured language program. (Millbury, MA). www.wilsonlanguage.com.

All of the preceding interventions include training programs in their usage, with more information found at their Web sites.

OTHER IMPORTANT RESOURCES

More research-based strategies and interventions to build literacy skills and support struggling readers and writers can be found in the following:

- Florida Center for Reading Research. This Web site includes presentations in pdf format and PowerPoints from faculty and staff at FCRR on the science of reading. www.fcrr.org.
- National Center for Learning Disabilities. This Web site has online publications and reports prepared by leading researchers addressing reading and writing challenges and interventions for students with LD. www.ncld.org.
- Reading Online. This Web site, provided by the International Reading Association, offers hundreds of articles on a range of topics in reading education. www.readingonline.org.
- National Institute of Child Health and Human Development. (2000, Apr.). *Report of the National Reading Panel: Teaching children to read: An evidence-based assessment of the scientific research literature on reading and its implications for reading instruction.* Washington, DC: Author. This report assesses the effectiveness of various approaches to teaching children to read.
- Reading for Blind and Dyslexic—Learning Through Listening. A nonprofit organization, RFB&D is the nation's educational library serving people who cannot read standard print effectively because of a visual impairment, learning disability, or other physical disability. It lends audio books in a broad range of subjects at all educational levels, from kindergarten to postgraduate studies. Nearly 75 percent of the people who use these audio textbooks have dyslexia or other reading-based learning disabilities. www.rfbd.org.

REFERENCES

Ackerman, P., & Dykman, R. (1996). The speed factor and learning disabilities: The toll of slowness in adolescents. *Dyslexia, 2,* 1–21.

Brozo, W. (2004). It's okay to read, even if other kids don't: Learning about and from boys in a middle school book club. *California Reading Association: The California Reader, 38*(2), 4–12.

Byrd, R., & Weitzman, M. (1994). Predictors of early grade retention among children in the United States. *Pediatrics, 93,* 481–487.

Cattas, H., Fey, M., Zhang, X., & Tomblin, J. (1999). Language basis of reading and reading disabilities: Evidence from a longitudinal investigation. *Scientific Studies of Reading, 3,* 331–361.

Cunningham, A., & Stanovich, K. (1997). Early reading acquisition and its relation to reading experience and ability 10 years later. *Developmental Psychology, 33,* 934–945.

Currie, P. S., & Wadlington, E. M. (2000). *The source for learning disabilities.* East Moline, IL: LinguiSystems.

Donahue, P., Voelkl, K., Campbell, J., & Mazzeo, J. (1999). *NAEP reading report card for the nation and states.* Washington, DC: National Center for Education Statistics.

Feldman, K. (2001, Nov.). *Supporting struggling secondary readers: Decoding, fluency and comprehension—what works?* CEC Annual California State Conference.

International Dyslexia Association. (1998). *Just the facts: Spelling.* Baltimore, MD: International Dyslexia Association.

International Dyslexia Association. (2000, May). *Just the facts—Dyslexia basics*. Baltimore, MD: International Dyslexia Association.

Lyon, G. R. (1998a). *Overview of reading and literacy initiatives*. Bethesda, MD: National Institute of Child Health and Human Development.

Lyon, G. R. (1998b). Why reading is not a natural process. *Educational Leadership, 55*(6), 14–18. www.ldonline.org/ld–indepth/reading/why–reading–is–not.html.

Lyon, G.R. (2000, Jan./Feb.) *Why reading is not a natural process*. Retrieved Feb. 10, 2006, from http://www.ldonline.org/articles/6396.

Mather, N., & Roberts, R. (1995). *Informal assessment and instruction in written language*. Hoboken, NJ: Wiley.

McCormick, S. (2003). *Instructing students who have literacy problems* (4th ed.). Upper Saddle River, NJ: Pearson Education.

Mercer, C. D., & Mercer, A. R. (1993). *Teaching students with learning problems* (4th ed.). New York: Macmillan.

Moats, L. (1995). *Spelling: Development, disability, and instruction*. Baltimore, MD: York Press.

Moats, L. (2001, Mar.). When older kids can't read. *Educational Leadership, 58,* 6.

National Center for Education Statistics. (2000). *Trends in educational equity for girls and women*. Washington, DC: U.S. Department of Education.

PBS. (2002). *Misunderstood minds. Writing basics, difficulties, responses*. Boston: WGBH Educational Foundation, 2002. http://www.pbs.org/wgbh/misunderstoodminds.

Posnick-Goodwin, S. (2005). In the march toward gender equity, girls surge forward, but boys fall back. *California Teachers Association: California Educator, 9*(6), 6–10.

Rhodes, L. K., & Dudley-Marling, C. (1988). *Readers and writers with a difference: A holistic approach to teaching learning disabled and remedial students*. Portsmouth, NH: Heinemann.

Rief, S. (2003). *The ADHD book of lists*. San Francisco: Jossey-Bass.

Rief, S. (2005). *How to reach and teach children with ADD/ADHD* (2nd ed.). San Francisco: Jossey-Bass.

Rief, S., & Heimburge, J. (forthcoming). *How to reach and teach all children through balanced literacy*. San Francisco: Jossey-Bass.

Shankweiler, D., Crane, S., Katz, L., Fowler, A. E., Liberman, A. M., Brady, S. A., Thornton, R., Lindquist, E., Dreyer, L. G., Fletcher, J. M., Stuebing, K. K., Shaywitz, S. E., & Shaywitz, B. A. (1995). Cognitive profiles of reading-disabled children: Comparison of language skills in phonology, morphology, and syntax. *Psychological Science, 6,* 149–156.

Snow, C. E., Burns, S. M., & Griffin, P. (Eds.). (1998). *Preventing reading difficulties in young children*. Washington, DC: National Academy Press.

Spache, G. D. (1981). *Diagnosing and correcting reading disabilities* (2nd ed.). Needham Heights, MA: Allyn & Bacon.

Stanovich, K. E., & West, R. F. (1989). Exposure to print and orthographic processing. *Reading Research Quarterly, 24,* 402–433.

Torgeson, J. (2003, Nov.). Keynote address at the International Dyslexia Association 54th Annual Conference, "Closing the Gap Through Intensive Instruction: New Hope from Research." San Diego, CA.

Weiner, S. (1994). Four first graders' descriptions of how they spell. *Elementary School Journal, 94,* 315–332.

Part 2

REACHING STUDENTS IN THE CLASSROOM AND AT HOME

Chapter 5

USING ACCOMMODATIONS, MODIFICATIONS, AND SUPPORTS

Our inclusive classrooms will always have some students who present with learning, behavioral, and social-emotional issues—children who are at risk and in need of attention and intervention. To reach and teach these students effectively, teachers need to employ appropriate instructional and management strategies and implement accommodations and modifications. Classroom teachers are not expected to know which are the best strategies and techniques to try or what are recommended practices for addressing the needs of our diverse learners without assistance and support. School support professionals, as well as administrators, must be available and willing to provide direct and indirect assistance to teachers and to share their knowledge and expertise in this regard. One of the means and vehicles for this effort is the student support team process.

STUDENT SUPPORT TEAM PROCESS

Most schools have a team process for assisting teachers in devising instructional and behavioral strategies and supports for students experiencing difficulties in general education (Rief, 2003, 2005). This is a site-based problem-solving team that is referred to by many names or acronyms; among them are SST (which can be the abbreviation for "student support team," "student study team," or "student success team"), SAT (student assistant team), SIT (student intervention team), IST (instructional support team), and TAT (teacher assistance team). In other districts this team may be called the "consultation team," "child guidance team," "child study team," "multidisciplinary intervention team," or something else. The SST process and protocol differ from district to district and school to school, yet usually there are many similarities.

The SST (the term we will use here) is not a special education process or procedure but rather a function of regular or general education. The purpose of the team is to strategize and problem-solve about individual students who are experiencing academic, behavioral, or social/emotional difficulty and develop and then monitor a plan of intervention.

SST is a process and forum for classroom teachers to meet with the school's multidisciplinary team to discuss and strategize about an individual student of concern. Typically, the team comprises various school support personnel, an administrator, and parents of the student. At the SST meeting:

- A review of the student's strengths and areas of concern or difficulties takes place, prioritizing one or a few areas for improvement.
- The team brainstorms possible supports, interventions, and strategies that can be tried to assist the student on the agenda.
- A few of those strategies or interventions are selected to implement for a period of time.
- An action (intervention) plan is developed for implementation.
- A follow-up date is set to review and monitor the effectiveness of the plan in addressing the concerns.

Depending on the support personnel assigned to the building and their schedules, the members of the team vary from school to school. Generally they include the classroom teacher or person who requested assistance, the team coordinator, and some standing members of the team, such as the school psychologist, school counselor or social worker, an administrator, and one or more teachers with expertise in teaching diverse learners (for example, a special education teacher or literacy specialist). There are also invited members to the team who may include the school nurse, speech/language therapist, adapted physical education teacher, and other special service providers who are asked to participate when the team will be discussing a specific student with issues involving speech/language, motor skill development, or possible health issues. The nurse, special education teachers and service providers, and curriculum and instructional specialists, such as literacy coaches or other reading, writing, or math specialists, may be among the standing or invited SST members in their schools. At the middle school level, at least one of the student's teachers (preferably more than one) participates in the SST meeting. That teacher should also have received input from other classroom teachers of that student to share with the team. If the intervention plan involves strategies that teachers other than the attending teacher are to implement, that plan must be clearly communicated to the other teachers as well.

The parents or guardians of the student being discussed are an integral part of the team. Their thoughts and involvement in the problem-solving process are very important. Team members must communicate to parents that their information on and insights into their child are valued and deemed necessary for identifying the child's needs and providing the appropriate support and intervention. (Chapter Nine elaborates on the need for home-school collaboration and partnership on behalf of the student.)

Some schools schedule initial SST meetings without the parents—for example, if a number of students are being discussed during the scheduled time frame or if it is deemed appropriate to meet first without parents to discuss sensitive issues. But parents should always be informed when their child is being discussed through SST and invited to participate—if not at the initial meeting, then for a follow-up meeting.

Benefits of the SST Process

This process has the potential of being a highly effective method for early intervention, providing needed support to struggling students and their teachers. The SST process:

- Provides the teacher with access to a group of colleagues who share information and expertise, enabling the teacher to better meet the individual needs of students.
- Assists the teacher in problem solving, strategizing, and developing a plan of appropriate classroom interventions.
- Facilitates student access to additional schoolwide and perhaps communitywide supports and safety nets as needed.

- Provides teachers with an expanded repertoire of instructional and behavioral strategies and adaptations and accommodations useful for students in the general education classroom.
- Provides the necessary prereferral intervention documentation if a referral for special education is needed.
- Provides an appropriate vehicle for making recommendations to parents as a team when a clinical (that is, medical or mental health) referral is indicated.
- Enhances the home-school partnership in efforts to collaboratively address student needs.

Before Requesting an SST Meeting

Prior to scheduling the SST meeting on a student, most districts require teachers to follow preliminary steps such as these:

- Implement some strategies or interventions (a few targeted strategies, for example, that address the areas of student difficulty).
- Determine and document the effectiveness of strategies tried.
- Collect work samples as examples of the student's performance.
- Establish communication with parents.

Teachers are generally asked to inform parents prior to an SST meeting about their observations regarding the student (positive ones as well as their concerns) and some of the strategies they have tried in order to assist the child. Teachers also elicit the parents' input and try to establish a partnership on behalf of the student. With these preliminary steps taken, the SST meeting is more productive. The team is in a position to recommend the next steps for intervention.

Request for an SST Meeting

Teachers will be asked to complete a referral or SST request form prior to meeting. The coordinator or facilitator of the SST will generally make a copy of the completed form to distribute to team members before or at the time of the meeting. A typical SST request or referral form asks the teacher to provide the following types of information:

- Student's identifying information (name, address, teacher, grade, parents' or guardian name, home phone, parents' cell phone)
- Student's strengths
- Concerns or description of difficulties the student is experiencing (academic, behavioral, social-emotional)
- Steps the teacher has taken to address those areas of concern (documentation of interventions or strategies tried and their effectiveness)
- Student performance indicators (grades, test scores, benchmarks)
- Parent contacts, dates, purpose, and outcome

The SST Meeting

During the SST meeting, one of the members facilitates discussion. Members of the team share pertinent information and observations regarding the student, as do the parents. The team typically examines available records such as the student's past report cards, assessment data, portfolio, work samples, attendance record, health records, and vision and hearing screenings. The team also discusses prior strategies and interventions that have been implemented.

After the classroom teacher shares information about the student's performance, and observed areas of strength and weakness, he or she may be asked clarification questions. The teacher may also be asked to identify the strategies and interventions that seem to work best and what he or she has learned to be effective in motivating and reinforcing the student.

The team next brainstorms possible strategies and interventions to address the areas of concern. A plan of action, generally consisting of a targeted goal or two for improved student outcome and a few strategies and interventions from the brainstormed list to achieve that goal, is decided on and written on the SST action plan.

A follow-up date to examine the effectiveness of the strategies and interventions is typically designated in the plan. This may be a follow-up SST meeting scheduled in a specified number of weeks or a less formal follow-up with the teacher, parents, and one or two members of the team as appropriate. Prior to the follow-up meeting, data are collected showing evidence of whether the intervention was successful in achieving the targeted goals.

It is highly recommended to use the SST process and attempt interventions (strategies, adaptations, accommodations) such as those that are found in the lists below for any students who are struggling or at risk. Most school districts' policy is for teachers to follow the SST process when concerned about an individual student, implementing various strategies and interventions to address the student's learning or behavioral difficulties—prior to making referrals for special education evaluation. The lists of strategies at the end of this section are all appropriate prereferral interventions that teachers may wish to consider for implementation and documentation.

For SSTs to be effective, they need to be priorities of the administration (of the same value as instruction). Meetings need to be scheduled on a regular basis, and all teachers must be trained in the SST procedures so they know how to access the team when they wish assistance with individual students. In schools with high numbers of low-performing and at-risk students, particularly large inner-city schools, in order to have SSTs that can begin to address the number of students in need of intervention plans, alternatives to one team per building should be considered. Some schools, such as those Sandra consults with in New York City, have found creative ways to increase the number and frequency of SST meetings without overburdening staff members. For example, some schools have more than one SST in the building, addressing academies or minischools, upper or lower grades, and other variations. Others have a tiered process, with a first tier of discussion and strategy planning taking place in grade-level teams and the next tier being the more traditional SST meeting.

Whatever the SST process is in any school, no teacher or parent requesting a student be discussed at an SST meeting should have to wait several months before a student is scheduled for a meeting. Efforts should be made to make the process efficient and timely. Note that parents and school personnel have the right under federal law to make a referral for special education, requesting an evaluation at any time if they suspect a student has a disability affecting his or her learning and school performance. It is not a legal requirement that they go through the SST process prior to making a special education referral. However, it is a requirement that there are documented interventions that have been implemented to address the student's areas of difficulty, and schools and districts typically frown on teachers' referring a child to special education without going through the SST problem-solving process.

ACCOMMODATIONS, MODIFICATIONS, AND SUPPORTS CHECKLISTS

The following lists contain a variety of strategies and interventions teachers should consider implementing when differentiating instruction and providing extra support for students in need. Most schools and districts require that teachers have tried various strategies and made some adaptations for struggling students prior to referral. Any of the following from the lists are possible accommodations and modifications that may be used when developing SST action plans, as well as 504 accommodation plans, and other individualized student plans, such as individualized educational programs and behavioral intervention plans. These lists, which come from my other books (Rief, 1998, 2003, 2005), are supplementary quick references in addition to the numerous strategies and more extensive suggestions provided in other chapters throughout this book.

Adaptation of Assignments and Instruction

☐ Modify or adjust the length of tasks and assignments.

☐ Reduce quantity of work required, while maintaining standards for accuracy and quality of work.

☐ Increase teacher modeling and use of multisensory instruction.

☐ Increase guided practice.

☐ Provide study guides, advanced organizers, partial outlines, and similar other aids.

☐ Use technology and games for skill practice.

☐ Provide highlighted texts that indicate key words or concepts and information.

☐ Introduce or preview new vocabulary before beginning new lessons.

☐ Use varied questioning strategies to elicit active participation.

☐ Increase the frequency and amount of direct feedback.

☐ Increase the amount of practice and review.

☐ Reemphasize main ideas and key points.

☐ Allow extra wait time or think time (at least five seconds).

☐ Provide direct, systematic instruction to build skills in areas of identified weakness.

☐ Monitor closely as the student begins assignments to ensure his or her understanding.

☐ Provide the student with a task card of things to do for independent seat work.

☐ Add color to increase focus on work (for example, a colored poster board under the student's work on the desk highlighting key words).

☐ Use eye contact and voice modulation to maintain attention.

☐ Structure assignments so that they are broken down into a series of smaller segments. Assign one part at a time, and provide corrective feedback after each part.

☐ Reduce the need for the student to copy from the board or book onto paper. Provide a photocopy or copying assistance instead.

☐ Back up oral directions with written instructions.

☐ Simplify complex directions.

☐ Provide extended time for completion of assignments as needed.

☐ Adjust the reading level of the assignment.

☐ Offer choices in assignments (for example, various topics and levels of difficulty, ability to work independently or with a partner or small group).

☐ Provide samples and models of at-standard and exemplary work.

☐ Provide a rubric detailing teacher expectations for the assignment, including the specific criteria that will be used to evaluate students.

☐ Allow controlled talking opportunities during instruction (for example, asking a peer partner for clarification, think-pair-shares, or structured cooperative group formats).

☐ Write a contract with the student with a reward provided for a specified number of tasks completed.

☐ Provide student graphs or charts to show the percentage of completed assignments.

☐ Use daily or weekly parent-teacher notes or a log book to communicate about the student's work performance and incomplete assignments.

☐ Use a timer with a reward for starting promptly on in-class assignments.

☐ Use an assignment sheet or things-to-do list (to check off completed work).

☐ Provide parents with a weekly progress report indicating their child's current grade and any missing, incomplete, or past-due assignments.

☐ Use a timer and a "beat-the-clock" system with rewards for completing a reasonable amount of work within a specified amount of time.

☐ Increase instructional assistance (from peers, teacher, assistants, and volunteers).

See Chapters Two, Three, Six, Seven, Ten, and Eleven for more strategies on this topic.

Adaptation of Materials

☐ Increase the rate and immediacy of feedback; for example, provide answer keys for immediate self-correction and use computer programs for drilling and practicing basic math facts.

☐ Allow use of a tape recorder to enable the student to listen as many times as needed, recording, for example, directions, test questions, lectures and class reviews, text chapters, and self-reminders.

☐ Structure materials to enhance the student's attention and focus. For example, block the page or fold it in such a way that only part of the text is shown at one time, or frame, highlight, underline, circle, or box in vivid colors the key information.

☐ Enlarge the print size and spacing on the page.

☐ Provide markers for the page when the student is reading—for example, strips of cardboard, index cards, colored transparency frames, and other tools such as the Easy Read Marker (www.sandrarief.com).

☐ Provide handouts that have fewer items on a page and are easy to read.

☐ Use hands-on activities, games, and puzzles that teach and reinforce skills.

☐ Use tactile materials (for example, salt and sand trays and pudding or frosting for writing and tracing with fingers on various surfaces and textures).

☐ Provide an array of learning materials and books that span the student's developmental levels (for example, books on a topic of study that range from an easy reading level through more challenging levels).

See Chapters Seven, Eleven, and Fourteen for more strategies on this topic.

Environmental Accommodations

☐ Establish a calm, predictable environment.

☐ Increase the structure of the environment.

☐ Provide preferential seating (for example, closer to the teacher and center of instruction).

☐ Reduce or minimize distractions: visual, auditory, spatial, and movement.

☐ Provide a study carrel or office area to reduce distractions during seat work.

☐ Provide privacy boards or other partitions for seat work and test taking.

☐ Use visual signals, for example, flashing lights and visual timers such as Time Tracker (www.learningresources.com) or TimeTimer (www.timetimer.com) to obtain attention to and alert students to approaching transitions, changes of routine, or remaining time to complete a test or task.

☐ Increase the use of a partner or buddy throughout the day to help focus the student's attention to task or check understanding of directions.

☐ Increase teacher proximity to student. Frequently move near off-task or disruptive students, and stand near students when giving directions or presenting lessons.

☐ Seat the student in close proximity to teacher (for example, where the teacher most frequently instructs or near the board or projection screen).

☐ Use visual or graphic depictions of routines, procedures, and steps.

☐ Reduce auditory distractions through the use of tools (for example, earphones, white noise music).

☐ Reduce clutter and visual distractions, especially in the direct visual field.

☐ Seat the student away from high traffic areas, windows and doors, center activities, or other areas of distraction.

☐ Seat the student among well-focused classmates.

☐ Use auditory cues (for example, ring a bell, chimes, or other instrument, or use auditory timers or clap patterns) to call students to attention before giving directions, signal transition time, and so forth.

☐ Record all assignments in a consistent place in the room (for example, on the corner of the board).

See Chapters Two, Three, and Six for more strategies on this topic.

Memory Supports and Accommodations

☐ Use visual or graphic depictions to help the student remember routines, procedures, or sequences of steps.

☐ Use mnemonics and association strategies to aid with memory of math facts, spelling, vocabulary, and other lessons.

☐ Use melody and rhythm to help with memory of information.

☐ Use checklists and things-to-do lists.

☐ After instructions are given, have partners clarify with each other what they are to do.

☐ Supply and use sticky notes for reminders, and encourage the student to place them in strategic locations.

☐ Significantly increase opportunities for review and practice.

☐ Provide memory aids for math, such as number lines, multiplication tables and charts, lists of steps and formulas, and a calculator.

☐ Provide checklists, task cards, reminders of expectations, and directions for independent work activities.

See Chapters Two, Three, Ten, Eleven, and Fourteen for more strategies on this topic.

Organization and Time Management Supports and Accommodations

☐ Provide an assignment calendar or planner or assignment sheet, and require assignments to be recorded daily.

☐ Provide direct monitoring and assistance (for example, by a peer buddy or teacher) to ensure assignments are recorded daily and taken home.

☐ Use a program that instructs students in organization and study skills, such as *Skills for School Success* (Archer & Gleason, 2003).

☐ Model the recording of assignments onto a calendar or planner.

☐ Have an end-of-day check by teacher for expected books and materials to take home.

☐ Provide handouts that are punched with three holes to place in a notebook.

☐ Color-code books, notebooks, and materials to help distinguish different subject areas and make finding them quicker and easier.

☐ Tape to the student's desk a daily or weekly schedule or things-to-do list.

☐ Limit the amount of materials on and inside the student's desk.

☐ Provide time and assistance for cleaning out and sorting students' messy desks, backpacks, notebooks, and lockers.

☐ Provide models of well-organized papers, projects, notebooks, and so forth.

☐ Provide in-class assistance with organization of space and materials.

☐ Provide bonus points and other rewards for being organized.

☐ Break long-term assignments into increments. Provide interim due dates and help with time management and monitoring of project time lines.

☐ Assist the student in determining the amount of time that assignments should take to complete.

☐ Modify homework as needed, being responsive to parent feedback.

☐ Provide the student direct assistance for getting started on homework assignments and projects at school.

See Chapter Ten for other organization, time management, and homework strategies and adaptations.

Writing Accommodations and Modifications

☐ Reduce the number of paper-and-pencil tasks.

☐ Provide a copy of another student's class notes to supplement the notes of struggling writers.

☐ Allow the student to use cursive handwriting or printing (whichever is easier and more legible to read).

☐ Allow the use of a computer for written tasks (and provide computer access).

☐ Provide options for demonstrating mastery of concepts and skills through alternatives to writing (for example, oral exams, projects, demonstrations, visual displays).

☐ Permit writing directly on the page or test booklet rather than having to copy answers onto another page or answer sheet.

☐ Allow the student to dictate responses while someone else records or transcribes them.

☐ Allow extra time for written responses.

☐ Have student try a variety of pencil grips and use one that is comfortable.

☐ Have student use a mechanical pencil.

☐ Provide a clipboard to anchor loose papers.

☐ Experiment with different sizes of graph paper and lined paper. Some children with writing difficulties can write more neatly and easily within smaller or narrower lines; others do better with wider lines.

☐ Provide models and rubrics of writing expectations.

☐ Provide graphic organizers for all writing requirements and genres.

☐ Provide direct assistance and support (for example, in proofing and editing, organizing ideas).

See Chapters Three and Eleven for more strategies on this topic.

Reading Accommodations

☐ Provide books on the topic of study and books of student interest available at the student's independent reading level.

☐ Increase the use of graphic organizers to aid in comprehension of text.

☐ Provide books on tape. Apply for books on tape through Recordings for the Blind and Dyslexic (www.rfbd.org).

☐ Provide direct, systematic instruction to build deficit skills and reading proficiency.

☐ Use assistive technology.

☐ Increase reading opportunities and instruction (for example, additional guided reading, read-alouds, phonemic awareness, phonics, and word study).

☐ Read directions aloud to the student and clarify his or her understanding.

See Chapters Three and Eleven for more strategies on this topic.

Accommodations for Testing

☐ Prior to testing, *review, review, review.*

☐ Provide students with handouts and test copies that are easy to read (typed, written in clear language, at least double spaced, clean copies, ample margins).

☐ Eliminate unnecessary words and confusing language on the test.

☐ State directions in clear terms and simple sentences.

☐ Omit some test items.

☐ Provide examples of different types of test questions the student will be responsible for on the exam.

☐ Administer frequent short quizzes throughout the teaching unit, reviewing the next day, and thus providing feedback to students on their understanding of the material.

☐ Read aloud the directions for the different parts of the test before students begin the exam.

☐ Provide extra credit and bonus point opportunities.

☐ Practice all types of testing formats, sharing and discussing test-taking strategies.

☐ Provide additional work space on the test, particularly for math tests.

☐ Write multiple-choice questions with choices listed vertically rather than horizontally (they are easier to read that way).

☐ Reduce the weight of a single test grade. Have several shorter and more frequent quizzes rather than a lengthy unit test.

☐ Allow students to retake the test orally after it is given in written form to add points to their score if they are able to demonstrate greater knowledge or mastery than shown on the written test (especially for essay questions).

☐ Do not penalize for spelling, grammar, and other mechanics on tests that are measuring mastery of content in other areas.

☐ Use privacy boards at desks during test-taking time.

☐ Read test items orally to the student.

☐ Administer the test to the student in a different location (for example, in a resource room).

☐ Administer the test to the student at a different time of the day from the rest of the class.

☐ Provide extended time for testing.

☐ Allow a calculator and multiplication charts and tables on math tests that are assessing problem-solving skills, not computation.

☐ Administer the test in shorter intervals in several sessions.

☐ Revise the test page format (for example, reduce the number of items on a page, enlarge the print size, or increase the spacing between items).

☐ Permit brief breaks during testing if needed.

☐ Permit the use of earplugs or some other device to block out auditory distractions during testing.

☐ Eliminate the need for students with writing difficulties to copy test questions from the board or book before answering.

☐ Provide a scribe.

Behavioral Accommodations

☐ Increase student monitoring and supervision.

☐ Use discreet private signals with the student.

☐ Provide student with cooling-off options (time and space to regroup).

☐ Provide the student with a two-seat option (for example, desk a or desk b) and different options for doing work in various locations or positions.

☐ Allow the student to move to another location in the room to regain control (student initiated or teacher prompted).

☐ Increase communication with parents—through more frequent conferences and planning meetings to build a partnership on behalf of student.

☐ Establish a home-school communication form or system for behavior monitoring.

☐ Buddy up with another teacher (for example, for providing the disruptive student time away in another classroom).

☐ Identify what will be most motivating as incentives for an individual student (for example, leadership roles, responsibilities, working to earn tangible or activity reinforcers individually or for the group).

☐ Increase the opportunity for positive reinforcement when displaying appropriate behavior, and increase the immediacy of reward schedule.

☐ Let the student know you are interested in helping him or her, talk with student about his and her needs, and encourage open communication.

☐ Give the student choices, and involve him or her in problem solving.

☐ Discuss inappropriate behavior with the student in private.

☐ Write a contract for student behavior, with the goal and a predetermined reward for success stated.

☐ Use role playing with the student to practice appropriate behavior.

☐ Use nonverbal cues, signals, and prompts to redirect and remind the student of behavioral expectations.

☐ Allow the student to stand up at the desk when having difficulty remaining seated, or use another alternative, such as sitting on a beanbag chair with paper attached to a clipboard.

☐ Use visual prompts (for example, a cue on his or her desk of behavioral expectations in pictures or a few simple words).

See Chapters Three, Six, and Nine for more strategies on this topic.

Social, Emotional, and Coping Accommodations and Supports

☐ Try to identify what is causing the student stress and frustration through private conference or close observation.

☐ Seek opportunities to involve the student in learning and practicing needed skills (for example, relaxation training, stress management, conflict resolution, anger management). Provide such instruction and practice through direct services of trained school professionals or refer the student to community service providers.

☐ Arrange opportunities for brief breaks to serve as diversions, for example, carrying messages to other classrooms or to the office.

☐ Call attention to the student's strengths and display his or her talents.

☐ Give the student class responsibility (for example, as a teacher's assistant, peer tutor, model, group leader) or other school responsibility, such as office helper or flag raiser.

☐ Consult with other teachers and support personnel (for example, a guidance counselor, nurse, assistant principal, special education teacher, or school psychologist).

☐ Increase communication with the parents.

☐ Assign a peer buddy who will be supportive and tolerant.

☐ Teach appropriate social skills, coping strategies, and problem solving.

☐ Positively reinforce the student's use and application of appropriate social skills and coping strategies.

☐ Pair the student with an upper-grade tutor or staff member as a mentor or special friend.

☐ Significantly increase positive interactions, frequency of encouragement, and feedback with the student.

☐ Use a point system or token economy for earning tokens (points, class "play" money) for targeted self-control behaviors that are redeemable for various rewards of choice.

☐ Provide opportunities for the student to take a break in order to calm down when he or she is feeling agitated or frustrated.

☐ Make extra efforts to build a relationship with the student and show an interest in his or her life.

See Chapters Three, Six, and Eight for more strategies on this topic.

SCHOOL SUPPORT STAFF AND EXPERTISE

There are various ways that school support staff, as well as administrators and others, may be able to assist teachers, students, and families. Sometimes as a result of the SST meeting, additional safety nets are recommended for the student that involve interventions and supports provided by someone other than the classroom teacher (for example, the counselor or reading teacher). Also, teachers or parents may bring their concerns to the attention of one of the support staff members, informally or as a first step prior to an SST meeting. It is important that teachers know who the school professionals in the building are, their room numbers, e-mail, and their school telephone numbers or extensions. It helps if teachers are provided a list, such as the With Whom Should You Consult? list shown below, which is filled in with the current information each school year. This is particularly beneficial for teachers new to the building. Teachers should always feel free to approach or contact a support staff member for information, consultation, and suggestions that would help the teacher better understand and be able to address the needs of individual students.

Possible Interventions

There are various ways that school support staff members may be of direct assistance to students, classroom teachers, and families. Roles of individual staff members differ by school; nevertheless, depending on scheduling, availability, and other factors, they may be able to provide some of the supports listed on pages 101–102.

With Whom Should You Consult?	
Questions/Concerns Related to:	**Speak with**
Hearing/vision	
Other health concerns	
Previous Student Support Teams/plans of action	
Academics (for example, modifications, strategies, materials)	
Gross motor/fine motor skills	
Speech/language	
Counseling	
Attendance/lateness	
Behavior	
Social-emotional issues	
ELL/second language	
Family/home issues	

Academic Support

☐ Provide modeling for teachers.

☐ Demonstrate and share instructional strategies.

☐ Suggest ways to modify assignments, make adaptations, and differentiate instruction.

☐ Observe students in the classroom, student work samples, and teaching style.

☐ Assist with academic screening.

☐ Provide materials and resources for teacher and student use.

☐ Assist in obtaining access to computers and other tools to enhance instruction or support students.

☐ Explore academic safety nets that students may access, such as organizational assistance, placement in an additional guided reading instruction group, or other school reading intervention program.

☐ Arrange teacher mentoring.

☐ Facilitate cross-classroom instruction and observation.

☐ Assist in finding cross-age tutors.

☐ Provide student support (direct or indirect; in class or out of class).

Health, Physical, and Attendance Support

☐ Conduct vision and hearing screening.

☐ Check medical records.

☐ Obtain a health and developmental history.

☐ Develop an attendance contract with incentives for improved attendance.

☐ Refer to appropriate agencies.

☐ Assist in obtaining eyeglasses or shoes for students in need.

☐ Observe the student.

☐ Provide AD/HD information, medication monitoring, or communication among the parent, teacher, and physician.

☐ Provide information or consultation regarding a student's health or medical needs.

☐ Arrange interagency communication.

☐ Serve as a liaison between teacher, physician, and parent.

☐ Attend parent-teacher conferences with the teacher as needed.

Behavior, Social, and Emotional Support

☐ Assist with behavioral contracts and incentives for the student.

☐ Provide crisis management.

☐ Observe the student.

☐ Model effective behavioral strategies to the teacher or student.

☐ Provide individual or group counseling.

☐ Assist the student with problem-solving and conflict-resolution strategies.

☐ Explore social-emotional safety nets appropriate for the student.

☐ Provide behavior modification resources.

☐ Maintain individual contact with the student to provide support.

☐ Arrange for interagency communication.

☐ Provide referrals to agencies.

☐ Attend parent-teacher conferences with the teacher as needed.

☐ Provide a time-out or time-away location and supervision.

☐ Conduct training, groups, and targeted strategies (for example, in anger management, social skills, stress management, or dealing with a crisis).

☐ Provide a functional behavioral assessment and development of behavioral intervention plans.

Communication: Speech/Language; English Language Acquisition

☐ Determine the student's language proficiency level.

☐ Assist with screening.

☐ Observe the student.

☐ Suggest or model strategies for English-language learners.

☐ Strategize and provide support with regard to the educational needs of English-language learners.

☐ Model techniques and strategies for children with speech/language difficulties.

☐ Provide materials and resources to the classroom teacher.

Family

☐ Conduct a home visit.

☐ Inform parents of the availability of supports, training, and other resources.

☐ Provide translation services.

☐ Assist with transportation.

☐ Provide referrals to agencies.

☐ Attend parent-teacher conferences.

☐ Help families link up with appropriate resources and agencies in the community.

☐ Help in organizing parent trainings on such topics as helping your child with homework or strategies and supports targeting parents of special population students.

Structuring for Success

When differentiating instruction and making every effort to address the diverse needs of students (especially special populations of children with disabilities and exceptionalities, English-language learners, and others), it is important for teachers to employ necessary adaptations and strategies for the classroom.

The previous lists should be helpful in considering what may be done with regard to adjusting some of the instructional and academic, environmental, and structural factors in the classroom. Among your school support professionals is a wealth of expertise. Teachers need to know those key professionals in the building and feel free to ask for their guidance, consultation, and support. The SST is a wonderful forum for tapping into the expertise of a team to develop and monitor an intervention plan for students in need. Schools should make every effort to ensure that the SST is structured for success and is a process that teachers view as helpful and worthwhile in addressing the needs of individual students.

REFERENCES

Archer, A., & Gleason, M. (2003). *Skills for school success.* North Billerica, MA: Curriculum Associates.

Easy Read Marker. San Diego, CA: Educational Resource Specialists. Available through www.sandrarief.com.

Recordings for the Blind and Dyslexic. www.rfbd.org.

Rief, S. (1998). *The ADD/ADHD checklist: An easy reference for parents and teachers.* San Francisco: Jossey-Bass.

Rief, S. (2003). *The ADHD book of lists.* San Francisco: Jossey-Bass.

Rief, S. (2005). *How to reach and teach children with ADD/ADHD* (2nd ed.). San Francisco: Jossey-Bass.

Chapter 6

MANAGING BEHAVIOR THROUGH SUPPORT AND INTERVENTIONS

Wouldn't it be wonderful if we could walk into each of our classrooms at the beginning of the year and know that our students were eager and motivated to do their best work, comply with our rules and procedures, treat one another with respect, and look up to us with high regard? Behavioral management is a vital issue for teachers, especially when classrooms have more and more students who exhibit challenging and disruptive behaviors. This chapter contains information and recommendations based on a number of sources, including literature on this topic, research on best practices, and years of experience (our own and that of numerous other well-respected administrators, teachers, and counselors who have shared with us the positive practices and behavioral interventions they use within their classrooms and schools).

UNDERSTANDING STUDENT BEHAVIOR

When students misbehave, it helps to understand that there are motivators to behavior: functions, goals, or needs that are being met by demonstrating those undesirable, inappropriate behaviors. Frequently these motivators are not within the student's conscious awareness, but nevertheless prompt the student to behave the way he or she does. Teachers who can determine or have a good idea about which of the student's needs are being fulfilled as a result of the misbehavior can make changes to prevent or reduce that inappropriate behavior.

Functions Served by Behaviors

The main functions or goals of student misbehavior are to get or obtain something, such as attention, power, status, access to something fun or rewarding, or stimulation, or to avoid or escape something, such as failure, fear, embarrassment, effort, punishment, pain, or discomfort.

There will be far fewer discipline problems and behaviors requiring correction and intervention if students' basic needs are being met within the classroom. Particularly with more challenging students, it is helpful to try determining what the student is gaining from the misbehavior, that is, which goals or functions are being met when misbehaving, and help the student meet his or her goals for appropriate rather than inappropriate behavior. For example, if the student's misbehavior results in attention from adults or peers (laughter, teacher providing direct interaction with the student at that time) and this is a student who is seeking attention, the result will be continuation of this type of misbehavior. It will continue because that behavior worked for the child or teen. The student's inappropriate behavior (clowning around) was rewarded or reinforced by obtaining attention (Rief, 2005).

Any behavior is sustained by reinforcement. If a behavior is rewarded, it will likely continue. Therefore, efforts should be made to withdraw attention from this student when he or she is misbehaving and ensure that there are numerous opportunities for him or her to receive a strong dose of positive attention from peers and adults throughout the day when he or she is engaged appropriately. In many cases, it also involves teaching the student replacement behaviors to use, such as ways to ask appropriately for help or signal the teacher that he or she is frustrated or needs a brief break, and being vigilant in reinforcing that student's use of the appropriate replacement behavior.

Environmental Triggers of Misbehavior

Some of the causes of misbehavior are manifestations of a child's inexperience, lack of awareness, or developmental immaturity. Our response to misbehavior needs to take these factors into account, which may involve addressing the misbehavior in different ways for different children.

Students may misbehave for any number of reasons. Certain conditions, times of day, settings, activities, events, and people can be triggers to misbehavior. We need to look below the surface to see what may be causing individual students to behave inappropriately. By teacher awareness of common triggers, or antecedents, to students' misbehaviors, we can be proactive and make adjustments that can prevent many behavioral problems from occurring or significantly reduce them. The best management strategy is to anticipate potential problems and avoid them through careful planning.

Some of the following antecedents are often triggers to misbehavior (Rief, 2003, 2005):

- *Environmentally based.* Uncomfortable conditions (too noisy, crowded, hot, or cold); certain settings (hallways, cafeteria, playground); a lack of structure (organization, predictability, clear schedule, visual supports)
- *Physically based.* When the child is not feeling well (ill, overly tired, hungry, thirsty); medication-related factors (for example, short-acting medication is wearing off, change of prescription or dosage)
- *Related to a performance or skill demand.* To remain seated an extended period of time, to read out loud or independently, to write in cursive neatly, to wait patiently for a turn, or any other behavioral or performance expectation that is frustrating or a struggle for that individual student
- *Related to specific activity or event.* Recess and other unstructured activity time, change of routine without warning, independent seat work, cooperative learning activities, when assigned tasks the student perceives as boring
- *Related to a specific time.* First period of the day, before or after lunch, transition times of day, late afternoons, Monday mornings
- *Related to a specific person.* In the presence or absence of . . . administrators; a particular teacher or staff member; a particular classmate, peer, or group of students; parents
- *Other.* When given no choices or options, when having difficulty communicating, when given no assistance or access to help on difficult tasks.

It is important to pay attention to antecedent conditions in the effort to help avoid, if possible, what tends to trigger reactive behavior from the student. If certain activities or performance demands set off a student who is easily frustrated by such tasks, teachers can take steps to avoid having the child turn to acting-out behavior in response to that performance demand. For example, providing the student with a buddy, making some adaptations to the assignment, or providing other various supports and accommodations may prevent that child from demonstrating acting-out behavior. If transition times of the day are known to be common problematic times, increasing the structure during changes of activity in the classroom, providing advance warning and cues before transitions, or providing direct assistance during those times can prevent the problem behavior.

SUPPORTING PROACTIVE CLASSROOM MANAGEMENT

Schools can do many things to support behavioral success. Effort on everyone's part to create a positive climate and culture in classrooms and school settings throughout the building is key. Every teacher should build classroom environments that are structured, welcoming, respectful, inclusive, and physically and emotionally safe, and reflect the commitment that each student belongs and can be successful. At the schoolwide level, the climate and culture can be improved significantly through adoption of a specific program (commercial or developed by the staff) that focuses on problem prevention throughout the building. All faculty are involved in teaching, modeling, promoting, and reinforcing the targeted prosocial behaviors and positive character traits and values, such as respect, responsibility, safety, cooperation, and perseverance, to the student population.

Schools support behavioral success when the schoolwide discipline plan is well thought out, has buy-in from the staff, and is consistently implemented. Provide adequate supervision during recess, lunch, before and after school, and passing periods and adult monitoring in all areas around the school campus that are identified as problematic. It is important that policies and rules are communicated clearly to all students, parents, and staff, with everyone accountable for student learning and behavior. All behavioral expectations and procedures must be taught, practiced, and reinforced within all environments of the school, and everyone—students, faculty, administrators, and parents—should be treated with respect.

It is important for teachers to receive professional development in classroom management practices and understanding and educating students with disabilities and various neurobiological and mental health disorders affecting learning and behavior. Providing for teacher mentoring and coaching and opportunities to share behavioral management strategies among peers is helpful. Teachers should be encouraged to bring students of concern, behavioral as well as academic, to their school's student support teams for strategizing and developing intervention plans (see Chapter Five).

There are many ways to support students with social, behavioral, and emotional needs. Initiate intervention when behavior problems first occur, involving parents early in the process. Carefully consider class placement for students, particularly those with disabilities and others who are known to be socially or emotionally fragile and vulnerable, overreactive, disruptive, or at risk for behavioral difficulties; then consider a change of classroom or schedule change for certain situations. Use peer mediation to settle conflict when possible, and provide counseling and guidance sessions of various kinds for students in need. Student interventions should be available for targeted students, such as conflict resolution, anger management, or social skills training, and pertinent issues affecting children's safety and social and emotional well-being, such as bullying and peer pressure, should be addressed throughout whole school, class, or small group programs and activities.

In addition, consider instituting a program at school in which teachers, administrators, support, and auxiliary staff "adopt" or mentor certain students in need of more attention and support. In fact, every child or teen should have at least one adult at school who takes a special interest in his or her life and success. (See Chapter Eight for more on this topic.)

PREVENTING STUDENT MISBEHAVIOR IN THE CLASSROOM

In most classrooms, students' behaviors can be managed through basic structuring of the environment with appropriate rules, consequences, and consistent enforcement (Rief, 2003, 2005). With a management system that focuses on prevention of problems and through mild interventions when problem behaviors do occur, most student misbehaviors can be brought under control. Following are general principles and strategies for preventing or minimizing behavioral problems and interventions to employ within the classroom. Start with the basics by establishing four to five rules that are positively stated, posted, and referred to frequently—for example:

1. Come prepared to work.
2. Follow directions.
3. Stay on task.
4. Keep hands, feet, and objects to yourselves.
5. Be kind and courteous to others.

1. Bring all needed materials to class.
2. Be in your seat and ready to work when the bell rings: pencils sharpened, paper and pencil out, and warm-ups started.
3. Obtain permission before speaking or leaving your seat.
4. Be respectful and polite to all people.

Class Contract

We agree to:

1. Practice safety.
2. Be respectful of others.
3. Follow directions and cooperate with each other.
4. Take responsibility for our learning.

Following are examples of schoolwide rules and expectations from two middle schools:

School A
1. Behave safely.
2. Be responsible.
3. Dress appropriately.
4. Show respect.

School B

- *Respect for People:* I will behave and cooperate in ways that help myself and others feel safe, respected, and cared about.
- *Respect for Learning:* I will be punctual and prepared for classes, listen carefully, participate, and give my best effort.
- *Respect for Property:* I will take pride in the care of my school. I will care for my own belongings and respect the property of others.

Structural and Environmental Variables

Effective classroom management involves careful planning, structuring, and establishment of a supportive learning environment. Through awareness of and attention to structural and environmental variables that affect student learning and behavior, teachers can significantly prevent or minimize behavioral problems in the classroom. Following are basic teaching strategies that establish the structure for success and address some environmental factors that will make a positive difference for students:

- Provide structure. Establish clear, reasonable rules and behavioral standards, routines, procedures, and guidelines.
- Explain the rationale for all expectations and procedures, and thoroughly teach, model, practice, and review them frequently.
- Externalize the rules (post them; use photos or pictures to depict them), and refer to the visual of the rules frequently.
- Provide specific, descriptive feedback to students—for example, "I see that Jody has her book open to the right page, and her paper and pencil are out. Jody is ready to work."
- Prepare for and structure transition times of the day, and provide extra help when there are unexpected changes of routine and unstructured situations.
- Arrange the environment for easy access to all parts of the room and students' desks and clear visibility of all students.
- Use proximity control: circulate among students, and stand next to the desk of a student who is prone to misbehavior.
- Change student seating; for example, move distractible students closer to the center of instruction or closer to the teacher for cueing and prompting and away from distractors.
- Provide more space if possible (for example, increase the distance between desks).
- Use music for transitions and for calming and relaxing students.
- Build a classroom environment with a sense of community, teamwork, and interdependence.

See Chapters Two and Five for more environmental strategies and accommodations.

Affective Variables and Personalized Efforts

The key to effective classroom management is building positive relationships and rapport with students and making a connection on a personal level. This requires teachers to be understanding, flexible, patient, and empathic. Children typically work hard and want to cooperate and please adults whom they like, trust, and respect:

- Smile, laugh, and communicate that you enjoy teaching and being with students; show through your daily interactions that you sincerely care about and expect the best from all of your students and would never give up on any of them.
- Acknowledge and validate what students are thinking and feeling.
- Avoid lecturing, nagging, and criticism.
- Enforce rules and expectations, but take into consideration factors that may require handling some situations differently.

Instructional Variables

There is no question that the best way to avoid students' misbehaving out of boredom, disinterest, or frustration is through positive instructional practices. Most teachers who are motivating and skilled instructors have few behavior management difficulties. Make sure to:

- Provide engaging, meaningful learning activities and instruction. This book is packed with ideas for instruction and specific activities.
- Plan well. The better we are prepared for lessons, the smoother classroom management will be. Lag time (when students are unoccupied and waiting for teacher direction) is when behavior problems often arise.
- Provide independent work that is developmentally appropriate and within students' capability of doing successfully without assistance or be able to access help in a short amount of time.
- Use effective and inclusive questioning techniques (such as those in Chapter Seven).
- Use differentiated instructional practices (see Chapter One), and make accommodations for different learning styles (see Chapters Two, Three, and Five).

IMPLEMENTING BEHAVIOR MANAGEMENT SYSTEMS

Teachers use a variety of group positive reinforcement systems in their classroom management practices. Such systems motivate and reward cooperative, rule-following behavior. There are several kinds of class reinforcement systems teachers may choose to implement to fit their style of teaching, comfort level, and the interest of their students.

Classroom Contingencies

Following are examples of some common group reinforcement systems (Rief, 2003, 2005).

Table or Team Points

Points are given when specific behaviors are demonstrated (for example, cooperation and teamwork, on task, all assignments turned in, area cleaned up, transitioning on or before allotted time). Table points may be used competitively or noncompetitively but more commonly are used competitively in classrooms. Points are awarded when the teacher observes tables or teams demonstrating the target behaviors: "Table 4, good job of cooperating and helping your teammates. You just earned a point." At the end of the week, the table or team with the most points earns the reward or privilege (or the top two tables may win the reward).

Tables that have students with more behavioral challenges seated at them may rarely win such a competition. This can cause frustration as well as resentment toward certain individual students in the group. It is important for all students to experience success, and the noncompetitive method of using table points may be preferable. With this method, whenever any table or team reaches a target number of points, they earn the reward or privilege. Then they start over again, so Friday is not necessarily the reward day of the week; it will differ for each team depending on when they reach their point goal.

Marbles in a Jar

Teachers (usually in primary grade classrooms) "catch" students engaged in appropriate behaviors. They call attention to the positive behavior of an individual student, group of students, or something the whole class did well. Then the teacher reinforces the positive behavior by putting a marble or similar other object in a jar (for example, a scoop of dried beans or of uncooked kernels of popcorn). When the jar is filled, the whole class earns a reward (for example, a popcorn party). This is a particularly effective technique for rewarding quick and smooth transitions. It also has the benefit of being a flexible technique for rewarding the whole group when an individual student accomplishes or demonstrates a particular behavior. "Nice job, Carolyn. You just earned the class a marble."

Chart Moves

A chart is created for the class or group. The class is reinforced for meeting a set goal by advancing one space on the chart each time they meet that goal. When the chart is filled, the whole class earns the reward. There are numerous types of charts that can be made. We recommend changing the chart frequently for novelty and to maintain students' interest. Dot-to-dot charts and any game board type of chart will work.

A particular goal or two is set—for example, all students are in their seats with materials ready by the morning bell or there are no observed incidents of a particular problematic behavior in a certain time frame (such as during writer's workshop, coming into class after lunch, each specified number of minutes of a class period with a timer set for that time frame). Each time the class meets that goal, a move is made on the chart, such as connecting to the next dot (on a dot-to-dot chart), advancing one square, or coloring in the next space on a class chart. Every move forward on the chart is a visual display of success.

Token Economy System

Students have the chance to earn tokens of some kind, such as points, tickets, poker chips, or class money for on-the-spot reinforcers. These tokens are accumulated and redeemable later at a class store, auction, or raffle for a desired reward. A menu of rewards, which include privileges as well as tangible items, is developed with corresponding price values attached. Students can spend their earned tokens, points, or money at designated times during class auctions or shopping at the class store.

Token economy systems also allow a teacher to fine or charge students (for example, ten dollars in class currency for leaving a needed book at home and having to borrow another; ten dollars for being late to class). Teachers must award generously and frequently for positive behaviors so that students, particularly those with AD/HD, are not overly fined for rule infractions or forgetfulness. This would result in frustration and loss of motivation, and the program probably would not be effective.

Probability Reinforcers

A raffle system is an example of probability reinforcers. Teachers pass out raffle tickets to individual students who are caught demonstrating target behaviors or meeting certain goals. The students write their name on the ticket and place it in a container. Drawings are held daily or weekly. Students whose names are drawn receive prizes or privileges. This system is based on the principle of probability, and students understand that the more tickets they earn, the greater their chance is of winning a reward.

Good Behavior Game

This is a research-validated approach first described by Barrish, Saunders, and Wolf (1969) for significantly decreasing disruptive behaviors in the classroom. There are a number of variations to the "good behavior game." It basically involves dividing the class into teams, with team numbers listed on the board. At specified times of the day, the game is played. A timer is set, and designated disruptive behaviors that occur during that time period result in a check mark or tally mark recorded under the team name. The teacher states the inappropriate behavior that resulted in that penalty. At the end of the time frame, any team with under a specified number of marks (for example, three penalties or fewer) earns a reward. Initially the time frame for playing the game is short, and the rewards are immediate for winning teams. Gradually the time frame is extended and reward times are not immediate; they are, for example, provided at the end of the day. (For information regarding this game and its implementation in Baltimore Public Schools, go to www.bpp.jhu.edu/publish/manuals/gbg.html, an online manual.)

Group Response Cost

Response cost techniques are an interesting means of improving and shaping behavior. They work differently from positive reinforcement systems in that instead of giving tokens or points for demonstrating the appropriate behavior, students work to keep the tokens or points that they are given up front. They are penalized by *losing* tokens for specific behaviors or rule infractions. Technically, being fined or losing tokens is a punishment. But this response cost program is designed so that if students have a certain number of tokens or points remaining at the end of the time frame, they met their goal and earn a reward.

A target behavior that the whole class is working to improve is selected—for example, being in their seats or otherwise in place unless they have permission to be elsewhere; using appropriate language, that is, no cursing or swearing; or waiting to be called on to speak. A certain number of points or tokens (for example, stars written at the top of the board, paper or plastic links on a chain, sticks in a cup) are automatically given at the beginning of each day, class period, or other time frame. The number of tokens given up front is determined after getting a baseline of how frequently the problematic behavior typically occurs. For example, if the target problem behavior (such as talking out without raising hands) generally occurs at least ten times in a class period, initially the class may start with eight tokens given at the beginning of the period. Then a point or token is removed or crossed out every time the inappropriate behavior (talking out) occurs. If there is at least one of the points or tokens remaining at the end of the time, the class has met the goal successfully and earns a preselected reward such as a move on the class chart or minutes earned toward a rewarding activity. In this example, if they started with eight points at the beginning of the period and had one remaining by the end of the class period, the talking-out behavior was improved by 30 percent (from ten times down to seven). The criterion for success is gradually raised. For example, next, only seven tokens are given at the beginning of the class period, then six, then five, and so on until the behavior has significantly improved to the point that the program can be discontinued or a different behavior may be selected.

There are many variations of response cost systems. The key is that students are working to keep what they have been given. One variation is that at the beginning of the day, the teacher may automatically give to the class fifteen minutes of free time or special activity time to be used at the end of the day or week. Specific misbehaviors that occur during the day will result in one minute loss of time from the free minutes given. The net positive balance will be awarded at the end of the day or week. Of course, the teacher has the discretion to add bonus minutes during the day for exceptionally good behavior to increase the motivation.

Rewards

Students should be involved in identifying a menu of rewards that would be motivating and fun to work toward earning. Following are some examples of social, activity, and material rewards and reinforcers that students can earn for incentive programs being implemented in the classroom or schoolwide.

Social Rewards

Potential social rewards are verbal praise, public recognition, positive telephone calls, notes, and e-mails to the student or parents. Earning a privilege of social status such as being team captain, class messenger, or teaching part of a lesson or time to work with or sit together with a friend are examples of social rewards.

Activity Rewards and Privileges

Earning the privilege of participating in various activities is a powerful reward for most students. Such activities can be classroom based: games, listening to music, drawing, working on a special project, accessing learning and interest centers, having the opportunity to use special materials or tools, do an Internet search, or being allowed time to catch up on work, with the teacher or peer assistance available if needed. Activity rewards might also be provided in other school settings, such as access to equipment or materials or playing a game in the gym, media center, or music room. Favorite student activities often involve participation in parties (ice cream, popcorn, pizza), movies, dances, or having breakfast or lunch with a teacher or other staff member. Special responsibilities may be considered activity reinforcers, such as tutoring a younger student, caring for the class pet, or assisting the teacher or other staff member with certain jobs.

Material Reinforcers

There are a host of possible material reinforcers students might earn. These are tangible items such as stickers, small toys, treasure box trinkets, baseball or football cards, special school supplies (such as pencils or erasers), and any kind of food snacks or drinks. Free tickets might be awarded to school sporting events, school plays, dances, or concerts. Material rewards may also include tokens such as class (or school) money, tickets, or points that are later redeemable at auctions or lotteries or purchasing items of choice at class or school stores. Special passes and certificates that students earn and can redeem when they wish are valued rewards. These might include homework passes (good for one assignment or one night of homework) or a bonus point coupon (good for five bonus points that can be added to quiz or homework assignment grade).

Class Meetings and Problem Solving

This is a system used to discuss and problem-solve issues happening inside and outside the classroom. Students write problems that have occurred on a problem board or clipboard. In some classes, the student needs to try at least one strategy for solving the problem before he or she is allowed to enter it on the board, and only at designated times of the day. On the form, the student writes his or her name and the person with whom he or she is in conflict, and then briefly explains what happened. As one counselor described this system, "This gives the child a place to temporarily dump the problem." At the end of the day, the teacher does a priority check: "Jeremy, was your problem resolved today?"

In many cases, the student will no longer have need of conflict resolution by the end of the day. Otherwise the situation is shared with the class, and the class decides on a consequence by consensus. Some teachers conduct regularly scheduled classroom meetings for a designated amount of time (for example, fifteen minutes twice a week or weekly or a half-hour weekly meeting). During these class meetings, if the problem still exists, the person accused of being involved has the chance to respond. Once again, if a rule has been broken by either party, the consequences are nominated by the class and voted on. In addition, the class shares suggestions for avoiding or dealing with such situations in the future. The teacher always screens the problems recorded and handles situations inappropriate for this format in other ways.

Some teachers instead have a special place in their room (on the bulletin board, the back of the door, or a desk) called the "parking lot." There may be a bag containing blank index cards, and another container for placing, or "parking," the cards that have been filled out—stating the problem. Students can fill out a problem card and place it in the parking lot to solve at a later time.

ADDRESSING STUDENT MISBEHAVIOR

In addition to positive reinforcement for appropriate behavior, teachers need to enforce consequences for misbehavior. Students need to know that if they break the rules and cross well-defined behavioral boundaries established in the classroom, there will be consequences. It must be kept in mind that the goal in providing any negative consequences is not to punish for the sake of punishing, but to teach students the need for and expectation they will take responsibility for their behavioral choices.

Corrective Consequences in Response to Problem Behaviors

Not every minor misbehavior should be or needs to be followed with a corrective consequence. Simple low-key responses such as signaling, nonverbal communication ("the teacher look"), reminding of the rules, warning, and ignoring of small infractions are appropriate before employing corrective consequences (Gootman, 2001).

Precision Requests

Rhode, Jenson, and Reavis (1995) recommend that prior to giving corrective consequences, the teacher first use a "precision request" with the student. Only if the student does not comply with the precision request is the consequence applied. This involves first making a quiet "please" request or command (such as, "Please get your materials out and start working"). This is made in close proximity to the student (approximately three feet distance) using a quiet voice and making eye contact with that student. Then, without saying anything for five or ten seconds, the teacher waits for compliance. If the student does not comply within that time, a second request is given using the word *need*—for example, "Now I *need* you to get your materials out and start working." If the student does not comply within five or ten seconds, the teacher implements a preplanned consequence.

Possible Corrective or Negative Consequences

Following are some possible negative consequences and strategies used for reducing misbehavior in elementary and middle schools. This list is not in any hierarchical sequence and serves only to provide examples of possible corrective consequences teachers may consider in addressing mild to moderate misbehaviors. All consequences should be given without lecturing or scolding. They should be delivered calmly, unemotionally, in a matter-of-fact manner:

- Last person to line up or be dismissed.
- Loss of time from participation in preferred activity in the classroom.
- Playground restriction from certain games or areas.
- Loss of some recess time (preferably no more than a couple of minutes). Some students, such as those with AD/HD, need to have opportunities to burn up their excess energy. Refrain, if possible, from using loss of recess or other physical activities as punishment for these children.
- Change of number card sent home (see explanation following).
- Write an apology.
- Change the child's seating or separate him or her from other students.
- Brief delay and owing time (for example, one minute of time owed for each incident of interrupting instructional time). Time owed can be paid back prior to being able to participate in a desired activity or before being dismissed at the end of the day. Even one minute of being delayed can be an effective negative consequence for a student eager to meet up with friends outside class.
- Time out for a period of time by being removed from class participation (within the classroom at a designated area; to a time-out area or desk in another classroom or other location under supervision in the school).
- Restriction or removal of privilege or desired materials for a period of time.
- Having to walk with or stand with a playground supervisor rather than participate.
- Undesirable task or chore assigned.

- Positive practice or "do-overs." For example, for an inappropriate behavior such as running in the hall, throwing materials, or speaking rudely, require the student to correct that behavior and perform it correctly and sometimes repeatedly (such as walking in the hall, picking up a thrown paper, asking a question politely).

- Filling out a think-about-it (problem-solving) sheet or Behavioral Improvement Report (see Form 6.1 at the end of this chapter).

- Loss of points or demerits.

- Being "fined" or losing tokens or tickets that are redeemable for rewards when using a token economy.

- Restitution, that is, fixing the problem. If, for example, the student broke something or made a mess in an area, the consequence is to repair or replace what was broken or to clean up the mess.

- Work center or detention.

- The student writes an e-mail home or phones to notify his or her parents of the behavioral problem at school.

- The teacher writes a note or e-mail or calls the parents to inform them of the student's misbehavior and behavioral problems.

- The student documents his or her own behavior in a class book or on a recording sheet or log.

- The student writes an apology letter.

- Behavioral contract.

- Team conference.

- Parent conference.

There are a number of corrective consequences that are options for teachers to enforce, as indicated above. Teachers should always address minor and moderate behavioral problems first through appropriate corrective consequences, prior to sending a student to the administrator or other school authority for discipline. Serious infractions such as fighting, assault, and other kinds of physical aggression are exceptions and should be referred immediately to administrators.

Numbered Cards

Some teachers use a system of briefly conferencing individually with specific students about their overall behavior for the day. Then the teacher assigns a number to be sent home at the end of the day to indicate to parents how well the student followed rules and expectations. Often this system is tied to a home-school reinforcement system. Students receive some predetermined rewards at home for good behavior days when they come home with a 1 or 2 card. They receive a predetermined consequence such as loss of TV time when the number card sent home is a 4 or 5. Numbers might represent the following teacher rating:

1	Very well behaved. Great day!
2	Good day
3	Fair day (so-so)
4	We had some trouble today.
5	We had a very difficult day.

Behavioral Improvement Forms

Many schools use a system of having students fill out a form describing the problem or situation he or she is in trouble for and identifying a more appropriate strategy or way to deal with the problem or situation if it were to occur again (see Form 6.1 at the end of the chapter). These forms help the student reflect on the situation and his or her own behavioral choices and take part in problem solving. Depending on the age or level of the student, these problem identification and behavior improvement forms vary. Some teachers, counselors, and administrators use forms that simply have the child write what happened, with whom the situation happened, and one alternative strategy to try if the situation arises again. Younger children, or those who have difficulty writing, could draw rather than write about the situation or more appropriate strategy for dealing with it. Counselors and teachers note that just this act of having the students identify the problem from their perspective is very helpful.

The form serves as a springboard for discussion when the student is then seen by the teacher, counselor, or administrator. Younger students can be asked, "Now tell me about your picture." As one counselor shared, "We're trying to teach students that if their behavior isn't good, they didn't make a fatal mistake. Having a chance to share and talk with somebody not directly involved with what happened that got them into trouble and what they can do differently next time is cleansing. It gives the child a fresh start. It allows an impartial person to listen, not respond out of anger or negativity, and credits the child with some dignity."

Step Systems and Discipline Hierarchies

Teachers at all grade levels often use a step system or discipline hierarchy of consequences for general management. In many schools, this is a consistent system used throughout the school as part of the schoolwide discipline plan. Although the specific steps and consequences vary, the general sequence is that for the first offense or infraction of rules, the student receives a minor consequence (for example, two minutes away from group). The next offense results in a stronger consequence (such as five minutes away from group). The third step in the hierarchy of consequences might be a longer period away from the group with a telephone call home to alert the parents to the problem and perhaps time away in a neighboring classroom or counseling center with work to do, or a problem behavior sheet to be filled out. The next step might be an office referral, which may include more significant disciplinary action, such as in-school suspension.

Here is an example from one elementary school classroom, set out in a step system:

1. Verbal warning
2. Second warning
3. Time out (five to ten minutes at the time-out desk in the classroom with a behavioral form to fill out)
4. Time away in a partner classroom (which also has a time-out desk), with work assigned for the student to do in the partner classroom
5. Parent telephone call
6. Office referral

Following is an example of a middle school discipline plan with a hierarchy of negative consequences. This plan is used throughout the school by all teachers, with flexibility with regard to the particular consequences assigned for levels 1–4:

- *First offense:* Conference with student.
- *Second offense, Level 1:* Teacher action and choice of consequences including but not limited to:
  - Time out in class
  - Detention with teacher after school
  - Detention in shared time place or class
  - Behavior journal

- Conflict busters referral (This is a conflict resolution program in the school. The conflict busters are a select group of upper grade students who have been trained in mediation techniques and in resolving conflicts when there is a dispute between students. It is a step students may take as an alternative to adult intervention. Students have the option of trying to solve their peer problems through conflict buster mediation assistance if they choose to do so.)
- Student writes a letter to parents or phones home with the teacher listening in or checking that the student has clearly communicated to the parents about the problem and his or her poor behavioral choices.
- *Third offense:* Teacher calls parent and explains steps taken for first and second offenses. Explains next steps if behavior continues. In addition, a behavior plan is set up with the student.
- *Fourth offense, Level 2:* Teacher action and choice of consequences assigned by teacher, including, but not limited to:
  - Mediation in class
  - Consult with support teacher
  - Time-out in buddy's class
  - Parent conference
  - Written plan
  - Detention after school for one day
  - Teacher can suspend from class for the day of offense and the following day
  - Lower citizenship grade
- *Problem continues, Level 3:* Consequences:
  - Counseling group referral
  - Detention room referral
- *Problem continues, Level 4:* Consequences:
  - Behavior contract in Student Services
  - Student support team referral
  - Saturday school assigned by administrator
  - In-school suspension assigned by administrator
- *Problem unresolved after all levels attempted, Level 5:* Referral to administrator for advanced intervention or action.

One of the keys to effective discipline is consistent follow-through. If the teacher lists on a discipline plan the specific predetermined consequences for various behavioral infractions (as in the example above), these prescribed consequences must be followed. In order to allow some flexibility with regard to which consequences to employ when needed, teachers may consider listing on the discipline plan a few possible consequences that may result for types or levels of behavioral infractions. This enables teachers to be consistent in enforcing a negative consequence according to the discipline plan but to be able to use their professional judgment at the time as to which consequence will be selected.

Alternatives to Suspension and Expulsion

For students whose behaviors are more significant and there is now administrative involvement, the administrator should consider a variety of alternatives to formal suspension. As one principal explained, "The only thing that suspension does that is positive is to document the severity of the problem and get the attention of parents when it happens. Formal suspensions always involve reentry conferences with parents as well to work out a plan for the student." It is important to keep in mind that for students who do not want to be in school, being suspended may have the unintended effect of rewarding that student rather than punishing him or her. In addition, being out of school makes it much more difficult for the student to keep up with classwork and achieve success.

Following are some alternative interventions that could be assigned by the administrator:

- Time-outs or time away in another classroom, counseling center, or office.
- Loss of activities.
- Saturday school (offered at some schools).
- In-school suspension. This has the advantage over out-of-school suspension in that it keeps the student in school and supervised rather than sending the student home, where he or she is often unsupervised and rewarded with the freedom to watch TV, use the Internet, and so forth. An in-school suspension must be absolutely dull, boring, and nonreinforcing for the student. It also requires that there be a physical place (a counseling center or office) where the student can stay and work with direct or indirect adult supervision. The student needs to be given work to do independently during the day. One school has teachers place all extra copies of papers they have run off in a box or tray in the work room for their grade and range of students' independent reading levels. Different packets of these materials can be prepared for students to work on independently during in-school suspension or extended time-outs.
- Parent shadowing of the student for the day or part of the day can be an effective alternative to suspension. Teachers of older students, particularly those in middle school, who have had a parent shadow their child find this strategy an excellent deterrent to future misbehavior. It is helpful to meet with the parent as a team or part of a team while the parent is at school as well and formulate a behavioral plan at that time.
- Modified schedule. This is an intervention that is used most often at the middle school or high school level when classes are changed for students who function better at certain times of the day. One school said that a particular student who had great difficulty functioning because of the high degree of his hyperactivity was scheduled with two physical education periods—one in the morning and one in the afternoon—which was a very helpful intervention for this student.
- School or community service. One middle school principal said that if students at her school are caught littering or defacing school property, she assigns them to be on the campus cleanup patrol. They need to help pick up trash around campus and do certain reasonable jobs assigned by the custodian during noninstructional time. Another middle school principal has a "gum patrol" to which students caught breaking the no-chewing-gum rule are assigned. The principal assigns any student referred for chewing gum to her Thursday afternoon gum patrol duty. She monitors their participation in scraping off gum found around the campus. Other kinds of school service assigned by the administrator may include shelving books in the library, helping in the cafeteria to clean up after lunch, or working in the computer lab to clean keyboards.

Problem Behavior in Other School Environments

In many cases, the most significant behavioral issues occur outside the classroom—on the playground, in the lunch area, in the restrooms, between classes—where there tend to be less structure and supervision.

Elementary School Playground

Following are recommended practices that schools have found to be effective in reducing the number of discipline problems that take place during these times:

- Increase the amount of supervision to allow adequate monitoring of students.

- Add more structure by teaching, practicing, and enforcing specific rules as to how supplies and equipment are to be used appropriately, checked out, and returned; signals for lining up to return to class; and so forth.

- Use a one-bell signal that signals everyone to freeze, then a second signal or bell for students to line up to return to class, preferably walking quickly.

- Provide several choices of activities that children can participate in during recess, allowing all students who wish to engage in activities the opportunity to play. It is helpful if certain areas of the playground are designated for particular games. Many discipline problems can arise out of frustration at having to wait without being able to actively participate. This is especially true for children with AD/HD.

- Make sure there is a variety of games, ideally ones that can run themselves with minimal adult supervision. In addition, there should be sufficient supplies and equipment (jump ropes and hula hoops, for example) to accommodate all children who wish to use them.

- If certain students or groups of students who play together at recess are frequently in conflict, assign an adult to target that group of students, adding more structure for and direct supervision of them.

- Have an option (if possible) available to students who are uncomfortable on the playground—perhaps open time in the library, the media center, or another area where students can read and play quieter games such as board games.

- Many schools have student conflict managers who have been trained, usually by the school counselor, to handle problems of younger students (not their own peers) that occur on the playground. They give the younger students a choice: "Do you want me to help you with the problem or get a grownup?" After approximately six weeks of training through sessions with the school counselor, these conflict managers shadow a senior conflict manager for a week or so. Then the senior conflict manager supervises the trainee. At a final meeting with the counselor, the trainees are asked if they think they are ready to begin the responsibility. Conflict managers on the playground have been highly effective in helping with resolving student problems.

- In some schools, the teachers or aides supervising on the playground are given a clipboard to carry with forms attached to fill out documenting behavioral problems that arise. When a problem occurs, it is first discussed with the child. If the behavior continues, students are often sent out of the activity to a supervised area, such as a bench or wall, near the playground. The teacher or aide fills out the form that designates the misbehavior and is later placed in the classroom teacher's mailbox. The classroom teacher decides on the action: (1) no action needed, (2) school service, (3) assign the student to write a letter to his or her parent, (4) parent call, or (5) referral to the principal.

- Many schools also reward students with helpful, cooperative behaviors on the playground (for example, with tickets to be used in weekly, biweekly, or monthly schoolwide raffles).

Some elementary schools have found that by having students play first during the lunch break and eat later, they are calmer when returning to class after lunch. However, one of the problems that schools with this system found is that some children are slow eaters or because of the long cafeteria line are late getting served and do not finish eating before it is time to go back to class.

Out-of-Classroom Behavioral Problems in Middle Schools

One middle school principal said her school significantly reduced behavioral problems during the lunch period by splitting the lunch, with all sixth graders eating at the same time as half of the eighth graders. At the second lunch period, all of the seventh graders ate with the other half of the eight-grade class.

Splitting up the eighth graders in this case was done because they had been hard to manage and problematic in large numbers. Using this "divide and conquer" strategy and providing a lot more equipment to use during lunch was beneficial.

This same principal found a creative way to reduce behavioral issues and improve cleanliness in the school restrooms by making separate sixth-, seventh-, and eight-grade restrooms and running school contests to see which grade could keep its restroom the cleanest. The winning class received special awards or privileges.

Other techniques have been recommended too:

- Increase adult supervision during passing periods and monitoring of all out-of-classroom building locations.
- Station teachers at the door to greet students as they enter class each day.
- Encourage parent participation, so parents are a visible presence on campus.
- Use music rather than bells for passing periods.

Interventions for Students with Chronic Disruptive Behaviors

Most classes have a few challenging students with whom it is easy to lose patience, become frustrated, and feel inadequate or unsuccessful in management skills. Often teachers view challenging behaviors as willful and deliberate and consequently respond to that student negatively and in a reactive mode to their behaviors. Nevertheless, it is important to look at each student individually and try to see past the behaviors to the whole child. A number of students who tend to be disruptive, aggressive, or oppositional have a disability or medical or mental health disorder of some kind (diagnosed or undiagnosed) such as AD/HD. Children with disabilities and brain-based disorders commonly have behavioral, social, or emotional challenges. There are physical reasons that they are impulsive or overactive or have difficulty calming and self-regulating their behavior, and they are not deliberate or intentional in nature. (See Chapter Three.)

Student Study Team Intervention

The *Report of the Surgeon General's Conference on Children's Mental Health* (Office of the Surgeon General, 2000) estimates that one in five children and adolescents will experience a significant mental health problem during their school years. These issues vary in severity, but approximately 70 percent of those who need treatment will not receive mental health services, which places them at risk for any number of academic and behavioral problems. This fact is an eye-opener for teachers and all other adults working with children. Students with disruptive behaviors as well as those who have internalizing symptoms (stress, anxiety, withdrawal, depression) need our recognition, attention, and intervention. Be aware that behavior communicates something the student is feeling or needing. That child's behavior could be communicating his or her embarrassment, anxiety, or fear of failure or looking stupid in front of peers and the student's need to escape those fears, uncomfortable feelings, or the environment.

Bring students who pose chronic behavioral problems in class, as well as other students you are concerned about for other reasons, such as learning, attention, or social or emotional difficulties who are not disruptive, to the attention of your student study team (SST). SSTs can be helpful in devising behavioral plans and social and emotional supports, as well as academic and instructional interventions. (Children with ADHD, ODD, and those with internalizing disorders such as depression and anxiety disorders and other mental health conditions are discussed in Chapter Three.)

SSTs can be helpful in devising behavioral plans and supports, as well as academic and instructional interventions. Refer these students to your school team for a multidisciplinary look at the child or teen and an examination of his or her school history. In doing so, you may be instrumental in helping to identify some students with unidentified and unmet special needs who have slipped through the system and need to be evaluated. There are more and more children who are now being diagnosed in middle school and high school with various disabilities and disorders, and finally receiving treatments and interventions that are making a significant positive difference in their lives. There is usually something going on with children who are defiant, oppositional, or aggressive. They are likely in need of counseling, various supports, and outside referrals. A team approach involving parents, teachers, counselor, administrator, social worker, school psychologist, or other school professionals is recommended to facilitate the student's receiving appropriate intervention.

Individualized Behavioral Programs and Monitoring Systems

For students with chronic behavioral problems for whom the classroom incentive systems are not sufficient to improve their behavior, an individualized program may need to be implemented for a period of time. Following are examples of behavioral programs and monitoring systems, all of which involve targeting one or a few (at most) behaviors to improve and rewarding the student's success, preferably at both home and school (Rief, 2003, 2005):

• *Home notes and daily report cards.* Home notes and daily report cards (DRCs) are excellent behavioral programs and tools for tracking a student's social, academic, or behavioral progress at school. They are highly effective for communicating between home and school and monitoring a child's daily performance. When parents are willing and able to consistently follow through with reinforcement at home for positive performance at school, it is a very powerful motivator for the student. Any means to forge a partnership between home and school and work together on improving specific behavioral goals is very beneficial.

Home notes and DRCs involve selecting and clearly defining one or more target behaviors to be the focus for improvement. The teacher is responsible for observing and rating how the student performed on the target behaviors during the day or class period. A chart is made, such as that in Form 6.2, Elementary School Daily Report form, at the end of this chapter. This includes the target behaviors and designated time frames for which the student is being monitored and evaluated. The form in this example has blank lines to be filled in with the specific time frames (for example, 8:30–9:20, 9:20–10:10, or by subject areas). It also has plus and minus signs for the teacher to indicate at the end of the period if the student did (plus sign) or did not (minus sign) demonstrate each of the three target behaviors during that specific time frame. At the end of the day, a total percentage score is determined for how successfully the student performed that day. If the student met his or her predetermined goal (for example, 70 percent success), it was a "good day," and the student earns rewards at home or school, or both.

The Middle School Daily Report form (Form 6.3 at the end of the chapter) is another example of a home note that involves teacher observation and rating the student's performance. On this form, the student's day is broken down into seven sections (first through seventh period), with a check-off for four behaviors: on time to class, brought needed materials/supplies, homework turned in, and participated appropriately. In addition, the teachers rate the student's attitude/conduct for the class period on a scale of 4 to 0 (with 4 being outstanding, 0 being poor). There is also room for class assignments to be listed, and it requires a parent or guardian signature.

Parents are responsible for asking to see the note or DRC every day and reinforcing school behavior and performance at home. "Good days" in school (as indicated by the home-school note or DRC) will earn the child designated rewards at home on a nightly basis. Bonus rewards for a great week (for example, at least three out of five good days initially) may also earn the child extra privileges on the weekend. It is recommended that parents back up the expectation that their son or daughter bring the note home daily by enforcing with some mild punishment (such as being fined or losing some TV time) on days the child "forgets" to bring the note home.

Home notes and DRCs can involve school rewards as well as home rewards. A small school reward (for example, stickers or earned time for a preferred activity) can be given to the child at school on a "good day." For a "good week" (initially three days and later raising the criterion to four days out of five of successful performance), the student can earn a special activity reward at school on Fridays. In some schools, the counselor or other adult provides the Friday reward for all students in the school on a behavioral program who had a "good week." Such rewards might involve a food treat like a popcorn party, a game of some type, or other activity the students find fun.

If the family is not able to follow through regularly with monitoring and reinforcement on a daily basis, it is best to do so at school. If the DRC is likely to get lost coming to and from school daily, then perhaps just a card that simply indicates "yes/no" or "met goal/didn't meet goal" can be sent home each day for parent notification of the student's performance and the actual DRC remains at school. The daily reward when meeting the goal can be provided at school. Parents are asked to praise the child daily when notified of a good day and to reward the child on the weekend with a special privilege if the child had a "good week."

It is important that reinforcement is provided consistently and as promised. A well-coordinated system between home and school is the most effective.

• *Contingency contracting.* This is a written agreement, usually among the teacher, student, and parent. The contract clearly specifies the required behavior that the student is to perform and the reward that will be earned if the student succeeds in meeting that behavioral goal. Sometimes the contract includes the negative consequence that will occur for failure to perform the required behaviors. All parties sign the contract and follow through on their end of the agreement.

• *Token programs.* Token programs use secondary reinforcers, or tokens, to provide students with immediate reinforcement for appropriate behavior, necessary for motivating children such as those with AD/HD to sustain the effort for behavioral change. When the student earns a designated number of tokens, they may be exchanged for a primary reinforcement such as a privilege, treat, or desired activity. These programs include any in which the student is earning points, tokens or plastic chips, moves or stickers on a chart, class money, or something else as an immediate reward for demonstrating the target behavior. The tokens are later redeemed for a more valued and motivating reward at school, home, or both.

• *Chart moves.* One or a few specific target behaviors are identified for a student to improve. A chart of some type is developed—for example, one with boxes for placing stickers, stars, stamps, teacher initials, or a dot-to-dot chart. Each time the student demonstrates the target appropriate behavior or meets the designated goal, a box of the chart is filled in, a dot is connected, or a move forward is made on the chart (depending on the type of chart used). When the chart is fully completed, the students earns a reward that is meaningful to him or her. The teacher may also provide a smaller reward when the student reaches a certain point or two on the chart, such as midway or the end of two rows, to increase the motivation along the way.

• *Self-monitoring.* It is helpful when trying to teach students to self-regulate their own behavior to involve them in self-monitoring. This technique gives them practice in paying more attention to their own behavior and thinking about and reflecting on their performance. Self-awareness often leads to improved performance. The technique can be as simple as asking a student to record on an index card each time the teacher warns him or her for a particular behavior, such as talking or being out of seat without permission. The warning can be given verbally or with a visual cue, but the student must note when it happens with a tally mark. At the end of the day or period, the number of warnings received for that behavior is counted and recorded. The goal for the student simply would be to try to do better the next day (receiving fewer warnings for that target behavior).

On the Self-Monitoring Behavior Log (Form 6.4 at the end of this chapter), the student rates his or her performance on a scale of 1 to 5 in pencil at the end of the monitoring periods. Note: As many of the seven available periods shown on the form can be used. The behavior being self-monitored can be something specific, like "on task doing my best work," or more general, such as "following class rules." The behavior selected for self-monitoring and rating needs to be written on the blank space under the form's heading. The teacher also rates the student but in pen. The student may receive points for each time the teacher's rating matches the student's self-rating exactly or if off by only one point. So, if the student's and teacher's ratings matched exactly or closely for all seven rating opportunities during the day on Form 6.4, the student could receive seven points. The purpose of this self-monitoring form is to help a student more accurately self-assess his or her behavioral performance. Earning points for matching the teacher's ratings is optional.

The Student-Generated Progress Report (Form 6.5 at the end of this chapter) is another example of a form students can use to self-evaluate their performance with regard to organization skills, effort, and behavior. There is no point value attached, but the teacher also is asked to indicate (with initials) whether he or she agrees with the student's assessment of his or her performance.

• *Involvement of school support personnel.* Teachers should consult with and draw on the professional expertise of the school's support staff (counselors, social workers, school psychologists, other members of the school's teacher assistance team or student support team) in helping with strategies and interventions for students with social, emotional, or behavioral issues. This help may take several forms: observing and strategizing regarding individual students; whole class or small group lessons or activities (for example, in social skills or conflict resolution); working individually with students; communicating with and working with families; support in developing, monitoring, designing, and implementing behavioral plans or interventions; troubleshooting issues with teachers; or facilitating referrals for evaluation or treatments in school or in the community. (See Chapter Five.)

RESEARCH-BASED MODEL OF SCHOOLWIDE POSITIVE BEHAVIORAL INTERVENTIONS AND SUPPORTS

The schoolwide positive behavioral support (SWPBS) approach was developed by researchers and collaborators at the U.S. Department of Education, Office of Special Education Programs Technical Assistance Center on Positive Behavioral Interventions and Supports (codirected by George Sugai at the University of Connecticut and Robert Horner at the University of Oregon). This approach is designed to support all students by establishing a continuum of preventive and positive interventions and systems. The intensity of these supports is increased as student behavior proves to be unresponsive to interventions (Sugai & Horner, 2005).

Based on a public health model of disease prevention, SWPBS emphasizes the implementation of a preventive schoolwide set of practices at which most students are expected to benefit. Primary or universal prevention consists of (1) a small number of operationally defined, directly taught, continuously monitored, and frequently acknowledged schoolwide behavioral expectations; (2) team directed data-based decision making, action planning, and implementation coordination; (3) clear and mutually exclusive definitions and procedures for classroom-managed versus administrator-handled rule violations; and (4) continuous evaluation, implementation adaptation, and professional development (Sugai & Horner, 2005).

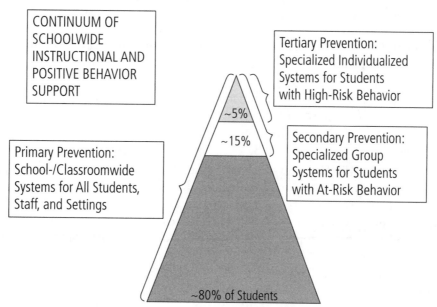

CONTINUUM OF SCHOOLWIDE INSTRUCTIONAL AND POSITIVE BEHAVIOR SUPPORT

Tertiary Prevention: Specialized Individualized Systems for Students with High-Risk Behavior

Primary Prevention: School-/Classroomwide Systems for All Students, Staff, and Settings

Secondary Prevention: Specialized Group Systems for Students with At-Risk Behavior

~5%

~15%

~80% of Students

Source: Walker et al. (1996); www.pbis.org. Used with permission.

Students whose behaviors are unresponsive to primary prevention practices, typically about 15 percent of the school population, are provided with interventions that increase social skills instruction, behavior monitoring and supervision, academic instructional adaptations, and teacher-to-student feedback, known collectively as secondary or selected interventions. Counselors, special educators, school psychologists, and others are involved in supporting teachers in the development, implementation, and evaluation of secondary prevention interventions (Sugai & Horner, 2005).

Tertiary or intensive interventions are directed to the small proportion of students (around 5 percent) whose behaviors are unresponsive to secondary prevention interventions. Multidisciplinary teams are used (student support, prereferral, teacher assistance, and others) to develop specially designed and individually implemented behavioral intervention plans. These plans are comprehensive (home-school-community), strength skill based (direct social skill instruction), function based (behavior analytic), and multidisciplinary (education, medical health, and mental health). To be effective, tertiary interventions must be team managed, and individuals with specialized behavioral skills and capacity must be involved directly with development, implementation, monitoring, and evaluation of individual student behavior intervention plans (Sugai & Horner, 2005).

To be successful, the SWPBS approach is led by a school leadership team comprising school administrators, general education grade and departmental representatives, special support personnel (such as special educators, school psychologists, and counselors), parents, students, and noncertified staff (such as security, custodial, office, cafeteria, and supervisory). This team reviews information on disciplinary referrals, academic achievement, staff and parent school climate satisfaction, and intervention implementation. Discipline patterns are particularly helpful in guiding action planning: rates of major and minor rule infractions, types of problem behaviors, location and time of day, and office referrals by students. The team uses these data to develop a schoolwide implementation action plan that considers primary, secondary, and tertiary interventions. Most schools start with primary interventions because of the emphasis on all students, all staff, and all settings. In addition, effective implementation of primary interventions assists in identifying which students might benefit from secondary- and tertiary-level interventions (Sugai & Horner, 2005).

Successful implementation of SWPBS has been associated with decreases in office discipline referrals; enhancement of school climate and staff, student, and parent satisfaction; increased opportunities to maximize academic instruction; and reductions in referrals for more intensive behavioral supports (Sugai & Horner, 2005).

Additional information about SWPBS is available at the center's Web site (www.pbis.org) as well as the following references and those listed in the References at the end of this chapter:

Horner, R. H., & Sugai, G. (2005). School-wide positive behavior support: An alternative approach to discipline in schools (pp. 359–390). In L. Bambara & L. Kern (Eds.), *Positive behavior support*. New York: Guilford Press.

Lewis, T. J., & Sugai, G. (1999). Effective behavior support: A systems approach to proactive school-wide management. *Focus on Exceptional Children, 31*(6), 1–24.

Safran, S. P., & Oswald, K. (2003). Positive behavior supports: Can schools reshape disciplinary practices? *Exceptional Children, 69*, 361–373.

Sugai, G., & Horner, R. H. (2002). The evolution of discipline practices: School-wide positive behavior supports. *Child and Family Behavior Therapy, 24*, 23–50.

Sugai, G., Horner, R. H., Dunlap, G., Hieneman, M., Lewis, T. J., Nelson, C. M., Scott, T., Liaupsin, C., Sailor, W., Turnbull, A. P., Turnbull, H. R. III, Wickham, D., Reuf, M., & Wilcox, B. (2000). Applying positive behavioral support and functional behavioral assessment in schools. *Journal of Positive Behavioral Interventions, 2*, 131–143.

Walker, H. M., Ramsey, E., & Gresham, R. M. (2005). *Antisocial behavior in school: Evidence-based practices* (2nd ed.). Belmont, CA: Wadsworth/Thomson Learning.

Walker, H. M., Horner, R. H., Sugai, G., Bullis, M., Sprague, J. R., Bricker, D., & Kaufman, M. J. (1996). Integrated approaches to preventing antisocial behavior patterns among school-age children and youth. *Journal of Emotional and Behavioral Disorders, 4*, 194–209.

Example interventions at each of the three levels follow.

Universal Interventions (Primary Prevention)

- Teacher training, for example, in proactive classroom management strategies and differentiating instruction to effectively teach diverse learners
- Schoolwide commitment to and leadership in building a positive, prosocial climate and culture throughout the school
- Social-emotional learning, social skills, or character education programs that are taught, reinforced, and implemented schoolwide by all school personnel in all school settings
- Clear schoolwide rules and behavioral expectations, safety plans, and procedures and processes for teaching and reinforcing the expectations and establishing and maintaining a safe and orderly environment
- Identifying specific locations and settings in the school that are problematic and providing more structure and support to minimize problems in these settings
- Establishing a schoolwide team to plan and oversee climate and problem prevention efforts and monitor the effectiveness of plans

Selected Interventions (Secondary Prevention)

- Teacher training and coaching in instructional and behavioral strategies for reaching and teaching students with learning, attention, and behavioral challenges
- A student support team process for effectively strategizing and planning for students at risk (classroom strategies and accommodations and appropriate schoolwide safety nets and interventions)
- Increased supervision, monitoring, and reinforcement
- Individualized behavioral interventions—for example, daily report cards, home notes, contracts, and reinforcement plans
- Self-management training and anger management
- Conflict resolution training
- In-school counseling

Intensive Targeted Interventions (Tertiary Prevention)

- Training educators about mental health disorders in children and strategies to help (for example, how to deescalate angry students)
- Crisis intervention training and skill development
- School case management practices of students with chronic or intense behavioral difficulties
- Functional behavioral assessments and behavioral intervention plans
- Clinical referrals
- Community-agency-family linkages

Universal interventions improve almost all students' behavior; have their greatest impact among students who are on the margins, that is, those students who are just beginning to be aggressive or defiant; and offer a foundation that supports the antisocial students throughout the day by reinforcing what they are learning in their more intensive selected interventions (Walker, Ramsey, & Gresham, 2003–2004). Once the environment is calm through universal interventions, the students who need more powerful interventions surface. The goal with these students is to decrease the frequency of their problem behaviors, instill appropriate behaviors, and make the children more responsive to universal interventions (Sugai,

Horner, & Gresham, 2002). The most severe cases—the most troubled children from the most chaotic homes—require intensive, individualized, and expensive interventions that are typically family focused, with participation and support from mental health, juvenile justice, and social service agencies, as well as schools (Walker et al., 2003–2004).

TIPS FOR DEALING WITH CHALLENGING OR DIFFICULT KIDS

The same basic principles described throughout this chapter with regard to preventing behavioral problems in the classroom and school environment are just as appropriate at home: increased structure, consistency, follow-through, and positive reinforcement of desired behaviors. Parents with a child whose behaviors are difficult to manage should be encouraged to seek help from the school and a pediatrician.

The following tips may be useful for all individuals working with difficult kids. Teachers may want to share them with parents as well (Rief, 2003, 2005).

- Plan a response and avoid reacting to challenging behavior, especially when you are in an emotional state. Do not feel compelled to give an immediate response in dealing with situations until you are in a calm, thinking state. Feel free to quietly and privately say to the child or teen, "We will deal with this after class [or after dinner]," or "I'm upset right now. I need time to think about this before we discuss the consequence of your behavior. I'll get back to you."
- It is okay to call for a break. Parents can go to a different room or take an exercise break. Teachers can provide the student with cooling-off options.
- Discuss, problem-solve, and negotiate solutions when both parties have had time to cool down and are in a calm, thinking mode.
- Realize that you cannot control anyone else's behavior.
- Change what you can control . . . : yourself (for example, your attitude, body language, voice, strategies, expectations, and the nature of the interaction).
- Physically relax your body before dealing with situations. Take a few deep breaths. Unfold your arms, and relax your jaw. Lower your voice. Cue yourself to be calm.
- Disengage from power struggles. Remember that you cannot be forced into an argument or power struggle. You enter into one only if you choose to do so (it takes two). Say, for example, "I am not willing to argue about this now. I will be free to discuss it later if you wish."
- Affirm and acknowledge the child or teen's feelings: "I see you're upset." "I understand that you are angry now." "I can see why you would be frustrated."
- Express your confidence in the child or teen's ability to make good choices. Communicate your hope that he or she will choose to cooperate. Provide choices: "I can't make you. . . . But your choices are either . . . or . . ."
- *Do not* take their behavior personally, take the bait, demand, or threaten.
- Avoid nagging, scolding, lecturing, and any head-on battles or confrontations.
- Try to maintain your sense of humor.
- Send "I" messages: "I feel . . . when you . . . because . . ."; "I want [or need] you to . . .
- Use the "broken record" technique. Respond by repeating your directions with the same words and calm, neutral voice.

- Use the words *however* and *nevertheless*—for example, "I understand you are feeling. . . . However . . ." or "That may be so. Nevertheless . . ."
- Take time to actively listen to the child. Be attentive. Listen without interjecting your opinions. Ask a lot of open and clarifying questions. Rephrase and restate what was said.
- Avoid being judgmental in your interactions.
- Show caring and empathy.
- Work together on establishing goals and identifying positive reinforcers that will be meaningful and motivating to the child or teen.
- Teach problem-solving strategies—for example, identifying the problem, brainstorming possible solutions, evaluating pros and cons, choosing one and trying it, reviewing effectiveness, and trying another if it was not working.
- If it appears the child is on the verge of a meltdown, try prompting him or her to use self-calming, self-regulation techniques (for example, deep breathing, counting backward, or relaxation techniques).

REFERENCES

Barrish, H. H., Saunders, M., & Wolf, M. M. (1969). Good behavior game: Effects of individual contingencies for group consequences on disruptive behavior in a classroom. *Journal of Applied Behavior Analysis, 2*(2), 199–124.

Gootman, M. (2001). *The caring teacher's guide to discipline* (2nd ed.). Thousand Oaks, CA: Corwin Press.

Office of the Surgeon General. (2000). *Report of the Surgeon General's Conference on Children's Mental Health: A national action agenda.* Washington, DC: Department of Health and Human Services.

Rhode, G., Jenson, W. R., & Reavis, H. K. (1995). *The tough kid book.* Longmont, CO: Sopris West.

Rief, S. (2003). *The ADHD book of lists.* San Francisco: Jossey-Bass.

Rief, S. (2005). *How to reach and teach children with ADD/ADHD* (2nd ed.). San Francisco: Jossey-Bass.

Sugai, G., & Horner, R. H. (2005). *School-wide positive behavior support: Practices and systems.* Center on Positive Behavioral Interventions and Supports, U.S. Department of Education, Office of Special Education Programs.

Sugai, G., Horner, R., & Gresham, F. (2002). Behaviorally effective school environments. In M. Shinn, H. Walker, & G. Stoner (Eds.), *Interventions for academic and behavior problems II: Preventive and remedial approaches* (pp. 315–350). Bethesda, MD: National Association of School Psychologists.

Walker, H. M., Ramsey, E., & Gresham, F. M. (2003–2004). Heading off disruptive behavior: How early intervention can reduce defiant behavior—and win back teaching time. *American Educator, 27*(4), 6–21.

Walker, H. M., Horner, R. H., Sugai, G., Bullis, M., Sprague, J. R., Bricker, D., & Kaufman, M. J. (1996). Integrated approaches to preventing antisocial behavior patterns among school-age children and youth. *Journal of Emotional and Behavioral Disorders, 4,* 193–256.

BEHAVIORAL IMPROVEMENT REPORT

Name: _____ Date: _____

What is the situation you were involved in? What rule(s) were broken?

_____

_____

_____

_____

How do you feel about what just happened?

_____

_____

_____

If a similar situation were to happen again, what would you do differently?

_____

_____

_____

_____

_____   _____

Student's Signature   Reviewed by [name of staff member]

Form 6.2

ELEMENTARY SCHOOL DAILY REPORT

_____ 's Daily Report

Goal _____ Date _____	stays seated		on task		follows directions	
	+	-	+	-	+	-
	+	-	+	-	+	-
	+	-	+	-	+	-
	+	-	+	-	+	-
	+	-	+	-	+	-
	+	-	+	-	+	-
	+	-	+	-	+	-
	+	-	+	-	+	-
	+	-	+	-	+	-
	+	-	+	-	+	-
	+	-	+	-	+	-
	+	-	+	-	+	-
	+	-	+	-	+	-

| | + | - | + | - | + | - |

| TOTAL | | | |

MIDDLE SCHOOL DAILY REPORT

Name: _____ Date: _____

Teachers: Write Y (yes) or N (no) by each behavior. Rate overall attitude/conduct on this scale: 4 = Outstanding, 3 = Very Good, 2 = Pretty Good, 1 = So So (can use improvement), 0 = Poor (intervention needed).

First Period   Class assignment
_____ On time to class
_____ Brought needed materials/supplies
_____ Homework turned in
_____ Participated appropriately
_____ Attitude/conduct
Teacher's initials _____

Second Period   Class assignment
_____ On time to class
_____ Brought needed materials/supplies
_____ Homework turned in
_____ Participated appropriately
_____ Attitude/conduct
Teacher's initials _____

Third Period   Class assignment
_____ On time to class
_____ Brought needed materials/supplies
_____ Homework turned in
_____ Participated appropriately
_____ Attitude/conduct
Teacher's initials _____

Fourth Period   Class assignment
_____ On time to class
_____ Brought needed materials/supplies
_____ Homework turned in
_____ Participated appropriately
_____ Attitude/conduct
Teacher's initials _____

Fifth Period   Class assignment
_____ On time to class
_____ Brought needed materials/supplies
_____ Homework turned in
_____ Participated appropriately
_____ Attitude/conduct
Teacher's initials _____

Sixth Period   Class assignment
_____ On time to class
_____ Brought needed materials/supplies
_____ Homework turned in
_____ Participated appropriately
_____ Attitude/conduct
Teacher's initials _____

Seventh Period   Class assignment
_____ On time to class
_____ Brought needed materials/supplies
_____ Homework turned in
_____ Participated appropriately
_____ Attitude/conduct
Teacher's initials _____

Parent signature _____ Date _____

SELF-MONITORING BEHAVIOR LOG

The behavior I am monitoring is _____ .

Student's name: _____ Week of: _____

Directions: How well did I do today? Rate yourself by circling a number between 1 and 5 using this scale: 5 = Great; 4 = Very good; 3 = Pretty good; 2 = Not so good; 1 = Poor. Use a pencil. Your teacher will also rate how well he or she thinks you did (using pen). See if you agree or almost agree about your behavioral performance.

Subjects/Periods	Monday	Tuesday	Wednesday	Thursday	Friday
_____	1 2 3 4 5	1 2 3 4 5	1 2 3 4 5	1 2 3 4 5	1 2 3 4 5
_____	1 2 3 4 5	1 2 3 4 5	1 2 3 4 5	1 2 3 4 5	1 2 3 4 5
_____	1 2 3 4 5	1 2 3 4 5	1 2 3 4 5	1 2 3 4 5	1 2 3 4 5
_____	1 2 3 4 5	1 2 3 4 5	1 2 3 4 5	1 2 3 4 5	1 2 3 4 5
_____	1 2 3 4 5	1 2 3 4 5	1 2 3 4 5	1 2 3 4 5	1 2 3 4 5
_____	1 2 3 4 5	1 2 3 4 5	1 2 3 4 5	1 2 3 4 5	1 2 3 4 5
_____	1 2 3 4 5	1 2 3 4 5	1 2 3 4 5	1 2 3 4 5	1 2 3 4 5

Teacher Comments:

Student Comments:

STUDENT-GENERATED PROGRESS REPORT

Following is a short progress report. Your child has evaluated himself or herself. My initials appear next to the evaluation if I am in agreement.

Behavior in class

_____ Exceptional, splendid, excellent!

_____ Good.

_____ Needs to improve.

Homework

_____ Wow! Everything's done

_____ Good. Almost everything is done.

_____ Help! I've gotten behind.

Class work

_____ Quality stuff!

_____ Pretty good.

_____ Could be better.

Notebook

_____ Neat!

_____ Okay.

_____ Messy!

Student's signature _____

Parent's signature _____

Date _____

Chapter 7

QUESTIONING AND ENGAGING STUDENTS

Being able to capture and hold students' interest and attention is not easy. Keeping all students engaged and motivated in daily instruction can be a monumental challenge to teachers and one that requires experimenting with a variety of approaches. This chapter addresses numerous strategies that increase students' engagement, motivation, and active participation in lessons. This includes techniques for obtaining and maintaining students' attention and interest, questioning methods and strategies that elicit a high rate of student response opportunities, instructional formats that increase student engagement, and types of questions recommended throughout instruction (particularly in a literacy classroom) that encourage deeper thinking and more meaningful discussion. In addition, questioning tips for parents are provided at the end of this chapter.

GETTING AND FOCUSING STUDENTS' ATTENTION

Before we can even begin instruction, we need to obtain students' attention and direct their focus to the task at hand. The following classroom strategies and techniques will enable you to do this (Rief, 1998, 2003, 2005).

Tips for Obtaining and Focusing Students' Attention

First arouse students' curiosity and anticipation. You may ask an interesting speculative question, show a picture, tell a story, or read a related poem to generate discussion and interest in the upcoming lesson. Try playfulness, silliness, humor, use of props, and a bit of theatrics to get attention and pique interest.

Storytelling, real-life examples, and anecdotes are also powerful means of capturing students' attention and hooking in listeners. Children of all ages love to hear stories, particularly personal ones, such as something that happened to the teacher when he or she was a child. At times you may want to add a bit of mystery by bringing in one or more objects relevant to the upcoming lesson in a box, bag, or pillowcase. This is a wonderful way to generate predictions and can lead to excellent discussions or writing activities.

Always model excitement and enthusiasm about the upcoming lesson to spark their interest, and clearly identify the objectives, content standards being addressed, and ultimate goals or outcomes to be achieved by the end of the session or unit. Whenever possible, activate students' prior knowledge and draw on their own experiences. Elicit discussion and use strategies that enable students to see the relevance of the lesson you are about to teach and make connections with previous learning or experiences. Also, when giving examples, use students' names, experiences, and other means of helping students identify with the topic being discussed.

After providing students with an overview of the major points they will be studying and their relationship to prior learning, post a few key points to be attentive to, listening for, and thinking about during the lesson.

Auditory Techniques for Getting Attention

Signal auditorily through the use of sound or music (for example, chimes, a rainstick, a xylophone, playing a bar or chord on a keyboard, or a few seconds of music on a CD). There are other instruments as well and toys that make a novel sound. Beepers or timers may also be used as an auditory signal.

Teachers frequently use a clap pattern to signal attention. You clap a particular pattern, and students repeat the clap pattern back to you or use a clear verbal signal (for example, "Freeze . . . This is important . . ." "Everybody . . . Ready . . ." or "1, 2, 3, eyes on me").

Visual Techniques for Getting Attention

Use visual signals to obtain attention, such as flashing the lights or raising your hand, which signals the students to raise their hands and close their mouths until everyone is silent and attentive. Gestures, demonstrations, and interesting graphics such as cartoons are helpful in engaging students' visual attention and interest.

Be sure to illustrate. You do not have to draw well to illustrate throughout your presentation. Do so even if you lack the skill or talent. Drawings do not have to be sophisticated or accurate. In fact, often the sillier, the better, and stick figures are fine. Any attempts to illustrate vocabulary, concepts, and other lessons focus students' attention and help in their retention of information. Also remember to point to written material you want students to focus on with a dowel, stick or pointer, or laser pointer.

Be sure not to have too many visuals, which can distract from the instructional focus. At times you may need to cover or remove some visuals. For example, erase unnecessary information from the board, and limit visual clutter when possible.

Being able to obtain students' eye contact is important, and so are seating arrangements that enable all students to see the board or screen. Students should be facing you when you are speaking, especially while you are giving instructions. Always allow students to readjust their seating and signal you if their visibility is blocked. Teach students (for example, those seated with desks in clusters who are not facing you) how to turn their chairs and bodies around quickly and quietly when signaled to do so.

Color is effective in getting attention. Make use of colored dry-erase pens on whiteboards, colored overhead pens for transparencies, and different colored print. Focus attention with colored highlighting tape or sticky notes. Write key words, phrases, steps to computation problems, and other material you want to highlight in a different color.

Overhead projectors have traditionally been among the best tools for focusing students' attention in the classroom because they enable the teacher to (1) model and frame important information, (2) block unnecessary information by covering part of the transparency, (3) face students and not have to turn his or her back on the students in order to write on the board, (4) avoid instructional lag time while writing on the board and erasing, and (5) prepare transparencies in advance, saving instructional time.

In addition, teachers can place novel objects on the overhead, such as a variety of math manipulatives and other overhead tools. It is motivating for students to write on the overhead. Cooperative groups, for example, can be given a transparency and colored pens and then share their work with the rest of the class at the overhead. Document cameras are wonderful tools now available in many schools. They look similar to an overhead projector, but are able to project images without need of a transparency. Any piece of paper, book, or 3-D object can be placed on the projector and shown to the class on the screen.

As schools become technologically advanced and modernized, more and more teachers have the benefit of PowerPoint and other multimedia tools such as interactive white boards at their disposal for daily classroom instruction. Instruction through PowerPoint presentations is highly engaging because slides can be created at the moment with a wide variety of backgrounds, colors, fonts, graphics, and animations. The visuals are powerful in engaging students' attention. PowerPoint presentations linked to the Internet—through pulling up images and information on the spot to create or enhance a slide or to download unitedstreaming (www.unitedstreaming.com) video clips directly into the PowerPoint, provide an extremely motivating means of instruction.

MAINTAINING STUDENTS' ATTENTION THROUGH ACTIVE PARTICIPATION

Keeping or sustaining students' attention requires active, not passive, learning (Rief, 1998, 2003, 2005). It also requires that teachers incorporate a variety of formats and activities woven throughout the lesson. Within a fifty-minute period of time, for example, the lesson may be formatted to include a mix of whole group instruction and end-of-lesson closure, with engaging ways for students to respond and participate; predominantly small group and partner structures for maximum involvement in learning activities; and some time to work on a particular task independently.

Keeping Students Engaged

To maintain students' attention, watch your pacing. Be prepared, and minimize instructional lag time. It is also important to use high-interest material and keep students actively involved and participating. For example, have students write down brief notes or illustrate key points during instruction.

Use study guides and partial outlines. While you are presenting a lesson or giving a lecture, students fill in the missing words based on what you are saying or writing on the board or overhead. Any kind of graphic tool for students to use accompanying verbal presentation is helpful. Jotting down a few words or filling in missing information in a guided format is helpful for maintaining attention.

Make all efforts to greatly increase student responses—saying and doing something with the information being taught throughout the lesson. This can be done, for example, through frequent pair shares: "Turn to your partner and . . . [summarize, share, paraphrase] your understanding," or, "With your partner, share and clarify any questions you still have about what we just discussed."

Cooperative learning formats with partners or groups are highly effective in keeping students engaged and participating during lessons. Teachers need to follow the proper structure of cooperative learning groups through assignment of roles and individual accountability. It is not just group work. Many students do not function well in groups without clearly defined structure and expectations.

Incorporate a variety of graphic organizers and techniques such as webbing, graphing, clustering, mapping, and outlining. Also, use computer programs for specific skill building and practice (programs that provide for frequent feedback and self-correction) and games for skill practice whenever possible.

Motivate all students to actively participate by differentiating instruction in the classroom. Provide many opportunities for student choices of activities and projects and ways to demonstrate their learning. Also provide options for projects and assignments: music, drama, art, construction, designing, writing, speaking, use of technology, research, and any other means of creative expression. Use learning centers, flexible grouping, interest groups, independent projects and study, and a variety of other instructional strategies, structures, and accommodations to differentiate instruction. Many of the chapters in this book provide differentiated strategies and activities to engage all students and maintain their attention, interest, motivation, and participation.

Keeping Students on Task During Seat Work

Some students have significant difficulty remaining focused and productive during independent and seat work times of the day (Rief, 2003, 2005). They may be distracted, forget what they are supposed to be doing, or lack some of the prerequisite skills to do the independent work without assistance. Following are some strategies to try:

- Provide guided practice before having students work independently on seat work activities.
- Check for clarity. Make sure directions are clear and understood before sending students back to their seats to work independently.
- Give a manageable amount of work that students are capable of doing independently.
- Make sure necessary supplies are available so students can work during independent time without excuses. Have extra materials available for unprepared students.
- Send students to their seat with a written task card or checklist. A task sheet (or things-to-do sheet) is also helpful. Have students cross out each task as they complete it.
- Study buddies or partners may be assigned for clarification purposes during seat work, especially when the teacher is instructing another group of students while part of the class is doing seat work. When part of the class has a seat work assignment while you are instructing other students (for example, during a reading group), set the expectation that students who have a question during seat work must ask their partner or classmates in their group first. Only if no one in the group can answer the question may the teacher be interrupted. Some teachers also assign one or more "experts" of the day for students to go to in need of help.
- Prepare some kind of signal to be used from the child's desk to indicate he or she needs help. One method is to provide a colored card that students place or prop up on their desks when they want to alert the teacher or any other adult who is scanning the room that they need assistance.
- Give other fail-proof work that the student can do in the meantime if he or she is stumped on an assignment and needs to wait for teacher attention or assistance.
- Scan the classroom frequently because all students need positive reinforcement. Frequently give positive comments, praising specific students who are on task. This serves as a reminder to students who tend to have difficulty.
- Do not give independent work that is very difficult before students have had sufficient guided practice.
- Try using a timer and "beat-the-clock" system to motivate completion of a reasonable amount of work. Reward for on-task behavior and work completed during short designated time segments. Although timers may increase the anxiety level of some students, many others respond well to the challenge and increase their work production when a timer is used.
- Provide study carrels and quiet areas for students who tend to be distracted during seat work.

QUESTIONING TECHNIQUES TO INCREASE STUDENT PARTICIPATION

One of the most important processes that takes place in a learning environment is that of asking and responding to questions (Rief, 2003, 2005). Many teachers inadvertently use questioning techniques that are exclusive of some students in the classroom. In many traditional classrooms, teachers ask a question and then call on an individual student to respond while the rest of the class is expected to sit quietly and listen to the interchange. In some classes, it is possible for days, weeks, and perhaps even months to go by with some students rarely sharing their thoughts or ideas verbally in class. Classroom teachers frequently do the following as well:

- First call on a student by name and then ask that student a question (automatically cueing the rest of the class that they do not need to answer that question).
- Ask a question and expect an immediate response without waiting for the student to process the question or have any think time before responding.
- Call on the same six or seven students habitually, often those whom the teacher can count on to respond with the answers the teacher wants to hear.
- Ignore many students, even when they raise their hand to respond.
- Call on low-achieving students with less frequency than high-achievers.
- Ask a low percentage of questions that require higher-level critical-thinking skills.

Typically teachers are unaware of their own pattern of questioning and are surprised, even appalled, when they monitor themselves as to which students they are calling on and with what frequency. In all classrooms, there are some students who are inattentive and easily distracted. There are also students who, for whatever reason, are reluctant to participate and are passively rather than actively involved in the lesson. Teachers who have the most success in engaging students are those who are skilled in the art of questioning. One of the most effective ways of ensuring that all students are actively engaged in the lesson is through specific questioning techniques that encourage high response opportunities, student accountability, critical and divergent thinking, and active participation, with everyone having a voice that is heard and respected.

General Questioning Tips

Following are a few general recommendations:

- Format lessons to include a variety of questioning techniques that involve whole class, group, partner, and individual responses.
- Before asking for a verbal response to a question, have all students jot down their best-guess answer. Then call for volunteers to answer the question verbally.
- Structure the lesson so that it includes the opportunity to work in pairs or small groups for maximum student involvement and attention. Use alternatives to simply calling on students one at a time; for example, have students respond by telling their partner or writing down or drawing their response.
- Ask questions that are open-ended, require reasoning, and stimulate critical thinking and discussion.
- Expand on students' partial answers: "Tell me more." "How did you arrive at that answer?"
- Wait until several hands are raised before calling on students to respond.

It is important for teachers to incorporate many techniques that enable students to have frequent response opportunities throughout instruction. There are a variety of strategies that are recommended for incorporating in lessons. Following are suggestions for whole group, small group, and partner responses that require active involvement of students.

Methods for Whole Group and Unison Responses

Teachers instruct through a variety of formats (whole group, small group, partner) throughout the day, and lessons are structured to use the most beneficial format to accomplish the different learning tasks. Although it is not recommended to overuse whole group instruction in a differentiated classroom, whole group strategies are necessary and advantageous at various times of the day or lesson (for example, in opening and closing activities, introducing concepts and topics to the whole class, and review and practice of information and skills taught). The following are some recommended techniques to keep all students actively involved during whole group instruction (Rief, 2003, 2005).

Choral Responses

Have students recite poems or share reading of short passages or lines from the text chorally (in unison). Singing songs or chants, reviewing (for example, irregular or sight words, or math facts), with whole class response to flash cards, or other such activities are examples of choral responses. During whole class instruction, make frequent use of choral or unison responses when there is one correct and short answer. While presenting, stop frequently and have all students repeat back a word or two. During choral responses, everyone in the group is involved and participating.

Direct Instruction Techniques

Explain to students that there will be times when you will be asking questions that everyone will be answering at the same time (rather than raising their hand and waiting to be called on to respond). Students are trained by modeling and practice to respond to a teacher question by calling out the answer in unison when they are signaled to do so. This method is used when there is only one correct answer and that answer is short.

Students are first focused to be looking directly at the teacher. The teacher holds out his or her hand as if stopping traffic (or arms up in the air), while presenting a question that has a short, single answer. The teacher continues to hold his or her hand still or arms in the air, pausing to give students time to think. Then the teacher gives a verbal signal (for example, "Everyone . . ." or "Ready . . ."), waits one second, and then immediately follows with a visual signal that has been previously shown to students, such as a gesture of dropping the raised hand. At that signal, students respond by calling out the answer in unison (Engelmann, Hanner, & Johnson, 1999; Archer, Gleason, & Vachon, 2000). The types of questions can include providing examples and having students identify if the example was a simile or metaphor, for example, or a proper or "improper" fraction. After students respond, a follow-up question for an individual response can be asked: "How do you know that?"

Another direct instruction method, the point-tap signal, is used when focusing on a visual stimulus—for example, reading together a list of words on the board or reciting answers to math facts shown on the overhead projector. The teacher points to a stimulus, such as an individual word on the list, and then pauses briefly for students to think and figure out the word. Then the teacher gives a verbal signal (for example, "What word?"), followed by a tap by a pointer next to the word. The students then read the word in unison, and continue in this manner to read the rest of the words on the list (Engelmann et al., 1999; Archer, Gleason, & Vachon, 2000). These direct instruction techniques greatly increase students' rate of response for these kinds of tasks. When incorrect answers are called out, the teacher can immediately correct the group and continue to practice without singling anyone out.

Hand Signals for Whole Group Responses

Unison responses can be obtained by having students use various hand signals—for example, thumbs up/thumbs down or open hand/closed hand responses from students indicating such things as: "yes/no," "I agree/I disagree," or any other "either/or" response. Finger signals can be used as well. Teachers can pose questions, wait for students to think, and when a signal is given, students hold up a designated number of fingers to match their answer. For example, teachers can do quick assessments using multiple-choice questions in which students hold up the corresponding number of fingers rather than write down their response. The choices can be listed on the board. After posing the question, allowing wait time, and then signaling, students hold up the number of fingers that correspond with the choices on the board.

Carolyn Chapman (2000) recommends a "Fist of 5" technique as a preassessment tool to find out what learners already know about a topic. Using a hand signal on a scale of 1 to 5, students self-assess: how well they know something. Five fingers mean the student believes he or she has a high degree of understanding, and one finger means a low degree.

Write-On Tools

Most students (particularly those with learning disabilities or AD/HD who often resist paper-and-pencil work) are motivated to work with colored pens and markers on dry-erase boards. Another way of eliciting unison responses is to ask the class a question, pause for thinking time, and ask students to write their answer on an individual dry-erase board, individual chalkboard, or other write-on tool. Then, after a teacher signal (for example, "Boards up"), students hold up their boards for the teacher to see and quickly assess which students understand and who needs extra help.

Students of all ages enjoy writing on the boards, which can be used in any content area for short answer responses (for example, solving individual math problems or equations or practicing spelling words). If used properly, they are also effective in checking for students' understanding and determining who needs extra help and practice. For dry-erase boards, a tissue serves as an eraser. For chalkboard use, it is helpful to store a piece of chalk inside a baby bootie or sock, which serves as the eraser. Write-on tools can be kept in each student's desk or passed out as needed.

Premade Response Cards

Preprinted response cards and fans are highly effective in engaging students in lessons. They are a hands-on and motivating format for answering questions, involving all students, and significantly increasing active participation. Any preprinted response cards should be easy for students to manipulate. These can be cards with a single-hole punch that are held together by a metal ring, cards that are held together by a brass fastener and opened up like a fan, or a single card made of card stock or construction paper that is divided into sections (halves, thirds, or quarters), preprinted with a choice of responses. The answer is indicated on this card by placing a clothespin on the student's choice of correct answer.

When the teacher poses the question, students select their answer by holding up the card of choice, placing their clothespin, or similar method of indicating choice. Cards should be designed with words or symbols written on both sides of the card so both the teacher and student can see when holding it up. Premade response cards or fans are useful at any grade level or content area to integrate into whole class questioning strategies (Heward et al., 1996).

Following are examples of some uses for premade response cards for reviewing material:

- The vowel sound heard in different words (a, e, i, o, u)
- The part of speech of a particular word within a sentence (noun, verb, adjective, adverb)
- The math process needed to solve a problem (add, subtract, multiply, divide). See the illustration.
- The final punctuation mark needed (period, question mark, exclamation point)
- Social studies terms or concepts (legislative, executive, judicial branch of government)
- The literary term that a given example demonstrates (alliteration, idiom, personification)
- Multiple choice (a, b, c, d)
- Greater than, less than, equal to

Teachers may wish to have the sectioned response card divided into three or four sections and laminated without anything written in the sections. These cards can then have multiple use by having students write in erasable marker the response choices for a particular lesson. A card, pen, and clothespin can be kept in each desk.

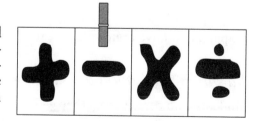

Methods for Small Group Responses

Much of classroom instruction involves small groups of students working together. Grouping patterns should be flexible, as discussed in Chapter Two. Small group active responses take place in any cooperative learning group structure. There are endless activities, learning tasks, and projects that are best accomplished in small groups—for example: creating a product together, solving a problem, brainstorming, analyzing, summarizing, conducting an experiment, studying and reviewing, or reading and discussing. Many of the activities throughout this book are intended and designed for small group format.

Methods for Partner Responses

Use of partners (pair shares) is perhaps the most effective method for maximizing student engagement (Rief, 2003, 2005). It involves turning to a partner for short interactions between two students. Pair-share formats are ideal for predicting, sharing ideas, clarifying directions, summarizing information, previewing information, drilling and practicing (vocabulary, spelling words, math facts), sharing reading of text, discussing reading material, and sharing writing assignments, among others. For example, the teacher could say:

"Pair up with your neighbor and share your ideas about . . ."

"Turn to your partner and . . ." After giving partners a chance to respond, ask for volunteers to share with the whole class: "Who would be willing to share what you or your partner thought about . . . ?"

"Turn to your partner [or person across from you or behind you] and discuss for a few minutes . . ." or, "Write down with your partner all the things you can think of that . . ."

"Help each other figure out how to do this."

Partner responses can be structured informally ("turn to a neighbor") or with teachers more carefully assigning partners. Partners can be numbered 1's and 2's, or A's and B's, so the teacher can assign different partner tasks—for example, "A's, tell your partner your prediction for the next page."

Partners can be used to check over each other's work before turning it in, combine ideas and resources for a joint project, take turns reading aloud or questioning and discussing a reading passage together, listening to and providing feedback on each other's writing, working out math problems together, checking that each other correctly recorded homework assignments in their daily planner, and numerous other tasks.

Consider allowing partners the opportunity to work together standing or moving to a location away from their desks. This is especially beneficial for students who need to be able to get up and move (such as those with AD/HD), while still having the expectation to be on task and working productively with their partners.

OTHER INCLUSIVE QUESTIONING STRATEGIES

To ensure that we are giving all students in the classroom fair and equal opportunities to respond, participate, and have their voices heard, consider using these inclusive questioning techniques.

Variation in Method of Calling on Students

Students who perceive that they will be required to participate and respond to questions remain more attentive. Sometimes teachers inadvertently neglect to call on certain students as frequently as others to contribute to class discussions or answer questions. One technique many teachers use to ensure they are giving all students in class an equal opportunity to respond is to write each student's name on a deck of cards or a tongue depressor stick. The cards or sticks are used to draw from when calling on students. Once a name is drawn, the name card or stick is put in a different stack or container. When using this technique, it is important that students not tune out and stop paying attention once they have had their turn. In order to prevent this from happening, it is good practice to draw names periodically from the discard pile of cards or sticks (those already called on) so students know they may be called on again at any time.

Students enjoy novel ways of being called on to respond such as: "Everyone wearing earrings, stand up. This question is for you." "Everyone who has fewer than six letters in their last name, you may try to answer this question." "Anyone who has a birthday in January, February, or March may answer this one." Students from that group may answer or have the option to pass.

Wait Time to Increase Student Participation

Provide sufficient wait time from when you pose a question until calling on the first student to answer that question. Studies first conducted by Mary Budd Rowe (1974) and others indicate the average amount of time teachers wait before calling on someone for a response is between one and three seconds (Sousa, 2001).

It is important to allow at least five seconds of wait time. Many students, particularly English-language learners and those with learning disabilities in auditory processing, need more time to process the question, gather their thoughts, and be able to express them. The partner strategies discussed previously are excellent means of enabling all students to share their thoughts and responses with another student before asking individual students to answer questions in a whole class format. This automatically builds in extra wait time and opportunity to think about the question and formulate an answer. Try rephrasing, ask probing questions, and wait longer for a response. Ask students if they need more time to think about their answer. Tell students who cannot answer the question at that time that you will come back to them later, and then do so.

Questioning Arrangements for Certain Students

Be sensitive to students who are often viewed by peers as poor students who rarely know the answer to questions asked in class. Be open to making a special arrangement in private with a student to help bolster his or her self-esteem. You may try telling the student to go ahead and raise his or her hand with a closed fist and you will not call on him or her at that time. When the child raises an open hand, you will make every effort to call on the student at that time. This technique is reported to be helpful in changing peer perceptions of individuals who seldom raise their hand and often have fragile self-esteem. Other classmates are not aware of the fist or open hand signal and notice only that the student appears to know the answer and wishes to contribute in class.

SOCRATIC SEMINAR

It is worthwhile to have teams of teachers trained in the method of Socratic seminar, a sophisticated method of leading dialogues in the classroom that focuses on understanding issues from various viewpoints rather than eliciting "right" answers or "covering" a topic. The Socratic method of teaching is based on Socrates' theory that it is more important to enable students to think for themselves than merely to fill their heads with the "right" answer. Students learn to think more critically, read more closely, and discuss ideas with clarity and confidence. The ability to ask the question that stimulates thoughtful and meaningful discussion is often more important than the answer (Cushman, 1992; Gray, 1989).

For a seminar, the teacher selects a short reading (a poem or article, for instance) that lends itself to ideas and issues worth discussing. It is the role of the teacher or seminar leader to formulate questions that have no single answer, can be answered best by reference to the text, and require the student to apply the text and ideas to himself or herself. Seminars are generally conducted with everyone seated in a circle. Students are trained to not raise their hand during the seminar, but to take turns and join in the dialogue. Everyone in the seminar must be familiar with the material being discussed. Often the teacher reads the passage aloud to the class before asking students to study it for a given length of time on their own (Cushman, 1992; Gray, 1989).

Student Responsibilities

There are guidelines, skills, and behaviors that are taught to students before engaging in seminars, such as the following:

- Listen respectfully.
- Stay on the subject.
- Come prepared to the seminar ready to participate.
- Refer to the text, and defend ideas from the text.
- It is all right to pass.
- Ask for clarification when you are confused about something.
- How to respond with statements such as, "I agree with . . . but I want to add . . ." "I disagree with . . . because . . ."

Teacher Responsibilities

The following strategies and recommendations will help ensure student participation and a successful seminar:

- At the beginning of the seminar, ask an opening question and then give students a certain amount of time to discuss in pairs or triads before beginning the group seminar.
- Allow at least five to seven seconds for replies to questions and then follow with a clarifying question.
- Rephrase a question if the students do not understand it.
- Ask for clarification—for the student to be more specific, to rephrase, or to elaborate, for example.
- Request that reasons be given for answers.
- Allow and encourage discussion of differences; draw out reasons and implications.
- Ask interpretive questions, divergent questions, and questions that are open-ended with many possible answers.
- Keep refocusing on the text.
- Ask students to paraphrase other students' responses and then respond or react to what the other student shared—for example, "Janet, what did you understand Michael to say just now? Can you say that in your own words? Do you agree with that? What evidence do you find in the text to support that?"
- Keep a record of who has spoken.
- Encourage students to speak up.
- Return to students who pass.
- Have closure by having students summarize a few points made during the discussion.
- Accept students' responses without labeling them right or wrong.
- Pause and allow time after a student answers a question, giving all students the time to consider the response. Then ask other students for their opinions about the response (Cushman, 1992; Gray, 1989).

Examples of Socratic Questioning

"In what ways are . . . and . . . alike [or different]?"

"What would you do [or say] if you were . . . ?"

"Can you think of an example to illustrate the point?"

"What if . . . happened [or were true] instead of . . . ?"

"In recent times, what well-known people are [were] like . . . ?"

"What would you do [or say] if you were . . . ?"

"How would . . . view this? Why?"

RECIPROCAL TEACHING

Reciprocal teaching (Palincsar & Brown, 1986, 1987) is a comprehension-oriented process that can be used throughout the curriculum for all grade levels and students and involves students in the cooperative process of prediction, question generating, clarification or defining of unfamiliar terms or phrases, and summarizing. Students are taught each of these strategies. After the students have learned the strategies modeled by the teacher and practiced as a group, they take over the "teacher role" in their cooperative groups. This is an excellent vehicle for teaching comprehension and training students in the art of questioning. They are responsible for working together to do the following when reading.

- *Predicting.* Have students look at the title, pictures, or any other clues to predict what the passage, article, or story will be about. Their predictions are confirmed or adjusted as they read.

  Examples: "Predict what the story [or article or passage] will be about in one sentence."

  "If you did not read the whole story today, predict what you think will happen next."

- *Generating questions.* Have students construct teacher-like questions that begin, "What do you think . . . ?" "Why does . . . ?" of "How are . . . ?" for example.

  Example: "Write three teacher-like or test questions about the story [or article or passage]. Write the answer and page number where the answer is found."

- *Clarifying.* Ask if there are any words used that they would like clarified or defined or that a younger child might need clarified.

  Example: "Write three to five words from today's assignment that your group [or younger children] would need to have clarified. After each word, write the page number where the word can be found. Look up the definition. Write the meaning of the word as it is used in the story [or article or passage]."

- *Summarizing. Example:* "Write a one-sentence summary of the passage or pages that were assigned for today."

ASKING THE RIGHT QUESTIONS

Good teachers are good questioners. They know how to pose questions throughout the day that require students to grapple with ideas, think critically, and produce thoughtful responses. This section highlights some of the more powerful thought-provoking questions that we recommend teachers use. First, we examine the challenge levels of questions based on Benjamin Bloom's *Taxonomy of Educational Objectives* (1984), which are well known by most educators.

Bloom's Taxonomy

Bloom (1984) describes six levels of thinking: knowledge, comprehension, application, analysis, evaluation, and synthesis. Following are some types of questions and activities that are at each of the six levels (knowledge being the least complex and synthesis the most complex).

- Knowledge: Tell, list, define, label
- Comprehension: Locate, explain, identify, describe, discuss, show, retell
- Application: Demonstrate, record, construct, illustrate, interpret, diagram, practice
- Analysis: Compare, contrast, categorize, classify, investigate, solve
- Evaluation: Judge, assess, justify, predict, determine, verify
- Synthesis: Compose, design, produce, transform, formulate

The questions asked of students depend on the kind of thinking (for example, linear or lateral) that we want them to engage in. We will examine types of questions and prompts that elicit lateral and linear thought processes.

Questions That Spark Lateral Versus Linear Thinking

Lateral thinking involves the type of questioning that encourages the unrestricted free flow of ideas—creative brainstorming sessions that explore a world of possibility. These thought processes are often prompted by asking, "What if . . . ?"—for example, "What if you could have one superhuman power? . . . What would you choose?" Such a question could generate a wide range of potential powers, such as "freeze time," "shrink or enlarge my body," "fly," "shoot lasers out of my fingers," or "breathe underwater." This kind of thinking could also be prompted by setting up scenarios such as: "What if you received two hundred dollars to start a business at the beach for the summer. What would you choose?" Again, this could lead to all kinds of responses ("sell ice cream and cold drinks," "rent out water sports equipment," "provide a babysitting service," "rent sun umbrellas"). If the idea of renting water sports equipment is the one chosen as most promising and exciting, how to execute that plan leads us to the next line of questioning . . .

Linear thinking involves the type of questioning that now recognizes a concrete goal and demands a plan of action to achieve that goal. Whereas lateral thinking explored a world of possibilities, linear thinking explores the step-by-step approach for executing the plan. There is now the shift from a "what if . . ." to a "how to . . ." frame of mind, as with these prompting questions: "With the two hundred dollars, what water sports equipment should we purchase?" "How should we go about advertising?" "Do we need to find a partner?" "Is there competition, and if so how will we stand out? Will we be cheaper than the competition? Will we provide different kinds of equipment from what is now available from the competitor? Will we provide for a longer time that the equipment can be rented?"

It is important to engage students in both kinds of thinking and questioning and to teach them how to ask themselves and their partners or groups appropriate questions to generate ideas and solve problems.

Questions for Deeper Understanding of Text

During the reading of books in the literacy classroom, the teacher guides students to construct meaning from the text through the art of questioning. Not only does the teacher model the kind of questioning he or she wants students to engage in as they read, but the children are also taught how to ask these questions to themselves and their classmates who are reading the same book. Following are questions that may be asked to elicit discussion, construct meaning from text, and enhance reading comprehension (Mooney, 1995; Schaffer, 1989):

"What do you think will happen next?"

"What do you think . . . is thinking?"

"Have you ever felt like . . . did when he or she . . . ?"

"Which character in the story would you choose as your friend? Why?"

"What message do you think the author is trying to get across?"

"What clues tell you that . . . was probably . . . ?"

"What other books have you read about a similar topic [theme, setting]?"

"What caused . . . to . . . ?"

"How do you think . . . and . . . were alike [or different]?"

"How was . . . different at the end of the book? What do you believe caused this change?"

"What effect did . . . have on . . . ?"

"According to the passage, what caused . . . ?"

"What do you think was the significance of . . . ?"

"Which character do you feel you know the best? Why? Read the text again to see what else you can find out about that character."

"As you reread, think about the techniques the author uses to . . . [create mood, portray characters]."

"Have you ever been in this situation?"

Chambers (1996) describes the "tell me" approach, which is a way of asking particular kinds of questions to encourage deeper thinking and more meaningful discussion in the classroom about books students have read. He points out the value of the question, "How do you know that?" to facilitate students' returning to the text to provide evidence.

Following are some of the "tell me" approach basic and general questions used during "book talk" that Chambers recommends:

"Was there anything you liked about this book?"

"Was there anything you disliked about this book?"

"Was there anything that puzzled you?"

"Was there anything that took you completely by surprise?"

"Were there any patterns—any connections—that you noticed?"

"When you first saw the book, even before you read it, what kind of book did you think it was going to be?"

"If the writer asked you what could be improved in the book, what would you say?"

"What will you tell your friends about this book?"

"What won't you tell them because it might spoil the book for them?"

QUESTIONING GAMES AND OTHER IDEAS

Many other chapters in this book share additional questioning strategies and examples for application. Here are a few more questioning ideas that teachers might want to use that are motivating for students:

- Play *Jeopardy* types of games with students, where the answer is provided and students need to determine the question.

  For example, review vocabulary words studied in class by playing "I'm thinking of . . ." The teacher states, "I'm thinking of a word that means curious." The child responds with, "What is 'inquisitive'?"

- Write terms on the board that are being studied in the content area. Students have to write a question that would have as an answer each of the terms.

- Firing squad: Three to four students come to the front of the classroom with prepared questions pertaining to a subject being studied in class. In quick succession, students "fire" questions to their classmates. If the student cannot answer it, he or she says, "Pass," and a new student is chosen.

- Display a bulletin board of "I wonder . . ." or "I always wondered why . . ." *Examples:* "I wonder why an older person's hair turns gray." "I wonder why the moon looks different colors on different nights." "I wonder how the memory of a computer works."

These types of questions can be generated individually, in partners, or in teams. This question board should be added to throughout the school year and could prompt writing assignments, Internet searches, and other research projects.

QUESTIONING TIPS FOR PARENTS

It is helpful for parents to learn effective means of questioning their children. Teachers may wish to share some of the recommended examples of questions to spark different kinds of thinking and questions for discussing books being read together at home. There are other kinds of questions as well to share with parents to foster better communication with their children. The following tips may be passed along to parents, perhaps at a back-to-school night, through a memo, or in a school newsletter:

Many of the common questions parents ask their children do little to elicit conversation or foster the kind of communication we would like to engage in with our son or daughter. For example, the typical queries, "How was school today?" "What did you learn in school today? "How are you doing in school?" "What's your favorite subject?" often result in little more than a shrug, one-word answer, or minimal response. Many times the questions we ask may sound like an interrogation, or we may not really listen with full attention to what our children are telling us. Sometimes such questions are more springboards to lecturing them about what they need to do, and it is easier and preferable for many children to evade such questions or discuss much about school with parents.

It is recommended to ask questions that indicate clearly that we are interested in the child's point of view: his or her feelings, thoughts, and perception of things. Asking good questions and being an active and thoughtful listener is important for building and maintaining those open lines of communication with our children. It helps, with regard to schoolwork, if parents know their child's teachers and take an interest in and are familiar with the classroom and what is being taught. Parents who are involved with the school have much more that they can talk about with their children with regard to school. Regularly look at your children's assignments and textbooks. That makes asking questions about what happens in class or what they are learning about a topic more sincere, and your child's answers to such questions more relevant. If you read with your child, the kinds of questions found above are helpful while you are reading together. In fact, if you have read the same book your son or daughter is reading in class or for home reading, it is a wonderful opportunity to try engaging in the type of "book talk" discussions, as described above with your child.

How we frame questions with regard to when our children misbehave also makes a big difference in our parenting style and relationships. To help our children develop in their problem-solving skills and to learn more responsible behavior, it is recommended to use language and ask questions such as suggested by Jim Fay and David Funk (1995): "How do you think we might solve this problem?" "Are there any other possible solutions that you can you think of?" "What would happen if you tried . . . ?" "What would be an appropriate consequence for . . . ?" "What can you do differently next time when you are feeling [angry, upset, frustrated] that will help you express your feelings without [hurting others, damaging property, breaking the rules]?" Offer limited choices, and ask your child to decide between those choices—for example, "Would you rather A or B?" or "You're welcome to A or B. What's your choice?" "Would you rather sit alone and not participate, or stop insulting your brother and join us in the game? [Fay & Funk, 1995].

Many adults (both parents and teachers) question children of all ages with, "Why . . . ?": "Why did you do this?" "Why did you do that?" Often the "why" question cannot be answered and is useless to ask. Try instead:

"What are you supposed to be doing right now?"

"What is your plan to . . . ?"

"What do you need in order to get this done?"

"How can we help you?"

REFERENCES

Archer, A., Gleason, M., & Vachon, V. (2000). *Rewards.* Longmont, CO: Sopris West.

Bloom, B. S. (Ed.). (1984). *Taxonomy of educational objectives: Book 1, Cognitive domain.* Reading, MA: Addison-Wesley.

Chambers, A. (1996). *Tell me.* Portland, ME: Stenhouse Publishers.

Chapman, C. (2000). *Sail into differentiated instruction.* Thomson, GA: Creative Learning Connection.

Cushman, K. (1992, Mar.–Apr.). Conversation in classrooms: Who are seminars for? *Harvard Education Letter.*

Engelmann, S., Hanner, S., & Johnson, G. (1999). *Corrective reading.* Worthington, OH: SRA/McGraw-Hill.

Fay, J., & Funk, D. (1995). *Teaching with love and logic.* Golden, CO: Love and Logic Press.

Gray, D. (1989, Fall). Putting minds to work—How to use the seminar approach in the classroom. *American Educator,* pp. 16–23.

Heward, W., Gardner, R., Cavanaugh, R., Courson, F., Grossi, T., & Barbetta, P. (1996). Everyone participates in this class. *CEC: Teaching Exceptional Children, 28*(2), 4–9.

Mooney, M. (1995, Sept.). Guided reading beyond the primary grades. *Teaching K–8, 26,* 75–77.

Palincsar, A. S., & Brown, A. L. (1986). Interactive teaching to promote independent learning from text. *Reading Teacher, 39,* 771–777.

Palincsar, A. S., & Brown, A. L. (1987). Enhancing instructional time through attention to metacognition. *Journal of Learning Disabilities, 20*(1), 66–75.

Rief, S. (1998). *The ADD/ADHD checklist: An easy reference for parents and teachers.* San Francisco: Jossey-Bass.

Rief, S. (2003). *The ADHD book of lists.* San Francisco: Jossey-Bass.

Rief, S. (2005). *How to reach and teach children with ADD/ADHD* (2nd ed.). San Francisco: Jossey-Bass.

Rowe, M. B. (1974). Wait-time and rewards as instructional variables: Their influence on language, logic, and fate control. *Journal of Research Science Teaching, 2,* 81–94.

Schaffer, J. (1989, Apr.). Improving discussion questions: Is anyone out there listening? *English Journal,* pp. 40–42.

Sousa, D. A. (2001). *How the brain learns.* Thousand Oaks, CA: Corwin Press.

Chapter 8

FOSTERING STUDENTS' SELF-ESTEEM AND RESILIENCE

Resiliency is the capacity to cope and feel competent (Brooks & Goldstein, 2001): to survive, progress through difficulty, bounce back, and move on positively again and again in life (Gibbs, 2001). The importance of human resilience and what can be done to strengthen children's resiliency has gained much interest in recent years. Research has identified some of the protective factors that enable some people who live through adversity and significant stress to become competent, successful, and emotionally healthy adults, while others who lived with the same or similar adverse conditions, environment, and risk factors do not fare well (Gibbs, 2001).

Some of the attributes of resilient children are described by Bonnie Benard (1991) and cited from the works of Garmezy (1991), Garmezy and Rutter (1983), Werner and Smith (1989), and Rutter (1979):

- Social competence: Prosocial behaviors such as responsiveness, empathy, caring, communication skills, and a sense of humor
- Problem-solving skills: Abstract and reflective thinking, flexibility
- Autonomy: An internal locus of control, a strong sense of independence, power, self-esteem, self-discipline, and control of impulses
- A sense of purpose and future: Healthy expectancies, goal directedness, orientation to the future, motivation to achieve, persistence, hopefulness, hardiness, belief in a bright and compelling future, a sense of anticipation, and a sense of coherence

In their wonderful book, *Raising Resilient Children* (2001), Robert Brooks and Sam Goldstein note that resilient children and youth:

- Are hopeful and possess high self-worth
- Feel special and appreciated
- Learn to set realistic goals and expectations for themselves
- Develop the ability to solve problems and make decisions

- Are more likely to view mistakes, hardships, and obstacles as challenges to confront rather than as stressors to avoid
- Rely on productive coping strategies that are growth fostering rather than self-defeating
- Are aware of their weaknesses and vulnerabilities but recognize their strong points and talents
- Have a self-concept that is filled with images of strength and competence
- Develop effective interpersonal skills with peers and adults
- Are able to seek out assistance and nurturance in a comfortable, appropriate manner from adults who can provide the support they need
- Are able to define the aspects of their lives over which they have control and to focus their energy and attention on these rather than on factors over which they have little, if any, influences

Brooks and Goldstein (2001) also refer to the importance of being a "charismatic adult"—an adult from whom a child gathers strength. Individuals who have had many risk factors in their lives and are now successful adults generally identify and can credit somebody (often a teacher) who, through his or her support, encouragement, special attention, and interest in that child made that difference. These adults conveyed their care and acceptance and were their advocates for them, especially in times of need. Their efforts and the relationship they built contributed significantly to the child's development of resilience and self-esteem.

As Brooks and Goldstein so poignantly remind us: "We can all serve as the charismatic adults in children's lives—believing in them and providing them with the opportunities that reinforce their islands of competence and feelings of self-worth. This is not only a wonderful gift to our children, but also an essential ingredient for the future. This is part of our legacy to the next generation" (p. 293).

STUDENT NEEDS FOR SCHOOL SUCCESS

All students deserve to come to school and have their needs met. This is vital to their learning and achievement, as well as to their development of resiliency and self-esteem:

- Children need to feel:
  - Safe and comfortable in the classroom environment, knowing that they will be treated with dignity and respect and not deliberately criticized, embarrassed, or humiliated in front of their classmates
  - Confident that their teacher cares about their needs and can be trusted
  - Part of a caring, inclusive community
  - Competent, capable, and respected
  - The importance of their own personal best efforts and self-improvement
- Children need teachers who:
  - Maintain high expectations yet provide support as needed—enabling students to achieve those expectations and standards
  - Help students develop self-discipline
  - Provide opportunities to voice their feelings, concerns, and ideas; make choices; and be involved in some decision making
  - Provide the opportunity to participate in school activities that nurture and showcase their areas of strength (what Brooks and Goldstein refer to as "islands of competence")
  - Model self-control, fairness, empathy, tolerance, a positive attitude, good communication, and problem-solving skills
  - Differentiate instruction to accommodate learning style differences in students
  - Make themselves available to their students

CLASSROOM STRATEGIES AND PROGRAMS TO PROMOTE SELF-ESTEEM

Among our responsibilities as educators is to enable students to experience and internalize positive feelings about themselves as capable, competent learners and valued, respected, cared-for individuals. We must provide students what they need to enable them to develop self-esteem. The following are ways to help in this regard.

Recognition and Appreciation

It is important for teachers to make every effort to communicate to each student that he or she is an important and valued member of the classroom and community. We should also teach students to extend themselves and show their appreciation and caring for others, as well. The following are ways to do so:

- Use questioning techniques and sharing methods that allow all students to have the opportunity to be heard and share with equity. (See Chapter Seven.)

- Send special messages or notes to students recognizing their efforts and behaviors you are pleased with and positive feedback on their work.

- Encourage students to write positive notes, thank-you letters, and get-well cards to other students, staff members, substitute teachers, guest speakers, and parents. Some elementary teachers maintain a center in their room with supplies and paper for this purpose.

- Encourage students to give social recognition and reinforcement to their classmates (for example, "high fives" and rounds of applause) and to themselves ("Give yourself a pat on the back" or "Take a bow").

- Help students recognize their strengths and competencies. Keep a record or profile of what students do well.

- Provide meaningful classroom job opportunities that allow all students the chance to contribute to their community. (See the multiple intelligence job descriptions in Chapter Two.)

- Designate individual students as "class experts" on certain topics or for specific skills that they shine in or have a special interest in.

- Provide many activities and opportunities for students to showcase their strengths; teach other students what they know how to do well; perform; share about their hobbies and interests; and so forth.

- Create a class book titled *Our Strengths,* with a page for each student. Students provide pictures or write about their strengths, interests, and positive character traits.

- Spotlight individual students for recognition such as through a Student of the Week program described below or something similar.

Student of the Week

Many teachers have a program in their classrooms aimed at recognizing individual students in the classroom and enabling classmates to learn more about that child. If you use this program, all students in the class must have a turn during the school year to be the recognized student. With this program, there is generally a bulletin board devoted to a different student each week. This "Student of the Week," "Student Standout," or "Student in the Spotlight" may be asked the week or weekend before it is his or her turn to be the featured student of the week to bring in pictures and any objects about himself or herself to display. Generally the student is asked to write a short autobiography; parents or guardians may also be asked to write a paragraph or two sharing positive things about their child. Some teachers ask students to fill out a form before their week. (See Form 8.1, Student Standout for the Week, at the end of this chapter.)

Some teachers pass out strips of paper (sentence strips) to each student in the class to write something positive about the student in the spotlight (for example, about character traits or attributes, what they think the student does well, what they like or appreciate about their classmate). The student in the spotlight can pass out additional strips of paper to family members, other school staff members, or friends from other classes to add to his or her collection. At the end of the week, these positive comments can be mounted on a poster or in some other fashion to take home. Teachers may want to ask all students to submit the paper strips of comments they have written to the teacher first (to make sure there are only positive comments) before posting or giving to the individual child.

Connection and Communication

In the effort to be inclusive of all students and establish a relationship in which each child feels cared about as an individual by his or her teacher, the following recommended strategies can build that personal connection:

- As students enter the room, welcome them with a smile and a personal greeting.
- Write students positive notes to place on their desks, attach to their work that you return to them, or e-mail or mail home (refer to them as postcards or "Happy Grams").
- If you know which students will be in your classroom before the beginning of the school year, make personal telephone calls to introduce yourself or mail or e-mail notes during the summer telling the students and their parents that you are looking forward to having them in your class.
- Call one parent each night (or as frequently as possible) with positive comments about the child's efforts.
- For every phone call made to discuss negative behaviors, make a few positive phone calls home to share good news with parents.
- Schedule brief individual conferences with each student throughout each grading period in addition to conferring with students during reader's and writer's workshops and other instructional periods.
- Have a regularly scheduled (weekly, monthly, or bimonthly) breakfast or lunch with different small groups of students. Teachers provide the food (juice, muffin or toast) or part of it (beverage or dessert). This special time allows everyone to talk about topics other than schoolwork in a pleasant way. It is a great opportunity to build positive relationships and connections with students.
- Using digitized photos or video or some other method, record students engaged in a variety of activities and showcasing their accomplishments. Display or present the album of pictures, videos, or PowerPoint presentation to parents and visitors to the classroom (such as during open house).

Words That Matter

Most of us will agree that the old adage "sticks and stones might break my bones, but words will never hurt me" is simply not true. Words and the message stated or implied through our verbal and nonverbal language can be hurtful and harmful, especially to those with fragile self-esteem. Following are suggestions for teaching, modeling, and cueing students to use positive language and communication with each other, critical to building a caring classroom community:

- Model how to use positive self-talk, especially to illustrate how to think positively, accept our mistakes, and not give up when frustrated.
- Point out students' errors in a way that is not demeaning and respects their efforts. On written work, take care not to mark up students' papers, especially with red ink. It is often helpful and respectful to indicate errors in the margins or on sticky notes when possible. When teaching students to peer-edit, train them and model how to share positive comments first—what they liked about the work (even if it is only a choice of one certain vocabulary word)—before making recommendations for improvement.

- Teach students how to make positive statements, compliments, and recognize and use esteem-building language. Enforce in the classroom that "in here, we say only positive things about ourselves and others; no put-downs or negative comments to or about others are acceptable."

- Teach students how to accept compliments appropriately as well.

- Discuss negative comments and how these words make us feel. Name those negative comments (for example, *put-downs, zingers*) and use a cue word or signal to remind students not to use esteem-hurting language.

- Some elementary teachers call positive statements or compliments "sparkles," "builder-upper words," or "fuzzies." They make a hand signal that indicates positive statements heard. Whenever the teacher or other students hear someone saying something positive to another student, they make the hand signal indicating they heard a "builder-upper statement." A list can be kept or chart made to record esteem-building language heard.

Some middle school teachers refer to their classroom as "home court." They teach students that "home court" means it is a supportive environment, filled with fans who are encouraging and cheering each other on. When any negative comment or put-down is heard, the cue to be more positive is to simply state, "Remember we're in home court."

SCHOOLWIDE STRATEGIES AND PROGRAMS TO BUILD RESILIENCE AND SELF-ESTEEM

There are many ways that schools engage students in activities and programs that build a sharing and caring community and strengthen resiliency and self-esteem.

Adopt-a-Student and Special Friends

Staff members at many schools make personal connections and efforts to be a special adult in the life of one student at that school. They go by various names, such as "adopt a student," "special friends club," or "staff-student mentoring." In such programs, all staff members have the opportunity to sign up to be a "special friend" or "adopt" a student for the year. Classroom teachers generally are not matched with a child from their own classroom. The adult provides attention to and interest in his or her particular student's life by talking with, really listening to, and getting to know that child; checking in regularly on his or her progress; providing support and encouragement; and other such ways. Some schools have a specific process of trying to identify a student who may be in need of adult connection and special attention—children who tend to be relatively anonymous to teachers and staff, as well as those known to have certain challenges in their lives—social or emotional, family, learning, behavioral—that may warrant extra support. Many schools arrange for some activities to take place as a group—for example, all participants in the program might have a special breakfast or picnic together or play a game together like softball.

"Caught Doing Something Good" and "Gotcha" Programs

Many schools initiate a "caught doing something good" or "gotcha" program. All staff members are given tickets to pass out to students (other than their own) whom they observe or catch in the act of doing something kind or helpful to others or performing a targeted social skill being practiced, such as courtesy or good manners. Tickets are either accumulated by students to use for purchase from a school store or are placed in a central raffle box for a weekly or monthly drawing, with the four to five students whose names are drawn receiving recognition and a reward of some type.

There are variations of this program and how it is implemented. For example, at one elementary school, each teacher keeps a box in the classroom for students to deposit any earned "caught being good" tickets (with their name written on the tickets). Every Thursday each classroom teacher selects three tickets from the box. The three students whose names were drawn from each class go to the cafeteria during the last twenty minutes of the day for their reward: a make-your-own ice cream sundae. In some secondary schools, students who acquire a certain number of "gotcha" tickets can redeem them for a free yearbook or other substantial reward.

Recognition Assemblies

Most schools have recognition assemblies throughout the year. Students have the opportunity to be recognized and rewarded at these assemblies for any number of reasons besides academic achievement: service, effort, cooperation, spirit, attendance, attitude, friendliness, showing growth and improvement, and others. Typically, parents and families are invited to the assembly, pictures are taken of the students for display in the building or in a school newsletter or Web site, certificates are issued, and often refreshments are served. All teachers and staff are urged to ensure that every student is targeted for recognition and has the opportunity to be among the "students in the spotlight" at assemblies during the year.

School Clubs and Organizations

School clubs and organizations provide opportunities for students to become involved in the school community and cultivate new friendships and interests. In so doing, they grow in their positive feelings about themselves. There are numerous club possibilities to address a wide range of interests and activities.

Some clubs are formed to target individual students who need extra attention and involvement at school and to reward those who are making efforts to improve themselves. One vice principal at a middle school formed a Hiking Club and a Builders' Club at the school. The Hiking Club is geared to students who have had problems that involved a lot of management or intervention from school staff but have managed to turn around in their behaviors, achievement, or attitude. Students are selected by any staff member to be in the Hiking Club. Twice a month, this group of students, along with the few staff members involved with this club, hike the trails of a regional park in the area. Then they stop for a soda, and the students are driven home. The Builders' Club is also a "prestigious" club of students who are recommended for acceptance by staff members who notice the student making a positive effort to improve citizenship. Some of the activities they do in the club are paint benches, decorate or paint the trash cans, plant trees, help construct things, and work in conjunction with the local Kiwanis Club to collect toys for a toy drive. One middle school social worker created a "Botanical Rescue Squad" of selected students responsible for the care of ailing plants throughout the building.

Helping and Caring for Others

Caring for something or someone and giving of oneself to help others without looking for or expecting anything in return is one of the most rewarding of human experiences. There are ways we can provide this experience at school. Many teachers have discovered the benefits of having a classroom pet, for example. For some children, the class pet strongly connects the child to the school and classroom, and the chance to play with, nurture, and care for the pet is a powerful incentive. In other classes, having a patch or area of a school garden to tend to is a wonderful esteem builder in that students are taking responsibility and making a contribution to their school environment in helping that garden grow.

School Buddies

Buddy up a child who has low self-esteem with a younger child as a cross-age tutor to that younger student. Cross-age tutoring and upper- and lower-grade buddy systems boost the self-esteem of all children. They build positive relationships, and older students are put in the position of being a helper and support to their younger buddy.

Buddy Assistance Folder

Many teachers pair students in the classroom as buddies for various activities and supports. The buddy assistance folder system described here is a wonderful use of buddies that can enhance a student's resiliency and self-esteem.

Students miss days of school for a variety of reasons. Whether it is for one day or for a week, when the student returns from an absence, the idea that someone missed him or her and was concerned about his or her well-being is a positive experience. The buddy assistance folder provides a list of assignments that the child may have missed and may contain activity sheets, bulletins, assignment, sheets, and little "miss you" notes from concerned students and the teacher. When a child returns from an absence, he or she might feel a bit disoriented because the class has continued on with its learning whereas the returning student probably has not. This folder may provide a student who has difficulty learning or does not want to be at school in the first place with a motivation to return to learn.

The folder is made of colored construction paper, a colored file folder, or a regular manila folder. If a plain manila folder is used, a piece of colored copy paper may be used for the form so it is a little more cheery and uplifting. The Buddy Assistance Folder form (Form 8.2, at the end of this chapter) is glued or stapled to the front of the folder. It is placed on the absent child's desk first thing in the morning after attendance has been taken. The teacher might say, "It looks as if Josh is absent today. Does anyone know why he is absent? If you are Josh's buddy, please pick up his buddy assistance folder from the tub, and make sure any important papers are put in there today."

To carry this one step further, the buddy could make a telephone call from the classroom later that day (or from home that evening) to check on the condition of the absent student, to see if there is anything that the child might need from school, or if there are questions about the day. This interaction should be set up and approved by parents at the beginning of the year to see if this would be an imposition on the family. Being the receiver of a voice mail or e-mail can help make a student's day better, again indicating that someone is concerned about the absence and that the child has been missed. We never know what small acts of kindness might keep a child coming to school and keep that student in school for the long haul.

Assigning buddies at the beginning of the year works well. That way there is no question as to who is responsible for the task. Keeping the folders in a prominent location in the room helps students remember what responsibility they have toward their buddy. There are reciprocal rewards for both the giver and the receiver in this system. Careful planning of buddies at the beginning of the year ensures a smooth buddy assistance relationship.

COMMUNITY MENTORSHIP PROGRAMS

The value and power of mentorship programs is well recognized, and businesses, organizations, and individuals in communities throughout the United States have embraced the effort. The following program, Lawyers Involved in Kids' Education (LIKE), is an example of one outstanding exemplar program taking place in Long Island, New York, involving a law firm and an elementary school: The East Meadow, Long Island, law firm, Certilman Balin Adler & Hyman, LLP, in association with the Mentoring Partnership of Long Island, has established a mentoring program called LIKE (Lawyers Involved in Kids' Education). The program's purposes are to establish mentoring relationships between attorneys and potentially at-risk elementary school children and to help the kids increase vocabulary and analytical skills through word games.

During the 2004–2005 school year, the program's inaugural year, fifteen lawyers from the firm met with an equal number of third and fourth graders at the neighboring Walnut Street School in Uniondale. The school administration selected children they thought had not reached their academic potential for whatever reason. The attorneys met with the children each Wednesday for an hour at lunchtime. Each attorney was matched with a child. Groups of three mentors were then matched with three kids so that if a mentor could not come on a particular day, another mentor would be present for the group. In addition to the fifteen full-time mentors, an equal number of substitute mentors signed up to fill in on an as-needed basis.

During the initial half-hour of each session, the mentors ate lunch with the students and talked about events in the children's lives. For the second half-hour each week, the mentors and kids played word games as a group. During the first session in the fall, the children learned about acronyms such as LIKE, and each group chose an acronym as a team name, for example, HOPE (Helping Others Perform Excellently) and SMART (Students and Mentors Are Really Terrific). Some of the word games were played in a team competitive setting. Others were played on an individual mentor-mentee basis. Although competition is sometimes frowned on by educators, the children enjoyed the competitive nature of the games. They rooted for their teammates when it was their turn to come before the group. They also enjoyed coming to the blackboard and being the scorekeeper.

The following games, among others, were played:

- *Jumble.* Letters from a word are scrambled, and the children need to unscramble the letters to make a word. They then use the letters to solve a riddle.
- *Password, One Minute Wonders,* and *Taboo.* In these similar games, a child is called up front and shown, in series, words that he or she needs to describe for teammates to guess. Each child is given one minute to describe as many words as possible. Once a word is guessed correctly, the child goes on to the next word and so on, until the minute is up. The teams take turns giving the clues. The mentees are the first to go, followed by the mentors. In Password, the child can give a one-word clue to have his or her teammates guess the hidden word. In One Minute Wonders, in contrast with Password, players are not limited to giving one-word clues; the child can describe the word or give examples (so long as he or she does not use a form of the word as a clue). Taboo is the same as One Minutes Wonders, except that there are two taboo words that the child cannot say in describing the hidden word.
- *Boggle.* The children are given a square with sixteen or twenty-five boxes within it and letters randomly written in each box. The children try to form as many words as possible within five minutes; words can be formed by letters that touch each other vertically, horizontally, or diagonally.
- *Mastermind.* The mentor coordinator has in mind a four-letter word (a clean one), and the children try to guess it by saying four-letter words. For each word guessed, the leader responds by stating how many of the letters in the word the child guessed are in the hidden word and how many of those letters are in the correct place in the word. The guessing goes on until the hidden word is discovered.
- *Cryptoquote.* A short famous quote or saying is encrypted so that each letter means a different letter, for example, "j" is "m" and "x" is "e," so that to write "me," you would write "jx." The kids need to determine the encryption to find the answer.
- *Pictionary.* A child is shown a word and must draw a picture so that his or her team can guess the word.
- *Balderdash.* There are two forms of Balderdash. In Initials Balderdash, the kids are given the initials of an obscure organization (for example, I.A.S.C.B.—International Association of Sand Castle Builders). The children try to be creative and use the initials to come up with an organization that sounds plausible. All of the children's answers, as well as the name of the correct organization, are then read to the group. The other kids try to guess which one is the correct answer. Points are given for a correct guess as well as for someone choosing the answer. In Word Balderdash, SAT words are used, and the children try to come up with a definition that others may think is the correct answer. Points are awarded for correctly guessing the definition or for having other kids guess the word.
- *Words from Words.* The children are given words that contain many letters (for example, *masterpieces*) and are asked to create as many words in five minutes as possible from the letters given.
- *Backward Hangman.* This is the traditional hangman game, but the answers are written backward. Also, instead of words, famous places or people are used.

At the next-to-last LIKE session, the students performed a mock trial for the mentors, their parents, and the school administration. The trial related to a child caught "cheating" on a math test by taking out a piece of paper from his or her desk during the exam. The paper, however, was only a note from the child's mentor that said, "You can do it!" The defendant was found not guilty.

At the final session of the initial school year, the children played one last word game. It was a cryptoquote that said (in encrypted code), "We've really enjoyed spending time with you. Have a fun summer.— The Mentors." The kids solved the puzzle as a group in two minutes. They first decided that the one-letter word in the quote was probably *a*. Then they figured out that the first word with the apostrophe probably ended in "e" and then decided that the word was probably *We've*. With that information, the leader started filling in some letters. One boy then yelled out, "The first word at the end is '*The*'"; then another said *Mentors*; then *really*; then *time*. The children were so excited—that they were all running up to the blackboard and shouting out the letters and words. Before you knew it, they had the puzzle solved. It was amazing to witness. At the end of the session, one of the kids yelled, "Group hug!" and a whole bunch of the kids ran over and gave the mentors a hug. It was a rewarding experience for mentee and mentor alike. For more information about LIKE, which expanded its scope during the 2005–2006 school year (with plans for the future), contact the co-creator and coordinator of this program: Fred Skolnik, Certilman Balin Adler & Hyman, LLP, fskolnik@certilmanbalin.com or go to the Web page. www.certilmanbalin.com

COMMUNITY SERVICE

Many schools seek opportunities for their students to reach out into the community and make a contribution. Providing a needed service and making personal connections with and helping others is highly rewarding, and the positive feelings children and youth gain through service enhance self-esteem.

- Depending on the location, some schools can partner with convalescent and nursing homes. The children can visit and talk with the residents or play games, make cards and pictures, and write poems and stories to deliver to the residents, sing and perform on holidays, and participate in other mutual activities.
- Students can work schoolwide on a project to help the homeless in the city. They collect clothing, toiletries, and blankets; bag food for delivery; and help in other ways.
- Many schools become involved in community projects. For example, at Benchley-Weinberger Elementary School in San Diego (where Julie teaches), there is an annual project of making quilts to donate to children in need in the community. With the help and commitment of the wonderful PTA parents, each class designs and makes its own special quilt.

It is very important to instill in children a sense of obligation and responsibility for helping others and involve them in community service projects whenever possible (through school, youth organizations, churches/synagogues, and as a family). Letting children experience the act of giving to others is a powerful means of building citizenship, character and values, and self-esteem.

INTERVENTIONS AND SUPPORTS

School counseling centers provide many services designed to build students' self-esteem, such as growth groups, new student orientation, teaching conflict resolution and social skills, coordination of agency services, and providing interventions for attendance problems.

Concerned teachers can refer students to support staff or to the student support team for assistance in helping students with a variety of needs. When children having a number of academic, behavioral, or social/emotional problems receive the appropriate intervention, they are enabled to achieve success and grow in self-confidence, resiliency, and self-esteem. Many children need help addressing physical, social, health, and medical issues, and speech/language and learning difficulties.

Universal schoolwide supports such as creating a positive, social climate and culture in the building, enforcing zero tolerance, and bully-proofing the school through proactive measures are important in developing the sense of safety, protection, trust, caring, and well-being that are necessary for student success.

PRINCIPALS' EFFORTS

One middle school principal we know established Principal's Forum. Students sign up to meet with her to discuss things they would like to see happen at the school or any problems and possible solutions. This is a way she keeps in touch with students' needs and concerns, and it promotes student self-esteem when they know the principal is listening to their issues, ideas, and recommendations.

Principals give positive attention and recognition to students in a variety of ways. They welcome students—with personal greetings (by name preferably) as they arrive at school or teachers send students to the principal's office for achievements and improved behavior. Principals call home or leave a voice message with the "good news" to the students' parents. Elementary school students are often given little treats such as pencils by the principal on their birthdays. Awards and certificates are awarded and pictures are taken of students who have met certain goals and deserve recognition. Students are showcased on designated office and school bulletin boards, in school newsletters, and in other ways.

Schools that prioritize the development of self-esteem and resiliency in their students have principals who make strong efforts to get to know their students, are approachable and supportive, and are committed and strong leaders who build an inclusive, positive school climate and culture. The impact is significant for everyone in the school community when the top administrator prioritizes, models, and leads the positive climate, culture, and resilience-building effort. When the leadership makes it clear that the focus in the school is "success for all," then staff and community generally follow suit. It is everyone's responsibility to ensure that students and staff members know they are valued and belong and will be treated with respect, shown appreciation, and given the support needed to meet goals and achieve success.

REFERENCES

Benard, B. (1991). *Fostering resiliency in kids: Protective factors in the family, school and community.* Portland, OR: Western Regional Center for Drug Free Schools and Communities, Northwest Regional Educational Laboratory.

Brooks, R., & Goldstein, S. (2001). *Raising resilient children.* Chicago: Contemporary Books.

Garmezy, N. (1991). Resiliency and vulnerability to adverse developmental outcomes associated with poverty. *American Behavioral Scientist, 34*(4), 416–430.

Garmezy, N., & Rutter, M. (1983, Nov. 21). How and why do some kids flourish against all odds? *Behavior Today,* pp. 5–7.

Gibbs, J. (2001). *TRIBES: A new way of learning and being together.* Windsor, CA: Center Source Systems.

Rutter, M. (1979). Protective factors in children: Responses to stress and disadvantage. In M. W. Dent & J. E. Rolf (Eds.), *Primary prevention of psychopathology, Vol. 3: Promoting social competence and coping in children* (pp. 49–74). Hanover, NH: University Press of New England.

Werner, E., & Smith, R. (1989). *Vulnerable but invincible: A longitudinal study of resilient children and youth.* New York: Adams, Bannister, and Cox.

STUDENT STANDOUT FOR THE WEEK

Student standout for the week of

_____

Student's name _____

Congratulations! You have the distinct honor of being Room_____'s Student Standout for next week. Please review the following items carefully, and come next Monday prepared to share them with your classmates.

1. Bring pictures of yourself at different stages of your life. These will be placed on the student standout board for the entire week. All pictures will be returned to you the following Monday.

2. Have your mother, father, grandparent, aunt, uncle, sister, or brother write a brief paragraph about you (for example, something funny that they recall, a favorite memory, or just some nice thoughts about you). See, even your parents get homework in this class!

3. Bring in an article of clothing or something that is special to you: a T-shirt, hat, uniform, or stuffed animal, for example—to help your classmates learn something new about you.

4. Have a friend make a list of the things he or she likes about you. Include it on your board.

5. Share your hobby with us during your special week. Bring your collection, special talent, or something else and share it with the class.

6. If you play an instrument, play something for the class.

7. Bring in your favorite game. You will have a special game time allocated to you. (It can be a computer game!)

BUDDY ASSISTANCE FOLDER

Buddy Assistance Folder for

_____

Hi! I'm your Buddy Helper. My name is _____. We missed you during your absence. Here are a few of the things that you missed and that you need to make up. If you need extra help to clarify the assignment, please ask me.

Monday _____

_____

_____

_____

Tuesday _____

_____

_____

_____

Wednesday _____

_____

_____

_____

Thursday _____

_____

_____

_____

Friday _____

_____

_____

_____

Other things you should know _____

_____

_____

_____

Chapter 9

INCREASING HOME-SCHOOL COLLABORATION AND PARENT INVOLVEMENT

A key element for school success is shared responsibility or partnership in education, involving the teamwork of school personnel, parents, students, and the community. The research is clear that children do better in school when parents are involved and take an active role in their children's education. According to the National Association of School Psychologists' Position Statement on Home-School Collaboration (2005), when families are involved in education, students demonstrate more positive attitudes toward school and learning, higher achievement and test scores, improved behavior, increased homework completion, greater participation in academic activities, improved school attendance, and fewer placements in special education. Educators report greater job satisfaction, higher evaluation ratings from parents and administrators, and more positive associations with families. Parents experience enhanced self-efficacy, better understanding and more positive experiences with educators and schools, improved communication with their children, and better appreciation for their role in their children's education.

The fact that when parents play a positive role in their children's education, they do better in school is true whether parents are college educated or grade school graduates and regardless of family income, race, or ethnic background. What counts is that parents have a positive attitude about the importance of good education and that they express confidence their children will succeed. Major benefits of parent involvement are more successful academic programs and more effective schools (Berla, 1991; Henderson, 1994; San Diego County Office of Education, 1994).

High-achieving schools—those whose students as a whole score at the high-performance levels—frequently have a very active and supportive parent community. We (both authors) have been fortunate to have taught at such a school for many years. Parents are an integral part of the school program. Their tireless efforts, commitment, and willingness to contribute in myriad ways have supported the school staff in providing a quality program for the children.

Finding ways to reach and encourage all parents to become more actively involved with the school and their children's education is a challenge for many schools. This chapter shares various efforts and strategies to do so, along with tips for forming a positive and collaborative relationship between home and school.

STRATEGIES FOR INCREASING PARENT PARTICIPATION IN SCHOOL ACTIVITIES AND FUNCTIONS

There are countless school events that serve to motivate and recognize students, attract parents and families to school, and increase involvement: literacy fairs, science fairs, art fairs, musical festivals, chorus programs, school or class plays, and performances of various kinds. Student performances and recognition activities are often the most well-attended school events. There is nothing that attracts families to school more than having the chance to see their child perform or receive an award or positive recognition from the school. Try to give every student the opportunity to be "on stage."

Provide interesting and motivational activities for the whole family to participate in and enjoy. There are many types of family workshops that are hands-on, interactive, and educational for both children and their parents such as family math (Stenmark, Thompson, & Cossey, 1986) events and the popular Poetry, Pretzels, and Popcorn Night described later in this chapter.

Some schools create events to engage faculty and parents in friendly, fun competitions with students. For example, in upper elementary or middle school, schools might have volleyball or softball games or tournaments or silly relay races or obstacle courses with faculty and parent teams versus student teams.

Multicultural fairs are popular in many schools, involving students, parents, and the whole community in multicultural activities. This often includes a variety of exhibits, games, dance, music, and other student performances, as well as food from several cultures and countries.

To attract parents to school functions, provide child care for younger siblings, transportation and translation for parents who need it, refreshments, door prizes, or something all families leave with at the end of the night. Involve the students in encouraging their families to attend school events by having them make personal invitations, and send reminders to parents or guardians about school functions and activities through personal telephone calls with voice messages, e-mail, and notes.

Invite parents and perhaps extended family (grandparents, aunts, uncles) to be guest readers or speakers and to share about their jobs or professions, cultures, interests, and hobbies, skills, and other parts of their lives that may be interesting to students. This is a wonderful way to show we value our students' families and welcome their participation and involvement.

There are other ways schools increase parent participation:

- Provide incentives to increase attendance. For example, classes with the greatest turnout to certain school functions sometimes receive a reward or privilege of some kind or students attending evening programs with a parent or guardian receive a "no homework tonight" pass.

- Make video recordings of school events for a lending library, so parents and family members who were not able to attend the program or event can view the programs if they wish.

- Have exhibitions of different kinds. One middle school has an eighth-grade exhibition every year during which students individually share with a community member about what they enjoyed learning that year, what was important and meaningful to them, and to view their student portfolios of favorite work samples for the year.

- "Shadow Your Student" half-day. At one middle school, parents follow their children from class to class on a shortened schedule and then all students and parents have a barbecue lunch together.

- Host volunteer appreciation celebrations of various kinds (teas, banquets, luncheons). Providing recognition and thanks to parents, grandparents, guardians, community members, and others who volunteered in any capacity during the school year are popular events in most schools.

- Encourage parent participation based on their interests. Send home the Parent Interest Form (Form 9.1 at the end of this chapter) to obtain this information, and invite parents to participate and volunteer in activities or ways that match their interests.

School Outreach Efforts

There are many ways schools can increase communication and reach out to assist the parents in their community:

- Some schools have parenting classes on topics such as "Helping Your Child with Homework/Study Skills," "Positive Discipline," and "Helping Your Child Be a Better Reader."

- Schools with informative, up-to-date Web sites or regular newsletters are making excellent efforts at communication. Individual teachers can create their own monthly newsletters or maintain a page on the school's Web site that parents may access, highlighting what is happening in class and projects and assignments.

- Homework hot lines are used in many schools. Teachers use their school voice mail to record homework assignments or keep them posted for access over the Internet so students and parents can check or double-check the assignments.

- One teacher sets aside one hour every other week during the evening for communication with parents by e-mail. Parents know when the teacher is sitting at home at the computer, available and willing to answer their questions by e-mail.

- In scheduling conferences with parents, providing scheduling options (for example, evenings or Saturdays) is helpful and appreciated.

- Some schools employ home-school liaison personnel whose job is to facilitate home-school interaction and collaboration, a valuable resource.

- Parent centers in the building are a means of making parents feel welcome and valued in school. This is generally a room specifically designed for parents—to meet, browse resources, and work on projects for the school.

- Many schools allow the community access to their facility. For example, one school provides classes such as English as a Second Language in the building, sponsored by the community college district. Classes are free of charge, and child care is provided.

- A number of schools partnering with agencies in the community, and often with funding through grants, are able to provide after-school tutoring, before- and after-school programs, parent institutes and classes, and provision of health and social services.

Poetry, Popcorn, and Pretzel Night

West Elementary School (Long Beach City School District, New York) developed a popular program: a special family evening of language exploration called "Poetry, Popcorn, and Pretzel Night." This is a fun, hands-on event, during which third-, fourth-, and fifth-grade students and their parents or guardians experience the joy and wonder of poetry together through selected shared poems and writing their own creations. This special evening was developed as an outgrowth of the school's "Bedtime and Books" night, a popular event for children who come back to school in their pajamas to listen to bedtime stories read by the principal and teachers. The "Bedtime and Books" program is targeted for grades K–2; while the children are interacting with the literature, their parents or guardians are getting literacy support from the school's reading teachers.

When families preregister for the "Poetry, Popcorn, and Pretzel" program, they are given a choice of fourteen poetry-related workshops from which they are to select their four top choices. From those four, each participating family is registered to attend two workshops. At least one adult must accompany every child or pair of children to all workshops.

On the evening of the event, after brief opening activities, children and their parents or guardians attend their first forty-minute workshop. At all workshops, parents and their children enjoy the poems shared by the facilitator and create their own original poems together. Prior to the second workshop of the evening, snacks are provided: pretzels, popcorn, and punch. At the end of the evening, each student leaves with a copy of the poems shared in his or her respective workshop. An anthology of the poems is later compiled by the school and distributed to each family that participated that evening—a wonderful memento and resource.

Among the workshops have been these:

- Alliteration Alley. Amaze and astound any aardvarks asking about alliteration.
- Amazing Animals. Combine animals and create animal parts poetry (such as "monkippos").
- Can You Haiku? Create and illustrate haiku using watercolors.
- Mmm Mmm Good. Read and write poetry with mouth-watering words, fantastic food, and oodles of onomatopoeia.
- Ship Shape. Read silly-shaped poems and watch ideas take shape.
- Color Me Beautiful. Enjoy and create colorful poems, and express them with watercolors.
- Colorful Language. Listen to and write descriptive poetry that draws pictures in your mind.
- Giggle Poems. Hold your sides while you make and master the giggliest poems.
- Limerick Lyrics. Feel the rhythm, and have fun with limerick poetry.
- Poetry on the Web. Surf the Web for great poetry Web sites and share them with friends.
- Poetry to a Beat. Get your drumsticks and cymbals out, and bang to the beat!
- Sports Cinquain. Have a favorite sport? Use this special form and describe it with poetry!
- There's a Monster in My Closet. Monster crazy? Don't be scared to read and make your monster grow poetically!
- There's No Business Like Show Business. Enunciation, dramatization, but no procrastination when reciting these poems out loud!

The fourteen choices of engaging workshops are presented or facilitated by the West Elementary School teachers and principal. For more information about this program, contact the program's coordinator: Arlyne Skolnik, at (516) 897–2215, 91 Maryland Avenue, Long Beach, New York, 11561; ASkolnik@lbeach.org.

PARTNERING WITH PARENTS OF SPECIAL POPULATION STUDENTS

Some school districts make significant outreach efforts to the parents of students with disabilities, those who are English-language learners (ELL), and those who are gifted and talented. (See Chapter Three for information and recommendations for reaching and teaching these special populations.)

At the School or District Level

Special programs, guest speakers, and resources specifically targeting parents of special population students may be provided at the school or district level. Teachers may also share recommendations and information with parents of special populations at the classroom level. Any number of meetings, materials, and activities to enable parents to better support their child's learning and success may be provided.

With Parents of English Language Learners

Bilingual facilitators and school and district personnel, translation of materials in represented languages, and parent liaisons representative of the linguistic and cultural diversity of the community are all important. Provide parent workshops and training, using concrete suggestions, guidance, and materials. Having resources in English and in parents' native languages that can be distributed at no cost or checked out from a lending library are also powerful means of supporting parents in the effort to become more involved in the education of their children.

With Parents of Gifted Students

Many schools have evening parent meetings to answer parent questions and discuss gifted programming at the school site. Often the school psychologist is available to talk to parents about gifted issues and the social-emotional aspects of gifted students. A district resource teacher with the gifted and talented program may present information about raising a gifted child, resources available through the district office, and enrichment opportunities in the community parents may want to access for their child. An example of one school's agenda for a parent meeting included the principal's welcome and introduction; a look at the third-, fourth-, and fifth-grade programs presented by classroom teachers of those gifted programs; a brief presentation on the importance of technology; a brief presentation on student-centered instruction and preparation for middle school; and suggestions and discussion among parents and presenting school staff.

With Parents of Students with Disabilities

Schools and districts are required under the federal Individuals with Disabilities Educational Improvement Act (IDEA 2004) and Section 504 of the Rehabilitation Act of 1973 to provide information to parents of children with disabilities or parents who suspect they may have a disabled child. Parents must be informed of their educational rights with regard to identification and evaluation, services and programs, due process, and other issues.

Districts are sometimes able to provide additional resources to parents of children with disabilities. Some, for example, have trained parent facilitators who provide guidance and support to parents in helping them navigate the special education process. These facilitators are generally themselves parents of a student in a special education program who have good interpersonal skills and have received training by the school district. They can provide parents with support such as attending individualized educational program (IEP) meetings with them if requested and being available to talk parent-to-parent regarding any questions or concerns. It is recommended that districts have lending libraries of materials and resources available for parents of children with disabilities to access, and provide parent workshops with knowledgeable speakers to address issues and topics of interest.

At the Classroom Level

For any student experiencing academic or behavioral difficulty, a critical intervention is to increase the communication between home and school and establish teamwork on the child's behalf. Students who have learning disabilities, AD/HD, Asperger's syndrome, or other special needs require far more frequent monitoring, reporting, and communication than will be necessary for other students in the general education classroom. Parents need to be willing to share information with teachers, ask how they can help, and try to support the classroom teacher in any way possible. Teachers need to be open and receptive to implementing the interventions and supports to help meet students' individual needs. They need to be sensitive to the input of parents and willing to make accommodations and modifications as appropriate.

Some students who exhibit behavioral challenges in the classroom will need behavior contracts, charts, and incentive and management plans devised to help them improve their conduct and self-management skills. These behavioral programs such as daily and weekly report cards (found in Chapters Six and Ten) involve home-school collaboration. They require close parental involvement to help reinforce the mutual expectations at home and school of appropriate school behaviors. The daily or weekly monitoring of the student's performance on targeted goals and behaviors is a joint effort, as is the rewarding of student success.

Students who have difficulty with study skills and do not follow through on homework assignments will need closer parental monitoring. In order for parents to be able to help, they need to know what the student has been assigned as homework and have the child bring home the necessary books and materials. Some students (such as those with AD/HD or LD) have significant difficulty and need assistance in this area. They often need extra monitoring and motivation to ensure assignments are recorded, needed materials follow them to and from school, and that homework is turned in. Chapter Ten has many strategies on this topic, including the Weekly Progress Report and the Daily Monitoring Form. The Middle School Daily Report (Form 6.3) is another example of a helpful form for home-school monitoring of study habits and behavioral performance.

Parents of gifted and talented and other high-achieving students are often concerned that their children in inclusive, heterogeneous classrooms may not be as challenged and enriched in their learning experiences as they need to be. To address this need, recommend the home extension activities at the end of this chapter particularly for families of gifted and high-achieving elementary students (although the list of forty-five activities provides fun extension and family learning options for any students and their families).

With Parents of All Students

Teachers need to reach out to all parents and be willing to extend themselves. Putting forth this extra effort is important to demonstrate to parents the teachers' commitment to their children's school success and desire to enhance home-school collaboration.

- *Parent-teacher conferences.* There is no substitute for parent-teacher conferencing on students. Teachers need to meet face-to-face with parents or guardians and have the time to discuss and answer questions, show work samples, and listen to parents talk about their child and any concerns. Such conferencing in person is most effective in gaining a better understanding of our students and how to best reach and teach them. For students experiencing difficulty in school, it is critical to meet and plan interventions together. Scheduling these meetings, which may involve other support staff or administrators as well as the teacher and parents, may not be easy. Sometimes it requires significant flexibility on the part of school personnel to accommodate parents' needs and circumstances when scheduling meetings. However, in order to help students, it is important to try doing whatever we can, even when it is inconvenient.

- *Progress reports.* All parents need to be kept informed about their child's school performance. Quizzes, test grades, and graded work should be sent home throughout the grading period so parents have feedback as to how their child is doing. Many middle and secondary school teachers use point systems to determine grades, and it is easy for students and parents to know how they are doing at any time throughout the grading period. If a parent requests more frequent feedback, in many cases it is relatively easy for teachers to provide.

It is highly recommended to keep some parents (particularly those of children with learning challenges) informed of their child's performance well in advance of when report cards are issued. If any student is falling behind, parents should be notified in a timely fashion and before the child fails. Forms for communication and monitoring of daily and weekly performance are beneficial and necessary for individual students but certainly would not be used as a whole class system. Various students from time to time may need some extra monitoring and communication between home and school through forms, such as Form 9.2, the Parent Report form, at the end of this chapter.

- *Reading logs.* Use of a reading log is another excellent means of involving both the home and school in motivating students to read and in monitoring out-of-school and independent reading. The student records the title of the book, along with the date and pages read, on a log. Parents are asked to sign the log, indicating that their child did that outside reading.

• *Interactive homework assignments.* Provide some homework activities that are interactive between parents and children and engaging for everyone. Examples might include The 100 Percent Smart Activity in Chapter Two (Activity 2.1) or some of the Home Extension Activities at the end of this chapter (Form 9.3). Offering choices of activities or project options that students may do with parent involvement and will be educational and fun rather than stressful or overwhelming is very beneficial.

COMMUNICATION TIPS FOR TEACHERS

To create a collaborative relationship between home and school, educators need to build positive rapport with parents and clearly communicate that we need and appreciate their assistance and involvement. It is important for teachers to maintain close communication with parents and keep them well informed. In fact, a study by Ames (1993) showed that parents of children whose teachers were high users of school-to-home communications reported greater belief in their ability to influence their children, viewed their children as more motivated, reported higher involvement with their children's learning, and evaluated their children's teachers as being more effective.

To establish and build a positive relationship with parents, communicate:

• In a manner that is respectful and nonjudgmental.
• That you welcome their partnership.
• Your acknowledgment that they are the experts on their son or daughter.
• That you value their input and any information and insights about their child.
• That you truly care about their child, are interested in working collaboratively, and intend to do all you can to ensure a successful school year.

In addition, be proactive:

• Call or write notes home communicating positive messages to parents about their child (what you appreciate about the student).
• Make yourself easily accessible, and let parents know when and how they can best contact you.
• Clearly communicate your expectations, goals, procedures and routines, homework policy, and how parents can best help.
• Reach out to parents by letting them know they are welcome at school and in the classroom, and seek ways for them to contribute that meet their comfort level and interest.

It is much easier to discuss concerns with parents once you have opened the lines of communication in a positive manner. In order to establish rapport with parents, it is important to recognize and speak about their child's areas of strength and competence. Make every effort to learn about the child, identifying his or her individual strengths, interests, and positive characteristics.

Clearly communicate to parents early in the year (beginning in the first days of school) and on an ongoing basis using weekly or monthly newsletters or something else regarding classroom goals, policies, expectations, activities, and special events. Always invite and encourage parent participation.

When you have concerns about a student:

• Make the personal contact and explain to parents what you are concerned about. Again, always try to indicate something positive as well.
• Describe how the child is functioning academically and behaviorally.

- State your observations objectively without labeling the behavior or child (such as "lazy," "apathetic," or "bad").
- Communicate your interest in doing everything possible to help the student do well in school.
- Ask parents if they have noticed any of the difficulties you have described or if previous teachers ever communicated these concerns in the past.
- Let the parents know what specific strategies and interventions you are using or will begin to implement to address areas of concern.
- Solicit parents' input, asking if they have any additional suggestions or information that can help you meet the student's needs.
- Really take the time to listen to what parents have to say, and communicate your interest and respect for their opinions, feelings, and goals for their child.

Be aware that parents are key members of any team meetings involving their child: a student support team, 504, or IEP team meeting. Realize how intimidating it can be for a parent to attend any such meeting in which a number of school people are discussing their child. Hearing that your son or daughter is struggling in school is not easy for any parent, and it often raises defenses, anxiety, anger, and fears. It is important to be sensitive and empathic to what parents may be feeling and take the time to listen to what they have to say. We must clearly communicate that the school is committed to working together in any way possible to help their child succeed.

COMMUNICATION TIPS FOR PARENTS

Schools may wish to share strategies and tips with parents to strengthen the communication and collaborative process. The following advice and recommendations for parents may be shared in a newsletter or other form of communication:

- Early in the school year, meet with the teacher, share information about your child, and establish the best means of communication (phone, e-mail, home-school notes) for how and when you can best be reached.
- Let teachers know you are interested, available, and accessible and want to support school efforts.
- Support teachers in reinforcing appropriate behavior and work production goals for your child.
- Ensure that your child is coming to school ready to learn, with adequate sleep and prepared with books, materials, and homework.
- Communicate closely, openly, and frequently with classroom teachers. Find out as much as you can about how your child is functioning at school and ways you can support him or her at home.
- Teachers and all school staff appreciate being treated with courtesy and respect.
- Become involved in the school community, and get to know staff members.
- If your child is having any school difficulty or if you have any concerns, please do not hesitate to contact teachers. It is important to resolve problems as soon as possible, and speaking with the teacher is an important first step.
- It is best to leave a message for the teacher to call you for a phone conference or to schedule a time for you to meet. It is much better to schedule such meetings by time and location in advance. Teachers will want the chance to speak with you without interruption or distractions rather than on the run.
- Please join efforts with us in providing the best learning environment and educational program for our students.

HOME EXTENSION ACTIVITIES

There are many ways teachers can involve families in fun, motivating activities that enhance and extend student learning. At the end of this chapter is a list of forty-five Home Extension Activities (Form 9.3). This list may be copied and distributed to families as suggestions for activities to complete at home.

REFERENCES

Ames, C. (1993). How school-to-home communications influence parent beliefs and perceptions. *Equity and Choice, 9*(3), 44–49.

Berla, N. (1991). Parent involvement at the middle school level. *ERIC Review, 1*(3), 16–20.

Henderson, A. T. (1994). *The evidence continues to grow—Parent involvement improves student achievement: An annotated bibliography.* Columbia, MD: National Committee for Citizens in Education.

National Association of School Psychologists. (2005, Apr.). *Position statement on home-school collaboration.* Bethesda, MD: National Association of School Psychologists. Retrieved Jan. 12, 2006, from http://www.nasponline.org/information/pospaper_hsc.html.

Rief, S. (2003). *The ADHD book of lists.* San Francisco: Jossey-Bass.

Rief, S. (2005). *How to reach and teach children with ADD/ADHD* (2nd ed.). San Francisco: Jossey-Bass.

San Diego County Office of Education. (1994). Parent involvement: The key to student success and community support. *San Diego County Office of Education, Notes from Research—A Research and Education Newsletter for Teachers, 2*(2), 1–6.

Stenmark, J. K., Thompson, V., & Cossey, R. (1986). *Family math.* Berkeley: Lawrence Hall of Science, University of California, Berkeley.

Form 9.1

PARENT INTEREST FORM

(WAYS TO BECOME INVOLVED IN ROOM _____)

Name: _____ Phone Numbers: _____

Best days to help: Mon. Tues. Wed. Thurs. Fri. Weekends

Best times to help: 7:45–9:45   10:00–12:00   12:00–2:00   evenings   weekends

Best times to call_____
Profession/work experience_____

My favorite kinds of books and materials to read: _____

I would feel comfortable helping in the following ways in the classroom or at home

_____ Math   Basic _____   Enrichment _____
_____ Reading
_____ Writing
_____ Research (helping students find resources: books, Web sites, or periodicals)
_____ Computer (troubleshooting, PowerPoint, locating Web sites for children, bookmarking Web sites, student research assistance, looking for computer programs for children)
_____ Art/crafts (drawing, painting, sculpture, wood, fabric)
_____ Dance (tap, jazz, ballet, modern, street, folk, or other)
_____ Music (voice, choir, accompaniment, piano, guitar, woodwinds, other)
_____ Speech (individual, debate, Toastmasters)
_____ Foreign language (Spanish, French, Italian, other _____)
_____ Science (living things, weather and space, matter and energy, helping with science experiments, other)
_____ Performing arts (dance, drama, live performances)
_____ Making a presentation to the class about your job, a trip, music, art, a craft or hobby
_____ Chess
_____ Stock market
_____ Classroom library organization
_____ Grant Writing
_____ Organizing and planning for special events such as field trips, guest speakers, programs

I have the following special talents/interests that are not listed above that I would enjoy sharing with the children.

_____

PARENT REPORT

Name: _____   Date: _____

	Excellent	Good	Satisfactory	Needs Improvement
Behavior				
Classwork Effort				
Homework				

Test scores:

_____

Comments:

_____

Please sign and return: _____

Parent/Guardian Signature

HOME EXTENSION ACTIVITIES

Parents often ask how they can help enrich and extend the educational process for their children without more busywork. Communication is essential to parent-child interaction. When you want some suggestions for how to work with your child and enhance your family's time together, consider some of the activities here: they are fun, provide family participation, encourage communication, and offer a wonderful learning experience. Although you probably already do many of these things, you may find this list helpful.

1. **Watch a program** with your child on the Discovery Channel or other educational programming station. Discuss what has been learned orally, and on a piece of paper have your child list some of the facts that he or she learned. Illustrations can also be drawn.

2. Watch a **sit-com** together. Discuss the humor of the show and what was funny about the actors and the situations they got themselves into.

3. Have a **"No Television Day"** in your home. Help your child to plan special activities for the family that everyone will cooperate in. After the experience, discuss the positives and negatives of the day, and have your child write them up based on the discussion.

4. Watch three to five **television commercials** with your child. Discuss the ways advertisers try to get people to buy their products. Make a list of the ways you discover. Compare and contrast the commercials, and have your child critically evaluate the methods the advertisers use.

5. Work on the **computer** with your child on educational programs. Enhance Internet skills by searching for information on topics that the class is studying. Read the pages, and highlight important information that might be shared with the class. Make a list of pertinent facts in the articles, or write a brief report highlighting the information.

6. Follow a **news story** with your child over two or three days. Use the information acquired from a news channel and in the newspaper or weekly periodical. Summarize the story orally or in written form.

7. Have everyone in the family read and **discuss a newspaper article** that might be of interest to each member.

8. Read a **Newbery Award–winning** book aloud to your child. Discuss reasons that this book won this prestigious award. Read another book that is not a Newbery Award winner, and talk about why this book probably did not receive the award.

9. Read the **classics** with your child. If your child is young, give him or her a copy of the *Illustrated Children's Classic* series while you read the authentic book. Talk about the story and why it has been popular for such an extended period of time.

10. Help your child select two or more books on the same theme or by the same author. Discuss the **similarities and differences between the books.** Have your child graphically organize the comparison—using a Venn diagram, webbing, or clusters, for example, or share the information learned in an oral presentation to the class or at home on a video.

11. Look for a **book of science experiments** from the classroom, school, or public library. Have your child select an experiment, and plan a family science night where everyone in the family performs a science experiment together and learns a new scientific principle.

12. Take a trip with your child to a **museum.** Help your child to synthesize the information learned through a reflective essay, video presentation, storyboard, photo essay, or discussion.

13. Help your child select an **interesting career** that he or she might like to pursue in the future. Select a person in the field to interview. Create ten interview questions, and schedule a time when that person can sit down to discuss the career with your child. Keep the interview questions and the responses gathered from the meeting, and take photos if possible.

14. Help your child **plan and prepare a meal** for your family. Make sure healthy choices are covered. Take your child to the grocery store to help buy the food and keep an estimate of the cost on the calculator while shopping. Use coupons if possible, and keep the receipt. After the meal is over, help your child to discuss the events or write up a reflection. Include photos if possible.

15. Think of a place where you and your child might **volunteer** some time, such as at a retirement home, serving meals to the homeless, or planting trees in the community. Talk about the importance of giving back to the community. Have your child evaluate the experience through discussion or in written form. Include photos if possible.

16. Have a **family get-together.** Ask the different generations to share a piece of music that they think everyone would like to listen to. Have a family discussion about how music has changed over the years and what likes and dislikes each member has for music of another generation. Have your child write a reflection of what happened and how the members of the different generations felt about the musical value of each set of music.

17. Attend a **religious or cultural event** that is different from your own. Help your child to appreciate the similarities and differences in the experience. Have your child take photos or draw pictures to show examples of what he or she saw. Have a discussion afterward, or write up a compare-and-contrast essay and tell how it aligns with your family's beliefs and experiences.

18. Go to **a movie, play, or recreational event** with your child. Have your child talk with you about the event, how it could be improved, and then write a summary of the time you spent together. Then decide on another event that you would like to attend together.

19. Have your child **interview** the oldest member of your extended family. Together, think of some interesting questions before the interview. Then discuss the interview, and have your child write a paragraph with the most important things that were learned. You may also make a tape (video or audio) of the interview, copy the tape, and send a copy to another younger member of the family.

20. Have your child write a **letter to a family member** whom your family has not seen for a while OR send a two- or three-minute voice tape to that person relating all the changes that have occurred since your last visit. The letter should be several pages in length and should contain factual information updating the other person on events in your child's life.

21. Have your child **write a script for a play** for presentation. Make sure there are at least two or three actors for the parts. Using family members and friends, dramatize the play, and present it on video. This play should be several minutes long and show character and plot development.

22. Help your child plan **to write an extensive chapter story** that will develop over a longer period of time. Encourage the use of a sequence planning sheet showing story development of the characters, setting, problem, solution, and dialogue. Have your child create the story on the computer.

23. Have your child **plan a video** showcasing all members of your immediate family and as many extended family members as possible. Ask your child to plan what each member should say and do on the video, remembering that this is a family biography to be kept for future generations of family members. Each family member should be interviewed, have a specific time segment, and the format should be the same for each family member.

24. Have your child create a **PowerPoint presentation** about your family history or some other subject of interest. When your family is all together, share it and keep it in the family archives.

25. Help your child to start **a hobby** or extend a current hobby. Give assistance in researching the hobby through books or on the Internet. Stress the importance of organizing the information in a thoughtful way. Encourage the child to make a presentation to his or her class, peers, or family members.

26. Introduce your child to the **art of photography**. Give your child a digital or disposable camera to take pictures of subjects of interest. Help your child put together a scrapbook of photos with captions underneath.

27. Have an **open mike night** with your family. Each person may sing, dance, present a play or performance, read a poem, recite a favorite passage from a book, or just talk about something of interest. If you have a microphone, use it for magnification of soft voices. Confidence is honed by presenting in front of family first and then to peer groups in classroom settings.

28. Have your child pick a **subject to talk about** at the dinner table and discuss thoughts, feelings, and insights into the topic. After your child has finished, have the rest of the family join in with their comments.

29. Have your child choose a subject such as school uniforms, animal rights, or kids' allowances and have him or her try **to persuade you** that something should be changed.

30. Play **a video game** together. Ask your child to introduce it to you and teach you how to play.

31. Play **board games** together to strengthen mathematic skills.

32. Have a five hundred- or thousand-piece **puzzle** laid out on a table for an extended period of time. Work it together or separately until it is finished.

33. Play **Scrabble, Boggle,** and other word games with your child. Word games extend language and vocabulary experiences.

34. Have family members **choose new words** that they have learned during the week to introduce to everyone else.

35. When you're on a vacation, have your child **write postcards** to family members or friends.

36. When you're on a trip, have your child **write daily journal entries**.

37. Have your child figure out the **mileage between important places** you visit by using the mileage scale on a map.

38. When your family is traveling in the car, have your child help you **navigate** by looking at the map, estimating the number of miles you still have to go, reading the names of the cities you travel through, telling you what the elevation is at certain points, and other information about the trip. Becoming familiar with map reading is an essential life skill.

39. Talk about **different kinds of music:** classical, jazz, blues, hip hop, rock and roll, country, alternative, gospel, and others. As a family, listen to different kinds for a week at a time. Listen together to distinguish the instruments that are being played and the change in the music that creates a mood or feeling of danger, anticipation, surprise, concern, or calm.

40. During a movie, pay attention to the **soundtrack**. See how music signals what is coming next in the movie. What mood does the music give to a particular segment?

41. **Save money,** count it, and wrap coins together as a family.

42. Use the **statistics (stats) in the sports section** of the newspaper to create weekly problems to solve. Follow players or teams, and have your child keep charts of the successes and failures. As a family, help your child to create sport stat questions that he or she might present to the class on the overhead.

43. Select **Survival Math Activities** from Chapter Fourteen that you think are appropriate for your child. Try some of the five-star activities that take extra family support.

44. Plan **a special outing** with your child, and discuss ways that the whole family can help to finance the trip.

45. Help your child learn about **perimeter** and **area** by measuring his or her own bedroom or another room in the house. (See Activity 11.1, Using Shel Silverstein's "Messy Room.")

Chapter 10

WORKING TO IMPROVE ORGANIZATION, TIME MANAGEMENT, AND HOMEWORK SUCCESS

Many students lack adequate organizational, time management, and study skills. There is a lot that both teachers and parents can do to help students improve in organization and time management, which are important life skills for success. This includes providing children and teens with structure, support, and training in:

- Organizing their materials and work space
- Time awareness
- Recording their assignments consistently
- Using and referring regularly to a planner, agenda, calendar, or assignment sheet
- Planning and prioritizing activities
- Making a schedule and following it
- Planning for short-term assignments
- Breaking down and systematically tackling long-term assignments
- Knowing standards of acceptable work
- Managing their time and meeting due dates
- Knowing what to take home and leave home daily
- Knowing what to take home and bring back to school
- Knowing when and where to turn in assignments
- Knowing and being prepared with the necessary materials for class and homework
- Homework monitoring: Making sure the homework is done, brought back to school, and turned in

WHAT TEACHERS CAN DO TO HELP BUILD ORGANIZATIONAL SKILLS

To be an organized student, it is necessary to have and maintain appropriate supplies and materials, as well as a system for carrying what is needed between home and school (Rief, 1998, 2003, 2005). It is also essential for students in the upper elementary and middle school grades to manage the paper flow (filing papers in a location and manner so they are quickly found and accessed when needed) and develop the habit of recording assignments and checking and reviewing those listed assignments and other things to do.

Supplies and Materials

It is highly recommended that schools have a policy requiring all students to carry a book bag or backpack and specific notebook (or alternative means for keeping papers) that travels to and from school daily. Beginning in the third grade, or by the latest the fourth grade, students should be required to use a three-ring binder in most cases. The binder contains colored subject dividers and a pencil pouch that fits in the rings and includes a few sharpened pencils with erasers and other small supplies and essentials. This notebook would also be the location for keeping a three-hole-punched calendar, agenda or planner, or assignment sheet for recording assignments and would have designated pockets and areas for papers to take home and leave at home and papers to return to school. It is not too early, even from kindergarten, for children to begin the habit of carrying a folder to and from school daily in their backpacks (Archer & Gleason, 2003). There are exceptions for some children, who would do better with an accordion folder or other alternative system to the three-ring binder, which is discussed below.

The three-hole-punched assignment sheets, or calendars or planners for recording assignments, should be placed in a prominent location of the notebook for easy access and reference. If a student is using a daily or weekly sheet for recording assignments, there should also be a month-at-a-glance page within the notebook. Whatever the student chooses for recording assignments (assignment sheets, agendas/planners, calendars), it is important to model, monitor, and reinforce daily and consistent use of these tools.

In addition, students should have a specific location in the notebook for storing homework assignments and other papers categorically. There are a variety of ways for doing so:

- Use colored pocket folders (single pocket or double) that are three-hole-punched and inserted in the notebook. For example, a red folder can be labeled "homework" and contain all homework (either one for all subjects placed at the front or back of the notebook or one red folder behind the tab for each subject). A different colored folder may be labeled for graded and returned papers or anything to leave at home.

- Some students prefer to use colored folders labeled "to do" and "done/turn in."

- Another option is use of large laminated envelopes that are three-hole-punched and inserted into the notebook for homework, assorted project papers, and other materials.

- Newton (2003) suggests colored tabs behind each subject area (for example, "daily work and notes," "tests or quizzes") to further organize within each subject area. She also recommends a three-hole-punched expandable file folder with the opening toward the binder rings to hold anything that becomes loose and items that are not three-hole-punched, such as index or note cards.

It is helpful to provide handouts to students that are always three-hole-punched to increase the likelihood that they will insert those papers in their notebooks. In addition, have available adhesive hole reinforcers students may use for ripped-out papers and plastic sleeves for papers to be inserted in the binder that you do not want to punch.

Teach your expectations for materials that students should have with them in class at all times (for example, sharpened pencils with erasers, notebook paper). Allow for natural consequences of not having needed materials. Do not reinforce poor study habits and "reward" students who are unprepared by giving or loaning them new, desirable materials or supplies. Instead, if they need to borrow from you, provide less desirable materials as substitutes. Some teachers keep recycled paper and a can of golf pencils or old pencils and erasers for this purpose.

You may want to keep spare supplies available so that time is not wasted with students searching or asking around to borrow from classmates. However, consider "charging" students (for example, they must pay you from their class money or tokens) or fining them in some way (points) for not being prepared and needing to borrow supplies.

To teach students how to use and maintain the three-ring-binder system, model how papers should be organized (for example, by placing them behind the tabs of the appropriate subject section of the notebooks). After showing them how to do so, have them practice and allow time for this. Students should also carry a supply of some clean notebook paper behind a separate tab of the notebook or within each subject section.

Notebook checks using the Notebook Check form (Form 10.1 at the end of this chapter) are recommended at the end of each week for the first four weeks of school. Reward students who pass notebook inspection with certificates, prizes, or privileges. Since this is a time-consuming task for the teacher, we suggest that, if possible, a parent volunteer or aide looks over the notebooks regularly. At some schools, the principal or assistant principal will occasionally drop by for a notebook check. Notebook standards and teacher expectations should be established early in the year. As the year progresses, most students are weaned from the checks, while others must continue with their use.

Accordion Folder Alternative

For most students, the three-ring binder is the best system for storing and maintaining their papers and is the preferred method for teachers and parents to work on training children to use. However, some students have a difficult time managing the three-ring binder, and their papers are typically shoved in the notebook without being placed properly in the rings or the correct sections. The child's backpack, desk, and locker are often filled with loose papers because the notebook system isn't working for him or her. An alternative method is the use of an accordion folder. Each subject is labeled on the tabs of the accordion folder, and the student can simply place the paper in that section. If the notebook is a requirement, then the student can later file papers, notes, and other materials in the notebook at home, but use the accordion folder as the daily system for carrying papers and the assignment sheet and calendar.

We recommend sequencing the sections in an accordion folder according to the order of the daily schedule or subject periods, or the subjects can be arranged alphabetically. The assignment calendar, planner, or sheet could be placed up front in the first pocket of the folder and note pads in the back. An outstanding book that explains this system and others is *The Organized Student* (2005) by Donna Goldberg with Jennifer Zwiebel.

Tips to Share with Parents Regarding Supplies and Materials

In addition to providing their child with a backpack or book bag, notebook, and other needed supplies for school, recommend that the child's materials and possessions be labeled with his or her name. To help with maintenance and organization, it helps to establish a routine (such as every Friday or Sunday nights) to sort through, clean out, and reorganize the backpack and notebook. Recommend that the child load his or her backpack at night and place it in the same spot before going to bed. To avoid early-morning rush and stress, it helps to establish the routine of getting organized and ready for school as much as possible the night before (for example, clothes to wear, lunch prepared, everything loaded into the backpack). This is another suggestion that may be made to parents, especially if morning lateness to school is an issue for their child.

Teachers may wish to share as well the importance of providing the necessary supplies for homework and keeping them readily accessible. Explain to parents that searching the house for homework supplies and materials is a frustrating waste of precious minutes and causes a major break in productivity, pulling children unnecessarily off task. To avoid this occurring, we recommend creating a homework supply kit.

Homework Supply Kit

A homework supply kit can be stored in anything portable, such as a lightweight container with a lid. Some children work at their desks, others on the kitchen or dining room table, and others spread out on the floor. With this system, it does not matter where children choose to study. The necessary supplies can accompany them anywhere. Following are some of the recommended supplies (depending on the age of the child):

Plenty of paper

Sharpened pencils with erasers

Pencil sharpener

Ruler

Crayons

Paper hole reinforcers

Self-stick notepads

Highlighter pens

Colored pens and markers (thick and thin points)

Stapler with box of staples

Paper clips

Single-hole punch

Three-hole punch

Dictionary

Thesaurus

Glue stick

Colored pencils

Clipboard

Index cards

Calculator

Work Areas in the Classroom

Many strategies can be implemented to help structure the work area to make it better organized and more manageable. Organize the classroom with clearly labeled shelves, files, and bins so that you and the students know precisely where things belong and can easily locate them. Clearly identify certain places in the room (trays, color-coded folders or boxes) where students consistently turn in assignments and store unfinished work.

Help students minimize the amount of materials and clutter on and in their desks by providing containers and other storage areas, and schedule regular times for students to sort and clean out their desks. Students with problems in organization need direct assistance sorting and recycling unnecessary papers periodically. Any adult or a peer buddy can be used for this purpose.

Tips to Share with Parents: Organizing the Child's Homework Area

Parents may appreciate recommendations for organizing their child's homework location. Suggest that together with their child, they choose a place in the home for homework that has adequate lighting, is comfortable for working, and is as free from distractions as possible. They should carefully examine the child's work space and make sure that there is a large working surface (desktop) that is free from clutter. If the child has a computer, it might considerably cut down on working surface area. Parents may consider placing the computer on a separate desk or table other than the child's working and writing desk area. In addition to the supplies and materials listed in the homework supply kit, we recommend keeping a three-hole punch and electric pencil sharpener in the homework area.

Visual Cues and Strategic Use of Color

The use of color is a powerful tool for organizing and calling attention to important information. Color-coordinate by subject area to make locating subject materials quicker and easier. For example, the color for science might be yellow: the science text is covered in yellow paper or has a yellow adhesive dot on the binding, the science notebook/lab book or folder is yellow, and the schedule with the science class period and room number is highlighted in yellow. So is the tab or divider for science in the three-ring notebook.

Prepare important notices, handouts, and project assignments on brightly colored paper, and use visual and pictorial cues for showing expected materials, daily routines, and schedule. Encourage students to use sticky notes for reminders to themselves. Have them adhere the notes to book covers, in their lockers, planners, and so forth.

Tips to Share with Parents: Visual Cues and Strategic Use of Color

Dry-erase boards are helpful to hang in a central location of the home for all phone messages and notes to family members. Suggest that parents also hang one in their child's room or bathroom for important reminders and messages. Recommend that parents write notes and reminders on colored sticky notes, and place them on mirrors, doors, and other places the child is likely to see. They should encourage the child to write himself or herself notes and leave them on the pillow, by the backpack, and other highly visible places. Explain to parents your system and rationale for color-coding subject-related materials, and encourage them to assist with color-coding their child's schedule, notebook, and other materials accordingly. Parents may also wish to color-code entries on a calendar (for example, school related, sports, social activities).

More Organizational Tips

Students need organizational models. Teach and provide models of how to organize papers (for example, headings, margins, spacing). Also, provide exemplars and models of well-organized, projects and science boards.

For students who have significant disorganization issues, various accommodations may be needed. For example, for those who have trouble remembering to bring books to and from school, consider providing a second set of books to keep at home. Some students will need to have someone (the teacher or another student) check at the end of the day or period that they have the needed books and other materials for homework. Buddy systems can be used for this, or you can check with the few students who need this support or accommodation. (See Chapter Eight on the use of buddy assistance folders for supporting students who are absent from school.)

To increase motivation for organization, consider rewarding student efforts in this area. For example, provide bonus points to students who, on request, are able to quickly locate a certain book or paper in their desk or notebook. The best motivator, however, will be the sense of well-being and satisfaction that comes from being organized, knowing where things are, and feeling in control.

WHAT TEACHERS CAN DO TO HELP WITH TIME MANAGEMENT

Time management—making efficient use out of the minutes and hours of our days—is a challenge for many of us (Rief, 1998, 2003, 2005). For some students, time awareness and time management pose significant problems, and they need a great deal of external structure and support in order to learn and gain competence in this important life skill.

Time Awareness

Lack of time perception or awareness can easily result in students' underestimating how much time they have to complete a task or arrive somewhere on time. For students who tend to be oblivious to deadlines and due dates (for example, many with AD/HD), this is not an issue of apathy about their schoolwork but part of their neurobiological disorder.

Any opportunity to practice time estimation is helpful in increasing such awareness. For example, challenge children to estimate how long it takes to walk to the office and back (without running), get dressed in the morning, or any other task. Make a game out of predicting, timing, and checking their time estimates for various activities.

Encourage self-monitoring during homework and independent seat work time in class by recording the start time on the paper. When the work period is over, have the child or teen record the time, noting as well how much work they got done. Self-monitoring and recording help some students better gauge their on-task behavior and work production and can be a motivator to improve their own performance.

Timers in the Classroom

Clocks, calendars, planners, and agendas are necessities for time awareness and management. In addition, electronic tools and gadgets are helpful in this regard. Timers are beneficial for both the home and classroom. There are various kinds ranging from inexpensive kitchen timers and sand (hourglass) timers to more sophisticated types. Digitized countdown timers that include seconds as well as minutes as very useful.

The company Time Timer (www.timetimer.com) manufactures and sells a unique type of timer: one that is excellent for helping children easily observe and recognize visually the passage of time (how much time has elapsed and is remaining before the time period ends). The timers are in the form of an analog clock showing in red the amount of time set for that period, and the red area shrinks as time elapses. For some children (including young ones) who have difficulty gauging time, being able to see the red area disappearing as time passes is very helpful.

Stokes Publishing Company (www.stokespublishing.com) produces some wonderful timers. Its TeachTimer can be used on an overhead projector or placed on a desk or table. The TeachTimer has many functions that teachers find useful. When it is set for a certain amount of time and projected on the overhead in the countdown mode (minutes and seconds), students can see in large numbers precisely how much time they have remaining before the alarm goes off. Warnings (for example, two-minute or five-minute warnings) can also be programmed into the timer.

Another recommended timer is the Time Tracker by Learning Resources (www.learningresources. com). This device looks like a traffic light and is illuminated from green to yellow, and finally red as the time period elapses. In addition to the visual colored cues, there is an option of programming auditory cues with various sounds.

Timers are valuable tools that can increase time awareness, alerting students to the time they have available for activities, transitions, and completing tasks. For most students, they are very helpful. However, some children may experience anxiety when they are timed. For those who find timers stressful, its use should be limited and another technique used instead.

Assignment Sheets, Calendars, and Student Planners and Agendas

Students need to be taught how to use a planner or assignment calendar and encouraged to write all assignments down. Parents and teachers need to communicate and maintain the clear expectation that all assignments are to be recorded and monitor that this is occurring. It is highly recommended that teachers model the writing of assignments on the calendar or planner using a projection (for example, overhead transparency) of the calendar. Take a few moments at the beginning or end of the subject period or school day to lead students in recording assignments on their calendar or planner. Also, post daily assignments in a prominent, consistent location, and maintain a visible, up-to-date monthly calendar of class and school activities.

Some experts recommend that students using an assignment calendar write the assignments on the day they are due, not the day they are assigned. So, for example, if on Monday students are assigned a math assignment that is due the next day, that math assignment would be recorded in the square for Tuesday on the calendar. Anita Archer, one of the authors of the popular *Skills for School Success* (Archer & Gleason, 2003) recommends this system. She also points out that due dates are when the assignments are to be turned in, not when students are supposed to "do" them.

Others recommend recording assignments on the day they are assigned, not the day they are due. Goldberg and Zweibel (2005) suggest that daily homework assignments be written down on the day they are given and that tests, quizzes, and major deadlines also be recorded on the day they are announced. At home that evening, the child should then transfer the information to the due date or test date and flag the top of those pages with a sticky note as a reminder.

Some students need extra help. Provide assistance to students who have difficulty recording assignments fully or accurately. Routinely ask table partners or groups seated together to check each other that everything is correctly recorded on their calendars. Directly check assignment calendars and planners for students who need this teacher monitoring, and provide support transferring due dates of any projects, tests, class trips, or important activities or events onto their monthly calendar.

The importance of recording assignments daily and consistently cannot be overstated. Many of us cannot consider managing our daily lives and myriad responsibilities without our planners or calendars. The sooner we build the habit and routine, the better. When the child or teen gets used to writing down assignments and important information in one place and referring to that record daily, this practice will help build skills that are valuable throughout life. The assignment sheet, planner, or calendar also serves as a powerful means of home-school communication and enables mutual monitoring and reinforcement of homework and school assignments. Shown here are examples of daily and weekly assignment sheets.

Todayís Date _____

Period	Assignment	Due Date
1		
2		
3		
4		
5		
6		
7		

Parent/Guardian Signature _____

Student Name _____   Week of _____

Assignment	Monday	Tuesday	Wednesday	Thursday	Friday	Weekend
Home Reading Parent initials in box each night	Read 30 minutes ☐	Read 30 minutes ☐	Read 30 minutes ☐	Read 30 minutes ☐	Read 30 minutes ☐	Read 30 minutes ☐
Home writing						
Word study						
Math						
Science Health Social studies						
Other						

Parent/Guardian Signature _____
Please sign and have student return to school every Monday of the following week

Comments/concerns _____

Schedules

Chapter Six discusses the importance of schedules and daily routines and procedures in the classroom. Schedules need to be highly visible and referred to frequently. We recommend that teachers walk through the schedule each day and point out any changes in the daily or weekly routine that will be taking place.

Encourage students and parents to carefully plan a weekly schedule, including an established homework and study schedule. Ask parents to help their son or daughter become aware of how much time he or she spends in a typical day on all activities from school dismissal until bedtime.

For students receiving special education and related services, write down their weekly schedule, and tape it to their desks. Keep accessible each of your students' special schedules so that you know at all times the days and times they are pulled out of class or when special service providers are coming to the classroom to work with the student. The Substitute Plan form (Form 10.2 at the end of the chapter), for example, includes information regarding students with disabilities in the classroom, their schedule of push-in and pull-out support from special educators, and other important information.

Tips for Teachers to Share with Parents Regarding Schedules

An important step that parents can take to help their child gain awareness and improve time management is to create a weekly schedule jointly. The parent would work together with the child in the scheduling process by first examining and tracking how time is spent during the entire twenty-four-hour day.

This includes morning routine before school, hours spent between school dismissal and bedtime, and time spent sleeping. After a few days of examining his or her daily schedule, the child should have a better sense of how much time he or she typically spends on routine activities: meals, sleeping, grooming, walking to class, watching television, talking on the phone, working on the computer, recreational and social activities, and study and homework time.

Next, parents schedule with their child a time for homework that best suits his or her individual learning style preference and other factors, such as best time of day, need for breaks, extracurricular commitments, and family activities. Some children like to come home and immediately get part or all of their homework done and out of the way. Others need a break before tackling any homework. Once the homework schedule is set, it is important to do whatever is possible to adhere to it as consistently as possible. Encourage parents to help their child when possible to plan a "things-to-do" list and estimate together how long each assignment or activity should take. The parent can assist their child in planning what assignments to do first, second, third, and so forth.

Many families find it beneficial to post a large calendar or wall chart in a central location of the home for scheduling family activities and events. Each family member may have his or her own color pen for recording on the calendar, and everyone is encouraged to refer to the calendar daily.

Ask parents to check to see their son's or daughter's assignment sheets or calendars or planners every day and to assist them, as needed, in transferring important activities and scheduling to the child's personal calendar or planner along with the school-related things they need to do. You may suggest that parents consider "no phone call" times in the evening, because calls often interfere with staying on schedule. In addition, you may wish to recommend the use of electronic devices with timers (such as vibrating watches or alarms) to help remember appointments and curfews and keep on schedule.

Morning and evening routines and rituals for getting ready for school and preparing to go to bed at night are helpful to many families. Clear reminders of the routine through the use of a checklist of sequential tasks to complete reduce the nagging, rushing around, and negative interactions at this time of the day. Checklists are great tools for time management and staying on schedule. It may be recommended as a tip to parents who wish to employ this technique to decide with their child on the steps of the routine and make a list in that order—for example:

1. Lay out clothes for tomorrow.
2. Shower.
3. Check master calendar and planner.
4. Load backpack and place by door.

Each task that is completed on the list or chart is crossed off (or if it is a permanent chart, a clothespin can be clipped on and moved down the steps of the routine as the task is completed).

Long-Term Assignments and Projects

Teachers and parents need to structure long-term assignments (for example, book reports, research projects) by breaking them into smaller, manageable increments. Assign incremental due dates to help structure the time line toward project completion. For example, assign separate due dates for stages of the project: getting a topic approved, outline submitted, research notes and resources listed, turning in first draft, and so forth.

It is important to call close attention to due dates and monitor student progress on long-term assignments. Post those due dates (and encourage parents to do so as well). Refer to the due dates and calendar notations frequently, and remind students and parents of them by using notes home, newsletters, e-mails, and other means of communication. Monitor progress by checking in with students—asking to see what they have accomplished so far—and provide a lot of feedback along the way.

Suggest to parents of students with time management difficulties that they closely monitor time lines and help with pacing (for example, by getting started promptly on going to the library and gathering resources), and provide them with multiple reminders and copies of project guidelines and due dates. When sending information home about long-term projects and deadlines, require students to bring back a tear-off section from the form with a parent's signature indicating that the family is aware of the assignment requirements and schedule. Teachers may still want to communicate further and speak directly with some parents to ensure that they are fully aware. In addition, make sure students have access to materials they need for the project. Some students have limited access and resources and will need more in-school help and support than others.

More Time Management Tips

Following are recommended strategies to ensure that students are well informed and aware of assignments and expectations, understand the importance of punctuality, and manage their time:

- Make sure that all assignments, page numbers, due dates, and other information are presented to students verbally and visually.
- Post all assignments in a consistent place in the room (for example, at the corner of the board or on a separate assignment board).
- Consider assigning homework at the beginning of a period rather than the end so students have plenty of time to record the information.
- Attach a "things-to-do" list on some students' desks; model and monitor the practice of crossing off completed items.
- Provide enough time during transitions to put material away and get organized for the next activity.
- Set timers for transitions. First state: "You have five minutes to finish what you are working on and to put away your materials." Then set the timer.
- Include "seated by beginning bell time" or some behavior indicating student's punctuality on the home-school monitoring system, such as an adaptation of the Daily Monitoring form (Form 10.3 at the end of this chapter), or on one of the charts or daily report cards from Chapters Six and Nine that you may be using with some individual students.
- If tardiness is an issue, try an individual contract to motivate the student to improve that behavior.

WHAT TEACHERS CAN DO TO SUPPORT THE HOMEWORK PROCESS

According to Tanis Bryan, Arizona State University researcher, "homework accounts for one-fifth of the time that successful students are engaged in academic tasks" (ERIC/OSEP Special Project, 2001). There are a number of ways that teachers can help support students and their families in the homework process and optimize the benefits of this substantial amount of learning time.

Homework is an important part of reinforcing and extending what students are learning in school. But in order for there to be any benefit to homework, teachers need to make the assignments relevant and purposeful. Be sure to assign homework to review, practice, reinforce, and extend skills and concepts taught in class. Do not give assignments presenting new information that parents are expected to teach their children. It is important to always collect homework and provide feedback when possible. It is frustrating to students and parents to spend a lot of time on assignments that the teacher does not bother to look at. Communicate with other teachers on your team as well. Students who have several teachers are often assigned a number of tests, large projects, and reading assignments all at the same time from their different classes. Be sensitive to this. Stagger due dates, and coordinate whenever possible with other teachers to avoid the heavy stress of everything being due at once.

There are many ways to try making homework assignments more motivating, such as by incorporating an element of play or fun in the task (for example, with a learning game to reinforce or practice a skill). Provide some homework assignments that are creative, and build in student choice. There are several activities throughout this book that exemplify motivating homework assignments. Consider as well providing incentives for completing and turning in homework, such as earning extra points or perhaps the privilege of being included in a class raffle at the end of the week.

One wonderful incentive that is being used successfully in classrooms is called Homeworkopoly (www.teachnet.com/homeworkopoly or www.homeworkopoly.com). This Web site has components teachers can download and use to assemble, laminate, and hang up in the classroom. It looks like a large game board that is similar in appearance to the Monopoly game board. Students who turn in their completed homework get to roll a die and move their individual marker that number of spaces along the game board. The markers can be dots made of Velcro with each student's name on their own dot. There are various opportunities along the way of moving around the board to land on special game squares, earning them small prizes or privileges when doing so. This is an ongoing game, with students continuing to move around the game board throughout the year. Teachers report that students are highly motivated for the chance to roll the die and move their marker.

Ensure that students are prepared to do their homework and know what to do. Be certain that you have explained the homework and clarified any questions. You may also assign study buddies so students have a partner with their phone number or e-mail address whom they may contact for clarification regarding homework assignments. In addition, you may need to supervise some students before they walk out the door at the end of the day, checking that they have materials, books, and assignments recorded and in their backpacks.

One of the most important ways you can help students and their parents keep on top of homework, tests, and long-term projects is to require the use of an assignment calendar or agenda. Then guide, walk through, and monitor the recording of assignments. If this is a daily expectation and routine, it will help everyone. With some students, require that parents initial the assignment calendar daily. This is a good way for you to communicate with parents as well. You may write a few comments or notes to the parent on the assignment sheet or calendar and vice versa.

Be aware that in many homes, homework is a great source of stress and conflict, particularly for students with AD/HD or learning disabilities. It often takes these children hours to complete what the average student in the class may easily finish in a matter of minutes. Parents should be encouraged to communicate this information to you if this is the case with their child, and you will need to work together collaboratively to solve homework problems.

For students with disabilities or others who may require accommodations and modifications, be willing to do so. Ask yourself: "What is the goal?" "What do I want the students to learn from the assignment?" "Can they get the concepts without having to do all the writing?" "Can they practice the skills in an easier, more motivating format?" "Can they practice the skills doing fewer?" (See Chapter Five for other suggestions with regard to accommodations and modifications in assignments.) Also, a goal can be set for improvement in homework performance (amount done or criteria for success) as part of an individual plan. The student can earn a reward for meeting the established goal, which may differ from that of the rest of the class.

It is important to communicate regularly with the parents of students who are falling behind in homework. Work out a system of letting the students and parents know that they are not getting the homework turned in—for example, through use of a form that includes a section for listing missing assignments, such as in Form 10.3, the Daily Monitoring Form, or Form 10.4, the Weekly Progress Report, at the end of this chapter. Teachers may want to call or e-mail home whenever a student is missing two or three assignments. That is far preferable than allowing a student to be missing several assignments and hopelessly behind in their work without parents being notified.

As with some of the tips suggested earlier that teachers may share with parents to help their children build skills in organization and time management, Form 10.5 at the end of this chapter, Homework Tips for Parents, can be provided to parents as well.

REFERENCES

Archer, A., & Gleason, M. (2003). *Skills for school success.* North Billerica, MA: Curriculum Associates.

ERIC/OSEP Special Project. (2001, Spring). *Homework practices that support students with disabilities.* Reston, VA: ERIC Clearinghouse on Disabilities and Gifted Education.

Goldberg, D., with Zwiebel, J. (2005). *The organized student.* New York: Fireside.

Newton, D. (2003). Teaching study skills and learning strategies to therapists, teachers, and tutors. *International Dyslexia Association: Perspectives, 29*(4), 27–29.

Rief, S. (1998). *The ADD/ADHD checklist.* San Francisco: Jossey-Bass.

Rief, S. (2003). *The ADHD book of lists.* San Francisco: Jossey-Bass.

Rief, S. (2005). *How to reach and teach children with ADD/ADHD* (2nd ed.). San Francisco: Jossey-Bass.

NOTEBOOK CHECK

Student's Name: _____   Date: _____

Evaluator's Name: _____

_____ Your notebook organization is outstanding. Thank you for being responsible in keeping your notebook orderly.

_____ Your notebook is in satisfactory order.

_____ Your notebook is not in satisfactory order. Please organize it tonight. You may have it rechecked again tomorrow.

Form 10.2

SUBSTITUTE PLAN

Substitute plan for _____

Grade _____ Date _____

Students with special needs _____

Schedule for special education students _____

_____

Auxiliary teachers _____

Classroom aide _____

Special events this week _____

Parent helpers _____

Behavior plan: We are currently using table team points. Students will receive points for getting a book out quickly, having their homework finished, working quietly, being on task, doing the right thing, and similar kinds of responsible acts. Give 1 point for each positive behavior. Team points are kept on the whiteboard at the front of the room. Use generously.

Flag salute, patriotic song: Team _____ is responsible for this.

For other assistance, see the classroom helper's chart at the front of the room.

Attendance is taken by the teacher.

SUBSTITUTE PLAN *(continued)*

Math _____ (time)   **Today's math concept** _____

Lesson introduction _____

Guided practice _____   Independent practice _____

Lesson summary _____

_____

Writing Workshop: _____ (time)

- Read-aloud/shared reading:

  Book or instructional piece _____

  Focus/purpose _____

- Assignment _____

  _____

- Independent writing _____

  _____

  Students to confer with today _____

  _____

Recess _____ (time)

Reader's Workshop _____ (time)

1. Shared reading/read-aloud selection _____

   a. Independent reading (30 minutes) _____

   Conferring with _____

2. Share-out _____

   _____

SUBSTITUTE PLAN *(continued)*

Guided reading/book clubs/literacy stations _____ (time)

_____

_____

_____

_____

Word study _____ (time)

_____

_____

_____

_____

Lunch _____ (time)

Daily language review/word study _____ (time)

_____

_____

_____

_____

SUBSTITUTE PLAN *(continued)*

Science/social studies/health _____ **(time)**

_____

_____

_____

_____

_____

Art/PE/music _____ **(time)**

_____

_____

_____

_____

_____

Additional classes or special events

_____

_____

_____

_____

_____

_____

DAILY MONITORING

Student Name _____ Date _____

Period	Turned In Homework		On Time to Class		Used Class Time Effectively		Behavior/Citizenship					Teacher's Initials/Comments
	Yes	No	Yes	No	Yes	No	5	4	3	2	1	
1	☐	☐	☐	☐	☐	☐	☐	☐	☐	☐	☐	
2	☐	☐	☐	☐	☐	☐	☐	☐	☐	☐	☐	
3	☐	☐	☐	☐	☐	☐	☐	☐	☐	☐	☐	
4	☐	☐	☐	☐	☐	☐	☐	☐	☐	☐	☐	
5	☐	☐	☐	☐	☐	☐	☐	☐	☐	☐	☐	
6	☐	☐	☐	☐	☐	☐	☐	☐	☐	☐	☐	
7	☐	☐	☐	☐	☐	☐	☐	☐	☐	☐	☐	

Behavior/Citizenship Key: 5—Great!   4—Good   3—OK/Needed some help   2—Needed lots of redirection   1—Poor/received referral

Missing Assignments/Overdue Work

Period 1		Period 5	
Period 2		Period 6	
Period 3		Period 7	
Period 4			Parent/Guardian Signature Date

Form 10.4

WEEKLY PROGRESS REPORT

Student's name _____ Room number _____ Week starting _____

Work Habits

___ Worked hard to complete assignments—Great job!

___ Participated and used time effectively most of the week

___ Work completion so-so this week

___ Poor work completion (class and/or homework)

___ Parent/teacher conference needed

Citizenship

___ Excellent behavior—tried hard most of the week

___ Acceptable behavior most of the week

___ Behavior so-so this week (some difficulties)

___ Behavioral problems—difficult week

___ Parent/teacher conference needed

Missing assignments that must be done listed on back

Teacher Comments	**Parent Comments**

Teacher's Signature _____ Date _____

Parent's Signature _____ Date _____

HOMEWORK TIPS FOR PARENTS

- Establish a routine and schedule for homework (a specific time and place), and adhere to the schedule as closely as possible. Don't allow your child to wait until the evening to get started.

- Choose a homework location that is quiet, with low traffic and few distractions, but accessible and easy for you to be able to monitor homework production, if your child needs this.

- Limit distractions in the home during homework hours (reducing unnecessary noise, activity, and phone calls, and turning off the TV).

- Provide healthy snacks and build in study breaks during the homework process.

- Assist your child in getting started on assignments (for example, reading the directions together, doing the first items together, observing as your child does the next problem or item on his or her own). Then get up and leave. Monitor and give feedback without doing all the work together. You want your child to attempt as much as possible independently.

- Use a timer if your child has difficulty staying on task. Often a "beat-the-clock" system is effective in motivating children to complete a task before the timer goes off. Ask to see the completed task, and reward if it was done with relative accuracy and neatness. Older students can be encouraged to self-reward for work completion each time they beat the clock.

- Praise and compliment your child when he or she puts forth good effort and completes tasks. In a supportive, noncritical manner, it is appropriate and helpful to assist in pointing out and making some corrections of errors on the homework. It is not your responsibility to correct all of your child's errors on homework or make him or her complete and turn in a perfect paper.

- Help your child study for tests. Study together. Quiz your child in a variety of formats.

- Make sure your child has the phone number of a study buddy—at least one responsible classmate to call for clarification of homework assignments.

- Explore various homework Web sites, such as http://www.yourhomework.com and http://www.homeworkplanet.com.

- The biggest struggle is keeping on top of those dreaded long-range homework assignments (reports, projects). This is something you will need to be vigilant about. Ask for a copy of the project requirements. Post it at home and go over it together with your child. Write the due date on a master calendar. Then plan how to break down the project into manageable parts, scheduling steps along the way. Get started at once with going to the library, gathering resources, beginning the reading, and so forth.

Part 3

Designing Curriculum to Hook in Students

Chapter 11

HOOKING IN RELUCTANT READERS AND WRITERS

The direction of language arts instruction has been changing. We have moved from a more traditional style of instruction to more of a whole language approach. Educators seem to have come to some consensus about the right way to teach literacy to children. The update is based on instructional strategies that are grounded in the researchers' best understandings about how language and literacy are acquired and developed and on how children learn best. It "combines the language and literature-rich activities associated with whole language with explicit teaching of the skills needed to decode words" (Honig, 1995). Balance has always seemed to make sense for many teachers, but as the pendulum swings back and forth, we have all taken on new learning and modified instruction to meet the trends. The longer we have been in the classroom, the more knowledge we have about what seems to work best for children. What we find most effective is balancing our instructional literacy program with the old, the new, the innovative and creative, current research-based practices, and good teacher judgment.

WHAT IS BALANCED LITERACY?

Balanced literacy is a philosophical idea that encompasses balance in instruction of all of the domains—reading, writing, listening, and speaking—along with balancing grouping of students and balance in the types of reading and writing opportunities we provide for students in the upper elementary and middle schools. Students in a balanced reading program are moved step by step from explicit modeling and instruction to guided practice and then to activities that position them into becoming independent learners. This model is referred to as "gradual release of responsibility" (Pearson & Gallagher, 1983). Students are supported through the process of reading aloud to shared reading to guided reading and finally to independence. The use of scaffolding or strategies that support students' own building of understanding (Walqui-van Lier, 1993) is used throughout the literacy block. Repeated modeling, embedding words in context, and activating prior knowledge are three scaffolding techniques that are prevalent in most classrooms. Providing these supports, plus adding teacher feedback, builds greater success for all students in all the domains. Even students with significant reading and writing difficulties are often able to meet reading and writing standards when they receive a high degree of explicit teacher modeling and guided assistance.

Some reading components of balanced literacy include (Harwell, 2001):

- Shared book experiences
- Reading aloud to children
- Oral language development and listening experiences
- Systematic vocabulary development
- Guided reading and book club experiences with special attention to comprehension
- Individualized reading lessons with attention to comprehension
- Individualized reading lessons with attention to the construction of meaning
- Sustained silent reading

An Overview of the Reading/Writing Workshop Components

Students in a balanced reading program are exposed to each of the following strategies to build meaning:

- Read aloud: These are opportunities for the class to enjoy reading for pleasure as the teacher demonstrates fluent reading from a variety of genres, authors, and quality pieces of literature, including fiction, nonfiction, and poetry.
- Shared reading: All students are given the opportunity to read or reread a text regardless of their reading level. They become engaged through charts, big books, transparencies, and multiple copies.
- Guided reading: Students have the opportunity to work in small groups reading and discussing their copies of the same text at their common instructional reading level. The teacher provides guidance and coaching, but the students do the majority of work. The text and the instruction are focused and specific to the needs of the children.
- Independent reading: Students read silently at their independent level, building reading stamina over time. They practice the strategies that they have learned from the minilessons taught by the teacher. They select their own books at their just-right level from a variety of levels and genres, assisted by the teacher only as needed.

A balanced writing program provides the same gradual release structures, building from full teacher responsibility and gradually releasing children to independence:

- Modeled writing: The teacher or other students model a particular structure or genre such as memoir, biography, or persuasive. The students observe the process.
- Shared writing/interactive: All students are given the opportunity to develop a piece of writing collaboratively with the teacher.
- Guided writing: The teacher guides students, typically in small groups, through the writing of part of their own piece, providing feedback and ideas for improving students' writing.
- Independent writing: The students write at their own independent level, building writing stamina and fluency over time. They practice the strategies that they have learned during the minilessons.

Having all of these components in place will help more students become proficient and advanced readers. The intent in this chapter is not to delve into each of these components but instead to look at a few ways that reluctant readers and writers can be motivated in literacy. Innovative ways of teaching can be implemented in the classroom that can nudge special needs students to address the standards.

Changes in Students' Reading and Writing Habits

In the primary grades, students have insatiable appetites for books and are motivated to read them because of the bright colors, large text, and phenomenally illustrative pictures. But what is there to captivate upper-grade students? The subject matter must be interesting and make connections to the students' lives so that they will continue to read as the books increase in difficulty, with more and more pages and chapters, many of which have very few supports to help challenged readers.

With an increased focus over the past ten years on the classroom library and on making literacy the center of instruction, an enormous change has occurred in how children enjoy reading and writing. Within classrooms, students are captivated by read-alouds, the beauty of words, and the pictures and reading in general, whereas in the past when a basal reader was used, students were not engaged in reading. The books are exciting, colorful, and interesting even in the upper elementary grades and middle schools. Children love to hear their teachers read to them, and there is research that backs up the fact. When teachers read stories to children and discuss the stories through literature activities, children read more (Morrow & Weinstein, 1982, 1986). Through these engaging books, many teachers and students have become more interested in the writer's craft and are looking more deeply at good writers or mentor authors and how they motivate us to read. More and more biographies of children's authors are being published, more book stores are spotlighting authors in book signing presentations, more DVDs and videotapes are being produced about authors' lives, and more books on tape allow students to hear the masterful writing style of numerous authors. Students are becoming more awe-struck by authors and their writing skills and are beginning to transfer some of those techniques into their own writing.

Today's world is fast paced. Television, movies, and videos are a much more attractive lure to students who are having difficulty reading. We need to show reluctant readers the importance of reading through meaningful and relevant approaches.

MOTIVATING STRUGGLING READERS AND WRITERS

The transition from picture books to chapter books can be difficult. When something is a challenge or overwhelmingly difficult, a certain percentage of students will give up. In every classroom, no matter how hard the teacher tries, some students are going to be reluctant readers and writers. These students have difficulty keeping focused for even short periods of time on the reading or writing task at hand. They are sometimes apathetic and often disengaged during the reading and writing period. Teachers in the upper grades must search for stories and other experiences that enthrall lower-achieving students, giving them a chance to be successful by building their self-esteem without defeating their self-images, and search for contemporary approaches that will hook them in to reading and writing. So what will motivate these reluctant learners?

Poetry

Poetry seems to bring out the best in children of all ages and can become a motivating avenue to teach many aspects of language. Poetry seems to breathe life and enthusiasm into the reluctant reader-writer. It gets them involved and makes them feel successful in some part of literacy. Children with limited English proficiency also seem to pick up and enjoy poetry because of its simplicity and brevity. Students who are high achievers seem to thrive on the humor, the memory of the verse, and the elements that make it so magical.

Every child seems to relate to Shel Silverstein's and Jack Prelutsky's lively, fun, child-centered poetry. Whether the poem is about not wanting to go to school, having too much homework, a father who snores too loud, or a four-leaf clover that brings bad luck, children tend to become active participants in the reading, listening, speaking, and writing of these poems. They smile, laugh, readily read, listen, and respond to this poetry because it relates to their interests, it is short and unintimidating, and it is enjoyable. For reluctant readers, there is not the threatening factor of too many words crammed on a page. The lines are fast moving and rhyming and have subjects that kids think about and are involved in regularly in their daily lives. Students who seem unable to stay focused because of factors in their lives outside school, or because of attention difficulties, or because they have low motivation in their learning style, tend to be quickly swept away in poetry because they can instantly be successful in the genre. (See Chapter Twelve.)

After reading many poems independently and through teacher read-alouds, modeling, and guided writing practice, students can create their own poems. Beginning with the understanding of what a stanza is and how the rhyming word comes at the end of the line, students have fun writing their own poems using Shel Silverstein and Jack Prelutsky as their mentor poets. Jack Prelutsky in a Meet the Author Series video (1992) tells children that most of his poems were based on stories from his own life. With challenged writers, teachers can write a few poems interactively on charts. The class may select a subject, and students can contribute their own lines with rhyming words. Although poetry is probably easier for challenged writers to create in free verse without rhyme, take small steps teaching couplets and simple quatrains. Rhyming limits expressive thought, but children love to attempt writing their own rhyming poems. An excellent book to tempt children with ideas for writing a variety of poems is *Fly with Poetry* (Harley, 2000), which addresses a variety of poem structures.

Getting Students Interested in Poetry

Beginning the day with a lesson on poetry is a cheerful way to start the morning. How can students not feel welcomed in a classroom where the day begins with something light, enjoyable, and stimulating?

For classroom use, overhead transparencies are made for many of the poems. The overhead printing is enlarged from its actual size. When dealing with a class size of thirty or more children, teachers need to be cautious when using the overhead projector so that students can read the text easily without straining their eyes. Care should be given to making the words large enough for all students to read. In the upper grades of elementary school and in middle school, students may move closer to the screen by placing their chairs nearer the front of the room or by sitting on a rug area directly in front of the screen. Older students in elementary school do not generally mind sitting on the rug if it is made available and used early in the year. Middle school children may be more uncomfortable sitting on the floor.

The use of overheads in these poetry lessons seems more beneficial than handing out individual copies of the poem because it gets students focusing collectively. Students are more likely to listen because they know that the poem will not be up on the overhead for very long but that it can still be reviewed if necessary. Also, a transparency is more economical than class sets of poetry papers.

Integrating Curriculum Through Poetry

Poetry offers many opportunities to teach important skills: rhyme, phonics, parts of speech (nouns, verbs, adjectives, prepositional phrases), listening, cooperation, poetry form, figurative language, imagery, and memory. In the following lesson plans, individual poems are used as a basis for teaching several of these skills. Lessons are spread out over two days, with a variety of activities for each.

Integrating Curriculum Through Poetry: Jack Prelutsky's Poetry

In order to teach the concept of imagery and to help ensure that children are making the transition from picture books to chapter books, Jack Prelutsky's poem "Michael Built a Bicycle" (from *The New Kid on the Block*, 1984) provides the perfect avenue to start. In this poem, Michael builds a bicycle that is overly accessorized.

Following is the plan for teaching basic imagery through this poem in grades 3 through 6. Middle school children may need more sophisticated poetry, although these poems can hold the attention of second-language (ELL) students and those with learning or attentional difficulties until grade 8. They may also be used for small group, guided reading, or writing instruction.

Day 1

1. The students are asked to listen carefully to the unusual items that Michael places on his bicycle.
2. The teacher reads the poem to the students while their eyes are shut. This is important so that they block out other stimuli in the classroom and concentrate on the poem.
3. The students have lined paper on their desks. At this time, they are asked to list as many items that they can think of that Michael has on his bicycle.
4. As they are making their list, the teacher again reads the poem.
5. The students are shown an overhead transparency of a basic bicycle frame.
6. They are given a piece of plain white paper and asked to draw a simple bicycle frame similar to, but not exactly like, the overhead on the screen.
7. They are asked to quick-draw a picture of what Michael's bicycle might look like, using the list of items they have just formulated.
8. After three minutes, the teacher asks for volunteers to draw some items on the overhead (bird cage, blender, bumbershoot, cassette deck) to motivate some of the students who are artistically hesitant to get started. Seeing a few ideas might be the catalyst for children who do not believe they can draw.
9. After ten minutes, the students are asked to stop their work. The students share their papers with their table partners (tables consist of four students each).
10. Volunteers are asked to share their pictures with the entire class at the rug area.
11. The students are asked to explain how this exercise is like making a transition from picture books to chapter books. (With pictures in a book, the illustrator determines what the reader will see. In chapter books with no illustrations, readers must fill in or create the illustrations or scenes in their own minds. The difference is similar to the difference between seeing a movie and reading a book.)

Day 2

12. A few overheads are made of the students' bicycle pictures to share with the entire class.
13. A discussion may ensue on why the pictures all look different. (We all have different artistic ability; we all perceive the words differently; we all heard different things while listening.)
14. The poem is presented to the whole class on the overhead projector. The students see how James Stevenson, the illustrator of Jack Prelutsky's book, *The New Kid on the Block,* visualized the poem.
15. The students read the poem from the overhead again, silently.
16. The students are each assigned one line of the poem to read independently in front of the class. They are given about thirty seconds to say the line out loud to themselves (in a whisper), and if they do not know a word or words, they ask their partner.
17. The poem is read in its entirety. Everyone participates, and because everyone has heard the poem at least three times when the teacher read it, each child should be able to read his or her part successfully.
18. The poem is handed out to each pair of students. They are to highlight the rhyming words and then read the whole poem alternating every two lines of poetry. This allows reluctant readers to be successful participants without being frustrated by having to read in front of too many other children.
19. Parts of speech are easily taught through poetry. Since this poem is rich in naming words, the teacher might want to take this opportunity to review the idea of common nouns. Students with limited English proficiency might be asked to recite the nouns in their own language, while locating the same words in English from the poem.

Jack Prelutsky's poems act as a springboard for teaching curriculum in the classroom. Reading and writing instruction is more engaging and the students may be more active participants as they are pulled into learning grammar and parts of speech through an approach that is fun for them. Who says that teaching language has to be dull? Reading and writing become more alive as these creative poems charge up the students in literacy activities.

In trying to meet all the standards, teachers sometimes forget to find time for creative writing. Challenged readers and writers need opportunities to write creatively. It might not always be the best writing, but the children enjoy it and become better writers as they experiment with their own ideas and try emulating mentor authors' craft. All of us need outlets for relaxation. Taking a break from more formal writing assignments can be very beneficial. If the schedule of the day is too tightly structured at school, encourage children to write creatively at home or in their free time. Like music and art, creative writing is a form of relaxation for many. Punctuation, grammar, reading skills, and creative writing can also be taught through the use of other Jack Prelutsky poems such as those listed below:

- "My Brother Built a Robot" (creative writing about robots and what a child might program a robot to do; construction of a robot)
- "A Remarkable Adventure" (creative writing: "What are your best excuses why your homework isn't done?")
- "I Found a Four-Leaf Clover" (verbs, creative writing: "What would happen to you if you found a four-leaf clover?")
- "Homework! Oh, Homework!" (memorization, writing: "How do you feel about doing homework? Create one homework assignment that you would like a teacher to give you. Explain why this assignment would be considered educational.")
- "Louder Than a Clap of Thunder" (comparisons, creative writing: "What is loud?")

Mentor authors use powerful words to build momentum in their poems. Prelutsky is no exception. The students should use these poems to help them build their own list of powerful words (verbs) in their own writing:

"I Should Have Stayed in Bed Today" (verbs)
"The Turkey Shot out of the Oven" (verbs)
"When Tillie Ate the Chili" (verbs)

Conversation is a difficult skill for upper graders and middle schoolers to transfer from their reading into their writing, and many class lessons must be spent on the skill of writing dialogue. A good starting point is the poem "Belinda Blue," in which Prelutsky uses conversation. Other sessions can build on this poem and include other mentor authors' use of conversation format.

Poems can build an initial foundation in grammar for students who are having trouble incorporating ideas such as prepositional phrases, descriptive words, and powerful verbs in their writing:

"Last Night I Dreamed of Chickens" (prepositional phrases)
"The Flimsy Fleek" (imagery, adjectives)
"Gussie's Greasy Spoon" (nouns)
"My Dog, He Is an Ugly Dog" (adjectives)
"If" (homophones)

Most children love to act out funny poetry. "Suzanna Socked Me Sunday" is perfect as a dramatization piece for students who are reluctant readers or for those who are not proficient at standing up before an audience.

All of these poems can be found in *Something Big Has Been Here* (1990), *The New Kid on the Block* (1984), and *A Pizza the Size of the Sun* (1996).

Integrating Curriculum Through Poetry: "The Messy Room"

Another poem that motivates even the most reluctant readers and writers in the classroom is "The Messy Room" by Shel Silverstein (From *A Light in the Attic*, 1981). This is a poem that students relate to for many reasons, but basically because at this age, most children do not keep their bedrooms particularly tidy. In fact, in many homes, the messy room is a source of contention between parents and their children.

The following lesson has been used successfully with third- through sixth-grade students.

Day 1

1. The teacher reads the poem to the students without the use of the visual. He or she prefaces the reading by saying, "Today I am going to read a poem by Shel Silverstein entitled 'The Messy Room.' Each of you should listen carefully and think about what you can see in this room."

2. The teacher asks the students to write down on paper or on a whiteboard what things they remember about this particular bedroom. About three minutes are given for this task. This is an excellent time for the teacher to observe which children are having difficulty with listening. Auditory children will find this task very easy, but the visual children will probably be challenged by the task.

3. The teacher reads the poem again to the students, and when he or she is finished asks the students to add to their list.

4. The poem is read a third time, and the students are allowed to add to their lists. They are asked to count the number of items they remember and place that number at the top of their page and circle it.

5. The transparency or poem itself is now placed on the overhead.

6. One by one individual students come up to the overhead and use an overhead marker to highlight the items found in the room. As one child is finished, he or she hands off the pen to a classmate of the opposite sex. This person now highlights a new idea and hands off to another student. This gets a number of students actively involved and encourages some of them who normally would not raise their hands to participate. Using the overhead pen does motivate some of the students to become involved.

7. A discussion is then held about auditory and visual learners. It can begin with a question, such as, "How many of you had difficulty remembering the poem when I read it only once to you? Twice? Three times? How many of you would have liked to have seen the poem from the very beginning?" Making students aware of how they learn is essential with students in grades 3 to 8. Students need to know their style of learning and how they can compensate if they are weak in one of their modalities.

8. Students are then asked to write a paragraph describing their own bedroom. Some ideas covered in that paragraph should be color, wallpaper, window coverings, size, shape, bedspread, stuffed animals, and other details. Ten minutes is given to this task. It is a quick-write. With this form of writing, students write nonstop for a short period of time, concentrating on the ideas that "pop" into their heads instead of being concerned about conventions of writing such as grammar, punctuation, or spelling. Keeping the pencil moving on the paper for the full amount of time is the emphasis. Students should write for the full ten minutes, and the teacher should also write, modeling good writing to the students. At the end of this time, all students are asked to turn to their partner and exchange quick-writes to read.

9. Students should be aware that a quick-write is not a final product. It is just a beginning. More time is needed to think about and expand the ideas. All students are asked to put finishing touches on their paragraphs at home and are encouraged to read their paragraphs to their parents.

10. The teacher might already have a more thorough paragraph written so that the students can hear what the teacher is expecting. Good teacher modeling is essential to good student writing.

Day 2

11. Students read their completed paragraphs to partners.

12. A discussion is held to compare bedroom neatness. The teacher may ask, "How does your bedroom compare with the child's in the poem? Do you think the person in the poem is a boy or a girl? Why? How many of you have messy bedrooms? How many of you have neat bedrooms? How many of you share a bedroom? How many of you get into arguments with your parents because of the messiness of your bedroom? How often do you have to clean your bedroom? How does it feel when you can't find something you need because your room is too messy? How does it feel when you get grounded or restricted because of the condition of your room?"

13. This questioning leads the students into discussing their own personal styles. The teacher can probably guess which students have messy bedrooms and which ones have neat rooms from how they keep their desks. A child's style is very noticeable. One job of the teacher is to make students aware of how they approach life. By doing so, they learn to understand and appreciate who they are.

14. The poem is now brought back onto the screen, and selected students are asked to read the lines. Since the students have all heard the poem several times, everyone should have some success in reading it orally. Choosing the best readers first does give the students a refresher course in listening to the poem. Since the purpose of presenting amusing poetry in class that everyone can relate to is to get students involved, everyone should have a chance to read some part of the poem orally. Use of partners is also helpful. Partner A reads the poem to partner B. Active participation by each student is a must. Limited-English-proficient students are able to enjoy and have fun with the shortness and content of this poem.

15. Students are now asked to write independently all of the pairs of rhyming words they can find in the poem. Selected students are asked to highlight them on the transparency.

16. Cooperatively in groups of threes, students are now asked to find as many naming words (nouns) that they can locate in the poem. The teacher may say, "I am looking for some other words that are like *room*. Find me at least ten other naming words [nouns: persons, places, or things]. You may find all of them if you want. You have five minutes. Remember that you can always test a naming word by putting 'the' in front of it, as in 'the room,' 'the underwear,' and 'the chair.'" (Balanced literacy entails teaching parts of speech, something that was not part of the whole language approach a few years ago. Students must have command of these parts, especially when they are dealing with a foreign language when they approach middle school. If we teach the basics of speech through pieces of literature, including poetry, students will have a better foundation when they do have opportunities to learn a new language.)

17. The students are now told that they will have one week to become more familiar with their own rooms. Their task is to measure their room and draw a sketch of it on graph paper or electronically, being careful to be exact. (This can be coordinated with the teaching of area and perimeter in math.) Some help may be necessary from parents. Extra tape measures may be borrowed from the teacher for students who do not have their own. Students may work together. Some students do not have bedrooms. We have to be careful to respect their need for privacy. Possibly letting them work with another student or having them create the perfect bedroom on their own, would make them feel more comfortable. (See Using Shel Silverstein's "Messy Room," Activity 11.1, at the end of this chapter.)

18. It is always helpful to have a guest speaker who is a builder, contractor, or architect. He or she can make children more aware of how to draw doors, windows, and closets to scale. It is surprising how children perceive the world. Many of them draw doors that stick out into the room, instead of seeing them from a bird's-eye view or from looking down on them. It is a good idea to have a model or sample of what you want. You will probably have to restate the idea several times that they are looking at their room from a position hovering above it.

The preceding two lessons integrate the curriculum so that students see the interconnection of the disciplines across instruction. Children build better connections and hold on to learning more soundly if the relationships of reading, writing, speaking, listening, math, and other academic areas are intertwined.

Setting Up a Poetry Corner or Center

Every classroom should have a place where students look at and review poetry books. The poetry center always seems to be popular. Students continue to borrow books from this center to take back to their own desks or to use during a "choice" period. As poetry is read, the teacher may ask the students to:

- Record and evaluate the poems on a special poetry log sheet they keep in their three-ring binders throughout the year. (See Activity 11.2, Poetry Log, at the end of this chapter.) Short, concise record keeping is an easy way for reluctant reader-writers to summarize and recall the poetry that they have read.
- Keep a file of poetry selections that students cut out of magazines, newspapers, or write themselves.
- Draw or illustrate their favorite poetry.
- Memorize a favorite poem.
- Share a poem with a partner.
- Dramatize a poem for the entire class.
- Write poetry of their own.
- Tape their reading of a poem, and listen back to their way of reading it.
- Read their favorite poetry to younger students at school or at home.
- Make a poetry board. Using a large white piece of tag board, students might copy (in printing or on the computer) a poem that they like, illustrate it, present it to the class, and display it on the bulletin board.

When the classroom is richly supplied with a large variety of poetry books for the students to use and enjoy and the teacher gives instruction in basic poetry, students readily use poetry to express themselves. Reluctant reader-writers have been known to write beautiful poetry. Having poetry in the classroom provides opportunities for all students to be involved in reading and writing. Students' success in short poetry reading experiences may open up the door to larger reading successes.

Hosting Poetry Parties and Poetry Nights

Often teachers have poetry parties in their classrooms where students memorize or read a poem of their choice. Some students write wonderful poems and read their own. Parents are invited to attend, and punch and cookies are served.

Many schools have special evenings when families are invited for a celebration of poetry. See Chapter Nine regarding the Popcorn, Pretzels, and Poetry event for families at West Elementary School in New York.

Using Nonfiction Poems

Poetry also comes in nonfiction form, and students can have fun with writing some of their own. Douglas Florian is masterful at presenting informational poetic text to children. His books contain poetry about animals, birds, insects, mammals and lizards, frogs and polliwogs. The classroom would benefit from having a collection of these books. Some children are not interested in rhyming poetry but are captivated by information. Reluctant readers and writers must have opportunities to experiment with reading and writing poems from both fiction and nonfiction.

Upper-grade and middle school teachers are always looking for new ways to slip in a little content throughout the day. Sara Holbrook has written *Practical Poetry* (2005), where she addresses how to promote content understanding and meaning making to meet the content standards in the areas of math, science, language arts, and social studies through poetry. The book provides a more functional use of poetry to meet the needs of today's curriculum.

Tongue Twisters

These silly phrases and hard-to-say rhymes provide fun language experiences for all students. Those who are reluctant reader-writers and speakers can become successful at reading, reciting and creating their own twisters.

Here are some examples from *Tongue Twisters* by Charles Keller (1989):

"Seven silly sheep slowly shuffled south."

"Eight apes ate eight apples."

"Sister Sarah shined her silver shoes for Sunday."

"Round and round the rough and ragged rock the ragged rascal ran."

Students may read the twisters from the board or from books. Beginning with one-, two-, or three-lined rhymes and then progressing to more difficult ones seems to be a logical order. When working with tongue twisters, students may:

- Start a file box or collection.
- Place one tongue twister on the board each week and say it to the class if they have mastered it.
- Work in partners to master the skill.
- Write tongue twisters of their own. Since tongue twisters use the literary element of alliteration, students might start with one example of their own using their name such as: "Mary mentioned money matters to her mother"; "Sue's sister sat sadly seeing the sinking ship"; "Jasmine jabbered joyously as the Jello jiggled." At the beginning of the school year, these can be written on brightly colored sentence strips and placed on the bulletin board next to the child's picture.
- Work with a book written in alliteration format, such as Kristin Pratt's *A Walk in the Rainforest* (1992) or Graeme Base's *Anamalia* (1987). These books are great read-alouds, and students can learn to appreciate the way they are written. This type of content format is a fun way to put new information into personal writing.

Comics

Children from all academic ranges can enjoy the use of the comics in the classroom. Reluctant readers view a comic strip as manageable because it is short and because pictures accompany the words, which give clarification to the meaning.

Stephen Krashen (1993) concluded that comics are linguistically appropriate, are not detrimental to reading development, and are conduits to book reading. He also mentioned that teachers should consider comics such as *Archie* (archiecomics.com) as a source for high-interest, low-vocabulary reading since they are written at the second-grade level.

There are many ways to entice children to read and write comics within the classroom. It is essential to have a large supply of comic strips from the Sunday newspaper. These may be laminated and used for both whole group and small group instruction. Having parents assist in the collection of comics is helpful so that there is more than one copy of each. Colorful comics tend to be more stimulating than black-and-white ones. In planning for instruction, teachers should select comic strips that are age appropriate for their students. Reluctant readers can become quite frustrated with complicated story lines even though the comics seem easy enough to read.

Small group instruction using multiple copies of one comic strip may be used with reluctant readers or with limited-English-proficiency students who have difficulty understanding more sophisticated strips. For whole class instruction, a comic strip may be placed on the overhead projector, read, and discussed.

A comic center may be set up for students to visit when their work is completed. Laminated comic strips may be used to read, summarize, and keep a record of. (See the Comic Strip Recording Sheet, Activity 11.3, at the end of this chapter.)

Students always enjoy creating their own comic characters and comic strips. This is sometimes harder than it seems, however. If it is approached by telling the students that comics are very short stories written in conversational form, then it may appear a little easier to grasp. Reluctant writers are less intimidated by the shortness of this story. Practice with this writing form and teacher and peer modeling will help build student success. As students finish their writing, they can share it with their classmates. Finished products can be displayed on the bulletin board.

Individual comic strips such as *Blondie, Dennis the Menace, Peanuts,* and other student favorites can be collected over several months. Cooperative groups may work together to see how the characters change or what their experiences are over a longer period of time. Reviewing comic strips in this way allows children to see that many characters do not change—that they keep their basic personalities over weeks, months, years, or even decades.

Children should be provided opportunities to read the comics out loud with partners and discuss them in cooperative groups. They might also like to act out and dress up like the comic character that they have read about or created themselves. Middle school students relate well to the Archie comic books, whose characters are relevant to them because of the age connection.

Limited-English-proficient speakers or learning disabled students may have difficulty understanding the humor in the comic strips. Therefore, small group instruction may assist them in translation or explanation of the meaning. It is helpful to pair students who speak the same native language when discussing figurative language. A student who is bilingual may be able to explain the true meaning of an expression to another limited-English-proficient student who translates literally instead of figuratively. This partner may be able to explain the humor in the comic in his or her partner's native language.

Word Study Using Archie Comic Books

If you can obtain enough comic books for each child, have students do a search of the types of words they can find in them that would be complicated for younger children. A list of words found in Archie comic books by upper-grade elementary students can lead to quite an interesting discussion and instruction. It would appear that these comic books produce a much higher level of vocabulary to challenge students than parents and teachers might think possible. Stretching and expanding student vocabularies can be done through comic books.

The following list of words were derived by sixth-grade students as they perused through Archie comic books. The list shows students that sophisticated words can be found in this light reading and help them infer that comics may be read for the development of richer vocabularies, as well as for enjoyment reading.

egotistical	inconvenience	vain
Victorian urn	dictator	seamstress
recoil	hideous	outmoded
sumptuous	primitive	rebellious
mediocre	syndrome	follicle
prohibitive	notorious	economics
impaired	temptation	disproportionate

peroxide	hospitality	chauffeur
punctuality	alma mater	commotion
embrace	petunias	Richter scale
charioteer	new fandangle	inhumane
malfunction	pharaoh	contraption
arrogant	impeccable	picturesque
conceivable	eternity	imperial looking
indefinitely	recuperate	frazzled
garish	punctual	fashionably late
hologram	resemblance	enabled
allotted	poltergeists	quaint
inanimate	executives	journalism

We highly recommend a wonderful book, *Teaching with Calvin and Hobbes* (1993), by Mary Santella-Johnson and Linda Holmen. The authors use some humorous *Calvin and Hobbes* comic strips to motivate upper-grade and middle school students while teaching a variety of skills: vocabulary, comprehension, figurative language, and problem solving. Reading and writing skills are the main focus. Copies of these pages can be made and students may study them independently, or they may be introduced as a whole class lesson. Some anthologies also have sections on comics.

Comic book instruction must be taught to some students explicitly. This might be a new genre for a few. Therefore, small group instruction may be a necessary starting place. One fourth-grade teacher, Dave, was surprised when he had a day set aside for choice reading. Several of his students did not know how to read a comic book. They were unfamiliar with the format and were not sure what to read first. The skill of reading from left to right and across one page at a time, then proceeding to the next page, had to be taught. Several children were reading across both the left- and right-hand pages without reading one page at a time. We take for granted that all students know how to access this type of format.

Graphic novels are another form of comic book that is gaining popularity in literature. Exposure to pieces of literature in graphic form is helping reluctant readers to gain access to more complicated story lines.

Candy Wrappers and Food Product Labels

Students can learn a great deal from looking at product wrappers. Labels from cans and wrappers contain a great deal of information such as:

weight (standard and metric)	date of expiration	scantron
serving size	ingredients	distributor
nutritional facts		

Teachers and parents should take opportunities to introduce this information to the children so that they learn to use it to become more aware of health issues in their daily lives. When reading these materials, students begin to see their value.

At the beginning of the school year, tell parents what you will be doing with can labels and wrappers of all types, and ask for their assistance in collecting them. Start a collection of these items. Have a labeled box where the students know where to place them. As you gather enough to start with, hand out one to each child, and instruct students why the labels are required by law to have certain information on them. Use the Wrapper/Label Information Sheet (Activity 11.4 at the end of this chapter).

You might want to begin a wrapper/label center. Encourage students to review the labels during their free time or at the centers. As students investigate and read the labels, they will be motivated to compare and contrast, look closely at nutrition facts, and become more conscious of how food relates to them.

You might want to invite the school nurse or a nutritionist to the class. As an expert, he or she can fill in some of the facts that will relate to the students' lives. A visit to a grocery store can be an educational field trip. Some grocery stores provide nutritionists who walk around the store helping students look at labels critically and encourage choosing nutritional snacks. Students can work in cooperative groups to locate foods with the best food value, least cost per ounce, best cost value, and so on. When they get back to school, they can share their findings on a poster board with the rest of the class and with parents.

Nutrition Guides from Fast Food Restaurants

As parents become more concerned about the food that their children are eating, restaurants are trying to appease consumers by providing important nutritional value of their food products that have come under attack in the last few years. For instance, Wendy's has an extensive nutritional guide. Children are able to determine the amount of carbohydrates, cholesterol, and other food value facts from this guide. If you can obtain five or six of these guides, you could set up a guided reading group to help more challenged readers gain an entry into this form of reading that will form strategic reading skills and address health issues at the same time.

Joke and Riddle Books

In the classroom, a good way to start each morning is to tell a joke or riddle or place one on the board for the class to ponder as attendance is being taken. Glen Singleton's books *1001 Cool Jokes* (2000) *and 1001 More Cool Jokes* (2002) provide a starting point for this study.

As children are looking for other books at home and in the library, they should be instructed on choosing jokes to share out loud that are appropriate for school—for instance:

- What has no beginning or end and nothing in the middle? (A doughnut)
- How much dirt is there in a hole exactly one foot deep and one foot across? (None. A hole is empty.)
- Why shouldn't you keep a library book on the ground overnight? (Because in the morning, it will be overdue [dew]).

Riddles and jokes motivate students to listen carefully and to think. They are tools to enhance reading, writing, listening, and speaking. For the reluctant reader, the teacher might ask a student to read one or two pages from a riddle or joke book in the classroom. That child must choose two riddles to present to the class in the morning on a specified day. If the child has difficulty reading the riddles, another student may be paired up to read with him or her. This gives silent and oral reading opportunities for the child and compels the child to read carefully and clearly. This short form of reading builds self-esteem and develops confidence in oral language presentation.

A riddle and joke fair where everyone contributes his or her favorites can be fun. Parents can be encouraged to bring in a few of their favorites as well, and refreshments could be served.

Some teachers have asked students to create a page for a classroom riddle book. The page could have five of the child's favorite riddles or jokes and illustrations to accompany them. Children can write them electronically or print them neatly.

In schools where there are cross-age big and little buddies, the older children can read from riddle books or create some of their own riddles to read to the younger children and add personal art, computer graphics, or photos cut from magazines or newspapers to them. The older students might be encouraged to tell riddles to their parents, brothers, and sisters and for the children whom they baby-sit. Connecting the joke and riddles with writing and reading activities can provide enjoyment to students who usually find reading and writing difficult.

Books About Idioms

There are many fun books for upper-elementary and middle school students, such as Terban's *Dictionary of Idioms* (1996) and *In a Pickle and Other Funny Idioms* (1983), that will help them process the meaning of idioms that they hear. For second-language students, these are the tricky and confusing parts about the English language. An idiom is a group of words that do not literally mean what they say. Each idiom has a special meaning, and someone who does not know that meaning will not be able to decode what the speaker is saying. Consider these idioms: to give someone the cold shoulder; in one ear and out the other; to put your foot in your mouth; to get up on the wrong side of the bed; to put the cart before the horse. English is full of idioms, and giving students practice with them can make a difference in your special population's understanding of what they hear and read.

Some teachers put an example on the board and call it the Idiom of the Day. Other teachers have competitions to distinguish idioms and their meanings. Still others ask students to draw pictures of the literal meaning and the figurative meaning of the sayings. Upper-elementary and middle school students might each bring an idiom to the class on different days and try to stump their peers. A chart may be kept, or idiom journal entries can be written down. Whatever the activities, working with idioms provides a foundation for word study that supports the second-language students in an enjoyable manner. These drawings and labels can build an interesting bulletin board that capitalizes on the use of drawing to get to explanation and understanding. (See the Idiom Activity Form, Activity 11.5, at the end of this chapter.)

Menus

As soon as kids are old enough to read, they love looking at menus and choosing their own meals. So why not continue with this interest as they develop into the years of adolescence? Menus are basically free, and if you start early in the year with your wish list for parents, you will receive a large supply of menus to keep in a container.

Here are suggestions for how teachers and parents can use menus to motivate children to read and learn other skills at the same time:

- Children choose a breakfast, lunch, or dinner of their choice from any menu on file. Younger children may use a calculator to add up the cost of each meal. The older children can also figure out tax and tip.

- The students take orders for their family members and their friends. Writing down the orders on a special receipt or tablet looks more official and will motivate some children because it is more like the real thing. Wait staff order forms can be found at some office supply stores and provide an enjoyable educational activity for children.

- After reading several menus, children can categorize them by types of foods, alphabetize them, or compare and contrast them as to which is the best buy. Graphs can be drawn to show the comparisons of several food items from two or three restaurants.

- Children may visit a restaurant and find out how the food items it offers have been selected and who designed the menu.

- Students may design their own menus and create their own restaurants, describing them in detail through the writing process, or creating them artistically through drawing, or a combination of both. See Let's Read a Menu, Activity 11.6, at the end of this chapter.

Letter Writing

Every classroom should have Michael Levine's *The Kid's Address Book* (2001), which contains over two thousand addresses of celebrities, athletes, entertainers, and other famous people. Children love to write to real people because they relate to them and are hopeful of receiving an answer. This book gets kids reading while they select a famous person, and then it moves them to write. This book can be used at home by parents or in the classroom at a center.

One way to motivate children to write is to give them the opportunity to communicate with someone they think is famous, such as an entertainer, celebrity, or athlete. Usually when children think they have a chance of communicating with a famous person through the mail, they are hooked into writing. That is one reason we have the Celebrity Letter Writing Station as a classroom experience. The following guidelines help in establishing such a station.

Providing Instruction

The teacher should provide instruction on what the behavior should look like at this station before giving the students access to the activity. What should the students be doing, and how should they be behaving? Without teacher-directed instruction, the students do not know the expectations.

Also, before having the station available to the students, it is essential that the teacher provide the basic instruction for correct letter writing format and addressing an envelope. Many upper-grade and middle school students are a little rusty with this form. Although letter writing is basic to all primary levels, it is also surprising how easily the students forget it as they progress in the grades. That is why it is essential to model letter writing as a reminder before letting the students work independently at this station.

Modeling the Writing

One way to do this is by the teacher modeling the writing of a letter. By modeling a letter, students see that the teacher has done it, so they have a foundation for writing their own letter. It becomes, "Oh, now I see how it's done! Now I can do it myself!" This teacher model could be written on a chart for all to see. It could also be written on an overhead for a shared reading experience. In this way, the students would not have a copy of the letter to use at the station as their model. If the students in the class are prone to copy from the teacher's modeling chart and seem unable to write without their own voice, then the teacher might not want this model letter up for all to see.

Another choice is to have the students co-create a letter. This would allow all students to have input into the writing and might sound more authentic to this age group. When students and teachers build their own work together in this way, challenged writers strengthen their understanding. This takes more time, but the students feel more connected in the process when they participate. This can also be charted or placed on an overhead for future study as the students take on the task independently.

Students could also have a copy of the teacher's modeling letter in their writing folders to keep throughout the year. That way the teacher's letter does not have to take up a lot of room on the classroom boards.

Suggested Materials

- *The Kid's Address Book* (1994), by Michael Levine. Multiple copies are provided at this station so that students have access to them. Students peruse the book, scanning to find one of their favorite people to write to. This book is updated every few years and is an essential source that children will not want to put down. There are several other books that are superb resources, but they are more costly: *The Ultimate Sports Address Book: How to Connect with 1000's of Sports Legends* (Mattison, 2002) and *The Ultimate Friend Book: More Than Your Average Address Book for Kids* (Eckstein, 2004).

- *The Jolly Postman and Other People's Letters,* by Janet and Allan Ahlberg (1986). This book gives an example of a variety of letters from well-known fairy tale characters. It also shows how to address an envelope. Students can use some of the models to create their own letters.

- *Dear Kalman: Smart, Peculiar, and Outrageous Advice for Life from Famous People to a Kid,* by Kalman Gabriel (1999). This is a collection of letters that a twelve-year-old boy received from famous people who answered his question about their advice for life. Students can look through this book to see that famous people do write back to students and that they have opinions about things that matter.

After the students finish writing their letters, a peer editor looks them over and offers suggestions. Students then hand in their letter to the teacher, and a copy is made to keep inside the student's writing portfolio. Letters are mailed, and the hope is that everyone will receive a response. Many students' letters are answered, and some even receive a photograph.

Teacher Extension Ideas

After the students complete this piece of writing, there are plenty of other ideas to supply this station with. For instance, let the boys and girls write welcome notes to new students, birthday cards, congratulation notes, permission slips, invitations for school events, "caught doing something good" notes, school newspaper articles, letters to families, letters to past teachers, pen-pal letters, letters to next year's students who will be in a particular grade, or letters to cross-age buddies. A fuller list of things to write about is provided in *If You're Trying to Teach Kids How to Write, You've Gotta Have This Book* (1995) by Marjorie Frank, which has over two hundred creative and innovative ideas for writing, including traffic rules, used car descriptions, vignettes, odes, headlines, critiques, and brochures.

Parent Tips

Children need to see that writing is part of their everyday life. Suggest to parents that they may have their children practice writing with more than thank-you letters; they might offer opportunities for kids to write postcards on trips, e-mails, shopping lists, supply lists for trips, poetry, dinner menus for the week, tooth fairy letters, directions to their house, instructions for babysitters, schedules for activities, calendar events, rules for the house, chore lists, letters to raise their allowance, and letters to grandparents about what's happening in their lives.

The Celebrity Letter

Student Directions
At this center you will . . .

- Look through *The Kid's Address Book* and the other books.
- Locate a person you are interested in writing to.
- Write a letter using correct letter writing format to the famous person. Be creative; add some of your own ideas to make the letter more interesting:
  - Tell something about yourself.
  - Tell how you know about him or her.
  - Say what you like or admire about him or her.

- Explain why you are writing.
- Consider whether there is something you will ask the person for.
- Are there any questions that you have that you would like answered?
- Have someone look over your letter and offer suggestions on how to make your ideas clearer and assist you in spelling or grammar.
- If necessary, rewrite the letter in better handwriting, or type it on the computer.
- Look over the correct envelope-addressing format in *The Jolly Postman*.
- Use a black or blue ballpoint pen to address your envelope.
- Address the envelope. Make sure your address is at the top left-hand corner and that the celebrity's address is in the middle of the envelope. Use a ruler to lightly draw parallel lines to guide your writing.
- Place your finished letter and unsealed envelope in the basket provided at the center.
- Don't seal the envelope so that we can make a copy of the letter to keep in your writing binder. If you finish, search for someone else you would like to write to or read some of the letters sent to Kalman Gabriel by famous people.
- What's next? Think of other letters you would like to write for other reasons. It might be to persuade, inform, or entertain.

World Record Books and Almanacs

Two other books that get students in grades 3 to 8 motivated are The *Guinness Book of World Records* and *Ripley's Believe It or Not!* which are published annually. Even the most unwilling reader may grab one of these books and become captivated about the world records and totally engulfed in the short factual information provided.

With a bit of teacher direction, students also find almanacs surprisingly interesting. Once given a chance, many children feel comfortable reading for factual information because these sections are short and manageable to read. See Activities 11.7 and 11.8, Almanac Research Sheet and Create Your Own Almanac Questions, at the end of this chapter.

Television Guide and Newspaper Movie Section

Television guides and newspaper movie sections present a great reading and writing experience for children in the classroom or at home and draw on the natural interest students have in movies and television. Activities that students may want to participate in are listed below:

- Have students highlight programs in the television guide that would be appropriate for young children and make a list of them and the times of day they are broadcast. Students write a paragraph explaining why they chose these programs.
- Students use the television guide for one day, and select three shows that their family members agree on and would like to watch together. As a family, they discuss the programs after watching them.
- Using a calendar, students write down a list of three programs each day for a week that they would like to watch if they were allowed to watch anything on regular television. They explain their choices. (See Activity 11.9, Let's Read a Television Guide, at the end of this chapter.)

- Using the newspaper movie section, students locate a movie that they and their family would like to see. They highlight the time that would be best for them to see it and find the theater that is nearest their home. How many times does it show each day? What number would students call or what Web site would they go to, to find out more information? What rating is the movie?

Taking this activity a bit further, the students may be asked to watch a television program that they have found in the television guide and explore the ratio of program timing to commercial timing. (See Activity 11.10, Televison Watching Observation and Evaluation Sheet, at the end of the chapter.)

Popular Music

Since music is the universal language, use it more to engage students in a group reading experience. By presenting the lyrics to the songs on the overhead projector or on sheets of paper, students enjoy reading the words as they sing with the vocalist on the CD. Having the students keep a notebook of the class's favorite songs is helpful so that they can be used again for future singing sessions.

Children's Magazines

Some students who do not like to read chapter books find magazines an excellent form of reading. *Sports Illustrated for Kids* is one magazine that many students find interesting because the articles are relevant to them. Other magazines of interest to children are:

National Geographic World	*Ranger Rick*
Boys' Life	*Cricket*
Kid City	*Zillions for Kids from Consumer Reports*
Kids Discover	*American Girl*

Caldecott Books

The Caldecott Award, established in 1938, is presented annually to the illustrator of the most distinguished picture book for children published in the United States.

Even in upper-grade and middle school classrooms, students like to reconnect to picture books. It is an enjoyable experience for students to review Caldecott books that are full of exquisite illustrations and stories of substance. Whereas these books must be read to children in the primary grades, the older children can enjoy reading the text themselves, as well as study and appreciate the depth and artistic techniques used in the illustrations. Having a Caldecott collection available can open up critical discussion on why these books have been selected for this distinguished award. Students can write their own picture books for younger students or to put into the school library. This can be an educational and engaging experience for upper-grade and middle school students. (See Activity 11.11, Caldecott Books Recording and Information Sheet, at the end of this chapter.)

Beginning to gather up a few of these award-winning books for classroom use is a practical idea. Our own personal favorites that can be used readily by classroom teachers in grades 3 to 8 are *Grandfather's Journey* (Say, 1994), *Smoky Night* (Bunting, 1995); *Snowflake Bentley* (Martin, 1999), and *So You Want to be President?* (St. George, 2001). Each of these books has appeal to older students and can be adapted for grades 3 to 8.

Making Big Books in the Upper Grades

After the class finishes reading some great Caldecott Award winners, it might be fun to borrow some of the big books from the primary grades and do the following activities. Big books have huge appeal to the younger students in the primary grades and the novelty of big books in the upper grades is worth having them available for the older children.

1. Have several class periods when students can read the big books silently.
2. Break the class into cooperative groups, and have each group present a big book to their classmates.
3. Discuss the reasons that young children enjoy big books and other picture books.
4. Have students pair up with other children who complement their skills to do a big book writing and illustrating activity. In other words, encourage those who love to write to pair up with someone who is a good artist. Discuss the importance of blending artistic and the creative writing skills.
5. Discuss subjects that are appropriate for primary children.
6. Give a review of lowercase and uppercase printing. Use the language book as a model for writing while on this project.
7. In pencil and on rough draft paper, have the students sketch out their story in words and pictures. They should have one page for every page they intend to have in their final big book. Use peer editing and correction.
8. Use white tag or white construction paper, twelve by eighteen inches, for the final draft.
9. Show students how to make a one-inch frame around each page using a ruler. This gives a finished look to the book. Frames should be drawn first on each page before any pictures or writing are done. The frame may be a solid line or a simple creative design, but should be exactly the same on all pages. One color of marker should be used.
10. Students should measure lines with a ruler at the bottom of each page for writing their text. The lines should be one or two inches apart depending on how many words the students have on each page. This is a great math lesson and involves concentration and planning.
11. Students write out and illustrate everything in pencil on their final paper. Many students want to type their story. In this case, a rough draft copy should be typed out first; editing may then be done. A large type size (24 or 36 point or even larger) will need to be used.
12. After proofreading, the students finalize the words in black marking pen (a thin-line pen) and color in the pictures using markers, crayons, colored pencils, or watercolors.
13. The pages are numbered at the bottom.
14. Students create a front and back cover for the book.
15. An "About the Author and Illustrator" page with pictures of the authors and illustrators is included at the end of the book.
16. It is a good idea to double the paper or have students write on only one side if they are using markers. Some markers leak through to the other side of the paper.
17. Each page is laminated and spiral-bound.
18. The books are shared with the younger children.
19. Students can "gift" their project to the school library or to a primary classroom especially if the students who created them are leaving the school to go onto middle school. They become a favorite part of the classroom or school libraries.

Using a Sequential Format Through Reading Recipes and Other How-to-Do Books

Some children can become absorbed in recipe books, especially if they have pictures. (See Activity 11.12, Let's Read a Recipe, at the end of this chapter.) This also helps students prepare for their survival math if they choose to follow a recipe and make it at home with their families. Following a step-by-step procedure can be helpful with real-life reading experiences using instruction such as doing an art project, creating paper airplanes, playing a game, or setting up a tent in the backyard.

BOOKS THAT APPEAL TO RELUCTANT READERS

Finding books that appeal to struggling readers is a challenge. To be hooked in, these readers need books that will hold their attention for read-alouds, shared readings, and independent reading sessions. Laura Backes, in her book *Best Books for Kids Who Think They Hate to Read* (2001), lists eight characteristics that give books reader appeal: humor, well-defined characters, fast-paced plot, concise characters, suitable text, kid relevance, unique presentation (nonfiction), and visual appeal (nonfiction). This book lists 125 books that will motivate children to read and is well formatted for easy browsing by teachers and parents.

A Long Read Made Easier

In the traditional bedtime story, there are only one or two children in a calm, relaxing setting, and the environment is perfect for concentration—the illustrations supporting the text and the adult supporting the story through talk and a cozy situation. In a class of thirty-five students, it is difficult for even the most focused student to always follow the longer stories that are read aloud in the class. Without support of some type, those students lose the essence of the book.

Beginning the school year with a genre study of short stories can draw in some of the reluctant readers. Short stories are less intimidating. Children see that they do not have to complete a thick Harry Potter book to feel successful.

One way to ensure that all students have access to a longer read is stopping the story at preselected spots and asking the children to turn to a partner and quickly review what has happened. The instructor can immediately see where the meaning has broken down. This form of turn and talk or partner check enables struggling readers a chance to hook back up with the storyline. The teacher reads it once; the partners talk about the story and check their comprehension; the challenged reader relays the information orally back to the teacher or the group. Everyone can jump back in where confusions might have developed.

Keeping track of the story on a classroom chart using one of the appropriate graphic organizers is an excellent way of supporting students. For instance, if a story is being read with a somewhat complicated plot, a simple sequence chart can be developed. Every day the chart can be reviewed so that all students have access to the story. Students can help generate the chart by deciding in pairs or triads what the main events were in the story. The organizer can be grounded in student suggestions.

Using Short Texts to Teach Comprehension Strategies

Using short texts such as picture books, short stories, magazine and newspaper articles, essays, and poems is helpful for supporting struggling readers. There are many reasons that teachers might choose to use short texts for instruction. Included in the list below are some reasons given by Backes (2001), as well as some brainstormed by fellow colleagues:

- They are short and easily read out loud, providing a common literacy experience.
- They are often well crafted, with excellent language and illustration.
- They can easily be reread when meaning breaks down.

- They provide many opportunities for modeling and thinking aloud.
- They are self-contained and provide a complete set of thoughts, ideas, and information for the whole class to think about.
- Teachers can provide students with anchor experiences through short-text reading that students use later to help comprehend longer or more difficult text.
- They cover a large range of topics, ideas, and issues.
- Although they are short, they are filled with sophisticated thoughts, issues, and information.
- They are easily assessable to the most students.
- They provide many opportunities for discussion.
- They become anchor texts that can be referred to throughout the year.
- Students can focus on the text because they are concentrated into small portions.
- They provide examples of models of strong writing.
- They provide myriad possibilities to look at different perspectives.
- They are filled with many literary elements.
- There are a large number of genres to expose students to choose from.
- They provide quick background knowledge for students who have not been exposed to specific life experiences.
- Different writing forms are exposed that students begin to use in their own writing.

Collections of Short Stories

Even someone who does not seem interested in reading may respond to a book of short stories. These short stories are more readable because of their brevity. Not all students are able to hold onto longer chapter books, even with a read-aloud, unless they are supported with charting and conversation about the book. Sometimes teachers begin the year with a short story genre study. Having a number of short story collections for read-aloud and for shared reading can introduce the class to many story elements and story structures in a short amount of time. If you have enough short story books, you can have every child read one for this genre study. This opens up discussions about the benefits of reading short stories and may be a catalyst for reluctant readers to choose more books of this type during independent reading time.

Although character and setting development may not be quite so detailed or elaborate in short stories, reluctant readers can become comfortable with these short versions and still learn a lot about narrative format. Middle- and high-achieving students also feel comfortable with these manageable and engaging texts.

Short Stories That Hold Older Children's Attention

Short story collections such as the following often appeal to reluctant readers in the upper grades and middle schools. They cover a wide range of interests and ability levels:

- *Girls to the Rescue* series, edited by Bruce Lansky (New York: Meadowbrook Press). In these stories, courageous girls are placed in dangerous situations and become heroines. These are inspiring stories selected with the help of girls ages seven to thirteen from across the United States. Many of the stories have girls from different cultures represented. The books provide positive female role models.
- *It's Fine to Be Nine* (New York: Scholastic, 1998). This book contains twelve stories about being nine years old and how each of these famous nine year olds faces the trials and tribulations of life as a nine year old. These are stories from Judy Blume, Beverly Cleary, and Jerry Spinelli. The book is best used in fourth or fifth grade because of the age of the characters.

- *The Scary Stories* series, by Alvin Schwartz (Philadelphia: Lippincott, 1986). Kids love these short stories that are sure to chill to the bone. They are best used in the middle school due to scary parts.
- *Animal Stories,* chosen by Michael Morpurgo (Glasgow: Caledonian International Book Manufacturing, 1999). All twenty of these stories are about the animal kingdom.
- *Aesop's Fables,* retold by Ann McGovern (New York: Scholastic Press, 1963).
- *Just So Stories,* by Rudyard Kipling. (New Jersey: Watermill Press, 1980). A wonderful collection of stories that tell how things came to be in the world.
- *Two-Minute Mysteries,* by Donald J. Sobol (New York: Scholastic, 1967). A mystery collection of seventy-nine very short stories that are filled with clues and suspense.
- *A Treasury of Pirate Stories,* chosen by Tony Bradman (New York: Kingfisher, 1999). These classic folktales and fables are excellent for reading aloud or for readers to enjoy independently. The stories are drawn from cultures around the world.
- *Detective Stories,* chosen by Philip Pullman (New York: Kingfisher, 1998). The detectives in these stories are skillful and brave. The collection helps students uncover clues to solve important cases. This is best used in the middle school grades because of the more difficult content and vocabulary.
- *Baseball in January and Other Stories,* by Gary Soto (San Diego, CA: Harcourt, 1990). These delightful stories are told from the viewpoint of adolescent Hispanic boys.

Series Books

Series books are supportive texts for all students, and a good supply of them should be part of the classroom library. Once we have read a good book, we often want to read the sequel. When students read one book in a series, the next book in the series becomes easier for them because they are already connected and familiar with the characters, the setting, and some of the events that have already drawn them into the story. A comfort zone has been established, allowing more challenged readers to become less intimidated by a new story that needs to be unwrapped. Each time we read a new book in a series, the familiarity makes the book easier to understand and gain meaning from. For less motivated readers, series books provide additional support that allows them to access more challenging books and be able to read and gain momentum. This ability to read more pages puts them at ease and makes them feel they are at the same level as less challenged readers. Upper-grade students want to keep up with their peers. Series books put struggling readers on a successful path to show their peers that they are not lagging behind.

A few series books that might initiate a classroom collection and address the reading abilities and interests of a group of children in grades 3 to 8 might include some of the following titles:

- *Goosebumps* (R. L. Stine), grades 3 and 4
- *The Babysitters Club* (Ann M. Martin), grades 3 and 4
- *Time Warp Trio* (Jon Scieszka), grades 3 to 5
- *A Series of Unfortunate Events* (Lemony Snicket), grades 3 to 5
- *Deltora Quest* (Emily Rodda), grades 4 and 5
- *Nancy Drew* mysteries (Carolyn Keene), grades 4 to 6
- *Sammy Keyes* (Wendelin Van Draanen), grades 4 and 5
- *Artemis Foul* (Eoin Colfer), grades 5 and 6
- *The Hardy Boys* (Franklin W. Dixon), grades 5 and 6
- *Harry Potter* (J. K. Rowling), grades 5 to 8
- *The Chronicles of Narnia* (C. S. Lewis), grades 5 to 8
- *Redwall* (Brian Jacques), grades 6 to 8

ACTIVITIES TO KEEP RELUCTANT READERS READING

This chapter has included many ideas for engaging students in reading. Regular reading is important for even the most reluctant students. These students must be able to take a good piece of literature and show understanding of what they have read. Through the following activities, students and teachers can keep the reading process moving and monitor students' progress in terms of understanding.

Organizing the Reluctant Reader and Writer

A child feels comfortable when he or she knows what direction the teacher will take in future instruction. Because each upper-grade and middle school student should have a three-ring binder, a list of the monthly genres of books that will be read is a helpful mental organizer. The Book Report Monthly Schedule (Activity 11.13 at the end of this chapter) can be reproduced on colored paper and then filed in the language arts section of the child's notebook so that it can be easily located for reference purposes. The child and the parent can stay abreast of the reading genres and projects that are expected for the entire year.

Creating a Bookmark

Every child loves to see the magic that appears on the pages of a colorful picture book. Younger as well as older children can be fully engrossed in a book with only a few words and illustrative images on the pages. But what happens when the child stops having the pictures to cue him or her into the story? It appears that about at the fourth-grade level, when books become void of illustrations, a segment of students becomes disinterested and unmotivated readers. The reading period becomes a time for daydreaming and getting lost in other thoughts. Without pictures and illustrations, some students turn off to reading.

What we want the students to learn is that no book is unconquerable. Although the picture books and short stories turn into chapter books, we want children to learn the skills to make reading manageable. The art of pacing and looking at a book in smaller chunks or manageable pieces is paramount in helping all kids to conquer a book.

The first week of school is the time to start. We talk about a reading scientific investigation. We become "read-i-o-logists." All the students use the same piece of literature, and every student reads for fifteen minutes. On the bookmark that is found at the end of this chapter (in Activity 11.14), the students each fill in the date, page started, and page ended in that fifteen-minute segment. Each child calculates the number of pages that he or she has read during the period. This gives him or her an understanding and sense of how many pages of a grade-level book he or she can read in a controlled period of time.

This experimentation continues for the full five days of the week. At the end of the week, the student averages the number of pages he or she reads and should better understand how to break up a book in the future so as not to leave it until the last minute. If the students see that on the average they can read ten pages in fifteen minutes, then they can figure out that reading a two-hundred-page book of their level will take them twenty fifteen-minute segments. They should learn that if they read for a half-hour segment, they can read that same book in ten sessions. Even in our own profession, we know that many of us have left a book until the night or weekend before the test or the book report is due and have had to power-read at the last minute. If we take the time in class to help students learn to pace their reading, not just for one week but several times throughout the year, we believe that the children will see themselves as more successful readers and realize that reading can be a journey that is fun and rewarding in itself.

It is important that the teacher occasionally evaluate the student's bookmark and check to see if the student needs to read for a longer period of time. This bookmark also helps parents to keep pace with the amount of reading their child is doing. It is useful for reading at home as well as in class.

Our goal is to have students read on a regular basis—not just during the class reading period. If students start viewing more sophisticated chapter books in small bites instead of big mouthfuls, we have begun to make them see that reading is conquerable.

These bookmarks can be duplicated on colored paper, used regularly by the students, and filed in a child's portfolio for evaluation by the parent, an aide or the teacher. See Bookmark, Activity 11.14, at the end of this chapter.

Demonstrating Understanding of Core Literature

Making meaning is the most important aspect of reading. Without understanding, reading is nothing more than word calling. Children need to have a variety of ways to show what they have learned from reading literature. Following are some creative activities to stimulate the reluctant reader/writer to show what he or she knows about his or her reading.

Creating a Report Card for the Main Character

This activity can be done in pairs, small groups, or independently. It is a good idea to use this activity before a report card period. Having students evaluate themselves and where they see their strengths and weaknesses on their own school's evaluation tool helps them see how a report card is designed. Children who are more independent can create their own categories for the main character in the book to be evaluated on (courage, survival skills, kindness, building skill, or physical strength, to name a few). Students who have more difficulty coming up with ideas of how to evaluate the character may work more closely with the teacher. Together they can brainstorm a list of possible categories for character strengths and weaknesses. Then each child can choose five or six to use for his or her own report card. (See Let's Create a Report Card, Activity 11.15, at the end of this chapter.)

Creating a Test

Because children are familiar with formal tests, this culminating book activity provides them with knowledge of questioning and how test makers might formulate test questions. The creation of the test works well in cooperative groups of three or four children. The option of working independently is also available. Each child or group of children is required to think up five true-false, five multiple-choice, and five short-answer questions that they think the other children in the room should be able to answer after reading a particular book. The book may be one that has been read aloud to the students, a story from an anthology that all the class has read, or a book from a book club or literature circle that several groups have read, possibly even from another classroom. It is essential that teachers model the basic types of questions. For the short answer–type questions, the students should create questions that are not one-word answers, but instead, questions that are thought-provoking and force their peers to think more deeply about the story, characters, plot, and setting. (See Create Your Own Test, Activity 11.16, at the end of this chapter.)

Finding Out Where in the World the Story Takes Place

While students are reading the book, they should have almanacs available to find out some basic information about the country or area they are studying and fill out the Literature/Geography Study Guide, Activity 11.17, at the end of this chapter. The students then locate the setting of the story on the world map and label it. (We suggest that students write in pencil first and then go over it in thin black marker to make the map look more polished.) Throughout the year, students keep their map in their notebook, so that they can update it as they read new books. At the end of the year, the class has a better grasp of world geography and should be able to locate on their maps the countries of the world that they have studied.

Locating literacy materials for engaging our most reluctant readers and writers is a large task. In today's inclusive classrooms, teachers need to look at catalogues and other resources. Most important, the materials that children have access to in their real lives will stimulate them to become more involved.

RESOURCES

Ahlberg, J., & Ahlberg, A. (1986). *The jolly postman and other people's letters.* Boston: Tine Wah Press.

Backes, L. (2001). *Best books for kids who think they hate to read.* Roseville, CA: Prima Publishing.

Base, G. (1987). *Anamalia.* New York: Henry Abrahms.

Bunting, E. (1994). *Smoky night.* San Diego: Voyager Books.

Cole, W. (1981). *Poem stew.* New York: HarperCollins.

Colfer, E. *Artemis fowl* (series). New York: Scholastic.

Dakos, K. (1993). *Don't read this book whatever you do!* New York: Four Winds Press.

Eckstein, K. J. (2004). *The ultimate friend book: More than your average address book for kids.* New York: Imagine Books.

Frank, M. (1995) *If you're trying to teach kids how to write you've got to have this book.* Nashville: Incentive Publication.

Gabriel, K. (1999). *Dear Kalman: Smart, peculiar, and outrageous advice for life from famous people to a kid.* New York: Quill.

Guinness world records. (2005). London: Guinness World Records.

Harley, A. (2000). *Fly with poetry.* Honesdale, PA: Boyds Mills Press.

Harwell, J. (2001). *Complete learning disabilities handbook* (2nd ed.). Upper Saddle River, NJ: The Center for Applied Research in Education.

Holbrook, S. (2005). *Practical poetry. A nonstandard approach to meeting content-area standards.* Portsmouth, NH: Heinemann.

Honig, B. (1995). *Teaching our children to read: The role of skills in a comprehensive reading.* Thousand Oaks, CA: Corwin Press.

Keller, C. (1989). *Tongue twisters.* New York: Simon & Schuster.

Korman, G., & Korman, B. (1992). *The D– poems of Jeremy Bloom.* New York: Scholastic.

Krashen, S. (1993). *The power of reading.* Englewood, CO: Libraries Unlimited.

Levine, M. (2001). *The kid's address book.* New York: Perigee.

MacLachlan, P. (1998). *It's fine to be nine.* New York: Scholastic.

Martin, J. B. (1998). *Snowflake Bentley.* Boston: Houghton Mifflin.

Mattison, C. (2002). *The ultimate sports address book: How to connect with 1000's of sports legends.* Union Lake, MI: Odyssey Publications.

Meet the Author Series. (1992). *Meet Jack Prelutsky.* New York: American School.

Morrow, L. M., & Weinstein, C. S. (1982). Increasing children's use of literature through program and physical design changes. *Elementary School Journal, 83,* 131–137.

Morrow, L. M., & Weinstein, C. S. (1986). Encouraging voluntary reading: The impact of a literacy program on children's use of library centers. *Reading Research Quarterly, 21,* 330–346.

Moss, J. (1989). *The butterfly jar.* New York: Bantam Books.

Packard, M. (2006). *Ripley's believe it or not!* New York: Scholastic.

Pearson, P. D., & Gallagher, M. C. (1983). The instruction of reading comprehension. *Contemporary Educational Psychology, 8,* 317–344.

Pratt, K. (1992). *A walk in the rainforest.* Nevada City, CA: Dawn Publications.

Prelutsky, J. (1984). *The new kid on the block.* New York: Greenwillow Books.

Prelutsky, J. (1990). *Something big has been here.* New York: Greenwillow Books.

Prelutsky, J. (1996). *A pizza the size of the sun.* New York: Greenwillow Books.

The Random House book of poetry for children. (1983). New York: Random House.

Rosenbloom, J. (1976). *Biggest riddle book ever.* New York: Sterling Publishing.

St. George, J. (2000). *So you want to be president?* New York: Scholastic.

Santella-Johnson, M., & Holmen, L. (1993). *Teaching with Calvin and Hobbes.* Fargo, ND: Playground Publishing.

Say, A. (1993). *Grandfather's journey.* Boston: Houghton-Mifflin.

Schwartz, A. (1986a). *Scary stories to tell in the dark.* New York: HarperCollins.

Schwartz, A. (1986b). *Scary stories: More tales to chill your bones.* New York: HarperCollins.

Silverstein, S. (1981). *A light in the attic.* New York: HarperCollins.

Singleton, G. (2000). *1001 cool jokes.* Dingley, Victoria: Hinkler Book Distributors.

Singleton, G. (2002). *1001 more cool jokes.* Dingley, Victoria: Hinkler Book Distributors.

Terban, M. (1983). *In a pickle and other funny idioms.* New York: Clarion Books.

Terban, M. (1996). *Dictionary of idioms.* New York: Scholastic.

Van Draanem, W. *Sammy Keyes* (series). New York: Scholastic.

Walqui-van Lier, A. (1993). *Literature review: Sheltered instruction.* Bilingual Teacher Training Program: Sheltered Instruction Institute. San Diego: San Diego County Office of Education Resources.

Wright, G. (1979). The comic book: A forgotten medium in the classroom. *Reading Teacher, 33,* 158–161.

Activity 11.1

USING SHEL SILVERSTEIN'S "MESSY ROOM"

Investigator's name: _____

Writing Assignment and Drawing a Map to Scale

1. Write a paragraph describing your own bedroom. Include such things as color, room arrangement, carpeting, closet size and space, stuffed animals, furniture, window coverings, wallpaper, bookshelves, and anything else. Tell whether it is neat or messy, and explain how and why it is that way.

2. Use a tape measure or yardstick to find these measurements:

   Length and width of the bedroom   L _____ W _____

   Area of the bedroom   (L × W) _____

   Perimeter of bedroom _____

   Length of the closet _____

   Length of the window(s) _____

   Length and width of the bed   L _____ W _____

   Door width _____

   Length and width of dresser   L _____ W _____

   Length and width of bookcase   L _____ W _____

   Length and width of nightstand   L _____ W _____

   Length and width of desk   L _____ W _____

   Other furniture   (L and W) _____

USING SHEL SILVERSTEIN'S "MESSY ROOM" (*continued*)

3. Draw a sketch of your room here; then use graph paper to draw your room to scale.

POETRY LOG

Name: _____

Date: _____ Today I read a poem entitled _____

Author: _____ It is about _____

_____

I liked/disliked the poem because _____

_____

Date: _____ Today I read a poem entitled _____

Author: _____ It is about _____

_____

I liked/disliked the poem because _____

_____

Date: _____ Today I read a poem entitled _____

Author: _____ It is about _____

_____

I liked/disliked the poem because _____

_____

Date: _____ Today I read a poem entitled _____

Author: _____ It is about _____

_____

I liked/disliked the poem because _____

_____

Activity 11.3

COMIC STRIP RECORDING SHEET

Name: _____   Date: _____

Directions

1. Read at least ten comic strips from the ones provided.

2. Record the necessary information.

3. Create your own characters, and make a comic strip of your own with four to eight frames. Add color and conversation bubbles.

Date: _____   Comic strip name: _____

Main characters: _____

Summary: _____

_____

Date: _____   Comic strip name: _____

Main characters: _____

Summary: _____

_____

Date: _____   Comic strip name: _____

Main characters: _____

Summary: _____

_____

Date: _____   Comic strip name: _____

Main characters: _____

Summary: _____

_____

Activity 11.4
WRAPPER/LABEL INFORMATION SHEET

Name: _____ Date: _____

In order to learn a little bit more about the nutrition facts in the food we eat, you are to research three labels or wrappers. You are to carefully look at the information on a (1) milk carton, (2) bread wrapper, and (3) a cake, cookie, or candy container. Record the information so that we can compare and contrast these items in class on the date indicated above.

1. Brand of bread _____ % of fat _____

Net weight of package _____ Cost _____

Serving size _____ Servings per container _____

Calories _____ Calories from fat _____

Total protein per serving _____

Total fat grams per serving _____ Total carbohydrate grams _____

List the first five ingredients: _____ _____

_____ _____ _____

2. Brand of milk _____ % of fat _____

Net weight of carton _____ Cost _____

Serving size _____ Servings per container _____

Calories _____ Calories from fat _____

Total protein per serving _____

Total fat grams per serving _____ Total carbohydrate grams _____

List the first five ingredients: _____ _____

_____ _____ _____

WRAPPER/LABEL INFORMATION SHEET (*continued*)

3. Brand of cake, cookie, or candy _____ % of fat _____

Net weight of carton _____   Cost _____

Serving size _____   Servings per container _____

Calories _____   Calories from fat _____

Total protein per serving _____

Total fat grams per serving _____   Total carbohydrate grams _____

List the first five ingredients: _____   _____

_____   _____   _____

IDIOM ACTIVITY FORM

Name: _____ Date: _____

Idioms are part of our everyday language, and they can often be confusing and difficult to understand because the group of words taken together usually has little or nothing to do with the meanings of the words taken one by one. They are particularly confusing to students who are learning English because we cannot use the literal words to figure out their meaning. There is a hidden meaning in the group of words that forms an idiom.

After listening to our discussion about figurative language, you are to make a list of twenty or more idioms that are part of our language. You can use the special idiom books that are in the basket, do research online, or talk with your family members. From your list of idioms, select two to represent in picture and word form. You will draw a picture of what the idiom means literally and figuratively.

Example 1: *You must have ants in your pants.*

Literal meaning: You have ants crawling up your pants.

Drawing: Boy sitting on the ground with lots of ants crawling up his pants.

Figurative meaning: You are overly active and cannot sit still.

Drawing: Boy jumping all over the place and not sitting still.

Example 2: *He saw the handwriting on the wall.*

Literal meaning: He is looking at handwriting that is written on a wall.

Drawing: Man is starring at a wall with handwriting on it.

Figurative meaning: A sign that something bad is going to happen: a warning of danger or trouble.

Drawing: The man is just about to be pulled over for a traffic ticket because he ran a red light and the police officer is going to stop him.

IDIOM ACTIVITY FORM (*continued*)

What to Do

Step 1: Take a piece of white 8½- by 11-inch paper, and fold it into eight sections.

Step 2: Write the idiom in the top square.

Step 3: Draw a picture for the literal meaning.

Step 4: Draw a picture for the figurative meaning.

Step 5: Explain what the expression really means.

Step 6: Repeat steps 2 to 5 for your second idiom.

Step 7: Use colored pencils to color in your pictures.

Step 8: Draw around your pictures with black, skinny marker so your pictures can be seen from a distance.

Step 9: Fold your paper to show only the pictures. See if a partner can tell what your expression is and what it means.

Step 10: Find a place on the bulletin board to display your work.

LET'S READ A MENU

Name: _____ Date: _____

You have $75.00 to spend at this restaurant. You may take as many of your friends with you as you would like, but everyone must have an appetizer, soup or salad, a main entree, dessert, and a drink. The object is to spend as close to $75.00 as possible! That must include sales tax and a 15% tip.

When you are completed, write a restaurant review. Name your restaurant and describe your experience at the restaurant — the atmosphere, food, and service. Attach your paragraph to this paper.

Restaurant Name: _____

Quantity	Food Item	Cost per Item	Total Cost
	Subtotal		$
	Sales tax		$
	Food total (+)		$
	15% food total (×.15)		$
	Total, including tip		$

Activity 11.7

ALMANAC RESEARCH SHEET

Name: _____ Date: _____

Using the almanac, find the answers to the following questions. Place the page number you found it on next to your answer.

1. Name the three highest **dams** in the world.

    a. Name _____ Where found _____ Height _____

    b. Name _____ Where found _____ Height _____

    c. Name _____ Where found _____ Height _____

2. What is the **world's fastest aircraft**? _____

3. Where and when was the worst **hurricane** in U.S. history? _____

    _____

4. Name four areas of the world where **typhoons** take place. _____

    _____

5. On what day is **Canada Day**? Why is it celebrated? _____

    _____

6. What was the name of the top sports show watched last year on **television**?

    _____

7. What night of the week do the most people watch **television**? _____

8. Who has had the most **home runs** in one season of baseball in the United States?

    _____

9. What is the average age for a first-time **marriage** in the United States for a man: _____ For a woman: _____

ALMANAC RESEARCH SHEET (*continued*)

10. What is **Lyme** disease? _____

11. Name the three largest **islands** in the world. _____

_____

12. Name the three **highest mountains** in the world. _____

_____

Activity 11.8

CREATE YOUR OWN ALMANAC QUESTIONS

Name: _____   Date: _____

1. Use your almanac to guide you in thinking up five almanac questions to ask a classmate.

2. Make yourself an answer key on a separate piece of paper so that you have the correct answer and the page number on which you found it.

3. Exchange papers with a partner. Have him or her answer your questions.

4. Check to see if your partner answered them correctly.

Question 1: _____

_____

_____

_____

Answer: _____   Page found: _____

Question 2: _____

_____

_____

_____

Answer: _____   Page found: _____

Question 3: _____

_____

_____

_____

Answer: _____   Page found: _____

Activity 11.9
LET'S READ A TELEVISION GUIDE

Name: _____   Date: _____

SATURDAY MORNING

Channel	6:00	6:30	7:00	7:30	8:00	8:30	9:00	9:30	10:00	10:30	11:00	11:30
69 KSWB	Paid Prog.	Paid Prog.	Liberty Kids	Capt. Planet	Yu-Gi-Oh!	The Batman	Xiaolin	Loonatics	Pokémon	Coconut	Johnny Test	Yu-Gi-Oh!
6 XETV	Paid Prog.	Paid Prog.	DoReMi	Mew, Power	Bratz 99307	Winx Club	G.I. Joe	One Piece	Sonic X	Turtles	NFL Helmet	Sm'th Jazz
39 KNSD	(5:00) Today (CC) 429524		News (CC) 59494				Tutenstein	Time Warp	Trading	Unleashed	Unleashed	Rescue
8 KFMB	(5:00) Early Show 908562		LazyTown	Go, Diego	Backyard	Dora ...	Little Bill	Little Bill	Backyard	Dora ...	Blue's Clues	Paid Prog.
51 KUSI	Paid Prog.	Garden	News 876388						EXTRA (CC) 66369		Estate	Travel/Style
10 KGTV	Paid Prog.	Paid Prog.	Good Morning 96543		Lilo & Stitch	Maggie	Family	So Raven	Suite Life	Phil, Future	Ca. Country	Paid Prog.
15 KPBS	Thomas	Bob Builder	Zoboomafoo	Dragon Tale	Arthur	Barney	Teletubbies	Boohbah	Caillou	Sesame Street 449369		Quilt in Day
35 UCSD	Planetary Interiors 43982		Healthcare 445098		White Coat	Genetic.	Autobiography 97291		Conv./History 43833		Controversy 30369	
49 XUPN	Paid Prog.	Paid Prog.	Paid Prog.	Paid Prog.	Paid Prog.	Paid Prog.	Paid Prog.	Paid Prog.	Paid Prog.	Paid Prog.	Paid Prog.	Paid Prog.
12 XEWT	Off the Air		Programa P.	Programa P.	Programa P.	Bob Esp'ja	Los Chicharrines 46901		Club Infantil	Mega Man	Programa P.	Programa P.
17 KBNT	Fuera Serie	Programa P.	Tu Desayuno Alegre: Fin 73765			Vivan los Niños	Grupo comparte. 95340		Voz y Voto	Tigritos	Vida TV La Fiesta 43299	
33 XHAS	Profeco	Programa P.	Programa P.	Programa P.	Dora	Dora	Jacobo Dos	Programa P.	Programa P.	Programa P.	Programa P.	Todo Bebé
28 KCET	Niños, Casa	P. Sésamo	Sesame Street 627630		Thomas	Jet Plane	Bob Builder	Postcards	Place, Own	Programa P.	La Plaza	Journal
A&E	Paid Prog.	Paid Prog.	Makeover	Old House	Old House	Old House	Old House	Old House	Flip This House 943369		Biography 196524	
AMC	"Angel and the Badman" ★★★ (1:40) 3119727				"Alvarez Kelly" ★★ (1966, Western) William Holden. (1:56) 6185253					"River of No Return" ★★ (1:31) 707098		
ANIM	Animals	Animals	Ani. Videos	Ani. Videos	The Most Extreme 462765		Crocodile Hunter 80901		Corwin's Quest 36543		Funniest Animals 56307	
AZNTV	Documentary 8464036		Discovery India 3128123		Chanakya (Hindi) 3196524		Paid Prog.	Paid Prog.	ICC Cricket	Cricket Classics 9535611		AZN Mast
BET	BET's Morning Inspiration 838456						The Parkers	The Parkers	The Parkers	The Parkers	106 & Park: Top 874949	
BRAVO	Actor Studio	B. Brown	Paid Prog.	Paid Prog.	Paid Prog.	Paid Prog.	Paid Prog.	Paid Prog.	Paid Prog.	Paid Prog.	Making Of	B. Brown
CMT	CMT Music 9266543										Top 20 Count. 5485185	
CNBC	Paid Prog.	Paid Prog.	Paid Prog.	Paid Prog.	Paid Prog.	Paid Prog.	Paid Prog.	Paid Prog.	Paid Prog.	Paid Prog.	Paid Prog.	Paid Prog.
CNN	Sat. Morning	Open House	Saturday Morning 320776		The Turnaround 970235		CNN Live Sat. 761974		In the Money (CC) 587727		CNN Live Sat. 590291	
COM	Paid Prog.	Paid Prog.	Duckman	Dilbert	MAD TV 5836920		MAD TV 5576017		MAD TV 5910727		MAD TV Ja Rule. 5923291	
COURT	Paid Prog.	Paid Prog.	Paid Prog.	Paid Prog.	Paid Prog.	Paid Prog.	Paid Prog.	Paid Prog.	Paid Prog.	Paid Prog.	Paid Prog.	Paid Prog.
CSPN1	(4:00) Journal 944388		C-SPAN Weekend 928340						C-SPAN Weekend 41673901			
CTN	Classic Arts Show 41524		Chronicles	San Diego	Oceanside	Birding	NASA	San Diego	Bears	Tai Chi	Ca. Country	To Earth
DISC	Paid Prog.	Paid Prog.	Paid Prog.	Paid Prog.	Paid Prog.	Paid Prog.	It Takes a Thief 487388		Robber/Century 941901		Bank Robberies 961765	
DISN	The Wiggles	Bear/House	Koala Bros.	Higglytown	Higglytown	JoJo Circus	Doodlebops	Charlie/Lola	The Wiggles	Lilo & Stitch	Lilo & Stitch	Brandy
E!	Bloomberg 243949		Scenes	Attractions	Scenes	The Soup	E! News Weekend 957630		Rich: Cattle Drive 506920		Next Door	Taradise
ESPN	SportsCenter (CC) 315104		SportCenter	College GameDay (CC) 438456			College Football: Teams TBA. (CC) (Live) 784475					
ESPN2	Bass Tech	Beat Charlie	Bassmasters 1689475		BassCenter	Sat. Kickoff	College Football: Teams TBA. (CC) (Live) 1904833					
FAM	Paid Prog.	Paid Prog.	Battle	Shinzo	Drgn Boost	Digimon	W.I.T.C.H.	Super Robot	Rangers	Fantastic 4	The Tick	Rangers
FOOD	Paid Prog.	Paid Prog.	Cooking	30-Min. Meal	Sara/Secret	Emeril	Low Carb	Calorie	Boil Water	Cooking	Sandra Lee	30-Min. Meal
FNC	(4:00) News 6418920		Bulls, Bears	Business	Forbes/Fox	Cashin' In	Weekend Live With Tony Snow 2311307				Fox News Live 7809185	
FSN	Baseball	Chris Myers	Pro Football Pre. 636388		Football	Paid Prog.	College Football: Southern Methodist at Texas A&M. (Live) 787036					
FX	Paid Prog.	Paid Prog.	"Stealth Fighter" ★ (1999, Action) (R) (1:27) 9761098				Married	Married	"70s Show	"70s Show	"70s Show	"Once ..."
HALL	Hillbillies	Hillbillies	Gilligan Isle	Gilligan Isle	"Finding Buck McHenry" ★★ (1:35) 7104494				"Just a Dream" ★★ (2002, Drama) (1:36) 4046017			
HBO	"Wyatt Earp" ★★ (1994) Portrait traces him from boy to lawman. (PG-13) (3:09) (CC) 39412562							"Breakin' All the Rules" ★★ 712814			Inside the NFL 392611	
HBO2	Pandemic	"Look Who's Talking Now" 12474307			(8:15) Indian 42874618		Boxing 4631814		Boxing 5180659		Making	"Doctor"
HGTV	Paid Prog.	Paid Prog.	Old House	Old House	DIY Rescue	Fix It Up!	New Spaces	H. Detective	Ground	Plants	Landscape	Gardening
HIST	History IQ	Vietnam	Automobiles 155098		20th Century 156727		Last Days WWII 829036		Modern Marvels 46543		Battlefield.Det. 66307	
ITV	Science	Series	Los Ninos	Place, Own	Series	My Food	NASA	Deviants	Series	Math	Rural Community 508388	
LAND	Gunsmoke 234291		Bonanza Worship. 207272		C. Burnett	Flip Wilson	TV Moments 955272		TV Moments 504562		Top 10	Confidential
LIFE	Paid Prog.	Paid Prog.	Paid Prog.	Paid Prog.	Paid Prog.	Paid Prog.	Paid Prog.	Paid Prog.	Paid Prog.	Paid Prog.	Head 2 Toe	Head 2 Toe
LMN	"Visitors of the Night" ★★ (PG) (1:36)				"Don't Look Down" ★★ (1:36)		"Obsessed" ★★ (2002) Jenna Elfman. (1:36) (CC)					"Crime ..."
MAX	"Movie"	"James and Giant Peach"		"Dodgeball: A True Underdog Story" ★★★ 84616098			"Surviving Christmas" ★★ 424272			"Hard to Kill" ★★ 4783543		
MAX2	"When the Sky Falls"		"Ice Station Zebra" ★★★ (1968, Suspense) (G) (2:25) (CC) 5580543				"Patriot Games" ★★★ (R) (1:57) 8505543				"50 First ..."
MPLEX	"Convicted" ★★ (1:36)		"Tora! Tora! Tora!" ★★★ (1970, War) Martin Balsam. (G) (2:24)				"Goldie and the Boxer" ★ (1:40)			"Quiz ..."
MSNBC	MSNBC Live 7648253		MSNBC Live 8899524		MSNBC Live 8890253		At the Movies 4315630		Headliners 9771475		Headliners 9751611	
MTV	Music Videos 384340				Real World	Real World	Real World	Real World	Real World	Real World	Reality	Laguna
NICK	Thornberrys	Hey Arnold!	Rock Power	Rugrats	Grown Up	Jimmy	SpongeBob	Catscratch	OddParents	Phantom	Avatar: Air.	Grown Up
NGC	Totally Wild	Totally Wild	Snake	Snake	UFOs: Seeing Is Believing The unexplained.				Crop Circles		Bigfoot Apelike creature.	
OLN	Bill Dance	Outdoors	Flyng	Journal	Buckmaster	Adventures	We Live	Alaska	Dream Hun.	RV Today	ATV Sport	Advent...

Television Listings Information provided by Tribune Media Services, Inc.

Using the television guide, answer the following questions.

Copyright © 2006 by Sandra F. Rief and Julie A. Heimburge

Activity 11.9

LET'S READ A TELEVISION GUIDE (*continued*)

1. What program would you be watching if you tuned to:

   Channel 8 at 7:00 A.M.? _____

   Channel 10 at 7:00 A.M.? _____

   Channel 39 at 7:30 A.M.? _____

   Disney at 8:00 A.M.? _____

2. On what channels and at what times would you see news? _____
   _____

3. On what channel and at what time would you see *Lilo and Stitch?* _____

4. If you tuned to Channel 69 at 8:00 A.M., what program would you see?
   _____

5. How long is the program *Dragon Tale*? What time does it begin, and what time
   does it end? _____

6. Name three shows that you might watch if you were interested in sports. Tell
   what time they are on. _____

7. Highlight five programs that you would be interested in watching on the television if your parents would allow you to do so.

8. Place an X next to five programs that would not interest you at all.

9. What do you think "CC" means in the parenthesis after the name of the program?
   _____

10. Name three movies that you could see on the Disney Channel between 6:00 A.M.
    and 11:00 A.M. _____

11. At what time and on what channel would you be able to watch *James and the
    Giant Peach?* _____

12. On what channels would you find Spanish spoken? _____

13. What would you be watching on HBO at 7:30 A.M.? _____

14. If you were interested in cooking, what channel would you watch? _____

15. What genre would you be watching on A&E at 11:00 A.M.? _____

238

TELEVISION WATCHING OBSERVATION AND EVALUATION SHEET

Name: _____ Date: _____

Name of television program watched: _____

_____

Time of Day: From _____ to _____.

1. Watch a television program for the full 30 minutes.

2. Use a stopwatch or a watch with a second hand. You'll probably need an extra pair of hands, so ask someone to assist you.

3. Time the actual program in minutes (do not include the commercials). How long was it? _____

4. What is the average length of a commercial? _____

   Why do you think each one is so short? _____

   _____

5. Time the number of minutes used for commercial time. _____

6. Make a list of all products advertised during the commercials. _____

   _____

   _____

7. Write a brief summary of the program that you watched. In other words, what is it about? _____

   _____

   _____

8. Write a short summary about one of the commercials that you watched. What will you remember about it? _____

   _____

   _____

   _____

CALDECOTT BOOKS RECORDING AND INFORMATION SHEET

Student's Name: _____

In the spaces below, you are to read 3 to 5 Caldecott Award winning books. Your teacher will set your guidelines. Pay careful attention to the illustrations, the text, the story itself, and the appeal it would have for younger children. In the "information" space, describe what the illustrations look like (for example, colors used, size, modern or old-fashioned looking). What medium was used to create them (paper collage, block print, water color, pen, photographs, other)? How did they relate to the story? What did they add to the appeal of the story? Do you think younger children would appreciate these illustrations? Why or why not? Try to decide why the book would have earned this most distinguished award. Enjoy.

Name of book: _____ Author: _____

Summary: _____

_____

_____

Illustrations: _____

_____

_____

_____

Name of book: _____ Author: _____

Summary: _____

_____

_____

Illustrations: _____

_____

_____

_____

Activity 11.11

CALDECOTT BOOKS RECORDING AND
INFORMATION SHEET (*continued*)

Name of book: _____ Author: _____

Summary: _____

_____

_____

Illustrations: _____

_____

_____

_____

Name of book: _____ Author: _____

Summary: _____

_____

_____

Illustrations: _____

_____

_____

_____

Name of book: _____ Author: _____

Summary: _____

_____

_____

Illustrations: _____

_____

_____

_____

Activity 11.12

LET'S READ A RECIPE

Name: _____ Date: _____

Directions:

1. Look through several cookbooks.

2. Find a recipe that you have never tried before. Make sure that it sounds delicious.

3. Read the recipe carefully, and then write it down in your neatest handwriting on a 3- by 5-inch index card.

4. Make a list of everything you would need to buy at the grocery store if you were really making this recipe.

5. Next to each ingredient, tell what the cost is. You may use the newspaper ads or actually go to the grocery store and price the ingredients.

6. If possible, actually make the recipe.

7. Write a paragraph telling in your words:

   a. Who you would invite over to share the dish you are preparing.

   b. Why you chose the recipe.

   c. How much time will it take you to prepare your recipe.

Name of the recipe I chose: _____

Name of the cookbook where I found it: _____

The ingredients and the cost of each:

_____

_____

_____

_____

_____

_____

_____

BOOK REPORT MONTHLY SCHEDULE

Month	Book Type	Project
September	Fiction	Sequence chart
October	Biography	Poster board
November	Nonfiction	Informational
December	Sport	Sell-a-book oral presentation
January	Newbery book	Book club—sharing with a small group
February	Five Caldecott Books	Create your own big book
March	Fantasy or science fiction	Book jacket
April	Mystery	Flowchart
May	Realistic fiction	Written report
June	Poetry	Poetry recording sheet

Activity 11.14

BOOKMARK

Use one of the bookmarks on this page to track your speed of reading for the next few days. Read for fifteen minutes to determine how many pages you read in that segment of time. Record the number of pages you read each day and that will help you to discover how long it will take you to complete a book.

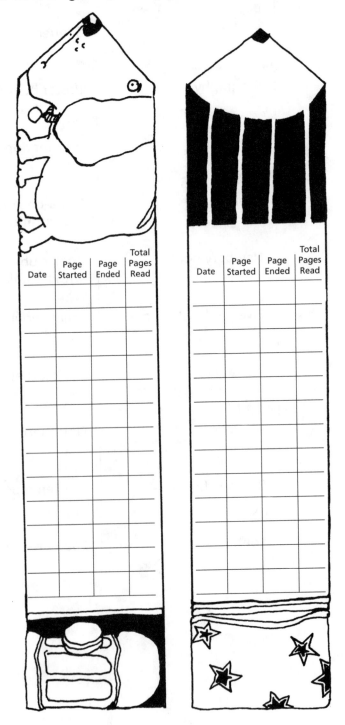

LET'S CREATE A REPORT CARD

Your name: _____

Date: _____

Book read: _____

Character evaluated: _____

Assignment

1. Review a copy of your school report card. Notice that there are categories your teacher is required to evaluate you on. You are to choose a minimum of six or eight categories to evaluate your character.

2. Your grading system for the academic subject is A, B, C, D, or F.

3. Your grading system for effort is E = Excellent, G = Good, S = Satisfactory, N = Needs Improvement, U = Unsatisfactory.

4. Evaluate the character in your book in subjects that are relevant to his or her book—for example, bravery, building skills, survival, kindness, swimming ability.

5. Give an academic and an effort grade for each subject you create.

6. Make a comment section for the teacher and the parent to respond.

7. Here is an example to guide you. You may make your report card similar to this, but be creative.

8. You may work alone or with partners.

LET'S CREATE A REPORT CARD (*continued*)

Report Card

Student's Name _____   Age _____

School Name _____   Date _____

Subject	Academic Grade	Effort Grade
Survival skills		
Building skills		
Bravery		
Acceptance of others		

Academic Grading Scale

A — Outstanding Progress
B — Very Good Progress
C — Satisfactory Progress
D — Unsatisfactory Progress
F— Failing

Effort Grading Scale

E — Excellent
G — Good
S— Satisfactory
N — Needs Improvement
U — Unsatisfactory

Teacher comments:

_____

_____

Signature _____

Parent comments:

_____

_____

Signature _____

Activity 11.16

CREATE YOUR OWN TEST

Name: _____ Date: _____

Book title: _____

Directions

You have just completed a novel in class. Create a test to show how well you have read and how well others in your class have read. Make sure your work is neat and that your questions are clearly stated.

1. Your test must include the following items:

   - 5 true-false questions: Example: This story took place in the Caribbean. True or false?

   - 5 multiple-choice questions: Example: Brian used which of these items as resources?

     A. Money

     B. A toothbrush

     C. A pocket knife

     D. A very heavy jacket

     E. All of the above

   - 5 short answer questions: They must be more than one- or two-word answers. They should involve thinking. Start your questions with the following words: *Who? What? When? Why? How?* Examples: How do you think Rick changed from the beginning of the book to the end? What were some of the reasons that Gilly was so mean to her foster brother? Why do you think Brian is prejudiced?

2. All the questions will be answered right on the test paper, so leave space for the answers.

3. Make an answer key on a separate sheet of paper.

4. Leave a space for the test taker's name.

5. Write your name at the bottom of the test.

6. You may write your test in neat printing or use the computer.

Activity 11.17

LITERATURE/GEOGRAPHY STUDY GUIDE

Name: _____ Date: _____

Book: _____ Author: _____

Country, state, or area studied: _____

Page on which it is located in the almanac: _____

Area in miles: _____

Type of government: _____

Population: _____ Capital: _____

Three largest cities: _____

Money used: _____

Major languages: _____

Major religions: _____

Education: _____

Three main products: _____

Three major exports: _____

What countries it trades with: _____

Locate this area on your world map. Label it. Also label the name of the book directly under the name of the area. Example: The Caribbean: *Timothy of the Cay.*

Use an encyclopedia or other reference book or go online to locate other information about this area of the world. Write five to ten facts your find (for example, about sports, typical foods, or music).

If needed, use a new sheet of paper and staple it to this sheet.

_____

_____

_____

_____

_____

Chapter 12

MAKING ORAL LANGUAGE COME ALIVE IN YOUR CLASSROOM

There is a real thrill at the utterance of a baby's first words—not only by the parents who oogle and oggle over those precious moments but by the child herself or himself, who seems to understand that she or he is going to get a lot of positive attention by making these sounds. Babies are rewarded for "talking." It seems natural that babies want to talk because they receive a lot of verbal stimulation that motivates them to form sounds and words. Parents write baby's first spoken words in baby books, and the list grows as the baby develops.

If oral language seems to be natural, then why don't all children share the same desire to engage in oral language as they get older? In fact, some children are so hesitant to speak in class that they rarely utter a word, preferring the safety of silence rather than having to speak up in front of their peers. While we must respect the child's personality, cultural background, and learning style, we must strive to pull each child into engaging in the oral language process.

Deficiency in our ability to present ourselves orally to those around us puts us in an awkward position in our adolescent and adult lives. Since communication comprises both speaking and listening, children must be made aware of its importance in their lives, not only in the present but also for their success in the future. Teenagers many times break off communication with their parents and turn more to their peers. Oral communication, no matter how small, must be kept open in these adolescent years. As teachers in the elementary and middle schools, we can do our part to keep the flow of communication open. This can be done by providing these enjoyable oral language experiences to children in the classroom that will motivate them to become good communicators:

- Videotaped presentations
- Tape recordings so that children can listen to and evaluate themselves
- Partner oral language experiences
- Cross-age oral language experiences with younger and older people
- Informal and impromptu role-playing situations

- Small discussion groups dealing with reading and writing
- Adult-child reading and writing conferences
- Student-student reading and writing conferences
- Parent-to-student oral language experiences
- Reader's theater presentations
- Puppet plays
- Poetry recitation and dramatic performances of poems
- Interviews
- Cooperative group assistance
- A variety of purposeful, formal speeches
- Book talks

MAKING TALK IMPORTANT IN THE UPPER-GRADE CLASSROOM

Discourse is an integral part of literacy instruction throughout the day. Children must be provided with an abundance of experiences that pull them into discussions and make them feel that their opinions, ideas, and thinking are important and that others are respectful of listening and responding to them. This is internalized through teacher and student modeling, demonstration, and role playing. Reluctant readers, writers, and speakers need excellent role models to lift their learning. In discussions about books and about the writer's craft, these students should be involved in the deep conversations that high-achieving students have. Through these mixed groupings, challenged readers gain entry into a richer understanding of literature that is beyond their independent level. They learn from other students' comments and elevate their own ability to converse intelligently about things they may not have been able to think about on their own.

GETTING STUDENTS TO USE ORAL LANGUAGE

In an upper-grade classroom, often the teacher wonders if anyone is actually "out there" sitting in the seats. Upper graders and middle schoolers progressively become less interested in telling what they know. This coincides with their need to blend in instead of standing out. A teacher who feels that the students are not participating in the classroom needs to pull the students into the instruction. Some ideas that might be used are:

- More opportunities for partner sharing and responses, making sure that every child is using oral language daily.
- Seating chart tally marks. When a child responds, the teacher makes a tally mark on the seating chart to show that the child has participated.
- Use of a deck of cards with student names on each card. The teacher draws one card at a time in order to ensure that every child during the day is called on.
- Handing out pencils or other small rewards when a child responds.
- Every child is handed a part to recite of a popular poem or song. Any child who has difficulty reading that part may ask for assistance from his or her partner before the presentation time begins.
- Having a set pattern of asking for responses (table 1, 2, 3), so that no student is left out of having the opportunity to use oral language during the day.
- Having students respond with answers to teacher questions as they are leaving the room ("Name three proper nouns." "Name three ways that you could use a paper clip." "Pay a compliment to

another person in the classroom." "Tell me one thing that you like about coming to school." "Tell me three things that you are truly thankful for.") Simple oral exercises that encourage students to talk and think can start a year out right.

Students need many opportunities to stand in front of a group and speak. Public speaking is one of the greatest fears among adults and one that we can help children to conquer. It is important to provide students the opportunity to practice this skill frequently in ways that are nonintimidating and even fun. How fortunate for students if their teachers, parents, and peers give them positive training, coaching, and encouragement.

Building Trust

Teachers must be sensitive to the discomfort and anxiety many people experience in public speaking and work to establish classroom environments that are safe and free of ridicule, criticism, and teasing. Within a classroom, children must develop a trust of their classmates and teacher.

Starting on the first day of school, students should have the opportunity to speak in front of their classmates. Following is an example of a short and effective oral language experience:

The class is divided into partner A and partner B groupings. Each child is given a set of questions to find out about his or her partner such as: "What do you like to do in your free time?" "What is your favorite sport?" "What kind of music do you like to listen to?" "What is your favorite subject in school?" Each child must speak and listen carefully to his or her partner. As partner A is speaking, partner B is jotting down the answers to the questions. Throughout the day, the partners are asked to go to the front of the room and personally introduce their partner to the rest of the class, using their notes as a guide. At this point in the year, many students just want to read off their paper with very little eye contact. Although this is uncomfortable for some, it is the beginning of a process that must be established in order to ensure the students feel that what they say is valued and that they will be listened to.

The teacher sets the tone of respect and trust for others. During the first week of school, the teacher might initiate a game such as: "One thing I think I'm really good at is . . ."; "Something I really could improve on is . . ." When the teacher makes these statements first about himself or herself, the student sees that the teacher has strengths and weaknesses. This opens up a child's desire to share a little more about himself or herself. In turn, the child offers the same two statements that show his or her strengths and weaknesses.

Encouraging Public Speaking in the Classroom

Classrooms should abound with opportunities for students to experience the enjoyment of speaking over time within the classroom setting. A teacher can use a variety of approaches to help students reach this goal.

Oral language is fundamental to the classroom. Having everyone participate and have fun with the English language should be our goal. We are a far cry from the days when oral language was not encouraged and children were supposed to be listeners, not participants. Today's classrooms should be filled with engaging conversations, vivid discussions, and lively talk. We believe in balance in oral language. A balance of enjoyable activities that bring the content and the rest of the curriculum to center stage, plus some more formal exercises, will create young speakers and listeners who will be prepared for a full life of engaging in oral language and be ready for and undeterred by speaking in their adult lives.

Quick-Talks

One way to get oral language rolling in the classroom with upper graders is to have a good-morning warm-up.

Each child is asked to speak constantly for fifteen, thirty, or forty-five seconds. This is something like a quick-write—only this is a quick-talk. We usually have one or two verbally comfortable students model this exercise first. It usually adds a bit of comic relief as these students mentally search for things to say nonstop.

Students must talk for the full amount of time. This works well after a vacation period. The teacher asks, "What did do you do over vacation?" Many upper-grade students would respond by saying, "Nothing." If you asked them to write about what they did, they would say something like, "We always have to do this." But if you make it a new experience and ask them to quick-talk, they have a pleasurable experience. After that warm-up, the students seem more eager to share with the rest of the class. This also might be the springboard to a writing assignment, but now they have a foundation on which to build. It should probably be noted to the class that most students will use one, long run-on sentence, connected, of course, with *and*.

Another idea is to have a quick-talk where the child cannot use the word *and for* the entire time. Now the exercise gets a little more complicated. Again, all the students want to try the activity, but it now has a purpose. Tape-recording a couple of students and letting them listen to themselves provides a memorable experience. (You might want to try this yourself on videotape. It's an eye-opener for teachers.)

To continue with this same idea, students might next be asked to speak for the entire number of seconds and may not say "uh" or "um."

Each verbal adventure is difficult at first, but children build their skill quickly. Because these exercises are enjoyable, even timid students are eager to try them.

Tongue Twisters

Another exercise that gets students motivated to use oral language is tongue twisters. You may want to have a weekly tongue twister on the board. Throughout the week, you may provide a time when students can practice the twister with a partner. At the end of the week, the students must either say the twister in front of the entire class or say it privately to another adult or a student representative. All students must participate, but the final product can be delivered in the manner chosen by the student. This opportunity provides a nonthreatening path for the limited-English-proficient student to participate. (See Chapter Eleven.)

Poetry

Poetry entices students to participate more enthusiastically. As we noted in Chapter Eleven, Shel Silverstein and Jack Prelutsky poems are wonderful to use with initial oral language experiences. Children who have inhibitions about orally presenting tend to lose them fairly quickly when humorous poetry is used.

Through these two poets, children learn that oral language encounters can be fun. Each child receives a copy of a poem that he or she must memorize and recite in front of the class. The teacher can be selective in giving students who have difficulty shorter poems to memorize and present. The children can be encouraged to dress up as a character in the poem or bring a visual aid to enhance the recitation. Multiple practice periods should be given for the children to practice their poems to another peer or to the wall. Wall reading is a strategy where the children stand alone and read in a soft voice to the wall, a window, a cabinet, or a bulletin board. All of the students in the class can read at the same time. There is a quite hum as children check their fluency, intonation, speed, and personal voice. Children learn quickly that practice improves the presentation. The outcome is a videotaped student presentation. As an assessment tool, the students themselves and their peers review the tapes. After looking at all the presentations, students are able to evaluate their own presentations more effectively and honestly by asking themselves, "How does my presentation compare with those of the other students?" Three other students plus the teacher evaluate a classmate's presentation.

Some teachers have regular poetry parties throughout the year to spotlight their students' oral language skills. The more practice the students get, the more confident they become. Each student is responsible for sharing a poem of his or her choice. Memorization of the poem is optional but strongly encouraged. If weather permits, these poetry parties are fun to do outside seated on blankets or carpet squares. Serving refreshments is a nice touch.

Some students prefer to read more serious poems and should be encouraged to seek them out. For instance, some poetry by Edgar Allen Poe or Shakespeare appeals to some children. A book tub filled with all kinds of poetry geared to your class's cultural backgrounds, gender preferences, and personal interests encourages poetry reading and writing.

Group Poetry

Sid Fleischman has contributed two books that are helpful in enticing children to read poetry aloud. His books *Joyful Noise* (1988) and *I Am Phoenix* (1985) are created for children to read together, sometimes simultaneously and sometimes with alternating voices. These are very supportive of reluctant speakers because they do not have to present the poem alone. Second-language students also have their needs met because the poems are short and concise and the scaffolding is there for them to branch out.

Formal Speeches

The previous oral experiences provide the foundation that fosters confidence in a child's presentation skills. As the year progresses, you may want to provide information and training about how to make more formal speeches. There are three basic types of speeches: speeches to inform, speeches to demonstrate, and speeches to persuade. It would be beneficial for upper graders to have the opportunity to present each type of speech during the year.

You should set the desired expectations and use the following guidelines:

- If the teacher models a good speech, the students will follow suit.
- Students should stay within the time allotment given: maybe one to two minutes at the beginning of the year and three to five minutes later in the year when students feel more relaxed.
- Visual aids are an important part of all speeches.
- Preparation should be evident.
- Students should have a brief written plan that they will follow when delivering their speech. (See Activity 12.1, Speech Plan Sheet, at the end of this chapter.)
- Notes can be used to glance at but not to read from.
- Practice in front of a mirror is beneficial.
- Teachers should have a student information sheet letting the students and parents know what the expectations are for the activity.
- A list of oral language experiences for the entire year helps students plan for the future events. (See Activity 12.2, Oral Language Monthly Presentations, at the end of this chapter.)

There are several steps in the process of giving a speech. In *Writers Express* (1995) David Kemper, Ruth Nathan, and Patrick Sebranek lays out the steps:

1. Pick the topic carefully.
2. Narrow your topic.
3. Gather enough information.
4. Prepare an exciting introduction.
5. Write an outline.
6. Write your speech
7. Practice your delivery.
8. Present your speech.

Careful consideration should be given to each step, especially in the planning stages. A good beginning is ideal for success.

Elements that can enhance the speech itself may also be introduced:

- Appearance (posture, stance, body movement, eye contact)
- Voice (tone, tempo, pitch)
- Diction (clarity)
- Rehearsal
- Gestures
- Humor
- Visual aids

One of the easiest forms of formal speech is the *how-to-do*. The children have been introduced to this nonfiction structure of books and have become familiar with it through several read-alouds and shared reading experiences. For instance, they may have shared a book about origami, survival, geometry, a special recipe, tying knots, or how to play a game. These examples help the boys and girls to obtain ideas for their own speeches. Children brainstorm ideas and chart them for classroom suggestions. (See Activity 12.3, An Oral Language Presentation: A How-to-Do Speech, at the end of this chapter.) Students should think of ideas that are of greatest interest to them.

With upper graders, you might think about providing monthly opportunities for the children to have formal, oral language opportunities that can be videotaped. At some schools, each child has personal videotape, and several times a year the child performs or presents a project for the camera. A child who enters a school where this is practiced would leave in fifth or sixth grade with a history or portfolio of all the oral language presentations he or she made throughout the elementary years. This taped portfolio is a wonderful keepsake for parents. To see the full development of a child's progress over the span of time would be a special gift indeed.

Having a full-time person to tape and organize these presentations would make this practice easier on classroom teachers. But there are several ways that a school might spearhead a similar plan of video production for each of the students in a modified and more cost-effective manner. Parents could be asked to send in their own blank videotapes or children could be videotaped only once during the year. A volunteer or nearby high school production class may be able to offer assistance. Another possibility is to begin the process with only one grade level at a time and add a new grade level each year. This experience is well worth looking into and lets students know that presentation skills and oral language are important life skills.

Newscasting

Newscasting is another means to inspire oral language. The class should be encouraged to watch a newscast on a local news station for the week preceding the activity or, if that is not possible for most students, the teacher might record a newscast and let the students watch it during class time. The first fifteen minutes are the most crucial. Students should evaluate and note the responsibilities of the anchorperson. They should also notice how the news team works together to report the news. How do they dress? What does the background look like? How do they present the news? Is the newscast relaxed or more formal? The students then meet in news teams that the teacher has formed. Usually heterogeneous groupings of about five people work best. As a team, they decide the responsibilities that each member of the group will have—for example:

- Anchorpersons
- Weather reporter
- Traffic reporter
- "Staying Healthy" reporter

- Restaurant reviewer
- Sports reporter
- Troubleshooter for consumers
- School reporter
- Other

Teams will enjoy deciding on props that can be used and colors or attire that the anchorpeople will wear. Weather reporters might want to use sticky notes to show weather conditions in other parts of the country and world on a map.

This process will probably take about a week of class time and some at-home research and practice. Most newscasts last approximately five to ten minutes. The students enjoy creating their own name for their television station and have a logo and sometimes a slogan to represent it. All news reports will be videotaped and watched by the class, and students will fill out self-evaluation forms and also evaluate their classmates.

Open Microphone

Some teachers hold an open mike session on the last Friday of each month. Children sign up for a slot of time if they are interested in presenting a song, a musical instrument, a poem, a dance, or any other type of performance. Usually it takes a little time to get everybody warmed up for the event. Some students are just made to be on stage. They are confident of their abilities to stand in front of an audience and show what they can do. Often there are a few children who read a poem, sing a song, or put on a skit. As time passes and the students get to know each other better, the performances grow in numbers and sophistication. Students you never thought would get up in front of the class do. Some gain their support from their peers who perform alongside them, giving them the extra push and footing that they need to build their confidence. By the end of the year, everyone seems to have something to offer, no matter how short and simple it is.

Open mike can be extended to a night performance for parents to see and, if they want, participate in. Several teachers make this available for their class and families. Some of the family members present poems they have written or perform together as a family.

There is a sense of pride on the children's faces as they see their own family members getting up on the stage and performing in front of their classmates. Administrators are also invited, and refreshments are served.

Interviewing

Throughout the year, students should be given opportunities to interview another person. One that always seems successful is interviewing the oldest member of one's family. Besides offering an avenue for bridging the generation gap, it also helps students to be more compassionate and sensitive toward older people. Another idea is for students to interview a World War II survivor or a person who served in another war or lived during these wars but was not in the military. (See Activity 12.4, Interview Planning Sheet, at the end of this chapter.) Some of the most compelling reports have been written after students have interviewed a person who lived in Europe during World War II or fought in the war. We can always learn from history, and when students hear it through personal contact, it comes to life. People who lived in a military area during wartime can be interviewed about the changes they had to make in their daily lives at that time. Curfews, blackout windows, and ration books can be better understood by talking with a person who lived through the historical moment.

Students may also interview a person who has been a survivor in other circumstances, such as being lost in the mountains, being lost at sea, being in a car accident, or having a particular health issue such as diabetes, knee surgery, or cancer.

In her "survival math" project, Natalie, a fifth grader, interviewed her mother about how she used math in her everyday life and why math was important to her:

My mom and I sat down while I interviewed her. We had fun and laughed. The best part was when we thought about all the things we wouldn't have if there wasn't math. We challenged each other to think of more and more things we wouldn't have. With more time, I wonder how many more we could have come up with!?! I made notes and from these notes my mom helped me to set up a chart.

I should do my best in math at school because I want to pass fifth grade and get better math grades. In the future, I want to be a veterinarian, which means I would have a lot of school and A LOT of MATH to learn. My mom thinks that I should do my best at math because it will give me a "solid foundation" in all aspects of life!! She said that without math there would be no calendars, no clocks, no measuring cups, no rulers or tape measures, no compasses, no maps with mileages, no scales, no calculators, no computers, no birthday, no dated holidays, no money, no betting on horse races, no thermometers, no gallons of gas, no pounds, no bank account, no stock market no postage stamps, no scoring of games, no speedometers, no clothing sizes, no weather predictions, no belt sizes, no physics, and no longitude and latitude!!!!!

Math is important to my mom for the following reasons:

1. She will always cook well as long as she follows the recipe and uses correct measurements.
2. She will keep her patients healthy by giving them the correct amount of medications at the correct times.
3. She will budget her money so her family can live comfortably and allow for savings.
4. She will always be timely thanks to the clock.
5. Shopping is more fun when you understand the amount you can save at a sale!
6. The calendar allows her to be at the right place at the right time.

Puppetry

It does not matter what their age, most students like to get involved in puppet shows. Whether the puppets are commercially created or personally created by the children, oral language seems simple with a puppet in hand. Students who are hesitant to speak up in class can have a miraculous lack of stage fright when they can hide behind a puppet or a puppet theater. Even older children have fun creating impromptu scripts. When a puppet center is set up in an upper-grade classroom, students gravitate to it. Students also enjoy making their own puppets from book sharing and for a culmination activity for book clubs. Stick puppets may be created and used by older students during book club culminating activities and other book responses.

Creating Scripts from Literature and History

One way to motivate students and to bring literature alive is to write a script for a reader's theater presentation. Students read a book and then break it down into parts so that several students can present the story together. Reader's theater is different from regular theater because the words rather than the action are the important focus, but students still enjoy using simple props, costumes, and actions. The audience enjoys the little extras too because it enhances the story. The boys and girls are happy that they do not need to memorize their parts, but some of them get into character and do learn their lines.

Students adapt a fiction or nonfiction piece into a script with roles for each of the characters. They should understand that their writing is an adaptation of the real piece. This means that the play is lifted from the original text and recreated in the student's own words. The writing of a reader's theater presentation is a good assessment tool so the teacher can see if the students understood the story. Any story can be put into this format. Students usually write a narrator part and individual parts.

It is important that the writers prepare well for their presentation by reading it multiple times until they are fluent. Presenters should know their parts well so that they convey the voice of the true character and feel comfortable with the part. Practicing out loud is helpful. Dialect or a special accent can be added to voices to bring even more fun to the part. Although each child needs to practice alone, the group should meet several times to practice together to bring tightness to the presentation.

As an assessment tool, you can learn a lot about a student's reading and writing abilities. Is the reader able to lift thoughts from one text and transfer it into another format? Can the reader comprehend the text? Can the learner read and write fluently? Is the writer able to use revision strategies? Can the learner generate new ideas for writing in a creative manner? Does the student have command of his or her presentation skills?

Students can engage in this activity through the following ways:

- Write their own.
- Use commercial reader's theater scripts for both fiction and nonfiction pieces of literature and content.
- Write variations of pieces of literature that they have read in class.
- Participate during station rotation.

Instruction on how to prepare for a reader's theater presentation should be given before actual use of the reader's theater scripts. One of the problems with this used as an independent station is that the children forget about using classroom voices. It is easy to get so involved and enthusiastic in the presentation that sometimes the station may need to be withdrawn from the rotation until the difficulty is under control.

A few suggestions to review with students about reader's theater presentations are:

- Act it out.
- Make the characters come alive.
- Change your voice.
- Use expression.
- Read the whole script silently first; know the whole story before selecting your part.
- Listen to your fluency. Does it sound as if you understand the character well enough?
- Speak up so you can be heard.

Many books are available with performances related to history or genre studies. Children can also be encouraged to write their own based on history, science, or general literature. A favorite station in the classroom is reader's theater. Often during book clubs, children choose this form for their culmination activity.

Role Playing

Another form of oral language experience is that of role playing. In this form, children imagine themselves as a historical or fictionalized character or in a different role such as a reporter or a senior citizen looking in on the situation. The acting out of a scene is usually done impromptu and allows children a chance to show what they know through drama and creativity. Many opportunities for allowing students to show what they know through acting can be offered during the week. Some students are more adept at using the drama form to show their understanding, but others can be nudged to this possibility.

In the book *Sounder* (Armstrong, 1970), children can take the parts of the mother, father, and boy as the father is being taken away to jail for stealing. In *Hatchet* (Paulsen, 1987), the students can take turns role-playing the pilot and Brian talking as they are flying at the beginning of the book. In *The Cay* (Taylor, 1969) one student may take the part of Phillip and one the part of Timothy as they first meet each other on the raft. In *The Great Gilly Hopkins* (Paterson, 1978) one child can become Gilly and another person can become the social worker or Mrs. Trotter. In *Because of Winn Dixie* (DiCamillo, 2000), two students can take on the roles of Opal and her father, the preacher, talking about keeping the dog. There are endless possibilities for children to show dramatically what they know in a cooperative setting. Because this dramatic presentation takes time, you need to look carefully at your schedule and incorporate longer sessions.

Telephone Role Playing

You can provide practice opportunities for telephone skills simulating different situations such as making reservations, requesting information, and setting up appointments. Discuss the importance of telephone etiquette and speaking clearly and politely. Assignments requiring students to use the telephone are helpful. (See the Survival Math Packet, Activity 14.14 in Chapter 14, for some suggestions of real-life purposes for using the telephone to obtain information.)

Hot Seat

This activity requires fully understanding a character in a book. After reading a chapter or an entire book, the students are asked to create three to five questions to ask the main characters about things they did in the story or about their actions or ways they treated other people. One person sits on the "hot seat" and becomes the character answering classmates' questions. All responses are in the first-person point of view. Students take turns becoming the character and responding to the questions. The lead-in lesson for this activity is how to create broad types of questions that cannot be answered in one or two words. The purpose of this activity is to check students' understanding of the main points in a story. Everyone loves this way of showing understanding of a book without having to write a summary. It is quick, fast-paced, and fun.

Hot seat can be done first as a whole class, but as everyone becomes more comfortable in the method, you might want to break the class into smaller groups. This is also a favorite idea for culminating activities for book clubs.

Asking Questions

Another way to get children talking is to ask questions that are fun to think about and play with and can ignite discussion in school and at home. *The Kids' Book of Questions* (Stock, 2004) is a perfect source for initiating conversation in your classroom. There are questions that children have thought about but possibly have never answered aloud. This book can be used with the whole class, at a literacy station, or in a small group setting with students who have difficulty participating in class discussions. In a small group setting, everyone has a comfortable place to express his or her thoughts without being intimidated. It is particularly helpful for second-language learners.

The following questions are representative of the 268 questions found in *The Kids' Book of Questions*:

211. After being given a truth pill, you are asked to describe each person in our family. What do you say? [back cover]
197. If you could e-mail any famous person and be sure they'd read and answer your note, whom would you write to and what would you say? [back cover]
108. If you knew you wouldn't get caught, would you cheat on a test by copying someone's answers? What would you think if you saw other people cheating? [back cover]

Some teachers use one of these questions every day to get the morning started. Students may talk with partners, or in groups of three or four. The rule is that everyone must contribute something to the conversation. Once the children have several days of practice, they are free in their discussions. Some personal questions are left until later in the year when everyone is more relaxed and more open in sharing their thoughts. Some questions may be too personal, so careful selection is suggested or students may pass if the question is uncomfortable for them or is inappropriate in any way. This book can also act as a springboard for students in writing their own questions. Possibly these questions could be placed in a box, and students could answer them when they are finished with an assignment or in their free time.

Often there are groups of students who like to share their conversations with the whole class. To get this activity started, a fish bowl method is used: all the students form a circle around another group of students and listen to the conversation. Through listening and watching, others can go off into their own small groups to continue the discussion.

The book can also be used by families at home at the dinner table to spur conversation or on trips in the car to make the time pass more quickly. Everyone in the family can identify a question that he or she would like to ask, and lively, interesting, or deep conversation can ensue.

Teaching Games

As the year progresses, students become more comfortable with orally presenting to others than their classmates. For instance, at one school, a multicultural fair was held in the spring. To combine multiculturalism and math strategy, Kathy Aufsesser, a fourth-grade teacher, brought her collection of multicultural games to share with the class. After she shared some of the history of each game, the students played the games. As an extension of this lesson, students were asked to share the games with their kindergarten buddies. Each child was asked to:

- Select a game he or she wanted to teach.
- Read the instructions carefully and figure out the correct rules.
- Present the game to another group of upper graders.
- Teach the game to their "buddies."

Students were given time in class to prepare. Oral language became important because the students now became the experts. They had to share their knowledge and make sure that they explained the rules correctly and that the rules were followed.

This school was fortunate to have many multicultural games from which to choose, thanks to a special teacher. When this is not the case, teachers can use games that the children are somewhat familiar with already (Monopoly, checkers, chess, Connect Four, and Uno, for example). Students explain the rules and make sure that all their classmates in the group follow them.

Games can also be set up on a rotation basis. Five games could be set up on one day, and the students in charge of teaching the games would have several groups rotate into their game. Then on choice game day, the students would have been exposed to five games.

Game days are enjoyable for all students because they are a break from the routine of the regular curriculum. Because they use mathematical strategies, once a month a game day could be set up in the classroom, similar to a math lab. Students could choose from the games they have been exposed to. When this less formal kind of oral interaction takes place, the teacher sees the children in a different light. Students who are reluctant to speak in class may open up in small groups and actively engage in conversation with their peers. More inhibited oral language students see this experience as less intimidating. Students who normally do not interact with one another now find a common need to converse in an informal, relaxed manner. (See Activity 12.5, Game Day Activity, at the end of this chapter.)

Science Experiments

As part of the assigned oral language for the year, science can be introduced. Model a simple science experiment in the classroom. (Students should be pulled up closer to the center of instruction because science experiments need to be closely observed.) Because students enjoy watching science experiments, almost everyone wants to have a front-row seat; therefore, we discuss the fifty dollar, twenty-five dollar, and ten dollar seats. Students earn the privilege of sitting in the fifty dollar seats by having exceptional behavior before the experiment is presented. Of course, the ten dollar seats are in the back row and students also "earn" those. By providing this challenge for the students, we make science experimentation a special period.

Students are asked to present a simple science experiment. Many books of experiments are nestled in the science experiment book tub. Students can also locate other books and choose their experiment from those. Books like *Homemade Slime and Rubber Bones* (Wellnitz, 1993), *Amazing Science Experiments with Everyday Materials* (Churchill, 1992,) and *Simple Science Experiments with Everyday Materials* (Mandell, 1990) are excellent sources to motivate students to become involved in child-centered, fun experiments. (See Activity 12.6, Science Experiment Planning Sheet: Oral Presentation, at the end of this chapter.) Additional science sources can be located in Chapter Thirteen.

Commercials

Students love to create their own commercials, which gives them an opportunity to be creative and dramatic at the same time. Because there is usually a product involved, they have a visual aide to help them throughout the presentation. Students may try to "sell" a book that they liked or they may take a product that they have at home that has been useful and try to "sell" it to their classmates. These two kinds of guided activities help students focus in on techniques to be used in promoting a product such as repetition, bandwagon, testimonial, emotional words, and other propaganda techniques. Once the students have tried out their presentation skills, they are ready to create their own products. A good starting point for commercial presentations would be to have the students preview several commercials at home. If this is not possible for most of the students, the teacher can tape a few commercials and bring them in for the class to preview and talk about together. Commercials can be given in partners or alone, with all students videotaped and then evaluated. (The commercials during the Super Bowl are the most extraordinary. See the Super Bowl Math Activity Packet, Activity 14.12, at the end of Chapter Fourteen.)

Book Talks

A book talk is like an advertisement: it is short and concise. Everything must be stated in a minute or two. If it goes on longer than that, the others become restless and inattentive. Teacher modeling of a book talk is essential so that everyone knows the expectations. A good book talk might involve:

- Talking about the title, the author, and the importance of the cover
- Giving a brief summary of the book without giving away the details or ending
- Relating this book to others the class is familiar with
- Reading a portion of the book that is interesting, funny, or exciting so that others get a sense of the book
- Sharing a bit about the main character or a main event that was engaging
- Sharing your feelings and opinions about the book and why someone else would like to read it

Book talks can go on all year long. In order to prepare for one, children can use sticky notes to write down a few brief notes to guide their thoughts, but they should be discouraged from writing a formal report to read from. A book talk should be informal but organized. Keeping track of students who volunteer for book talks is important. All students should have a chance to participate in this experience. Children who are apprehensive about sharing might be paired up with a stronger orator who will take the lead in the partnership. Another way to support reluctant speakers is for you to take the lead and partner up with one of them. This gives them the feeling that their teacher is at their side and available for support. Gradually all students should be able to participate independently.

Conferring with Students

Teachers can learn a lot about a child's oral language skills by sitting down with him or her on an individual basis during a reading, writing, or portfolio conference. On a one-to-one basis, children talk more freely and seem to be less inhibited. For instance, during a reading conference, a teacher or other adult can informally evaluate how well a child has read a book that he or she has chosen. Basic questions such as, "How's your reading going?" or a statement such as, "Tell me about your reading," can draw students into conversation.

Since children talk differently to other children than to an adult, it is also a good idea to allow students to conference with their peers. Reading and writing conferences can be set up in peer partners. The same basic questions can be used with partners as with the teacher.

Conferences for portfolio selections are good opportunities for a teacher to listen to a child's oral language skill. Providing experiences where a child is verbally relaying reasons for choosing selections for a portfolio adds reflective insight into a child's ability to organize and evaluate his or her own work.

Speech of the Month

At the end of this chapter in Activity 12.2 you will find a list of types of speeches that you might involve your children in. Over time, students will begin to feel comfortable in establishing themselves as a speaker. For students who are reluctant to stand up in front of an audience, you might need to let them give their presentation to you personally instead of in front of the whole class. Sometimes teachers allow reluctant speakers to come in during recess or lunch to give their performance without their classmates present. Other teachers allow the reluctant speakers to choose two or three friends to be their audience. We must be cognizant of the fear that some students have in expressing themselves in front of a large group. Accommodations need to be made to ensure that all students are comfortable in their speaking abilities.

After-School Speakers' Club or Drama Club

In some schools, a teacher becomes the sponsor of a speakers' club or a drama club. Identifying students who would benefit and enjoy a club setting to experiment with oral language activities will build confidence and poise in students. Both of these clubs would be beneficial to the school and provide an enjoyable path to communication. Having guest visitors to assist in the process will liven up the club. If you know of a contact member of a local Toastmasters Club or a drama club from the local high school, college, or university, possibly you can set up a partnership that would be advantageous to both the school and the organization. These students may be able to earn volunteer hours by assisting you. Using the many resources in the community will help build confidence and bring intrinsic rewards to both the participants and the volunteers, as well as add a new element of knowledge and instruction.

The Art of Storytelling

Storytelling is a powerful means of communication—a gift that more and more teachers are recognizing the need for and learning how to bring into the classroom. Few other activities can captivate an audience of any size or age as completely as the oral telling (not reading) of a good story. Catherine Farrell (1987) describes what happens in a storytelling session: "Time seems to stop. The teller creates an environment free from distractions, maintains continuous eye contact and speaks directly to the listeners. The images from the story appear to hang in the air, and the silence in the classroom deepens. All the students become engrossed in the shared experience of literature. The heightened attention to a literary work created by storytelling has many teaching possibilities. . . . As teachers discover the compelling nature of storytelling as a teaching method, they will be greatly rewarded for their efforts."

Many children have never heard a story told in the oral tradition. The benefits of storytelling to students are numerous. It promotes good attention and inner concentration, and invites active involvement. It encourages visualization and the active use of imagination. It develops children's sense of story and listening skills. It is an excellent vehicle for motivating students, particularly distractible, harder-to-reach students. It has been our experience that even the most inattentive, distractible child is quiet and captivated while listening a good, short story. What a wonderful gift to our students if every teacher learned one or two stories, and slowly over the years developed his or her repertoire of stories that can be shared in the classroom and as a visiting storyteller to other classes in the school as well.

There are several ways to learn a story. Many storytellers recommend the following:

1. Select a story. A picture book of a folk tale that appeals to you may be a good place to start, or choose a short story from an anthology.
2. Read the story several times.
3. Block the story out by drawing the main points or making a graphic organizer such as a flowchart or story map to depict the scenes and sequence of events. Then visualize each sensory detail, watching like a silent movie the scenes unfold.
4. Read the story aloud, and keep practicing until you feel confident that you know it.

It is not recommended to try learning the story word by word. Some storytellers make an outline and list the main events in order.

We have had the good fortune of taking classes on storytelling offered at one of our local universities and having the pleasure and privilege of hearing many outstanding professional storytellers from around the country perform and share their craft. Here are some of their strategies for learning a story to tell.

One storyteller, a multisensory learner, tape-records herself reading the story and plays it back several times. To make the story her own, she first flushes out the story line in a few sentences. Then she draws the action on butcher paper to get a sense of the story's flow. She draws cartoons to help herself visualize the story, so that if in the telling she forgets where she is, she can picture the scenes. She then takes the script, which she has typed out, and highlights some of the language in different colors to help her remember what she wants to include in the telling (for example, yellow for descriptive vocabulary, blue for action words). As Milbre Burch shared, "If the story is good enough to learn, it's good enough to do your homework on."

Storyteller Carol Birch recommends picking stories you like but cautions not to memorize them—just tell them in the order of the pictures you see, and be sure to amplify the humor or pathos of the characters when telling the story.

Gay Ducey, a historical storyteller, says that powerful historical storytelling begins with a story from history that fires you and the interest to want to tell it. We can teach the vital life force of what history is. As the storyteller, you are an emissary of the time period or person. She recommends picking a story from your favorite historical period and telling it through the lens of a narrowed theme such as one family, which will give the story more intimacy. Choose a point of view and a voice. Ducey recommends finding the underrepresented events in history. Fascinating historical stories can be found in magazines, newspapers, travel guides, and numerous sources.

Teachers need to be willing to take the risk of trying their hand at storytelling. It is risky to perform in front of an audience, yet a good teacher does so all the time—catching the interest of students and reeling them in. We highly recommend giving it a try. Once you have experienced it, it becomes much easier each successive time the story is told. Your students will be appreciative of your efforts, and it is so very rewarding.

Children as well should be given the opportunity to tell stories to their peers. Upper-grade students can be taught to apply the same recommended techniques to learn a simple story to tell and should be allowed to perform to a small group if they are not comfortable telling their story to the whole class. Teachers should model storytelling to students before asking students to take the risk.

An easier way to elicit informal oral sharing of personal stories is to have students work in cooperative groups. In sharing sessions throughout the week, provide prompts to the students to trigger sharing personal experiences—for example, "Can you remember a time you were ever locked out of your house or somewhere else?" "Can you remember a funny incident with a pet?" "Have any of you ever been in a car that ran out of gas or broke down on the road somewhere?" "Have you ever lost something that didn't belong to you?" "Tell about a visit from a relative to your house."

In telling sessions with prompts such as these, not everyone will be able to share a story, but it is equally as beneficial to hear a story as to tell one. Some children are so bashful or uncomfortable sharing in even a small group that after listening to the students in small group, they may wish to orally share with a partner instead of the group. By first sharing and listening to others share stories, students are better able to transfer their stories into written form. Donald Davis, a professional storyteller, recommends this technique as an important step in helping students learn to write stories. Students briefly write down some of the stories they shared in small group (story starts) and save them. After they have collected a few, they are asked to select one to work on writing into story form. Davis suggests telling students as they are writing to "fatten up" their written stories with the necessary words to recapture the story they told.

ASSESSING ORAL LANGUAGE

Because of the complexity of oral language assessment, teachers should look for direction from their own school district's standards. In some districts, children are evaluated as beginning, developing, or independent learners in the area of listening and speaking. The California State Standards for listening and speaking call for fifth graders to:

- Deliver focused, coherent presentations that convey ideas clearly and relate to the background and interests of the audience. They evaluate the content of oral communication.
- Ask questions that seek information not already discussed.
- Interpret a speaker's verbal and nonverbal messages, purposes, and perspectives.
- Make inferences or draw conclusions based on an oral report.
- Select a focus, organizational structure, and point of view for an oral presentation.
- Clarify and support spoken ideas with evidence and examples.
- Engage the audience with a appropriate verbal cues, facial expressions, and gestures.
- Identify, analyze, and critique persuasive techniques; identify logical fallacies used in oral presentation and media messages.
- Analyze media as sources for information, entertainment, persuasion, interpretation of events, and transmission of culture [p. 132].

The domains of speaking and listening must be threaded throughout the day and connected with the domains of reading and writing. Through modeling different kinds of oral language presentations, including one-on-one conferences, pair-share opportunities, small group conversations, whole group discussions, and book clubs, students see clear examples of the types of presentations.

Because oral language is somewhat difficult to evaluate in a formal manner, teachers must assess children more informally through observation and by taking anecdotal records as the process unfolds. There are several detailed continuums that address oral language skills. Because speaking/listening is only one area of the language arts program, it is somewhat difficult to assess every child on all the areas at the same time. Some teachers start with a small target group of students, such as their second-language learners or children whom they have concerns with, and assess the full spectrum of skills at each report card period. Other teachers assess each child on a limited basis using only a few skills on the continuum. Choice of formal assessment is sometimes dictated by an administrator or school district.

Students should be involved in the process of evaluation. Through the use of the video camera or tape recorder, students can listen to themselves and see how they compare to the others. Peer evaluation of oral presentation is also helpful. When students see good modeling, they can build their own oral language skills and grow as successful oral communicators. In all aspects of oral language, students should use self-evaluation, peer evaluation, and teacher evaluation. Including the parents in evaluation is also important. Possibly sending a parent evaluation form while a child is practicing for a monthly oral language presentation would be beneficial. We should strive to bring parents into the evaluation process. (See Activities 12.7 and 12.8 Oral Language Teacher Evaluation and Oral Language Peer Evaluation, at the end of this chapter.)

REFERENCES

Armstrong, W. (1969). *Sounder.* New York: Scholastic.

Churchill, E. R. (1992). *Amazing science experiments with everyday materials.* New York: Sterling Publishing.

DiCamillo, K. (2000). *Because of Winn-Dixie.* Cambridge, MA: Candlewick Press.

Farrell, C. (1987). *Word weaving: A guide to storytelling.* San Francisco: Word Weaving.

Five easy-to-read plays based on classic stories. (1999). New York: Scholastic.

Fleischman, P. (1985). *I am Phoenix.* New York: HarperCollins.

Fleischman, P. (1988). *Joyful noise.* New York: HarperCollins.

Famous Americans: 22 short plays for the classroom (gr. 4–8). (1994). New York: Scholastic.

Kemper, D., Nathan, R., & Sebranek, P. (1994). *Writers express: A handbook for young writers, thinkers, and learners.* Willingham, MA: Great Source Education Group.

Mandell, M. (1990). *Simple science experiments with everyday materials.* New York: Sterling Publishing.

Paterson, K. (1978). *The great Gilly Hopkins.* New York: Dell.

Paulsen, G. (1987). *Hatchet.* New York: Puffin Books.

Stock, G. (2004). *The kids' book of questions.* New York: Workman Publishing.

Taylor, T. (1969). *The cay.* New York: Avon Books.

Wellnitz, W. R. (1993). *Homemade slime and rubber bones.* New York: Tab Books.

TEACHER RESOURCES

Chambers, A. (1995). *Booktalk: Occasional writing on literature and children.* Stroud, UK: Thimble Press.

Chambers, A. (1996). *Tell me: Children, reading, and talk.* Portland, ME: Stenhouse Publishers.

Cranston, J. W. (1991). *Transformations through drama: A teacher's guide to educational drama, K–8.* Lanham, MD: University Press of America.

Cresci, M. M. (1989). *Creative dramatics for children.* Glenview, IL: Scott, Foresman.

California State Department of Education. (Ed.). *Recommended literature, grades nine through twelve.* Sacramento, CA: Author.

Five easy-to-read plays based on classic stories. (1999). New York: Scholastic.

Fountas, I., & Pinnell, G. S. (2001). *Guiding readers and writers, grades 3–6.* Portsmouth, NH: Heinemann.

Juskow, B. (1991). *Speakers' club.* San Luis Obispo, CA: Dandy Lion Publications.

Reading for life: The learner as a reader. (1996). Wellington, NZ: Learning Media.

Reeves, R., Swinburne, L., & Warner, J. (1998). *Readers' theater.* New York: Steck-Vaughn.

Routman, R. (1991). *Invitations.* Portsmouth, NH: Heinemann.

Sylvester, D. (2003). *Current events: Contemporary issues for classroom debates, discussion, and writing.* Santa Barbara, CA: Learning Works.

West, T. (2001). *Twenty terrific mini-plays that build reading skills.* New York: Scholastic.

Willhelm, J. D. (2002). *Action strategies for deepening comprehension.* New York: Scholastic.

Wolf, J. M. (2002). *Cinderella outgrows the glass slipper and other zany fractured fairy tale plays.* New York: Scholastic.

Wolf, S. (1993). What's in a name? Labels and literacy in readers' theater. *Reading Teacher, 46*(7), 540–545.

Writers Inc. (1996). *School to work.* Lexington, MA: Heath.

Young, T., & Vardelk, S. (1993). Weaving readers' theater and nonfiction into the curriculum. *Reading Teacher, 45*(5), 396–406.

Activity 12.1

SPEECH PLAN SHEET

Presenter: _____ Date: _____

Title of presentation: _____

Materials and equipment I will need:

1. _____

2. _____

3. _____

Outline of my topic:

1. _____

2. _____

3. _____

4. _____

5. _____

6. _____

Answer the following questions:

1. I practiced my speech about _____ times.

2. I practiced my speech with _____.

3. I feel prepared for my speech. Yes _____ No _____

4. I could do better by _____

5. I really feel I have done my best. Yes _____ No _____

6. I deserve a (an) _____ on this speech because,

_____

_____

_____

Activity 12.2
ORAL LANGUAGE MONTHLY PRESENTATIONS

Month	Presentation Type
September	Magazine article: 1 minute, alone
October	Hobby or special interest: 1 to 2 minutes, alone
November	Mystery person, place, or thing: 3 to 5 minutes, alone or pairs
December	Teach a game: 5 to 10 minutes, cooperative groups
January	Biography book report: 2 to 3 minutes, alone
February	Demonstration speech: 3 to 5 minutes, alone
March	Science experiment: 3 to 5 minutes, alone or pairs
April	News team: 5 to 10 minutes, team project
May	Persuasive speech: 3 to 5 minutes, partner debate or alone
June	Poetry: Memorization, 1 to 2 minutes

AN ORAL LANGUAGE PRESENTATION: A HOW-TO-DO SPEECH

For the month of _____

What to Do

You are to become an instructor. You are to choose a subject that you are truly interested in. Remember the KIS rule (Keep It Simple). You will be expected to speak for 1 to 3 minutes. You may use an outline while you are in front of the class, but do not write things out word for word.

Here are a few examples to get you started thinking:

- How to French-braid hair
- How to set up a two-person tent
- How to apply makeup
- How to draw a person's face
- How to make an origami frog
- How to throw a football correctly
- How to draw a cartoon character
- How to eat an Oreo cookie
- How to make finger Jello
- How to make the basic knots with rope

These are just a few suggestions, and knowing your talent, I'm sure you've got many more ideas. For more suggestions, ask your family for help. They would like to get involved.

Requirements

1. Hand in your plan sheet to have it approved by the teacher.
2. Gather your materials together, and come prepared on your assigned day.
3. Practice your speech at home.
4. Speak for 1 to 3 minutes. (You may request extra time before your presentation.) You will be timed.
5. You must have a visual aid.
6. You may have an assistant, but you must do your own speech.

AN ORAL LANGUAGE PRESENTATION:
A HOW-TO-DO SPEECH *(continued)*

Grading

You will be evaluated on the following:

- Your visual aid
- Eye contact
- Evident preparation
- Speed of your delivery
- Loudness of your voice
- Enthusiasm
- Content and information
- Posture and poise

There will be a sign-up on the door for your presentation date and time. Sign up early. It's easier to get it over with and not have to worry.

INTERVIEW PLANNING SHEET

Sometimes when you do research, you will want to get a more personal look at your subject. For instance, if you are trying to find out something about World War II, you might find out a lot by reading a book or an article in a magazine or online. For a more personal touch, you might want to interview a person who lived during that period of time.

A good interview takes some thinking. Because you do not want to waste your subject's time, you should always be prepared before you do the interview.

Try to think of some meaningful questions that bring out the best in the person you are interviewing. These questions should make your subject feel comfortable. Make sure the questions are appropriate and show sensitivity. When you are finished with the interview, thank the person for helping you.

Interviewer's Name: _____ Date of interview: _____

Person being interviewed: _____ Place of interview: _____

How you know this person _____

Question 1: _____

_____

Answer: _____

_____

_____

_____

Question 2: _____

_____

Answer: _____

_____

_____

_____

INTERVIEW PLANNING SHEET *(continued)*

Question 3: _____

_____

Answer: _____

_____

_____

_____

Question 4: _____

_____

Answer: _____

_____

_____

_____

Question 5: _____

_____

Answer: _____

_____

_____

_____

Activity 12.5
GAME DAY ACTIVITY

Scheduled day: _____

In the next few weeks, you will be asked to sign up to explain a game to a small group of your classmates. You may select a game that you already know or one that you would like to learn.

Here is what you need to do:

- On your scheduled day, you will need to be the "expert" on your game.

- The game that you choose should be simple enough to explain in approximately ten minutes.

- You must obtain the game from home, a friend, a neighbor, or a relative. You can also borrow one from our game center.

- You must carefully read the game rules and possibly even highlight the most important rules.

- You should play the game *before* you present the game to your classmates. This will assure yourself of being prepared if your group has questions.

- On Game Day, you will present your game two times. Two different groups of your classmates will rotate into your game teaching session. You will be the teacher.

- Learn your game well, practice, and be prepared.

Name of the game you have chosen: _____

SCIENCE EXPERIMENT PLANNING SHEET: ORAL PRESENTATION

Names of students: _____

Briefly describe your experiment: _____

_____

_____

_____

What will your question be? _____

_____

Hypotheses: Predict what you think will happen.

I think that _____

_____

_____

Procedure:

Step 1: _____

Step 2: _____

Step 3: _____

Step 4: _____

Step 5: _____

Scientific principle behind the experiment: _____

_____

Materials needed: _____

_____

Conclusions (Findings): _____

_____

_____

ORAL LANGUAGE TEACHER EVALUATION

Presenter's name: _____

Evaluator: _____

Evaluate with a +, √, or −:

Time taken: _____

Visual aid: _____

Eye contact: _____

Evident preparation: _____

Speed of delivery: _____

Loudness of voice: _____

Enthusiasm for subject: _____

Content: _____

Posture/poise: _____

Comments: _____

_____

_____

Note: Preceding the presentations, the class should discuss how the presentations are to be evaluated. A list of positive comments and constructive suggestions can be formulated by the students, so that negative comments do not become overwhelming. At least five classmates should evaluate the presenter using the peer evaluation sheet on page 274, along with the teacher. After the presentation, the evaluators' copies are given to the presenter.

ORAL LANGUAGE PEER EVALUATION

Presenter's name: _____

Evaluator: _____

Time taken: _____

Evaluate with a +, √, or −:

Visual aid: _____

Eye contact: _____

Evident preparation: _____

Speed of delivery: _____

Loudness of voice: _____

Enthusiasm for subject: _____

Content: _____

Posture/poise: _____

Comments:_____

_____

_____

Presenter's name: _____

Evaluator: _____

Time taken: _____

Evaluate with a +, √, or −:

Visual aid: _____

Eye contact: _____

Evident preparation: _____

Speed of delivery: _____

Loudness of voice: _____

Enthusiasm for subject: _____

Content: _____

Posture/poise: _____

Comments:_____

_____

_____

Presenter's name: _____

Evaluator: _____

Time taken: _____

Evaluate with a +, √, or −:

Visual aid: _____

Eye contact: _____

Evident preparation: _____

Speed of delivery: _____

Loudness of voice: _____

Enthusiasm for subject: _____

Content: _____

Posture/poise: _____

Comments:_____

_____

_____

Presenter's name: _____

Evaluator: _____

Time taken: _____

Evaluate with a +, √, or −:

Visual aid: _____

Eye contact: _____

Evident preparation: _____

Speed of delivery: _____

Loudness of voice: _____

Enthusiasm for subject: _____

Content: _____

Posture/poise: _____

Comments:_____

_____

_____

Chapter 13

REVVIN' UP THE CONTENT AREAS

Since the original version of this book was written in 1996, a lot has happened to open up the world of nonfiction, informational, and expository texts within classrooms. Those of us who had begun our journey of expanding our classroom libraries were feeling a little smug with all those books that students could get their hands on easily. It was amazing to find out that the vast majority of *my* [Julie's] books were fiction. I was drawn to fiction, so shouldn't it be that all of students would be drawn to it too? Thinking back over the years, it wasn't just that I liked fiction; in fact, there was a limited selection of good books available for classroom libraries that supported nonfiction. Besides, I had a textbook for social studies, science, and health, as well as a weekly student newspaper and the local newspaper. That just about said it all—that's the way I taught it, and that's the way almost everyone else taught nonfiction. What could I have been thinking?

In these ten years, the nonfiction portion of our state testing has increased. Children are expected to know how to read a variety of informational texts in various formats.

Looking through the California state-adopted anthology (Houghton-Mifflin, 2003), the statistics were astonishing. Out of the main stories in fourth grade, one-third of the selections were nonfiction; in fifth grade, the nonfiction selections rose to two-thirds. Increasing numbers of nonfiction selections are also found in middle school texts, as well as in standardized testing. So just as math reform has taken us into a new arena, we must ratchet up our understanding of how nonfiction works and ensure that students understand it well enough to navigate through the complexity of the information.

According to Pearson Education (www.pearsonlearning.com), about 80 percent of everything that we read as adults is nonfiction. Nonfiction permeates our adult lives through such sources as directions, maps, teacher guides, cookbooks, television guides, magazines, computer directions, the newspaper, bulletins from myriad places, notices, e-mails, and junk mail.

The initiation of a unit on nonfiction is begun in the same manner as a unit on fiction. The process entails read-aloud, shared, guided, and independent reading; accountable talk; and rich, deep conversations about the reading. There is no isolation between the reading and writing of nonfiction. The two blend together.

NONFICTION: WE'RE ALL IN THIS TOGETHER

Love of information is already built into young children by the time they enter kindergarten. They come to school curious about the world around them, with questions about everything for which they want answers. The only thing holding them back is their inability to read.

Therefore, it is essential that parents and primary teachers make nonfiction a priority and incorporate it in their young children's lives. This will ensure that there is scaffolding already in place so that upper grade and middle school students feel more comfortable navigating through more complex informational texts.

In the *Reading/Language Arts Framework for California Public Schools Kindergarten Through Grade Twelve* (California Department of Education, 1999) for reading, writing, listening, and speaking, nonfiction instruction is called out starting as early as kindergarten. Some of the grade 3 to 8 California reading standards are listed here:

Grade 3: Use title, tables of contents, chapter headings, glossaries, and indexes to locate information in text [p. 92].

Grade 4: Identify structural patterns found in informational text (for example, compare and contrast, cause and effect, sequential or chronological order, proposition and support) to strengthen comprehension [p. 114].

Grade 5: Understand how text features (for example, format, graphics, sequence, diagrams, illustration, charts, maps) make information accessible and usable. Analyze text that is organized in sequential or chronological order. (Write research reports and persuasive letters in writing.) [p. 129].

Grade 6: Identify the structural features of popular media (such as newspapers, magazines, online information) and use the features to obtain information [p. 146].

Grade 7: Understand and analyze the differences in structure and purpose between various categories of informational materials (for example, textbooks, newspapers, instructional manuals, signs). Locate information by using a variety of consumer, workplace, and public documents. Analyze text that uses the cause-and-effect organizational pattern [p. 161].

Grade 8: Compare and contrast the features and elements of consumer materials to gain meaning from documents (for example, warranties, contracts, product information, instruction manuals). Analyze text that uses proposition and support patterns [p. 176].

From these standards, the importance of setting priorities for instruction in reading is clear, as is the awareness that with the reading comes the transfer of the learning into the writing. Expository writing standards must also be addressed in all grades.

Since each grade level has standards to meet, everyone needs to do his or her part. Just because a particular standard is called out at one grade level does not mean that the standard is taught only at that level; it can be introduced earlier. It would be disappointing for a fifth-grade teacher to be solely responsible for teaching persuasive texts. It is the responsibility of the primary and intermediate grades to find some persuasive texts in fiction and nonfiction that implant that word *persuade* into the child's head.

What Is Nonfiction?

Nonfiction gives real information about the world around us. It comes in many forms (essays, letters, diaries, and picture books, to name a few), but its purpose is always to describe, inform, or persuade. By giving us facts, ideas, and principles, an author can explain difficult and complex concepts. Nonfiction may look confusing to novice readers because it looks different from what they are already familiar with: narrative. For instance, there are real pictures or photographs, headings, captions, bold print, colored print, diagrams, tables, charts, graphs, as well as many other special features. Teaching students how to read nonfiction is critical for the reading-to-learn stage of older children. Nonfiction must be documented. The information must be verifiable from other sources and accurate (Fountas & Pinnell, 2001).

Nonfiction Is Important

The world around us is filled with lots of information, and curiosity about these things starts early in life. Little children are always asking questions about the physical world and asking why things happen. For young children, nonfiction helps them understand their physical world better. Answers to their questions can be found in books. Older students can find answers to more complex questions and gain a better understanding of the content in textbooks, encyclopedias, and magazine articles. Knowing how to read nonfiction can also help children perform better on tests. In the upper grades, students have developed hobbies and passions that they strive to find out more about. Once a child learns that the pursuit of information can be discovered through inquiry into the subject in nonfiction sources, the world opens up for him or her and satisfies the thirst for knowledge.

For some children, nonfiction has always been their favorite genre, but teachers have not been equipped with the basics to support their needs. Research indicates that boys are more inclined to read informational texts, magazines, and newspaper articles; that they like to read about hobbies, sports, and things they might do or be interested in doing; and that they read less fiction than girls do (Smith & Wilhelm, 2002). Keeping a balance in our classroom libraries and in our instructional practices can cater to all of our special populations.

The inclusive classroom must have a large variety of different levels of materials to meet the challenges of the students' needs. All classrooms need to provide multiple entry points into the content material that the standards address. The students cannot be expected to rely on a textbook as their main source of information. They need supplementary materials and scaffolding or strategies that support building their own understanding. For high achievers or gifted and talented students, supplemental materials must open up and expand their inquisitiveness at a more sophisticated level. The textbook for them is limiting and provides only a glimpse into subject matter.

Teacher Modeling and Instruction

Reading nonfiction takes a different form from reading narrative texts. Children who fly through narrative pieces with ease sometimes hit a wall in informational texts. The skills and strategies that are used do not necessarily transfer from one genre to the other. There are new features, structures, and vocabulary that can cause a stumbling block for older students and cause confusion, frustration, and even a sense of despair. It is important that teachers model how to read nonfiction, and to do this, they must know themselves what they do as readers before trying to teach students. Understanding information in texts may be learned only, or learned best, through teacher and peer modeling and plenty of practice with decreasing amounts of scaffolding (Armbuster, Anderson, Armstrong, Wise, Janisch, & Meyer, 1999).

As in narrative, teachers should use excellent nonfiction to demonstrate to students what quality informational texts look and sound like. Certain authors have established themselves as masters of their craft and can be used as mentors who may be referred to over and over again throughout the year. Students should know the craft of these authors; through reading and listening to their writing. They can mimic or demonstrate this craft in their own writing. In other words, they borrow ideas and incorporate them into their own writing craft, hence becoming stronger writers themselves. Teachers can begin to build their own nonfiction collection of grade-level titles by looking carefully at their state standards, perusing catalogues and spending time in bookstores and libraries, and working collaboratively with their grade-level colleagues in the selection process.

Types of Expository Texts

Children need to be exposed to a variety of forms in nonfiction. Learning Media (1998) suggests the following:

Letters	Diaries
Advertising and propaganda	Descriptions
Explanations	Instructions
Tables	Forms
Reports	Notices and signs
Catalogues and directories	

There are many entry points for introducing nonfiction in the classroom. Much of what you need is already there or easy to obtain through your resources. Make sure that you have a large variety of material to hook in both reluctant readers and gifted and talented students, and everyone in between:

- *Anthologies.* Many states have adopted an anthology, which is a collection of numerous readings covering poetry, short stories, excerpts, and complete works of fiction and nonfiction. In the California state-mandated anthology for fourth grade, there were twenty-one featured works, with about one-third of the content nonfiction (three nonfiction, two historical fiction, and three biographies).
- *Biographies and autobiographies.* These factual accounts of famous persons' lives are enjoyable to most children. They find pleasure in reading about interesting people and getting to know them in a personal way. There are many levels of biographies that can be accessed by every ability and interest group of students. The sequential structure of this form is predictable and easy to understand for even our most challenged readers. See Activity 13.1, A Biographical Journey, at the end of this chapter.
- *Trade books.* These books are usually found in bookstores and libraries and are produced for the popular market. There is an abundance of these in nonfiction.
- *Picture books.* Picture books combine small amounts of text with illustration. There are many excellent nonfiction picture books for older readers, many of which act as excellent models for meeting social studies and science standards. Picture books can play a significant role in getting across content to reluctant readers.
- *Newspapers.* These can be very beneficial for small group work and are relatively low cost. Local papers often participate in the Newspapers in Education program that bring newspapers into the classroom for no charge.
- *Magazines.* Articles in magazines such as *Time for Kids* and *Weekly Reader* tend to be short, concise, and student friendly, with a high-interest level that can hook in challenged readers. There are usually personal interest stories that tap children's interest and those that stimulate ideas for their own writing for reluctant writers. Teachers may ask parents for a yearly subscription for the class or may obtain money for magazines through their PTA, school foundation, principal, or other sources.
- *Real-life functional texts.* School bulletins, bus and trolley schedules, nutrition guides from fast food restaurants, schedules for the students' soccer and dance performances, recipes, and instructions for playing games are just a few real-life documents that are useful and practical ideas for introducing children to nonfiction.
- *Digital sources.* Technology is changing rapidly and bringing students closer to possibilities for nonfiction access. Student use of the Internet and availability of CD-ROMs and DVDs opens up new avenues of updated research possibilities.
- *Big books.* Although there is a limited supply of big books for older children, they can be powerful tools during shared reading. Three nonfiction big books that children have been exposed to in the upper grades are: *Should There Be Zoos?* (Stead, 2002), The *Children's Giant Atlas of the Universe* (Ridpath, 1993), and *How Your Body Works* (Henderson Publishing, 1997).

- *Poetry.* Poets are beginning to see the beauty of nonfiction poetry to draw in students. Doug Florian has numerous books of poetry that introduce students to animals and nature through poetry, among them *In the Swim,* (1997), *Mammalabilia,* (1986), *Insectopedia* (1998), *and Lizards, Frogs and Polliwogs* (2001).

- *Historical fiction books.* This genre of books can ease students into nonfiction. Information is embedded in stories that have memorable, fictionalized characters and plots based on historical events.

- *Narrative nonfiction.* Many authors are using this form of nonfiction to capture the interest of children through narrative or story-like texts. Reluctant and struggling readers find this form of nonfiction more palatable than more standard nonfiction. Examples are Jane Yolen's *Letting Swift River Go* (1992) and Lynne Cherry's, *A River Ran Wild* (1990). The blending of narrative and nonfiction makes informational reading seem friendlier. Some publishers have introduced same-topic paired books: one text is fiction and the other nonfiction. These help reluctant readers see differences in the ways in which the two genres are formatted around one topic.

- *Graphic nonfiction books: Comic type.* Reluctant and struggling readers can access nonfiction through this avenue. These look like comic books and are a fun, motivating format for many reluctant readers. Capstone Publishers has graphic nonfiction books on the *Titanic,* Salem witch trials, King Tut, and the Boston Tea Party. Students can replicate this format easily in their own writing and have fun with it.

- *The Mini Page.* The Mini Page, a syndicated (Universal Press) four-page nonfiction tabloid that appears in over 500 newspapers, is a wonderful nonfiction resource for more challenged readers in grades 3, 4, 5, and 6. It addresses many state and national educational standards. It has a major topic that is considered each week, such as the Olympics, or for a number of weeks such as presidential elections, Black History Month, or the U.S. Constitution. The content is concise, easy to read, and full of current photos and activities for children to use. It is a good idea to laminate these pages or put them in plastic sleeves for protection. (For more information regarding this resource, go to www.nieonline.com.)

- *Songs from history.* The Voices of America series is a package of CDs or tapes with a reproducible book of songs for children to sing from different historical periods and informational narration that explains the era and makes history come alive. The series contains *Pre-Colonial Times Through the Revolutionary War; The Young Nation Through the Civil War; The Westward Expansion of the United States.* Students enjoy singing these songs and learning history through them.

- *Historical scripts.* Students internalize nonfiction when it comes in different forms. Commercial historical plays are written for students to perform. This provides oral language opportunities to break down complicated concepts through acting out the parts.

SOCIAL STUDIES AND OTHER TEXTBOOKS: A DEEPER LOOK

One important type of nonfiction not yet addressed but found in almost all classrooms is the textbook. The moan of children's voices when the teacher says, "Take out your social studies textbook," is unforgettable. These books can be dull. Textbooks should be used as a resource, not the only resource. Social studies and science are supported by numerous other supplemental books and magazines that keep students involved and engaged in the content.

Learning How to Read a Textbook

Textbooks can be confusing and complicated for any reader, let alone a struggling reader. The publishers have a lot to cover and think it all has to be covered by the end of the year because there are social studies and science standards that need to be met. Children must learn that reading nonfiction is much different from reading fiction. They may need to slow down, reread more often, or read parts out loud to themselves to gain more clarity and greater meaning. They may need to survey the pages first before reading; they may need to skim and scan; they need to learn about text structures and text features to aid them in navigating through complex-looking pages. The good thing about a textbook is that it is predictable and repetitive and the chapters are usually set up with a similar structure; thus, learning to read from a textbook is a manageable task.

Dip-In/Dip-Out Technique

Teachers approach a textbook in a number of ways. In some districts, a textbook is a resource and students learn that the entire book will not be read from cover to cover. Instead it will be dipped into and out of and other resources and supplementary materials such as trade books, picture books, historical novels, and periodicals will be used to address the standards. Therefore, these students will come to realize that a textbook is a resource and will not *need to be read* from cover to cover.

In other classrooms, the textbook is used as the main source of information that addresses the standards and will be read in its entirety.

The manner in which a textbook is approached is driven by the district, the state, or the individual teacher. For many children, especially those who have difficulty with reading, a textbook is a monumental task.

Although the most current textbooks are colorful and packed with information, the size alone can dismay a child. A book that has about six hundred pages, plus a resource section of approximately another one hundred pages and weighs about five pounds, can intimidate children. Many students in grades 3 to 8 are working with and carrying around not one textbook but three or four—one each for reading, science, math, and social studies. Any book that is that big and has a hard cover is suspect to some children, except, of course, a Harry Potter book.

Making the Textbook Easier for Struggling Readers

Students need to know that a textbook is not a thing to fear. Let them peruse it leisurely in a relaxed setting. Let them pull out the interesting parts and mark them for further study. If you see that reluctant readers are truly interested in a topic, try to locate other books and materials to support their inquiry at a later time.

Have the children do the following things in a social studies text:

- Preview the entire book. Mark three pages that look interesting with sticky notes. Share the notes and pages with a partner.
- Read about the things you found above, and write three things that are new to your thinking today. Share it with a partner.
- Find a picture that is interesting. Read the captions underneath it, and share what you have learned with another person.
- Count up the number of colors you see in the headings. Try to figure out how the book is formatted.
- Locate a map that intrigues you. Look at the key, and try to figure out what it means.
- Look up three new words that are in boldface print. Use the glossary. Share these words with a peer.
- Find a picture of a child your age. Write down the page number, and tell why that child is shown.
- Locate a song, and tell what it is about.
- Find a picture of something old. Learn why it has been included.
- What's the most interesting thing that you found that you might want to pursue more in other books or materials?
- Go on a scavenger or feature hunt to locate parts of the book that will support your learning.

Have the students do the following things in the science book:

- Look for three things that are interesting to you. Mark them with sticky notes. Share them with a partner.
- Find three new science words that you are unfamiliar with. Look them up in the glossary, and share them with a partner.

- Look for an experiment that you might like to try. Mark it. Read it through, and talk with a partner about it.
- Scan the index, and locate three things that you would like to learn more about. Write them down and the page numbers they are found on. Locate them in the book. Mark your pages for further study possibilities.

Helping Students Access Content Material in the Textbook

Making sure that struggling students have additional supports in place before beginning any study, activity, or project that extends the concepts of the textbook is essential for their success. A few suggestions are listed here:

- Have important Web sites bookmarked for easy access.
- Locate less challenging information in less complex books.
- Locate "just right" books before the study begins.
- Pair two students together you know will need additional help on the same project; then support them in a guided reading group.
- Have volunteer parents, grandparents, or other family members assist them on locating resources.
- Have a child who has completed his or her research assist the struggling student.
- Have the school librarian locate less challenging books for the child on their topic.
- Make copies of materials so that the student can highlight information instead of just taking notes.
- Have the student talk about information he or she has gleaned from other sources, and have an adult scribe write down these thoughts on paper.

Reader's Theater Scripts

In one fifth-grade classroom, the children wrote reader's theater scripts using the organizational format of the textbook. Each child or pair of children was assigned a part or small section of a chapter with an important event in it. This event was maximized with additional research from other sources and was put in script format form for a performance. The students worked in teams to tie the performance together with transitional words and phrases. They brought props and costumes to make the performance more authentic. All the parts were videotaped for parents and family members to watch.

Rewrite of a Textbook

In another classroom, students were asked to recreate a section of the textbook by using the main headings and subheadings. With a partner, they were asked to choose a section that they were interested in and to rewrite the segment by making it more kid-friendly, that is, simplifying the information. They were also asked to use other sources that might clarify the textbook information and add details that would make it more interesting. A copy of each of the student's sections was assembled into student-prepared packets, and these were handed out to each student. The fact that the students were writing to their own peers elevated the level of the writing. The packet was an excellent tool for review of the whole chapter.

Wax Museum Presentation

In the fourth-grade team of Kathy Aufsesser, Jan Armstrong, and David Van Slyck, students looked through the textbook to locate the names of famous Californians who were spotlighted. A list was compiled, and students were asked to choose a person they wanted to research in greater depth. They were first required to read the information in the textbook and then take notes. They discovered that the textbook did not develop the key historical figures very thoroughly, so they would have to look further into the person's life using other sources, including biographies, autobiographies, and memoirs. After their inquiry was completed, the students wrote speeches to introduce themselves, developed props, and created costumes. They stood perfectly still in waxed museum style, but when a visitor came and pushed the small red dot in front of them, the historical character "came alive."

Historical Fiction: An Entry Point for Social Studies Content

Many teachers have begun to use historical fiction to accomplish a twofold goal: teaching students about embedded nonfiction (real historical information that is incorporated in a narrative-type text) in reader's workshop and presenting content in an interesting way. Historical fiction presents ordinary, everyday characters that boys and girls can relate to. They are fictionalized and carry many of the problems and conflicts that children today face. Children who connect with these characters can readily make sense of a historical account and begin to feel what it must have been like to live during the time period. They have great difficulty, though, understanding the idea of what two hundred years ago means when they cannot understand what life was like even seven, ten, or thirteen years ago. They have no reference point for understanding historical longevity.

Integrating literature into the content areas hooks in all readers and gets them involved in knowing about history through characters that seem real. Many times historical fiction is told from the first-person point of view instead of the impersonal third person. Personalized accounts are always more believable and easier to relate to, especially if the main character is about the reader's same age. Writers of historical fiction have had to do a great deal of research to write about a historical period or event, so we assume that the facts that are embedded in these stories are real.

Although many students do not pick up historical fiction to read on their own during independent reading, teacher direction can nudge them into this genre with vast rewards. Through historical fiction, children are immersed in the time period and gain a lot of background information about what it was like to live in the past. Care needs to be taken to make sure that children know that not everything that is written in historical fiction is true. There is a fine line between what is true and accurate and what is fictionalized in this blended literature. During a read-aloud of a good piece of historical fiction, the teacher must guide the students in extrapolating the real from the made-up portions of the text. The same holds true for narrative nonfiction texts: much of the text is in story form, and some students have more trouble than others figuring out what is real and what is not.

Historical Fiction in Julie's Classroom

Historical fiction can be used for read-alouds and shared reading to bring content into the reader's and writer's workshop. Following are suggestions for some specific mentor or touchstone texts that I refer to over and over again in my classroom and that support the language arts and social studies standards.

- *The True Confessions of Charlotte Doyle* (1990), by Avi. Although this book and our exploration unit do not fit perfectly with each other, the knowledge of the ship and the nautical terms that this book contains make it a perfect entry into nonfiction. There are plenty of important facts that come from the book that we can sift through together. We start a chart that has two columns— "Things That Are Really Part of History" and "Things That Are Fictionalized"—and continue it through our study.

As we develop this list, the students become more aware of the characteristics and restraints of this genre. But they are also able to see the hardships of being a crew member during history. The compelling characters bring history to the forefront: the children can see history unfolding through the connections they are making with the characters. Student writing parallels the book talks that are propelled by the characters and setting.

- *The Thirteenth Floor* (1995), by Sid Fleischman. Our study of the New England colonies is next. Through this piece of historical fiction, we begin to understand the hardships of living in colonial times. The students can identify with the characters and can compare their lives now with lives then. They also use their social studies textbook to add information. Using the two sources helps students to synthesize the blended information into their own first-person account.
- *Sing Down the Moon* (1970), by Scott O'Dell, and *The Sign of the Beaver* (1983), by Elizabeth Speare. Our study of historical fiction next turns to Native Americans and the gender perspective. The girls read *Sing Down the Moon* and the boys read *The Sign of the Beaver*. Combining the information from the textbook and other sources, students gather a well-rounded knowledge of the Native American life. Many students want to read both of these books and are given the chance after they have looked deeper and gained an understanding of the time period from a gender perspective.

During this time, we also use *The Ledgerbook of Thomas Blue Eagle* (1994), by J. Grutman, as a read-aloud to go deeper into the plight of Native Americans. The class then writes their own stories and illustrates them in the fashion of the book. (See Activities 13.2 and 13.3, Native American Poster Board Project and Native American Poster Project Rubric, at the end of this chapter.)

- *The Fighting Ground* (1984), by Avi, and *Sarah Bishop* (1980), by Scott O'Dell. These books can also be used as whole class gender book clubs by looking at the Revolutionary War through the eyes of a girl and a boy. I introduce both books, one at a time, as read-alouds. I then assign the books as a book of the month that can be read at home. I want the students to support each other as they work through these books, so as each assignment is finished, the girls meet to discuss their book and the boys meet to discuss their book, both under teacher supervision.

I hand out the following information sheet so that parents and students understand the assignment:

Reading Book Information and Schedule for
Sarah Bishop and *The Fighting Ground*

In the next three weeks, I have assigned you a Book of the Month. This selection has to do with the Revolutionary War period of history. In order to get a better understanding of this period of time, I am asking you to read the assigned book at home for your 20–30 minutes of nightly reading. This book will help you to comprehend the social studies book more fully by giving you a fictional look at the subject. The main character is a girl/boy and I would like you to figure out how you would have reacted to the same situation that she/he found herself or himself in. On the scheduled date, you should have read the pages indicated so that you can discuss the section with your group and do your assigned job. Make sure you use sticky notes to help you stay tuned into your reading.

Student groupings and scheduled dates for communicating about the books are placed on a chart and posted so that students can refer to them as the study progresses.

The groups that finish early read the other book too. There is a lot to be gleaned from both of these excellent books.

DISCOVERY THROUGH NONFICTION: RESEARCH IN THE CLASSROOM

Ultimately we want students in the upper-grade classes to seek out and pursue an interest or a passion—something that they have always wanted to study or learn more about and to stay with it for an extended period of time—to become an expert in the field, so to speak. Throughout the year, there will be opportunities provided for children to question and research areas of interest that take them deeper and more fully into an area that they want to explore.

We take research in small, guided steps in the classroom. Children need to know what the standard is going to be and have some guidelines for setting their path. Your job as a teacher is to get to know your children well and what they are interested in. Some of them say that they're not interested in anything, but we all know better.

Leading into Independent Research

Before students can enter into a unit of inquiry independently, they need an opportunity to test their wings in a guided or shared experience. Below are some entry points for beginning miniprojects to help ease them into using nonfiction for independent study.

Native Americans

Students become immersed in the study of Native Americans through U.S. geography, locating where the major tribes lived on a map, and discussing the ways different tribes lived due to environmental conditions. Then students begin their study of major tribes of the United States. In pairs or triads, they begin researching their chosen tribe using marked Web sites, books, and additional material. (See Native American Poster Project, Activities 13.2 and 13.3, at the end of this chapter.) Some children need less complicated projects with more partner support, and others can take a more independent role. Gifted and talent students need to be challenged to a higher level of research.

For struggling readers and writers, we put together a small group that receives a great deal of guided support. We use the book *If You Lived with the Sioux Indians* (McGovern, 1974) or one of the other Native American books in this series. The book is set up in a question-and-answer format and is simplified for older readers, although it has a reading level of third grade. The book is full of information that is explicit and easy to transfer into their own writing. We also pull several sources from other books that are at a just-right level for these challenged readers and writers. We encourage a minimal amount of writing taken on sticky notes. From the notes, the students write their own personal words about five subject areas that they are most interested in.

Exploration

Early in the year in conjunction with the reading of *The True Confession of Charlotte Doyle* by Avi and a simulation of what a sailor's life was like on board a sailing ship during the 1800s, our exploration unit takes place. This project has been formatted in a more complex manner for students who need to be accelerated in their study, such as those who are highly motivated, high achievers, and gifted and talented children. For more challenged readers and writers, the packet may be modified to meet their needs. For instance, it may be done in partners or with more guided teacher practice for more support, or the teacher may assign only certain activities and delete others or students can make some choices as to what portions they will do. (See Activities 13.4 and 13.5, Explorer Notebook Student Packet and Explorer Notebook (Group) Student Check-Off List, at the end of this chapter.)

The Great Kapok Tree and the Rain Forest

While studying biomes of the world, fourth graders learn about protecting their environment. Through reading several books, including *A North American Rain Forest Scrapbook* (1999) by Virginia Wright-Frierson, *A Walk in the Rainforest* (1992) by Kristin Joy Pratt, and *The Great Kapok Tree* (1990) by Lynne Cherry, the class begins to think about their part in keeping rain forests safe for the animals and for the future generations to enjoy. Together, the class creates their own ABC rain forest book using Kristin Joy Pratt's book as their model and watercolors. Independently or in partners, students work on one page of the alphabet. They each research a rain forest animal more thoroughly and write their own text.

Other activities provide engagement and interaction with the text of *The Great Kapok Tree*:

- Big idea: Have the students brainstorm the big idea or author's message of the book, such as, "People are able to change the destruction of the rain forests."

- Performance: You need a narrator or two and a group of enthusiastic children. Have them retell the story through the animals' eyes, write a reader's theater script to perform, or write a poem about the animals. You can also break the class into small groups. Have the students each take a part. Without practice or a script, let the student ad-lib the roles of the rain forest animals.
- Writing: Take a viewpoint of one of the animals of the rain forest, and write from its own perspective.
- Research: Using books and the Web, students can research one of the animals mentioned in the book and write a report about it.

For another more guided activity using this book, see Activities 13.6 and 13.7, Sample Starters for the Diary Entry for *The Great Kapok Tree* and Rubric for *The Great Kapok Tree,* at the end of this chapter.

Revving Up Research Skills

Fundamental research skills need to be taught to all children beginning in the primary grades with the organization of simple facts and developing into a more sophisticated and complex study in the upper grades and middle school. Research needs to be appropriate to the grade level as delineated in the state standards. Probably one of the most important skills students will need in order to be successful as adults is the ability to access and use the abundance of information and resources available. Technology has changed our ways of researching because our information is current and updated, sometimes to the minute. The important thing for teachers to remember is that research is a skill that needs to be taught. It cannot be learned through osmosis.

Teacher-Directed Research Instruction: The Mini-Research Project

In the upper grades and middle school, students should be given basic instruction in research skills collectively as a starting point. They should receive clear, structured, and guided instruction and modeling of the procedures and steps involved in research, and they should become familiar with the teacher's expectations and standards before beginning their own independent work.

In October, students are always captivated with scary, or mysterious-sounding places of the world, so capitalize on their curiosity and excitement. Depending on the knowledge level of the class, an approach that might be taken in grades 3 and 4, and can be modified for grades 5 through 8, would be to build research skills in reading and writing through a nonfiction mystery genre study. Since only the classroom teacher knows the special needs and interests of his or her students, the following lesson may be relevant for all, some, or only a very few students in an inclusive classroom. It addresses a basic foundation or starting point for developing research skills.

- Hand each child copies of three articles about the Loch Ness Monster: one from an encyclopedia, one from a book, and the last from an Internet article. Each child should have the same materials.
- The children place each article in a different colored folder with a label indicating the source it came from.
- Stress that different facts could be discovered if three different sources are used. Not all research information agrees with one another. Synthesizing these resources and putting the information into your own words is the hard part.

red construction paper folder	yellow construction paper folder	blue construction paper folder
Loch Ness article from a book	Loch Ness article from an Internet article	Loch Ness article from an encyclopedia

- One of the articles should be read aloud by the teacher. It is helpful if a transparency is made of the article and placed on an overhead projector. This is an excellent opportunity to model to students how to highlight important information on which they will take notes. The students must be aware that usually they will not be able to highlight information they find in a book that is not their own. Therefore, they must take notes on paper, note cards, or on sticky notes and keep them in an organized manner.

- After the article is read, instruct the students on note taking. Teacher modeling of his or her thinking is the best way to show students how to take notes. Explain that when note taking, everyone must keep the notes organized. For any material that is read, students need to record the title of the book or article, the author, and the page where the information was found. That is probably enough for the intermediate grade levels or children who have learning difficulties. As children progress into the middle school, they will be required to do more complete referencing.

In this mini-research project, the students are asked to color-code their notes and bibliographical information. For instance, if the Internet article on the Loch Ness Monster is in a yellow folder, a yellow dot is used to identify notes taken from that article. The bibliographical information from the material is also colored-coded with a yellow dot. The intent of this system is that the students will begin to see the connection between the materials they use and the information they keep.

- All students receive a Research Note-Taking Sheet (Activity 13.8, at the end of this chapter). Throughout the Loch Ness Monster study, these notes become their guide for writing the research paper.

- All students receive Information About Bibliographies (Activity 13.9 at the end of this chapter). On this sheet, students find the correct form to use for referencing their papers. This should be kept in a folder. Students are again reminded to use the color-coding dot to show the book, encyclopedia article, or Internet article that they are referencing.

- The students continue the process by repeating the steps for the encyclopedia and the book they use.

- Because each child has a copy of the same article, this might be another step to include, especially for students who have trouble determining what information is important.

Notebook Paper

Notes

yellow dot →
blue dot →

Notebook

Bibliography

red dot →
blue dot →
yellow dot →

Yellow Construction Paper Folder

Loch Ness Internet article

- Take notes from the source using the color-coding method. A red dot on the note-taking sheet is used to indicate that the information has been taken from the book, and a red dot is used on the bibliography page to connect the reference information, the book itself, and the note taking.

- Blue dots are used to connect the note taking with the bibliography reference and the encyclopedia.

- Three index cards are handed out to each child, who writes the bibliographical information on each card (for the book, the article, and the encyclopedia).

- These cards are glued down by the author's last name in alphabetical order on an 8½- by 11-inch piece of colored construction paper. This will be labeled "Bibliography" and included with the rest of the mini-research paper.

- As the students complete their highlighting and note taking, structure a simple outline for the students to use to guide their paragraph writing:

  A. Introduction—hook in your reader

  B. What is it?

  C. Physical characteristics

  D. Location where it is found

  E. Evidence that has been found

  F. Other interesting information about Loch Ness monster

  G. Concluding paragraph

  The children use this basic format because all of the information can be found in the materials preselected by the teacher.

- The teacher writes a sample introductory paragraph for the students. This modeling helps the students to see how an introductory paragraph will hook in readers and make them want to read more. Now the children are asked to write their own introductory paragraphs. The teacher should have students volunteer to share their paragraphs. Having student samples read aloud or, even better, presented on the overhead and read aloud to the entire class—is useful to students who are having difficulty initiating their own. Some students may need to basically copy the teacher's example or one by a classmate.

- The second paragraph is co-created as a class. Students create a topic sentence, and then the class adds details and ideas that complete the paragraph.

- The third paragraph is written in pairs or triads. One child records, while the other two review their notes and find the information to complete the topic. Having the children write this paragraph on a large piece of lined tag board or lined newsprint gives more examples for the rest of the class to review together. The overhead projector is also helpful in making student copies available for their peers to see. These cooperative group pieces can be rotated around for other groups to read.

- The fourth paragraph can also be written cooperatively and reviewed as a class. The more examples the students have, the easier the process is for all students.

- The last two paragraphs can be written independently by the students. Because there have been a lot of scaffolds used to this point, the teacher should release the responsibility of the work to the individual students. Through using the teacher-guided paragraphs, co-created paragraphs, and the cooperative group paragraphs, the students are now ready to develop their own. Pair-sharing of the paragraphs or oral reading by individuals for the rest of the class can be used to assure the students that what they have written is factual and sufficient.

- Because all the students have exactly the same materials to use for this mini-research project, they can see how their peers used the information differently to make more detailed or complete paragraphs. All students should be able to write a one- to two-page bare-bones paper with the notes they have taken. Some students will be able to extend their writing because they are able to look through all three references and draw that information altogether to write thorough paragraphs.

Each child is writing at his or her own developmental level with the skills that he or she has at this time.

- Since this is a rough draft, students are encouraged to write on every other line of the paper so they can make corrections and additions easily.
- When they have finished their rough drafts, all students read their paper to a partner and peer-edit with that partner.
- The teacher reviews rough drafts.
- The students rewrite the rough drafts in neat handwriting or using the computer, being sure to number the pages. The finished paper should have these parts:
    - Cover
    - Title page
    - Outline
    - Research paper
    - An "extra"
- The suggested paper's length is one to two pages. Think carefully about what your goal is in teaching research skills. It is important that you do not encourage your students to copy information, and long research papers do encourage copying. When a report is kept short, students are more likely to write the paper in their own words, and that is what we want to teach children to do. The word *plagiarism* should be discussed with students, and some of the consequences for plagiarizing in the academic and business worlds might be noted.
- After the paper is completed, instruct the students how they can embellish or extend their paper by adding little extras—for example:
    - A hand-drawn map of where the Loch Ness Monster has been seen
    - A newspaper or magazine article giving more information
    - An illustration of or picture of the Loch Ness Monster (drawn or copied)
    - A diorama or model of the Loch Ness Monster

This mini-research project establishes some necessary groundwork and structuring for students. Because they have received guided instruction and modeling of the process, they are now more skillful in writing research papers.

Students may further their interest in mystery by delving into another mysterious creature or places. They may work on a special mystery project individually or independently. A few research ideas are included at the end of this chapter in Activities 13.10 to 13.13. Later, students may use the skills they have practiced to develop a project for a Discovery Fair.

The Discovery Fair

A discovery fair is a developmental process where students become totally emerged in the excitement of research. They choose a topic that is of interest to them, and then they actively pursue their subject. By the end of the research period, children have the tools to explain information about their topic to others, and through their growth of research skills, each becomes an "expert" who motivates other students to learn more about the subject. The process encourages active participation by all students and allows them to become more skillful at researching at their developmental level of understanding. The goal in a learning fair project is to spread excitement about the wonderful world we live in and introduce the resources that are available to pursue the world through research.

How much time to allow for a discovery fair is an individual choice. Plan on a period of about four to six weeks. Depending on how much skill the students have to begin with and how much time the teacher will actually spend using class time, the time can be extended or shortened accordingly. Class work periods should be built into the project so that you may observe how the students are progressing and who needs help. Twenty- to thirty-minute periods of class time several times a week usually work well with older students. As the end of the project nears, longer work periods may be needed. Some work will need to be done as homework.

Getting Started

To begin, the teacher should inform the parents and students about the project early in the year. Most schools have a back-to-school night where the teachers explain their program for the year. This is a perfect opportunity to broach the topic. It gives everyone a stretch of time to be thinking about what subjects are interesting to the students. As students take trips or visit monuments, parks, and museums, they can be searching for topics of interest.

About a month before the project begins, the teacher should hand out a parent letter so that parents are informed again about the project. A tear-off sheet for the parent to sign and return to school assures the teacher that all families have been informed.

The students and the teacher should create a bulletin board with suggestions for research projects. Students can look through back issues of *National Geographic,* encyclopedias, library books, magazines, newspapers, and computer Web sites to generate interesting topics.

Brainstorming sessions are good opportunities for students to hear about topics that they might want to pursue. With partners, the students can create a list of possible topics. Topics can be written on large charts or can be placed on sentence strips and added to the bulletin board.

The more time a teacher spends at the beginning of this project by helping students think of subjects for their research, the easier the whole process will be. If students have a topic they are genuinely interested in, they will be motivated to continue seeking information.

Because students self-select their topics, they have ownership in the project. The opportunity for choice should be built into assignments for older students. When they buy into their work, they are much more enthused about it. (See Activity 13.14, Research Topic Suggestions, at the end of this chapter.)

The decision must be made if students will work with partners or independently. This choice may be made by the teacher for the whole class or for some of the students or by the students themselves. With older children, working independently may be the preferred way. Many high-achieving students prefer to work on their own. In the inclusive classroom, the teacher sometimes makes the decision for special students who need more guidance. For instance, a teacher may pair up two second-language students who would have difficulty on their own and give them extra support during the process through additional adult help. It is the teacher's professional judgment of the students' needs that will set this choice in motion.

Since the students have already been taken through several mini-research projects as a class, they have a solid foundation to begin. The groundwork has been laid, and the process is ready to begin.

Materials and Resources

A class trip to the library is a good starting point. Contact the librarian at your school and at the nearest public library. Students can take a field trip and learn how to locate materials for their reports.

Most school districts have a central media center to order materials. Students can look through catalogues to see what is available. They may learn how to order these materials and preview them for their classmates. Films, videos, CD-ROMs, study prints, and other audiovisual materials can be ordered, and the students can become skillful in this aspect of research.

Parents should be asked to volunteer their time for helping students who do not have much parent assistance from home. Research is difficult in the initial stages, and some students need individual attention to get started. Not all students are self-starters. Parent volunteers can work individually with students who require extra help at any stage of the research. Peer tutoring can also be arranged, such as in a K–8 school, where eighth graders might volunteer to help a fourth grader or a third grader might get assistance from a sixth grader in developing research ideas.

Deadlines

The students should be aware of the importance of deadlines. As you fill out the Discovery Fair Due Date Schedule, Activity 13.15 at the end of this chapter, be sure that all students are given ample time to complete each part of the project. You also need to provide consequences for students who do not meet the due date. The importance of a due date should be emphasized. Monitoring these dates can be time-consuming; therefore, ask for assistance from a student monitor, an aide, or a parent volunteer. A chart might be set up in the room, and as students complete an activity, they may receive a dot, a star, a check mark, or a sticker.

Discovery Fair Packet

All students should receive their own copy of the entire Discovery Fair Essentials, Activity 13.16, at the end of this chapter. This should be kept inside a folder for use throughout the project. Each child has all of the information at his or her fingertips so that there are no misunderstandings about what the expectations are between the school, the home, and the child. An electronic copy can also be provided on a school Web site or classroom link. This provides a place for parents and students to look if their packet is misplaced.

Reviewing the Student/Teacher Evaluation Form

Before the project begins, the students should review Activity 13.17, the Student/Teacher Evaluation Form, at the end of this chapter. Going through the three parts of the project and making sure that the students know what is being asked will answer many questions. The students can always refer back to this form when they are not sure of the guidelines.

Introducing Extras

Students need to be shown what a graph, a chart, a map, an illustration, and other extras should look like. Therefore, you must model some examples. Samples of student projects saved from previous school years provide excellent examples of what students can do to enhance their project. These student sample copies may be filed for future use. (See Activity 13.18, Research: Add Some of Those "Extras," at the end of this chapter.)

Daily Student Logs

During the first few weeks of research, the students receive a twenty- to thirty-minute period of class time to work on their projects. This allows you to observe who is having difficulty and who is off and running. Students really motivate each other. There always seems to be someone who is out in the front of the pack. These are the students who provide motivation for the rest of the class. Daily updates, reviews, and sharing opportunities give eager students an intrinsic reward for their hard work. Students who are lagging behind are given a little encouragement and assistance in getting started. Filling out the Research Daily Log (Activity 13.19 at the end of this chapter) at the end of each work period helps students to reflect on what they have accomplished and focuses them on the time it has taken to accomplish that task. You can collect the daily logs each week and evaluate them.

The Display Board

The students will present their information visually on a display board, which may be viewed by their peers, parents, and students from other classrooms. This is a good idea for an Open House or other parent visitation. The teacher may determine the size of this display board, the visual representation and culmination activity for the research.

A good starting place for obtaining the boards is the site supply room. Chipboard panels twelve by eighteen inches work well for the board. This material is often available at school sites and can be taped together on the back side and covered with butcher, wrapping, or contact paper. Sometimes two panels provide a large enough area to tell the story of the research, but some students may require a larger surface provided by three panels. Some students like to purchase their own preformed display boards from office supply stores.

The boards can be recycled each year. Students take home their butcher paper with their display of materials, but the chipboard remains at school for use by other students the following year.

As the students are researching, they can also be working on preparing materials for their display boards. During the class work periods, the students can make maps, graphs, charts, and other extras.

Many students like to type their written information for the display board. Since the display board has a large surface area and needs to be seen from a distance, students usually use a larger type size than they do for their research paper. If they do not type their written work, they may print the material on five- by seven-inch note cards.

All work is in rough draft form until it is glued onto the display board. Note cards written in pencil and typed material must be peer corrected and approved by a teacher. All written work must be redone in thin black marker, so that it is readable from a distance.

Students should not glue any materials to the display board until all parts are completed. Many children have not had experience thinking through a whole project and begin gluing without understanding what the finished project will look like. Organizing and spacing the information can mean the difference between an eye-appealing project and one that has been thrown together without forethought. Third and fourth graders have less experience with big projects and therefore need more guidance, whereas fifth through eighth graders can understand the need for waiting until everything is completed so that the finished project looks planned and organized. There should be a minimum of background space left showing. Laying out the materials on the board first, playing with their placement, and then asking someone else to assess the placement contributes to a more sophisticated-looking finished board.

Allowing children to choose their own background color paper and two foreground colors of construction paper gives each child ownership of his or her project. To enhance the eye appeal, each item that is going to be placed on the board is framed or backed with a piece of colored construction paper. Some students double-mount their items. For the older students in grades 5 to 8, skill in the use of the paper cutter may be taught so they can create even borders for the items they have used. In grades 3 and 4, parent helpers may assist in the framing of the information. The students may also cut their frames with scissors that have different patterns or with regular scissors. The form of framing should look age appropriate.

After all parts are self-corrected, peer corrected, and adult corrected, students arrange the items on their board. No gluing is allowed until an "expert spacer" gives final judgment. This person helps the student make sure the materials that are being used are spaced evenly on the board, with little background showing.

Gluing down of materials is now permitted. Students need to be reminded that less is more in the case of glue. Even upper graders do not always have the concept that gluing can ruin a perfectly good project. Since rubber cement is not allowed in many schools because of its toxicity, glue sticks are preferred over white glue.

All gluing is done in class. This project is to be the student's work, not his parents'. Since a discovery fair ends with a presentation to parents, the unveiling of these projects is not done until the open house or parent night. It is important that the final product be done in class so that it is a surprise to the students' parents.

The Oral Presentation

As a culmination of this process, the students need an audience to demonstrate their knowledge and accomplishments through presentation to their peers. As the students complete their research and display boards, time must be built into the program to practice the oral presentation. Here are some tips for this process:

- All students should practice with a partner.
- All students should deliver their presentation to the entire class. The peers should have the opportunity to evaluate their classmates. (Activity 12.8 in Chapter Twelve is a peer evaluation form.) It

is a good idea to have at least three students evaluate each presenter. The presenter receives these evaluations. Teachers should review the standards and model constructive praise and criticism of presentations.

- Use of the video camera is an excellent evaluation tool. Students should have the opportunity to see themselves in action as they present.
- Another classroom can be invited in to rotate through the discovery fair.
- Parents are invited to walk through informal presentations of the topics. Cookies and punch can be served. This is a perfect way to get all parents to visit the classroom.

Project Evaluation

All students received a rubric before the project began that let them know what they needed to do and the number of points each part was worth. As the project develops, the student should continue to refer back to the rubric. This assures them of understanding the guidelines and standards that are expected of them.

On the rubric, the point values are added up and the individual teacher may grade the project as he or she sees fit (such as 90 to 100 percent is an A, and so on). The teacher evaluates each paper, display board, and oral presentation.

The students are taught how to evaluate themselves, making a comparison with the other students' projects. The video camera puts things into perspective. Students are able to observe how theirs is unique or different from their classmates'. Some students are hard on themselves, while others are overly boastful. Through peer, self, and teacher evaluation, each student should begin to develop a realistic view of how his or her project compares with those of other class members. A final grade is given, and the teacher makes comments.

THE SCIENCE CONNECTION

Science Verse (2004) by Jon Scieszka begins with a teacher telling his class, "You know, if you listen closely enough, you can hear the poetry of science in everything." One student believes he has been cursed because he hears nothing but science verses that sound like well-known poems. The book, a sequel to *Math Curse* by the same author, is an ideal book for getting science started in the first weeks of school.

State standards for science for upper-elementary and middle school students are lofty, and science instruction needs to begin promptly at the start of the year. In California, for example, science standards are tested in the spring of fifth grade and again in the ninth, tenth, and eleventh grades. In eighth and tenth grade under the No Child Left Behind Act, students are again tested. This testing puts a lot of pressure on elementary school and middle school teachers to teach the grade-level standards that build the foundation for the testing and make sure the students are grasping the content. We need not think of science as a curse but instead as a rewarding and exciting adventure of exploration and discovery. In an inquiry-based, hands-on science class, children are excited about the subject. There is dialogue, experimentation, and wonder. Many upper grade and middle school students name science as their favorite subject in school. Having a teacher who loves science and knows how to teach it in an intriguing way is the best method to get children to love science. Unfortunately, not all of us are science experts, and even though we try, science is not our strongest area.

Teachers always have a captive audience when they are demonstrating a scientific principle through a simple experiment. Many students view science as a magic trick and question how an experiment really worked. Building scientific investigation skills is really very simple because all life is one big investigation. We must teach students the importance of being observers in the world around them. As they become better observers, they are becoming keener in scientific observation skills.

Impact of Television

Many upper graders and middle school children are fascinated with science. Programs like *CSI* (Crime Scene Investigation) and *NCSI* (Navy Crime Scene Investigation) are developing large audiences, including older children. Students are beginning to talk about becoming scientists to help solve problems in crime. There is an intrigue about investigating and using clues to get results. These programs are on fairly late in the evening and contain some grisly images not intended for children to see. Parents talk about not allowing their children to watch these shows, yet many of them do. The complexion of science is changing, and new careers are developing that are holding children's attention.

Developing a Science Program in the Classroom

Although many school districts have adopted a science curriculum with kits that include numerous hands-on activities and active learning science experience such as FOSS (Full Option Science System), other districts have to rely on more teacher-created materials. Below are some basic principles and ideas to keep in mind for developing a science program with a minimum amount of expense:

- Science should be fun. Children are naturally inquisitive and should enjoy investigating the world around them.

- Children should see that science is related to other areas of the curriculum, such as art, math, and social studies. Helping children learn about different branches of science that connect the world to each of them is an important process.

- Science materials should be easily accessible.

- If we want students to investigate, we should provide science experiments based on common household items and easily acquired materials.

- A science station can be made available for students during the day. Simple materials can be laid out on a table—possibly one new experiment per week. When students complete their work during free choice time or before or after school, they can experiment with the materials and learn to follow easy-to-read instructions that explain fundamental principles of biology, chemistry, and physics. Students who have difficulty with more complicated reading assignments may find science experiments, with their step-by-step instructions, less threatening. Teaching about this structure through a variety of books and articles is strongly suggested. Many children who have learning disabilities are comfortable with hands-on experimentation. Because many of the experiments are also illustrated, these challenged students can find a greater degree of success.

- Schools without abundant science materials can request assistance and materials from parents. Inexpensive materials such as plastic cups, spoons, measuring spoons and cups, jars, washers, corks, food coloring, balloons, tongue depressors, baking soda, small bowls, and cornstarch can be stored in shoe boxes or plastic containers in the classroom. A parent letter requesting donations of supplies early in the school year can get any classroom started.

- A science cart can be accessible for all teachers to use. A parent may be interested in volunteering time to gather together and replenish simple materials for science. All teachers may check out the cart. Having the cart housed in an area where teachers see it frequently will remind them of the materials that are available. Old microscope kits are also very valued.

- Inviting guests with expertise in science into the classroom is always helpful. Many parents are excited about sharing their field of interest with the students. If the teacher is somewhat limited in science knowledge, asking for assistance from a parent is a step in becoming more confident. Parents who are interested in dissection have offered some of our best science lessons. Having a person who is willing to share this expertise with the students is a real bonus.

- Students love to conduct science experiments. As we noted in Chapter Twelve, children can make a science experiment into a presentation. For instance, during one month, all students could be required to present an experiment for their oral language experience. Students can work alone or with partners, and the teacher can videotape the presentation.

- Science experiment books should be available in the classroom for students. Books such as *Homemade Slime and Rubber Bones* (1993) by William R. Wellnitz, *Simple Science Experiments with Everyday Materials* (1992) by Muriel Mandell, and *Cool Chemistry Concoctions* (2005) by Joe Rhatigan and Veronika Alice Gunter can hook in reluctant readers. These books are inexpensive and at appropriate levels for all elementary grades. Janice VanCleave's *Experiments* series books such as *Janice VanCleave's 202 Oozing, Bubbling, Dripping and Bouncing Experiments* (1996) and *Janice VanCleave's 203 Icy, Freezing, Frosty, Cool and Wild Experiments* (1999) are excellent resources for gathering ideas. The procedures are easy to follow and provide many experiences that students will enjoy doing themselves or watching someone else do.

- Trade book baskets or tubs should be filled with all levels of interesting and engaging books for students to peruse during their free time. Books like, *Oh, Yuck! The Encyclopedia of Everything Nasty* (2000) by Joy Masoff, Gail Gibbon's science books, and books that support the science standards for your state in the forms of narrative nonfiction as well as traditional nonfiction should be incorporated.

Designing an Observational Study in Science

As children reach the middle and upper grades as well as the middle school, it is important that they be given the opportunity to design a question and pursue an answer to it scientifically. Many children enjoy the behavioral sciences. Watching and observing the actions of people is fairly easy to do. As students generate their list of interests, you can assist them in forming an experiment. Students can be guided in their discovery that almost anything can be turned into a science project and that science *is* fun!

Todd, a fourth-grade teacher, had his students list all the things that they were interested in and then developed a class chart entitled Things We Might Like to Investigate Further. Everyone contributed at least one idea, except one boy who said he was not interested in anything. Several girls stated that they liked to "hang out" at the mall. The teacher then suggested that they design a science project that allowed them to spend time at the mall as a threesome. They came up with the idea that they would like to observe what age group of people would bend down to pick up certain denominations of coins. They used pennies, nickels, dimes, and quarters. The girls knew this experiment would have a cost that they would have to bear, and they also knew that they would not see their money again. They each placed seven dollars into the experimental pot. At the mall, they observed people and found out that older people bent down most often for all denominations of money, while younger people bent down most often only for the quarters. The girls enjoyed the company of each other and the idea that they were at their favorite location. They were able to observe over a hundred subjects, and a four-hour session was an enjoyable and educational experience.

Another experiment at the mall involved a mother and her daughter who watched shoppers as they exited the mall. They kept a tally of each shopping bag carried out of the mall. At the end of two hours, they had observed over 150 people and identified what store had been visited most often. A third experiment at the shopping mall was designed by two boys who wanted to find out when couples were shopping, which one (male or female) carried the bag. They observed 125 couples.

What about the boy who said that he did not like to do anything? Todd asked him if he would just like to sit in a lawn chair and watch the traffic on his street. He agreed that that was just about like doing nothing. He sat by a stop sign in his neighborhood and observed cars to see who made complete stops, who stopped but went over the crosswalk lines, and who did not stop at all. This boy was involved in science even though he liked the lazy form of participation.

When kids feel that they can put together an experiment that is enjoyable and relevant to the world around them, then they become more interested in pursuing a finished product. Not all science experiments require huge amounts of apparatus. Many students view science as a complicated subject that requires extensive research, documenting, observation, and equipment. When students start seeing that the principles they learned in the primary grades can be examined more extensively in the upper grades, the task becomes easier. Creating behavioral science experiments can be one choice for students, while others might want to engage themselves in more traditional topics. See Student Interest Survey Form for Observational Investigation; Observation Study; and Observation Project Information Sheet, Activities 13.20 to 13.22, at the end of this chapter.

As in the case of the discovery fair described earlier in this chapter, some teachers may want to give their students the experience of a science experience involving observation, research, scientific investigation, a display board, and an oral presentation. The entire class may concentrate on any form of science including behavioral. Other teachers may want to give the students choice of pursuing science or choosing research in other areas of the curriculum. A true discovery fair takes in the interests and choices of each child. Therefore, a child might investigate the topic of earthquakes or weather phenomena, while another child may study politics (What Does It Take to Be a U.S. President?), history (Was the Boston Tea Party Really a Party?), or music (A Look at Music Through the 1950s).

Involving students in other enjoyable science experiences, and capitalizing on that natural curiosity of investigation and observation in the upper grades will establish some fundamentals of a lifelong interest in scientific pursuit.

Extending the Science Book into New Frontiers

The textbook is one form of gathering information. As is the case in social studies, the book must provide interesting, colorful, and engaging access for the students. Many textbooks, however, are formatted in a structure that does not hook many of our challenged readers. The textbook publishers are keeping current with the needs of all readers and –the newest books are including many contemporary features such as quick experiments, step-by-step longer experiments, Web sites to visit, updated text features, interesting fact sections, and other motivating sections to grab reluctant readers' interest. Other materials should be included to support the textbook, such as picture and trade books.

The Big Storm (1993), an awarding-winning book by Bruce Hiscock, is an upper-grade picture book rich with illustrations and text that is content oriented but told with a narrative flair. The text flows from the west coast to the east coast over the course of a week. The class gets the idea that a storm that is in their city leaves and goes elsewhere, taking many forms throughout its travels. Students have fun retracing the steps of this storm from the point of view of a bird flying east with it. The writing takes children through the weather content and allows them to have fun writing weather details in narrative form. Students are asked to watch several segments of the weather on the news for several days. They take brief notes to remind themselves how the weather portion is reported to the public. If there are students in the class who do not have a television at home, the teacher can record several segments for the whole class to observe and discuss during the school day.

Students choose one weather condition found in the book *The Big Storm* that they are most interested in and put together weather teams to present more information about it. They may use their textbook, nonfiction trade books, online encyclopedias, weather videos, and other resources to assist in the assignment. The weather forecasting teams prepare a TV weather show explaining the weather condition and the ways people deal with it. They can use maps, props, and costumes to make it look more authentic. The individual team reports can be videotaped for other classrooms, parents, or administrators.

Another idea to try is letting students themselves become the weather condition and explain their view or perspective about what they are. This may be written or in oral presentation form. Giving students a choice of how to show that they own the information is affirming for the child and makes an excellent assessment tool for the teacher.

Other Ways to Get Students Involved in Science Activities

The Einstein Anderson science mysteries are excellent books for children who love science. The main character is a supersleuth who uses his brainpower to solve science mysteries. Although these are currently out of print, your school or public library might have them available. If you cannot find these books, try getting used copies of them online. They can also be found in anthologies. A few books included in this series written by Seymor Simon are *Wings of Darkness* (1998) and *The On-line Spaceman and Other Detectives* (1998).

Science songs aligned to the National Education Standards can be found in the Musically Aligned Science Songs CD Packet, available at musicallyaligned.com. This active music has songs such as "Decomposers," "We Are the Rocks!" and "Electricity to Move." They engage students in examining the physical, life, and earth sciences. These CDs scaffold learning and instruction in each grade level.

Another idea for upper grade classrooms is NASA's S'COOL (Student Cloud Observation On-Line). According to fifth-grade teacher Linda Bryson of Rochester, New York, students all over the world participate in this program, helping NASA interpret and confirm the images that satellites send back to earth. They make cloud observations and report them online while learning weather concepts and authentic science research. If you are interested in this program, visit www.larc.nasa.gov/SCOOL.

Following are some upper-grade explorations that are engaging and enjoyable.

The Pumpkin Investigation

A pumpkin investigation is a good activity for the end of October. Parents are asked to donate a small pumpkin for a team of two to three students to investigate and other materials for the activity. (See Activities 13.23 and 13.24, Becoming a Pumpkinologist and Pumpkin Investigation Letter to Parents, at the end of this chapter.)

This lab can be set up on picnic tables in the lunch arbor, cafeteria, auditorium, or on a grassy knoll. Tables should be covered with butcher paper, and students may use plastic gloves if they want. The students, working in small groups, spend the first part of the period examining the pumpkin and using their observation skills to look for blemishes, colorization, size, shape, and other features. They are each given a packet to work from and a blue book (the type commonly used for exams in college) to record their observations and findings. Encourage students to focus on their own pumpkin, but also to look around and do some comparison with other pumpkins. This comparison observation is a major part of the investigation since the pumpkins are different sizes. Make sure that you have a few parents who are willing to help.

If you do not have time to do an investigation like this, start smaller. Bring in about eight oranges all with different shapes, sizes, and hues. Do the same type of research as described for the pumpkins as a whole class; do the illustrations and descriptions; cut the oranges open; and have the students do brief write-ups with their findings and conclusions.

Investigation with Plants

Finding enough time in a busy teaching schedule to prepare an entire discovery or science fair project is sometimes impossible. So as the end of the year approached, Shira Maltz, a fifth-grade teacher, decided to scale down the research and focus specifically on plants, building an understanding of both qualitative and quantitative observation skills. She also wanted to allow the children to have some choice in their experimentation. Knowing that students enjoy observing plants, she added some sophisticated scientific language to the students' vocabulary and more challenging charting for all students to work on.

She modeled an experiment on a chart so that the students could see her thinking process and her observations over several days. She kept this chart up in the classroom for the students to see.

Students were paired in two-person heterogeneous teams with one high-achieving student and one medium- to low-achieving student. She assigned members of the team questions that they had brainstormed as a class and charted what questions they had about plants that would help them design a scientific investigation of their own over a ten-day period. Following is the student-generated brainstorming chart:

> ### What Kind of Science Fair Project Can We Create Using Plants?
> - Will feeding plants colored water change their color?
> - Do plants grow better toward artificial light?
> - Does overwatering kill plants?
> - Will a plant grow in water only?
> - Which fertilizer works best?
> - Does fertilizer even work on flowers?
> - Do flowers really grow toward the light?
> - What grows better toward light: plants or flowers?
> - Does weed killer kill flowers?
> - What type of soil works best for growing plants?
> - Does leaf size affect how fast a plant grows?
> - Can outdoor plants grow inside?
> - Does one seed brand grow better than another?

The students then created their own projects and kept accurate records of their observations. When the ten days were over, students shared their findings. (See Activities 13.25 and 13.26, Plant Observation Team Sheet and Science Project Student Evaluation, at the end of this chapter.)

The Inventors' Showcase

This is an exciting San Diego County adventure for children to get involved in. Students use their science skills to solve problems, think creatively, experiment and work with data. All grade levels K–12 can participate. The Invention Convention (Houghton Mifflin, 2000) is another national competition that is similar to this local event. Both include similar formats:

1. Learning about the inventors
2. Finding an idea
3. Researching and planning
4. Developing, testing, and marketing something new

Many books about inventors and their inventions are used for read-alouds and shared reading experiences to ground students in the curriculum such as *Book of Lists* (Buckley & Stremme, 2003); *Inventions That Rocked the World* (Mason & Stephens, 2004); and *Incredible Inventions* (Griffiths, 1996). This scientific unit of study takes about three to four weeks. On a designated date, the inventions are officially judged and awards are presented. Student winners move on to the next level of participation. Some past winners were: a baseball cap that had a light shining down on a girl's face so that her deaf mother could read her lips at night; a collapsible skateboard; a pacifier that had a built-in thermometer; a stackable washer/dryer that automatically dropped the clothes into the dryer after the wash cycle was over. Look online for additional information on either of these competitions.

Squid Dissection

In Linda Lemen's, Janet Manen's, Linda Sheeler's, and Michele Janette's third-grade classrooms, there is an excitement that is present every spring when the squid dissection lab begins. Students sit in partners with a squid on their desks. Charts abound in the room, and there is an abundance of narrative and expository books about squid along the perimeters of the classrooms. Parent helpers are in place, and an enthusiastic third-grade teacher is ready to instruct her students on how to dissect a squid. Each child has a squid packet and is guided through the process step by step. There is a lot of partner interaction and involvement from the children in the discussion. This lab situation is repeated with all third-grade classrooms. Expert teachers provide instruction for teachers who are less comfortable with the instruction. Teaming can be advantageous to all the students at a site. Teach your strengths, so that your students get the best of your expertise.

The parents help with the cooking preparation of the squid so that all students can taste the squid. Preparation is done outside due to the strong aroma. The day has been a memorable one that students remember for years to come.

The Challenger Space Center

In 1986 the families of the space shuttle *Challenger* 51-L crew helped create a program to perpetuate the lives of their loved ones who died in the tragedy on January 1986. The outgrowth is an exciting simulation for upper-grade and middle school children. Students take on roles of the shuttle program—half of them in ground control and the other half in the space shuttle. This program inspires and educates students about the mysteries and wonders of space and science. Problem solving, communication, and decision making are stressed before, during, and after the simulation takes place. There are forty-four international operating centers. The cost of the program is a little steep, but it is well worth the money. The Challenger Center for Space Science Education Web site is an excellent link to astronomy and space science and also has student activities for teachers to download. Challenger Center information is available at www.challenger.org or at 1250 North Pitt St., Alexandria, VA 22314.

REFERENCES

Armbruster, B., Anderson, T., Armstrong, J., Wise, M., Janisch, C., and Meyer, L. (1991). Reading and questioning in content area lessons. *Journal of Reading Behavior, 23,* 35–59.

Armstrong, W. (1969). *Sounder.* New York: Scholastic.

Avi. (1984). *The fighting ground.* New York: Trophy.

Avi. (1990). *The true confessions of Charlotte Doyle.* New York: Avon Books.

Buckley, J., Jr. & Stremme, R. (2003). *Book of lists.* Santa Barbara, CA: Shoreline Publishing.

California Department of Education. (1999). *Reading/Language Arts Framework for California Public Schools Kindergarten Through Grade Twelve.* Sacramento: Author.

Cherry, L. (1990). *The great kapok tree.* Orlando, FL: Harcourt.

Cherry, L. (1992). *A river ran wild.* Orlando, FL: Harcourt.

Doeden, M. (2005). *The sinking of the titanic.* Mankato, MN: Capstone.

Fleischman, S. (1995). *The thirteenth floor.* New York: Bantam Doubleday Dell.

Florian, D. (1986). *Mammalabilia.* Orlando FL: Harcourt.

Florian, D. (1997). *In the swim.* Orlando, FL: Harcourt.

Florian, D. (1998). *Insectopedia.* Orlando, FL: Harcourt.

Florian, D. (2001). *Lizards, frogs, and polliwogs.* Orlando, FL: Harcourt.

Fountas, I. C., & Pinnell, G. S. (2001). *Guiding readers and writers grades 3–6.* Portsmouth, NH: Heinemann.

Gibbons, G. (1996). *Caves and caverns.* New York: Voyager Books.

Gibbons, G. (1997). *The moon book.* New York: Scholastic.

Griffiths, N. (1996). *Incredible inventions.* New York: Scholastic.

Grutman, J. (1994). *The ledgerbook of Thomas Blue Eagle.* Palm Beach, FL: Lickle Publishing.

Hiscock, B. (1993). *The big storm.* Honesdale, PA: Boyd Mills Press.

How to draw . . . (series). London: Usborne Publications.

How your body works. (1997). Fairfield, IA: Henderson Publishing.

Learning Media, Ministry of Education. (1997). *Reading for life: The learner as a reader.* Wellington, NZ: Learning Media.

Mandell, M. (1992). *Simple science experiments with everyday materials.* New York: Sterling Publishing.

Masoff, J. (2000). *Oh, yuck! The encyclopedia of everything nasty.* New York: Workman.

Mason, J., & Stephens, S. (2004). *Inventions that rocked the world.* New York: Scholastic.

O'Dell, S. (1970). *Sing down the moon.* New York: Bantam Doubleday Dell.

O'Dell, S. (1980). *Sarah Bishop.* New York: Bantam Doubleday Dell.

PBS Kids. www.pbskids.org

Pearson Education, Inc. wwwpearsonlearning.com.

Pratt, K. J. (1992). *A walk in the rainforest.* Nevada City, CA: Dawn Publications.

Rhatigan, J., & Gunter, V. A. (2005). *Cool chemistry concoctions: 50 formulas that fizz, foam, splatter and ooze.* New York: Sterling Publishing.

Ridpath, I. (1993). *The children's giant atlas of the universe.* Melbourne, Australia: Hamlyn Children's Books.

Scieszka, J. (2004). *Science verse.* New York: Viking Press.

Simon, S. *Einstein Anderson* (series). New York: HarperCollins.

Smith, M., & Wilhelm, J. (2002). *Reading don't fix no chevy's.* Portsmouth, NH: Heinemann.

Speare, E. G. (1983). *The sign of the beaver.* New York: Bantam Doubleday Dell.

Stead, T. (2002b). *Should there be zoos? A persuasive text.* New York: Mondo Publishing.

Taylor, T. (1969). *The cay.* New York: Avon Books.

Taylor, R. (1991). *Journey through inventions.* New York: Smithmark Publishers.

Traugh, S. *Voices of America* (collection). Cypress, CA: Creative Teaching Press.

VanCleave, J. *Experiments* (series). Hoboken, NJ: Wiley.

VanCleave, J. (1996). *Janice VanCleave's 202 oozing, bubbling, dripping and bouncing experiments.* San Francisco: Jossey-Bass.

VanCleave, J. (1999). *Janice VanCleave's 203 icy, freezing, frosty, cool and wild experiments.* San Francisco: Jossey-Bass.

Wellnitz, W. R. (1993). *Homemade slime and rubber bones.* New York: Tab Books.

Wright-Frierson, V. (1999). *A North American rain forest scrapbook.* New York: Walker Publishing.

Yolen, J. (1992). *Letting swift river go.* Boston: Little, Brown.

TEACHER RESOURCES

Allison, L. (1977). *Blood and guts.* New York: Scholastic.

Almeida, D., & Cullum, A. (2002). *American history playhouse.* New York: McGraw-Hill.

Base, G. (1986). *Animalia.* New York: Harry Abrams.

Five plays. (1995). Middleton, WI: Pleasant.

Harvey, S., & Goudvis, A. (2000). *Strategies that work.* York, ME: Stenhouse.

Hoyt, L., Mooney, M., & Parkes, B. (2003). *Exploring informational texts.* Portsmouth, NH: Heinemann.

Janisch, C., & Meyer, L. (1991). Reading and questioning in content area lessons. *Journal of Reading Behavior 23,* 35–39.

Kramer, S. P. (1987). *How to think like a scientist: Answering questions by the scientific method.* New York: HarperCollins.

Kristo, J. V., & Bamford, R. A. (2004). *Nonfiction in focus.* New York: Scholastic.

Lindquist, T. (1997). *Ways that work: Putting social studies standards into practice.* Portsmouth, NH: Heinemann.

Lindquist, T., & Selwyn, D. (2000). *Social studies at the center.* Portsmouth, NH: Heinemann.

Richards, R. (1992). *101 science tricks.* New York: Sterling Publishing.

Routman, R. (2003). *Reading essentials.* Portsmouth, NH: Heinemann.

Schanzer, R. (2004). *George vs. George: The American Revolution as seen from both sides.* Washington, DC: National Geographic.

Schwartz, D. (2001). *Q is for quark: A science book.* Berkeley, CA: Tricycle Press.

Stead, T. (2002). *Is that a fact?* Portland, ME: Stenhouse Publishers.

Walqui-van Lier, A. (1993). *Literature review: Sheltered instruction.* Bilingual teacher training program: Sheltered Instruction Institute. San Diego: San Diego County Office of Education.

West, T. (2001). *Terrific mini-plays that build reading skills.* New York: Scholastic.

Yolen, J. (1999). *The Mary Celeste: An unsolved mystery from history.* New York: Scholastic.

A BIOGRAPHICAL JOURNEY
A FAMOUS PERSON IN HISTORY
A POSTER BOARD

You are about to embark on a biographical journey. You will be taking a trip through another person's life, either someone who lived in the past or someone who is currently living. This individual should be worthy of remembering for a contribution he or she has made to our lives or someone else's life.

Hereís What You're Going to Do

1. Select a biography—that's a story of someone's life. There are so many interesting people to choose from. Here are a few to get you thinking: Bill Cosby, Elvis Presley, Harry Houdini, Judy Bloom, Michael Jordan, Wyatt Earp, Clara Barton, Princess Diana, Mark Twain, Louis Pasteur, George Bush, Martin Luther King.

2. In the next few weeks, read the book you have chosen. Remember to pace yourself. Don't leave it until the last minute—that's called procrastination. Use your bookmark to record your reading habits.

3. While you're reading your book, also read information about your person in the encyclopedia, an almanac, or another reference book.

4. Make a list of ten facts about his or her life. Keep that list until you have completed the book.

5. Find five important dates in this person's life. You will be making a short time line in class.

6. Locate a picture of your person. It should be bigger than an encyclopedia picture. Put this picture or book on my desk with a sticky note letting me know what picture needs to be copied.

7. Select two colors of construction paper. One is for the background and should be 12 by 18 inches. The other is for the foreground color for your poster that will be used for the following cards:
   - A name card (9 by 2 ½ inches) with the name of famous person
   - A date card (9 by 2 inches) with the birth and death dates of the person
   - A fact card (9 by 6 inches) with six to ten important facts about your person
These cards should all be the same color.

8. Frame the picture of your famous person on a piece of paper the same color as your cards above.

9. Do not glue anything onto your mini-board yet. You want to make sure that you have proper spacing on the board and that things are not too crowded or too sparse.

10. In pencil, write out the information you need for your cards.

11. Have someone proofread it.

12. Go over your words in fine-line black marker.

13. Erase your pencil marks.

14. Space out your information cards on your background construction paper.

15. Prepare a mini-talk (2 to 3 minutes) for your classmates about your famous person. Your biography poster board will be your visual aid. You may want to use another prop or dress up as the person.

16. Also use your time line to show a little about your famous person.

A BIOGRAPHICAL JOURNEY (*continued*)

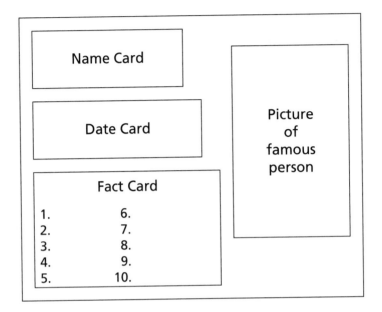

Name Card

Date Card

Fact Card

1. 6.
2. 7.
3. 8.
4. 9.
5. 10.

Picture
of
famous
person

NATIVE AMERICAN POSTER BOARD PROJECT

Name: _____ Date: _____

Basic activities: We have been talking about Native Americans in the continental United States. You have each selected a tribe that you are interested in researching. We have also been talking about topic sentences and how real writers write information paragraphs. Now it is your turn to put your knowledge from your research into gear. Using the research skills that we learned in class, you will now branch out on your own independently.

- Choose one of the U.S. Indian tribes found in another state. A few examples are Navajo, Zuni, Blackfoot, Pawnee, Chippewa, Iroquois, Pueblo, Hopi, Cherokee, Seminole, Sioux, Apache, and Nez Percé.
- Locate materials, books, Web sites, and other references that will help you to become more familiar with your tribe. Make a list of these sources.
- Take notes as you read, or highlight the information if you have your own copies.
- Think about the important information that would make you feel that you truly know this tribe of people.
- Look over the rubric so you know what is expected.
- Organize your ideas in a logical way.
- Include at least *five* of the categories below or think of other areas that you would like to find out more about.

food	music
travel	ceremonies
war/weapons	religion
clothing	games
crafts	jewelry
language	shelter
hunting	education
government	important people

- Write about each of five or six categories on a 3- by 5-inch index card or type them up on a 3- by 5-inch piece of paper. (Of course, you can always do more, but make sure they'll all fit on the piece of paper provided. The paper will be 12 by 18 inches.) If it takes you more than one card to summarize your information, you may staple two or three cards together. Make sure you summarize in your own words. You will need a topic sentence for each card and at least five detail sentences, and most likely more.
- Include a map of where your tribe lives. If you don't have a blank one, ask your teacher for one.

Activity 13.2

NATIVE AMERICAN POSTER BOARD PROJECT *(continued)*

- Design a Native American border for your poster display. Use the ideas that you have seen in class.
- Include at least one hand-drawn illustration. You may also include other pictures if you have room.
- Neatly glue down your information in an organized manner on a piece of paper that your teacher gives you in class.
- Show that you have become an expert by sharing your poster and your bonus activity with your classmates.

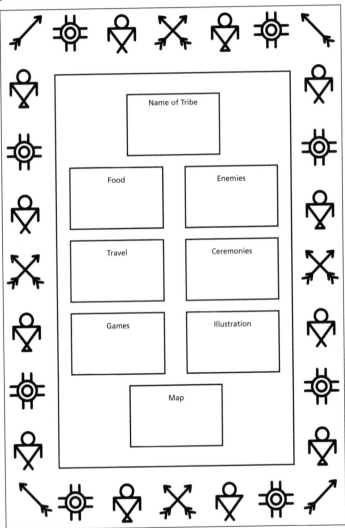

Bonus Activities

Choose at least one of the following activities to help you learn about your specific tribe or another Native American tribe:

1. Create a game that children of your tribe might play. Try to use real materials that the people would have used. Share the game with your class. Use the reference books in the classroom to give you some ideas.

2. Create a piece of jewelry that your tribe members might have made themselves. You may use authentic materials such as shells, beads, or feathers. If you can't get the materials, draw the design on a piece of paper using color, and label what materials you might use if you had them.

3. Watch a video that illustrates what Native American life was actually like. Make sure your parents approve of it. If possible, ask them to watch it with you. Make a sequence chart to show the main points about the video.

4. Write a story about an adventure that a girl or boy of your tribe might have had.

5. Write a poem about something in your tribe's natural environment. Some ideas you might think about are the wind, streams, eagles, buffalo, forests, seasons, rain, flowers, mountains, lakes, snow, and sky.

6. Think of the words in the song "Color of the Wind" from the Disney movie *Pocahontas.* Create your own song that shows the importance of the environment in the life of your people. Perform it for your classmates.

7. Create your own Native American musical instrument. Make sure that it looks authentic and that your tribe might have had the materials to make it. If you cannot obtain the materials, draw a design of it, and identify what materials you would use if you had them.

8. Draw pictures of tools and weapons that your tribe members used for hunting, weaving, cutting skins, and making a shelter. Label each.

9. Design an Indian village in a box or on a piece of tag board paper to demonstrate how your Indian group lived. Write an explanation of what is happening in your village. Label the parts.

10. Perform a ceremony or dance that your tribe may have performed. You may want to dress in a costume.

11. Make a chart to show what your tribe's language looked like. Seek out information to learn how to pronounce the words. Help your classmates to learn a few words.

12. Interview a Native American. Compose ten questions that you would like to know about his or her life and culture. Try to take a snapshot during the interview.

13. Visit a museum that has a display of an Indian group. Jot down eight to ten new things you learned about the tribe, and share this information with your classmates.

14. Make a food that your tribe members might have eaten. Share it with your classmates.

15. Plan a visit to your class by a Native American. Assist him or her in deciding what information to cover about his or her culture. Make sure your teacher approves and can assist with the schedule.

16. Visit a public cultural presentation, ceremony, or program at a local Indian reservation. Summarize your visit.

17. Learn five to ten words or phrases in sign language. Present them to the class.

NATIVE AMERICAN POSTER PROJECT RUBRIC

Name: _____ Date: _____

You have at least five well-written paragraphs (mini-reports) that include lead and detail sentences about your Native American tribe.

5   4   3   2   1

Your poster report clearly shows pacing, planning, and organizational skill.

5   4   3   2   1

You have a labeled map that clearly shows where your tribe lived.

5   4   3   2   1

You have included a minimum of one quality hand-drawn illustration and two other illustrations of your specific tribe. Each illustration is labeled with a statement about its importance.

5   4   3   2   1

Your poster is neatly written or typed, is neatly glued, is well spaced, is visually appealing, and is quality work.

5   4   3   2   1

You have at least one bonus activity that is grade-level quality and is properly labeled.

5   4   3   2   1

Your oral presentation shows knowledge of your subject, is well organized, and shows adequate preparation.

5   4   3   2   1

Total number of points _____

Overall letter grade _____

Comments

Activity 13.4

EXPLORER NOTEBOOK STUDENT PACKET

Name: _____ Date: _____

We will be studying European explorers of the 1400s and 1500s in the next few weeks. You and your team will become the experts on your explorer. You may find a brief overview of your explorer in your textbook, but you will also have access to many books, maps, diaries, articles, and Web sites that will provide you with more information. One period each day will be provided in class to work on this project, for a total of about eight in-class work periods. Some work will need to be done at home.

Basic Activities

Do these as a team:

- Read at least three articles about your explorer from the materials you received in class. Prove that you read the information by highlighting the important facts that you need or by taking notes right on the paper. This should be done as a group, so that everyone has access to the same facts. The more that you read about your explorer, the more of an expert you will become. You may read other materials at home or gather more information online.

  Papers that you have used should be handed in with this project.
- Take notes on an individual copy of the explorer CD. This is your personal copy for note taking.
- Complete the team CD report on your assigned explorer on an enlarged circle resembling the CD on this paper. Make sure that everyone has done his or her part.

  Due Date: _____

Activity 13.4

EXPLORER NOTEBOOK STUDENT PACKET *(continued)*

- One choice is to write a public announcement letting the people of your village know about your voyage. Include where you are going, who is paying for your voyage, information about your crew, and what you expect to find. Be descriptive, and use an illustration. Due date: _____

The second choice is to write or draw a "want ad" to help attract crew members for the voyage. Make it look authentic. Use parchment paper that is provided in the room. You may even want to burn the edges of your paper at home with the help of an adult to make it look more authentic. Due date: _____

Write a journal entry essay explaining about your crew, the ship, problems you faced on the voyage, and the weather. Because you have read widely, you should be able to fill in a bit of the information with your creativity. Since you know where your explorer traveled, you should know something about his surroundings and the land. Also include information about the area explored: animals, food, plants, and human life that he might have encountered. For instance, if he traveled in the Bahamas, you would know that it is a tropical area, that people wore few clothes, and that they ate fruits. You may draw pictures of what he might have seen. Use parchment paper. Due date: _____

- Design a group cover for a folder that includes all of your team members' names, your explorer's name, the date, and an illustration. All of your work will be placed inside and be evaluated.

Individual Activities

Choose two of the activities below:

- Create a time line showing your explorer's life events.
  Due date: _____

- Create five interview questions that you would ask your explorer if you met him in person. The questions should not be yes or no answers, but should ask about how the person felt about events and people during his lifetime.
  Due date: _____

- Draw a free-hand map showing your explorer's voyage. If he made more than one voyage, draw the lines of the voyages in different colors. Use the parchment provided in class. Make sure you include a map key and a compass rose.
  Due date: _____

- Write a "report card" for your explorer. Give him grades of A to F in the following five categories: leadership skills, treatment of others, contributions to history, organization and planning, and intelligence. You may want to add a few more categories that you think he should be graded on. Next to each grade, justify (give reasons) why you gave the grade you did. You may give any grade as long as you justify it.

EXPLORER NOTEBOOK STUDENT PACKET *(continued)*

- Draw a four-frame cartoon showing your explorer's life, voyages, and contributions to our lives.

- Draw pictures of technological instruments that helped sailors find their way on the high seas at the time your explorer lived. Label each, and tell how it was used.

- Put together a model of a ship used during this time period.

- If you have a historical ship near where you live, visit it, and write a summary of the things you learned.

- Compose a sea chantey. Make the words go along with some work that is done on the ship. In other words, it should have a work rhythm. Put the chantey to a favorite tune.

- Pretend that you are the captain of a ship. Write a three-day diary of what might have happened during that part of your voyage, or write an essay in the first person about the problems that a captain had.

- Find a recipe for hardtack or another authentic ship food. Write down the recipe, and make copies for your classmates. Then prepare the food for your classmates.

- Research the part that pirates played during the period of exploration. In words and pictures, describe a pirate's life.

- Create a list of rules that you as the captain expect your crew to follow. Make it into a poster that can be hung up on the ship for all the crew to see. Also include a list of punishments a captain might give for not following the rules. Use parchment paper, if available.

- Write a story about a mutiny on the high seas.

- Make a thorough drawing of a vessel that would have sailed during the 1400s and 1500s. Label the main parts. Make sure the drawing is quality work. You may use color or you may keep it in sketch form.

- Make up a skit to show the interaction between a captain and a crew member. Dress your part, and thoroughly role-play your character. You may put it on videotape.

- Write a poem about an explorer using the following formula or one of your own format:

  Line 1: Explorer's name

  Line 2: Two adjectives that describe the explorer, joined by *and* or *but*

  Line 3: A verb and an adverb showing the explorer in action

  Line 4: A simile or metaphor describing the explorer's action in line 3

  Line 5: An "if only" phrase that expresses a personal wish related to the explorer.

- Create a sea monster or serpent that an explorer might tell stories about when he returns home. Write a story explaining where, when, and how the monster was spotted and how it affected the journey.

EXPLORER NOTEBOOK STUDENT PACKET *(continued)*

- Research another explorer, this one of more modern times. Write a short paper telling others about the explorer and what contributions he or she made to our lives.

- Pretend that you are a cabin boy or girl on a ship during your explorer's time. Write a creative story telling about the difficulty of your trip and how the captain and other crew members treated you.

- Plan an expedition to a place that you might want to explore in the future. Explain the following: what place would you like to travel to; equipment and materials needed; weapons needed for protection; types and amounts of food; number of people in your expedition and what skills they would need; anticipated dangers; what you hope to find; length of the expedition; and cost of the expedition.

Activity 13.5

EXPLORER NOTEBOOK (GROUP) STUDENT CHECK-OFF LIST

Group member names _____

Explorer name _____

_____ Explorer Round Information CD
_____ Wanted poster
_____ Group explorer "expert" presentation
_____ Explorer questions
_____ Additional information from other sources
_____ Use of the map
_____ Individual world map and explorer route
_____ Note taking and highlighting sheets

Please note below how you think you worked as a group. Who helped the most? The least? Did everyone do his or her part? (This will be kept private.)

_____

_____

_____

_____

_____

Tell what you think you did that went above and beyond the rest of the team. In other words, tell me what you did to help your group. Be specific. Examples could be Internet research, took home the group organizer, did the wanted poster, wrote a script, read a book about the explorer, worked well as a team.

_____

_____

_____

_____

_____

Overall group grade: _____   Overall individual grade: _____

Activity 13.6

SAMPLE STARTERS FOR THE DIARY ENTRY FOR
THE GREAT KAPOK TREE

Paragraph One

Dear Diary,

What a day this has been! I was out with my buddy working on cutting down a kapok tree and I had to rest because of all the hard work. While I was sleeping, I dreamed of all these animals, and did they have some stories to tell me about not cutting down their tree! Let me tell you about them.

Dear Diary,

I'm not sure what really happened today while I was sleeping, but let me tell you what I was dreaming about.

Dear Diary,

Today while I was cutting down trees in the forest, I got very tired and fell asleep. As I was napping, I heard strange voices of animals telling me about the importance of this tree. First of all, there was a boa constrictor that said . . .

Dear Diary,

This tree must be really important to the animals of this forest. While I was sleeping, I thought I heard voices telling me why I shouldn't cut down their tree.

Paragraph Two

I learned so many things today.

I thought I was so smart when I was cutting down the tree, but I learned so many things from the animals. Let me tell you a few things about what I learned about the animals and myself.

I learned a lot about myself today.

Paragraph Three

I thought it would be so easy to cut down this tree, but now I know that I can't ever cut one down again. I feel upset because . . .

I feel so sorry for the animals in the rain forest because . . .

I am angry that so many animals are becoming homeless because of the careless cutting down of the trees.

I am sad for the animals of the forest because . . .

I am glad that the animals let me know how important their home is because . . .

RUBRIC FOR *THE GREAT KAPOK TREE:* POINT OF VIEW RESPONSE TO LITERATURE

PORTFOLIO ENTRY

You are to take the point of view of the man in the forest. Write a diary entry that you (the man) might have kept on the day the story takes place.

Paragraph One describes your day in the forest—what you were doing there, why you fell asleep—and summarizes what the animals whispered in your ear. (You don't need to tell about all the animals, just two or three.)

5   4   3   2   1

Paragraph Two tells what you learned about yourself and the animals that lived in the rain forest.

5   4   3   2   1

Paragraph Three tells about your new feelings about the forest, the animals, and yourself. (Use your own feelings here from your prior knowledge and past learning.)

5   4   3   2   1

Your paragraphs are organized and have at least five sentences.

5   4   3   2   1

Your final draft is neat and uses correct spelling, capitalization, and punctuation.

5   4   3   2   1

Your work is grade-level quality.

5   4   3   2   1

Total points earned _____   Student's name _____

Activity 13.8

RESEARCH NOTE-TAKING SHEET

Student's Name _____

On this sheet of paper, you will begin to record information for your research report. While you are reading from the many books provided, jot down some important facts that you want to remember. (You may need three, four, or even more lines to write down your notes.) In the column on the left, write down the author's last name, and in the middle column the page number that you found it on. If you need more space, staple this sheet to any other pieces of notebook paper where you take notes. You'll use these notes to assist you in writing your research paper.

Author's Last Name	Page Where Found	Notes

INFORMATION ABOUT BIBLIOGRAPHIES

1. A bibliography is a list of the books, encyclopedias, pamphlets, magazines, and other reference materials that you use to form your ideas for your research paper.

2. While you are taking notes about your subject, you should make a list of the resources you are using.

3. There is a prescribed way to list materials in your bibliography.

   a. Alphabetize items in your bibliography according to the last names of the authors or, where there is no author, the first important word in the title.

   b. When an entry takes more than one line, indent all the lines after the first.

   c. Follow the style in these examples:

   BOOK: Author [last name first]. *Title.* City where the book is published: Publisher, date.
   Example: Smith, Mary. *Making Hearts with Children.* San Diego, CA: Gordon Press, 2006.

   ENCYCLOPEDIA: "Article Title." *Title of the Reference Book.* Edition. Year published.
   Example: "Art." *World Book Encyclopedia.* 2005 ed.

   ONLINE SOURCE: Author [last name first]. "Title of Article." Title of file. Publication date. Name of computer network. Date of electronic retrieval. Electronic address.
   Example: Adams, Marissa. "Making Hearts with Construction Paper." *Art in America Quarterly,* April-September 2003. Retrieved January 25, 2006, from http://www.art.new. com.

To write this report, you will need to use at least three references or sources. You should have at least one encyclopedia, one source from the Internet, and one book. You might also have a magazine or pamphlet.

As you start to take notes, jot down the important information about the source that you are using. When you are finished, rewrite the bibliography following the guidelines given above.

315

MYSTERY PLACE OR MYSTERY CREATURE RESEARCH REPORT RUBRIC

Name: _____ Date: _____

You have chosen a topic about a mysterious creature or place in the world and have received a note-taking and bibliography packet. You have also had an opportunity to use the Internet to access materials for this report. After taking notes and underlining key facts for your report, start to write your report. Use this rubric as a guide. Depending on your topic, your paragraphs may be slightly different.

1. Introduce your topic. Make sure that you explain why you choose this topic and what you expect to find out as you perform your research.

    1   2   3   4   5

2. Discuss the importance of this place or creature. Tell what it is and where you would find it. Give important details about why this place is important in the world of mysterious things.

    1   2   3   4   5

3. Discuss some of the strange events that have taken place here or with this creature. You might discuss investigations that have taken place to see if this is a real creature or if the area really is mysterious.

    1   2   3   4   5

4. Discuss the theories or explanations that scientists give about this place or creature. According to the experts, is this real? Is this really mysterious, or is there a logical explanation?

    1   2   3   4   5

5. Tell what you think about this place or creature. Form your own opinion, and explain your own thoughts now that you have become the expert. Do you believe that this is real or not real? Pose questions of your own if possible.

    1   2   3   4   5

6. Write a concluding paragraph. You might start it with, "In conclusion . . ."

    1   2   3   4   5

Include all of these with your report:

*   A picture or drawing of your creature or place.
*   A map to show the exact location of your creature or place.
*   A title page with your name, date, and the title of your report.
*   A list of all the books and other resources that you used (the bibliography).

7. Your work is grade-level quality and has few errors in spelling or grammar.

Total points earned _____

Activity 13.11

WHAT YOUR MYSTERY RESEARCH REPORT SHOULD INCLUDE

Name: _____ Date: _____

Since every mystery subject area is different, individual reports will differ. This sheet will give you an idea about what you should include. Please make sure that you are taking notes from three different sources. Many books are available in the classroom, and Internet sites are set up for your use. Your report should include all of the areas listed below, but you may want to include other things not listed that you find interesting. Some of the ideas may be combined into one paragraph. The paper should be approximately *two typed pages* in length.

- What is it?
- Where do you find it?
- What history does it have?
- Why is the area mysterious?
- Theories that explain it. How do others explain the mysteriousness of this subject? What is your opinion, and why?
- Interesting, weird, strange, or fascinating facts about your subject not already mentioned.
- What feelings or thoughts do you have about your subject now that you have read widely about the subject?
- How has this research affected your thinking, and why is the subject important to you and to others throughout the world?
- Can you make any connections to other topics, events, or personal experiences?

You must also include:

- One quote from one of your sources
- An illustration, chart, graph, or map (a visual aid)
- A bibliography with three sources of information (see your Mystery Folder research packet for the correct setup of information)
- A set of notes from your reading and all pages of the research packet from your Mystery Folder
- An attractive, well-done cover page (include your name, grade, date, and the title of your report)

MYSTERY RESEARCH PROJECT RUBRIC (INDIVIDUAL)

Name: _____ Date: _____

Information provided in the research paper

       1   2   3   4   5

Organization and neatness of research paper

       1   2   3   4   5

Spelling, grammar, and punctuation

       1   2   3   4   5

Use of time in class

       1   2   3   4   5

Map

       1   2   3   4   5

Cover

       1   2   3   4   5

Illustrations

       1   2   3   4   5

Overall quality of the project and neatness

       1   2   3   4   5

Extra activities _____

Total points earned _____

Activity 13.13
MYSTERY POWDER OBSERVATION SHEET

Name: _____ Date: _____

At this center you are to observe and explore the mystery powders in the containers. Explore through the use of all of your senses. All of these powders can usually be found in your kitchen or bathroom. They are edible. Record your results. Write a brief but detailed explanation of each powder. Use descriptive words; use the thesaurus if you have difficulty. Remember that a good detective has to keep detailed notes.

Mystery Powder 1 _____

_____

Mystery Powder 2_____

_____

Mystery Powder 3_____

_____

Mystery Powder 4_____

_____

Mystery Powder 5_____

_____

Mystery Powder 6_____

_____

Mystery Powder 7_____

_____

Mystery Powder 8_____

_____

Mystery Powder 9_____

_____

Mystery Powder 10_____

_____

Mystery Powder 11_____

_____

Mystery Powder 12_____

_____

Mystery Powder 13_____

_____

Note to the teacher: Here is a list of possible powders that you might want to include. You may include this list of powders or leave them off the student activity sheet.

Choices: granulated sugar, powdered sugar, salt, baking soda, baking powder, cream of tartar, NutraSweet, flour, baking soda tooth powder, dairy creamer, pancake mix, garlic powder, onion powder

Activity 13.14

RESEARCH TOPIC SUGGESTIONS

Name: _____ Date: _____

Here are some topic suggestions for your discovery project:

1. Gravity
2. The Butterfly and Its Life Cycle
3. Thunder and Lightning
4. Orthodontics—How It Works
5. All You Want to Know About Ice Cream and More
6. The Poisonous Snake and How It Affects Us
7. The Great Houdini—Why Does His Fame Live On?
8. Earthquakes—Nature Shakes the Earth
9. Police Dogs and Their Training
10. How Does a Person Become a U.S. President?
11. A Close-Up Look at the Game of Soccer
12. The History of Rock and Roll
13. Dreams and What They Mean
14. Dyslexia and How It Affects a Person
15. Right Brain/Left Brain—What Are the Characteristics?
16. I Want to Be an Astronaut—Here's the Real Scoop
17. The Life Story of an Ant—Why Do We Need Them Anyway?
18. The Black Hole
19. The Story of Elvis Presley and His Impact on the Music World
20. The Beatles and Their Impact on the Music World
21. Twins: The Tale of the Two of Us
22. What Is ADD?
23. Mummification and Why the Egyptians Used It
24. What Is an Atom?
25. Japanese Relocation in the United States During World War II
26. Mosquitoes
27. Bacteria
28. All You Wanted to Know About Poison Ivy and More
29. Chocolate
30. I Want to Be a Psychologist
31. Yellowstone National Park
32. Bubblegum
33. Rock Climbing
34. Moto-cross
35. Snowboarding

DISCOVERY FAIR DUE DATE SCHEDULE

Due Date _____ Research Activity _____

_____ Narrow your choices to one subject
_____ Visit the library to find books on your subject
_____ Note taking—First check
_____ Note taking—Second check
_____ Note taking—Final check
_____ Topic outline—Main topics
_____ Topic outline—Main topics and subtopics
_____ Bibliography index cards
_____ Final form of bibliography
_____ Rough draft check—First three paragraphs
_____ Rough draft check—Second three paragraphs
_____ Rough draft check—Third three paragraphs
_____ Rough draft check—last paragraphs
_____ Title page
_____ Research paper cover
_____ Display board sketch
_____ Final research paper (cover, title page, outline, research paper, bibliography, and "extras")
_____ Lettering for display board
_____ Pictures, graphs, maps, and other extras framed on construction paper

DISCOVERY FAIR ESSENTIALS

1. This project consists of three parts: the research paper, the display board, and the oral presentation.

2. All parts should be neatly written in cursive writing or typed.

3. The research paper should be _____ to _____ pages in length. It should be written in your own words. It should include the following things:
   - An attractive cover
   - A title page
   - A topic outline
   - A bibliography (at least three sources should be used)
   - "Extras" (see the attached "extras" sheet)
   - Numbered pages

4. The display board will consist of three panels. The total size is _____ by _____. You may design items for the board at home, but the final placement of materials will be done in class. *No gluing* will be done before the board has been checked by the teacher. Try to limit the number of "copied" pictures that you use. Make your own materials, such as maps, charts, and graphs. A combination of written descriptions and graphics should be used. Tell the story of your subject in words and pictures.

5. The oral presentation: See the Student/Teacher Evaluation Form to see what items you will be graded on.

STUDENT/TEACHER EVALUATION FORM

Name: _____ Date: _____

Written Report
Title _____ (5 points)
Cover _____ (5 points)
Neatness _____ (10 points)
Information _____ (20 points)
Introduction _____ (5 points)
Conclusion _____ (5 points)
Bibliography _____ (5 points)
Outline _____ (5 points)
Spelling/grammar _____ (10 points)
On time _____ (10 points)
Pages numbered _____ (5 points)
"Extras" _____ (10 points)
Ink/typed _____ (5 points)
Total points _____ (100)

Oral Presentation
Total time taken _____
Knew information well _____ (10 points)
Well prepared _____ (10 points)
Looked at audience _____ (5 points)
Spoke loudly _____ (5 points)
Used notes well _____ (5 points)
Posture of delivery _____ (5 points)
Answered questions well _____ (5 points)
Stayed within time limit _____ (5 points)
Total points _____ (50)

Display Board
Good use of color _____ (5 points)
Straight positioning
of lettering _____ (5 points)
Pictures and other graphics well framed _____ (5 points)
Neatness of written and drawn materials _____ (10 points)
Good spacing of items _____ (5 points)
Personally created materials _____ (5 points)
Spelling, grammar, and punctuation _____ (5 points)
Lettering, gluing, erasing _____ (5 points)
Use of preparation time in class _____ (5 points)
Total points _____ (50)

STUDENT/TEACHER EVALUATION FORM (continued)

Final grade _____

Written report _____
Display board _____
Oral presentation _____
In-class work habits _____
Teacher's comments:

RESEARCH: ADD SOME OF THOSE "EXTRAS"

Name: _____ Date: _____

You may want to add some of the following things to your project to make it come alive. Try to make them "home grown." In other words, make them yourself—don't just use photocopies from your sources. Add those personal touches that show your reader more about your subject. Here are some things you can add to make your research paper more interesting.

1. Make your own map of the area you are researching.
2. Add a chart that tells more about your subject.
3. Take a survey; then draw a graph showing your results.
4. Interview an expert.
5. Invite a guest speaker expert to talk with your class about your subject.
6. Find a newspaper or magazine article about your subject.
7. Preview films, videos, and sound strips from the library or other school supply or materials center.
8. Add music to your presentation.
9. Dress up in costume to get more "into" your topic.
10. Make a diorama or model.
11. Make a special food associated with your subject.
12. Take snapshots of some aspects of your report.
13. Make a PowerPoint presentation to enhance your research.
14. Draw an illustration or picture of some aspect of your research.
15. Make a time line to show the progression of time for your subject.

RESEARCH DAILY LOG

Name: _____

Research topic: _____

Keep a daily record of the time you spend working on your research project. Keep an accurate account of what you accomplish during your work time. Your teacher will be reviewing this log with you occasionally.

Date	Time Begun	Time Ended	Tasks/Accomplishments

STUDENT INTEREST SURVEY FORM FOR OBSERVATIONAL INVESTIGATION

Name: _____ Date: _____

Answer the questions below. By doing so, you will begin to gather your thoughts on what interests you. This may help you to create a science question that you would like to pursue.

1. If you were not at school today, what would you be doing right now?

   _____

   _____

   _____

   _____

2. When you get home today, list two things you will probably do. _____

   _____

   _____

   _____

3. If you could write one question right now about anything in the world, what would you ask? _____

   _____

   _____

   _____

4. Pick one of the things that you are interested in, and write two questions about it. _____

   _____

   _____

   _____

Activity 13.21

OBSERVATION STUDY

Name: _____ Date: _____

You will need to allow yourself a chunk of time to do this observational experiment. Try not to leave this until the last minute. You may do this project at school, at home, or in the field (a mall, grocery store, gas station, intersection).

The focus will be on *observation*. The ideas that follow are what I call *behavioral*—that is, observing the way people act in certain situations:

At the Mall . . .

- Watch couples at the mall. Design an experiment to see who carries the bags while shopping: male or female.
- Observe the bags that people carry at the mall. Design an experiment to see which is the favorite store based on what bags are being carried.
- Drop coins (penny, nickel, dime, quarter). How quickly does someone pick up these coins after they have been dropped?
- What age group is most likely to pick up a coin at the mall?
- What kinds of foods do people eat at the mall? Observe those walking around, or go to the food court area.
- Sit at a bench, and watch people pass by for fifteen minutes. Tally the number of children (boys and girls) and adults (men and women).
- When a man and woman are going to a movie, who buys the tickets?
- How many woman wear jeans? Compare the number to those who wear dresses and skirts?
- How many men wear shorts compared to long pants?

At an Intersection . . .
- What kinds of vehicles (vans, pickups, sedans) tend to signal when turning?
- At a crosswalk, how many cars stop behind versus in front of a crosswalk?
- What is the most popular car type or color that passes?
- What is the most common state license plate?

At the Grocery Store or Gas Station

- When a man and a woman are shopping together, who pushes the basket?
- How many people do major shopping compared to light shopping?

OBSERVATION STUDY *(continued)*

- Do more women or men pump their own gas?
- How many people pay their bill with cash compared to credit card, debit card, or checks?

At School

- Give fifty students a taste test to see which drink, cupcake, or some other food of your choice is the most preferable.
- Show students pictures from magazines of different foods on cards to determine what food they would select as their favorite.
- Show students pictures of faces of people. Ask them which one they would prefer as a friend or neighbor.
- Color cookie dough with blue, red, and green food coloring. Which color cookie do people select the most?
- Compare two brands of one kind of cookie or similar other product. See which one children of different ages prefer.
- Which do more students at your school prefer when given the choice: a nonfat version of a product or a regular version of it?
- Sit in one spot for a certain amount of time. Count the colors of the shirt, blouses, and T-shirts that people are wearing. Besides plain colors, there may also be combinations of color or a multicolor category.
- Count the number of children who are wearing jeans as they walk by you.
- How many children have blond hair? Black hair? Brown hair?

These are just a few ideas. Try to create something of your own. Have fun with this!

Requirements

- Use a large sample of subjects—between twenty-five and fifty.
- Try to collect all your data on the same day.
- If possible, take snapshots of your experiment as you are working. This will be a record of your experience and will help you remember what you observed and how you gathered your data.

OBSERVATION PROJECT INFORMATION SHEET

Name: _____ Date: _____

1. State your question: _____

   _____

2. What is your prediction/hypothesis? _____

   _____

3. Make a list of the materials you will need to carry out your experiment:

   _____

   _____

   _____

4. List the steps that you will take in order to carry out the experiment (the procedure):

   _____

   _____

   _____

   _____

5. Write in summary form what you find out—that is, your conclusions or findings.

   _____

   _____

   _____

   _____

   _____

   _____

   _____

BECOMING A PUMPKINOLOGIST: AN OBSERVATION AND HANDS-ON INVESTIGATION

Date of Investigation _____ Pumpkinologist's Name _____

Partner's Names _____

You are about to embark on a scientific investigation or science lab. You will be a new kind of scientist called a *pumpkinologist*. You will see that you have a few things to research online and through reference books. You will keep all of your notes and research information in a small notebook called a *blue book*. (This is the book that college students use when they take a test.) Your teacher will evaluate each section of this lab on a five-point basis.

One Week Before the Investigation

Find out everything you can about pumpkins. Make a bulleted list of the things that you learn about pumpkins over the course of the week. We will compile a class list and chart it. You may earn up to five points for your information. Make sure you write down the reference where you got your information.

Possible points _____ (5)

First Half-Hour of the Investigation

- Look carefully at your pumpkin. Turn your pumpkin to one side, and draw exactly what you see. Make sure you have the correct shape, number of creases, blemishes, coloration, gouges, stem color, and so on. Color your picture with pencils.

- Make a list of ten or more words and phrases that describe your pumpkin, such as *bumpy, oblong, imperfect, bright orange, perfectly round, blemished on one side, one side is flat.*

- Make some predictions about the circumference and weight of the pumpkin and the number of seeds you think will be inside.

Possible points _____ (5)

BECOMING A PUMPKINOLOGIST: AN OBSERVATION AND HANDS-ON INVESTIGATION (continued)

Second Half-Hour

Outside of the Pumpkin

Find answers to as many questions as you can during this half-hour:

1. Does the pumpkin float? If it does, how does it float in the water? How much is above the waterline and below the waterline? Does it float straight up, on its side, or bottom up?
2. How many creases does it have?
3. What is the circumference?
4. Where are the creases closest together?
5. How do you know what side the pumpkin rested on while it was growing?
6. Does the stem tell you anything about how the pumpkin grew?
7. What do you notice about the creases from the outside?

Inside of the Pumpkin

1. Do the seeds line up with anything on the outside?
2. How are the seeds arranged inside the pumpkin?
3. How do seed size and pumpkin size compare? Look at other pumpkins to find your answer.
4. Are all the seeds the same size? Compare yours to several other pumpkins.
5. Where is the pumpkin shell the thickest?
6. How much empty space is in the pumpkin?
7. Describe the smell of the pumpkin.

Possible points _____ (5)

Third Half-Hour: Seed Counting

1. Take all of your seeds out of the pumpkin.
2. Put the seeds in groups of twenty-five for fast counting.
3. You will get an approximate number of seeds for your count—some will drop and get lost. Do the most accurate count possible.
4. Put the seeds in the plastic bags and label them with your name and number in permanent marker.
5. Record your information on the classroom chart.

Possible points _____ (5)

BECOMING A PUMPKINOLOGIST: AN OBSERVATION AND HANDS-ON INVESTIGATION *(continued)*

Fourth Half-Hour

1. Write up a summary of your findings.
2. Assign someone to roast the seeds at home for everyone.

Possible points _____ (5)

The Next Day

1. Share your findings.
2. Draw conclusions from the class chart.
3. Discuss the benefits of the investigation.
4. Eat your seeds.

Possible points _____ (5)

Total Points _____ (35)

PUMPKIN INVESTIGATION LETTER TO PARENTS

Dear Parents,

On _____ (date) morning we will be scientifically dissecting pumpkins to learn more about these orange wonders. The purpose is to find out through investigation, observation, questioning, and thinking all about them. Math, science, social studies, and language arts will be used to discover the pumpkin's secrets. We will be using the area outside the cafeteria. Thanks to each of you who have already donated a pumpkin for this event.

So that each child has success, I would appreciate it if your child could bring some of the following items to school on _____ (date). Please mark the item with your family name:

- A scoop or large spoon
- A tape measure
- Serrated pumpkin carving knife (usually with an orange handle)
- Small plastic bags with ziplock bags for the pumpkin seeds
- An old shirt or apron to protect clothing

Some children really dislike getting seeds and pulp all over their hands, so you have any clear, thin plastic food handler gloves, please also send them. I will have a few on hand also.

If you're interested in helping us out, plan to be here about _____ on _____ (date) morning. We can use all the help we can get.

Sincerely,

_____

[Your name]

PLANT OBSERVATION TEAM SHEET

Team name: _____

Question: _____

	Quantitative Observation		Qualitative Observation	
	Plant A	Plant B	Plant A	Plant B
Day 1				
Day 2				
Day 3				
Day 4				
Day 5				
Day 6				
Day 7				
Day 8				
Day 9				
Day 10				

Hypothesis: What might happen? Give two or three possibilities.

_____

_____

_____

Experiment Design: What steps did you do?

_____

_____

_____

_____

SCIENCE PROJECT STUDENT EVALUATION

Name: _____ Date: _____

1. One thing that I learned by doing this project is _____

_____

2. What I liked most about this activity was _____

_____

3. What I liked least about this experience was _____

_____

4. What I think I could do better if I attempted this again would be _____

_____

5. I feel successful about this assignment because _____

_____

6. I estimate the time spent completing this project was approximately _____

_____

7. I would like my teacher to know _____

_____

8. If I were to give myself a grade on this activity, I would give myself a/an
   _____ because: _____

_____

_____

Chapter 14

MOTIVATING STUDENTS TO BE SUCCESSFUL MATHEMATICIANS

We all know people who are logical-mathematical learners. They are skillful at manipulating numbers, problem solving, and analytical reasoning. They are good at interpreting data, figuring out things, and exploring abstract patterns and relationships. They are strong in math and science (Gardner, 1983).

Then there are math teachers like Mrs. Fibonacci in the *Math Curse* by Jon Scieszka (1995) who are so passionate about their subject that they instill in their students the thought, "You can think of almost everything as a math problem." This teacher makes us realize that there is math all around us, day in and day out: lunch, social studies, health, science, and physical education. She is absolutely right because in today's world, virtually every job requires some mathematical thinking and reasoning. So if our world is filled with math, how is it that so many children are still having difficulty understanding and making sense of it in our schools, and why do more than two-thirds of American adults fear and loathe mathematics (Burns, 1998)? What about this generation of students? Will their parents pass on this fear to them, or will the spell be broken through the new reform?

Why do so many students have a negative attitude toward math as they reach the upper grades? They did not when they were in kindergarten through third grade. Math was fun to them. In a 1995–1996 study of 500,000 students, U.S. fourth-grade students scored above average among the forty-one participating nations, whereas eighth graders scored below the international average and significantly below average at the twelfth grade (U.S. Department of Education, 1997). More recent research points to the same fact. What happens to that excitement that is so apparent in math at the primary grades? We are fortunate that reform has been happening, but there's still a long way to go.

RECENT REFORM IN MATH INSTRUCTION

The National Council of Teachers of Mathematics (NCTM) has led reform in mathematics instruction. This reform movement is reaching not only the United States but has spread worldwide to the entire mathematics community.

NCTM Standards

The NCTM Standards (2000) emphasize the need to prepare all students for algebra beginning in kindergarten and progressing through each grade. Gagnon and Maccini (2001) summarize these standards setting forth goals of learning that encompass valuing mathematics, becoming confident problem solvers, and learning to communicate and reason mathematically.

According to *Principles and Standards for School Mathematics* (NCTM, 2000), in order for high-quality mathematics to take place, there must be high expectations set and strong support given to all students; mathematics must be looked on as an integrated whole, not as isolated facts; professional development must be encouraged so that teachers know how students learn and plan instruction accordingly; and students can and must learn mathematics with understanding. Furthermore, teachers must use a variety of assessment techniques to meet their students' needs, and technology such as calculators and computers must be considered essential tools for helping students learn.

Teachers will inform their instruction by helping students navigate through problem-solving experiences, giving reasons and proof for their answers, writing and explaining their thinking aloud, making connections to the real world, and using a variety of representations to show their understanding. (The current NCTM Principles and Standards for School Mathematics can be found at www.nctm.org.)

Applications for the Classroom Teacher

Math is cooperative, hands-on, and a lot more fun than it used to be. Looking back at how many of us learned mathematics when we were in school, this is a huge shift in the way instruction needs to look in classrooms today. Many of us were taught in a teacher-directed way. We watched the teacher, listened to the teacher, and then did numerous problems that made many of us dislike math. Doing twenty-five long division problems at night sent many of us into a tailspin. The more problems that were assigned, the more likely we were to make computational mistakes. It is no wonder that many teachers are so comfortable with the teacher-directed approach. Teaching in the old way was easier: the answers were either right or wrong. Once the lesson was taught, all the teacher had to do was take out a red marking pencil and put the dreaded red checks on the missed problems. Many of us today have adverse reactions to red pens and pencils because the check marks made indelible markings in our mathematical brains.

The transition to new ways of math instruction will take time and administrative patience. Small steps are better than no steps at all. Putting child-centered practice into the math program will be monumental and highly rewarding. We will begin to see change as we encourage students to listen to each other and learn that there are different ways to solve a problem and that individual reasoning and problem solving are valued. Change is always difficult, but once we see the benefits and rewards for students, we too will be gratified knowing that we are changing to meet the needs of our students who live in a changing word.

The Rush to Be Ready for Standardized Testing

In 2001 Congress passed the No Child Left Behind Act, which mandates every state to test children in every grade beginning in third grade. This puts pressure on all educators to be ready for the test, sometimes putting demands on children to hurry up and learn. If all the curriculum is not taught, then how will the students be ready to be assessed? For every teacher and administrator, students have to do better than last year because our worth is being determined by how well our students do in testing. There has been an increased demand for higher achievement and proficiency in mathematics. Math content is becoming increasingly complex at earlier ages (CEC, 2003). Every teacher from kindergarten on must do his or her part to ensure that all students are meeting their grade-level standards by the end of the year.

According to Sousa (2001), about 6 percent of school age children have some form of difficulty with processing mathematics. So how can we make sure that they too are proficient and successful in math?

According to Van de Walle (2004) well over 80 percent of the classrooms are using traditional, teacher-directed textbooks. This type of program, using a textbook for the basis of instruction, will help students learn skills needed for high-stakes testing, but will it teach them understanding of the concepts and prepare them for their future problem solving and higher-order thinking? Probably not. The fast-paced instruction to make sure that all the standards are taught before testing begins puts a lot of pressure on teachers to keep teaching from the textbook and instructing with formulas and other devices to rush learning. Unfortunately, this pace does not teach depth of understanding, so students have not internalized the concepts and often mix up formulas and skills and forget important math strategies to use. When children do not have number sense firmly in place and have shaky understanding of the standards, how can they do well on a test?

Van de Walle discusses both traditional and nontraditional (reform curricula) programs. He characterizes these latter programs as having student engagement, making sense of mathematical ideas through exploration and projects, encouragement of written and oral communication, the importance of teacher training and supportive activity guides, and using teacher resources and consumable materials for students instead of textbooks. Looking at this information makes us wonder why so many classes continue to do so much test preparation. Perhaps what we need to think about is that good math teaching of the big ideas gives students a foundation that will help them in all life math problems, including those that they find on tests.

When traditional programs are compared to reform curricula or nontraditional programs, Van de Walle (2004) points out that in these reform programs, students perform much better on problem-solving measures and at least as well on traditional skills as students in traditional programs. He cites many sources that support this idea (Arc Center, 2002; Bell, 1998–1999; Boaler, 1998; Fuson, Carroll, & Drueck, 2000; Reys, Robinson, Sconiers, & Mark, 1999; Riordin & Noyce, 2001; Stein, Grover, & Henningsen, 1996; Stein & Lane, 1996; Wood & Sellers, 1996, 1997).

The Balancing Act in the Math Classroom

As is the case in all aspects of instruction, math needs to be approached in a balanced way. For older students, the hands-on approach and the more directed textbook drill-and-test approach must reach a happy medium: students must be exposed to some of each in order to be comfortable in real-world situations and on standards-based assessments. Teachers must use the tools required of them through their state and city mandates, but they must also keep in mind the needs of their students and how to reach them on a personal level. No one program or activity can reach all students' mathematical needs. Therefore, using a variety of materials, resources, and teaching tools is by far the best way to accommodate the diverse needs within the upper-grade classroom. In truly inclusive classrooms, student mathematical needs can have a huge span of a few months to several years. Sometimes gifted students are several years above grade-level math standards, whereas sometimes they have voids in their understanding that need to be addressed. Every student has voids and challenges. Just because a label of "smart kid" has been placed on a student does not mean that the student excels in all academic areas. (See the multiple intelligence section in Chapter Two.) For instance, a student may be well above grade level in reading but may be somewhat deficient in math. Meeting all of our students' challenges is a daunting task but what teaching is all about.

A textbook is used in the majority of classrooms across the United States; therefore, students need to know how to use a textbook and how the format is set up. Teachers will need to show students how to navigate through a math text, so that they can use all of the supports the text can give when they are working independently. For organizational purposes, some classes hand out assignment sheets on a weekly basis so students know what they have to complete. The daily assignment, project assignments, dates of tests and quizzes, problems of the day and week, extra credit, family math activities, and other math puzzlers are placed on this sheet. Students keep records on this sheet indicating what they have accomplished and how well they have done by figuring a ratio and a percentage score. This information helps them pace their day and week. Parents appreciate knowing what their children are doing and what the teacher's expectations are. (See Activity 14.1, Math Assignment Sheet, at the end of this chapter.)

Balancing the paper-and-pencil tasks with the more child-centered, hands-on approach for problem solving encourages exploration and investigation. No matter what, math has to make sense and so does instruction. In today's math classes, the goal must be seeking understanding, not just rote memory of a formula or procedure. Why do you invert a fraction and multiply and to question *why?* It is because our teachers did not learn the *why* when they were in school. By using a variety of materials and resources, including the textbook, by the time our students reach the secondary level, they should thrive in math and not let it intimidate them. It is important that all students, no matter what their level in math, have materials available to them that will help them access the big ideas. For instance, in Carolyn Hasselbar's fifth-grade room, the students might approach a problem with the use of 100s charts that are protected with plastic

sleeves and can be written on with whiteboard markers, large chart-sized graph paper, a variety of math manipulatives, and whiteboards and pens. Having appropriate materials at arm's reach can provide entry levels into problem-solving tasks.

SETTING UP THE CLASSROOM

Teachers must set up the classroom environment at the beginning of the year to let students know right away that math is going to be a vital part of every day. Students should be able to observe signs of the importance of math just by looking around the classroom.

Literature for Read-Alouds and Math Centers

In the past decade or so, there has been a plethora of books that act as springboards for math lessons. Many of them are picture books that are colorful and engaging, providing motivating stories that capture the interest of the students and focus attention on math concepts and skills. These books provide an effective way to encourage talking about math ideas. Using interesting books with a math theme provides a new avenue to hook readers into math. Even reluctant math students can focus on math through a read-aloud. Many of the books can be used for launching a new concept or a review of an idea that the children are still grappling with. Never discount the power that a picture book can have in getting across an idea. Many times these books can bring greater understanding and creative thinking into the math workshop. To get the students off to a great start, read *The Math Curse* by Jon Scieszka. This book gets children thinking about math experiences in their own lives. Through books, we truly open up the world of math to all students.

Listed below are a few books that have proven to be worthwhile additions to the math program for older children:

Esio Trot, by Roald Dahl (New York: Puffin, 2002).

Grandfather Tang's Story, by Ann Tompert (New York: Crown Publishers, 1990).

How Much Is a Million? by David M. Schultz (New York: Lothrop, Lee & Shepard, 1985).

Marvelous Math, by Lee Bennett, Hopkins (New York: Aladdin, 2001).

Millions to Measure, by David M. Schultz (New York: Scholastic, 2004).

Once upon a Dime, by Kelly Allen (Watertown, MA: Charlesbridge Publishing, 1999).

Sadako and the Thousand Paper Cranes, by Eleanor Coerr (New York: Dell, 1993).

Sir Circumference and the Dragon of Pi, by Cindi Neuschwander (Watertown, MA: Charlesbridge Publishing, 2000).

Sir Circumference and the Knights of the Round Table, by Cindy Neuschwander (Watertown, MA: Charlesbridge Publishing, 1997).

Sir Circumference and the Great Knight of Angle Land, by Cindi Neuschwander (Watertown, MA: Charlesbridge Publishing, 2002).

The Best of Times, by Greg Tang (New York: Scholastic, 2002).

The Complete Paper Airplane, by Michael Shulan (Mahwah, NJ: Watermill Press, 1979).

The Grapes of Math, by Greg Tang (New York: Scholastic, 2001).

The Greedy Triangle, by Marilyn Burns (New York: Scholastic, 1994).

The Hershey's Fraction Book, by Jerry Pallotta (New York: Scholastic, 1999).

The King's Chessboard, by David Birch (New York: Puffin Pied Books, 1988).

The Librarian Who Measured the Earth, by Kathryn Lasky (New York: Little, Brown, 1994).

The Man Who Counted: A Collection of Mathematical Adventures, by Malba Tahan (New York: Norton, 1993).

The Math Curse, by Jon Scieszka (New York: Viking, 1995).

The Number Devil, by Hans Magnus Enzensberger (New York: Holt, 1998).

The $1.00 Math Riddle Book, by Marilyn Burns (Sausalito, CA: Math Solutions, 1990).

The Warlord's Beads, by Virginia Pilegard (Hong Kong: Pelican Publishing, 2001).

The Warlord's Puppeteers, by Virginia Pilegard (Hong Kong: Pelican Publishing, 2003).

The Warlord's Puzzle, by Virginia Pilegard (Hong Kong: Pelican Publishing, 2000).

Twizzlers, by Jerry Pallotta (New York: Scholastic, 2001).

What Is a Polygon? by David Alder (New York: Holiday House, 1998).

Math Manipulatives to Have on Hand

A classroom that is ready for math adventures, explorations, experiences, and investigations should have a large variety of materials for children to get their hands on quickly. Plastic see-through tubs with lids are perfect storage bins for some of the materials such as rulers, protractors, compasses, colored pencils, and calculators. You can find a large variety of these bins at teacher supply stores or in their catalogues. Finding the size for your needs is a personal choice. The storage containers should be neatly labeled for child availability. For other items, such as counters, tiles, pattern blocks, base-10 blocks, and unifix cubes, use sturdy ziplock plastic two-gallon freezer bags.

Charts: Support for All Learners

Until recently educators have had to rely on commercial charts, chalkboards, and whiteboards to support and scaffold classroom instruction. Often, though, these charts blend into the wall and are not used for anything except filling bulletin board space. Nevertheless, personalized teacher-created or student and teacher co-created charts (charts created by students and teachers) can be effective in helping support learners in all areas of the curriculum. When students have input into the charts, they are more apt to use them for their learning. When a substitute, parent, or administrator visits a classroom, good charting helps them size up what is happening in that room. In math, the charts support the learning that is being worked on and gives additional places to locate information for help with meaning and understanding. There might be personal charts showing process and progress in thinking, brainstorming charts, vocabulary charts to support the unit of study, and procedural charts that show step by step how a problem can be broken down. These act as reminders of learning for students who need visual cues.

Contrary to commercial charts, teacher/student charts are personalized. They show the thinking that has been going on in that particular classroom. Many teachers write what the child commented on the chart and then put the child's initials or name next to the entry. This gives ownership to that child's thinking, and because it has been recorded, the class may return to it the next day or a week later. Because the child's name is mentioned, that child may want to change his thinking on a future day and when the chart is revisited, changes and reflections can be made. It is a good idea to keep the charts up for the duration of the unit. They act as a beneficial review of concepts that children need before an assessment or test. One teacher told a story of a student who was taking a standardized test. She was staring at a cleared-off space where a procedural chart had been recently. When she was asked what she was looking at, the fourth grader said, "I'm trying to remember what information was on that chart. I need it now!" She *was* able to retrieve the chart information and did respond on the test with the correct answer. The impact on her was profound. Charting had affected her learning.

Charting can be time-consuming and takes up a lot of space. Teachers must make decisions on how much is enough. If the room becomes overly crowded with charts, they lose their effect, and the clutter can be counterproductive. For space constraints, some teachers cut chart paper in half or use smaller-sized paper. For time constraints, it does not have to be done every day—just when it is relevant. Charting does not have to be perfectly neat; it is a record of discussions that you take on the run. Sometimes children make their own charts in small groups or by themselves. Charting provides the scaffolding and support to reinforce math learning.

Math Word Walls

Many classrooms maintain a list of math words on a portion of their word wall. The internalization of the math words comes through use and application. Words that are being discussed such as *denominator, numerator, multiples,* and *factors* are placed on the wall when they are introduced. Sometimes quite a few words are presented during a lesson, such as in a geometry unit. Many of those words might be familiar to the students, but some students still need to have a visible reminder of their meaning. The word wall acts as a reminder of the most recent lessons and is a scaffold for students who need them. Many times these words are also written in the students' math journals or on flash cards, but the more the student sees and uses the word, the more the word will become part of his or her vocabulary.

In most upper-grade classrooms, there is a short, "kid-friendly" definition attached to the word. Sometimes when a definition is taken directly from the glossary of a textbook or a dictionary, it is still confusing to the student. A simplistic, rewritten definition in words that children can connect with and remember can be more manageable for students to understand. The word wall should be adjusted or modified on a daily or weekly basis. Some words may stay up for a long period of time, and others will be used briefly and taken down quickly. In some classrooms, students are responsible for putting the new words up on the wall, and in others the teacher is responsible. If the majority of students understand a word, it does not need to stay on the wall. When a word is on the word wall, there is no excuse for not spelling it correctly in writing. Word walls give students a place to look to find the word they need for writing or speaking. If there is not enough wall space to create a separate math word wall, then using a chart with related words and definitions is the next best thing.

Having a math dictionary such as *Mathepedia* (Randall et al., 2000) can be helpful when a word cannot be located in the textbook glossary. Having a few copies of the dictionary on hand is even better.

SUPPORTING CLASSROOM LEARNING

On the first day of school, students begin to assess whether their class is a good or a bad place to take risks in math and whether this is going to be a comfortable or uncomfortable place to spend a year. Students size up the other students, the teacher, and the classroom environment. These first days and weeks of school are vital in establishing a safe, respectful, child-centered classroom. Children need to feel free to take risks and to know that they are not going to be made fun of or laughed at for giving a wrong answer or for making mistakes.

Developing Classroom Community

It is well worth the time to model for students how to listen, respond to one another, and think out loud. Kind, caring, and courteous responses are encouraged and rewarded. The teacher and the students can model role-playing situations of active listening. What does it look like, and what does it sound like? The students may format a chart as a reminder of this protocol. Talk and thinking out loud must be taught and valued. The idea that everyone has something of worth to bring to the discussion and that diverse ways of thinking strengthen each other's ability must be firmly implanted. Respectful thinking and listening must be taught and practiced. Teachers can see if active listening is taking place because children will be responding, gesturing, nodding with affirmation, looking perplexed, or restating what they have heard.

It is essential to give multiple opportunities to talk with others about math ideas. For that reason, changing students' seats regularly is helpful in building community. The students quickly learn that sometimes they are the leader or expert in a key mathematical concept, and sometimes they will be the learner or follower. Sometimes they will be on similar mathematical journeys, and at other times they will be on opposing journeys. Students must learn that everyone is responsible for helping others to understand new concepts and that learning is not just one teacher with one student. Students must see themselves as "experts" whose ideas and learnings should be shared with others who do not understand.

The cooperative learning environment is rewarding. Students become more active, self-directed, and communicative. Academic achievement and discipline often improve when children feel successful and interested in the tasks they are performing (Walter, 1996). Cooperative learning experiences are built into the daily math routine and instruction:

- *Partners.* Working in pairs, one student works a problem while the other coaches. Roles are then reversed. After a couple of problems are completed, partners pair up with another set of pairs and compare answers and check one another (Kagan, Kagan, & Kagan, 2000). Choosing partners should be quick and uncomplicated. In the upper grades, they should be more random than assigned. The teacher might say, "Turn to the person next to you. Choose who will be a partner A and who will be partner B. Partner A will be the *doer.* You will do the division problem on the whiteboard first. Partner B will be the *coach* or *overseer.* You will be responsible for seeing that your partner is doing the problem correctly. Let your partner do the problem by himself or herself first. Then look it over and make suggestions or talk him or her through the problem where thinking has broken down."
- *Group and teams.* Teams of four work a problem together and check each other's understanding on one or more problems. Then the team breaks into two pairs and continues to work together to solve the next couple of problems. Students then continue independently working similar problems (Kagan, Kagan, & Kagan, 2000). When students are working like this, they may want to work on a larger piece of paper with markers so that the work is easily visible to everyone. Then it can be placed on the board with magnetic clips for easy sharing with classmates.

Teachers should provide for lots of interactive work with partners, triads, and quads. Children are less likely to feel intimidated in small groups.

This give-and-take of responsibility and cooperation gives all students an opportunity to feel successful, and if they are struggling with a concept, they have group support to get them through the hard parts. These steps from teacher direction and modeling, to student sharing and cooperation, to independent application foster a gradual release of responsibility (Pearson & Gallagher, 1983) that is applied to instruction in all other areas. The model calls for teacher demonstration and modeling, guided practice (the structure and scaffolding to support exploration), independent practice, and then application and follow-up. In other words, everybody has to do his or her part to allow individuals to take on the responsibility for his or her own learning and application of skills taught.

Following are ways to build a strong math community in your classroom:

- Let the students know how important math is to you. Model your thinking about how math has influenced your life. Tell about the good times and bad times that you have had in your math history. Let students know (or at least think) that you love math. Talk about your learning styles and how you learn math yourself. What do you do when something mathematical doesn't make sense to you?

- Promote self-esteem by calling on math-challenged students when you know that they have learned a concept and can verbalize it to others.

- Students who have difficulty in number and operations and algebra strands may be spotlighted in geometry, graphing, probability, and measurement. These strands may provide less of a challenge and allow students to shine as mathematicians.

- *Fishbowl* around students who know what they are doing in math. Call out the word *fishbowl*, and students drop what they are doing and form a circle around the students you want to model some mathematical idea.

- Read lots of books about math and students who like math—create a community of readers about math.

- Have a center for math books that you have read and that you want to read. Have kids share the books to let them see that math is alive and well in your room.

- Have fun with personalizing math story problems. Add the students' names and special interests to the story problems. For instance, if you have students who love baseball, skateboarding, extreme sports, shopping, or special kinds of books, incorporate those interests and topics into math problems to be solved.

- Capitalizing on a student's strengths and interests can hook in even the most reluctant mathematician.

- Show students that you value their thinking, and impress on the class that everyone has something to offer. Reward acts of constructive working partnerships.

- Personalize children's comments when charting math by putting their name or initials next to their idea.

- Take lots of pictures of the students, and put their pictures near their math work on bulletin boards or next to their math goals for the week, month, or year.

- Allow students to help plan and organize events such as parties, field trips, cafeteria menus, author's writing celebrations, and parent visitations. This helps children organize and work with numbers, dates, and data in a mathematical sense.

- Have the students show what they know through their strongest modality: visual, auditory, or manipulative. This might include drawing, graphing, writing, acting-out demonstrations, and singing. Be open to all aspects of a child's personality. Let them show you what they know.

- Let all students feel that they can be an expert or teacher. When a child shows a promising practice, let him or her be the teacher of the minute and take over teaching the lessons.

Engaged Students, Noisy Students

Math classes today look much different from math classes five to ten years ago. Math is now active and engaging. Students must be involved learners. They should be talking, interacting, involved in conversations, leaning over desks in cooperative groups, thinking out loud, manipulating objects, creating charts, and drawing. Math can be noisy. For some teachers, that is an uncomfortable feeling because their math training was teacher-directed and independent work.

It is important for the individual teacher to set up parameters of the noise level that is appropriate for that classroom. Management techniques should be carefully thought through and consistently enforced. Some teachers allow the ripple effect to take place—in other words, let the conversation die down gradually. For instance, the teacher may give countdown intervals of five minutes, three minutes, and one minute so that students can summarize their thinking and gradually wrap things up. Signals might be used for stopping conversation: clapping rhythms, a bell, lights off, an Indian rain stick or other musical instrument or apparatus, a one-word command, or a backward countdown. Each signal is personalized, but the students will be aware of it and know that it means *stop*. Through reinforcement and consistency, the class will respond appropriately to the signal. Hands-on math is noisier than worksheet and textbook use; therefore, a teacher must establish clear standards for use of manipulatives.

If children are to learn math deeply, they must be given the chance to talk about math and bounce their ideas off each other. Purposeful noise will be part of the math class of the present and most likely of the future.

Of course, there must always be time for thoughtful reflection and quiet individual work. Assessment is used for all types of classroom work, whether it is cooperative or individual. Students learn quickly that some sessions are done alone and others are cooperative.

INSTRUCTIONAL PRACTICES

Much of the teaching of mathematics has changed over the past ten years. With the changes come questions of what is still appropriate to use and what needs to be eliminated or altered. Balancing the math program with a variety of good teaching practices that provide hands-on, mental, and computational experiences, plus time for problem solving and some of the basics, gives students a wide variety of opportunities to build a solid foundation for mathematical success.

Mental Math and Estimation

Marilyn Burns's research (1987) indicates two ideas that can help inform classroom instruction:

- More than half of real-life math situations call for mental math.
- Much of real-life math requires only an estimate or approximate answer instead of an accurate answer.

She indicates that by the time children leave elementary school, they should be able to do mental calculations with all numbers up to one hundred. We need to carve plenty of time within the school and home day to focus on mental computation and balance it with paper-and-pencil tasks.

A fun lesson for children to tackle with their families at home (based on Burns, 1987) is figuring out how much of their real-life math requires an exact answer and how much requires an approximate answer. As children begin to see the math needs of adults, the importance of approximating and mental calculations becomes clearer. Consider a visit to the grocery store. Let's say that a family has twenty dollars to spend at the store. As they are shopping, the student and parent might mentally add up, through approximation, how much the basket of groceries will cost. Next, they can check their answers with a calculator, using rounded-off prices (to the high side) instead of the actual cost. Then they can get an actual answer at the checkout stand. This situation is similar to the shopping adventure activity mentioned later in this chapter, which is done as a field trip. Life is truly one big math adventure, so use it to motivate children to look at math in their real life through mental approximations.

Other activities can be looked at in this same manner:

- Estimating mentally the cost of dinner when they are at a restaurant
- Estimating mentally the cost of a CD at the music store if the sign says it is on sale for 25 percent off the regular price
- Estimating mentally the number of miles it is to a particular location based on reading the miles on a road map
- Estimating and mentally adding the cost of the items they want to purchase at a store (children should have their own money to spend, so that they can weigh the cost of the items and determine if they really want it)

Problem-Solving Strategies

Teachers need to model problem-solving behavior whenever possible, exploring and experimenting with students. It is also important to ask questions that encourage critical thinking and the discovery approach:

"How did you solve the problem?"

"Why did that approach work [or not work]?"

"Can you think of another way to solve the problem?"

Teachers must also take the time to teach students specific steps for problem solving.

Upper-grade and middle school students should already have a foundation in these strategies and can help co-create a class chart that could be used for further study and support. Let the students come up with their own ideas first, but if they are at a loss for ideas, guide them to use some of the following problem-solving strategies.

- Read the problem out loud.
- Read the problem more than once before beginning.
- Restate the problem in your own words.
- Draw pictures, diagrams, and sketches representing the problem.
- Cross out irrelevant information.
- Circle, underline, or color-highlight the numbers that are important.
- Write the kind of answer needed (for example, miles per hour, degrees, dollars or cents).
- Use objects and manipulatives.
- Construct a chart or table.
- Act it out.
- Make an organized list.
- Look for a pattern.
- Make a model.
- Work backward.
- Eliminate possibilities.
- Guess (estimate) and check.

Messy Math—or Not?

A relatively recent shift of thinking is the idea that math can be messy. As students are exploring, investigating, and trying out their thinking on paper and with manipulatives, their daily work might not look as orderly and concise as we are used to. Many times the students are asked to draw a table, graph, or chart that organizes their information, but it is done informally and in a hurry and is not perfected. Just as in the writer's workshop, boys and girls write many pieces but take only a few through the full writing process. In math, many assignments and activities are rough sketches, quick drawings, and informal representations of thinking. Of course, they need to be readable, neat enough to share, and organized for finding when they are revisited, but they do not all need to look like cookie-cutter math projects. Thinking is messy. Our aim is to help students figure out their own ways to attack problem solving—the way that works for them.

There is, of course, a time when math needs to be neat, especially when computing must be correct and accurate. Some talented math students have difficulty with computation. They make careless mistakes and sometimes cannot even read their own numbers. Students need to be made aware when messy is appropriate and when it is not. If there are students having problems with organizing their work and are missing problems because of careless or unreadable writing of numbers, you might try using these alternatives (Rief, 2005):

- Encourage students to write and solve their computation problems on graph paper rather than notebook paper.
- Turn notebook paper sideways, with the lines running vertically rather than horizontally. This makes it much easier for students to keep numbers aligned in columns and reduces careless errors.
- Provide lots of space on tests and activity pages so that the work is not all scrunched together.
- Fold papers into eighths or fourths, and have the work contained in that space.

Use of Calculators—or Not?

Calculators are outstanding tools to facilitate and widen children's problem-solving skills, improve the use of mental math and estimation skills, and learn about the importance of place value, the correct operation, and the correct order of operations. They are useful for collecting, displaying, and analyzing data and discovering patterns. The fact that they also reinforce decimal notation of fraction, ratios, and percentages is a huge bonus for upper graders.

Campbell and Stewart (1993) found that calculators aid in "stimulating problem solving, in widening children's number sense, and in strengthening understanding of arithmetic operations." They can help students learn basics, such as numbers, counting, and the meaning of arithmetic operations. Students also show greater ease in problem solving when using calculators, since they focus less on computational recall and algorithmic routines and more on the other parts of the problem-solving process. Appropriate calculator use "promotes enthusiasm and confidence while fostering greater persistence in problem-solving" (Campbell & Stewart, 1993).

Math warm-ups can focus on using the calculator and getting used to how it works. Class discussions must center on reasonableness of solutions because students need to know how to read the calculator. Teachers need to ask key questions like, "Does that make sense?" "Is that reasonable?" "How do you know that is right?" Children and adults make lots of mistakes using the calculator. There are so many questions to answer: "Where does that decimal go?" " Why is there no 0 after the 8 in .8?" "How can I figure out percent when there are so many numbers in .37562?" Rounding, estimation, and equivalent fractions must be understood in order for the calculator to be valuable.

Calculators cannot serve as a substitute for good teaching or for the use of concrete materials or manipulatives in the classroom. They should work in concert with good math instruction while learning skills and strategies. Manipulatives and calculators should always be readily available for student use as a regular part of the classroom environment in elementary and middle school (Van de Walle, 2004).

Students should understand that there is a time for using a calculator, a time for using paper and pencil, and a time for mental math. A combination of these may be required for some calculation tasks. But on a standardized test, calculators might not be permitted, so paper and pencil, backed up with mental approximations, must be used. The fact that most adults do not keep a calculator with them all of the time should be pointed out. That means that many adults rely on mental math and approximations. How often do children see people in the grocery store or at the mall whipping out their calculators? That might be an interesting observation that could be calculated. It might also be pointed out that some mathematical professionals, such as tax consultants and financial advisers, and parents who are trying to balance their checkbooks use calculators. As children see a need for calculators, they will use them.

One other point to make is that kids are kids. They are going to make mistakes as they enter numbers into the calculators. They are going to forget which number needs to be put in first in a division problem. They are going to forget or misplace the decimal in the different operations. They input numbers quickly, do not check the numbers on the screen after they input them, and are not sure how to round off numbers. What happens when they get a decimal answer for a division problem and need a whole number or fractional remainder? Although there are a lot of questions, calculators are a valuable tool in our world.

Math Facts: Still Important?

Children still need a solid foundation in the basic facts and skills. If children get into the upper grades and middle school and have not developed some rudimentary understanding or memory of the basics, math is a puzzle to them. It is very difficult to have success with more advanced mathematical concepts and skills without the basics. Lacking the basics, students struggle to apply the skills of estimation to problems involving fractions, decimals, and percentages (those involving tax, tip, buying, banking, and so forth) in the real world.

Learning the basic multiplication facts is usually expected in the third grade, but some students struggle with them through the upper grades and even into middle school. Some educated adults even admit to not knowing all of them and having to work forward or backward from ones that they do know.

Some students have memory weaknesses that disable them from holding onto the facts. Poor mastery of basic facts should never prevent students from being taught grade-level math curriculum and higher-level concepts. Provide compensatory tools to help them past this hurdle while continuing to teach, practice, and review math facts on a regular basis in short sessions. A variety of strategies will help older students still having problems in mastering multiplication facts learn them: rhymes, raps, songs, finger plays, and other mnemonic devices (Rief, 2005).

So that they are not hampered from working with their classmates on more complicated problem solving, many teachers allow these students to use a "cheat sheet": a basic fact sheet that is laminated or placed in a plastic sleeve for protection. Other teachers encourage and allow the students to use a calculator. Both tools are used regularly and are kept at the child's desk. Calculators are always available for all students, but more confident math students choose to use them only on a limited basis.

Math Centers in the Classroom

To vary the math program and expose students to the use of their math skills in a more informal way, the teacher may provide a center day or a math lab where students choose or rotate into math-related centers. Depending on the teacher's schedule, this special math day may be once a month or even once a week for a thirty- to forty-minute session. This is the time when students apply all of their math skills. Students who have special academic talents should move beyond exploration of basic skills in these centers and study math in greater depth and complexity.

Math Center Possibilities

- Graphing center: Students find a large number of graphing pictures to create from numbered pairs. All developmental levels of graphing skills are stimulated by easy to more complicated pictures, including positive and negative integers.
- Math manipulative center: Students explore math manipulatives like geoboards, pattern blocks, pentominoes, and tangrams.
- Math game center: Students play games that teach math skills such as Othello, Sorry, SMath, Trouble, Mastermind, Pente, 50 in One, Uno, Dominos, HI-Q, Qubic, and Math Pentathlon.
- Restaurant center: Students choose from a variety of menus and order a meal, figuring tax and tip. Actual order receipts may be used to make the center seem more official for the students.
- Card center: Students play a variety of card games to enhance their mathematical strategies and skills, such as Concentration, Crazy Eight, and Rummy. Books such as *Deal Me In* (Golick, 1973) are readily available for other game suggestions.
- Computer center: To build their skills in math, students use a variety of math programs ranging from easy to more difficult games and activities or may visit benchmarked Web sites that are approved for student use. Some recommended math Web sites include:
  - MathStories at http://www.mathstories.com
  - A+ Math at http://www.aplusmath.com
  - National Library of Virtual Manipulatives at http://nlvm.usu.edu/en/nav/vlibrary.html
  - Cool Math 4 Kids at www.coolmath4kids.com
  - Funbrain at www.funbrain.com.
- Calculator center: Students have a variety of calculator activity cards, puzzles, books, and games to explore.
- Math art center: Students have a variety of art and math activities to create using geometry, tessellations, perspective drawing, number pictures, and line and angle drawings. (See Activity 14.2, Geometry Design Project, at the end of this chapter.)
- Measurement center: Students use a variety of measuring tools, including liquid and linear, metric and standard, to measure the world around them. The centers include rulers, yardsticks, metric sticks, containers, measuring cups and spoons, and tape measures.

Games and Other Activities to Help Students Practice

Children love to play games and can practice their math skills as they play. The first two games here, PIG and the 24 Game, are especially good for helping children sharpen mental math skills. Others, such as the student store activity and the pizza party, require students to apply math skills to real-life situations that are relevant to them.

PIG and the Practice of Mental Math

The object of this game is to add numbers on a die and be the first person to get a score of 100 or to have the highest score in ten rounds. The whole class can play the game together, or small groups of four to six can play at centers.

To begin, the teacher or another caller rolls one die. Students add the numbers on the die mentally. The caller then rolls the die again, and students add the numbers to what they have already. At any time, they may raise their hand to let the caller know that they are recording the total number of points they have added and are finished with that round. After writing down a number, a student's score is frozen for the remainder of that round; other students continue. When the teacher or caller rolls a one, the round is over. (If the one appears on the first roll, all children write down a zero for that round, and the next round continues.) Any student who has not recorded a number when the one is rolled must write down a zero for that round. All students begin play again with the next round.

The game continues for ten rounds or until someone reaches one hundred points. If ten rounds are played, the person with the highest score wins. Students keep their scores mentally but may add their scores for the rounds together with paper and pencil. (See Activity 14.3, Pig Score Sheet, at the end of this chapter.)

The 24 Game

This game is played with a set of cards printed on both sides, each with a different set of four numbers. The single-digit cards have numbers from 1 to 9. Double-digit cards have numbers from 1 to 24.

The object of the game is to reach 24 with all four numbers that are on a card. You can add, subtract, multiply, and divide. You must use all four numbers, but use each only once. The secret of the game is the science and language of patterns. Children love this game, and it can be played by students of all levels, from the most challenged to the most talented math students. The game comes in levels: add/subtract, multiply/divide; factor/multiples; double digits; variable; fraction/decimals; integers; algebra/exponents. The 24 Game editions are available through educational dealers and suppliers and at www.24game.com.

Student Council Student Store Activity

In one fifth-grade classroom, students are given the opportunity to run the student store. They work in five teams of six students each month to order items to sell to students from grades K–5. They are given a budget of a hundred dollars for ordering the supplies that they think will sell best. They establish a price for each item and clearly mark it. The student store is open every Friday, and each team is responsible for one month of sales. Occasionally students buy items from local stores. They are also in charge of marketing their products in creative ways. The money is counted up, recorded, and handed to the school secretary. A chart of how much each team earns for the month is kept in the classroom, and at the end of the sales period, the team that has earned the most wins a trip to a fast food restaurant. Discussions are lively and team oriented. Math concepts are clear and understandable. Everyone wants his or her team to win.

The service project is something that is fun to watch with students selling to students. The fifth graders have to mentally add up how much the items will cost the students. All items are multiples of twenty-five, so they are fairly easy for the students to calculate without calculators. In fact, calculators are not allowed. The younger children are mentally calculating the cost of the items they have in their hands. Everyone is having fun with math.

Pizza Party

In the same fifth-grade classroom, a pizza party is given every year to celebrate the results of test scores from the previous year. The class is broken up into cooperative groups. The assignment is to plan a class pizza party. No rules are established except that everyone must have something to eat and drink and the maximum amount that can be spent is fifty dollars. Some students try to find deals in the newspaper or use coupons or even have their moms make pizza from scratch, while other teams just go with the least expensive pizza they can find. Some students poll the class to see what kind of pizzas are the favorites. Many students use the telephone to find out about the best deals, and some go online.

Coming to consensus is the difficult part. A team of three adults is chosen by the class to evaluate which party would be the best buy to cover the needs of the class. Every team hands in its plan and makes calculations on a large piece of colored paper for everyone to look at and discuss. A lot of work goes into this plan, and it is not as easy as it seems. Children are encouraged to use their calculators and to have someone check their work. Only a few teams ever get their computation totally correct.

Decks of Cards in the Classroom

Many students who are puzzle and game players tend to feel more comfortable in math. Their first games taught basic skills and concepts of numbers, such as one dot on the die meant the player could move his or her playing piece one spot, two dots meant moving the marker two spaces, and so on. Game playing builds number confidence. Cards have educational and instructional value, and they also provide opportunities for children to interact in a fun and nonthreatening way. In her book *Deal Me In*, which is still in print and is an invaluable tool for math programs, Golick (1973) points out numerous skills that are used in playing cards. If parents question the use of cards in the classroom, this book will give intelligent responses to counter any disagreements.

Many other skills and strategies associated with playing card games are gleaned from this book. Golick (1973) divides the games into categories for developing different skills:

Fast verbal or motor reaction	Language building
Thinking	Motor skills and social skills
Notions of probability	Numerical sequence
Number concepts	Computation
Visual discrimination	Visual and auditory memory
Rhythm	

Upper-grade students in particular enjoy these card games:

Snap	Flashlight
Havana	Put and Take
Pisha Paysha	Go Boom
Crazy Eight Goof	Kings
Fan Tan Spit	Hearts

Deal Me In and other card game books are set up at the math center. When students are finished with their work or have a special math game day, they look through the books to find games that they are interested in and teach classmates how to play.

Keeping track of the many decks of cards can be a problem, so when a new deck is added, the cards can be marked with a symbol such as a heart, a star, or a happy face. This helps to keep decks together when the decks are the same design or pattern. An even better idea is to buy different designs. Cards are going to get lost and ruined, but they are inexpensive and easy to store. Staying away from card games that involve betting is strongly suggested.

ASSESSING STUDENT WORK

Math assessment is ongoing: it can be formal or informal; on the run or contemplated; individual, small group, or large group. Teachers must be observers of children and good listeners. Some assessment takes no more than a mental check of faces and the expressions on them. Walking around the room and listening to the conversations and the way that individuals are responding to each other and watching what children are doing are the best ways to assess. Teachers should always be on the move and observing who is showing understanding and who is not.

One-on-one conferring is probably the best way to find out who understands and who does not, but it is also the most time-consuming and logistically is not always practical for every new concept. Letting the whole class know that they are all teachers and should be involved in teaching others is critical. One teacher cannot attend to every question or confusion. In some classrooms, teachers turn over the instruction to the students by allowing them to be the teacher-for-the-minute (or minutes) to demonstrate and explain to their classmates how they solved a problem. They take control of the teaching process. An overhead pen in hand gives such empowerment. Providing this opportunity also communicates to students that their ways of solving problems are listened to and valued.

"We're all in this together" is a motto that can be integrated into the whole day. There are always students who want more of your time than is acceptable. The rule in some classes is that you must ask at least three other students for help before coming to the teacher, or everyone at the table or in the team must have the same question before a teacher is asked for help. This makes students responsible to others and encourages them to take on the learning and teaching in the classroom.

Written assignments can be used to assess students also. They allow the teacher to read them at another time to see who is showing understanding and who is not. Because written assignments involve more planned and organized thinking, they are a way for students who are somewhat quiet verbally to show what they know. Written products or directions can also be read by other students and questioned critically or discussed in order to resolve confusions. They may be used on the overhead or read aloud for modeling purposes. Children must become familiar with the idea that there are several ways that you can assess their work—orally, on paper, or through manipulating objects. The best assessments involve all three.

At the end of the year, it is informative to have students evaluate their learning in written form. How have they grown in math during the year? What have they learned? How have they changed their thinking about math? What new strategies will they use? What are their future goals? These are only a few of the questions that can guide student writing. Teachers can use a simple form or allow students to write freely about their math development during the year. (See Activity 14.4, End-of-Year Math Evaluation, at the end of this chapter.)

Assessment Through Testing

More formal assessments include weekly tests of concepts, district assessments that are given quarterly or each trimester, and standardized testing. Students need to practice these kinds of tests so they know how to take them.

Here are some ideas to make an in-class unit test a less intimidating and less stressful situation:

- Walk around as students are taking the test and put C's next to the problems that they have correct. This allows them to see the positives and gives them more time to reflect on their answers that are not correct.

- Have helpers correct the papers as individuals finish. Give the paper a score for the first round; then give the students a chance to work on the missed problems again. Average the two scores together to get a composite score.

- Let the students see the test the day before it is given, or use sticky notes to mark the areas in the textbook that will be tested.

- Vary the way the test is given, such as a take-home test, a partner test, an open book test, or a call-a-friend test. Students can also make up their own tests for the class. Changing the testing format can give children more confidence in test taking.

- Make up tests based on the problems that the students have already practiced. The boys and girls have already seen the problems, so they have a second chance to do them again. Typically a child who does not understand the problem when he or she did it the first time probably will get it right if he or she sees it again.

- Have parents initial tests to show that they have seen the work their child is doing. Make them aware of any problems their child is having in math. Math is not just an in-school activity.

- Send home a parent bulletin or a weekly or biweekly newsletter to communicate your ideas about math and what their child is doing in math. Let them know when a test is coming up.

- Teach students how the math text is set up or structured. Explain what the different colors used for subheads and features mean and how to find vocabulary that they have forgotten. Reviewing the procedures and trying out some of the problems the night before a test can ease a child's mind.
- Revisit the classroom charting.
- Give a teacher-made practice test, or use one in the textbook. The class may do it in partners or individually, or may take it home if they want more time. The next day, choose half of the problems that they did on the practice test and have them redo them for a formal assessment.
- If individual children do not do well on the assessment, provide small group or guided group time after school, before school, or at recess when they can come in to clarify their problem areas.
- Be accessible for children who need extra time. Ask another teacher to take your class for a video, extra physical education, or music for a few minutes so you can work with certain students who are experiencing difficulty. You might offer to take another teacher's students who are in need of help. If you cannot carve time out of your day, you might want to extend your day for after-school accommodation.
- Seek out adults who love math, and ask them to volunteer some time helping students who did not do well on the test. One-on-one time will benefit these students.
- Keep a team of math student experts who are responsible and helpful to other students. Pair them with a child who did not do well on the test, and have them work with the child. Have them initial the problems they have gone over with the child so that you know what has been retaught.
- Analyze problems that students miss to determine where their understanding breaks down. Then teach those targeted skills.

Math Notebooks and Journals

There are a variety of ways to organize student math work. One way is to have all the students keep a spiral notebook for computational problems and daily work. It can also be on notebook paper (wide-lined paper is preferred to the college rule because it has a larger space for students to write in) and stapled together in a construction paper folder. Or it can be lined paper stapled together. Some teachers use college blue books for daily work for each unit of study. They are easy to punch holes in, put in three-ring binders, and carry home at night for assessment, but children lose them more easily because they are small. Some teachers use journal-type notebooks with a hard cover. These are a little less manageable because of their bulkiness but can be useful if a system is worked out for assessing only four or five at a time.

The method you use is a personal choice, but the main idea is to keep all the work together so that it may be referred back to during the day, week, or unit. There is so much paperwork that teachers have to glance over in the course of a day or week that single sheets of unattached math paper can easily get lost, especially if it is plain white.

For writing in math, some teachers use hardcover math journals or composition books so that the students easily distinguish between daily work and writing that is assessment oriented. Journals are where students record what they are pondering and learning. They might write reflective or summarizing entries about their learning, thinking, reasoning, questions, and understandings or misunderstandings of the math lesson or unit. For instance, at the end of the day, a teacher may have the students write how to change a ratio into a percentage using their math test score, how to figure out sales tax without a calculator, or how to determine if a number is prime or composite. Writing and representation should be encouraged so that students can expose their thinking. Teacher modeling will help students know what the expectations are and how they need to support their thinking in their writing journal. A pre- and posttest could be given to check understanding. This would give an idea of what the students know and what needs to be taught. When the majority of the class can explain on a preassessment how to multiply double-digit numbers by double-digit numbers, maybe they do not need to spend a lot of whole class time on the concept, and the instruction can be adjusted accordingly. Students who need help with the concept can be supported in a small group for additional help.

Writing takes organization and prethinking of ideas. Giving students time to talk about and then write about their thinking builds confidence. For instance, a lesson on changing fractions into decimals may be taught first through a variety of instructional methods. Then the students can summarize orally what they have learned. Finally, they summarize their thinking by writing their thoughts down as if explaining it to their parents at the dinner table that evening. Instruction, exploration, talking about, writing about, and then talking about it again give the basic support that children need to internalize a concept. Repetition helps firm up an idea. At home, parents can be encouraged to listen to their children talk about math concepts. In fact, instead of a steady stream of computation problems for homework, children can be expected to explain new concepts to their parents and then the parent can sign off that it has been explained thoroughly. By taking their math journals home, students will have the reminders of their in-class learning for backup. This also helps the parents know what their child is learning and if more support is needed.

Students may start the year letting you know a little about their math history so that you can learn where their attitudes and feelings are coming from.

In order to motivate students to write in their math journals, teachers may initiate the writing with a few basic math prompts (Rief, 2005):

- Today I learned about [or how to] . . .
- The most important ideas I learned today are . . .
- I am still confused by . . .
- I discovered that . . .
- The mathematical rule for this problem is . . .
- The way I remember [how to] . . . in my head is . . .
- The tricky part of this problem is . . .
- The thing you have to remember with this kind of problem is . . .
- The steps I used to solve this problem were . . .
- I could use this type of problem solving when . . .
- I was frustrated with this problem because . . .

USING RESOURCES

A familiar complaint of many teachers seems to be that there is never enough time to meet the mathematical needs of all the students in the classroom. Activating some valuable resources may provide a supportive environment that will benefit everyone involved.

Volunteer Help in the Classroom

As students progress into the upper grades and middle school, parents often do not feel comfortable helping out in their child's classroom during math time. The complication of the higher level of math skills and the newer ways of teaching with manipulatives are foreign to many parents, and they are uncomfortable with assisting with the unfamiliar. With the huge span of abilities within upper-grade and middle school classes, one-on-one time with an adult is always valuable for both the teacher and the students. Finding just the right job or form of assistance for parents is an art; honing in on their exact abilities and skills and keeping them within their comfort zone is well worth the time to figure out. Here are ways you can use volunteers during the math period:

- Check a student's progress on different kinds of problems.
- Help students create and label graphs and charts.
- Go over problems missed on recent assessments or tests.
- Help students work on a survival math project, especially if they do not have help at home.
- Assist in the use of a protractor or compass.
- Help students make flash cards with math vocabulary.
- Preview math computer games with a pair of students.
- Give individual attention to challenged math students.
- Work on enrichment possibilities for stronger math students.
- Assist students in creating charts for classroom instruction purposes.
- Work with children who have not mastered traditional (analog) clocks and telling time.
- Work with students with measurement.
- Work with students counting back change.
- Have students read story problems aloud and decipher what the question is asking.
- Have students who have difficulty with writing dictate their learning or transcribe work that cannot be understood without child input.
- Look for Web sites that students can visit for math activities and information.
- Help students with basic facts.
- Help students write math goals.
- Glance through math journals to check understanding.
- Help locate and administer computer Web sites and math games.
- Walk around and spot-check students' computation, marking correct answers with C's.

More Support in the Classroom

Some schools have a high school nearby and are able to arrange a last-period elective class that can include community service. High school students taking this elective may spend their last hour assisting elementary students with math. Both ages enjoy the cross-age tutoring experience. Upper elementary students relate well to teenage tutors and therefore greatly benefit and enjoy working on their math with these high school students.

Collaborative teaching (regular and special educators coteaching and working together) is also effective for providing intensive assistance to students during math instruction. Resource teachers have schedules that coincide with classroom teacher schedules, and both work side-by-side assisting students who need additional help.

Use students who have strengths in math as class "experts" whenever appropriate. Sometimes during independent practice time, the teacher chooses a team of math experts to assist others. When a new concept is introduced, the teacher is only one of several people who help students with learning and understanding the concept. One concept that always needs additional helpers is double-digit division. A class is made up of those who know or almost know how and the ones who have little or no idea of what to do. With so many challenged students, a teacher will do well to have a team of experts supplying lots of support—possibly one expert for every two students who need help.

Establish math jobs in the classroom. (See the section on multiple intelligence jobs in Chapter Two.) For example, enlist students to help with the following:

- *Computer Math Researcher.* Researches Web sites and computer programs that will be supportive to students in math. Checks in with computer lab teachers for resources.

- *Math Aide.* Someone who is eager to assist students having difficulty in math.
- *Math Center Manager.* Someone who will keep the math station resources, books, and materials organized. Introduces new books that are purchased. Looks through math catalogues to suggest new games and math books that the class should order.
- *Math Materials Distributor.* Hands out math manipulatives, graph paper, protractors, rulers, compasses, and other math materials as needed.

Encouraging Math Throughout the School

Math should be a priority throughout the school, not just in the classroom. Collaborative planning, innovative ideas, and utilization of the whole staff can establish a schoolwide math community:

- If you are uncomfortable teaching math, see if you can departmentalize and teach your area of strength while another teacher teaches math for you.
- Begin a student store at your school so that students can buy things and learn about money.
- Help the custodian chalk the playing field with correct line measurements.
- Have the nurse talk with your students about how she uses math and why it is important in her career.
- Talk with the physical education teacher about how math is important to him or her.
- Ask the music teacher how math influences his or her career.

Getting Parents to Support Their Child's Math Needs at Home

Establishing a math environment at home is also an important step in setting children on a successful math course. There are a multitude of everyday math experiences that parents may participate in with their children. The following list of suggestions might be added to a parent letter at the beginning of the school year nudging parents to be more proactive in creating a home connection in mathematics:

- Use special family events to teach about math concepts.
- Encourage children to use money, and make sure that they know how to count out change.
- If the child is not using a traditional (analog) clock, give him or her double doses of clock opportunities, such as having a check-out sheet of when each student leaves home or starts an activity; having a family member ask him or her what time it is at different intervals during the day, and by having the child be responsible for announcing the time a few minutes before lunch or dinner. Having parents work with a child on clock skills and giving cross-age tutoring opportunities for the child to teach what they do know about time to a kindergartner or first grader can also build skill.
- Make up little problems about math while you are waiting for dinner, a movie, or a ride at an amusement park such as: "How many minutes are in two hours?" "If one ticket costs twenty-four dollars, how much are four tickets?" "What time do we have to leave home if we need to get to school at 8:30?" "How many quarters are in three dollars?"
- Solve puzzles together. "If a ticket costs twenty-four dollars, how much are four tickets?" "What time do we have to leave home if we need to get to school at 8:30?"
- Use the grocery store, gas station, and restaurant for sources for mental math problems. "If one pound of potatoes is thirty-nine cents, about how much would three pounds of potatoes be?" "If one gallon of gas is $2.98, about how much will ten gallons cost?" "About how much money should we leave the wait staff for a tip?"

- Sing songs about the multiplication basic facts.
- Teach your child how to read a map, and predict about how many miles your trip will be.
- Encourage your child to share his or her school math learning with you. (You might learn something new.)
- Have your child help a younger sibling with math homework.
- Talk to and show your child what things you do that are math oriented.
- Play math games and board games together. Let your child be the scorekeeper or banker.
- Cook or work in the garage together.
- Play card games together.

For more ideas use the survival math activities at the end of this chapter. If it is not a school project, adapt and adjust the activities to your personal family needs.

ADDRESSING THE NEEDS OF SPECIAL POPULATIONS

All children need to feel successful and be active participants in classroom math experiences. This can be a monumental task for teachers with large numbers of students who are challenged in mathematics. Special accommodations and modifications should be put in place to ensure that all students are able to access the math curriculum.

Accommodations for Second-Language Learners

Making math accommodations for second-language students is needed. Whereas ten or fifteen years ago, second-language students were very comfortable with computational math, today with so much of the work being word problems, these students are at a disadvantage because they have not only the math content vocabulary to learn, but also basic everyday English words. In order to accommodate these students, we need to provide lots of scaffolding through drawings and other visible realia to bring these problems to life. Having another child who is bilingual paired with the student can be one way to provide support. Acting out the problem or providing gestures can assist the child also. Teachers need to make sure that all supports are in place to compensate for the lack of language. According to Terri Walter (1996), students who are acquiring a second language need certain conditions to enhance their learning:

- *Attention to background knowledge and experience.* Tapping into student prior knowledge and experience is a highly effective way of developing understanding.
- *Real and purposeful context and language.* Solve problems that they are interested in and are relevant.
- *Comprehensible language.* Language is acquired when messages are understood (Krashen, 1981; Krashen & Terrell, 1983). Students must understand the intent of the message, not necessarily every word that is spoken.
- *Low anxiety.* The classroom must be a safe and supportive environment in which students feel free to take risks and recognize that their risks will be rewarded.
- *High interaction.* Active participation and interaction increase learning (Kagan, 1986; Enright & McCloskey, 1988; Cummins, 1989, 1993; Long, 1982).
- *Support through a variety of models.* The second-language learner must be supported through interaction with a variety of English-speaking models and through their primary language models. Cooperative and collaborative groups must be used throughout the day.

Modifications and Accommodations for Students Who Struggle

Some students do poorly in math computation because they have difficulties copying and organizing math problems. They may be deficient in visual motor integration skills—causing them significant difficulty when aligning numbers, writing within the space given on the page, remembering which number gets carried up when regrouping, and so forth. Some students have a disability in their memory skills; no matter how hard they try, they may be unable to commit math facts to memory. These students should be provided with accommodations to help them bypass these disabilities so that they can be successful with their classroom math.

Many students with learning disabilities or AD/HD make numerous careless errors in their computation but are often quite strong in mathematical reasoning and math aptitude. To help these students, teachers should:

- Provide many kinds of manipulatives to help students visualize and work out problems.
- Allow and encourage the use of calculators.
- Give a choice of computing with a calculator, paper and pencil, or mentally.
- Allow extra time on math tests so students are not rushed and make careless errors.
- Encourage writing and solving computation problems on graph paper rather than notebook paper. Experiment with graph paper of varying square sizes.
- Allow students to write and solve problems on notebook paper held sideways, with lines running vertically rather than horizontally. This makes it much easier for students with difficulty to align numbers, thereby reducing careless errors.
- Reduce the number of problems assigned (those on the first half of the page, even- or odd-numbered problems only).
- Reduce the amount of copying required by photocopying the page or writing out the problems on paper for certain students.
- Color-highlight processing signs for students who are inattentive to change in operational signs on a page.
- Provide a large work space on tests. If necessary, rewrite test items on other paper with lots of room for computation.
- List steps clearly.
- Provide models of sample problems.
- Provide a chart of multiplication facts and tables for student reference.

Challenges for High-Achieving and Gifted Students

All students have strengths and weaknesses, even the most brilliant. Some gifted and talented students are not proficient in mathematics. Often teachers and parents think that just because their child carries a label of *gifted and talented,* that means he or she is gifted in everything. In the upper grades, any student who is experiencing difficulty in math may need extra support in all or some of the mathematic strands. They may have voids that everyone assumes they should have mastered. We must be careful to fill in these voids and make sure that these students are supported in their learning also.

Challenge is something that all students need in order to forge ahead in any area of the curriculum. We must give gifted students more opportunities to venture further, deeper, and more elaborately into an area of study and seek connections, relationships, and associations between, within, and across subject areas. These terms of depth and complexity can be applied to all areas of the mathematics program. High-achieving and gifted students' math programs should provide:

- A rigorous academic curriculum
- Learning centers that offer varying degrees of depth and complexity

- Tiered lessons and assignments to build math readiness skills
- Pretests in math, with those achieving high scores given alternate (challenge or enrichment) activities during the instruction sessions leading up to the posttest
- Daily activities that provide advanced problem solving
- Expectations for more complex survival math projects to be chosen and completed with a higher level of sophistication and thoroughness
- Opportunities to set up competitions in chess and the 24 Game
- Curriculum compacting
- Enrichment or challenge activities in problem solving that require high-level thinking strategies
- Independent study of famous mathematicians, principles, and books about math
- Additional opportunities to learn about math occupations
- Additional resources that enrich the basic math program
- High-level books that approach math topics and issues for the library
- Books containing activities that challenge student thinking

MAKING MATH RELEVANT THROUGH REAL-LIFE EXPERIENCES

Mathematical concepts should be taught in a manner that can be connected to the way that they would be used in real life. A child who understands the importance of why a math concept is used is a step ahead of the game. These children say to themselves, *I need to learn this because I am going to need it as an adult—not just because my teacher says it is important.* Teacher talk needs to link a concept or mathematical idea with its importance in the real world.

It is also important that we integrate the teaching of mathematics with other subject areas to show students the connections that math has with science, social studies, music, art, physical education, and health. Again, making the curriculum have meaning in the lives of older children helps them to see math as a tool to be used on a daily basis, not as a separate subject area that is used only in math class. When we begin to show the connections between math and sports, cooking, reading music, working on cars, purchasing items, taking medicine, and creating pieces of art, students will become more interested in understanding how math pertains to them and their survival in the real world. Although textbooks are getting more user friendly and more relevant in creating math problems that connect the students with real life, few students grasp the relevancy of math from a textbook.

We must show students that math is everywhere in our world, and that to be deficient in it hampers us and makes our lives more difficult. As we enable children to see math work in their own world, engaging them in useful, relevant, and purposeful problem solving, students buy into the math program.

Upper-grade teachers need to bring the real world into the classroom, but also take the students out into the real world to face the challenges of being consumers. In this section, you will find ways that upper-grade and middle school students have been exposed to math other than through a textbook—ways that make math more enjoyable and meaningful for them. Students are given the chance to interact with their environment and try to make practical use out of what the textbooks are trying to get across (often with little success or understanding of concepts).

Math Is Everywhere You Look

Begin the school year with a Math Is Everywhere You Look project, asking students to look around their environment and find examples of how math is used. In small groups, students brainstorm a list of at least twenty-five items that would use math. Examples from students' lists include music, clocks, putting up wallpaper or installing flooring, playing games, sewing, shoe sizes, cooking, tools, the microwave, sports, coupons, cereal labels, bus and train schedules, medicines, and mileage for traveling. The assignment is extended to the home, where students are to add more ideas with the help of their parents. Getting parents involved in their child's math experience is very worthwhile.

After the students have generated their lists, they are asked to elaborate on eight to ten of the items in writing. In addition the students cut pictures out of magazines or newspapers, draw their own pictures, take snapshots, or use graphics from the computer. (A disposable camera is always available in the classroom for students to use.) A variety of these types of illustrations adds the element of balance and allows each child to approach the project in his or her own individual style. (See Activities 14.5 and 14.6, Math Is Everywhere You Look Assignment Sheet and Math Is Everywhere You Look Evaluation Form, at the end of this chapter.)

Katie, for example, drew a picture of a measuring cup. She wrote underneath her picture, "I need to know how to use a measuring cup so I can measure ingredients in a recipe. Knowing fractions and how to add them in case I want to double a recipe is also important. I need to know liquid measurements, too. Some recipes have you measure liquids in ounces. I need to know how many ounces are in a cup in order to do that."

The Math Is Everywhere project stretches students' thinking by building on experiences and knowledge they already have. Aaron, a sixth grader, approaches the project using baseball team standings. Aaron wrote the following about sports from the newspaper: "These are the baseball standings from the Sports Section in the newspaper. There are records, numbers and percentages listed on it. For example, our San Diego Padres have a 60 (w) and 63 (l) record. Their percentage is .488 and they are 4½ games behind (GB) the 1st place Colorado Rockies. The use of math gives us the knowledge to understand percentages, read numbers, etc."

This project provides an opportunity to impress on students that a due date is when the project must be handed in. A discussion of the real world of work and how a boss would not tolerate it if a major project was not prepared by its due date is helpful in getting this point across. We do a great disservice to upper-grade students by not enforcing a due date. On the due date or the day after, students share and evaluate their project with their peers. An important part of any student project should be self-evaluation. This is when the children look at other students' projects and constructively assess their own work. Seeing how other students approached their activity assists all students in seeing how they might approach their project in a different way the next time.

Graphing for Everybody

Teaching graphing skills and how to make a graph of their own is essential in the upper and middle school years. Finding examples of easy-to-read graphs from newspapers and magazines and placing them on overheads or on a document camera for the entire class to see is a good starting point. Students begin to understand that graphs show comparisons and let us see things in a visual way that unlocks information and organizes it into relationships that are easily understood. Students tend to comprehend bar graphs more readily than other forms of graphs and tend to make them more often when given a choice. Children must begin to realize, though, that other types of graphs fit some situations better than others. Using examples from different sources opens up discussions on why certain types of graphs might have been chosen by the creator to represent the particular information being shared.

On the first day of school, a teacher may quickly assess some pertinent information about the students in the classroom. This is done by handing the children several sticky notes on which to write their names. Then the children post their names under the heading *Girl* or *Boy* on the chart paper. This immediately lets students see the classroom population according to gender. A heading such as *What School Did You Attend Last Year?* could be placed on the board, and a list of schools where the class may have originated from the previous year also helps the class quickly make connections that would otherwise take more time. With younger students, *What is your favorite kind of ice cream?* might be a good starting point. Again, each student would be given sticky note to write his or her name on. The categories could be: *Chocolate Chip Cookie Dough, Mint Chocolate Chip, Coffee, Cookies and Cream, Peanut Butter, Neapolitan,* or more standard flavors such as vanilla, chocolate, and strawberry or other favorites. Students then place their sticky note with their name on it under the favorite category. This bar graph then becomes the basis for discussion, comparison, and contrast. Great discussions come from graphing.

Math tends to make more sense when relationships begin to take shape. Students are able to verbalize or write about what they can see. For instance, a third grader may say, "I see that more students in our classroom like chocolate chip cookie dough ice cream than cookies and cream." An upper-grade or middle school student may write, "Twenty out of thirty-two fifth graders in Room 8 prefer chocolate chip cookie dough ice cream. This is a 20:32 ratio. It can also be stated 20/32 or in reduced form as 5/8. It can be restated as 63 percent (or in decimal form as 63.25) of our class prefers chocolate chip cookie dough to the other kinds of ice cream." A more skillful and thorough approach is given as the children developmentally learn new math concepts.

Younger children might be given more opportunities to use pictographs and bar graphs, whereas older children may be encouraged to use circle and line graphs. Making graphs with regular graph paper and compasses and protractors should be encouraged with the older students, but they should also become skillful at making computer-generated graphs. There are times that informal (hand-drawn) graphs will suffice and other times when more precise formal graphs should be developed. Graphs with positive and negative integers also need to be introduced as the students become more skillful.

Students can develop their own questions and survey their classmates to apply what they already know about graphing. Developing their own question, hypothesis, procedure, conclusions, and findings is an important step for collecting data in a fun way. This also leads to a more complete understanding of the scientific process and shows how math and science fit together. (See Activities 14.7 to 14.9, Graphing Can Be Fun, Question Possibilities for Graphing Projects, and Graphing Project Design Form, at the end of this chapter.)

Low- or No-Cost Math Materials from Newspapers and Pamphlets

Teachers should be looking for materials that are not too costly for enhancing their math programs. Newspapers offer many ideas for math centers or activities, for example. Television and movie guides can generate questions and activities. For instance, cooperative groups can plan a one-day schedule for a primary student's television viewing. They should write out a chart with the time of day, the channel, and the program listed. Another group may want to plan out a television-viewing schedule for students of their own age, using only appropriate programs that all their parents would agree to.

In most grocery stores, *AutoTrader* magazines and *Home-Buying Guides* can be found at no cost. These guides can also be used in the classroom. Students may be asked to locate a car that they would like to buy for less than twenty thousand dollars. The idea that most teenagers cannot afford a new car can generate discussion. The issue of insurance and the difference between boys' and girls' insurance premiums and the reason that boys' insurance is more costly can be pondered. The concept of sales tax, registration and licensing fees, tires, maintenance, and gasoline enlighten the students as to the high cost of owning a car. Writing can be drawn into this math lesson with a composition about car ownership. Students can write about why they chose a certain car, how they would earn money to buy and maintain the car, the responsibilities of being a driver, and the reasons that there are age restrictions on drivers. Students can also make graphs and charts to show comparisons of car prices. They can cut out a picture of the car they chose from the book and paste it to a piece of paper, giving them a visual point of reference to start their writing assignment. In cooperative groups, the students may share their choices and writing. The opportunity to brag about the special accessories their car has, the great deal they got, and the excitement of being an owner takes the outside purchasing power into the classroom math setting. Some students who do not own a family car now have gone through the experience of "buying" a car. This gives them the opportunity to dream a little.

The same holds true for buying a home. Through the *Home Buying Guides*, students develop a sense of how costly homes are. Special features such as fireplaces, swimming pools, large pieces of property, and location become not only a practical reading lesson but also a practical math experience that students enjoy. Comparing and contrasting home prices through charts and graphs make children appreciate how costly a home is. For some whose families do not own their own homes, this may offer them an understanding of why their parents cannot afford a home, and for those who do own a home, they may develop a greater appreciation for what they have. As in the car buying activity, students can write about "their home" by telling why they chose it, what they will do to pay for it, how they will maintain it, and what other costs owning a home entails.

Having a parent who is a real estate agent visit the classroom can help students realize another career they might want to pursue. An agent can help a class get hooked into the online multiple listings. This will give them access to current information regarding homes, condos, and townhouses that are on the market.

Consumer Math Field Trip

One upper-grade experience that students can be given is a buying trip to a variety store, which can be an eye-opener for them. When the students are asked to shop with a team and follow certain guidelines, they find themselves in the real world of currency and consumerism. Each team of four students is given $8.00, or $2.00 per person; they have thirty minutes of shopping time to buy five to seven items with the money. The goal of this assignment is to come as close to spending the full $8.00 without going over it. (There is almost always a group that hits it right on the button.) Any groups that go over the allotted amount are disqualified from the grand prize (usually ice cream treats and certificates).

It is always a good idea to preface this trip by giving the store a call and making sure the manager knows exactly what the purpose of the trip is. The employees then become part of the process, and students must ask questions of the employees instead of relying on their teacher or the parents.

Before the trip is taken, the classroom teacher must have given instruction about taxable and nontaxable items, addition and subtraction of decimals, use of the calculator, special charges for recycling plastics and aluminum cans (recycling value), and working cooperatively. Several constraints are added to the process to make it more structured: time (thirty minutes of shopping time), the ceiling of $8.00 per group ($2.00 per person), all items must be evenly divisible by the number of students in the group, and all groups must buy five to seven items. Of course, no toy or real weapons can be purchased. Although students complain about the restrictions, more time, money, or items just complicates the experience.

Sales tax and recycling charges cause the most challenges, and students need a lot of practice working on these two things before going on the trip. The students get so charged up in this whole process that they do not seem to bicker about what they actually buy, although they are encouraged to buy items that are useful to the entire group.

This experience is a teambuilding event usually at the end of the year. At this point, the students should be fairly comfortable with the math concepts that they are now able to apply to the real world and also fairly comfortable with their classmates. Students must come to consensus on the items they buy and anything that is packaged must be divisible by the number of students in the group. For instance, a package of sixteen pencils could be divided up evenly and fairly by four.

The store employees are always helpful—and sometimes too helpful at the checkout: in their eagerness to give suggestions to the students, they often give too much help. The agreed-on rule is that once the students are at the checkout stand, there can be no switching of items.

When the students return to school, they are asked to fill out a form to show how they spent their money and display their purchases for the rest of the class to see. The other teams informally investigate each of the other team's purchases to see who got the most desirable items. Then the items are divided up among the team members. Each person receives a plastic bag with a ziplock to hold his or her purchase. At this point, the class decides which group received the most for its money. There is usually one group that makes astonishing purchases, and everyone is envious of their wealth of items.

The last part of this exercise comes when students are asked to summarize and evaluate and reflect on their experience. Self-evaluation reveals many important ideas for the teacher. Students are asked to write three paragraphs showing their understanding of the importance of this adventure.

Here are some students' comments about this experience from past years:

"I thought it was fun roaming around choosing things you wanted. The only problem was that we always didn't agree on some items, but after the half-hour shopping spree, we had to come to some agreement, and fast."

"On my team we weren't very organized, but we wouldn't buy an item unless the whole group agreed on it."

"My classmates are a lot different when they are not in school. I liked getting to see them in a different light."

"I liked the fact that no adults helped us because it made the adventure more fun. I think this was a very creative way to get us to learn math."

"I liked this project because it was adventurous and exciting. I thought we could have had more time to shop and more money. This was much better than a boring math lesson."

The parents who accompanied the class gave the experience rave reviews. They were pleased to see what the children were doing. By the time students are in the upper grades, some field trips become redundant. This particular experience is worthwhile and unique, and the children, parents, and teachers were thrilled with the learning that transpired. (See Activities 14.10 and 14.11, Parent Letter for the Shopping Adventure and the Shopping Adventure Recording Sheet, regarding this activity at end of this chapter.)

For schools that are not near an inexpensive variety store, you might want to try using the catalogues or ads from the newspaper or stores in your community. Although real money would not be used, the basic math concepts can be covered in this manner.

Super Bowl Math

It is important to capitalize on mathematical moments. Since the Super Bowl is the single most watched event in the United States and has the highest rate for advertising, why not use it to enhance students' math ability? Although not everybody is interested in football, the Super Bowl does motivate some more reluctant math students and helps to extend the math understanding of some higher-achieving students. This project's intent is to inspire children to get involved in an activity and find out how money, scores, advertising, attendance, roman numerals, height, weight, time, weather, statistics, and other math skills are used in this event. Parents tend to enjoy this project because it gives their child a focus during the Super Bowl, and when parents get involved in their child's education, the child feels that it is important.

Although much of the packet is math, there are other skills that can be developed or extended: writing, mapping, geography, interviewing, illustrating, vocabulary development, oral language, and spelling. (See Activity 14.12, Super Bowl Math Activity Packet, at the end of this chapter.)

Survival Math

Life is filled with many math opportunities and experiences. Sitting at a restaurant waiting for their order to come up, a grandfather and his grandson sat together talking about fractions. The grandson was about six years old. The grandfather talked about the quarters he had in his hand and how four of them had the same value as the dollar bill that he had in the other hand. He talked with the boy about how two quarters could also be referred to as fifty cents or half a dollar, how three quarters could be called *three-quarters of a dollar,* and how one quarter could be called *one-quarter of a dollar.* The little boy was fascinated. This initial introduction was just enough to keep the cross-generational pair engaged in an important life skill dialogue—just enough time for a six year old with a short attention span. How insightful this grandfather was in introducing his grandson to the concept of fractions in casual conversation.

Making math come to life and engaging students in real-world math experiences is just what survival math is all about. This project is an outgrowth of many years of searching for how to teach math more meaningfully and help students realize the concerns their parents have when they say, "We can't afford that this month" or "We don't have the money." Those comments by parents do not seem to make sense when students do not see the connections. Most children think that parents can write a check for anything at any time. They do not realize that there has to be money somewhere to cover their purchases. With the wide use of credit cards, students think you can say, "Charge it" and that covers everything.

Through the activities suggested in the survival math packet (Activities 14.13 to 14.18 at the end of the chapter), students begin to feel a part of their world by opening bank accounts, practicing check writing, using the telephone or online services to check out the cost of airfare and bus fare, reading schedules, going grocery shopping, and watching the rise and fall of gasoline prices during the month. These activities provide the opportunity for students and parents to work together in the discovery of math in our world. Parents begin to feel a sense of importance in helping their children to understand the financial world of adulthood. Children and their parents interact and participate in relevant and meaningful activities to let students know why they have to understand key concepts in the textbook: if they do not, survival in the real world is significantly more difficult.

Depending on the teacher's and students' needs and interests, five to ten activities are required by the end of the school year. Students may hand them in any time before the due date.

On a regular basis, the teacher showcases a number of student projects that have been turned in. These examples serve as models for the other students and motivate them to complete their own quality activities. (Some student examples are provided later in this section.) Each child places his or her completed activity in the math section of a personal portfolio after it has been shared with classmates, self-evaluated and teacher evaluated, and spotlighted on the bulletin board.

These activities also provide excellent problem-solving opportunities. The beginning of every math period can start with the use of one of these personalized activities. For instance, Jennifer brought in a list of coupons she and her mother cut out and used when they went shopping for groceries. They saved $13.13 by using the coupons. She told the class that the store she shopped at doubled the coupons. The teacher now had an opportunity to capitalize on the personal activity and teach the entire class some problem-solving strategies. She asked the students to take out their calculators and figure out how much money was saved when the coupons were doubled. She further stretched the students' minds by asking, "If Jennifer saved this much money for one week, how much could she and her family save over a year's time?" It turned out that few of these sixth graders knew how many weeks are in a year. After establishing that fact, the students discovered that Jennifer's family could save $682.76 per year. That seemed to make a real impression on them. The class then tried to think of what they would buy if they had that much more money to spend on other things besides groceries.

Another activity that Jennifer did was to fill out order forms for magazines she would like. One of the orders she placed was for *Cricket*, a child's magazine of literature and poetry. The cost of the subscription for one year was $26.79. The teacher asked the class, "If Jennifer purchased *Cricket* for one year at $26.79, how much does it cost per month?" In the sixth-grade class, the students were perplexed by the question. One of the students thought she had the correct answer when she decided to multiply the price per year by twelve. The entire class agreed with her until, through questioning by the teacher, she realized that amount would be the cost for twelve years of subscriptions, not one month. The students finally realized that the operation to use was division, but the idea did not come easily.

We must train students through problem-solving strategies to look at word problems as puzzles to solve. We take each of the parts and find how they fit together. We must also train students to look for reasonable answers. The sixth grader above knew, after some teacher direction, that her answer was not reasonable and did not make sense.

In this process of showing students the faults in their process of deduction, teachers must be careful not to make students feel incompetent because they make mistakes. We must carefully show students that through mistakes, they will learn to think more thoroughly and reasonably. This same type of questioning could have been set up in the classroom in cooperative groups or in partners, giving students the opportunity to talk through the problem together. This allows students to feel less afraid of failure.

Another strategy to use with survival math activities would be to give the students the basic foundation of the problem such as "*Cricket* magazine subscription, $26.79 per year, 12 issues, Jennifer's order" and have the students come up with a word problem for their classmates using the information.

This process of working with the facts and generating their own questions gives students a chance to see the parts and feel secure in putting together the whole. Knowing how test makers create the questions is helpful in understanding word problems. Teachers should provide opportunities throughout the year to have students problem-solve, but also to create their own problems for others to solve. (See Activities 14.13 to 14.18: Survival Math Parent Letter, Survival Math Packet, Survival Math Rubric—Teacher Evaluation, Survival Math Record Sheet, Survival Math Checklist, and Survival Math Peer Evaluation Form.)

A Whole-Group Weather Project to Start the Year

To ensure that all students know my (Julie's) expectations, I spend a lot of time at the beginning of the year going over past students' projects. We use them as a warm-up segment.

Our first project, Number 74 on the Survival Math Packet, due at the end of September, is a guided practice activity. I take the class through the steps of the activity very slowly; we use the newspaper weather section to chart the daily weather in San Diego for ten days. (This connects literacy with math and initiates conversations about current events and the use of the newspaper, a skill we also work on in writing.) Students make predictions of what they think the average high and low will be for the ten days. They then learn how to make a double-line graph showing the highs and lows for the ten days. This is quite a challenging task for many fifth graders. In conclusion, we prepare a write-up to summarize our findings. Our discussions have depth and rigor. In conjunction with this math activity, we study the weather in our science books and through numerous other resources and experiments. This ties math in with science and shows children the math-science connection.

The following fifth- through eighth-grade student activities are representative of the kinds of projects students might hand in. They can act as examples for you to use with your students to begin your own survival math program. Saving your own classroom examples will provide you with more models for future classes. The numbers in the examples, which are the student's write-ups on the activity they chose, refer to the items on the Survival Math Packet, Activity 14.14.

Make Versus Buy: Project #31, by Hailey S.

My project is project #31. This project has you go to a fabric store, find a pattern you like, and to see how much it costs to make it. I chose this project because I thought it would be really fun (and so did my mom). I am going to be a devil for Halloween so I thought it would be interesting to see how much it would cost to make it verses [sic] buying it pre-made.

The first thing I did was go to Joann's. I found a devil pattern in a Simplicity catalog. The pattern number was 4461. I looked in the big Simplicity drawer and searched for the pattern. When I found the pattern I looked at the back and wrote down what I needed to make the costume. I needed fabric for the dress, cording for the belt, stuffing for the horns and a headband, and thread. Then I went around the store looking for each item and wrote down the prices. Some of the items were on sale so I wrote down the sale price and the regular price so I could compare them. The fabric and the cording were only sold by the yard so I had to multiply the cost by how much I needed. I only needed 1 oz. of stuffing for the horns but the smallest amount available was a 10 oz. bag. I didn't actually buy the materials to make this costume because I had already bought a devil costume from Joann's last month. I came home and put my data into two tables and added up all the items including sales tax. One table shows how much it would cost to make the costume at regular price and the other table shows how much it would cost to make with the items that were on sale. I also included the cost of the costume that I bought.

During this project I learned how to calculate the cost of fabric, calculate sales tax, and how easy or hard it can be to make something. I also learned that it cost more to make this costume than it does to buy one. Sometimes it may be cheaper to make something than to buy it, but not in my case.

Regular Price

Item	Regular
Simplicity Devil Costume Pattern #4461	$ 13.95
Red Festive Foil Fabric (3 3/4 yds. @ $6.99 yd.)	$ 26.21
3/8" Cording (1 3/4 yds. @ $1.99 yd.)	$ 3.48
Fun Stuff Fiberfill Stuffing (10 oz. Package)	$ 1.99
Headband	$ 2.49
Thread	$ 1.49
Sales tax (7.75%)	$ 3.84
TOTAL	$ 53.45

Sale Price

Item	Total	Sale
Simplicity Devil Costume Pattern #4461	$ 8.37	$13.95 @ 40% off
Red Festive Foil Fabric (3 3/4 yds. @ $6.99 yd.)	$ 13.11	50% off
3/8" Cording (1 3/4 yds. @ $1.99 yd.)	$ 3.48	NA
Fun Stuff Fiberfill Stuffing (10 oz. Package)	$ 1.00	$1.99 @ 50% off
Headband	$ 2.49	NA
Thread	$ 1.49	NA
Sales tax (7.75%)	$ 2.32	
TOTAL	$ 32.26	

Store Bought

Item	Total
Devil Costume	$ 24.99
Sales tax (7.75%)	$ 1.94
TOTAL	$ 26.93

The Cost of Having a Pet #2 by Nick K.

- I chose this project after reading through the entire packet.
- I began by constructing a list of the pros and cons of owning a dog.
- I drafted a list of questions for a veterinarian.
- I drafted some questions for the San Diego Humane Society.
- I called a veterinarian (my uncle) to ask him some questions.
- I called the Humane Society to ask my questions.
- I took notes on the information that I had collected.
- I did Internet research on several sites to make sure my information was correct.
- I calculated the costs of owning a dog for one year.
- I modified my list many times so it would be as accurate as possible.
- I collected some clip art from the Internet to create the cover page of my project.
- I gathered some thoughts to begin my persuasive letter.
- I completed my persuasive letter.
- I summarized what I have learned in my conclusion.
- I put my project into final form by putting it together into a book.
- I formatted the components of my book until I was satisfied with them.

Pros of Owning a Dog

A friend who will always be there for you
Someone to teach you responsibility
Keeps vermin out of the house
Can act as a guard for the house
Someone to keep you company
Can protect you when walking alone
Someone to alert you of possible trouble
A reason to exercise
A reason to keep the house clean
Someone to love
Someone to grow up with

Cons of Owning a Dog

You must pick up after it
Must pay for food and other supplies
Must walk it early in the morning and late at night
Must find someone to take care of it while you are away
Must pay for veterinarian checkups
Must feed and take care of it
Must train it and keep it out of trouble
Must pay for emergency vet care
Needs constant attention
Puppies destroy things while teething
Is at least a ten-year commitment

Average Costs of Owning a Dog for First Year

Expenses	Pound Dog Amount	Breed Dog Amount
Adoption fees (includes microchip, shots)	$100–$150	Purchase fees: $450–$1,200
Additional puppy shots#	$160/year	$160/year
Puppy training#	$60/year	$60/year
Fecal exam and worming	$25/year	$25/year
Rabies (one, then every three years)	Included in fees	$20/year
Distemper/Parvo inoculations	Included in fees	$60/year
Spay (one-time expense)*	$50–$175	$50–$175
Neuter (one-time expense)*	$45–$110	$45–$110
Heartworm check/preventive	$50/year	$50/year
Food	$400/year	$400/year
License	$10/year	$10/year
Emergency vet care	$250/year	$250/year
Microchip	Included in fees	$35/year
Miscellaneous/accessories	$30/year	$30/year
Total estimated expenses		
For puppy (male)#	$1,130–$1,245	$1,595–$2,410
For adult dog (male)	$910–$1,025	
For puppy (female)#	$1,135–$1,310	$1,600–$2,475
For adult dog (female)	$915–$1,090	

*Only one of these two would apply, depending on the gender of the animal.
Prices vary depending on the veterinarian and the size of the dog.
#Refers to items that only apply to a puppy.
Sources: Humane Society of San Diego, www.cbrrescue.org; veterinarian Patrick Kelly.

Persuasive Letter

Dear Mom and Dad,

I know that I have begged you for a dog for a long time. I also know that one of the reasons that you have resisted my pleas is your well-justified concern that I have not understood how a big a responsibility I was taking on. This time, my request is different because it is informed by research. I have calculated every cost associated with getting and keeping a dog. I have a complete and honest list of the good and bad things that relate to having a dog. I hope that you will conclude that I am ready to own a dog.

I know that we can manage having a dog because I will care for it all the time, even if it means doing so all by myself. I understand that every dog-related responsibility will be mine.

There are numerous reasons I would like to have a dog and why having a dog would be good for all of us, and they are in my list of "pros." I also recognize that there are cons, the biggest one being that Grandpa does not like dogs. Nevertheless, I feel that the family can easily conquer every con to having a dog by working as a team.

Finally, I know that getting and keeping a dog also costs money. On average, even a dog from the pound can cost nearly $1,000 per year after purchase or adoption. Although that sounds like a lot of money, it translates into a cost of about $3.00 per day—less than a Starbucks coffee!

It is my personal theory that the decision to have a dog cannot be made simply by considering the cons versus pros. No matter how many cons or pros there are, the pros greatly outnumber the cons because of the love a dog is capable of giving.

Mom and Dad, please take this request into consideration. My two siblings and I would adore a dog. We will start to show you that we can be responsible around the house and try to be as neat and tidy as possible. Then we will be completely ready to take on the challenge that awaits us in having a dog.

     Sincerely,
     Nick

[*Note:* After completing this project, this student successfully convinced his parents to buy him a dog.]

Gas Pricing: Project #18, by Jenny L.

I Chose This Project Because . . .
I have a few reasons why I chose this project. One is the fact that it was a good one to start with because it looked simple. We also go to my piano lessons once a week. The reason why that matters is because the project asks for the collected data each week for three weeks, and the stations are near-by my piano lessons location. I also wondered how often gas prices change in a variety of stations.

What Did I Do and How Did I Do It?
Every Wednesday, starting on 9/21, up until 10/05, I grabbed my data table sheet and headed out the door to piano lessons. When we passed by the gas stations, my brother Gavin told me the prices so I could track them. After three weeks of gathering data, I made a final table by hand, and then plotted it using Excel (a computer program).

Evidence of Where I Obtained My Information
My mom and brother were with me when we went to my lessons and, therefore, are my witnesses. Her sworn statement is below:

     I solemnly swear that my daughter, Jennifer Anne Laird, went to the gas stations and collected the data for her charts. [The student supplied her mother's signed statement.]

Summary of What I Have Learned

I have learned a lot by doing this project. I can now answer my question (how often gas prices change): very often! I have also done math to detect the mean, or average, for each station. The results are below:

- Chevron: $3.07 (without diesel) $3.12 (with diesel)
- ARCO: $2.99
- Exxon: $3.07 (without diesel) $3.11 (with diesel)
- Union 76: $3.14

If you buy 60 gallons of gas from ARCO every month the annual cost would be around $2152.80, on average. I was surprised that diesel is the most expensive. This project was fun, and I will do more things like it by myself in the future.

Station	Chevron			ARCO			Exxon			Union 76		
Week	1	2	3	1	2	3	1	2	3	1	2	3
Unleaded	$2.95	$2.93	$3.03	$2.89	$2.85	$2.89	$2.96	$2.94	$3.01	$3.03	$3.03	$3.03
Unleaded Plus	$3.05	$3.03	$3.13	$2.99	$2.99	$2.99	$3.06	$3.04	$3.11	$3.13	$3.13	$3.13
Super Unleaded	$3.15	$3.13	$3.23	$3.09	$3.09	$3.09	$3.16	$3.14	$3.21	$3.25	$3.25	$3.25
Diesel	$3.19	$3.23	$3.39				$3.18	$3.18	$3.37			
Nondiesel sum/average	$27.63/$3.07			$26.87/$2.99			$27.63/$3.07			$28.23/$3.14		
Diesel sum/average	$37.44/$3.12						$37.36/$3.11					

Support for Students Who Have Difficulty Planning and Organizing

There are always a few students who have difficulty choosing, getting started, and pacing themselves on these projects. When there are students who do not have enough parent support at home, there must be some classroom supports in place that offer assistance for these children. Here are a few suggestions that might give more success to special students who need a little more guidance and direction:

- Keep a big three-ring binder of copies of previous students' work samples, marked "Great Survival Math Activities from Past Students." The students can read through them during literacy center time and obtain ideas for their own projects.

- Have a box of readily available items for use on these activities: tape measures, graph paper, rulers, disposable cameras and instant cameras, newspaper ads, newspapers, magazines, bookmarked computer Web sites, math books, blank checks, *Auto Trader* magazines, catalogues, home buying and selling catalogues, and telephone books for the students to use if they do not have help at home. Encourage others to bring in math staples to ensure that all students can access the activities.

- Use the students who complete their survival math projects before the due date to help organize students who cannot seem to get started. I also use parent volunteers to assist students who have difficulty getting started.

- Bring in copies of your own utilities bills, and have a parent volunteer, the resource teacher, a student teacher, an aide, a high school volunteer, counselor, or other school employee who is not busy at the time to work with the student.

- Keep an ongoing survival math bulletin board posted in the classroom so that students can look at examples as an inspiration.
- Give a ten-day countdown so that everyone has a project finished by the due date and can share the activity on the same day.
- Send home a weekly or biweekly newsletter/update or personal reminder to keep parents informed. Also note, "If your child needs help, please indicate that on the form below."
- Make your own car available so that a student can keep a daily record of the miles driven in a three-week period of time.
- Have helpers assist students with the reading of the packet.
- Suggest the following activities for students who are remiss at getting started: 3, 5, 9, 15, 26, 27, 28, 29, 34, 35, 40, 41, 55, 59, 63, 66, 67, 68, 75, 76, 77. These activities are less complicated than others.

Students who would like to contribute new ideas to this project, please have them e-mail us at julieheimburge@cox.net or www.sandrarief.com.

Changes in Survival Math Since 1996

Over the years, students have become more sophisticated in the types of activities that they are producing and the way they are doing their researching. Most children have access to a computer and the Internet; consequently many of them are shopping online instead of honing their verbal skills by using personal contacts or phone calls. Newspapers are being replaced by online Web sites that have up-to-the-minute information. More students are creating their own activities based on things that are relevant to their own lives. Many students are combining activities such as check writing with a shopping spree or using coupons with the cooking activity. Students are using their family trips to figure out gas mileage and keeping track of mileage by estimating mileage on a road map and figuring out time zones as they pass through them.

Parents are more involved than they were in 1996. They are beginning to see that math can be fun and interesting and that their support is giving their children a new outlook on math. Teachers have modified and adjusted rubrics to fit their own needs and the needs of their children.

I hand each child a personal hard copy of the survival math packet, but I also include it on our classroom Web site so that students and parents can refer to it if theirs got lost. Teachers using this book have permission to put it on a class Web site for student availability, as long as proper acknowledgment is included for this book.

Survival Math or Consumer Math on a Smaller Scale

For some schools and classrooms, the survival math packet is not practical for any number of reasons. In this case, an in-class mini-survival math project might be feasible. A teacher can bring all of the materials needed for a fun project into the classroom and the students can work on engaging math activities using menus, house and car magazines, pamphlets, catalogues, and newspaper guides. These consumer stations can be set up and the students can rotate into them in the classroom. Several in-class mini-survival math projects can be found at the end of this chapter: Activity 14.19, Math in the Real World, and Activity 14.20, Using a Menu to Solve Math Problems. For Activity 14.20, you will need to obtain multiple copies of a menu from a nearby restaurant. Make sure that the menu is at an appropriate ability level for your students.

Holiday and Special Events Math Activities

It is always a good idea to capitalize on the special holidays and events in your students' lives and in the real world. Making math fun and relevant for the holidays enriches the basic math program and makes math meaningful. Two activities that use multiple sources other than a textbook to check understanding of taxable and nontaxable items, decimals, and calculator use can be used at the holidays: Activities 14.21 and 14.22, Thanksgiving Math Project—Simulation and the Gift Giving Math Project for December, at the end of this chapter.

OTHER TIPS FOR TEACHERS

The world is filled with possibilities for math instruction. The more input given by parents and by the community at large, the greater gain there is for the students. Math instruction becomes everyone's responsibility. It is up to teachers to seek out engaging math experiences for the classroom, the home, and the real world and to add them to their program. Good school-home-community communication creates motivated math students. The following list highlights a few opportunities:

- Have a math career day. Invite people from the community and elsewhere in your area whose jobs involve a great deal of math. Have name tags and bottles of water (and perhaps other refreshments) for the visitors. Plan a rotation of students so that each student will hear at least three speakers who talk about the importance of math in their occupation. Every career uses math in some way: stockbrokers, surveyors, pharmacists, doctors, engineers, waiters, and limo drivers, to name a few.

- At the beginning of the year, have an inventory ready to hand out to your children's parents. Find out what their interests and strengths are. At least several of the people will be able to offer math expertise. Try to find out what they can offer you in the way of math support or interests.

- Communicate regularly with parents about their child's math. Let them know what assistance you are able to give and how they can help at home.

- Encourage parents and family members to work with their child on math skills. Make this interaction fun.

- Encourage children to share math vocabulary with their families.

- Have a problem of the week to help families interact with problem solving.

- Ask students to create their own story problems biweekly to share with the class or a partner. These problems should be personalized to include their family members' names and events that have taken place in their own family settings.

- Ask family members to look for math puzzles, problems, jokes, riddles, videos, music, pictures, and words and share them with you.

- Ask families to share graphs and charts from the newspaper that explain something of interest to their children. Cut them out, and ask the child to talk about it the next day in class.

REFERENCES

A+ Math. http://www.aplusmath.com.

Arc Center. (2002). *The Arc Tri-State Student Achievement Study*. Available: www.comap/elementary/projects/arc/.

Bell, M. (1998–1999, Winter). Problems with implementing new curricula: The example of the K–6 everyday mathematics curriculum. *UCSMP Newsletter, 24*, 1–2.

Boaler, J. (1998). Open and closed mathematics: Student experiences and understandings. *Journal for Research in Mathematics Education, 29*, 41–62.

Burns, M. (1998). *MATH: Facing an American phobia*. Sausalito, CA: Math Solutions.

Burns, M. (1987). *A collection of math lessons for grades 3–6*. Sausalito, CA: Math Solutions.

Burns, M., & Silbey, R. (2004). *So you have to teach math?* Sausalito, CA: Math Solutions.

Campbell, P. F., & Stewart, E. L. (1993). Calculators and computers. In R. Jensen (Ed.), *Early childhood mathematics: NCTM Research interpretation project* (pp. 251–268). New York: Macmillan.

CEC. (2003, January). Teaching *math* to students with disabilities. *CEC Today, 9*(5), 1–13.

Charles, R., Kelly, B., Brummett, D., Wortzman, R., Harcourt, L., & Barnett, C. (1995). *Addison-Wesley Quest 2000: Exploring mathematics—grade 4.* Menlo Park, CA: Addison-Wesley.

Coolmath 4 Kids. www.coolmath4kids.com.

Cummins, J. (1989). *Empowering minority students.* Sacramento: California Association for Bilingual Education.

Cummins, J. (1993). *The acquisition of English as a second language.* Presentation article/handout for California Education Association, San Diego, CA.

Enright, D., & McCloskey, M. (1988). *Integrating English: Developing English language and literacy in the multilingual classroom.* Reading, MA: Addison-Wesley.

Funbrain. www.funbrain.com

Fuson, K. C., Carroll, W. M., & Drueck, J. V. (2000). Achievement results for second and third graders using the standards-based curriculum. *Journal for Research in Mathematics Education, 31,* 277–295.

Gagnon, J. C., & Maccini, P. (2001, Sept./Oct.). Preparing students with disabilities for algebra. *Teaching Exceptional Children, 34*(1), 8–15.

Gardner, H. (1983). *Frames of minds: The theory of multiple intelligences.* New York: Basic Books.

Golik, M. (1973). *Deal me in.* New York: Jeffrey Norton.

How Stuff Works. www.howstuffworks.com

Kagan, S. (1986). Cooperative learning and sociocultural factors in schooling. In *Beyond language: Social and cultural factors in schooling language minority students.* Sacramento: California State Department of Education.

Kagan, S., Kagan, M., & Kagan, L. (2000). *Reaching standards through cooperative learning—English/language arts.* Port Chester, NY: National Professional Resources.

Krashen, S. (1981). Bilingual education and second language acquisition theory. In *Schooling and language minority students: A theoretical framework.* Sacramento: California State Department of Education.

Krashen S., & Terrell, T. (1983). *The natural approach.* Hayward, CA: Aleman Press.

Long, M. (1982). Input, interaction, and second language acquisition. *TESOL Quarterly,* pp. 207–225.

MathStories.com. http://www.mathstories.com

National Council of Teachers of Mathematics (NCTM). (2000). *Principles and standards for school mathematics.* Reston, VA: Author.

National Council of Teachers of Mathematics. (2001). *Principles and standards for school mathematics navigations* (series). Reston, VA: Author.

National Library of Virtual Manipulatives. Salt Lake City: Utah State University. Available at http://nlvm.usu.edu/en/nav/vlibrary.html.

Pearson, P. D., & Gallagher, M. C. (1983). The instruction of reading comprehension. *Contemporary Educational Psychology, 8,* 317–344.

Randall, C. et al. (2000). *Mathepedia.* Reading, MA: Addison-Wesley.

Reys, B. J., Robinson, E., Sconiers, S., & Mark, J. (1999). Mathematics curricula based on rigorous national standards: What, why, and how? *Phi Delta Kappan, 80,* 454–456.

Rief, F. S. (2005). *How to reach and teach children with ADD/ADHD* (2nd ed.). San Francisco: Jossey-Bass.

Riordin, J. E., & Noyce, P. E. (2001). The impact of two standards-based mathematics curricula on student achievement in Massachusetts. *Journal for Research in Mathematics Education, 32,* 368–398.

Scieszka, J. (1995). *The math curse.* New York: Viking.

Sousa, D. A. (2001). *How the special needs brain learns.* Thousand Oaks, CA: Corwin Press.

Stein, M. K., Grover, B. W., & Henningsen, M. (1996). Building student capacity for mathematical thinking and reasoning: An analysis of mathematical tasks used in reform classrooms. *American Educational Research Journal, 33,* 455–488.

Stein, M. K., & Lane, S. (1996). Instructional tasks and the development of student capacity to think and reason: An analysis of the relationship between teaching and learning in a reform mathematics project. *Educational Research and Evaluation, 2*(1), 50–80.

U.S. Department of Education, Office of Educational Research and Improvement. (1997). *Pursuing excellence: A Study of U.S. fourth grade mathematics and science achievements in international context.* NCES 97-255. Washington, DC: U.S. Government Printing Office.

Van de Walle, J. A, (2004). *Elementary and middle school mathematics—Teaching developmentally.* Boston: Pearson Education.

Walter, T. (1996). *Amazing English!* Reading, MA: Addison-Wesley.

Wood, T., & Sellers, P. (1996). Assessment of a problem-centered mathematics program: Third grade. *Journal for Research in Mathematics Education, 27,* 337–353.

Wood, T., & Sellers, P. (1997). Deepening the analysis: Longitudinal assessment of a problem-centered mathematics program. *Journal for Research in Mathematics Education, 28,* 163–168.

TEACHER RESOURCES

Bresser, R. (2004). *Math and literature.* Sausalito, CA: Math Solutions.

Burns, M. (1992). *About teaching mathematics.* Sausalito, CA: Math Solutions.

Burns, M. (1998). *MATH: Facing an American phobia.* Sausalito, CA: Math Solutions.

Golick, M. (1973). *Deal me in.* New York: Jeffrey Norton.

Hiebert, J. (1996). *Making sense: Teaching and learning mathematics with understanding.* Portsmouth, NH: Heinemann.

Krashen, S. (1993). *The power of reading.* Englewood, CO: Libraries Unlimited.

Stenmark, J., Thompson, V., & Cossy, R. (1986). *Family math.* Berkeley, CA: Lawrence Hall of Science.

MATH ASSIGNMENT SHEET

Studentís Name: _____

Week of: _____

Day	Assignment	Completed	Corrected	Ratio (Number correct/ number possible)	% Correct
Monday					
Tuesday					
Wednesday					
Thursday					
Friday					

Comments _____

_____

Copyright © 2006 by Sandra F. Rief and Julie A. Heimburge

Activity 14.2

GEOMETRY DESIGN PROJECT

Name: _____ Date: _____

Create the following geometric shapes following the step-by-step instructions.

Design 1: Hexagon Design

- Set your compass at a radius of 3.
- Draw the circle.
- Place the point of the compass on the circumference of the circle without changing the setting of 3.
- Form a small arc that barely crosses over the circumference of the circle.
- Where the arc and the circumference meet, put a point. Mark it with a letter *A*.
- Place the point of the compass on point *A* of the circumference and form another arc. Mark it *B*.
- Continue doing this until you have six points on the circumference of the circle.
- Place a dot where each of the six points crosses the circumference. Mark them *A, B, C, D, E, F.*
- Use a ruler to draw chords to connect the dots. You should have six.
- Use a ruler to draw all of the diameters that you can locate. You should have three.
- Make chords to connect all of the rest of the points. You should have six.
- If you have done this correctly, you should have two big triangles that have geometric shapes inside them.

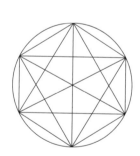

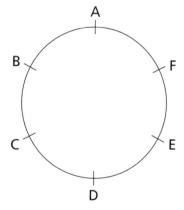

GEOMETRY DESIGN PROJECT *(continued)*

Design 2: Flower Design

- Set your compass at a 1½ inch opening.
- Place the point of your compass anywhere on the original circumference, and form a full circle around this point. Mark it *A*. Do not change the setting.
- Place the point of the compass again on the original circumference of the circle where the circumference of the new circle crosses the original circle. Move in a clockwise position. Mark it *B*. Draw a new full circle.
- Continue this until you have completed six full circles.
- You should have a flower-like shape formed in the middle of your original circle.
- Your outside should be scallopy looking. You should have formed seven circles including your original.

Design 3: Smaller Triangles

- Set the compass at 3 inches.
- Draw a diameter line as your starting point.
- Using your protractor, measure off segments of 45 degrees on the circumference of the circle. You might have to extend your lines so that you reach the circumference. You should have nine arcs on the circle.
- Place a point where each of the arcs touches the circumference.
- Join all of the points with chords. There should be eight of them.
- Join each point with all other points. There should be seven diameters and chords radiating from each point of the circle.
- Color in each space geometrically with color. Limit your colors.

Completing the Project

- Color each of the designs with colored pencils or crayons. Be sure to concentrate while you're coloring, so that symmetrical shapes are colored the same. Each person's design will look different. Repeating colors make for a more balanced design.
- Use a permanent medium-point black marker to carefully go around your pencil marks to enhance your colors. Use a ruler for the longer straight lines. Be careful to let the marker dry so that it doesn't smear.
- Think through the process of creating your geometric shapes.
- Cut around the circumference of each of your circles with scissors so that you have three circles, all about the same size.
- Using a 5- by 8-inch index card, explain what you have learned about geometry design using a compass and protractor. For your write-up, use some or all of the following words from your learning. You either used the words as you were designing or you "saw" the words in your final product. Underline the words you use:

GEOMETRY DESIGN PROJECT *(continued)*

triangle
squares
ruler
point
geometric shapes
radii
chords
arcs
rectangle
quadrilaterals
scalene triangles
accurate measurement

isosceles triangle
compass
circle
protractor
circumference
diameter
symmetrical
flower-like
central angle
circumference
equilateral triangles

- You might want to use a free-hand diagram in your write-up to clearly show what you mean.

- You might use a topic sentence such as, "I learned a lot of mathematical vocabulary as I was creating my geometric designs."

- Here are a couple of examples to help you out. Of course you do not want to use these as your own—that would be plagiarizing.

Sample A: In order to create geometric designs, I must know how to use a <u>compass</u>, <u>ruler</u>, and <u>protractor</u>. To make the original circle shape, I used a compass. A <u>compass</u> is a simple tool used to make a perfect *circle*. How to use a compass is kind of tricky. You put the pointy side at a <u>*center point*</u>. At the top there is a little handle, and you spin the compass. When you're starting to learn how to use it, your circles look bumpy—that's why you have to practice.

Sample B: When I look at my designs I see a lot of <u>*geometric shapes*</u>, including <u>*isosceles triangles*</u>, <u>*squares*</u>, <u>*equilateral triangles*</u>, <u>*rectangles*</u>, and <u>*circles*</u>. If I colored them correctly, I can see these shapes are <u>*symmetric*</u>, just like in nature. I learned a lot about geometry while I was doing this assignment. I didn't know math could be so fun. As I worked with the <u>*compass*</u>, I actually could feel the words like <u>*circumference*</u>, <u>*chords*</u>, <u>*diameter*</u>, and <u>*radii*</u> that I had tried to learn earlier. Now they make sense.

- Mount your designs on a long, skinny piece of black paper, approximately 31½ by 8 inches. This will show off the designs better.

- Double-mount your designs on a larger piece of a bright color that you have used in your designs such as yellow. The approximate size is 9 by 32 inches.

- Show your designs off by putting them on a bulletin board.

Activity 14.3

PIG SCORE SHEET

Game 1

Round	Number of Points on This Round	Cumulative Score
1		
2		
3		
4		
5		
6		
7		
8		
9		
10		
11		
12		
13		
14		
15		
16		
17		
18		
19		
20		
21		
22		
23		
24		

Game 2

Round	Number of Points on This Round	Cumulative Score
1		
2		
3		
4		
5		
6		
7		
8		
9		
10		
11		
12		
13		
14		
15		
16		
17		
18		
19		
20		
21		
22		
23		
24		

Play continues until a player reaches the highest cumulative score over 100 at the end of a round.

END-OF-YEAR MATH EVALUATION

Name: _____ Date: _____

Important things I have learned in math this year: _____

_____

_____

_____

_____

How I think I have improved in math this year: _____

_____

_____

_____

_____

Goals for my summer math learning: _____

_____

_____

_____

_____

MATH IS EVERYWHERE YOU LOOK ASSIGNMENT SHEET

Name: _____   Date: _____

1. This week you will become a math detective.

2. Look around you carefully every day.

3. Make a list of at least twenty-five things you see in your life that involve math: for example, clocks, scales, radios, gasoline pumps, mileage signs, and medicine bottles.

4. Look for pictures in magazines, newspapers, catalogues, cookbooks, and other such resources of things that use math: for example, pictures of televisions, telephones, watches, menus, and rulers. You may also draw your own pictures or take snapshots of these things.

5. You have two choices for what to do next.

Choice 1: Glue the pictures of eight to ten items on separate sheets of 8½- by 11-inch notebook paper. Under each picture, write three to five sentences telling why you selected this picture and how it ties into math. Here is an example:

Picture of an ad for Air Max Moto IV shoes by Nike.

This is a coupon for "Air Max Moto IV" Nike shoes. We used this coupon to get this pair of shoes for exactly $15.01 off the price. The regular price for this pair of shoes was $75.00, but with this coupon, we got them for $59.99. We still had to pay more because of the state sales tax. The use of mathematics gives us the answer to what $15.01 off is. It also helps us to understand the use of money.

Choice 2: Make a collage on 12- by 18-inch construction paper, and write a one- to two-page summary explaining your collage choices.

6. Add an interesting math cover sheet, or put these pages into a folder with a catchy math title and an illustration.

MATH IS EVERYWHERE YOU LOOK EVALUATION FORM

Name: _____ Date: _____

1. I spent about _____ hours/minutes on this project.

2. I think I did a/an _____ job on this assignment.

3. I think my grade should be a/an _____ because

_____

_____

4. Compared to the rest of the class, I feel _____

_____

5. I asked for help from _____

6. I'd like my teacher to know this about the Math Is Everywhere assignment:

_____

_____

GRAPHING CAN BE FUN: A MATH PROJECT

What Will I Be Doing?

YOUR FAVORITE DESSERT?

1. Choose a question from the Question Possibilities for Graphing Projects sheet. You will use this to do a survey of your classmates to find out what they like. Each person in the class will select a different question. If you think of another question that you would like to investigate, ask your teacher for approval.

2. You will make a prediction/hypothesis card on a 3- by 5-inch index card. Write at least one or two sentences to predict what you think will happen in your survey and tell why you believe your prediction. Make sure you print it neatly. Have a spelling expert check your work before you finalize it with thin black marker.

3. You will receive a class list with everyone's name on it. So that your research is valid, after you survey one classmate, you need to cross his or her name off your list. Only survey the people who are available to you. Some students may be absent or out of the classroom at the time of the survey. Make sure you approach as many classmates as possible during the time allotted.

4. You will need six other index cards, each with one of the following labels: Question/Problem, Procedure, Research/Data (The Survey), Findings/Conclusions, Materials, and Your Name. Your writing should fill up each card. Don't leave wasted space. Each card should be neatly printed and spell-checked. If you hand-write the cards, start with pencil first, and after everything has been spell-checked, write over the pencil with thin black pen. If any pencil is still showing, erase it thoroughly. If you use a computer, make the font large enough to fill a space the size of a 5- by 7-inch index card. Divide your data/research card into four sections to show your data or statistics in four different mathematics ways: Section 1: Number of people responding in each category; Section 2: Ratio or fraction form; Section 3: Decimal form; Section 4: Percentage form. For your Findings/Conclusion card, you will write up a narrative telling about your data and what you found out from your survey. Be sure to include percentages, decimals, and ratios for your findings. Also, let the observer know if your prediction was correct or incorrect.

GRAPHING CAN BE FUN: A MATH PROJECT *(continued)*

5. You may make a line, picto, bar, or circle graph to show your results. First make a rough draft in pencil. Check with your teacher that you are correct at this point.

6. You are now ready to make a final draft. Use colored pencils to make your lines, pictures, bars, or sections on your graph. All words must be in thick black marker.

7. You will receive a colored file folder to display all of your work. On the right-hand side of your file folder will be your Question, Prediction/Hypothesis, Procedure, Research/Data, and Findings cards. On the left-hand side of the folder will be your graph, and your Name Card.

8. Make sure that your materials are securely glued onto the file folder and your work is top quality.

QUESTION POSSIBILITIES FOR GRAPHING PROJECTS

Look at the list of questions below. Highlight five of them that interest you most, and then choose one for your project. You will be given the opportunity to take a survey of your classmates during math period. As a good mathematician and scientist, you must be sure that your findings are valid. Double check to see if your tally marks add up to the number of students that you surveyed. Do your percentages add up to 100 percent? Do your ratios equal one whole (for example, if you surveyed 30 people, do your category ratios add up to 30/30 or one whole)? Do your decimals add up to 1.00?

1. What is your favorite color?
2. What kind of pets do you have at home?
3. What is your favorite fast food restaurant?
4. What is your favorite sports car?
5. What amusement park is your favorite?
6. What is your favorite kind of ice cream?
7. How many people live in your house or apartment?
8. What color cars do the students have in our class?
9. What is your favorite sport to watch?
10. What time of day do you watch the most television?
11. What topping do you like on your pizza?
12. What is your favorite department store?
13. What grocery store do your parents shop at most often?
14. What kind of books do you prefer to read?
15. What is your favorite color?
16. What color eyes do you have?
17. What color hair do you have?
18. What is your favorite brand of cereal?
19. How often do you brush your teeth each day?
20. What is your favorite way to relax?
21. Where would your favorite place to travel be?
22. What is your favorite music group?
23. In what month is your birthday?
24. What time is your bedtime?
25. How many hours of sleep do you usually get on a school night?
26. What is your favorite type of dessert?
27. What is your favorite professional baseball team?
28. What is your favorite professional football team?
29. How many years have you gone to this school?
30. Which middle school will you attend?
31. Can you roll your tongue?
32. Which kind of earlobe do you have?
33. What state were you born in?

QUESTION POSSIBILITIES FOR GRAPHING PROJECTS *(continued)*

34. What country did your ancestors come from?
35. How many brothers and sisters do you have?
36. What is your favorite kind of music?
37. How many inches tall are you?
38. What is your favorite radio station?
39. What is your favorite video game?
40. Which is your favorite kids' movie?
41. Which is your favorite television program?
42. What is your favorite vegetable?
43. What is your favorite food?
44. Are you right- or left-handed?
45. What size shoe do you wear?
46. What is your favorite thing to do?
47. What is your favorite kind of candy?
48. What time do you arrive home from school?
49. What chores do you do around the house most often?
50. How much allowance do you get each week?
51. How many cars do you have in your family?
52. What is your favorite tourist spot?
53. What is your biggest pet peeve?
54. What is your favorite sport to watch?
55. What time do you get up in the morning on school days?
56. What is your favorite holiday?
57. Who is your favorite male celebrity?
58. Who is your favorite female celebrity?
59. Who is your hero?
60. What is your favorite brand of shoe?
61. What is your favorite magazine?
62. What is your favorite time of day?
63. What is your favorite kind of music?
64. Who is your favorite cartoon character?
65. What is your favorite kind of soda?
66. What is your favorite brand of clothing?
67. What is your favorite sports utility vehicle?
68. Who is your favorite female vocalist?
69. Who is your favorite male vocalist?
70. Which is your favorite mall to shop at?
71. What language would you like to learn most?
72. What is your favorite musical instrument?

Activity 14.9

GRAPHING PROJECT DESIGN FORM

Name: _____ Date: _____

Question/problem: _____

_____

Prediction/hypothesis (what you think you will find out and why?): _____

_____

_____

What will your main categories/choices be? _____

_____

Materials: _____

_____

Findings: Use tally marks to show your survey results:

Category 1: _____

Category 2: _____

Category 3: _____

Category 4: _____

Category 5: _____

Provide a written statement of your findings using decimals, ratios, and percentages:

_____

_____

_____

Research/Data Card (Change your results into ratios, decimals, and percentages.)

Findings/Conclusions: Was your prediction correct? Explain why or why not.

_____

_____

_____

GRAPHING PROJECT DESIGN FORM *(continued)*

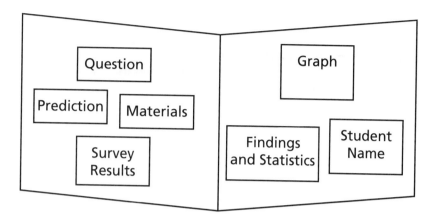

File Folder

Requirements

1. Completely fill out the project design form.
2. Have all of your work checked by a "spelling expert."
3. All written work should be done in pen (permanent black thin marker or typed in an appropriate size that is large enough to read from a distance).
4. All graphs should be drawn on paper using a picto, line, bar, or circle graph.
5. Index cards may be framed with colored construction paper or borders may be drawn around the cards with felt tip markers.
6. When you glue your work into the folder, REMEMBER: less is better.
7. You will be responsible for orally sharing your results with your classmates.
8. Freestanding graphing folders will be displayed on desks for peer observation.

Activity 14.10

PARENT LETTER FOR THE SHOPPING ADVENTURE

Dear Parents,

Next week as part of the math program, our class will be participating in a field trip to better acquaint us with real-life math survival skills. My hope is that at the end of the trip, the students will feel more confident in their ability to spend money meaningfully. On the date of _____ from the time of _____ to _____ , the class will participate in a shopping adventure at _____ [name of store].

Here's how the experience will work:

1. Each child will bring $2.00 to pool with the other three members of their team.

2. The team will have a half-hour to shop together.

3. The team will make decisions as to what to buy.

4. The team must purchase between five and seven items. All purchases should be appropriate. No guns or weapons may be bought. When shopping, consideration should be given to how the items can be divided up in four ways fairly.

5. The team must use a calculator to keep a tally of their desired purchases. A notepad and pencil may be used. The store manager has been contacted, and the employees are aware of this project. They should be asked politely for any needed assistance. Parents accompanying the students may help to clarify questions that arise but should not offer extensive help. The students should be problem solving as a team.

6. The team must figure out the cost of the items, plus the sales tax and other charges, before going to the register. After checking out, the team may not reenter the shopping area to take back or repurchase items. The total must be as close to $8.00 as possible without going over. Teams that go over their allotted amount of money are disqualified from receiving the first place award. The award will be determined by the teacher.

7. When the team returns to school, they will compile a report describing why they purchased the items, how much each item cost, and how they will divide the purchases. They will make a display of what they purchased and show how the sales tax was figured out. The class will then vote on the team that got the most value for their dollar. Adult judges will assist in the evaluation for the grand prize.

Through this experience, I hope the students learn to figure out sales tax correctly, use a calculator, work as a team, and learn how to purchase items in an intelligent way. As they will be representing _____ School in the public view, I hope they will be courteous shoppers.

We will need drivers to help us with the experience. Please let us know if you might be available for the one hour period of time.

Thank you,

_____

[Your name]

SHOPPING ADVENTURE RECORDING SHEET

Group Name _____   Date of Event _____

The students will write in the item name and the price of the item on the line.

Name/Price of Taxable Items	Name/Price of Nontaxable Items
1. _____	1. _____
2. _____	2. _____
3. _____	3. _____
4. _____	4. _____
5. _____	5. _____
6. _____	6. _____
7. _____	7. _____

Subtotal _____   Total _____

Sales tax _____

Grand total _____

SUPER BOWL MATH ACTIVITY PACKET

Name: _____ Date: _____

Since this is Super Bowl Week, you will be asked to keep your eyes and ears open so that your can see how heavily influenced this game is with math facts and statistics. You have been given some pertinent information in class having to do with statistics from *The Guinness Book of World Records,* and your notes can be helpful to you for some of the information below.

   You may find the answers to these questions by watching television, listening to the radio, reading newspapers and magazines, or asking people who already have the information. Of course, many things may be learned by just looking at the Super Bowl itself on Sunday.

   Answer as many questions as possible. Some questions can be answered right now, while others will need to wait until during, or even after, the game ends. Don't get stressed if you can't find an answer. Just do your best. Try to make this a fun, fact-finding mission, and get everyone looking for answers. We'll discuss our findings when we return to school the day after the Super Bowl.

   You will be evaluated on how many activities you have completed independently, the neatness of your work, the effort you put into your activities, and the quality of your work.

Pregame Activities

   Score Prediction:

      NFC Champions: _____

      AFC Champions: _____

1. How many Super Bowls have there been? _____

2. What was the *point spread* predicted before the game began? _____

3. How much is airfare from the airport nearest where you live to the Super Bowl city?

   _____

4. How many miles is it from where you live to the Super Bowl? _____

SUPER BOWL MATH ACTIVITY PACKET (*continued*)

5. How many miles are between the two Super Bowl Champions' cities? _____

6. If an average hotel room in the Super Bowl city is $300.00 per night, how much would it cost two families, each with their own room, to spend three days and nights there? _____

7. If it cost a person on the average $30.00 a day for food in the Super Bowl city, how much would it cost two adults to eat meals for three days? Show your calculations.

_____

8. Give the names, numbers, and positions of two offensive players and two defensive players of your favorite Super Bowl team. _____

_____

9. How much money does the Super Bowl ring cost that every player receives for participation in this game? _____

10. How much money will a Super Bowl player earn if he is on the winning team?

_____ The losing team? _____

11. If 50,000 people each buy one soft drink ($3.00) and one hot dog ($4.00) at the Super Bowl, what is the total amount spent by all of these people for food?

_____

12. How many feet high is the goal post? _____

13. Using the facts given to you in class or by looking them up in the encyclopedia under *football*, find the perimeter and area of a football field.

Perimeter: _____

Area: _____

SUPER BOWL MATH ACTIVITY PACKET (*continued*)

14. Write the first 50 roman numerals:

_____

_____

_____

15. What is the number in roman numerals of this Super Bowl? _____

16. What are the weight and length of the football? _____

17. What geometric shape is a football? _____

18. What is the name of this year's Super Bowl stadium? _____

19. What is the face value of a Super Bowl ticket? _____

20. How are Super Bowl tickets distributed? _____

21. How many tickets is each player allocated? _____

22. Take a survey of ten to fifteen friends and family members of all ages before the game to find out which team they predict will win. Make a chart to show the results.

23. Find out the height and weight of five football players in this Super Bowl. Write down their names and their height and weight.

24. Create three math questions for your classmates using information about the Super Bowl that you have acquired through your pregame research. At the end of each question, write the correct answer upside down. Use the back of the paper if you run out of room.

_____

_____

_____

SUPER BOWL MATH ACTIVITY PACKET (*continued*)

During-the-Game Activities

1. What was the score of the Super Bowl game at the end of each of the following times?

   Quarter 1: _____

   Quarter 2: _____

   Quarter 3: _____

   Quarter 4: _____

2. What is the temperature (Fahrenheit and Centigrade) at game time in the city where the Super Bowl is being held? _____

   Where you live? _____

   In the home city of the NFC champs? _____

   In the home city of the CFC champs? _____

3. How many people were in attendance at this year's Super Bowl? _____

4. How many people will the Super Bowl hold? _____

5. How much did it cost to advertise for one minute of time during the Super Bowl?

   _____

6. What companies did the most advertising during the game? _____

   _____

7. What was the highest amount you heard that anyone spent on a ticket to go to the Super Bowl? _____

SUPER BOWL MATH ACTIVITY PACKET (*continued*)

8. How many touchdowns were made by each team?

   NFC champs: _____ AFC champs? _____

9. What was the *aggregate score* of this year's Super Bowl? _____

10. Did the score of this game make any records as far as the greatest or narrowest *victory margin*?

    _____

11. Give the name and team name of the heaviest person mentioned during the game:

    _____ The tallest person: _____

12. Listen to the ages of the players mentioned. Who is the oldest, and what position does he play?

    _____

13. Which AFC and NFC player has played in the most Super Bowls, counting this one?

    _____

14. What time does the Super Bowl begin in the Super Bowl city? _____

    Where you live? _____

    In the home cities of both the NFC and AFC champs? _____

15. Which professional team has won the Super Bowl the most times? _____

    How many times? _____

16. Using a stopwatch or second hand on your watch, time one commercial break. List each advertiser, and the number of seconds each used for commercial time. Using the figure $2 million per 30 second segment, figure out how much each commercial segment cost the advertiser. _____

    _____

    _____

SUPER BOWL MATH ACTIVITY PACKET (*continued*)

Postgame Activities
Two of these activities are required:

1. Create a collage (9 inches by 12 inches) on construction paper showing how math is used in the Super Bowl.

2. Write a paragraph (½ to 1 full page) telling how math has been used in the Super Bowl. Attach it to your collage.

3. Make a list of at least five other math-related facts that you have learned about having watched the Super Bowl or from reading or listening to news programs.

4. Plan a menu for a Super Bowl party. Tell what you would buy and what the total cost would be. You may want to use the food section of the newspaper to help you out. Show a picture of what you want and how much it will cost. Create an invitation to the party. Include the where, when, and who part of the invitation.

5. Draw a map of the United States. Locate where you live, the city where the Super Bowl is being played, and the two cities where the championship teams are located. Label them.

6. Write a paragraph describing one of your favorite commercials that ran during the Super Bowl. Tell why you think it was worth the company's money to run it.

7. Write a paragraph telling why so many people have Super Bowl parties and what the benefits are to the people who attend.

8. Interview a person who went to the Super Bowl. Tell what this person thought were the high points of the trip, and get an estimate of how much the trip cost. Ask questions about the Super Bowl city, the fans, the stadium, the weather, traffic, and anything else that interests you.

9. Write a paragraph telling which Super Bowl team is your favorite, and why you like it.

10. Draw illustrations of both of the teams' football jerseys. Use color.

11. Write a paragraph about the half-time show. Be complete in your detail, including costumes, music, celebrities, and other special features.

12. Make up a word search with the teams in the NFL. Have someone try to locate each with a highlighter.

13. Scramble up to fifteen Super Bowl words (example: rtreuaackqb = quarterback). Have a partner unscramble them.

14. On a map of the United States, locate fifteen professional football team cities. Show where they are, and label them.

15. Make up your own idea to show how math is important to the Super Bowl.

Activity 14.12

SUPER BOWL MATH ACTIVITY PACKET (*continued*)

Self-Evaluation

1. What did you enjoy most about this Super Bowl math project? _____

   _____

   _____

   _____

2. What did you learn from doing it? _____

   _____

   _____

   _____

3. How did you go about finding the answers to these questions? _____

   _____

   _____

4. Did anyone help you to find answers? _____

   Who? _____

   How did that person help? _____

   _____

   _____

5. How much time do you think you put into completing this packet? _____

   _____

6. What was the most difficult part of this activity? _____

   _____

   _____

SURVIVAL MATH PARENT LETTER

September 200 _____

Dear Family Members,

Please look over this Survival Math Packet with your son or daughter. Help him or her to select activities that sound interesting and that your family can work on together to better understand math in the real world. Make this a fun event.

Choose carefully by reading through all the activities first, but also realize that there are amazing math problems out there waiting for you to tackle. You can create activities to relate to your own family's life.

Our class will be doing activities for the year. Our first one will be done together in class so that the students know my expectations.

Thank you,

_____

[Teacher's Name]

Survival Math Due Dates

First Reporting Period

Friday, September _____
   (in-class project)

Friday, October _____

Second Reporting Period

Friday, December _____

Friday, January _____

Third Reporting Period

Friday, February _____

Friday, April _____

- -

Please return the bottom portion with your child to class.

We have reviewed the *Survival Math Packet* with our child and have selected the following activities to work on during the year. We also have reviewed the due dates. The activities we have chosen are _____

_____

Child's Signature: _____

Family Member's Signature: _____

SURVIVAL MATH PACKET (EXPERIENCING MATH IN YOUR EVERYDAY LIFE)

What Will You Be Doing?

Throughout the year, you will be responsible for doing several of these math activities that connect you with the wonderful world of math. There are over eighty activities to choose from. How will you ever limit your choices? Your teacher will decide how many activities you will choose for the year. It may be one a month, one bimonthly, or several for each report card period. A couple of them will be done in class to help you know what an activity should look like. But the others will be done at home. I hope you will get your family involved too.

Activity Essentials

You should include the following parts on each activity. Everything should be neat and well organized.

- A cover sheet or label at the top of the paper with your name, date, and project number

- A reason that you chose this particular project

- Chart, graph, table, or other graphic representation of your findings

- An explanation of what you did and how you did it

- Evidence or proof of where you obtained your information

- A summary telling what you learned

More Specific Instructions

1. Some activities are more difficult to research and will take more time to do. They are worth more points. You should get started on the activity long before its due date. Don't procrastinate.

2. You will be graded on a 10-point system. Each activity is worth from 1 to 10 points. The highest score is a 10. Receiving a 10 on an activity means that you have gone well beyond what someone your age normally would do, you have put out extra effort, and you have extended the activity to its fullest. Of course, it also means that your work is easy to read and understand.

SURVIVAL MATH PACKET (EXPERIENCING MATH IN YOUR EVERYDAY LIFE) (*continued*)

3. If you can think of some other math life skills activities that will give you a better understanding of your personal math world, feel free to create your own. Just make sure you check with your teacher first.

4. Stars (*****) indicate the amount of involvement you will give to your project:

***	Minimum involvement necessary	Usually can be done with very little adult help, time, or extra materials
****	Extra involvement necessary	Usually takes some extra materials, transportation, communication by phone, and/or some extra time
*****	Maximum effort needed	Usually takes research transportation, parent involvement, and/or additional time and effort

5. The key word(s) is in **bold letters** so that you can scan the activities quickly to find something that you might be interested in pursuing.

6. Your audience is your teacher and your classmates. You will be responsible for sharing your activities with them the day after the due date—so don't be late.

7. You will be keeping all of your activities in a math portfolio or special folder so that you'll have them all together to look back at.

8. You will keep a record of your activities on the *Survival Math Record Sheet.*

SURVIVAL MATH PACKET (EXPERIENCING MATH IN YOUR EVERYDAY LIFE) (*continued*)

Survival Math Activities

1. Make a prediction about how much it costs to own your **pet.** Keep track of how much money your family spends to feed and take care of it. You might include pet supplies, pet food, litter, toys, medication, vet bills, and pet insurance. List what your pet needs for a month. Calculate how much it costs to own your pet for an entire year. Were your predications correct? *****

2. If you do not have a **pet,** research the cost of having the one that you want. Include the cost of the animal and the supplies and equipment you will need. Try to think of all the concerns that your parents would have against the pet. Write a persuasive letter to your parents trying to convince them that you should have this pet and showing them the research that you have done. *****

3. Prepare a grocery list with your parents. Then go to the **grocery store,** or if you can't get to the store, go online. Select five items to do a comparative price check. That means that if you have spaghetti on your list, compare three different brands of spaghetti. Make sure the weight on the package is exactly the same and that the item is a very close match. Tell the name of the store you shopped at in the title of the chart. Use a chart similar to the one shown below. *****

Item Comparison

Name of Market _____

Item #1 Spaghetti Prices

Anthony's Spaghetti	$1.19
American Beauty Spaghetti	.99
Lady Lee Spaghetti	.89

Item #2 Tomato Soup

---

4. Select any ten **grocery items** your family normally uses. Make a comparison chart showing the difference in price at three different grocery stores. You may go online for your shopping adventure or you could use newspaper ads. *****

SURVIVAL MATH PACKET (EXPERIENCING MATH IN YOUR EVERYDAY LIFE) (*continued*)

Item	Von's	Food 4 Less	Albertson's
1 gallon of Dreyer's chocolate ice cream			

5. Ask your parents to share the **cost of groceries** for your family for one week. Include the cost of the food for the nights you eat out in restaurants and fast food takeouts. Figure out the approximate cost of food for your family per week, per month, and per year based on the information you have. Are you surprised at your findings? ****

6. If you are in Girl Scouts, Boy Scouts, or another organization, use your **money-making projects** to create a survival math activity. You could show the results of the cookie/peanut/magazine/gift wrapping drive for yourself and for the whole organization. Find out how that money was spent. ****

7. **Tutor** or assist a younger child with his or her math homework such as telling time, multiplication facts, or counting change. Make a schedule for yourself and the child. Make sure you spend ten 10- to 15-minute sessions with your student. Have an adult initial each session. What do you think your tutee learned from you? ****

8. Go to a **restaurant** with your family. (This should not be a fast food restaurant.) Ask for the bill at the end of the meal. Check to see if the waiter or waitress has added the bill correctly. Check to see if sales tax is added to it. How much tip should be given to the waiter or waitress? Then pay the bill for your parents to see if you get the right change back. Obtain a menu if possible. Keep a record of what the dinners were and how much each cost. Figure out the average cost of each person's dinner. ****

9. Fill out three **catalogue order forms** from a store of your choice. Make sure that your work is neatly filled out and accurate. Include a picture of what you are ordering. If you don't actually buy anything, hand in the form. If you are planning a real order, make a copy to hand in to your teacher. Don't forget sales tax and shipping cost where applicable. Glue all of these to a piece of paper to hand in. ***

10. If you are in a **competitive sport,** figure out how much it costs for the uniforms, equipment, fees, transportation, gas, and food for the season. *****

11. Think of a **hobby** that you are interested in. Figure out how much money this hobby will cost you for a week, for a month, and for a year. Show the cost on a chart or diagram. Include your supplies and the cost of each. *****

SURVIVAL MATH PACKET (EXPERIENCING MATH IN YOUR EVERYDAY LIFE) (*continued*)

12. If you travel to school by car or bus, figure out how many **miles** the round trip is. Find out how many days you are actually in school. Based on your information, how many miles do you travel per week, per month, and per school year? ***

13. Help your family figure out how many **miles per gallon** your family car gets on a long trip. You can do this by filling your tank at the beginning of the trip and recording your odometer mileage. When you stop for gas again, fully fill the tank. Divide the number of miles that you have traveled by the number of gallons you have used. ****

14. If you receive an **allowance,** figure out how much you will receive in a week, a month, and a year. Tell how you will use your allowance in a responsible way. You may also include approximate amounts you will receive in gifts. Make sure your calculations are correct; recheck your totals with a calculator. ***

15. Keep a record of how many miles your family's **cars** travel in a three-week period. Record the mileage at the end of each week. Find the average number of miles that the cars traveled per week. At that rate, figure out how many miles your cars will travel in a year, two years, five years, and ten years. Show your calculations. *****

16. Find out what the costs of **renting an economy, midsize, and luxury car** are at a local rental agency. Compare these with another agency's prices. If there are extra charges for mileage and gas consumption, what are they? If you are taking a trip, try to use the information to help you prepare for it. ****

17. Save the money you earn from **recycling** cans. Tell how much a can and a two-liter bottle are worth, how many cans you collect, what the bottles and cans weigh (if your state weighs them), and how you think you will spend your money. If you find a double redemption coupon, use it. ****

18. Follow the price of a gallon of **gasoline** from three service stations. Compare the price for unleaded, unleaded plus, and super/premium unleaded at three different service stations over a three-week period. Compare the rise and fall of gas prices during this time. Make a chart similar to the one below, or draw a graph to show your comparisons. ****

SURVIVAL MATH PACKET (EXPERIENCING MATH IN YOUR EVERYDAY LIFE) (*continued*)

Station	Shell			Chevron			Union 76		
Week	1	2	3	1	2	3	1	2	3
Unleaded									
Unleaded Plus									
Super Unleaded									

19. Go to the bank with your parents. Open a **savings account** if you do not have one. Find out how much interest the bank will pay you for having your money in your account. What does *interest* mean? Make a copy of your application or paper work, or fill out a deposit slip to show you know how to fill it out correctly. What is the minimum amount you must have in order to open a new account? Try to put a small amount of money away in your account each month. ****

20. If you already have **a bank account,** make a real deposit or a pretend deposit. Fill out a deposit form at the bank. If you can, fill out a duplicate form, and hand it in to your teacher. Also fill out a withdrawal slip to show that you know how to fill out that form. Include the slips in your final project. Discuss how the bank teller assisted you and if you think he or she was a courteous employee. ****

21. Go to a travel agency or online to find out how much a **trip** to a place you would like to travel would cost for you and your family. Include a brochure or online ad, or make up a brochure of your own to advertise the place. Do you need air fare? What about accommodations and food? How much would your trip cost altogether? ****

22. If your school, church, or social group is going on a **special trip or outing,** think of ways that you can help your family defer the cost. Make a list of the things that you could do to earn money so you can attend. Do some of the things on the list, and record how much money you earn. Ideas might include baking and selling cookies, selling or planting flowers, mowing lawns, or pulling weeds. ****

23. Go to two **car agencies,** and price the cost of a new car that your family would like to have. Include a brochure for each of the cars that you look at. List the special options that you would like on the car. Write a paragraph about your favorite car and what you like about it, or make a collage of cars that you would like to have. ****

SURVIVAL MATH PACKET (EXPERIENCING MATH IN YOUR EVERYDAY LIFE) (*continued*)

24. Call an **airline**, talk with a travel agent, or go online. Find out how much it costs you to travel to a place you and your family would like to go. Compare the price with one other airline. Find out if each airline offers any special deals. What is the best deal you can find, and how much would it cost your family to take this trip? You could do the same thing traveling by bus or train, or you could compare the price for all three. *****

25. If you're going on a **family car, plane, or train trip,** use this as a math experience. Keep track of the cost of the gas, food, accommodations, and any other costs that your family will incur. *****

26. If your parents are willing to share the information with you, find out how much money your monthly **gas (or oil) and electric bills** are. Look over the bills, and find out if you pay more for the gas (or oil) or more for the electricity. If all your bills were equal, what would the cost be for an entire year? Divide the bills by the number of days in the month, and find the average cost for use each day. You may want to compare your consumption last year with what you used this year. ****

27. If your parents are willing to share the information with you, find out how much your monthly **water bill** is. See how many gallons of water you actually used during the billing period. How often is your family billed? Write it down. Divide it by the number of days of use, and find out how much an average day of water use is for your household. Find out how much difference there is between the amount of water you used this year compared with last year in the same time frame. Make a list of ways that you can conserve water. ***

28. If your parents are willing to share the information with you, find out how much the basic service is for your **telephone** per month. Also find out the amount you pay for long-distance calls and special services. Divide those amounts by the number of days in the month, and find out how much your average phone bill is per day. If you have a cell phone in your family, compare its costs to those of your land line. ****

29. Go to a store of your choice or go online, and treat yourself to a **shopping spree.** Select five items you would like to buy. (You do not really need to buy anything.) List the items you have selected, how much they cost, and figure out how much sales tax you would have to pay on the total. You may want to combine this activity with the check writing activity, and write out a sample check. You may want to select birthday presents for members of your family. ****

30. Predict how much you think your **clothes** will cost you for the entire school year based on what your family spent on clothes for the start of your school year. Show your results. If you wear uniforms, take a look at how much they cost for the entire year. ****

SURVIVAL MATH PACKET (EXPERIENCING MATH IN YOUR EVERYDAY LIFE) (*continued*)

31. Go to a **fabric store.** Choose something to make from a pattern catalogue, such as an apron, T-shirt, curtains, or shorts. Figure out how much fabric you will need and how much it will cost. Don't forget to get any accessories you might need. If you can, make the item. Compare the price of the item with one you can find in a store. Show the price of each of the items, how much fabric you bought and its cost, and how much the sales tax was. *****

32. Pretend that you have $10,000 to invest in the **stock market.** Choose five to ten stocks that you might be interested in acquiring. Research how the value of these stocks fluctuates for three weeks. Show your results. *****

33. Go to two **real estate open houses** in the same area of your town or city. Obtain a sheet that shows how much each house costs. Which house would be the better buy? Divide the cost of the house by the square footage of the house to find out how much the house costs per square foot. For instance, if the house costs $500,000, you would divide that by the square footage of 2,500 square feet (500,000 ÷ 2,500 = $200 per square foot.) ****

34. Go to the **public library.** Ask about its fines for overdue books for both children and adults. Figure out how much an adult would have to pay if the book was overdue for 5, 10, 15, and 20 days. Figure out the fine for a children's book for the same period of time. What are overdue fines for other items, like tapes, CDs, and videos? ***

35. Find out how much the **minimum wage** is in the United States. Considering that an average adult works 40 hours a week, calculate how much a person making minimum wage would make in one week, one month (4 weeks), and one year (52 weeks). Remember that this does not show the actual amount a person would take home because of taxes, but it is an approximation. ***

36. Find out how much each of the major **theme parks** costs in your state. Make a list to show the amount you would pay to get into each of the parks with no discounts—just the admission price. List the parks and the costs of admissions. After you have the correct prices, figure out how much admission to each of the parks would be for your entire family. You might want to include the parking price also. *****

37. Compare the price of a regular hamburger, a regular order of french fries, and a medium soda for three **fast food restaurants.** List the restaurant and the cost of each. Figure out the price of these items for you and your family at each place. If you can find a coupon for one of the restaurants, compare the individual item price with the coupon price. How much do you save? Include the coupon and, if possible, a menu or advertisement from the restaurant. *****

SURVIVAL MATH PACKET (EXPERIENCING MATH IN YOUR EVERYDAY LIFE) (*continued*)

38. If you were going to have a pizza party and eight of your friends were going to be invited, figure out what the menu would be and how much your party would cost. ****

39. Keep track of the scores of your favorite **baseball team** for ten games. List each of the games, who played, and what the score was. Figure out the average (mean) number of points the team scored during these ten games overall. Also identify the median score and the mode. You may need to review those math words in the glossary of your math book. ****

40. Go to several **fast food restaurants** or look online for a list of food items and the number of calories each has. Plan a meal for yourself with between 500 and 700 calories. Do the same for another family member. Which food item has the most calories and which the fewest calories? What food choices do you think are healthy? Figure out how much each of the items you want would cost. ****

41. Obtain a schedule for the **subway, trolley,** and/or **bus** in your city. Tell how close to your home the pickup point is and the exact place you can catch the ride. How much is the fare for each mode of transportation? Find out how far it is to the main part of your city. Also tell the time involved in making those trips. If you want to ride the trolley, subway, or bus, write a paragraph about the experience. Include a schedule if you can. ****

42. How much is the per-mile fare for a **taxi** where you live? Is there a difference in pricing between taxi companies? If so, tell the difference in prices of three taxi companies. What other charges is a person responsible for when taking a cab? Figure out how far it is from your house to the airport and how much it will cost for that ride. *****

43. Go to the **post office** (or look online) and find out the least expensive way to send a package to New York City from where you live. What is the rate? Figure out how much packages weighing 2 pounds, 5 pounds, and 7.5 pounds would cost to send. Find out what the differences are in the service you will get. Write the information in paragraph form. If you would prefer to find out about another city where you have family or friends, change the location from New York to another city.****

44. Find out how much an **18-hole round of golf** would cost at two local golf courses. See which one is the better deal. Also compare the cost of using a golf cart at both courses. Find out the time of day when the prices are the least expensive, and figure out how much money it would cost for your entire family to spend the day golfing and using a golf cart. You might also like to estimate the cost of clubs, shoes, and gloves. ****

SURVIVAL MATH PACKET (EXPERIENCING MATH IN YOUR EVERYDAY LIFE) (*continued*)

45. Research two **bowling alleys.** Find out which one has the better value for playing two lanes of bowling for each member of your birthday party group. Your party will consist of ten eleven and twelve year olds. Remember that you also need to include the price of bowling shoes for each partygoer. Tell the name of the bowling alley, where it is located, and the cost. ****

46. You are researching the best price for taking five of your friends to the **movie** for a party. Find the best price for three movie theaters close to your own house and the best time of day to go. Also include the price of one small box of popcorn and one small soda for each of your five friends, plus yourself. *****

47. For your birthday party, you may take seven friends with you to the **skating rink.** Find out how much money it will cost the eight of you to go skating. Also include the price of one hot dog and one medium soda for each member of your party. You may want to compare the price of two skating rinks in order to get the better deal. Show your mathematical figures on paper. ****

48. Cut out **coupons** for your parents using the Sunday newspaper for two weeks. Keep them in a plastic bag or shoebox. Have your parents go through them with you and select the ones they will use. Keep a list of the name brand, item, and amount of the coupon. How much money will you save on the grocery bill for that two-week period? If you saved that much every two weeks, how much would that be for a month? A year? ****

49. Find out the cost of season tickets for the next season for your favorite professional or local college **football team.** Compare the price of the most expensive seats and the least expensive seats for your own family. How much does parking cost at the stadium of this team? How much is that altogether for an evening at a sports event? ****

50. Figure out the cost of feeding your family for **dinner** at your local college, professional, or high school stadium. Tell what stadium you are attending. List each food item and its cost. Make sure you have the actual cost of the food items at this year's prices. ****

51. Find out how much it costs to rent a **limousine** for four hours and for eight hours. What is the maximum number of people that it can take? If you had the maximum number of people in the limo, how much would it cost per person? Write a paragraph telling what you would do if you took a limo ride for four hours. *****

52. Research the actual amount of **sales tax** you would pay in each of five states, including your own, for items costing $10, $100, $1,000, and $10,000. You will need to find out what the sales tax is in each state. Figure out the difference in total price if you purchased the item in each of the five states. *****

SURVIVAL MATH PACKET (EXPERIENCING MATH IN YOUR EVERYDAY LIFE) (*continued*)

53. Compare the cost of an **oil change** for your car at three different locations. Name each of the businesses you check out. If someone in your family changes his or her own oil, find out how much he or she saves. ****

54. Find out the difference in cost of **car insurance** for a sixteen-year-old boy and a sixteen-year-old girl. Find out the difference in cost for a student with good grades and a student without good grades. You may want to check out several insurance companies. List the companies and how much the insurance is for each person. *****

55. What is the cost of a **fishing license** in your city and country for an adult for a day and for a year in both fresh water and salt water? What is the age that a person needs to be to obtain a fishing license? Tell where you would fish and what kind of fishing you would do. ****

56. Make an investigation into your **kitchen.** Look for items that show measurements. List them. Write a paragraph telling how measurement is used in the kitchen and what you would do if we didn't have measuring spoons and cups. ***

57. **Measure your bedroom** (length and width). Find the perimeter and area of the room. Decide how many square feet of carpet you would need (area) and how much wallpaper border you would need to go around your room (perimeter). You could also figure out how much paper you would need for wallpapering the whole room. Don't forget to exclude doors, closets, and windows. If you actually do redecorating, take pictures and share them. ****

58. Preview a **cookbook.** Prepare a good item where measuring cups and spoons are used. Write your recipe on a note card. If you can, share the food item with your classmates, and provide the recipe for each student. Make a list of ingredients you need to prepare the food. If you do this before the due date, let your teacher know if you are bringing in food. ****

59. Find out how much it would cost to have your local **newspaper** delivered to your house for a month. Compare it with what you would pay if you purchased it daily at a newsstand for a week, month, and year. ***

60. If you have a sports arena in your city, find out how much **season tickets** are for a team that plays there, or for three other events that take place there during the year. Also find out how much it costs to park in the parking lot. ****

61. How much is a season ticket for one of your local **college teams** for students and for nonstudents? How many home games will there be? Divide the number of home games into the price of the season ticket. What is the average cost per game for students and nonstudents? ****

SURVIVAL MATH PACKET (EXPERIENCING MATH IN YOUR EVERYDAY LIFE) (*continued*)

62. If you are a musician, tell how **music** is influenced by math. Talk with your music teacher about the time signature, metronome, and other mathematical terms. Write up your findings. ***

63. **Interview** a person who works in a job where mostly numbers are used. Get a detailed description of the job, why math is important to the job, what education the person needed, how much math the person had to take in school, and what the person likes or dislikes about the job. Before your interview, write up at least six to eight good questions that you might want to ask the person you interview. Be prepared for the interview. When you are complete, write a summary of the interview. ****

64. If you live in a large city, find out the cost for season tickets for the **ballet, opera,** or **symphony** for the most expensive and least expensive seats. Also find out how many performances there are in a season and the programs presented. Attend one of the performances, and write a paragraph describing the experience. Don't forget to share the program guide with your teacher and classmates. *****

65. If you have a **junior theater or other children's theater** where you live, find out how much season tickets are for you and your family to attend. Is there a difference between the adult price and child's price? What plays will be presented and on what dates? ****

66. Choose three of your favorite **magazines.** Fill out three subscription forms. What is the cost of each for a year? Either make a copy of the forms or hand in the forms for your teacher and classmates to see. ***

67. Ask your parent to show you the correct way to **write out a check.** If your parents have an extra check, write a pretend one and hand it in to your teacher. If you can't use a real check, copy one, or make up a check of your own to show that you know how to write one correctly. Hand in at least three checks made out to different businesses and for different amounts. You might want to pair this activity up with a buying spree (see activity 28). ****

68. **Interview your parents.** Ask them why they think math is important to them. Ask them to tell you how they use math every day in their jobs, at home, and in their personal lives. Also ask them why they think you should do your best in math at school. Make a list of five to seven reasons math is important to them. ***

69. Ask your parents to assist you in looking through the **tools** in your garage, basement, or car or truck. Find out how the tools involve measurement. Look for the metric numbers. Write a paragraph telling how tools in your home are involved in math and what parts of math you need to know before you can use them effectively. ***

SURVIVAL MATH PACKET (EXPERIENCING MATH IN YOUR EVERYDAY LIFE) (*continued*)

70. Think of something that you and a family member or other adult can build together, like a doghouse, bird feeder, fence, planter box, cabinet, or clock. Go to a building supply store, and look for the materials that you might need for the project. Figure out how much material you would need to build it. How much would the materials cost? You might want to draw a diagram of what you plan to build and when it is finished take pictures and share them with your classmates. Tell what you learned about math and working as a team member from this **construction project.** *****

71. If you have **auto racing** events where you live, go to one. Keep track of the times of ten of your favorite cars. Figure out the average speed of the drivers. ****

72. Take six to eight photographs of **math in your world,** such as a calculator, a clock, a coupon for a department store, the back of a cereal box, or a gasoline pump. Write captions underneath each photo to show its math importance and write several sentences to tell how math is involved. ****

73. Compare the **values of eight to ten currencies.** Tell what each is called, from what country or area it comes, and how much it is worth in U.S. dollars. Share the information with your class. If you have samples of any of these currencies, bring them to share also. *****

74. Predict what you think the average **temperature** (highs and lows) will be where you live. Look through the weather section of the newspaper or online for ten days. Compare the high and low temperatures in graph form. ****

75. Follow the highest **temperatures** and the lowest temperatures in the United States for ten days. Locate those areas on a map. ****

76. Study the **time zones** in the United States. Choose ten major cities across the United States, and tell what time it is compared to where you live. ****

77. Look at the scale at the bottom of a **map** of the United States. Using a ruler and the scale, figure out approximately how many miles it is from where you live to ten U.S. cities. If possible, find the exact number of miles it is to those cities. How close were you to your measurements. What may have caused the difference? ****

78. Make a comparison chart of the **metric system** and the U.S system of measurement. How are they similar? What things are different? What countries use our system? Name other countries that use metric measurement. Choose ten items to measure in both systems. ****

SURVIVAL MATH PACKET (EXPERIENCING MATH IN YOUR EVERYDAY LIFE) (*continued*)

79. You are looking for the best price on your favorite **CDs.** List the five CDs you want to purchase. Compare the price of these CDs at three different music stores. Show your comparison in chart form. ****

80. Find out how much it costs to **camp overnight** for your family at one of your county or state parks. Also, how much does it cost at a local tourist-type **hotel** where you live? Figure out the difference for a week of vacation at both places. *****

81. **Make up your own activity.** Check it with your teacher before you get started. *** to *****

SURVIVAL MATH RUBRIC—TEACHER EVALUATION

Name: _____   Date: _____

Cover sheet with name, date, project number included; neatly done—may include illustration or border	2 points	_____
Reason that this project was chosen	2 points	_____
Data shown/graphic representation (graph, table, chart)	3 points	_____
Explanation of what you did and how you did it	4 points	_____
Summary (what you learned)	3 points	_____
Neatly done with few or no spelling errors	2 points	_____
Activity shows planning and organization	2 points	_____
Oral presentation of the activity (tell/show what you did; don't read your paper)	2 points	_____
Total points	Total points	_____

Comments: _____

_____

_____

SURVIVAL MATH RECORD SHEET

Student's Name:_____

Month	Active Number and Key Words	Approximate Time Spent on Preparation	Self-Evaluation (1–10 points)
September			
October			
November			
December			
January			
February			
March			
April			
May			
June			

SURVIVAL MATH CHECKLIST

Name: _____   Date: _____

Please check off all the parts that you have completed and respond to the questions so that you are aware of your progress and your teacher can evaluate your project more thoroughly.

_____ My survival math is completed on time.

_____ I have listed the number of the activity, my name, and the date.

_____ I have given a reason that I chose this activity.

_____ I have given a graphic representation of the activity (chart, graph, table, etc.).

_____ I have explained what I did and how I did it.

_____ I have summarized what I learned.

_____ My work is neat and has been checked for spelling and grammar.

_____ My activity shows planning and organization.

This project took me about _____ minutes/hours to complete.

Is there anything you could do to improve on this activity? Please explain your answer.

_____

_____

Who helped me with this activity and how they helped:

_____

_____

SURVIVAL MATH PEER EVALUATION FORM

As an evaluator, you will try to locate all the parts covered on a classmate's survival math. Please check off the parts you find and offer at least three positive and constructive comments as feedback.

Evaluator's Name: _____   Student's Name: _____

_____ The paper is on time.

_____ The activity number, student's name, and date are listed on the paper.

_____ There is a reason why this activity was chosen.

_____ There is a graphic representation to show the findings.

_____ There is an explanation of what was done.

_____ There is an explanation of what was learned.

_____ The activity shows planning and organization.

_____ There is good spelling, grammar, and neatness.

_____ The oral presentation showed mathematical understanding.

Other comments: _____

_____

_____

MATH IN THE REAL WORLD

Name: _____ Date: _____

You will be rotating through thirteen shopping stations for the next few days. You will use the materials that are provided for you at each station. You must stay at the station for the full 20- to 30-minute segment of time, so don't hurry, but don't dally either. The purpose of this activity is to immerse you in the real world of math. You will also be doing skimming and scanning, reading and writing. Since you are not old enough to really buy the expensive stuff, you will have the opportunity to buy it in class through catalogues, menus, car magazines, home catalogues, store catalogues, grocery store advertisements, vacation brochures, and other odds and ends. Good luck on your selections and calculations.

1. Buy yourself a **new car or truck.** Your price may not exceed $25,000. Use your calculator to figure out the cost of sales tax in your state. (If this were a real purchase, you would also have to pay other fees, but not for this activity.) What accessories does the car have that you think are good? Cut out the picture and the price, and tell why you want this car and why you think it is a good deal. Create a personalized license plate for your car with no more than seven numbers and letters if you have time.

2. Use the catalogues, pamphlets, and ads from the paper to **purchase a new outfit for school** or weekend wear. You have $50.00 to spend. Make sure you include shoes.

3. Choose **a new house** for you and your family in an area of where that you would like to live. It may cost up to $1 million. Cut out the picture and the price, and write the reason you chose this house out of all of the ones you had to look at. Tell how many bedrooms, baths, and square feet there are in the house. Is there a pool? What area is it in? If you can, figure out how much commission the real estate agent will receive if he or she gets a 6 percent commission. You'll be surprised on this one. Be careful with the decimal point. If you forgot how to figure percentage, there is a chart to look at in the basket.

4. Use **the grocery store ads,** and choose food for your family dinner tonight. Write down the items and the price of each. Make sure that you have chosen nutritious food and that you have covered all the food groups even though they may not be something you would normally choose. If your state does tax food items, make sure you add tax. Try to stay under $20.00.

5. Use the newspaper to find out the name of a **movie** that you would like to see. Select three theaters that are close to your house or to the school. Write down their addresses and the times that the movie is playing at each theater. When is the bargain hour?

MATH IN THE REAL WORLD (*continued*)

6. Look at the **television schedule** from the newspaper. Select five TV shows that you would like to see during the school week. Tell what times they are on and how long the show lasts, plus what channel it is on. If you have time, select three shows that you would like to watch on the weekend, and write down the same information.

7. Look at the **menus** in the basket. Choose a lunch for you and a friend. Do not go over $15.00. Fill out the order form. Add sales tax on the food, and decide how much you should leave the waiter or waitress for a 15 percent tip. If you have forgotten how to figure tax or tip, there is a copy of how to do it in the basket.

8. You are to buy five items for the **student store.** Look through the school catalogues, and select items that you feel kids would love to buy. Write down the price, and figure out how much each one would cost separately because they come in a multi-item packages.

9. Look at the classified ads, and **locate a job** that you might be interested in. Look at the dark bold headings to get you into the correct category. Cut out the ad, and write a reason or two that this job interests you.

10. Look though the **furniture ads.** Select at least five pieces of furniture that you would use for your bedroom or living room. How much would all the pieces cost? Don't forget the tax.

11. Use the pet store catalogues or flyers to help you buy **pet supplies** for the pet that you already have or one that you want to get. If you can find an ad for a pet, you can buy that too. Cut out the ads that name the product and the price. You should have at least five items. Did you remember to include tax?

12. Use the Yellow Pages of the **telephone book** to locate three caterers who could take care of the food for a class party. Figure out what kind of food you would want and then find someone to cater. Write down the address and telephone number of the one you choose. Why did you select this caterer?

USING A MENU TO SOLVE MATH PROBLEMS

Name: _____ Date: _____

Materials needed:

- Menu

- Waiter/waitress receipt form

- Pencil

- Health book

- Dictionary

Basic Activities

1. Which items from the menu would you order for lunch if you were on a low-fat diet? What is their total cost?

2. Which items would you order for lunch if you were allergic to dairy products? What is their total cost?

3. Which items would you order for lunch if you were a vegetarian? If you were a vegan? What is their total cost?

4. Suppose you were treating a friend to lunch and had $15.00. What would the two of you order? Write up a receipt to show the cost. Make sure you multiply your total cost by _____. This is the amount you must add on to your cost. It is sales tax. What is the total cost of lunch including sales tax? Have a member of your group check your figures. Include a tip for your waiter or waitress of at least 15 percent of your total.

Extra Activities

1. Suppose your family went out to lunch to celebrate your birthday. What would each person order? What would be the total cost of lunch? Don't forget to add your tax. Find out the amount you tip the wait staff for good service. Also add this onto your bill.

2. Make up a problem about ordering lunch from the menu. Exchange problems with a classmate and solve.

THANKSGIVING MATH PROJECT—SIMULATION

Name: _____ Date: _____

Materials Needed

- One colored piece of 12- by 18-inch paper (you can get this from your teacher when you are ready to start)

- One index card for your items and prices

- Grocery stores ads from the newspaper

What You're Going to Do

- You have $75 to spend for a Thanksgiving dinner.

- Using grocery ads from the newspaper, create a poster showing what foods you would choose, how much of each food you would need, and the cost of each item.

- You will use a mathematical table to show your items and the totals.

- Glue your ads and your totals onto your construction paper. Be neat.

- Try to get as close to $75.00 as possible, but do not go over.

Things to Remember

- If your state taxes food, remember to add the tax. If your state does not tax food, you still have to add tax on your nonfood items like plates or table decorations. Tax is currently _____%. That means on the taxable items, you need to multiply the cost by that percentage in order to get the actual cost.

- Use your calculator, and ask for help from your parents.

- If you do not get a newspaper, ask your relatives, neighbors, classmates, or teacher for some ads.

- Don't wait until the last minute. Pace yourself. Talk with your parents about your choices.

- Have fun and enjoy the shopping experience.

- If you buy soda in cans or bottles, do not forget to include the recycling charge, if your state has such a fee.

Activity 14.22

GIFT GIVING MATH PROJECT FOR DECEMBER

Name: _____ Date: _____

Materials Needed

- Shopping ads (for example, from the newspaper, mail, store ads)

- One piece of construction paper

- One 5- by 8-inch index card

The Math Project

- You have $100.00 to spend. Try to get as close to that amount without going over.

- Make a list of the people you would like to buy gifts for.

- Look through the advertisements.

- Select a gift for everyone on your list.

- Cut out the gift ads with the prices.

- Add up your total.

- Make sure to add sales tax to items that are taxable.

- Use a calculator to find your totals. Be careful when you input your numbers: the calculator does what you tell it to. Incorrect input = incorrect output.

- Have an adult check your calculations.

- Display your work in an organized and neat manner.

- Have fun.

Chapter 15

MAKING THE MOST OF MUSIC AND ART IN THE CLASSROOM

With the back-to-basics approach to education and the concern for high-stakes test scores, some schools have been forced to significantly reduce the time for the music and art programs. In the primary grades, students are involved in singing, movement to music, and artistic expression often on a daily basis. Due to the dense amount of content material that needs to be covered before high-stakes testing by upper grade and middle school teachers, it is often difficult to find time to address the music and art standards. Some teachers in low socioeconomic elementary and middle schools have reported that art is not allowed during the school day and children may not use crayons, colored pencils, and markers for even illustrating stories or for enhancing their literacy projects. We must all work within the confines of our school, administrator, and district guidelines, but we must also cover the standards that our state has adopted. It is sometimes a fine line that we must walk in education. Howard Gardner (1983) specifically emphasizes the need for music and art in students' lives (see Chapter Two). Many students have talent in these areas, and they must be fostered and stimulated in order to provide the balance that they need in their education.

PROVIDING BALANCE BETWEEN WORK AND RELAXATION

All students need balance to their day, but for our challenged learners, we need to provide time away from content to rest and relax their brains. Music and art are those enhancers that help keep reluctant readers progressing forward.

We are in a new era of understanding how the brain works and how students learn. New brain research is adding discoveries, and we have new knowledge to help us be better instructors. Students today are dealing with a huge amount of stress in their lives. Although school cannot reduce all of it, a teacher can provide an environment that allows children to have periods of time to relax and learn techniques and skills to help them balance their own lives away from school.

It is very important in the balanced classroom to provide many right brain/left brain activities during the day. During testing, for instance, students need opportunities to rest the spheres of their brains.

421

Songs, poetry, art, and drama provide those outlets and can be used to take a break from stressful testing sessions. Music can be a powerful means for creating a mood that is calming, energizing, motivating, and inspiring.

Using Resources

Many new and updated resources are available for teachers who are willing and able to make music and art a priority in the classroom. Bookstores are filled with brightly colored, motivating, and interesting books about the arts that children will be drawn to whether they are situated in a book tub or provided as ongoing read-aloud selections. Many states have music and art textbook adoptions with supplementary materials to accompany them to provide support for the state standards. This is the best of times for filling your classroom with exciting music and art experiences for children.

Setting Up Music and Art Book Baskets

A balanced classroom provides many selections of books for children to reference throughout the year. Book baskets that support the arts are available for children to pique their interest. A wide variety of fiction and nonfiction, picture books and novels, should be provided. Students can be encouraged to choose books from these baskets during choice time. Read-alouds by the teacher from the fine arts should also be encouraged because these books can support learners who have specific interest in these areas. Letting children know that you value their special talents sends a strong message that the classroom is set up for everyone. Web sites that are of interest to students interested in the fine arts are also bookmarked.

Getting to Know Artists and Musicians

Kathleen Krull in her *Lives of . . .* series introduces children to the great artists and musicians of the world. Children learn funny, sad, intriguing, and unusual facts about the artists and musicians. *The Lives of the Artists—Masterpieces, Messes and What the Neighbors Thought* (1995) and *Lives of the Musicians—Good Times, Bad Times and What the Neighbors Thought* (1993) can be used for biographical study. Students are also introduced to *The Lives and Times of the Great* Writers—*Comedies, Tragedies and What the Neighbors Thought* (1994) during the literacy block. As part of this study, students look at the illustrations in these books, which are caricatures of the real people. While the students are learning about the musicians, examples of their music are played during work periods and during writing workshop. While learning about the artists, the students are exposed to art prints, enabling them to connect the artist with the artwork. To culminate the unit, the students write brief reports based on the information from the book and research that they do independently and then create large-size imitations of Kathryn Hewitt's caricatures. Transparencies are made and students reproduce them on large tag board and color them appropriately. (Students can also be encouraged to create their own without the use of the overhead projector.) The poster illustrations are showcased with their reports in the classroom, in the auditorium, or on bulletin boards throughout the school. These older students exhibit much pride in their products.

Using Special Resources

At the beginning of the year, formally or informally survey your children's parents, grandparents, and other family members. Through conversations and newsletters, get the word out that you are looking for valuable resources in music and art. Try to find out about their special talents. Do not be afraid of asking for support in both music and art. (See Form 9.1, Parent Interest Survey.) Some parents may play instruments, paint, or compose. These parents are valuable assets to your class to introduce your students to new experiences.

MUSIC IMPLEMENTATION

Music makes the world a happier place to be—that includes the school. Unfortunately, as children approach the upper levels of the elementary school, music in the classroom diminishes. Teachers without music backgrounds may not feel comfortable teaching music; therefore, this part of the curriculum is left out. Music has a place in the primary classroom, but what about in the middle and upper grades in elementary and middle schools?

Music affects our moods and emotions. If we went to see a movie and there was no music to accompany it, we would be disappointed, and there would not be the same impact on our emotions. We would feel let down because we have come to expect music to enhance the movie and to cue us to the rise and fall of the events. Even in early silent movies, organ music was played to awaken the senses and to set the tone. Music makes the movie. Whether a movie is scary, sad, exciting, happy, or suspenseful, watching it without music can truly have an impact on our state of mind. Try an experiment with your students. Have them close their eyes or turn away from a Disney movie. Have them only listen to the music and see if they can predict what is going on. Older children are very good at this. They are able to understand the importance of music to enhance the storyline of the movie.

Disney's *Peter and the Wolf* cartoon video introduces children to instruments of the orchestra. Each character is paired with a particular instrument, and the students can hear the instrument as the character appears. The duck is the oboe, the cat is the clarinet, Grandpapa is the bassoon, the hunter is percussion instruments, the wolf is the brass, and Peter is the string family.

Research About Music

Music has therapeutic effects and can enhance learning, with numerous benefits in the classroom, home, and other settings. Research such as Sousa (2001) indicates that there are cognitive, health, and emotional benefits that can be gained through music. Our experience and that of many other teachers supports the value of listening to music and of learning to play a musical instrument.

Research shows that learning is easier and quicker when the learner is in a relaxed, receptive state. The heartbeat of a relaxed individual is sixty to eighty beats per minute. Much of baroque music closely matches the relaxed heartbeat of a human being in an optimal learning condition. Baroque melodic chord structures and instrumentation assist the body in accessing an alert yet relaxed state (Schuster & Gritton, 1986).

An easy way to introduce music, one of the eight intelligences, into the classroom is to have it as background music. Learning style research shows that many students perform better at their work if there is baroque music playing during work periods. The introduction of music does tend to add the dimension of relaxation to the classroom. One popular artist is Gary Lamb (wwwgarylamb.com). Many of his musical compositions are based on a tempo of approximately sixty beats per minute, the same as a resting heart rate. This tempo centers and calms us.

David Sousa, in his book *How the Special Needs Brain Learns* (2001), suggests the following:

- If you are using music as background to facilitate student work, choose music that plays at about sixty beats per minute. If the music is accompanying a fast-paced activity, choose eighty to ninety beats per minute. To calm a noisy group, choose music at forty to fifty beats per minutes.
- Music played at the beginning or end of the class can contain lyrics because the main purpose is to set a mood, not get focus. But if students are working on a learning task, lyrics become a distraction [p. 235].

Gordon Shaw and his colleagues at the Mind Institute have discovered the link between music and brain function. Their research in the 1990s showed that music training improves spatial reasoning skills—the ability to recognize patterns and plan ahead multiple steps in space and time. Their research in 1995 also confirms that listening to Mozart improves spatial reasoning and that this effect can increase with repeated testing over days.

Music seems to help us with recall and memory. We can remember facts such as states and their capitals or multiplication tables more easily when we put them to music or rhyme (Rief, 2003).

Laura Erlauer in her book *The Brain-Compatible Classroom—Using What We Know About Learning to Improve Teaching* (2003) suggests ways to use music in the classroom based on Sousa's research (1995):

- To calm students, such as for testing situations. Playing baroque music slows the heartbeat and clears the mind for concentration and thinking.

- To excite students, use uplifting songs to spark enthusiasm and energy and to perk up, rejuvenate, and inspire them.

- To improve students' long-term memory and recall. When students are having trouble memorizing information, have them create a song to help them remember the information or use commercial tapes or CDs such as Multiplication Rap & Hip-Hop, by Twin Sisters Productions (www.twinsisters.com).

Gardner (1993) suggests that music can enhance children's enjoyment and understanding of mathematical concepts and skills. Of all the academic subjects, mathematics seems to be most closely connected to music as it involves concepts basic to music such as patterns, counting, ratios/proportions, and sequences (Sousa, 2001).

According to Walter (2004), "Evidence shows that music (and the language encoded within it) enters the brain and is processed differently from spoken language. This might help us understand why lyrics are remembered for years. The pattern and flow of language within gives students opportunities to develop language in a non-threatening, meaningful, and fun way" (p. 39).

Using Music in the Classroom

There are many ways to incorporate music in the school day, some within the classroom and others on a schoolwide basis, some focusing specifically on music and others using music in conjunction with other curriculum.

Student Writing About Music

Sometimes teachers can be directive in asking students to write about the arts and the importance they play in their lives. Students can give insight into their musical lives through their writing experiences. You will learn the kinds of music that they listen to and what parameters their parents set for them.

Claire, a fifth grader writes, "Music affects my life by soothing me. It's important to me because whenever I feel angry or whenever I've had a bad day, I just plop on my bed and listen to music. I am introduced to all sorts of music because my parents play music they like which includes classical and music from when they were kids. I think my parents have encouraged me a lot to listen to music and play the piano. I'm glad that they have pushed me to play because it has really made a difference in my life."

Rachel, another fifth grader, writes, "Music affects my life by cheering me up when I'm sad and giving me something to do when I'm bored. When I'm doing homework or when I'm in the car, I like to listen to music. Music is a kind of art that inspires me and keeps me motivated. It is calming. I usually fall asleep while I'm listening. I play piano/keyboard and I love it! It gets tricky, sometimes; I feel like quitting, but it's worth it! I really like pop and country music."

Taking a survey of your students' favorite kinds of music and favorite musical artists gives you insight into their interests and contributes to music discussion and writing opportunities.

For her survival math activity (see Chapter Fourteen), Emily explored the effect of math in music. She created two charts to show the value and comparisons of the notes and rests. She wrote, "Piano playing is one of my hobbies and that is why I chose this activity to do. I am trying to figure out why playing an instrument boosts your grades. Playing an instrument is supposed to help connect the left and right part of the brain, which is just asking for good grades for math and music. Playing piano is just like doing fractions. One whole note is four beats, four-quarter notes, or 0.25. One half note is one-half of a whole note, or 0.5. There are also such things as sixteenth notes, and an eighth note. A measure is a space between two bars. A time signature is a sign that tells you how many beats in a measure there are." Emily shows a representation of her explanation on another page, pointing out her vocabulary on a piece of sheet music.

Music Centers

A music center may be available to students with a variety of activities. Having a keyboard for students to play is also fun, and with guidelines, students can play and work out simple tunes as time permits. The Orff-Schulwerk approach to musical teaching calls for engagement, movement, and improvisation through the playing of a variety of instruments. It was conceived by the German composer Carl Orff (1895–1982). His approach was developed for children and was based on his belief that the easiest method to teach music was to draw out the children's natural skill in rhythm and melody. He designed a special group of instruments, including glockenspiels, xylophones, metallophones, drums, and other percussion instruments to encourage musical expression. The American Orff Schulwerk Association (AOSA) is a source of information for this approach and may be reached through mail at P.O. Box 391089 Cleveland, OH 44139-8089. During choice time, before or after school, students may want to explore their musical skill through the instruments.

Music Performances

Opportunities for students who possess musical talent should be made available. Once or twice a year, small performances for their peer group can be informally made. Children who want to play an instrument should be encouraged to participate. Students who want to sing should also have the chance. It is important for the teacher to draw out these students who might be unwilling to show their talent. Showcasing students in this way can be beneficial. Some of the students who are musical are not confident in other areas of the curriculum. As the teacher prepares to plan for these special occasions, he or she must call attention to the talent that these students possess. The poise and ability to stand in front of others to perform is something to be commended.

On a larger scale, some schools have a talent show for students. The talent show is coordinated by a group of parent volunteers or, in middle school, possibly by a student leadership group. After-school practice sessions are held to polish the acts, and any child who wants to participate can. Through gentle guidance, children are sometimes combined into groups so that everyone can be successful. Sometimes "canned" acts (ones that are prewritten or already scripted and are provided by the adults that are in charge) are suggested so that those who want to participate but do not have an act of their own will be able to perform. A talent show can be a popular event.

Open Microphone

Some classrooms offer opportunities for students to pursue their musical talents, with every other Friday afternoon being an open mike day. Children are encouraged to read poetry, sing, prepare skits, play musical instruments, and perform in a variety of genres. During this time, the students may perform solo or in pairs or triads.

Some teachers have a microphone so that students feel as if they are performers. Entry-level microphone systems can be purchased at a reasonable cost. They can also be useful during other parts of the day or when a teacher's voice becomes hoarse. Students love a microphone to amplify their voices. Some schools purchase wireless microphones for their teachers so that all students can clearly hear the instruction. For challenged learners, this amplification may help them to focus better on their teacher's voice.

Contemporary Music in the Classroom

Singing is an enjoyable part of any day. Bringing appropriate songs into the classroom that students listen to on the radio is one way of relating to their interests. Most children by the middle and upper grades like to sing with the songs on the radio. They know the words and are able to repeat them verbatim. It is essential that we provide some opportunities for children to sing on a regular basis in school. Contemporary songs delight the children especially if they already know them from the radio. The Disney Channel is a source of popular music for students to listen to and sing along with.

Rhythm Instruments

Older children also enjoy playing the rhythm instruments that they used in the younger grades. Occasionally the teacher should provide these for experimenting with rhythm to contemporary songs. Older children can also construct simple rhythm instruments. Giving them the chance to share their newly made instruments with younger children is a rewarding experience for them.

A class set of plastic eggs with rice inside is excellent for keeping rhythm during music. They may be held together with tape or glue. This is an inexpensive way to have students participate with instruments if others are not available.

Music of Different Generations

Another rewarding musical experience is pairing students up with a nearby senior citizens group. Once a month or more often, students and seniors participate in an exchange. The seniors can be paired with small groups of children—to share their interests, hobbies, family life, pictures, and jobs. They might bring the music from their generation and share it with the students. Together the seniors and the students can enjoy the simplicity and "silliness" of the songs of the 1920s, 1930s, and 1940s. In this way, students and seniors bridge the gap between the generations in a language that is understandable to both. The final outcome of a program like this is an appreciation of and respect for the music of other eras. Music does tend to bring people closer together in enjoyable, nonthreatening experiences.

Cross-Age Singing

An upper-grade class can be paired up with a primary-grade class. The positive value of this exchange is long lasting. Part of this program is the interaction of the children through musical experiences. The older students sing with the kindergarten and first-grade children. This gives the upper graders a lot of enjoyment, bringing back fond memories as they reconnect to the songs that made their primary years so musically rich.

School Chorus

Having a school chorus can build the musical intelligence of a large population of children. Meeting once or twice a week with a teacher who is especially interested in music, children experience a wide variety of music. The community appreciates special performances that allow children to express their love of music. If this large an endeavor is not available to the school, possibly the formation of smaller afternoon or lunchtime music clubs is an option. Parents, other volunteers, and other school personnel may help in these efforts.

Interest Classes

To tap the musical intelligence of the school community, "wheel" or "interest" classes can be set up in the upper grades. Children can choose music as an option for a period of time, or all children can be rotated at some point into that group. Teachers who have a strong interest in music can share their talent with many students, and teachers who are uncomfortable teaching music can share their interest with another group of children. This team teaching approach of using everyone's special talents and strengths makes everyone a winner.

Multicultural Music

Many schools serve a diverse multicultural population. There is no better way to bridge the cultures than through music. Teachers may center their music program on the music of the different cultures represented in their classroom or in the school at large. Having children bring in and share the music of their culture should be encouraged, and the children in the classroom should begin to appreciate and respect the shared music experiences that bring cultures closer together.

At some schools, a multicultural fair is held to honor diversity. The individual classrooms perform dances, songs, and games of their representative populations. The upper graders research each of the countries that is represented and then go to the primary classrooms to impart their knowledge. Each upper-grade group makes a flag and locates currency samples for their country. The parents provide food from their cultures. Building good relationships between cultures and taking pride in their diversity begins with the simple elements of music and dance. The world looks smaller and less complicated when music is added to the children's school lives. If your class is not very diversified, bring in music from other cultures yourself.

Welcome parents to share their musical talents, and if they play unusual instruments, have them explain the instrument and play it.

Oldies but Goodies

"Oldies" captivate the older students. The simple words and melodies are easy to sing. The older students seem to enjoy the songs. Many of the selections can be downloaded online or CD collections of oldies can be purchased at music stores. Upper-grade students chose these as some of their favorites:

- "Yakety Yak" (Coasters)
- "Surfin' USA" (Beach Boys)
- "Celebration" (Cool and the Gang)
- "Be True to Your School" (Beach Boys)
- "Mission Impossible" (Lalo Schifen)
- Theme from *Rocky*
- "Takin' Care of Business" (Bachman-Turner Overdrive)
- "We Are Family" (Sister Sledge)
- "Don't Worry Be Happy" (Bobby McFerrin)
- "Hit the Road Jack" (Ray Charles)
- "All Shook Up" (Elvis Presley)
- "Bridge over Troubled Water" (Simon and Garfunkel)
- "Change the World" (Eric Clapton)
- "Fun, Fun, Fun" (Beach Boys)
- "Don't Be Cruel" (Elvis Presley)
- "Great Balls of Fire" (Jerry Lee Lewis)
- "Kokomo" (Beach Boys)
- "La Bamba" (Ritchie Valens)
- "Louie, Louie" (Kingsmen)
- "Twist and Shout" (Isley Brothers)
- "What the World Needs Now" (Jackie De Se Shay)
- "You Talk Too Much" (Joe Jones)
- "Rock Around the Clock Tonight" (Bill Haley)

Patriotic Songs

In many classrooms, students sing a patriotic song each morning. With so many military men and women serving in other countries, most students know someone who is in the military. The short segment of time to commemorate all personnel serving abroad is a small way to show our pride in being Americans. Children can be given a notebook with patriotic songs that have been duplicated for them. One person each morning can choose a song and set up the CD player.

Music Genre of the Month

In some classrooms, teachers introduce a type of music each month and support it through the artists and other resource materials that will allow students to grasp the genre. For instance, you might start out in September with classical music, exposing students to the greatest musicians of all time, such as Bach, Beethoven, and Mozart. Books about each of the artists can be read aloud, and the music of each can be played throughout the day. By the end of the month, students will appreciate the music of the great composers.

Each month then introduces the different genres of music such as musicals, blues, country, gospel, rock and roll, electronic, reggae, and hip-hop and rap. By the end of the year, students will have developed a musical background that they can feel comfortable with.

A good Web site to visit with a list and explanation of the different categories of music is www.Answers.com.

Sources of Information About Music

One magazine that can help teachers find music for their students that is lively, engaging, and fun is *Music K–8,* a quarterly magazine that provides music, CDs, and Boomwhackers. (colorful plastic tubes that can be used to play melodies, rhythms, or chords). *Music Express* comes with a teacher's guide that is very helpful in viewing what the whole program offers. Subscribers obtain a free choreography video.

The following Web sites provide music information:

- Essential Musical Intelligence, www.essentialmusicalintelligence.com.
- American Music Therapy Association, www.musictherapy.org.
- National Association for Music Therapy, www.namt.com.
- National Association of Music Merchants, www.namm.com.
- Advanced Brain Technologies, www.advancedbrain.com.
- TV Tunes Online, www.tvtunesonline.com/.
- American Symphony Orchestra Leagues' "get acquainted with the orchestra," www.playmusic.org.
- Musically Aligned: Science songs. www.musicallyaligned.com. Science songs that have been created to help students learn and recall key content area information at grade-level standards.

The Importance of an Inspiring Teacher

Whatever level our music ability is, we as classroom teachers must continue to provide experiences for children in music. To leave this important experience out of the lives of students is to neglect one of the basic intelligences. To enhance and balance a highly academic day, music may be the much-needed element that gives a challenging or unmotivated student a short reprieve so that he or she can regroup, take a breath, and go on.

A powerful and uplifting movie is *Mr. Holland's Opus,* the story of a music teacher who is an inspiration to the teaching profession. By looking carefully at the needs of his students, he was able to design a program that motivated his students in a more contemporary way, using rock and roll as the focus. Through his innovative teaching, he helped many of his students to be more successful in school and to seek a higher level of education.

One Teacher's Approach to Music in the Upper Grades

In Steve Guadarrama's fifth-grade class, students are given opportunities every day to use the right side of their brain through musical expression. Sometimes that experience is formal, but more often it is informal. The room environment abounds with the sight and sounds of music. If you look around on the desks and throughout the room, you will see musical instruments. There are congas, a keyboard, tuned hand drums, a xylophone, a glockenspiel, and myriad other rhythm instruments, all to be used at appropriate times.

Steve demonstrates how to play each instrument and sets up a firm management system at the start of the year. Students understand that his hand signal means "no playing." After the instruments are taught, students are allowed to experience the instrument during the open play periods, which take place before school and the last few minutes of the school day. Students are encouraged to make up songs and present them to the class. It is not uncommon to hear a keyboard, guitar, drum, and singing all in concert with each other with an unfamiliar melody that students have enjoyed creating.

In this classroom, you will also hear the melodic sounds of recorders. Steve teaches all of the students to play, and students take the recorders home to practice. Parents are pleasantly surprised to hear the improvement as the students progress from the first week to the presentation time.

Students in this classroom prepare for three performances: a parent program with all students playing the recorders with some vocal accompaniment in November, a multi-instrument and vocal accompaniment performance in February during the schoolwide multicultural fair, and open house, which provides all visitors with another concert with vocals and recorder. The pride that the students feel is apparent on their faces as they perform.

Grading and Assessing Music

To see the smiles and energy that is exuded on the students' faces through music participation is an assessment in itself. A music focus in elementary schools should seek to develop an enjoyment and appreciation for different styles of music presented in a variety of formats and by different artists. Many teachers grade students on enthusiasm and participation whether students are involved in an instrumental program, chorus, rhythms, recorder playing, reading music, learning key musical concepts, or singing along with a recording. In Steve Guadarrama's class, a student who loves music (and most of them do) receives an effort grade indicating that. If they repeatedly do not bring their instrument to practice and have a poor attitude and interrupt the enjoyment of music for the others with inappropriate behavior, then the grade is lowered. Some teachers give a notation on their grading sheet (a plus or minus sign or a check mark) as they observe the children during the lesson. This serves as a reminder for report card assessment in music. A music grade in the middle and upper elementary classrooms often is an effort grade, not attached to academics.

Depending on the middle/upper elementary or middle school music class configuration, teachers may need a more formal grade for the report card. Since band and chorus are offered at many schools, teachers assess the students on their performance and their participation level. In this case, each child needs to be assessed individually through a solo audition or performance. Does the child play his or her part correctly? Is there evidence of practice? Does his or her performance affect the whole band or chorus positively or negatively? How does his or her performance contribute to the whole sound of the group? Is he or she attentive and actively engaged in instruction? Does he or she contribute new or creative ideas to enhance the standard of the performance? All of these questions are scrutinized through the lenses of objectivity and subjectivity. Teachers set standards for their students and make sure they have clear understanding of how they will be graded.

ART IMPLEMENTATION

When we take a look at Gardner's eight intelligences, we realize that all of us are not equal in our ability to present ourselves artistically to the world around us. It does not take much effort for a child in the elementary school to realize that some of their classmates see things differently from the other children: they draw things the way they really look. These children have natural ability or talent and possess a high percentage of art smartness, or spatial intelligence. They perceive, manipulate, and recreate forms in the world around them. Clearly some people are better at art than others. This is the case with both students and teachers.

A few characteristics of students who are art smart or spatial learners are listed here (see Chapter Two for a more extensive list):

- Have clear visual images when thinking about something
- Read maps, charts, and diagrams more easily than text
- Enjoy art activities
- Draw accurate representations of people or things
- Get more out of pictures than words in reading
- Doodle on school work
- Love working with their hands on projects like crafts, sewing, or clay

Nevertheless, those who are not naturally artistic must be exposed to many experiences in art so that they can become better at expressing themselves in this form. Everyone can develop skill in their spatial intelligence by participating, focusing, and putting out some effort. Everything in life is difficult to someone; the degree of difficulty depends on the person. For example, learning to visualize the world takes a lot of practice for some people. As we develop an eye for detail, the world becomes less complicated and comes together in meaningful ways. A child who is asked to draw something from memory often is lost and frustrated because he or she has not learned to carefully observe the world in detail.

Much of what we can do is dependent on our personalities. Some people have a more global view of life, and detail for them is more difficult to comprehend, whereas others have keener observational skill and readily see detail around them. Those of us who are more global need to be taught to experience the wonders of the detailed world. In a typical classroom, we have a small percentage of students at both ends of the spectrum: artistically talented and artistically frustrated or challenged. The majority of the classroom falls in the middle.

It is the goal of the teacher to provide each child a sense of success in his or her art development. Every child deserves the privilege of growing in the ability to picture the world on paper or in another art form. The teacher needs to provide appealing and exciting lessons that encourage children to desire growth in their art development. All students may not be equal in their ability, but everyone can learn to enjoy their own success in art.

An example of a student who fully typifies a success story in art is Jeff. At the beginning of the year, he had no interest in art and was frustrated at any type of art that was given. He became angry and frustrated when he could not create anything to his satisfaction. Quiet guidance by the teacher did not help him. Something destructive would always happen to his project before it was finished (it got torn, mashed up in his desk, or stepped on). He said he hated art and did not want to be forced to do it. Around January, all of a sudden he started gaining confidence. The turning point was a project of a large-scale bug done in thin black pen, with the inside textured with many different forms. He had finally found an art project that he could truly become engaged in and one in which he enjoyed and felt successful with. Jeff was able to identify with this idea, gain confidence, and appreciate his originality. From that day forth, he completed every project with excellent effort and participation. His Georgia O'Keeffe flower was a real favorite. When a World War II project came about and he was able to select from several possible projects, he chose to draw planes and ships. And he took great pride in knowing his work was appreciated and praised by his teacher and classmates.

We must look at art as an integral part of a child's education, not as a frill that can be left out. Art continues to play an important role in a child's development. We must see art as one of the eight intelligences that must be cultivated so that children will be well balanced.

Illustrative and Expressive Art

Teachers need to give children opportunities to use their illustrative capabilities in all areas of the curriculum, not just during art period. With whole language, children should be given many experiences in drawing their images of the characters, the setting, and the plot. During social studies, science, and math periods, drawing should be encouraged to provide better understanding of the material being taught. Many children show their understanding of ideas through drawing, and teachers need to allow this form of informal assessment in the classroom. A child who may not be able to explain things easily in words may show his or her capabilities in drawing or picture form.

The classroom teacher should have a balanced art program between illustrative (drawing) and expressive (creative) art. In expressive art, students develop a sense of originality. The process of the piece of work is far more meaningful than the final product. Children need experiences where ownership is sought because they can pursue their personal style that stems from their own heart and not from the teacher's direction. They need to be confident in knowing that their work is cherished and valued. They should show pride by wanting credit for the idea that they have created.

You can provide experiences in art where samples are shown, but the children know that they can modify, adapt, investigate, and explore new approaches or directions within the guidelines of the project. You must instill a feeling that risk taking, originality, and uniqueness are valued and appreciated. When this idea manifests itself, students feel successful knowing that what they have done is worthwhile and enjoyable.

Fifth-grade teacher Pat John, an art consultant, provided a lesson that offered a great deal of individual expression, gave children choice, and was open-ended, and everyone was successful. The lesson was based on the unique style and technique of the artist Georgia O'Keeffe. O'Keeffe chose to explore flowers during her career and to do so looked closely at a small subject, placed it under a personal microscope, and enlarged it. Here is how to implement a similar project:

- Allow children to look at pictures of numerous flowers. This helps them to recall what flowers in nature really look like.
- Give students a 12- by 12-inch piece of white paper and a piece of chalk. Looking carefully at one of the pictures, they draw the flower in chalk from their own perspective. Allowing adaptation and modification from the child's eye is valued. Most students do not get frustrated with this process because the subject matter is recognizable and designed for success.
- As they appraise their preliminary chalk drawing, they can make changes.
- Give the children limited direction on how to use color pastels and some simple shading techniques. It is up to the child to choose the colors he or she likes, even if the picture presents the flower in one color. Experimentation is part of expression. There is no wrong way to feature this flower. The flower does not have to be whole. It can flow off the page.
- The children paint the background in a mixture of white and turquoise paint. All the backgrounds are the same color so that the combined flowers from all students in the classroom form a mural-like bulletin board.
- After the picture dries, the students outline the flower with a mixture of half black tempera paint and half white glue that they gently squeeze out of an applicator bottle with a pointed nozzle.

Students, parents, and teachers are amazed how lovely every one of the products turns out. Each child was allowed and encouraged to observe, explore, experiment, and express a simple idea creatively.

Teachers should also be looking for art ideas to accompany their content areas of the curriculum. In math, geometry lends itself to symmetry, color, and pattern development. Giving a child a compass, protractor, a ruler, and a little direction offers a more structured view of artistic design.

The Art and Literature Connection

With the abundance of wonderful pieces of literature with illustrations abounding, children are very attuned to art and its importance to picture books. The picture books that children had read to them as primary students are now available to them as upper-grade readers—they can read the words themselves. It is important that teachers of middle and upper-grade and middle school students point out and evaluate the types of illustrations that are used by author-illustrators like Bill Peet, Roald Dahl, and Chris Van Allsburg. Discussion on the importance of how skillful a person needs to be to take someone else's writing and create the illustrations also provides several interesting mini-lessons. Someone other than the author illustrates most picture books. This leads into conversations as the students create their own picture books, forming pairs with someone who may be more skillful at the writing of the story and the other person who is more skillful at drawing the illustrations. Assessing students' feelings about their own strengths and weaknesses for the multiple intelligences is a foundational point for creating partnership pairings for author-illustrator big books. (See Chapter Eleven for details on big book production.)

Allowing students to listen carefully to a descriptive section of a piece of literature such as *Charlotte's Web* (1952) and how E. B. White describes the barn in Chapter Three of that book opens up an opportunity for children to close their eyes and visualize what they hear. Then the students can take a piece of paper and draw what they saw in their mind's eye during the description. Many stories and poems for upper-elementary and middle school students can be read without showing them the pictures. With a few exceptions such as second-language students, they no longer need the pictures for support. Reading a description of a character and having the students draw what they think that character looks like challenge students to use their illustrative skill. Displaying these illustrations on the bulletin board shows students how one or two paragraphs of text can create such different impressions. To build visualization skills for second graders, Terri Roseman masked the cover of the book and had the students enjoy the beauty of the text without the support of the pictures. On a second reading, she uncovered the illustrations. Creating pictures in our minds is an art form that also creates stronger readers.

The Teacher's Role During an Art Period

Not all of us are artists, and this lesson can be a challenge for us as teachers. We need to seek out classes, read guided sequential art lessons manuals or books, and ask for suggestions and ideas from fellow teachers. Before presenting any lesson to our classes, it is imperative to try out the lesson ourselves. This will give us a better sense of the pitfalls of the lesson and where the children might falter. If you are a novice artist, this will help you understand how the children who are less than eager to try art will feel. This also gives you an additional sample for the children to look at. It is always a good idea to have more than one sample to present to children before the lesson begins. Since our goal is to give children ideas without their feeling the need to copy our sample, three samples is a good number to use. As children begin to feel more confident and freer to express themselves and take risks within the guidelines of the lesson, they will not feel the need to copy the sample. This usually takes place as the children develop and mature naturally.

During the work period, you should be observing, assisting, asking questions to refocus students on their process, making constructive suggestions, and checking to see if students have followed the basic parameters of the technique or skill being taught. Since one of our goals should be to see students becoming progressively more skillful at their developmental level, you should set standards and strongly encourage students who are frustrated or have a slump on the project to complete their work.

Children delight in seeing their teachers involved in the lesson too. It is fun and enjoyable for teachers to try the lesson again with their students. Sitting with the students and making yourself another sample of the lesson gives credibility to the project and lets children see that even though you might not be a skilled artist, you are nevertheless putting in effort and enjoying the activity.

Your role in the art process should also be to encourage students throughout the lesson. Students will receive your praise of their work with pleasure if they believe that you are being honest. While you are observing the work period, you will probably want to offer some suggestions to students who are experiencing difficulty or have not understood the assignment. Questions such as, "What do you think would happen if you tried . . . ?" or "If you were to add another color, what would it be?" might direct students to be more successful in the end result.

The Art Environment

It is important for students not to be restricted by the time allotted for the art project. Your objective should be that students enjoy the art so much that they want to complete what they have started. Too often we put constraints on the students because there is only a forty- to fifty-minute time frame for art. Special consideration should be given to students who do not finish their project during the class time. Extra class time may be required, or the student might take the project home to complete.

You need to treat each child's work as something of value. If the teacher says at the end of the period, "Fold your picture in half and place it in your backpack," the child never sees the work as valued or important. As often as possible, children's work should be displayed on a bulletin board. Every child should sign the picture to show pride of ownership. Framing each child's work in construction paper contributes to that child's sense of worth as an artist.

During the art period, teachers and students sometimes feel that this is a time to socialize. In some classrooms, the art period becomes a social buzz time when children spend more time chatting with their friends than focusing on the project they are working on. The art period should be a relaxing time for everyone. Research shows that people who work quietly as they delve into an art project are more focused; less distraction gives the person a greater feeling of success and pride at the end of the project. Soft music contributes to relaxation and focusing. Music also tends to eliminate some of the self-consciousness that students feel when they are around their peers. Some children are uptight and restricted in their ability to express themselves freely, but music tends to lift these concerns and allows them to relax. Those who find art challenging know those feelings of frustration and concern. When someone feels incompetent in any area, feelings are intensified, and fear sets in because no one wants to be laughed at for being unskillful.

Resources

Developing a collection of art prints and pictures is easier than you think. Ask parents to save calendars, nature magazines, and greeting cards, and anything else you let them know you are looking for. Over the course of a few years, your collection will be bulging, and you'll have them to use, to the children's delight. Enlisting the assistance of volunteers who are willing to share their art expertise in small groups throughout the year is always a good idea. Teachers should be seeking out ways to identify skillful parents and community members who can bring their talents to share with the children in the classroom. (See Form 9.1, Parent Interest Form.)

The public libraries should be used extensively to access books to demonstrate the style and art forms prevalent in the works of famous artists and in periods of history.

Some schools are fortunate to have a talented art consultant, such as Pat John in the San Diego Unified School District. Some schools hire her for monthly lessons for each classroom, whereas other schools hire her for one, two, or three lessons per year per teacher. Funding for her consulting is often paid for by PTA funds. Individual teachers also use additional school funds that are available to them or personal funds to hire her for classroom art projects. Her method is to center a lesson on a famous artist and his or her personal art technique such as Seurat (dots), O'Keeffe (enlarging an item—making it bigger than life), and Grandma Moses (folk art). Study prints and samples are used to focus the students on each artist's style. Books are also available from the public library with large pictures to use for class lessons.

Ideas for Art Lessons

There are several paths to obtaining ideas for art lessons for your students. One of them is *Scholastic Art,* which is endorsed by the National Gallery of Art and correlates with the National Content Standards for the Visual Arts. This bimonthly magazine brings a class:

- Classic and contemporary artists
- Art history lessons
- High-quality reproductions
- A "Masterpiece of the Month" poster
- Studio workshops
- Student "Artist of the Month" profile

Students will learn to appreciate artists through the six monthly issues that help balance a classroom art program.

Two monthly magazines that are of significant assistance to classroom teachers are *School Arts* (MagsontheNet.com) and *Arts and Activities* (www.artsandactivities.com).

Samples to Show Children

It is a good idea to use student samples. The children relate to ideas from their own peer group better than to an adult's ideas. An adult perspective of art is more difficult for a child to connect with. Following are some suggestions for obtaining samples from students and others:

- Ask a child who finishes early to make you another picture. That makes a child feel good about himself or herself. The fact that you will use the sample to show other children in the years to come is a positive charge.
- Make color copies of your best student work for use the next year.
- Borrow samples from other teachers.
- Take pictures of children's work.

Art in the Classroom

Most children love to draw. Too often, though, this form of art is limiting and constrained. Children want to make things look exactly the way someone else made it without thinking of how to modify or change it to become their own idea. Some children who cannot make their rendering of the picture look like the model become frustrated and give up. Children who are perfectionists also become frustrated because they think their art can never be as good as what they are looking at. If we as adults are asked to draw a house, my house looks very similar to what the person next to me draws. That is the way we learned to draw a house from our own teachers when we were in elementary school. It is our hope today that our students will have a foundation to see that all houses do not look the same. We want children to learn some basic ideas of drawing and be given the freedom to modify and enhance their drawing skill. We should encourage children to reflect their own unique awareness and view of the world in their pictures and other art.

Students who have difficulty writing or putting their ideas into words should have an opportunity to show what they know through drawing. For instance if you are working on a Native American unit, a culminating option for a reluctant reader or writer might be to draw pictures of the weapons, art forms, or artifacts and dwellings of a particular tribe, with captions attached for clarification instead of writing a full paragraph about these areas. The child might also be asked to tell about these pictures so that the other students can see the learning that has taken hold. This show-and-tell experience gives access to all students, no matter what their academic level.

During math time, students should be encouraged to draw pictures to help them understand the question, clarify, and explain their thinking—for instance, when a word problem like this one is given: "Your family is giving you a party for your birthday. They order 6 pints of ice cream from Stone Cold. If you served ¼ of a pint of ice cream to each guest, how many guests can be served? Work the problem next using ½ or ¾ of a pint." Most students have difficulty with word problems, so urging students to create or draw pictures to explain their thinking is important. Drawing offers a clearer view of what the question asks and gives us a reference in case our thinking goes awry.

Picture books offer a variety of artistic media and techniques that illustrators use. Exposure to watercolor, collage, pencil or pen sketching, and printing allows children to see different ways of illustrating that bring the story to life. As students read books about famous artists, they should be encouraged to try the art techniques used.

In science and health, children should be encouraged to draw diagrams of such things as the process of photosynthesis, the water cycle, weather patterns, diagrams of human and animal bodies, cells, plants, and what they observe in an experiment or under the lens of a microscope.

During quiet time when students concentrate on listening to music, they may draw pictures that display the effect the music has on their thinking. What pictures are elicited during certain segments of a piece of classical, contemporary, country-western, jazz, hip-hop, bluegrass, or new age music? What colors and images are brought forth? A plain piece of paper can be filled with the images that present themselves as music is played. This is an eye-opener with students who sometimes have very little to say in other academic subjects.

The classroom setting is a place to discover a new dimension of your students' thoughts. Art provides an avenue for students to create, imagine, arrange, and improvise ideas that are not formed in other academic instruction.

Drawing Opportunities

There should be many opportunities for students to draw. Art books in an art center give students ideas for drawing. No pressure is placed on them to draw things exactly as shown in a book. This center should be filled with books that children may use to draw from, such as *How to Draw Monsters, How to Draw Horses,* and *How to Draw People.* The public library is a fine source for these types of materials.

Children need many opportunities to follow steps and put together parts to understand relationships in the world. When asked to draw a horse from memory, many students have no idea where or how to start. They have limited relational memory. How long is the tail of a horse? Is it longer or shorter than the neck? Is the body wider than the legs are long? Children need to have experiences that build understanding of size, shape, and relationships of body parts. A good idea is to have numerous pictures of what you are having the students draw. All teachers should accumulate illustrations and keep them in a file, so that when they ask students to draw certain things, there are examples. So that students do not copy, these pictures should be handed out to look at before the drawing begins, allowing time to observe what the image looks like, and then collected. This gives children a feeling of comfort because now they have something to recharge their memory of the item.

Multicultural Literacy Chalk Walk

First, students read books that take place in settings in countries other than the United States. On a large map in the auditorium, students place a "little book" (a colored piece of paper about the size of a postage stamp) in the general area of the setting of the book. The "little book" has the title of the book, the author, and the name of the location where the story takes place. Each child has at least one "little book" to place on the map. Through this activity, students can see the locations of the books that the whole school has read.

Students are assigned a location at the school site, usually on the playground, to illustrate their selected book in chalk. They may work with a partner or work alone. The size of their chalk spot can be 18 by 18 inches or 24 by 24 inches. Every child in the school participates. Parents and the students walk around the school to visit the chalk illustrations of good pieces of literature that represent other people's cultures.

Photography

One project that helps students tackle art is photography. Many county and state fairs have competitions for children's photography, and the school is an avenue to motivate students to try something new. With digital cameras and inexpensive disposable cameras, children have art at their disposal. In the upper grades and middle school, a photo opportunity is one way to focus students on a specific subject. Almost all upper-grade students have difficulty limiting their subject in writing. With a photography project, students are forced to choose and concentrate on a specific, narrow subject. Looking closely at a subject and observing the limited world is more difficult than it seems.

Start out by having a professional photographer visit the classroom and present his or her way of observing the world. A photographer can share pictures from his or her portfolio and address the skills and education that a career in photography might entail. Use the Activity 15.1, Photography Project, at the end of this chapter.

Read-Aloud First, Art Lesson Second

Students enjoy being introduced to an artist or art technique through a picture book or a piece of non-fiction about the artist. Many art lessons are preceded by a piece of literature that inspires students to take on the artist's style or technique while learning more about the artist himself. One example is the study of Vincent Van Gogh through using the book *The First Starry Night* (1997) by Joan Shaddox Isom. Together the classroom teacher and the art teacher, Pat John, coordinate the two and provide students with a lesson that shows the connection between art and literacy. The art lesson contained the following steps:

- Listened to a read-aloud entitled *The First Starry Night* by Joan Shaddox Tsom about Van Gogh
- Discussed factual information about Van Gogh and how he was not fully appreciated until after his death
- Wrote paragraphs about special friendships that they had in order to identify with the main character in the story
- Using the same technique as Van Gogh, created "starry night" illustrations of their own versions of this famous picture

We must be careful in not always tying art to literature. Students need to have opportunities to create for themselves, just as they need to write creatively and not always be guided by the teacher into doing exactly what the teacher wants.

Support for Other Content Areas

Art lessons can be supported with pieces of non-fiction in the content areas. For instance, when students are studying exploration, Pat John developed a ship-in-a-bottle lesson using construction paper and black permanent pens. Students used more detail while drawing the rigging. The lesson was preceded with a shared reading lesson on how messages in the bottle related to wind and ocean currents and how bottles were used historically. She also has designed scrimshaw lessons to support this unit. When studying Native American Indians, the students dabble in making parfleches and ledgerbook drawings, which they understand much better through a piece of nonfiction for read-aloud or shared reading.

One School's Approach to the Arts: Benchley-Weinberger: Application for California Distinguished School K–5

One section of the application for the California Distinguished School Award addressed the visual and performing arts. Benchley-Weinberger, a K–5 school, approached the application is this manner.

Music, art, and drama are highly respected and celebrated by teachers who understand and appreciate the relationship that academics have with these special areas of the intelligence spectrum. It is the intention of all teachers to educate the whole child, therefore developing a well-rounded individual prepared for all life encounters. Students are encouraged to use all of their seven intelligences therefore, giving them outlets that accompany the stresses of academics as they approach their middle and high school years. Most children are involved in a very intense curriculum and teachers set high standards academically for all children. The visual and performing arts are encouraged throughout the school and provide the balance of a high quality program that educates the whole child. Students are given a wide range of opportunities to develop their spatial, musical, linguistic, and interpersonal skills.

Often projects and learning centers within the classrooms are developed to include all of the intelligences. A child may have a project where he or she can choose a culmination activity based on his/her area of interest. For example, while studying World War II, through the Newbery Award winning book *Number the Stars* by Lois Lowry, students might be given the choice to show their knowledge of the period of time by acting out a scene from the book, making up a reader's theater and performing it with expression, drawing pictures of the clothing of the period or military ships, or through demonstration of the music of the era. In other words, artistic, dramatic, and musical talents and skills support the curriculum. The teachers believe that this extra creative support enhances learning across the curriculum. Students learn to appreciate the importance of art, music, and drama and see how they interconnect with the other disciplines. In math students are encouraged to draw illustrations to better understand the concepts of fractions and problem solving. In science students have opportunities to draw what they see in microscopes or in observations as they do hands-on experiments. These are sources of data collection and enhance scientific principles. In literature, students learn to appreciate the richness of illustrations and can use their own illustrations as they try to comprehend chapter books more thoroughly. They also discuss the differences between mediums used in their text and illustrations seen in their read-alouds, independent reading selections, the anthology, and big books. Students are encouraged to draw "mental pictures" for comprehension purposes while reading a selection in a chapter book. Students who understand the importance of illustrations to the reading process more easily comprehend the plot and sequence of a story. With the number of special needs students that are serviced each year, students use the artistic outlet as a form of assessment when they have difficulty expressing themselves in writing or on tests. Upper grade and primary students with second language concerns often use drawing to show their understanding of the subject matter.

Art abounds in the classrooms and on the school bulletin boards, in the cafeteria, and in the front office. Art showcases student work that connects with a certain thematic teaching unit or with a well-known artist's style. An annual art fair is presented at Spring Open House to showcase student work to show spatial intelligence. Parents assist the teachers and the art consultant in hanging the show. Upper grade students delve into evaluating a piece of art at the art show showing their understanding of the method or style of art. This year B/W will focus its attention on multiculturalism. At Open House, students and parents will be part of an *Art and Literacy Art Walk* featuring student multicultural art work, games, music, and food. Artwork will be centered on picture books that represent the cultures of the students at the school. Each grade level will represent a continent and will choose activities, including literature, music, art, and games around that section of the world.

The PTA sponsors each classroom with two lessons throughout the year from an art consultant, Pat John. Additional lessons are purchased out of Gifted and Talented funding, parent support, or individual teachers' own money. Art lessons concentrate on the lives of master artists, followed by a project focusing on a related topic. Focus is sometimes on the type of materials the artist used, his/her style, or even the subject of his/her art. Master artists include Monet, Matisse, Picasso, Cézanne, and Van Gogh to name just a few. The children are exposed to many forms of multicultural art that reflect the student population including African American folk art, Mexican arts and crafts, arts from China and Japan, and Native American art. Forms of art such as impressionism, surrealism, and cubism are also subjects of focus. The special mediums of watercolor, crayon, colored pencils, and pastels also provide areas of study. The art lessons also take on the literacy focus using picture books such as *Anasi, An African Tale, The Girl Who Loved Wild Horses,* and *Liang and the Magic Paintbrush.*

Students participated in a field trip to the Mengei Museum featuring Native American art and art of Mexico, which enhanced their understanding of the themes of Native Americans and Early California history. They also attended the UCSD [University of California at San Diego] Art/Music Festival, giving them the opportunity to visit a university campus.

Special guest speakers were provided by the PTA to show students the connection of art in the memorization of academic material such as social studies and science. Students have had their work exhibited in the Young Art Exhibit at the San Diego Museum of Fine Arts in Balboa Park. Student work is also showcased in Union Bank, our Partner in Education. Each year students donate their personalized classroom quilts to charity organizations. The students choose quilt ideas. Each child has his/her own square and designs a piece to go with the theme of the classroom idea. Quilts are paraded around the playground during School Spirit Day and are on display at Open House. Some are selected to be exhibited at the Del Mar Fair.

Many opportunities are given to children to act out or dramatize both informational as well as creative events. For instance, fifth graders are participants in the monthly News Broadcast networked to all classrooms. This is but one aspect of the communication focus of our school. Students sing, anchor, dramatize, and report important events of the school and the community through creative means. School Spirit Assemblies spotlight songs and skits for the month. All students participate in these programs when their classroom is showcased at the assembly.

The Talent Show is grandiose. Students start planning for months before the event. All students may participate. Parent volunteers assist and form groups for those students who want to perform but don't have an act. The Lewis Middle School Auditorium is used and is filled to capacity, bringing in many of our cross-city families. The event is attended by many people from other schools and the community-at-large because of its numerous years of past success.

Upper grade students have also had the chance to perform in the San Diego Opera's presentation of *Hansel and Gretel.* The students paint the scenery, handle the stage crew responsibilities, and perform the entire play on the school site. The performances were well attended by parents, relatives, and other community members. Fourth and fifth graders had occasion to attend the *Theater of the World* presentations at San Diego State University.

Many classrooms attend plays performed regularly by Junior Theater, Christian Youth Theater. Many of our students and former students perform in these plays and continue their education at the School of Performing Arts in San Diego.

The importance of music in the lives of students is generated through several avenues. Background music is used to help students focus while they are writing or doing art. Baroque, as well as classical music is often played during work periods. Many classrooms have set up centers with music as the focus. Students often have opportunities to listen to music at a listening post. Upper grade students attend the Grossmont College Dance Performance each year, which focuses on multiculturalism. This connects them with the college community in our area of the city. Each year in December, all classes participate in a holiday singalong focusing on music representing multicultural beliefs. The principal and resource teacher accompany the singing with guitars. A multicultural fair is held during the year and classrooms choose music through song and dance to represent their country. During thematic study, music from the periods of colonial times, Revolutionary War, and westward expansion is sung. Sea chanteys are learned and new ones created as students attend the Star of India Overnight which is a historical simulation that gives a hands-on, living-history experience enhancing the California State Framework for Social Studies.

Individual classrooms delve into famous musicians such as Bach, Mozart, and Beethoven through biographies and pieces of literature. Students research famous composers, write reports, and put together displays featuring these men and women. The individual classrooms perform square dancing and other folk dancing presentations throughout the year.

An instrumental music program has been established in the school for fifth graders. Once a week, a guest music teacher visits the school and instructs students with real instruments including violin, trumpet, percussion, and clarinet. This program has revitalized the students participating in the middle and high school orchestras and marching bands.

We are proud of our ability to maintain high academic standards in the San Diego City Schools. Our test and portfolio scores are among the highest in the district. Our waiting list is long. We believe that our success is due to the value we place on a balanced program that educates the whole child, stressing high academic standards that are supported by the enrichment, appreciation, and respect for the visual and performing arts.

Grading and Assessment

Since many teachers are not formally trained in the area of art, it is difficult to grade or evaluate the finished product. A simple form of evaluation might be for the teacher to use two statements on the back of the project or on a sticky note: "Something I really liked about your picture is . . ." or "A suggestion I would like to make is . . ."

A system using a plus or minus sign might also be used to let children know how they applied the skill they were being taught. Formal grading of art in the elementary school seems to discourage students in their ability to be expressive and creative. They can become more concerned about pleasing teachers than in pleasing themselves. Since evaluating art is subjective, teachers must be careful in grading art because it can be the discouraging factor that squelches a child's enjoyment and confidence in a relaxing pastime.

For assessment purposes, teachers are encouraged to start a student art portfolio. The teacher should keep on file the student work so that the students and parents can see a development of art ability throughout the year. Because of the lack of space, schoolwide art portfolios have not gained a lot of momentum. Can you imagine the excitement children would feel if when they exited the school as fifth, sixth, or eighth graders, they were given a history of their development in art since kindergarten? Only one or two pieces of work each year could be saved, much of it chosen by the child himself.

The importance in art should be placed on the process of the art, not the product. Too often we forget that our focus should be on the enjoyment of art. Children should be evaluated on their effort and participation, not on the product itself. As long as children stay within the guidelines of the skill being taught, they should be allowed to make choices so as not to be too restricted by the teacher's control.

BOOKS FOR MUSIC AND ART CENTERS

Children's Books for the Music Center

Anderson, M. T. (2001). *Handel, who knew what he liked.* Cambridge, MA: Candlewick Press.

Burleigh, R. (2001). *Looking for bird in the big city.* Orlando, FL: Harcourt.

Christensen, B. (2001). *Woody Guthrie.* New York: Knopf.

Cutler, J. (1999). *The cello of Mr. O.* New York: Dutton.

George-W., H. (2001). *Shake, rattle and roll.* Boston: Houghton Mifflin.

Guthrie, W. (1998). *This land is your land.* New York: Scholastic.

Kroll, S. (1994). *By the dawn's early light.* New York: Scholastic.

Krull, K. (1993). *Lives of the musicians.* Orlando, FL: Harcourt.

McGill, A. (2000). *In the hollow of your hand—Slave lullabies.* Boston: Houghton Mifflin.

McDonough, Y. (2003). *Who was Wolfgang Amadeus Mozart?* New York: Grosset and Dunlap

Pinkney, A. (1998). *Duke Ellington.* New York: Scholastic.

Ryan, P. M. (2001). *When Marian sang?* New York: Scholastic.

Children's Books for the Art Center

Andrews-Goebel, N. A. (2002). *The pot that Juan built.* New York: Lee & Low Books.

Anholt, L. (1998). *Picasso and the girl with the ponytail.* Hauppauge, NY: Barron's Educational Series.

Brenner, B. (1999). *The boy who loved to draw.* Boston: Houghton Mifflin.

Hamm, J. (1982). *How to draw animals.* New York: Perigee Books.

Ison, J. S. (1997). *The first starry night.* Watertown, MA: Charlesbridge Publishing.

Krull, K. (1995). *Lives of the artists.* Orlando, FL: Harcourt.

Winter, J. (1998). *Georgia.* Orlando, FL: Harcourt.

Winter, J. (1991). *Diego.* New York: Knopf.

Scholastic voyages of discovery. (1994). New York: Scholastic.

Series Books

Artists in their times (series). New York: Scholastic.

How to draw . . . (series). Australia: Usborne Publications.

Mason, A. *In the time of . . .* (series). London, WI: Aladdin Books.

Smart about art (series). New York: Grosset & Dunlap.

Venezia, M. *Getting to know the world's greatest artists* (series). Chicago: Children's Press.

Young artist (series). Australia: Usborne Publications.

REFERENCES

Buck, D. (1991). *Patriotic songs and marches* [CD]. Long Branch, NJ: Kimbo Educational.

Buck, D. (2002). *Celebrate America* [CD]. Twin Sisters Production. Long Branch, NJ: Kimbo Educational.

Erlauer, L. (2003). *The brain-compatible classroom—Using what we know about learning to improve teaching.* Alexandria, VA: Association for Supervision and Curriculum Development.

Gardner, H. (1983). *Frames of mind: The theory of multiple intelligences.* New York: Basic Books.

Isom, J. S. (1997). *The first starry night.* Dallas, TX: Whispering Coyote Press.

Lamb, G. *Gary Lamb music.* San Clemente, CA: Kagan Publishing.

Multiplication Rap & Hip-Hop. www.twinsisters.com.

Oxlade, C. (1997). *Cameras.* New York: Anness Publishing.

Rief, S. (2003). *The ADHD book of lists.* San Francisco: Jossey-Bass.

Rief, S. (2005). *How to reach and teach children with ADD/ADHD.* San Francisco: Jossey-Bass.

Schuster, D. H., & Gritton, C. E. (1986). *Suggestive accelerative learning techniques.* New York: Gordon and Breach.

Shaw, G. (2003). *Keeping Mozart in mind.* Irvine, CA. Reed Elsevier.

Sousa, D. (2001). *How the special needs brain learns.* Thousand Oaks, CA: Corwin Press.

Traugh, S. (1993a). *Voices of American history: Precolonial times through the Revolutionary War.* Cypress, CA: Creative Teaching Press.

Traugh, S. (1993b). *Voices of American history: The young nation through the Civil War.* Cypress, CA: Creative Teaching Press.

Traugh, S. (1993c). *Voices of American history: The westward expansion of the United States.* Cypress, CA: Creative Teaching Press.

Walter, T. (2004). *Teaching English language learners.* West Plains, NY: Pearson Education.

White, E. B. (1952). *Charlotte's web.* New York: Harper & Row.

TEACHER RESOURCES

Brookes, M. (1986). *Drawing with children.* Los Angeles: Jeremy P. Tarcher.

Carratello, J., & Carratello, P. (1994). *Focus on composers.* Huntington Beach, CA: Teacher Created Materials.

Krull, K. (1992). *Gonna sing my head off—American folksongs for children.* New York: Knopf.

Mind Institute. (2003). *Math success for every student* [Brochure]. Costa Mesa, CA: Author.

Reznick, C. *Imagery for kids—Discovering your special place* [CD/audiocassette]. www.imageryforkids.com.

Trudeau, K. (1997). *Mega memory.* New York: HarperCollins.

Walters, C. (2005). *Multi-cultural music—lyrics to familiar melodies and native songs.* Minneapolis: T. S. Denison.

PHOTOGRAPHY PROJECT

Name: _____   Date: _____

In the past few days students have had the opportunity to hear about the art form of photography from several experts. We have also looked through magazines and books about photography. We have discussed the art of taking pictures and have been given tips on how to capture the best shots. Each student will create a photo essay through words and photographs.

- Students will take a series of pictures focused on one specific topic. The focus could be such things as shoes, hats, balls, trash, chairs, doors, bridges, windows, arches, phones, signs, tires, hubcaps, a specific kind of fruit or a combination of fruit, feet, a letter or number in words or symbols, items of a particular color, things that relate to math, or things that show Greek influence.

- Students who need cameras will receive them on Friday. They may use part of their spring vacation to search for special photo opportunities. Looking throughout our community for shots will be a family adventure, or you can stay right in your own home. We will need the cameras or the processed film back right after spring vacation.

- Students will look through their photographs and select their best nine to twelve pictures. They will glue these on a long, narrow piece of black paper, which the teacher will provide.

- Students will write a narrative or poetic expression to accompany their photos. This should be typed up and framed on a black sheet of paper. The paper should be half a page to a full page in length.

Have fun!

Photography Project Selection Form

Child's Name _____

Parent's Signature _____

Some students may want to use their own family's camera: regular, disposable, digital, or something else. If you have a camera or want to buy your own disposable camera, please use that as an option. The disposable cameras do not always yield high-quality pictures. I will purchase just the number that are needed, so please let me know if you need one by _____. The disposable cameras will have twenty-four exposures.

PHOTOGRAPHY PROJECT (*continued*)

Please check the following that apply:

_____ My child would like to work alone.

_____ My child would like to work with a partner.

_____ We would like a camera.

_____ We will use our own camera or buy our own disposable camera.

_____ We will have our own pictures developed at a photo store.

_____ We would like our pictures developed for us.

The subject my child has chosen is _____

Photo Tips to Help You with Your Photo Essay

- Most cameras have a limited range of focus. With disposable cameras, you should be at least four feet away from the subject. Do not take pictures any closer because they will be out of focus.

- Holding the camera properly is very important. To avoid taking pictures of your fingertips, hold the camera by the sides.

- Disposable cameras have a built-in flash. You should always use it whether you're indoors or outdoor. By using it outdoors, the flash will help fill in the shadows on faces and will help during low-light situations.

- Try taking pictures framed as both horizontal and vertical.

- When taking a photo, try to fill the frame as much as possible by getting the subject completely in it. *Tip:* Take a few steps backward to get more in the photo.

- Sometimes you may want to frame your picture with foliage or a doorway.

INDEX

A

Academic language skills, 57

Academic performance: art portfolio, 439; Asperger's syndrome impact on, 53–54; grading and assessing music, 429. *See also* Evaluating; Support measures; Teacher interventions

Acceleration strategy, 62

Accommodations: adaptation of materials, 94; of assignments and instruction, 93–94; behavioral, 98–99; environmental, 26–28, 94–95; IDEA legislation on providing, 36, 45; for math instruction, 357–359; memory supports and, 95; for organization and time management, 96; reading, 97; social, emotional, and coping, 99; for students with Asperger's syndrome, 55; for testing, 97–98; writing modifications and, 96–97. *See also* Learning; Special population students

Accordion folders, 179

Accountability, 8

Activities: art curriculum, 434–439, 442–443; auditory/visual cues addition, 28; auditory/visual distraction reduction, 27–28; behavioral management, 128–132; Gardner's multiple intelligence theory instruction using, 18–19,

31–34; Home Extension Activities, 169, 172–175; homework, time management, and organization skills, 189–196; increasing parental involvement, 170–175; math instruction, 349–351, 359–420; music curriculum, 425–428, 438–439; oral language development, 250–274; reading and writing development, 225–248; resilience and self-esteem building, 159–160; science curriculum, 296–297, 316–336; social studies curriculum, 281–292, 301–315. *See also* Curriculum; *specific activities*

Activity rewards/privileges, 113

AD/HD (attention deficit hyperactivity disorder): bipolar disorder overlap with, 51; challenges associated with, 44; common characteristics of children/teens with, 42–43; comprehensive evaluation for, 45; considering learning style elements for, 24; cooperative learning benefits for, 8; described, 40–41; distinguished from giftedness, 64; DSM-IV and DSMIV-TR on characteristics and symptoms of, 41–42; graphomotor skills deficiency and, 81; homework stress as issue for, 187; instructional strategies/accommodations for, 47–48, 358; math difficulties associated

with, 44, 358; multimodal treatments for, 45–46; ODD as common coexisting condition with, 49; previous names for, 41; questioning strategies for students with, 139, 140; reading difficulties associated with, 78–79; statistics and risk factors for, 43–44; strategic seating arrangements for, 27; time management challenges and, 44, 181; types of, 41; Web sites on, 66, 67; writing difficulties associated with, 81, 82. *See also* Special population students

ADHD and LD: Powerful Teaching Strategies and Accommodations (video), 47

AD/HD multimodual treatments: behavior modification/management strategies, 46; counseling, 46; educational support, 46; medical/pharmacological intervention, 46; overview of, 45–46; physical outlets, 46; support groups as part of, 46

Adolescents. *See* Teens

Adopt-a-student program, 153

Affective filter hypothesis, 56

African American gifted students, 65

After-school speakers' club, 261

Ahlberg, A., 214

Ahlberg, J., 214

Aitken, K., 53

Other Books of Interest

How to Reach and Teach Children with ADD/ADHD: Practical Techniques, Strategies, and Interventions, Second Edition

Sandra F. Rief

Paper   ISBN: 0-7879-7295-9

www.josseybass.com

It is both a pleasure and a privilege to provide this strong and unequivocal endorsement of so informative and consumer-friendly a book as this one. Grounded in the latest science of ADHD, filled with exceptionally detailed advice . . . parents and educators will find this book to be exceptionally useful in raising a successful ADHD child.

—**Russell A. Barkley**, Ph.D., professor of psychiatry,
Medical University of South Carolina,
and author, *Taking Charge of ADHD*

Finally, it's here! This is the much-anticipated new edition to the best-selling book that has served for over a decade as a resource for teachers, school professionals, parents, and clinicians. *How to Reach and Teach Children with ADD/ADHD* is filled with practical strategies and techniques to improve the academic, behavioral, and social performance of students with ADHD. The book is easy to read, includes the most current research-based information about ADHD, and outlines effective treatments.

Sandra Rief offers myriad real-life case studies, interviews, and student intervention plans for children with ADD/ADHD. In addition, the book contains best teaching practices and countless strategies for enhancing classroom performance for all types of students. This invaluable resource offers proven suggestions for:

- Engaging students' attention and active participation
- Keeping students on-task and productive
- Preventing and managing behavioral problems in the classroom
- Differentiating instruction and addressing students' diverse learning styles
- Building a partnership with parents and much more

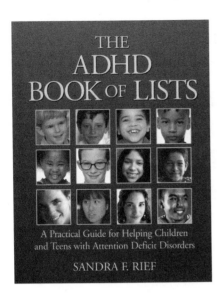

The ADHD Book of Lists: A Practical Guide for Helping Children and Teens with Attention Deficit Disorders

Sandra F. Rief

Paper   ISBN: 0-7879-6591-X

www.josseybass.com

When Sandra Rief writes about ADHD and educational issues, people listen! Rief, widely recognized as the leading authority on these topics, has an extraordinary gift for identifying key challenges and providing practical, effective tips for helping children succeed in school. Her latest book, The ADHD Book of Lists, *is another indispensable tool for both parents and teachers! As the author of two popular books on ADHD, I always use Sandra's books as primary references.*

—**Chris A. Zeigler Dendy**, author, *Teenagers with ADD*
and *Teaching Teens with ADD and ADHD*

The ADHD Book of Lists is a comprehensive, reliable source of answers, practical strategies, and tools written in a convenient list format. Created for teachers (K–12), parents, school psychologists, medical and mental health professionals, counselors, and other school personnel, this important resource contains the most current information about Attention Deficit/ Hyperactivity Disorder (ADHD). It is filled with the strategies, supports, and interventions that have been found to be the most effective in minimizing the problems and optimizing the success of children and teens with ADHD. The book contains a wealth of information to guide in the management of ADHD in school and at home. In addition, *The ADHD Book of Lists'* 8½ inches by 11 inches lay-flat format is filled with reproducible checklists, forms, tools, and resources.